Informatik aktuell

Herausgeber: W. Brauer
im Auftrag der Gesellschaft für Informatik (GI)

Paul Müller
Reinhard Gotzhein
Jens B. Schmitt (Hrsg.)

Kommunikation in Verteilten Systemen (KiVS)

14. Fachtagung
Kommunikation in Verteilten Systemen
(KiVS 2005)
Kaiserslautern, 28. Februar – 3. März 2005

Eine Veranstaltung der Gesellschaft für Informatik (GI)
unter Beteiligung der Informationstechnischen Gesellschaft
(ITG/VDE)
Ausgerichtet von der Technischen Universität Kaiserslautern

Herausgeber

Paul Müller
Reinhard Gotzhein
Jens B. Schmitt
Technische Universität Kaiserslautern
Fachbereich Informatik
Postfach 3049
67653 Kaiserslautern

Bibliographische Information der Deutschen Bibliothek
Die Deutsche Bibliothek verzeichnet diese Publikation in der Deutschen Nationalbibliografie; detaillierte bibliografische Daten sind im Internet über http://dnb.ddb.de abrufbar.

CR Subject Classification (2001): C2, C4

ISSN 1431-472-X
ISBN 3-540-24473-5 Springer Berlin Heidelberg New York

Springer Berlin Heidelberg New York
Springer ist ein Unternehmen von Springer Science+Business Media

springer.de

Printed in Germany

Satz: Reproduktionsfertige Vorlage vom Autor/Herausgeber
Gedruckt auf säurefreiem Papier SPIN: 11382409 33/3142-543210

Vorwort

Die Fachtagung „Kommunikation in Verteilten Systemen" (KiVS), die zum ersten Mal 1979 in Berlin durchgeführt wurde und seither in zweijährigem Rhythmus stattfindet, blickt 2005 auf eine 27-jährige Tradition als wichtigstes Forum der Community im deutschsprachigen Raum zurück. Nach der letzten erfolgreichen Konferenz 2003 in Leipzig befasst sich auch die 14. GI/ITG-Fachtagung KiVS 2005 an der TU Kaiserslautern mit einer großen Vielfalt von innovativen und zukunftsorientierten Fragestellungen. Sie spannt dabei einen Bogen von verteilten Anwendungen über Netzwerk- und Middleware-Aspekte bis hin zu eScience und Grid. Die KiVS 2005 dient der Standortbestimmung aktueller Entwicklungen, der Präsentation laufender Forschungsarbeiten und der Diskussion zukunftsträchtiger Ansätze für die Kommunikation in verteilten Systemen.

Aus den 97 eingereichten Beiträgen hat der Programmausschuss 24 Arbeiten zur Präsentation ausgewählt. Zusätzlich werden 13 weitere Einreichungen im Rahmen von Kurzbeiträgen und Praxisberichten vorgestellt. Begleitet wird die Fachtagung von Tutorials zu Themen wie *UMTS-Technologie/3GPP IMS für NGN*, *Netzwerksicherheit – verteilte Angriffserkennung im Internet* und *Kontextbezogene Systeme* sowie von einem Workshop zu *Peer-to-Peer-Systemen und -Anwendungen*. Diese inhaltlichen Schwerpunkte werden abgerundet durch eingeladene Vorträge aus der Industrie.

Ein besonderes Ereignis im Rahmen der KiVS 2005 stellt die 25-Jahrfeier der Fachgruppe Kommunikation und Verteilte Systeme (KuVS) dar. Die Fachgruppe Kommunikation und Verteilte Systeme wurde unter dem Arbeitstitel „Rechnernetze" 1979 in Berlin gegründet und dann im Rahmen der GI und ITG als gemeinsame Fachgruppe KuVS etabliert.

Mit der TU Kaiserslautern wurde eine junge Universität mit einem renommierten Informatik-Fachbereich mit der Ausrichtung der Tagung beauftragt. Zukunftsorientierte Studiengänge, praxisnahe Ausbildung und modernste Infrastruktur – das sind die Rahmenbedingungen, die Studierende an der TU Kaiserslautern vorfinden. Darüber hinaus profitieren die Studierenden von den zahlreichen renommierten Forschungseinrichtungen, die unmittelbar auf dem Campus angesiedelt sind und im Bereich der angewandten Forschung eng mit der Technischen Universität kooperieren. Dazu gehören beispielsweise das Deutsche Forschungszentrum für Künstliche Intelligenz (DFKI), die Fraunhofer-Institute für Experimentelles Software-Engineering (IESE) und für Techno- und Wirtschaftsmathematik (ITWM) sowie das 2005 zu gründende Max-Planck-Institut für Softwaresysteme.

Dem Programmausschuss sei an dieser Stelle für die zeitaufwändige Arbeit im Vorfeld der KiVS 2005 herzlich gedankt. Unser Dank gilt auch dem lokalen Organisationskomitee, insbesondere Frau Ulrike Hahn und Herrn Markus Hillenbrand, die wesentlichen Anteil an der Vorbereitung, Organisation und Planung haben. Und nicht zuletzt sei auch den Sponsoren gedankt, ohne deren Beitrag die Konferenz nicht in dieser Weise hätte ausgerichtet werden können.

Kaiserslautern, im Februar 2005

Paul Müller
Reinhard Gotzhein
Jens B. Schmitt

Organisation

Die 14. Fachtagung Kommunikation in Verteilten Systemen KiVS 2005 wird vom Fachbereich Informatik der Technischen Universität Kaiserslautern organisiert und in Kooperation mit der Gesellschaft für Informatik (GI) unter Beteiligung der Informationstechnischen Gesellschaft (ITG/VDE) in Kaiserslautern veranstaltet.

Exekutivkomitee

Vorsitz:	Paul Müller (TU Kaiserslautern) Reinhard Gotzhein (TU Kaiserslautern) Jens B. Schmitt (TU Kaiserslautern)
Organisation:	Markus Hillenbrand (TU Kaiserslautern) Ulrike Hahn (TU Kaiserslautern)

Programmkomitee

Sebastian Abeck	Universität Karlsruhe
Heribert Baldus	Philips Research Aachen
Gerold Blakowski	FH Stralsund
Torsten Braun	Universität Bern
Berthold Butscher	GMD-FOKUS Berlin
Georg Carle	Universität Tübingen
Joachim Charzinski	Siemens AG München, INC
Reinhold Eberhard	DaimlerChrysler AG
Jörg Eberspächer	TU München
Wolfgang Effelsberg	Universität Mannheim
Anja Feldmann	TU München
Stefan Fischer	Universität zu Lübeck
Kurt Geihs	TU Berlin
Boudewijn Haverkort	Universität Twente
Heinz-Gerd Hegering	Universität München
Ralf G. Herrtwich	DaimlerChrysler AG
Sven Hischke	Deutsche Telekom AG
Uwe Hübner	TU Chemnitz
Klaus Irmscher	Universität Leipzig
Peter Kaufmann	DFN-Verein Berlin
Ulrich Killat	TU Hamburg-Harburg
Hartmut König	BTU Cottbus
Paul J. Kühn	Universität Stuttgart
Winfried Lamersdorf	Universität Hamburg
Ralf Lehnert	TU Dresden
Christoph Lindemann	Universität Dortmund
Claudia Linnhoff-Popien	Universität München
Steffen Lipperts	Deutsche Telekom AG
Lothar Litz	TU Kaiserslautern
Norbert Luttenberger	Universität Kiel
Herman de Meer	Universität Passau
Peter Merz	TU Kaiserslautern
Christian Prehofer	DoCoMo Euro-Labs
Erwin Rathgeb	Universität Duisburg-Essen
Hartmut Ritter	Freie Universität Berlin
Kurt Rothermel	Universität Stuttgart
Alexander Schill	TU Dresden
Otto Spaniol	RWTH Aachen
Ralf Steinmetz	TU Darmstadt
Heinrich Stüttgen	NEC Europa
Ralph Urbansky	TU Kaiserslautern
Lars Wolf	TU Braunschweig
Bernd E. Wolfinger	Universität Hamburg
Adam Wolisz	TU Berlin
Martina Zitterbart	Universität Karlsruhe

Sponsoren

DaimlerChrysler AG
dpunkt.verlag GmbH
Enterasys Networks, Inc.
fgn GmbH
Fraunhofer-Institut für Experimentelles Software Engineering IESE
IBM Deutschland GmbH
Ministerium für Wissenschaft, Weiterbildung, Forschung und Kultur Rheinland-Pfalz
NEC Deutschland GmbH
PfalzKom GmbH
Profi Engineering Systems AG
Siemens AG
SUN Microsystems GmbH
TU Kaiserslautern

Inhaltsverzeichnis

I Verteilte Anwendungen

II Neue Middleware-Ansätze

III Drahtlose Netze

IV Leistungsmessung und -bewertung

V Methoden und Werkzeuge

VI Preisträger

Teil I

Verteilte Anwendungen

A Service-Oriented Peer-to-Peer Middleware

Jan Gerke[1] and Burkhard Stiller[2,1]

[1] Computer Engineering and Networks Laboratory TIK, Swiss Federal Institute of Technology, ETH Zurich, Switzerland

[2] Department of Informatics IFI, University of Zurich, Switzerland

Abstract Today, peer-to-peer (P2P) networks, e.g., filesharing networks like Gnutella, are specialised towards specific purposes. New P2P networks have to be created and installed to support new purposes. Furthermore, current P2P networks are almost impossible to use in business processes, because their lack of control makes them too unreliable. This paper addresses these problems by introducing a new middleware for P2P networks. The middleware supports the deployment and use of services inside a P2P network, independent of their purpose. It follows a modular design, thus allowing adaption through plug-ins. It includes negotiation mechanisms which can be used to configure a service according to a specific need. Furthermore, the middleware makes use of strong identities and offers mechanisms enabling the management of services through market forces, thus allowing the creation of legally enforceable contracts. Thus, it allows to reliably compose services into new value-added services. This paper also briefly describes the middleware's implementation and application in filesharing and wireless LAN scenarios.

1 Introduction

Recent years have seen two new trends in the Internet: Peer-to-Peer (P2P) networks and Service-orientation. On the one hand, pure P2P networks are completely decentralised, which makes them extremely fault-tolerant. However, existing P2P networks, e.g., filesharing networks like Gnutella [1] or instant-messaging networks like ICQ [2], are dedicated to specific purposes and do not allow to adapt their services to a user's need.

On the other hand service-orientation, especially the Web Services approach [3], which is driven by large companies like Microsoft and SUN as well as the World Wide Web Consortium supports the implementation of services of any kind. However, current approaches like .NET [4] contain centralised control mechanisms, giving the central controller enormous power over the complete system and its participants. A completely decentralised service platform would avoid this problem, and thus, pose lower entrance hurdles to new service providers. Furthermore, it would make it possible to reserve and release resources on short notice, thus also reducing the risk and effort involved in offering new services. Therefore, in [5] we proposed a service-oriented P2P architecture which merged the benefits of both approaches.

A service-oriented P2P network offers the potential of composing services, which are offered in a free and decentralised service market, into new services. However, this potential can only be fully used, if service compositions can rely on the services they are composed of. Thus, the delivery of services must be guaranteed, and it must be possible to adapt them to a service composition's need. As means to achieve this we propose to introduce service negotiations and service contracts into the service-oriented P2P network.

In this paper we present a middleware, which enables our architecture. It creates a service-oriented P2P network, which is not dedicated to a specific purpose and which is managed through market forces, i.e., the available supply of services and the demand for these services. Our middleware consists of modules with a fixed API, thus allowing the implementation of modules as plugins. It allows to adapt services to a user's needs through a negotiation process and supports legally enforceable service contracts, thus making it possible to build reliable service compositions.

This paper is structured as follows: Section 2 introduces the overall architecture and describes how the middleware approach is used to create the service-oriented P2P network. Section 3 presents the modular design of this middleware and Section 4 describes the negotiation of services and the service contracts. Section 5 briefly describes our implementation of the middleware and the service negotiation. Finally, Section 6 concludes the paper and identifies future work.

2 P2P Service Architecture

Our P2P network is not a physical network, but is built on top of of the Internet. This implies that the peers are Internet hosts and the links of the P2P network are end-to-end (e2e) connections through the Internet between such hosts. Thus, the set of hosts taking part in the P2P network and the e2e connections between them form an overlay network on top of the Internet, consisting of peers and links (cf. [5]). Thus, the notion of terms like 'link' or 'neighbour' is different in the Internet and in the overlay network. It is assumed that the connections provide e2e quality of service guarantees when required by services, regardless of the technology used to provide these guarantees, e.g., IntServ or DiffServ.

Every peer inside the network can provide and request services to and from other peers. We define the term service as functionality which is offered by a peer to other peers, and which can be accessed through input and output interfaces. Services are described through service descriptions, including service functionality and interfaces, but also characteristics such as terms of usage, e.g., prices and methods of payment. Services can be used by applications, which are programs running on peers which are not provided as services themselves and offer user interfaces.

A peer providing a service to another peer is acting as a service provider, while a peer which is using a service from another peer is acting as a service consuming peer. A single peer can take on both roles successively or even at the same time, if he provides a set of services to a set of peers and uses a set of other services from another set of peers. The service usage is always initiated by the service user, thus a service provider can not supply unrequested services to users or even demand payment for services delivered in such a fashion. Due to the dynamic nature of P2P networks, the duration of a service usage is restricted, i.e., it is not possible to rely on the availability of a certain service for weeks or months.

The service usage follows a one-to-one relationship between service user and provider, i.e., neither do several service users use the same service instance, nor do several service providers together provide a service to a user directly. Several service users can still use the same service at the same time, but in this case several service instances are created by the service provider and the services usages take place independently. Furthermore, a service provider can use services from other service providers, in order to provide a new value-added service to a service user. However, there will be no direct relation between these additional service providers and the service user. Examples of all variants of service usage described here are shown in Figure 1.

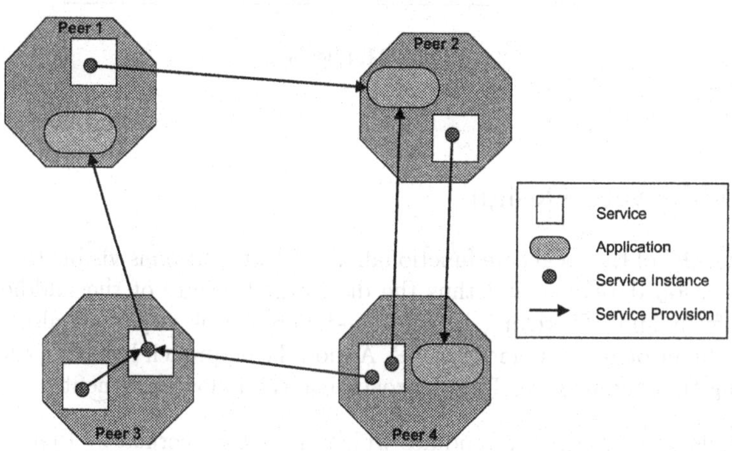

Fig. 1. The usage of services

In order to provide its functionality, a service needs to access local resources on the peer it is executed on. These resources can be external applications, hardware resources like computing power or storage space, or content like audio or video files. Services are executed in a runtime-environment on peers. Apart from executing the services, the peers must also manage and control the services and build and maintain the basic P2P network, e.g., through the creation of the overlay network. These tasks are carried out by the *core functionality* of each peer. Different implementations of this core functionality can exist on different platforms and access the local resources through platform dependent interfaces. However, all implementations follow a common standard of protocols to communicate with each other and offer a uniform interface to applications in the form of APIs (Application Programmers Interfaces). Thus, platform dependent details are hidden from the application and its programmers. Together, the core functionalities of all peers act as a middleware (cf. [6]), which makes it possible to treat the collection of all peers as a single service-oriented P2P network. Our view on the middleware is shown in Figure 2. Through the middleware the services running on the peers can be accessed, including their remote execution. Thus, services can become part of distributed applications.

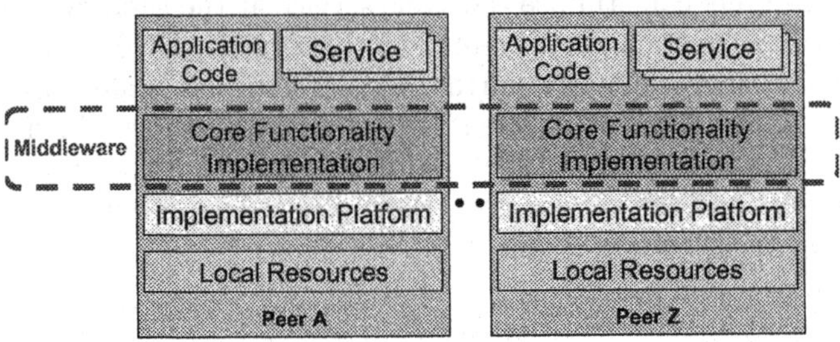

Fig. 2. Middleware

3 Middleware Design

Only the API of the local core functionality implementation is visible to a service or application developer and thus the distributed nature of the middleware is hidden from him. Therefore, in the remainder of this paper we also refer to the core functionality as 'middleware'. A modular approach has been chosen for designing this middleware. This approach has the following benefits:

- Details are hidden from modules which are not concerned by them.
- Implementors don't have to consider the complexity of the complete middleware but only the less complex single modules.
- It facilitates maintenance, especially plugging in new modules.

Our P2P middleware consists of six modules as shown in Figure 3. These modules belong to three different groups. The central group are the Service Support modules, namely the Service Negotiation and Service Management module. These modules are responsible for managing all service related information, i.e., all Service Descriptions and SLAs, and for controlling service execution. In order to enable the management of the services through market forces, additional functionality is provided by Market Management Modules, namely Pricing to determine the price of services in the market, and Accounting and Charging to collect information about service usage and calculate charges based on this information. Finally, the Enabling Modules provide basic functionalities needed to enable the P2P network and offer support to the other modules. The Search module is used to search and find services in the P2P network, and the Security module provides encryption and identity management to all other modules, especially access control to the Service Negotiation module.

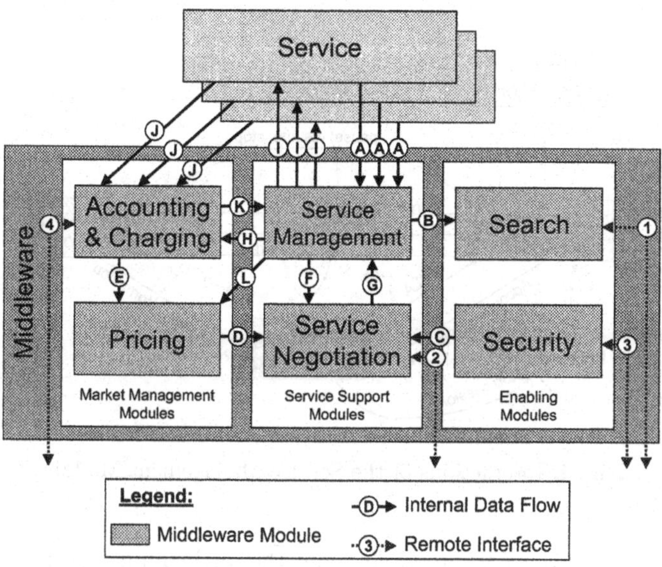

Fig. 3. The Modular Middleware

In Figure 3 an arrow going from a module A to a module B denotes a data flow from module A to module B. Dotted arrows denote remote interfaces, i.e., a module of one peer communicating with a module of the same type on another peer. When a new service is deployed, it sends its description to the local Service Management module via *interface A*. From there the service description is forwarded to the Search module via *interface B*. Thus, whenever a remote peer searches a service via the remote *interface 1*, the Search module can compare the requirements stated in the received service description to the service descriptions it has stored. If this comparison leads to a match, the remote peer can decide to negotiate the terms of service usage via the remote *interface 2*. In this case, the Service Negotiation module will first let the Security module check the remote peer's access rights. The results of this check are returned via *interface C*. In order to perform this check, i.e., to authenticate the remote peer, the Security module may contact other peers via the remote *interface 3*. The Pricing module calculates an appropriate price for the service requests and sends it to the Negotition module via *interface D*. In order to do so, it can retrieve information about past peer behaviour from the A&C module via *interface E*. Furthermore, it can be configured by the Service Management module via *interface L*, e.g., to support a new service or to adapt to a change in the service market. In order to make such decisions, the Service Management module can also retrieve information about the past from the A&C module via *interface K*. If a service negotiation is successful, the negotiation module uses *interface G* to send the final SLA to the Service Management module to start the service delivery. The resulting process of service delivery is shown in 4.

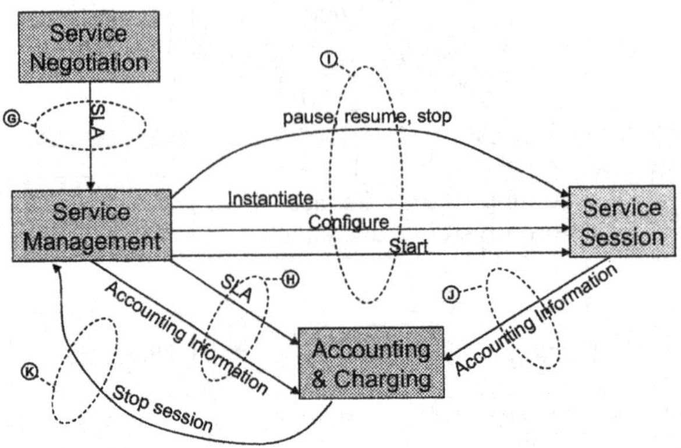

Fig. 4. Interactions of the Service Management Module

After informing the A&C module about the forthcoming service delivery via *interface I*, the Service Management module instantiates, configures and starts a new service session through *interface I*. During the service delivery, the service session reports its status by sending events to the A&C module via *interface J*. The A&C module compares these events against the SLA and informs the Service Management module via *interface K* when necessary, e.g., in the case of an SLA breach or when the service session has finished. The Service Management module controls the service delivery via *interface I*, e.g., stops it in the case of an SLA breach. For special purposes the A&C module can contact remote A&C modules, e.g., to receive an immediate payment through tokens (cf. [7]).

4 Service Negotiation

In general, after candidate services have been discovered by the Search module, there are two ways to achieve a legally binding SLA. Either reverse auctions or bilateral negotiations can be used. However, it is unlikely that all candidate services are exactly the same. This makes it at least difficult to compare them in a classical auction where only the price may change. Furthermore, service users may have to adapt service parameters individually, which is not supported by classical auction mechanisms. Therefore, the middleware supports bilateral negotiations instead of auctions, similar to the real world case of inviting service offers, e.g., when building a house.

In order to negotiate the terms of service usage, a potential service user sends service requests to his local Service Negotiation module. This module then contacts the Service Negotiation module of the potential service provider via the remote interface 2 which is encapsulated within the Service Negotiation modules. The Service Negotiation module of the potential service provider processes these requests and sends back its answers via the same remote interface. A potential service user will try to settle for a service which fulfils his requirements while implying only small or no costs. At the same time he will try to keep his search and negotiation effort low.

4.1 Service Level Agreements

A negotiation consists of a series of service requests by the potential user and service offers by the potential provider. Of special importance for the Service Negotiation protocols is the data contained within these messages. These are the SLAs specifying the terms of a service provision, which are needed to request the service and to act as enforceable contract if the negotiation is successful. Otherwise the negotiation is aborted by either of the involved parties. Every SLA states the terms of service usage, including parameters like bandwidth for transmitting data or the Tariff the service provider will use to calculate charges for the usage of the service. Since the final SLA needs to be legally enforceable, it has to be signed by both parties. Thus, it can't be forged later on and can act as proof of the contract and its terms. After the SLA has been signed, the service can be provided and used.

In order to fulfil the SLA, the SLA must be specified in a formal way which the middleware modules can interpret. However, it is must also be possible to generate another presentation of the SLA which can be easily read and understood by human users. Every SLA contains the following information:

- Identities: The service user and the service provider must be specified through identifiers which are unique within the complete P2P network.
- Authentication: The SLA must be electronically signed by the service user and the service provider.
- Service Description: The SLA must contain the service description which was valid at the time of the negotiation.
- Service Parameters: During negotiation the service user and the service provider can negotiate various service parameters, e.g., the bandwidth a video streaming service will use. These parameters have to be specified in the SLA by key/value pairs.
- Duration: The duration of the service delivery phase has to be specified. This can happen in different forms, e.g., a fixed start and end time, a fixed duration or even an unlimited duration with a possible service abort by either user or provider. Terms of duration extension can also be specified.
- Payment: The SLA must also describe whether the service provider charges money for the service usage and how much. Various charging schemes can be employed, e.g., a fixed amount has to be paid for the service usage or the

amount is proportional to the time the service is used. Another important information is how the service user will pay for his service usage, e.g., by bank transfer, by credit card or by electronic online payments.

4.2 Service Provider Side

On the provider side, the Service Negotiation module uses three other modules during the execution of its task. The Security module checks identities and provides access control for the requesting user via interface C. The Pricing module calculates appropriate Tariffs for the requested service and sends them to the Service Negotiation module via interface D. Finally, the Service Management module accepts or rejects a service request or even sends a counter proposal through interface F. If the terms of service usage are successfully negotiated, the agreement is sent to the Service Management module via interface G, including all parameters agreed upon. In order to illustrate the use of the Service Negotiation module on the provider side, the sequence chart in Figure 5 shows the interactions taking place.

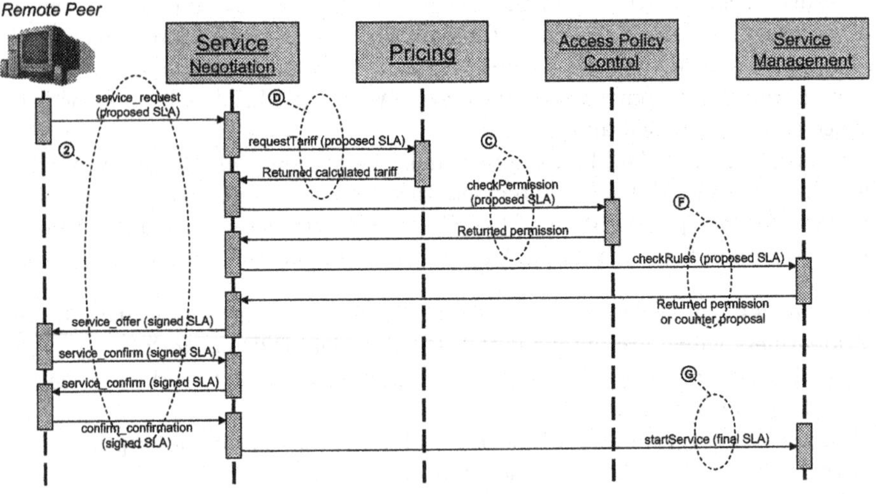

Fig. 5. Service Negotiation on the Provider Side

The sequence chart also shows an important implementation detail: The middleware modules do not carry out continous activities. An activity is ended after sending a message to another module. Responses to the message always start a new activity. This prohibits the waste of local resources and enables the modules to efficiently support parallel requests coming in from different peers or middleware modules. The interactions of the Service Negotiation module are described in detail in the following.

1. After an promising service has been found during the Service Search phase, its potential user sends a service request to the Service Negotiation module of the peer which provides this service. This service request includes a detailed description of the service parameters in form of an initial SLA.
2. The Service Negotiation module forwards this SLA to the Pricing module, in order to obtain a suitable Tariff for the requested service or to decide whether a Tariff proposed by the potential user is economically acceptable.
3. The Service Negotiation module forwards the SLA to the Access Control within the Security module, in order to determine whether the potential user has the right to use the requested service.
4. The Service Negotiation module forwards the SLA to the Service Management module which checks whether the service request can be fulfilled. According to the outcome of this check, it then accepts or rejects the SLA and sends its decision back to the Service Negotiation module. Additionally, it can make a counterproposal by changing the SLA.
5. The Service Negotiation module sends the SLA back to the requesting peer after having made necessary adaptions to it. There are two extreme cases. On the one hand the Service Negotiation module might not make any adaptions at all, indicating that the service can be provided as requested. On the other hand the Service Negotiation module might send back a very short or even empty SLA, indicating that the service will not be provided to the requesting peer at all. Otherwise, steps 1 to 4 may be repeated several times.
6. If the SLA offered by the provider satisfies the user, he sends a confirmation message back to the provider. In order to have a legal proof of the agreement, he signs this SLA by encrypting it with his private key. The provider can then verify it with the user's public key.
7. The provider also confirms the agreement by signing the SLA accordingly and sending it back to the user.
8. The user confirms that he has received the confirmation, thus finishing a three-way handshake and indicating that he is ready to receive the service.
9. The Service Negotiation module orders the Service Management module to start the requested service with the service parameters specified in the SLA.

4.3 Service User Side

On the other hand, the Service Negotiation module on the user side interacts directly with the user or a user agent acting on behalf of the user. This interaction does not take place via an internal middleware interface. Rather, it is an interaction between the middleware and application code (cf. Figure 2), which implements a graphical user interface or a user agent. Initially, the user or his agent starts the negotiation by contacting his local Service Negotiation module. During the negotiation he is informed whenever a new service offer or service confirmation arrives from the service provider. He then reacts upon this message by either sending a new request, confirming the offer or confirming the confirmation. In order to illustrate the use of the Service Negotiation module on the user side, the sequence chart in Figure 6 describes the interactions which take place on the user side during a successful negotiation. They are described in more detail in the following.

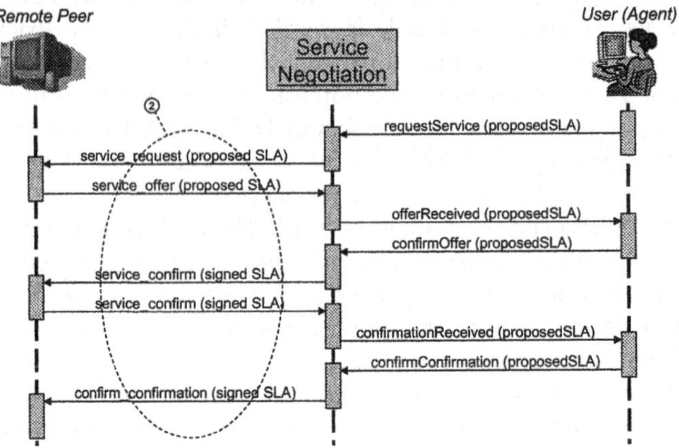

Fig. 6. Service Negotiation on the User Side

1. The user creates an initial SLA describing the terms of service usage he is aiming for. He sends this SLA to his local Service Negotiation module, which forwards it to the service provider via an encrypted communication channel.
2. Via the same channel the local Service Negotiation module receives a service offer from the provider, which is specified in an SLA. This SLA is forwarded to the user, so that he can decide how to proceed.
3. If the user agrees to the offer he received, he instructs his local Service Negotiation module to confirm the offer. The Service Negotiation module does this by signing the SLA describing the offer with the user's private key and sending it to the provider.
4. The local Service Negotiation module receives back the SLA which has now also been signed with the provider's private key. It forwards this enforceable contract to the user, who is thereby informed that the provider has confirmed the contract and he can await service delivery.
5. Finally, the user instructs its Service Negotiation module to confirm the provider's confirmation. Thus, the Service Negotiation module signs the SLA a second time and sends it to the provider. This three-way handshake ensures, that now user can avoid paying for a service by claiming he never received the provider's confirmation.

4.4 Security Considerations

The Security module provides access control functionality to the Service Negotiation module via interface C. In order to provide its functionality, the Security module implements cryptography and authentication mechanisms. For this purpose it utilizes key management mechanisms. Its encryption functionality is also used to ensure privacy, i.e., to provide secure communication channels between two peers, which are used during the whole negotiation process and can also be used by other modules, e.g., for communicating with remote A&C modules or for the service communication itself. Furthermore, the Security module allows a peer to sign an SLA using its private key and others to verify this SLA using the corresponding public key. Thus, the SLAs represent enforcable contracts which make service delivery reliable enough to create service compositions. Carrying out key management requires communication with remote Security modules, e.g., key management. This communication takes place via interface 3 which is encapsulated within the Security module.

5 Implementation and Evaluation

An extended version of the middleware [10] has been implemented as a prototype within the MMAPPS project [11]. The implementation is based on the JXTA framework [12], which was used as an implementation platform to provide the basic P2P networking functionality, including unique peer IDs, message routing through rendezvous peers and pipes as a communication channel between two peers. The only drawback of using JXTA which was discovered during the implementation, was the search mechanism which turned out to be difficult to extend to support generic service descriptions.

The service negotiation protocol has been based on encrypted bidirectional JXTA pipes provided by the Security module. So far, key management in the prototype has been done by hand. While public key infrastructures (PKIs) could be used to carry out this task, this would introduce a centralised component into the P2P network. This can be avoided by making use of a decentralised key management infrastructure, similar to a Web of Trust [8] built upon OpenPGP [9]. The SLAs exchanged through the negotiation protocol take the form of XML documents which contain key-value pairs which transport generic information (e.g., peer ids) as well as service specific information (e.g., the name of a file to download).

Based on the middleware implementation several demonstration scenarios where created by the MMAPPS consortium. First of all, two classical filesharing applications have been created which are based on files which are offered by downloading services. The difference between the two filesharing applications lies in the charging applied to the service. The first only uses local charging, not resulting in any form of payment, similar to current filesharing networks. On the other hand, the second makes use of a token-based accounting and charging scheme which has been described in [7]. The middleware has also been used to implement a collobaration platform for radiologists, where radiologists exchange and evaluate x-rays and reports done by their colleagues. Furthermore, the middleware has been used to implement a scenario where WLAN access has been offered in a P2P fashion [13]. All scenarios have been described in detail in [14].

The middleware performed well in practical tests of the scenarios described above. The modular nature of the middleware and the fixed APIs of the modules allowed application designers to use it efficiently. Furthermore, the negotiation protocol and the SLAs supported the exchange of service specific data without any adaptions to the middleware. No significant network overhead created by the middleware was noticed. This was to be expected, as the middleware design itself does not impose any significant additional network load in comparison to existing P2P networks, since additional communication for service negotiation only occurs between pairs of peers and only when a service is about to be used. However, the question of scalability of service searches is another matter and currently depends on the underlying JXTA platform. The MMAPPS project has investigated scalable mechanisms for service search (cf. [15]), but these have not yet been implemented as a middleware Search module.

6 Summary and Conclusions

In this paper we have presented the design of a middleware which enables a service-oriented P2P network. A modular approach has been chosen, which makes it easy to adapt and extend the functionality through plug-ins. The middleware modules create the basic P2P overlay network by providing distributed search, but also enable the provision and use of services through the use of service descriptions, the negotiation of service level agreements (SLAs), and the execution of services. Furthermore, mechanisms for managing identities and encrypting communication are provided, which are used for access control and for ensuring privacy during service negotiation and the exchange of accounting information, as well as the service communication itself. They also enable the creation of legally enforceable service contracts by requiring service users and providers to sign final SLAs, thus allowing the creation of reliable service compositions. The provision of pricing, accounting and charging functionality enables the management of services through market forces.

The middleware has been implemented based on the JXTA framework. It has been used in two filesharing and a wireless LAN scenario, giving a strong proof-of-concept of the middleware design. More applications based on the middleware are currently being developed within the MMAPPS project, and will be used in field trials with real users. This will further demonstrate the practical applicability of the middleware.

Our middleware design allows the use of one P2P network for various services, eliminating the need for the design, implementation and installation of a new P2P network for every new application. Furthermore, it allows to find and compare similar services in a distributed service market. Since every peer taking part has a strong identity, it is possible to create legally enforceable contracts, which enables the management of services through market forces and the reliable composition of services into new value-added services. Future work includes the detailed evaluation of the middleware in user trials, the replacement of the search mechanism offered by JXTA to improve scalability and service matching, and the support of n-to-one services, like swarm delivery of files (cf. [16]).

The authors want to thank their partners from the MMAPPS project for their valuable input to this work, especially to the implementation of the middleware modules, and their colleague Arno Wagner for his help in writing this paper.

7 References

1. Clip2: The Gnutella Protocol Specification v0.4; http://www9.limewire.com/developer/gnutella_protocol_0.4.pdf, 2004
2. ICQ Inc.: What is ICQ? - About community; http://www.icq.com/products/whatisicq.html, 2004
3. World Wide Web Consortium: Web Services Activity Statement; http://www.w3c.org/2002/ws/Activity, 2004
4. Microsoft Developer Network: .NET Framework Product Overview; http://msdn.microsoft.com/netframework/technologyinfo/overview/, 2004
5. J. Gerke, D. Hausheer, J. Mischke, B. Stiller: An Architecture for a Service Oriented Peer-to-Peer System (SOPPS); In Praxis der Informationsverarbeitung und Kommunikation (PIK), No. 2, 2003
6. P. Bernstein: Middleware: A Model for Distributed Systems Services; In Communications of the ACM, pp. 86-98, February, 1996
7. D. Hausheer, N. Liebau, A. Mauthe, R. Steinmetz, B. Stiller: Towards A Market Managed Peer-to-Peer File Sharing System Using Token-based Accounting and Distributed Pricing; TIK Report Nr. 179, ETH Zrich, TIK, August, 2003
8. R. Khare and A. Rifkin: Weaving a Web of Trust; In security special issue of the World Wide Web Journal, Volume 2, Number 3, Summer 1997
9. J. Callas, L. Donnerhacke, H. Finney, R. Thayer: OpenPGP Message Format; RFC 2440, November 1998
10. J. Gerke (Editor): Specification and Implementation of the Peer-to-Peer Middleware (Final); Deliverable D10 of the MMAPPS Project, 2004
11. MMAPPS Consortium: MMAPPS - Market Management of Peer-to-Peer Services; Project homepage, http://www.mmapps.org, 2004
12. Project JXTA: JXTA Framework; URL: http://www.jxta.org/, 2004
13. E. Efstathiou and G. Polyzos: A Peer-to-Peer Approach to Wireless LAN Roaming; The First ACM International Workshop on Wireless Mobile Applications and Services on WLAN Hotspots (WMASH 2003), San Diego, California, USA, September, 2003
14. J. Farr (Editor): Specification and Prototyping of Peer-to-Peer Services; Deliverable D14 of the MMAPPS Project, 2004
15. V. Darlagiannis, A. Mauthe, R. Steinmetz: Overlay Design Mechanisms; To appear in the 3rd issue of 2004 of the Journal of Network and Systems Management, Special Issue on Distributed Management, 2004.
16. MetaMachine: eDonkey2000 - Overnet; http://www.overnet.com, 2004

Token-Based Accounting for P2P-Systems

Nicolas C. Liebau[1], Vasilios Darlagiannis[1], Andreas Mauthe[1] and Ralf Steinmetz[1]

Multimedia Communications Lab, KOM
Darmstadt University of Technology, Germany
[Nicolas.Liebau|Vasilios.Darlagiannis|Andreas.Mauthe|
Ralf.Steinmetz]@kom.tu-darmstadt.de

Abstract This paper presents a token-based accounting scheme for decentralized autonomous systems, such as peer-to-peer systems. The scheme uses tokens as proof of resource or service usage. Conforming to the peer-to-peer paradigm, the tokens are issued using a decentralized mechanism. Within peer-to-peer systems the proposed accounting scheme can be used to overcome information deficits. Thus, it constitutes the basis for coordination and control mechanisms as well as for pricing in commercial scenarios in fully decentralized systems. The presented scheme is compared against an alterative approach showing the advantage of the token-based scheme in terms of communication costs.

1 Introduction

The design of the first peer-to-peer (P2P) systems was based on the assumption that participating peers share their own resources with other peers while they benefit from resources that are shared by others. Through resource replication and utilization of otherwise unused resources, P2P systems can provide higher robustness and host more content/information at lower costs than traditional client/server-based applications. Actual P2P file sharing systems like eDonkey2000 [2] host huge amount of content. Users of P2P file sharing applications are accepting performance constraints compared with client/server systems because they are retrieving content at virtually no cost. One reason for this reduced performance of P2P systems is in the opportunistic behavior of the participants who try to maximize there own utilization. Participants try to benefit as much as possible from the resources provided by the other members of the system; however, they try to avoid providing resources themselves. The most familiar example is the free-riding phenomenon in P2P systems [4]. This behavior pattern is fostered through the strong anonymity and the enormous lack of information in P2P systems. Actions cannot be traced back to users. Therefore, resource or service usage and provisioning is not attributable to users. Thus, it is hard to give incentives for resource provisioning, or, as a further step, to implement and enforce rules about participant behavior in the system. The result is the aforementioned weaker performance of P2P systems in comparison to a client/server alternative. The weaker performance also makes P2P systems unattractive for commercial applications.

To overcome this disadvantage the lack of available information must be resolved. An accounting mechanism for P2P systems is required to provide the missing information. Using this information, coordination of the available resources becomes feasible in order to improve the overall system performance. Coordination can be achieved e.g. through the introduction of rules and rule enforcement supported by the information an accounting mechanism has been collecting. However, the design of such mechanisms for decentralized autonomous systems is not trivial because the control mechanism cannot be decoupled completely from the accounting mechanism. The absence of a controller that analyzes the gathered information and coordinates the system entities requires that the accounting mechanism includes the coordination functionality. Thus, the accounting mechanism itself must enable the ability to constraint the participants' behavior.

For a distributed accounting system that also enables coordination, it is required that the collected accounting data is held in a robust and secure way so that no important information is lost. Further, the accounting information must be collected and held in a trustworthy manner. If the information is used for system coordination, participants may be tempted to modify information for their own benefit. Moreover, the accounting mechanism should be scalable and the net benefit of using it should be positive across the complete system. If the accounting mechanism is supposed to be used in different scenarios it should be flexible to support different kinds of coordination mechanisms.

To tackle the discussed problem this paper proposes a token-based accounting scheme. Tokens serve as signed receipts for transactions between peers. Further, tokens represent the transaction history of peers and allow for monitoring and control of the account balance of all participants in a system by means of appropriate aggregation mechanisms.

2 Related Work

There are several design alternatives for distributed accounting systems. Essentially, accounting data is collected in form of receipts. The information stored in a receipt can vary from a single number to detailed transaction data. For the purpose of coordination, for every peer the data stored in its receipts is aggregated to an account balance. The balance determines if a peer is allowed to use further resources from the system or if it first has to provide more own resources. However, a major characteristic that distinguishes different accounting schemes is the location of the stored receipts.

Local Accounts. Using local accounts, a receipt is generated for each transaction and participating peer. Receipts are stored locally on the peers. To enhance the trustworthiness of receipts they can be signed by the transaction partner. P2P accounting systems using local accounts scale well because there is no communication with further parties. Today local accounts are used e.g. in eMule's credit system [3] to determine other peers' position in the local download queue. This mechanism tries to achieve local fairness; global coordination is not its goal. With local accounts all information about a peer is derived directly from the peer itself. Even if the receipts are signed by the transaction partner, fraud is easily possible through malicious collaboration.

Remote Accounts. This alternative tries to overcome the trust problem of local accounts by storing accounting information at third party peers. Each account is located at set of "account peers" to achieve robustness. The account peers are usually organized in a Distributed Hash Table (DHT) for efficiency reasons. In [5,11,19] this approach is applied. In [5] issued tokens are used as a kind of a virtual currency, which is transferred between the remote accounts during a transaction. For trust reasons receipts can be signed either by transaction partners or (ideally) by multiple trustworthy peers. The trust level in such a system is high. This is achieved through additional network traffic per transaction for querying accounts, signing receipts, storing receipts and keeping the accounts consistent.

Central Accounts. This alternative uses a central network administrator to collect receipts and to distribute the usage of network resources among the participants in a fair way. For instance, for Grid Computing such a system is presented in [6]. However, our goal is to avoid central elements in P2P systems.

Token-based Systems. An alternative to using receipts is to use tokens. Tokens are issued receipts why their availability could be limited. Peers spend tokens with other peers to receive a service. If a peer runs out of tokens the peer is not eligible for using more system resources. The tokens must be protected against forging and double spending. Storing tokens is not different from normal receipts. Often tokens are used as a virtual currency. Doing so, the trust problem of local storage is bypassed, because these tokens do not contain any accounting information that might be altered. Token-based systems require that the token issuer is trustworthy. There are three alternatives for the token issuer: (a) Each single peer can issue tokens. This way the trust problem is bypassed. However, introducing rules and rule enforcement become impossible because there is no control on the amount of tokens issued. Such an approach is shown in [15]. The authors claim that eventually a completely free stable market will develop. Further, in [18] self-issued tokens are used for accounting in Grid Computing. (b) A central, trusted "bank" issues the tokens. Mojo Nation uses this solution as well as some existing micro payment schemes like NetCash [13]. A micro payment scheme especially tailored to P2P systems is presented in [20]. The goal of this work is to reduce the load on the central broker. However, the use of a central entity is contrary to our goal of designing a decentralized P2P system. (c) A quorum of peers signs the tokens using a shared private key. If the private key is kept secret such a system combines scalability and trustworthiness. This solution is used in the presented approach.

3 The Token-Based Accounting System

Prerequisites. The token-based accounting system assumes that users can clearly be identified through a permanent id, (e.g. through a private/public key pair proven through a certificate issued from a certification authority). Depending on the application scenario, alternative approaches like [1] are also applicable. Apart from the certification authority it is intended to avoid any central element.

Further, we assume the use of a reputation mechanism in the P2P system. This system is used to publish fraudulent behavior that technical mechanisms cannot detect. The reputation mechanism assigns a reputation value to each peer that represents the trustworthiness of the peer. A possible solution is presented e.g. in [12].

3.1 Overview

The primary goal of the proposed system is to collect accounting data and to enable system-wide coordination of resource service usage based on the collected information. To enable the usage of receipts for coordination in a distributed system, the receipts must have the basic characteristic of the resources and services they represent, i.e. they must be scarce. Therefore, the receipts must be issued. Accordingly, every user has a limited amount of receipts it can use in transactions. Thus, in the presented approach tokens are used rather as issued receipts than as a virtual currency. As a result, the tokens must not have the characteristics of micro payments of anonymity and untraceability [8]. Therefore, tokens have a clear owner that is contained in the token. This enables local tokens storage. Otherwise (if anonymity should be maintained) untraceable tokens have to be stored at trusted remote accounts to control double spending.

Each peer holds an account with a specific amount of tokens clearly issued to it. A peer spends a token by sending it to its transaction partner in order to receive a service. Accordingly, when a peer provides a service it collects foreign tokens from other peers. Peers cannot spend foreign tokens. Using the token aggregation process, peers exchange the collected foreign tokens against new ones. To achieve trustworthiness new tokens are signed with the systems shared private key using threshold cryptography [10]. Thus, a token must be signed by a quorum of peers to become valid. The token structure ensures protection against forgery, double spending and stealing. The three basic protocols of the token-based accounting system are *Token Aggregation*, *Check for Double Spending*, and *Payment*.

3.2 Token Structure

Figure 1 shows the information contained in a token. A new unused token contains the first 5 information fields starting from the right hand of the figure. The issuing date and time in milliseconds together with the serial number and the owner id serve as unique identification of a token. This is required to enable the detection of double spending. Further, this way double spending can be traced to the owner. During the creation of a batch of new tokens the serial number is randomly selected for every token. Thereby, guessing which tokens exist in the system becomes hard. The account id is used to allocate a token clearly to a specific application. Cross application usage and trade of tokens is possible. This field is optional. The fifth field contains the signature of the information contained in the first four fields, signed with the system's private key. This prevents forgery.

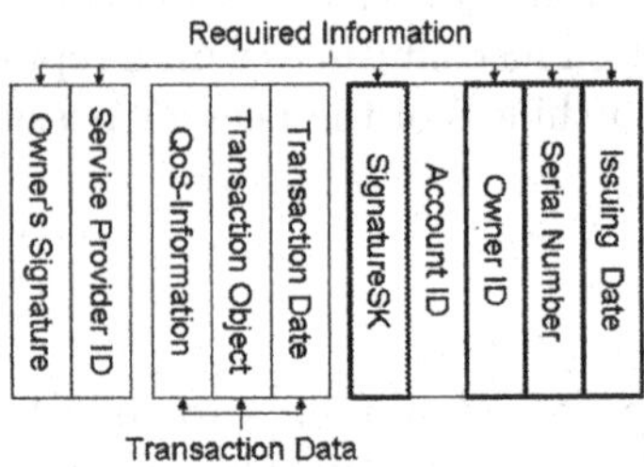

Fig. 1. Token Structure

Since a token is basically a receipt, it contains further information about the transaction for which a token is used. The service consumer is the token owner.

Before the owner sends the token to the service provider, it also adds the service provider's id to the token as well as information about the transaction (such as transaction object, date and information about the quality of the service provisioning). The owner finally signs the complete token using its private key. Subsequently, the contained information cannot be changed by the service provider. The required information in a token is the information needed for unique identification, i.e. the system signature, the service provider as well as the service providers signature. This prevents tokens from being stolen. Because unused tokens contain the owner, only the owner can spend them. Used tokens are signed and contain the receiver of the token. Only the receiver is allowed to exchange tokens against new, own tokens. A token has no intrinsic value; it rather presents an accounting event. The value of a token is determined in the token aggregation process.

3.3 Token Aggregation

The Token Aggregation process is used to exchange foreign tokens a peer collected for new tokens issued to that peer. The eight-step Token Aggregation procedure is shown in Figure 2 (a).

First the *exchanging peer* EP locates a *trusted peer* TP (1). Trusted peers are eligible to exchange tokens and possess one part of the system's private key [10]. EP sends its N collected foreign tokens $(Fn_1, ..., Fn_N)$ to TP (2). TP checks the foreign tokens for their validity. Only tokens signed by the owner and spent only once are valid for exchange.

Using the aggregation function $M = A(Fn_1, ..., Fn_N)$ TP calculates the amount M of new tokens EP must receive in return for the foreign tokens. The aggregation function is public and can take any form. TP now creates M new, unsigned tokens $(Un_1, ..., Un_M)$ (3).

To sign the new tokens with the system's private key using threshold cryptography [10] TP now locates further trusted peers (4). EP is not allowed to choose the quorum of trusted peers itself. This alleviates the problem of potential collaboration and fraud. The number of required trusted peers to sign a token is determined by the used secret sharing scheme. The system's trustworthiness increases proportional with the size of the quorum of trusted peers.

TP sends the new tokens to this quorum of trusted peers (5). Each peer of the quorum signs now the tokens with its part of the system's private key (6). The resulting partial tokens $(Pn_1, ..., Pn_M)$ are transmitted back to EP (7). Finally, EP combines the partial tokens to new complete tokens $(Tn_1, ..., Tn_M)$ (8).

It is important to mention that the aggregation function adds an additional degree of freedom to the system. With an appropriate aggregation function specific economic systems can be implemented.

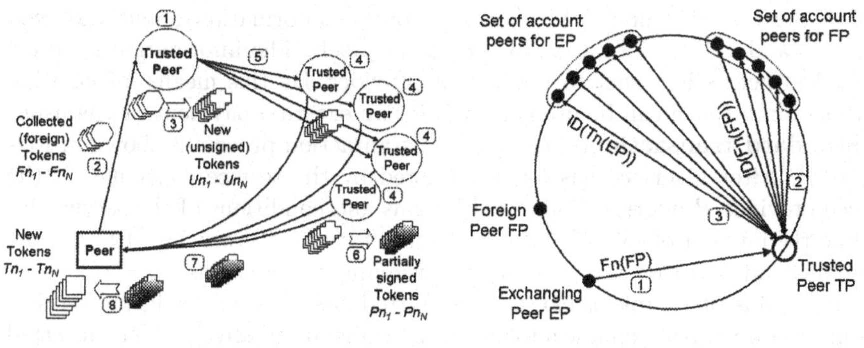

(a) Token Aggregation Process (b) Check for Double Spending

Fig. 2. Token Operations

3.4 Check for Double Spending

To check for double spending a token must be clearly identifiable. To facilitate the check in an efficient manner, for every peer (the account owners) there is a set of account holding peers, i.e. the *account holder set*. The account holder peers are organized in a DHT manner, such as Pastry [17] (see Figure 2 (b)). Account holders hold a list of tokens currently issued to the account owner. The list is filled with the required information during token aggregation. After new tokens have been created (Figure 2 (a), step 3), TP sends a list of these new tokens to the exchanging peers account holders (Figure 2 (b), step 3).

During the token validity check of the token aggregation process, TP will ask the account holders responsible for a token, if the token is valid (Figure 2 (b), step 2). The account holders will remove the token from the list. Accordingly, if the token is not in the list, it is an invalid token. TP will discard such a token and the P2P system's reputation mechanism will be informed about the incident.

In order to avoid message manipulation, every message sent to the account holders must be signed with the senders private key. To keep the list between the account holders consistent, all account holders for one specific account exchange the list whenever the set of account holders change. This takes place only when peers of that set join or depart from the system. Consistency checks are only necessary, if the sender does not receive all confirmation messages.

3.5 Transactions

During transactions the token-based accounting system accounts for resource usage, service usage, or a combination of both. Service usage is valued differently than resource usage. A service for example detects water marks in pictures. Since special software is needed to provide such a service, it is valued higher than the sum of the used resources. A token can contain information about the used resources and value information of the service itself. The information is added to a token before it is sent to the service provider. By this means information contained in a token can be used as basis for an external payment mechanism.

Standard transaction. The standard transaction process is shown in Figure 3 (a). After a service has been requested by the service consumer C, the service provider P informs C about the terms and conditions of the service, including the number of tokens P it expects in return for the service. If C accepts the terms and conditions, the service provisioning phase begins.

During this phase tokens can be transmitted before, after, or during the service provisioning. For example a token can be transmitted after 1 MB transferred or after 1 minute service received. Before a token is transmitted, C fills in the required accounting information. C has no intention to falsify the information, because it influences only the token exchange of P. Then C signs the token with its own private key and sends it to P. P checks the signature of the received token using C's public key, which can be contained in the token as owner id or transmitted with the service request. Thus, it can be verified, that the token sender is also the token owner.

P can choose not to continue to provide the service, if the contained accounting data was incorrect. As a result of each transaction C's own token balance decreases and P's foreign token balance increases.

Trustable transaction. In a scenario where tokens are used as virtual currency, a more trustworthy settlement process might be required. Here, the transaction party that delivers last has an incentive to cheat the other party. It still receives the full benefit but does not have to deliver its part of the deal. Therefore, we have designed and implemented a trustable payment procedure that eliminates the incentive to cheat for the transaction partners. In addition, double spending of tokens is not only detectable, but becomes impossible. Figure 3 (b) shows the procedure. After a service request is received, P notifies C about the conditions and terms of the transaction, including the required amount of tokens. C answers with the token ids of the tokens it intends to spend for the transaction. Now P contacts the account holders responsible for C *AH(C)* and checks if the tokens are valid. *AH(C)* mark in the token list these tokens as "*planned to spend*". Using the same tokens in another transaction becomes impossible. If all tokens are valid, P informs C that the transaction phase can begin. C starts the transaction by sending an unsigned token to P. C loses the token. However, since it is not signed by C, P cannot exchange it against own tokens. P has no incentive not to provide the service. Therefore, P now provides the agreed service. Because C already lost the token, it has no intention keeping the token for itself. C will sign the token and send it to P. If C should fail to send the signed token, P can present the unsigned token to *AH(C)*. The possession of the token proofs that the transaction had started and the token will be removed from the list and is finally lost for C. The aforementioned reputation system provides further incentives against such malicious behavior. On the other hand, if both peers are consenting to cancel the transaction, C does not lose its tokens. The "*planned to spend*"-mark just needs to be removed from the tokens in the token list at *AH(C)*.

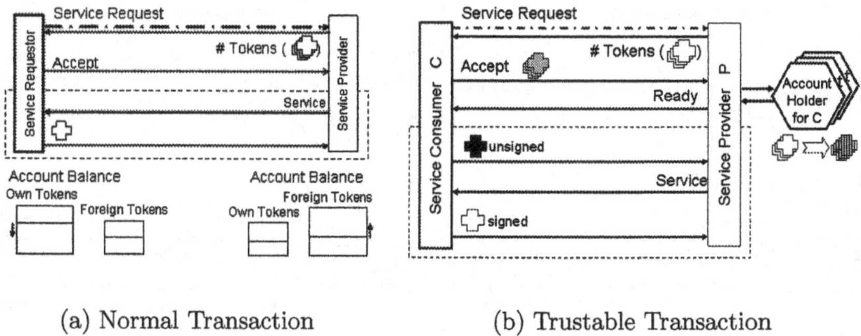

(a) Normal Transaction (b) Trustable Transaction

Fig. 3. Transaction Procedures

4 Trust & Security Considerations

It is crucial for the use of an accounting mechanism that the information it provides is correct. Therefore, the token-based system has been designed to provide a high degree of trust for distributed systems.

Robbery. Tokens were designed to eliminate robbery. Tokens contain the owner id that cannot be changed without detection through the system signature. Spent tokens contain the token receiver secured through the owner's signature.

Forgery. The system signature on each token ensures that the basic token data cannot be changed and that no peer can create tokens itself. Thus, the system signature prevents forgery and is crucial for the trustworthiness of the system. Accordingly, fraudulent collaboration of trusted peers must be avoided.

This can be achieved if in a quorum of trusted peers is at least one trustworthy peer. The probability of a quorum consisting of at least one good peer can be determined using the hypergeometric distribution. The resulting probability p defines the trust level of the system according to:

$$p(T, t, p_g) = \frac{\binom{T \cdot (1 - p_g)}{t}}{\binom{T}{t}}, \text{ where } \begin{array}{ll} T & \text{number of trusted peers} \\ t & \text{quorum size} \\ p_g & \text{percentage of good peers} \end{array}$$

Figure 4 shows the required quorum size for specific trust levels. Moreover, because the trusted peers are not aware which other peers belong to a quorum, having only bad peers in a quorum does not mean that this results in fraud. The chosen trusted peers must also collaborate. Thus, the quorum peers must know which other peers have been chosen for the quorum.

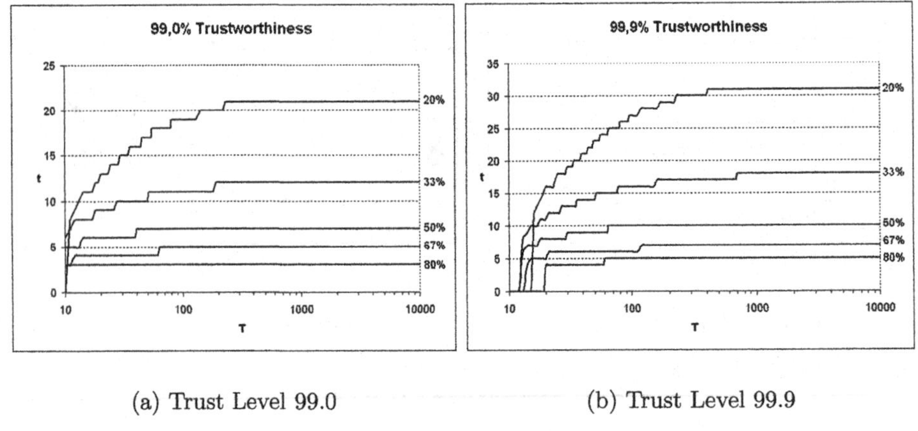

(a) Trust Level 99.0 (b) Trust Level 99.9

Fig. 4. Required Quorum Size for Trust Levels by Percentage of Good Peers

Furthermore, peers can only become trusted and receive a part of the shared system private key, if their reputation is above a specific threshold value. Accordingly, the proportion of bad peers among the trusted peers can be assumed less than the proportion of bad peers in the whole system. The actual trust threshold value depends on the used reputation system.

Additionally, threshold cryptography provides different proactive mechanisms to secure the key from being compromised. The key parts will be updated periodically using proactive secret sharing [16]. This makes the old key parts obsolete without changing the actual key. The system's public key remains the same. Further, a new system key will be created periodically using the decentralized method presented in [7]. This is enforced through tokens being valid only for a specific period of time. Therefore, the unique token id contains the creation date and time. Outdated tokens can be exchanged for new tokens using the Token Aggregation process. If the system's private key is kept secret the system can be considered secure.

Double Spending. The verification for double spending relies on the data hold at the account holders. Thus, users might try to corrupt their token list at the account holders. This is avoided by not allowing peers to send any queries or enquiries to the account list. Rule breaches are reported to the reputation system. Further, the token list at the account holders is a positive list. If a peer plans to double spend a token, it has to avoid that the token is marked in the list as planned-to-spend and later removed from it during token aggregation; though in both actions the peer is not involved.

Malicious peers trying to remove tokens from the token list of another peer must guess token ids of existing tokens. That is very hard because the creation date and time in milliseconds and the random serial number have to be guessed correctly. Therefore, this kind of messages is obvious malicious behavior and will be reported to the reputation system.

In P2P systems (even if using a DHT) it cannot be guaranteed that a remote account at the account holders is never lost. In such a case the account owning peer would not be eligible to receive services anymore. Since in the token-based system the tokens are stored locally, users can secure themselves against loss by making a backup of their tokens. The loss of an account at the account holders will just influence the ability to check for double spending. Since a peer can not notice if its remote account is lost, it must assume that double spending would still be detected. Hence, it will be discouraged to cheat.

5 Performance Analysis

We have implemented the token-based accounting system based on JXTA 2.2.1 [14]. Measurements of message sizes were used to simulate the accounting scheme with the simulator presented in [9].

To study the performance of the token-based accounting system two use cases have to be distinguished - costs for maintenance and costs for transactions.

Maintenance. Maintenance costs arise from keeping the remote accounts consistent and from the requirement to keep the systems private key secret. This involves calculating key updates at one quorum of trusted peers and distributing new key parts afterwards to the rest of the trusted peers. Table 1 summarizes the complexity of the maintenance actions, where k denotes the size of the bank-sets and a (t, T) secret sharing scheme is used, where T denotes the number of trusted peers in the system.

Transactions. For the analysis we assume a conservative ratio of 67% good peers in the system. Further, we set a trust level of 0,1% which results in a quorum size t of 6 trusted peers. Furthermore, we set the account holder set size k to 4. We model a file sharing scenario, where for 1 MB download 1 token is required and the average file size s is 5 MB. Users exchange tokens in different

Table 1. Account Holder Set & System Key Maintenance Complexity

Account Consistency		System key related operations	
node arrival	O(k)	key update calculations	$O(t^2)$
node departure	O(k)	key update distribution	$O(t^2)$

batch sizes b. The trustable transaction procedure is used. If n transactions are carried out the average number of accounting messages M sent in such a scenario results in:

$$M(n, k, t, b) = n(2s + 2k) + \frac{ns}{b}(1 + 2k\frac{b}{s} + 2k + 2t)$$

For 100 transactions exchanging 500 tokens with a batch size of 20 results in 3125 messages. Simulating this scenario the token-based accounting system creates an additional overhead of less than 1% (for the mentioned example it is less than 3,5 MB overhead for file transfers of 500 MB). Figure 5 (a) shows the generated traffic for different batch sizes and up to one million transactions. As it can be expected, the overall traffic generated by the token-based accounting system is reduced as the batch size increases. However, the effect levels off after a batch size of 20. Figure 5 (b) shows the influence of increased quorum size. The effect is not strong. Even with a very high trust level (t=18) the system still generates not more than 1% of overhead. The effect of size of account holder set for the generated traffic is very small and therefore the graph is omitted here.

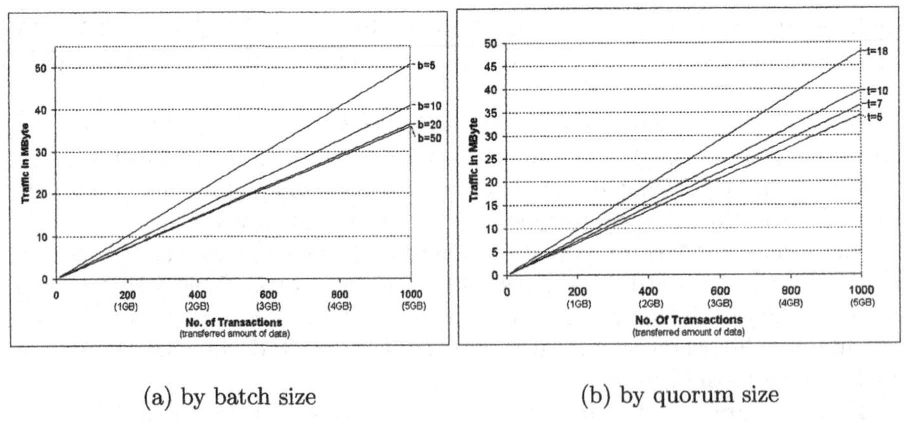

(a) by batch size (b) by quorum size

Fig. 5. By Token-Accounting Scheme Generated Traffic

6 Summary & Conclusions

One of the biggest challenges for a wider deployment of P2P systems is to retrieve, collect and use information about the resource utilization within the system. It is crucial that the information is secure and reliable while the core features of P2P are still maintained.

This paper presents a flexible and trustworthy token-based accounting scheme for P2P-systems. Its purpose is to collect accounting information of transactions. This information can be used to coordinate the behavior of the system's entities to achieve a higher system performance. Further, the collected information can be used as basis for pricing and price finding processes. Moreover, this builds the foundation for the development of a market within P2P systems. Further, the collected accounting information could be the basis for a payment system to support commercial applications.

Since the responsibility of creating tokens is delegated to a randomly selected quorum of peers, fraudulent behavior is prevented. Only if all peers in the quorum would be malicious, tokens can be forged. Also, a trustable payment mechanism is available that does not require to involve a third party. Thus, this approach is especially scalable.

The token-based accounting scheme is very flexible through the introduction of the aggregation function. Here the exchange ratio of used tokens against new tokens can be defined by the usage policy. Thus, different economic models can be implemented.

The further steps to investigate next are detection of the need for a system key update or system key creation procedure. Also the economic behavior of the system with respect to inflation and deflation will be evaluated using simulations.

References

1. Crypto-id project. http://crypto-id.jxta.org/, 2004.
2. edonkey2000. http://www.edonkey2000.com, 2004.
3. emule project. http://emule-project.net/, 2004.
4. E. Adar and B. A. Huberman. Free riding on gnutella. First Monday, volume 5, number 10, Oktober 2000.
5. A. Agrawal, D. J. Brown, A. Ojha, and S. Savage. Bucking free-riders: Distributed accounting and settlement in peer-to-peer networks. Technical Report CS2003-0751, UCSD, June 2003.
6. A. Barmouta and R. Buyya. Gridbank: A grid accounting services architecture (gasa) for distributed systems sharing and integration. In *17th IPDPS, Workshop on Internet Computing and E-Commerce*, Nice, France, April 22-26 2003.
7. D. Boneh and M. Franklin. Efficient generation of shared rsa keys. *Journal of the ACM (JACM)*, 48(4):702–722, July 2001.
8. D. Chaum, A. Fiat, and M. Naor. Untraceable electronic cash. In *CRYPTO '88*, volume 403 of LNCS, pages 319–327. Springer Verlag, 1990.
9. V. Darlagiannis, A. Mauth, N. Liebau, and R. Steinmetz. An adaptable, role-based simulator for p2p networks. In *Proceedings of MSV'04*, pages 52 – 59, Las Vegas, Nevada, USA, june 2004.

10. Y. Desmedt and Y. Frankel. Threshold cryptosystems. In *CRYPTO '89*, volume 435 of LNCS, pages 307–315. Springer-Verlag, 1989.
11. D. Dutta, A. Goel, R. Govindan, and H. Zhang. The design of a distributed rating scheme for peer-to-peer systems. In *Proceedings of the Workshop on the Economics of Peer-to-Peer Systems*, Berkeley, California, June 2003.
12. S. Kamvar, M. Schlosser, and H. Garcia-Molina. Eigenrep: Reputation management in p2p networks. In *Proceedings of the 12th International World Wide Web Conference*, 2003.
13. G. Medvinsky and B. C. Neuman. Netcash: A design for practical electronic currency on the internet. In *Proceedings of the 1st ACM CCS Conference*, November 1993.
14. Sun Microsystems. Project jxta.
15. T. Moreton and A. Twigg. Trading in trust, tokens, and stamps. In *Proceedings of the Workshop on the Economics of Peer-to-Peer Systems*, Berkeley, California, June 2003.
16. T. Rabin. A simplified approach to threshold and proactive rsa. In *Proceedings of Crypto*, 1988.
17. A. Rowstron and P. Druschel. Pastry: Scalable, distributed object location and routing for large-scale peer-to-peer systems. In *IFIP/ACM Middleware*, pages 329–350, Heidelberg, Germany, November 2001.
18. W. Thigpen, T. J. Hacker, L. F. McGinnis, and B. D. Athey. Distributed accounting on the grid. In *Proceedings of the 6th JCIS*, pages 1147–1150, 2002.
19. E. G. Sirer V. Vishnumurthy, S. Chandrakumar. Karma : A secure economic framework for peer-to-peer resource sharing. In *Proceedings of the Workshop on the Economics of Peer-to-Peer Systems*, Berkeley, California, June 2003.
20. B. Yang and H. Garcia-Molina. PPay: Micropayments for Peer-to-Peer Systems. In *Proceedings of the 10th ACM CCS Conference*, Washington D.C., October 2003.

Epidemic Dissemination of Presence Information in Mobile Instant Messaging Systems

Christoph Lindemann and Oliver P. Waldhorst

University of Dortmund, Department of Computer Science,
August-Schmidt-Str. 12, 44227 Dortmund, Germany
http://mobicom.cs.uni-dortmund.de

Abstract This paper presents an approach for exchanging presence information between users of an instant messaging system in a mobile ad hoc network. As major feature, presence information is transferred when mobile users get in direct contact, similar to the spread of an infections disease. By exploiting node mobility, presence information is epidemically distributed throughout the network, effectively overcoming network partitions. We show how to apply the Passive Distributed Indexing Protocol, which implements a general-purpose lookup service for mobile applications building upon epidemic data dissemination, for implementing the exchange of presence information. The effectiveness of the approach is illustrated in a simulation study using the network simulator ns-2. Building upon the results, we present the architecture of a mobile instant messaging system that supports the widely adopted Extensible Messaging and Presence Protocol (XMPP), an IETF standardized protocol for instant messaging.

1 Introduction

Pervasive computing devices such as Personal Digital Assistants (PDAs), mobile phones, and notebooks can be found in every situation of human life. Beside using these devices for the management of personal information, an upcoming application is message-based real time person-to-person communication, better known by the term instant messaging. Beside communication, instant messaging systems enable a user to track the presence state of his contacts, i.e., to determine in real time whether a peer user is currently online and available for a chat. Many instant-messaging systems have been developed for the wired Internet, including the AOL instant messager, the Microsoft instant messager, ICQ, or the Jabber instant messaging network. The rapid adoption of the protocol used by the Jabber network resulted in standardization efforts within the Internet Engineering Task Forth, that lead to development of the Extensible Messaging and Presence Protocol (XMPP, [14], [15]).

Unfortunately, the mechanisms defined by the various approaches to instant messaging are not well suited for self-organizing networks of mobile devices, so called mobile ad hoc networks [12] for several reasons. On the one hand most systems require a centralized server for managing communication and presence information. Unfortunately, in a MANET in general no devices with extraordinary capabilities exist, that are suited to implement centralized functionality. On the other hand, limited transmission range and node mobility lead to frequent partitions of the network, which hinder the communication with nodes providing centralized functionality. However, as shown by Grossglauser and Tse node mobility does not only hinder communication in MANET, but also supports cost-effective information exchange by epidemic dissemination [4].

In previous work [9], [10], we introduced a distributed lookup service, denoted as Passive Distributed Indexing (PDI) and proposed consistency mechanisms for keeping the distributed index coherent. PDI stores index entries in form of (key, value) pairs in index caches located in each mobile device. Index caches are filled by epidemic dissemination of popular index entries. That is information is transmitted when nodes get in direct contact, similar to the transmission of an infectious disease between individuals. By exploiting node mobility, PDI can resolve most queries locally without transmitting messages to nodes outside the radio coverage of the inquiring node. Thus, PDI can effectively cope with network partitions. For keeping index caches coherent, we introduced two consistency mechanisms for PDI index caches: (1) configurable value timeouts implementing implicit invalidation and (2) invalidation caches implementing explicit invalidation. Simulation results showed that with the suitable integration of both invalidation mechanisms, more than 95% of results delivered by PDI index caches are up-to-date for numerous application scenarios.

In this paper, we show how to apply PDI for implementing a mobile instant messaging system, which relies on epidemic dissemination of presence information in a MANET. As basic concept, the system employs PDI query messages for polling presence information, and a combination of lazy invalidation caches and value timeouts to provide presence state consistency. Performance results show that in systems with more than 50 participating users this approach resolves the presence state of contacts in more than 70% of all cases, with stale results in below 10% of the cases. Motivated by these results we outline the architecture of a mobile instant messaging system that is compliant to the XMPP protocol. The system satisfies all of XMPP's basic requirements, such as message exchange, exchange of presence information, maintenance of subscriptions and roosters, and blocking communication.

The remainder of this paper is organized as follows. Related work in epidemic data dissemination is discussed in Section 2. To make the paper self-contained, Section 3 summarizes the basic concepts of PDI. Section 4 discusses how PDI can be employed to implement the exchange of presence information in a mobile instant messaging system. Performance curves illustrating the effectiveness of this approach are presented in Section 5. Section 6 outlines the architecture of an XMPP compliant instant messaging system based on PDI. Finally, concluding remarks are given.

2 Related Work

As a first approach to epidemic information dissemination in mobile environments, Papadopouli and Schulzrinne introduced seven degrees of separation (7DS), a system for mobile Internet access based on Web document dissemination between mobile users [13]. To locate a Web document, a 7DS node broadcasts a query message to all mobile nodes currently located inside its radio coverage. Recipients of the query send response messages containing file descriptors of matching Web documents stored in their local file caches. Subsequently, such documents can be downloaded with HTTP by the inquiring mobile node. Downloaded Web documents may be distributed to other nodes that move into radio coverage, implementing an epidemic dissemination of information.

Using a related approach, Goel, Singh, Xu and Li proposed broadcasting segments of shared files using redundant tornado encoding [3]. Their approach enables nodes to restore a file, if a sufficient number of different segments have been received from one or more sources. In [8], Khelil, Becker, Tian, and Rothermel presented an analytical model for a simple epidemic information diffusion algorithm inspired by the SPIN-1 protocol [5]. Both systems implement a push model for information dissemination. That is, shared data is advertised or even actively broadcasted without a node requesting it. Hanna, Levine, and Mamatha proposed a fault-tolerant distributed information retrieval system for P2P document sharing in mobile ad hoc networks [6]. Their approach distributes the index of a new document to a random set of nodes when the document is added to the system. The complete index of a document, i.e., all keywords matching it, constitutes the smallest unit of disseminated information. Recently, Small and Haas proposed an epidemic approach for collecting information in a hybrid network consisting of mobile nodes and fixed infostations [16]. Their architecture, denoted as Shared Wireless Infostation Model (SWIM), actively transfers information among wireless nodes on each contact, until information is unloaded to one of the infostations.

Opposed to all related work on epidemic data dissemination in mobile networks, PDI cannot only be employed for document and information sharing, but also for numerous other mobile applications. The ability of PDI to implement search functionality in a mobile peer-to-peer file sharing application has been demonstrated in [9]. In this paper, we show how PDI can be applied to disseminate presence information in a mobile instant messaging system.

3 Epidemic Data Dissemination by Passive Distributed Indexing

To keep the paper self-contained, we recall the basic concepts of PDI as introduced in [9] [10] in this section. All functionality described below is specified in an upcoming Internet draft [11], and thus ready to be used in various mobile application. PDI is designed for a system consisting of several mobile nodes, e.g. mobile users equipped with notebooks or PDAs and wireless network interfaces as illustrated in Figure 1. All mobile nodes collaborate in a shared application that uses a distributed lookup service. Radio coverage is small compared to the area covered by all nodes, e.g., less than 5% of the covered area. Typically, communication is performed using several intermediate hops as in mobile ad hoc networks (MANET, [12]). Subsequently, we assume IEEE 802.11x in the ad hoc mode as underlying radio technology [7]. However, we would like to point out that PDI could be employed on any radio technology that enables broadcast transmissions inside a node's radio coverage.

PDI implements a general-purpose lookup service for mobile applications. In general, PDI stores index entries in the form of pairs (k,v). Keys k and values v are both defined by the mobile application. For example, in case of a file sharing application, keys are given by keywords derived from the file name or associated

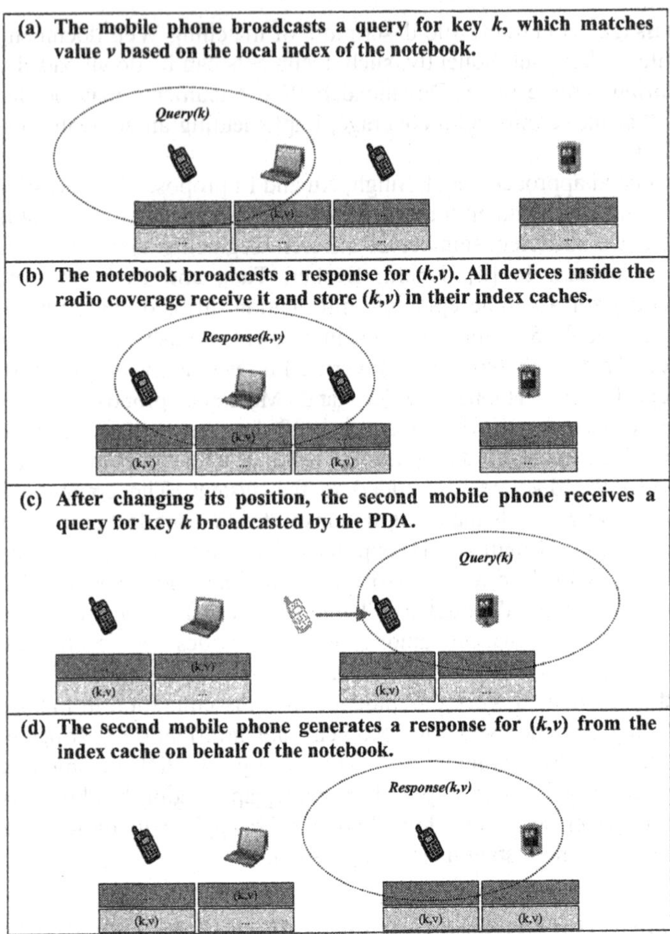

(a) The mobile phone broadcasts a query for key k, which matches value v based on the local index of the notebook.
Query(k)
(k,v)
(b) The notebook broadcasts a response for (k,v). All devices inside the radio coverage receive it and store (k,v) in their index caches.
Response(k,v)
(k,v)
(k,v)
(k,v)
(c) After changing its position, the second mobile phone receives a query for key k broadcasted by the PDA.
Query(k)
(k,v)
(k,v)
(k,v)
(d) The second mobile phone generates a response for (k,v) from the index cache on behalf of the notebook.
Response(k,v)
(k,v)
(k,v)
(k,v)
(k,v)

Fig.1. Illustration of epidemic information dissemination with PDI

meta-data. Values are given by references to files in form of URIs. PDI does not require a one-to-one matching between keys and values. However, some mechanisms implemented in PDI require that a value is unique in the system. That is, it is only added to the system by a single node. This can be easily achieved by extending values by unique node identifiers. A node n may contribute index entries of the form (k,v) to the system by inserting them into a local index. In Figure 1, the local index is drawn as the first box below each mobile device. We refer to such an index entry as supplied. The node n is called the origin node of an index entry. For example, the notebook shown in Figure 1 is the origin node of the index entry (k,v). A key k matches a value v, if (k,v) is currently supplied to the PDI system. Each node in the system may issue queries in order to resolve a key k to all matching values v_i (see Figure 1a). A node issuing a query is denoted as inquiring node.

Queries are transmitted by messages containing the key to resolve. Query messages are sent to the IP limited broadcast address 255.255.255.255 and a well-defined port, using the User Datagram Protocol UDP. Using the IEEE 801.11 ad hoc mode, all nodes located inside the radio coverage of the inquiring node receive a query message. Each of these nodes may generate a response message. A response message contains the key from the query and all matching values from either the local index or a second data structure called index cache which is drawn as a second box below the mobile devices in Figure 1. To enable epidemic data dissemination, PDI response messages are sent to the IP limited broadcast address 255.255.255.255 and a well-defined port, too. Thus, all mobile nodes within the radio coverage of the responding node will overhear the message (Figure 1b). Not only the inquiring node but also all other mobile nodes that receive a response message extract all index entries and store them in the index cache (see Figure 1b). Thus, the distributed index is maintained in a passive way. In Figure 1, index caches are drawn as the second box below mobile devices. Index entries from the index cache are used to locally resolve queries, if the origin nodes of matching values reside outside the radio coverage of the inquiring node (see Figures 1c and 1d). Obviously, the index cache size is limited to a maximum number of entries adjusted to the capabilities of the mobile device. The replacement policy least-recently-used (LRU) is employed if a mobile device runs out of index cache space. By generating responses from index caches, information is disseminated to all other nodes that are in direct contact, similar to the spread of an infectious disease.

To extend the dissemination of information beyond the radio coverage of the inquiring node, PDI includes a message forwarding mechanism. When message forwarding is enabled, queries are relayed a certain number of hops specified by the inquiring node in a time-to-live field (TTL_{query}). Similarly, response messages are forwarded TTL_{query} hops. Since response messages may be considerable larger than query messages, PDI incorporates a concept called selective forwarding. That is each node that receives a response message will search the index cache for each index entry contained in the message. When an entry is found, in most cases the node itself has already responded with this index entry. Therefore, forwarding this index entry constitutes redundant information. Using selective forwarding, each relay node removes all index entries found in its local index cache from the response message, before the message is forwarded.

Caching index entries in mobile devices may introduce inconsistency. PDI incorporates a message-based explicit invalidation mechanism to remove stale index entries for a given value v from the index caches. Flooding is a straightforward way to propagate invalidation messages. Unfortunately, a flooded invalidation message might not reach all nodes in case of network partitions. Subsequently, stale index entries remain in index caches of nodes not reached by invalidation message. To cope with this problem, we introduced a passive approach for epidemic propagation of invalidation messages denoted as lazy invalidation. Each node maintains a data structure called invalidation cache. When a node receives an invalidation message for a value v it does not only relay it, but stores v in the invalidation cache for epidemic dissemination of invalidation messages. Cached invalidations are sent when a node receives a response containing a stale value. To cope with stale information due to sudden departures of nodes, we introduced the concept of value timeouts. Value timeouts limit the maximum time an entry (k_i,v) for a given value v will be stored in an index cache. Value timeouts rely on epidemic dissemination of recent timeout information for each value. Simulation results showed that with the suitable integration of both invalidation mechanisms, more than 95% of results delivered by

PDI index caches are up-to-date for a mobile peer-to-peer file sharing application [10].

4 Applying PDI for Mobile Instant Messaging

Recall that a major function of an instant messaging system is the monitoring of the presence state of users participating in the system. That is, a user is able to determine if one of his contacts is online, busy, free for chat, etc. Such information is denoted as the presence state of a contact. In state-of-the-art instant messaging systems, e.g., in systems that use the Extensible Messaging and Presence Protocol (XMPP, [14],[15]), the instant messaging software will notify the user when a contact changes his presence state. XMPP specifies the usage of dedicated servers that send presence state updates to all other users that have a particular user on their contact list, if this user changes his presence state. Unfortunately, when implementing an instant messaging system in MANET, a centralized approach using a dedicated server for communication of presence state cannot be employed. An alternative solution might communicate presence state directly between the users using direct connections. Nevertheless, frequently occurring network partitions will hamper this solution, as we will show in Section 5.

To cope with these shortcomings of MANET, we employ epidemic dissemination of state information based on PDI.. We assign a unique identifier to a user, denoted as his instant messaging identifier (IM-ID). Each mobile user contributes his current presence state to the system as only value. The value matches only a single key, given by the user's IM-ID. Note that this results in a one-to-one matching of keys and values. The IM client software periodically polls the presence state of each contact on a users contact list, using a PDI query for the user's IM-IDs. Presence information received in PDI response messages will be displayed to the user. Subsequently, on a presence state change of one user, the client software will not explicitly notify other users, but sends a PDI invalidation message for the old present state, and subsequently contributes the new state to the system. The invalidation will be disseminated epidemically, using lazy invalidation caches. For additionally increasing the coherence of reported presence states, the client software uses a value timeout, which is set to the average time between presence state changes. The client software can easily calculate this time. We will show in the Section 5 that this methodology enables the determination of the current presence state in many cases. In Section 6, we show how to implement an entire XMPP compliant instant messaging system based on PDI.

5 Simulation Study

5.1 Simulation Methodology

In this section, we show that PDI can be effectively employed to implement a communicate presence information in an instant messaging system in MANET. For this purpose, we conduct simulation studies based on the network simulator ns-2 [2]. We have developed an ns-2 application implementing the concept of PDI as described in Section 3. An instance of the PDI application is attached to each simulated node, using the UDP/IP protocol stack and a MAC layer according to the IEEE 802.11 standard for wireless communication. All MAC layer parameters are configured to provide radio coverage with radius of 125m for each mobile node. We assume that N mobile nodes, for $N = 20, 35, \ldots 110$[1], move in an area of 1000 m × 1000 m according to the random waypoint mobility model [1]. Maximum node speed is 1.5m/s and a pause time between two movement epochs is 50s. The random waypoint model is commonly used to mimic the movement of pedestrians.

To model a mobile instant messaging application implementing the concepts described in Section 4, we assume that each mobile user maintains a list of his/her favorite contacts. Each user u is on the contact list of each other user with probability Cu^{-1}, where C is a constant. I.e., the social contacts are described by a Zipf distribution. To account for state changes, we assume that users change availability state in intervals of exponentially distributed length with mean 300s. On a state change, the contributed value expires and is replaced by a new one. Furthermore, function we assume that users arrive and depart with exponentially distributed arrivals. Arrival rates are chosen such that 30% of the nodes arrive and depart during a simulation run.

We conduct transient simulations starting with initially empty caches. For each run, total simulation time was 2 hours. To avoid inaccuracy due to initial warm-ups, we reset all statistic counters after a warm-up period of 10 min. simulation time. For each point in all performance curves, we performed up to 100 independent simulation runs and calculated corresponding performance measures at the end of the simulation. In all curves 99% confidence intervals determined by independent replicates are included.

5.2 Performance Results

Before looking at PDI performance, we provide some evidence that the random waypoint mobility model applied in a simulation area of one square kilometer result in sparsely connected networks for all considered numbers of nodes. Figure 2 plots the number of partitions and the number of nodes that are in each other's transmission range (i.e., the node degree), respectively, as a function of the number of nodes. We find that even for a high number of nodes, the network comprises of about 4.8 partitions on average. Clearly, the number of partitions is highest for the lowest node density, i.e., on average about 10.16 partitions for 20 nodes. Note that the high number of partitions implies that neither an approach using a central presence server nor an approach relying on direct communication of presence information among the nodes can be applied. Fortunately, with increasing number of nodes the average node degree increases. That is, each node encounters an increasing number of direct contacts per time unit, fostering epidemic dissemination of presence information. Thus, Figure 2 implies the conjecture that PDI is well suited to implement dissemination of presence information in such scenario.

---

[1] Note that 20 nodes constitute a small community, while a community of 110 IM users on a square kilometer is fairly large.

To confirm this conjecture we illustrates the accuracy of the presence information returned by PDI in Figure 3. accuracy is measured by hit rate *HR*, i.e., $HR = H_F / K_F$, where H_F denotes the number of up-to-date presence information and K_F the total

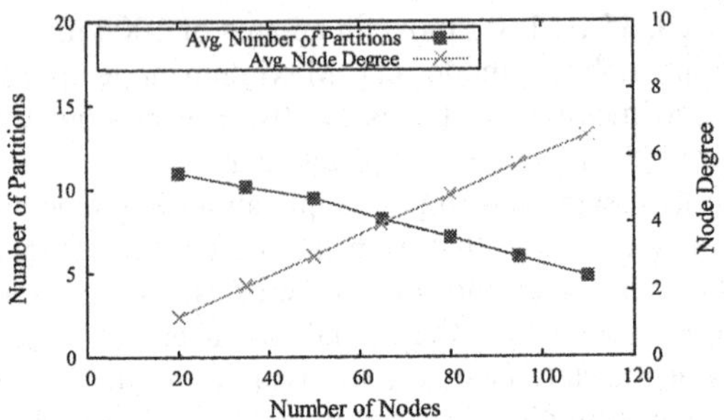

Fig. 2. Connectivity statistics for the considered scenarios.

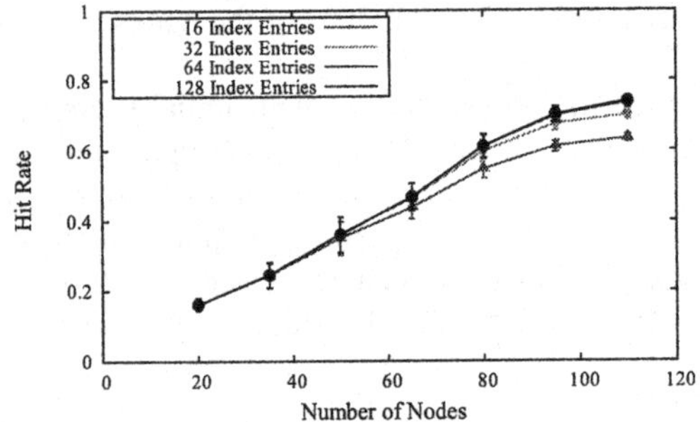

Fig. 3. PDI Hit rate for different index cache sizes.

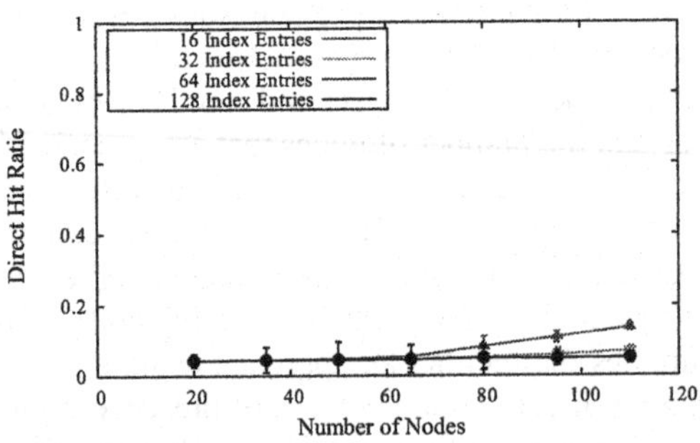

Fig. 4. Direct hits received for different cache sizes.

number of all up-to-date information currently in the system. Note that hit rate can be compared to the information retrieval measure recall. Figure 3 plots hit rate as a function of the number of nodes for different index cache sizes, i.e. 16, 32, 64, and 128 index entries. We find that for low number of nodes, the hit rate is independent of the index cache size, since all presence information fit into the smallest index cache. Nevertheless, the low node degree in such scenarios limits the epidemic information dissemination, resulting in hit rates of about 0.2. Recall from Figure 2 that node degree increases linearly with the number of nodes, resulting in a hit rate increasing up to 0.73 for 110 nodes. Note that increasing index cache size beyond 64 entries does not increase hit rate even for high number of nodes, since value timeouts limit the

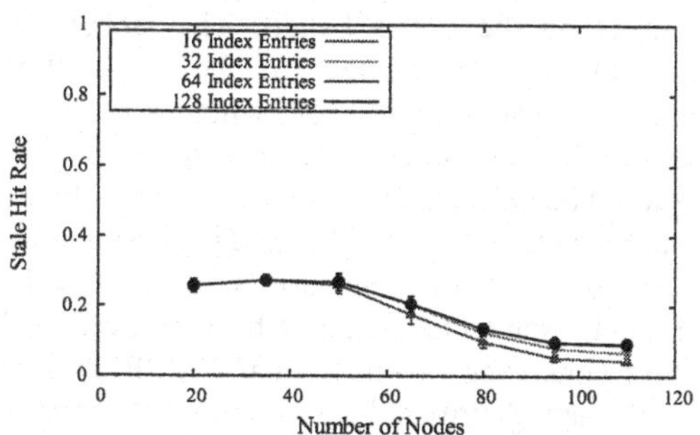

Fig. 5. Fraction of responses containing a stale presence state.

time an index entry is stored in a large cache [9]. We conclude from Figure 3 that PDI provides reasonable hit rates for scenarios with more than 50 nodes. To further illustrate the benefit of PDI, we plot the direct hit rate, i.e. the relative number of up-to-date hits received from the origin nodes of each reported index entry, in Figure 4. We find that direct hit rate is constant at about 0.05 for all number of nodes. Only for small index cache sizes and high node densities, direct hit rate increases due to increasing network connectivity. Recall that connectivity fosters selective forwarding. For larger index caches, selective forwarding filters out the direct hits if a nearby index cache, reducing bandwidth consumption. We conclude from Figure 4 that PDI increases hit rate by more than 14 times for scenarios with a high number of nodes.

In a last experiment shown in Figure 5, we illustrate coherence of the results returned by PDI. Coherence is measured by stale hit rate *SHR*, i.e., $SHR = H_S / (H_S + H_F)$, where H_S denotes the number of stale hits returned on a query. Note that stale hit rate is related to the information retrieval measure precision by $precision = 1 - SHR$. We find that stale hit rate is about 0.2 for scenarios with few nodes, which is somewhat higher than in P2P file sharing applications [9]. Nevertheless, stale hit rates drops below 0.1 for scenarios with 110 nodes, indicating that PDI will report only few stale presence states in a mobile instant messaging application.

6 Implementation of a Mobile Instant Messaging System Based on PDI

Motivated by the results obtained from the simulation study, we have designed an entire mobile instant messaging systems based on PDI. The system is compliant to a proposed standard for instant messaging in the wireline Internet, namely the Extensible Messaging and Presence Protocol (XMPP Core, [14]) together with its extensions for instant messaging (XMPP Messaging and Presence, [15]). [16] defines extensions to the core XMPP protocol specifications that enable a user to establish sessions, exchange messages and presence information with other users, manage subscriptions and items in a contact list, and block communications to or from specific other users. Development of XMPP originates from the popular Jabber instant messaging system. Thus, the user identifiers used in XMPP are denoted Jabber Ids (JIDs). A JID is of form *user@domain/resource*. Here, the jabber domain typically specifies server that manages a users contact list and relays IM communication messages on the user's behalf. The jabber resource specifies the device that the user employs to connect to the IM system. A JID of form *user@domain/resource* is denoted as full JID, whereas *user@domain* is denoted as bare JID. Full JIDs can be associated with a priority, which specifies to which resource a message should be delivered if it is addressed to a bare JID.

Note that, due to the structure of JIDs, [14] and [15] rely on one or more dedicated nodes running server software to manage user's contacts and communication. As shown in Section 5, such architecture cannot be employed in MANET. Thus, we propose an architecture consisting of one virtual XMPP enabled IM Server, which physically comprises of many distributed server entities (DSEs). One DSE is running on each mobile device participating in the IM application. To connect to the IM system, users can configure any XMPP enabled IM client to connect to the local DSE. Similar to communications between the IM client application and the DSE, the DSEs use XMPP for message-oriented communication with other DSEs. As a novel feature, DSEs use PDI to implement efficient resolution of JIDs to presence and device address information. An overview of the system is shown in Figure 6. In the remainder of this section, we show how the distributed IM server employs PDI to implement each of the features described in [15].

Session establishment: [15] requires that a user establishes a session by logging in to the XMPP server managing his jabber domain. The user is identified by his JID and a password. Similarly, in the mobile IM system, a users logs in to the DSE running on his personal mobile device, using his JID and password. Account information is stored by the DSE and password protected to ensure confidentiality when the mobile device is lost. Furthermore, account information contains a user certificate signed by a trusted certification authority. The certificate is used to authenticate and encrypt messages exchanged between DSEs.

Message exchange: According to [15], XMPP messages are transmitted using TCP connections. Similarly, the mobile IM system uses TCP connections that are established using a state-of-the-art MANET routing protocol. Before a TCP connection can be established, the DSE must resolve a user's JID to the device IP address of the terminal running the user's DSE. This is done by issuing a PDI query for a key given by the user's JID. The query is resolved to a value representing the user's terminal address. Furthermore, a PDI query is used to resolve bare JIDs to full JIDs. Note that it may happen that the PDI queries cannot be resolved, i.e., the recipient of a message is currently unavailable or unreachable. In this case, the message is stored by the local DSE. Subsequently, the DSE periodically employs PDI to poll for recipients of stored messages.

Exchange of presence information: As in the simulation study, the mobile IM system uses PDI queries to resolve JIDs to presence information. Encrypting the information with the public keys of all intended recipients ensures confidentiality of presence information. When a user logs in to the local DSE according to [15], the IM client sends initial presence information to the DSE. The DSE stores the presence state and responds to PDI queries by remote DSEs that try to obtain the presence information for the JID. When the user changes his presence state, the client notifies the DSE. The DSE generates a PDI invalidation message for the last presence information and responds to successive presence queries using the new presence state. Furthermore, a value-time-out implicitly invalidates old presence information. A DSE

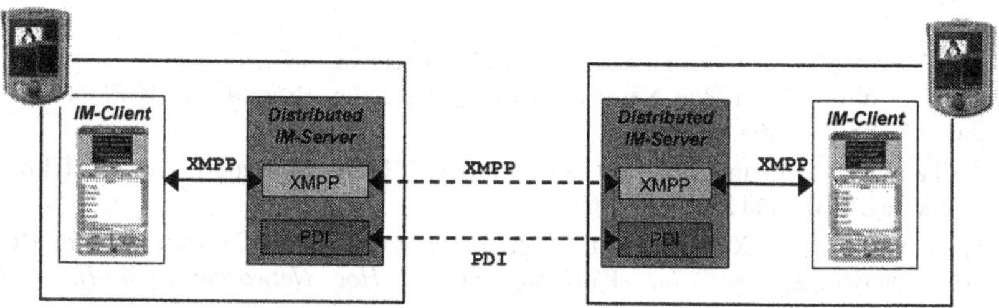

Fig.6. Architecture of a PDI-based distributed instant messaging server.

periodically polls the presence state of all contacts in the rooster of a user and send presence updates to the client in case of a presence state change.

Managing subscriptions and roosters: According to [15], a user must be authenticated by another user in order to see the user's current presence state, a process denoted as subscription. Subscribing a presence state requires a two-way handshake using XMPP messages. Again, before message transmission JIDs are resolved to device addresses using PDI. Presence subscriptions are stored in roosters together with contact information. [15] requires that a user that is logged on to a server using multiple resources (devices) has a consistent view of his rooster from all resources. Unfortunately, a user might be logged on with different clients on multiple mobile devices, i.e., using multiple DSEs. DSEs periodically poll for local users that are also logged on remote devices using PDI queries for users JIDs. If the user is discovered with a resource currently managed by another DSE, the DSEs synchronize the roosters using XMPP communication.

Blocking communications: [15] defines privacy lists that enable users to allow or deny users to view presence state and send or receive messages based on JIDs, servers, or resources. The current implementation the mobile IM system does not support privacy lists. However, consistent privacy lists can easily handled by the mechanisms used for rooster management.

Conclusion

In this paper, we demonstrated that the Passive Distributed Indexing protocol can be applyed for epidemic dissemination of presence information in mobile instant messaging systems. The main contributions of this paper include: (1) Presentation of a basic concept for using PDI for dissemination of presence information, (2) performance results that show that the presented concept provides more sufficient up to date results in a system with more than 50 users, and (3) the outline of a entire PDI-based mobile instant messaging system that is compliant to the Extensible Messaging and Presence Protocol XMPP.

We are currently developing a software prototype of the distributed IM server in Java according to the concepts described in this paper. Future work includes field-based performance studies based on this software prototype in order to mature the design of the distributed IM server.

References

1. J. Broch, D. Maltz, D. Johnson, Y.-C. Hu, and J. Jetcheva, A Performance Comparison of Multi-Hop Wireless Ad Hoc Network Routing Protocols, *Proc. 4th ACM MobiCom 98*, Dallas, TX, 85-97, 1998.
2. K. Fall and K. Varadhan (editors), *The ns-2 manual*, Technical Report, The VINT Project, UC Berkeley, LBL, and Xerox PARC, 2003.
3. S. Goel, M. Singh, D. Xu, and B. Li, Efficient Peer-to-Peer Data Dissemination in Mobile Ad-Hoc Networks, *Proc. Int. Workshop on Ad Hoc Networking (IWAHN 2002)*, Vancouver, BC, 2002.
4. M. Grossglauser and D. Tse, Mobility Increases the Capacity of Ad-hoc Wireless Networks, *IEEE/ACM Trans. on Networking* **10**, 477-486, 2002.
5. W. Heinzelman, J. Kulik, and H. Balakrishnan, Adaptive Protocols for Information Dissemination in Wireless Sensor Networks, *Proc 5th ACM MobiCom 99*, Seattle, WA, 174-185, 1999.
6. K. Hanna, B. Levine, and R. Manmatha, Mobile Distributed Information Retrieval for Highly-Partitioned Networks, *Proc. 11th IEEE Int. Conf. on Network Protocols (ICPN 2003)*, Atlanta, GA, 2003.
7. IEEE Computer Society LAN MAN Standards Committee, *Wireless LAN Medium Access Control (MAC) and Physical Layer (PHY) Specifications*, IEEE Standard 802.11-1997, New York, NY, 1997.
8. Khelil, C. Becker, J. Tian, and K. Rothermel, An Epidemic Model for Information Diffusion in MANETs, *Proc. 5th ACM Int. Workshop on Modeling, Analysis and Simulation of Wireless and Mobile Systems (MSWiM 2002)*, Atlanta, Georgia, 2002.
9. C. Lindemann and O. Waldhorst, Consistency Mechanisms for a Distributed Lookup Service supporting Mobile Applications, *Proc. 3rd Int. ACM Workshop on Data Engineering for Wireless and Mobile Access (MobiDE 2003)*, San Diego, CA, 61-68, 2003.
10. C. Lindemann and O. Waldhorst, Exploiting Epidemic Data Dissemination for Consistent Lookup Operations in Mobile Applications, *Mobile Computing and Communication Review (MC2R)* **8**(3), *Special Issue on Mobile Data Management*, 44-56, 2004.
11. C. Lindemann and O. Waldhorst, *Passive Distributed Indexing (PDI)*, Internet Draft (Work in progress), 2004. (forthcoming).
12. Internet Engineering Task Force Working Group Mobile Ad hoc Networks (MANET). *http://www.ietf.org/html.charters/ manet-charter.html*
13. M. Papadopouli and H. Schulzrinne, Effects of Power Conservation, Wireless Coverage and Cooperation on Data Dissemination among Mobile Devices, *Proc. 2nd ACM MobiHoc 2001*, Long Beach, NY, 117-127, 2001.
14. P. Saint-Andre, *Extensible Messaging and Presence Protocol (XMPP): Core*. IETF Internet Draft, January 2004.
15. P. Saint-Andre, Extensible Messaging and Presence Protocol (XMPP): Instant Messaging and Presence. IETF Internet Draft, January 2004.
16. T. Small and Z. Haas, The Shared Wireless Infostation Model – A New Ad Hoc Networking Paradigm (or Where there is a Whale, there is a Way), *Proc. ACM MobiHoc 2003*, Annapolis, MD, 233-244, 2003.

Dynamic Software Deployment with Distributed Application Repositories

Stefan Paal[1], Reiner Kammüller[2], Bernd Freisleben[3]

[1]Fraunhofer Institute for Media Communication
Schloss Birlinghoven, D-53754 Sankt Augustin, Germany
stefan.paal@imk.fraunhofer.de
[2]Department of Electrical Engineering and Computer Science, University of Siegen
Hölderlinstrasse 3, D-57068 Siegen, Germany
kammueller@pd.et-inf.uni-siegen.de
[3]Department of Mathematics and Computer Science, University of Marburg
Hans-Meerwein-Strasse, D-35032 Marburg, Germany
freisleb@informatik.uni-marburg.de

Abstract. The deployment and installation of Java applications in a distributed environment is a complex task, particularly for unmanaged nodes in large scale deployment scenarios as found in the Internet. A promising remedy is *dynamic software deployment* which does not require particular user intervention but is supposed to install application components on demand. While related approaches like Sun Java Web Start use fixed deployment and application configurations, we present in this paper a dynamic and customizable deployment approach based on so called *Java class collections*. The realization of our proposal is presented and the use of the approach in an ongoing research project is demonstrated.

1 Introduction

In distributed application scenarios such as the Internet, an application must be deployed and installed on every node that may be used to run the application. Although this task can be done manually for a limited number of known applications and managed nodes, it tends to be too complex for large scale and dynamic deployment scenarios as found with distributed Internet applications [1]. A possible remedy is *dynamic software deployment* offered by approaches like Sun Java Web Start [2]. Instead of installing the application components on each node, they are deployed into particular application repositories. From there, the required application components are dynamically retrieved and installed when an application is requested. Updated components are automatically downloaded each time the application is started, which keeps the local installation up-to-date without user intervention. While the employment of application repositories releases administrators from manually maintaining local application installations, it introduces other issues such as the synchronization of multiple and separately managed application repositories. In this context, a basic problem is the dynamic lookup, the identification and the selection of matching components across different application repositories. Compatible components may be shared by various installations on the same node and do not have to be individually downloaded for each application, as done with Sun Java Web Start. The deployment process can typically not be modified by the application or by the customer when using a fixed configuration file like the JNLP file used by Sun Java Web Start or the web archive used for Java Servlets [3].

In this paper, we present a customizable approach for the dynamic deployment of Java applications using distributed application repositories. It is based on the separation of application and platform configuration and utilizes so called *Java class collections* [4] to define customizable groups of Java classes independent of their actual packaging. The class collections can be decorated with additional attributes such as versioning information or vendor name. We outline how these attributes are used to dynamically lookup Java classes matching a given application and platform configuration. We illustrate the transparent employment of the approach for managing different versions of an application without modifying legacy code or JAR files. Finally, we demonstrate its use in an ongoing research project.

The paper is organized as follows. In section 2, we depict the objectives and requirements of dynamic software deployment with respect to Java applications and consider existing solutions. Section 3 presents our approach using distributed application repositories and Java class collections. In section 4, the application of the approach is demonstrated. Finally, section 5 concludes the paper and outlines areas for further research.

2 Dynamic Software Deployment

In this section, we illustrate the objectives of dynamic software deployment with respect to Java applications in distributed scenarios like the Internet, examine the resulting requirements and discuss related work.

2.1 Objectives

The basic objective of dynamic software deployment is the installation of applications on demand without extra user intervention. New applications are not immediately installed on an application system but are put in an application repository by the deployer. In turn, the repository can be queried by the application system of the customer for new applications which can be dynamically installed on request, as shown in fig. 1. As a result, the application repository separates *application deployment* from *application installation.*

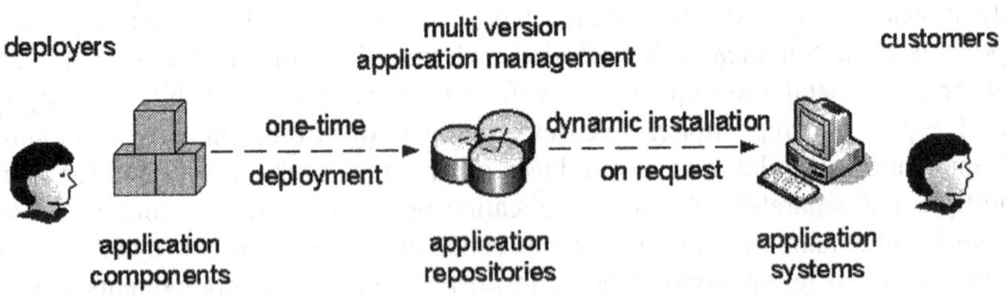

Fig. 1. Dynamic Software Deployment and Installation

If the application repository is concurrently used by several deployers and customers, application components are likely to be uploaded and requested in multiple versions. In this context, there may also be more than one application repository which offer the same application components. A particular objective of dynamic software deployment is the identification of the best matching application component and its dynamic installation, e.g. resolving possible dependencies to other components.

2.2 Requirements

The following requirements have to be addressed by application repositories supporting dynamic software deployment in distributed environments:

Version Management. An application and its components typically exist in different versions which may be concurrently requested by various application systems. An application repository should be able to identify, store and return different versions of the same application component. In addition, dependencies to other components should be covered by the version management as well as the identification of compatible components.

Distributed Repositories. The employment of distributed application repositories allows the introduction of particular features needed for large scale deployment scenarios, such as caching and fault tolerance. An application repository should be able to communicate and synchronize itself with other repositories. It should provide transparent access to other application repositories and hide the actual distribution behind the scenes.

Concurrent Deployment. Application components may be concurrently deployed to various application repositories. In addition, there are often different versions of the same component. The lookup of a suitable application component should return the best matching component and version. Once a common version has been installed on an application system, it should be shared among applications and not downloaded again for each one.

Deployment Customization. The deployment of application components is initially defined by the deployer. If alternative components become available, the customer as well as the application should be able to dynamically adjust the deployment process. This would enable the custom selection of best matching components and support self-configuration with respect to the capabilities of the current node, such as the screen resolution.

Transparent Application. An important requirement concerning dynamic software deployment is its transparent application with respect to existing components and installations. The application should not be aware of the dynamic deployment process. In turn, the application system does not have to know from which application repository the application components are actually downloaded.

2.3 Related Work

In the following, we limit our discussion of related work to dynamic software deployment of Java applications. In this context, the deployment and composition features are usually implemented by providing a customized Java class loader [5]. After the start of the Java application system, it replaces the native system class loader and is subsequently used to retrieve Java application classes from particular class repositories. Due to the large diversity of class loader variants, we group them into supporting native, standard and custom deployment approaches.

Native Deployment Approaches

The native deployment approaches are basically characterized by using the Java system class loader. They do not require any particular Java Virtual Machine (JVM) or application framework. Typical application repositories are built using native JAR files which have been deployed into a locally managed directory. The basic problem of this approach concerning dynamic software deployment is its limitation to local file systems and the static configuration. Once started, the JVM can not be easily reconfigured to consider additional JAR files that were not added to the CLASSPATH. Furthermore, the system class loader does not provide reasonable version management, as depicted in [6]. It simply loads the first occurrence of a class found in the CLASSPATH matching the name of the required class. For the same reason, there is no support for sharing Java classes among different application installations and their synchronization across various nodes. Finally, there is no way to address a group of application classes spreaded across various JAR files without actually repackaging them into another JAR file. This complicates the distribution and reuse of Java classes and JAR files shared across different applications.

The Standard Deployment Approach

There is a common specification for Java class distribution called Java Network Launch Protocol (JNLP). It is the official proposal of Sun Corp. to dynamically deploy Java applications in a distributed heterogeneous environment like the Internet. While JNLP itself is a public specification of Sun, there are various implementations available, such as Sun Java Web Start or Quest Deploy Director [7]. Common to all is the introduction of a particular JVM that is equipped with a custom class loader. Instead of processing the environment setting CLASSPATH, the JVM retrieves and processes a JNLP configuration file from a remote application repository during startup. The JNLP file contains web links to the required JAR files which are dynamically downloaded. The major application of JNLP is its integration as a plugin in a web browser which is started when the user follows a link to a JNLP file. It supports local caching of downloaded JAR files and checking for updated versions which are transparently downloaded when the application is started the next time. However, the version management is not customizable by the user, e.g. selecting an arbitrary version other than the latest. Downloaded JAR files are not shared by different applications but separately downloaded. The JNLP file is typically located on the server and can not be modified by the customer. And finally, distributed JNLP application repositories are not synchronized and can not query other repositories for missing JAR files. Although the JNLP approach can be extended with a server-side repository handler, it is still an approach for fixed and well-known deployment configurations [2].

Custom Deployment Approaches
Besides the native and standard deployment approaches there are several custom approaches such as Jakarta Tomcat [8], Apache Avalon [9] or Power Update [10]. While the first one represents a servlet engine and is used in server-side scenarios, the second one is an application server and the last one is supposed to manage auto-updating of Java clients. There are further custom deployment approaches which mainly focus on particular application features, e.g. extracting files from a WAR file or dynamically compiling updated JSP pages. In general, custom approaches tend to be specific for a certain application scenario (e.g. Java servlets) but fail for different ones, e.g. Power Update supports thick Java clients but lacks support for servlet engines. The hot deployment feature of Jakarta Tomcat offers the dynamic update of running servlet installations but is not usable for regular Java applications.

3 Distributed Application Repository

In this section we present our proposal to deal with dynamic software deployment of Java applications with distributed application repositories. After presenting the conceptual approach, we highlight its realization and illustrate its use. A discussion at the end compares the listed requirements with the provided features.

3.1 Conceptual Approach

One of the fundamental problems of Java application deployment is the missing support to explicitly address a certain group of Java classes, e.g. representing the latest version of an application component or query for compatible Java classes. In previous work, we introduced so called Java class collections [4] to select and group certain classes from various JAR files without actually repackaging them. The major idea is the provision of additional descriptions which contain extra properties such as the vendor and version of the related Java classes. A custom class loader processes these descriptions and dynamically retrieves related Java classes without modifying the application. Based on this work, we present our proposal for a distributed application repository which does not rely on ambiguous JAR files but is able to manage different versions of the same class using Java class collections. As shown in fig. 2, a distributed application repository is built of interconnected configuration registries and class repositories. It hides the actual deployment, distribution and retrieval of application components from the deployer and the customer, respectively.

First, native JAR files are uploaded to a class repository and associated with a unique tag which is used to address this JAR file and to identify copies across distributed class repositories. In this context, a JAR file is no longer referenced by its location or by its name but by its unique tag. The actual location of a suitable copy is determined during runtime depending on the current distribution scenario, e.g. loading the JAR file from a caching class repository server in the local network.

Next, groups of Java classes are composed using the Java class collection approach. They address selected JAR files by using their tags and are as well tagged with a unique identifier. As outlined above, they are additionally marked with a set of properties which describe the class collection and can be used to lookup compatible variants. In particular, the separation of class deployment and collection composition supports the distribution of native JAR files without considering their use in a certain application scenario.

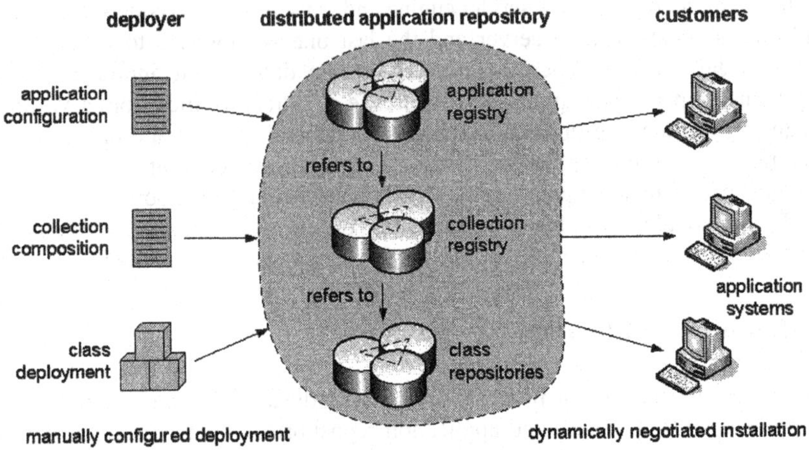

Fig. 2. Conceptual Approach

The application configuration contains information about the class collections required by the related application such as the vendor and the version of a class collection. It introduces another abstraction level to configure applications without binding it to a certain class collection or JAR file. Instead, suitable class collections are determined on request considering the current requirements of the application and the features of available class collections. In addition, platform constraints such as the display resolution can also be evaluated and used to customize the deployment depending on the capabilities and configuration of the target platform.

3.2 Realization

The deployment approach has itself been implemented in Java and uses various XML based repositories to store, retrieve and share the deployment and configuration data. While applications can download and process the XML descriptions from the repositories on their own, we added a collection resolver that resides on a repository server and can be shared across various clients. It represents the access point to the distributed application repository and accelerates the actual lookup and download of the Java classes from diverse repositories. A custom class loader is used to trap class loading requests and to customize the deployment process according to the application configuration. It uses the collection resolver to lookup a suitable class collection and to determine the location of the related JAR files, as shown in fig. 3.

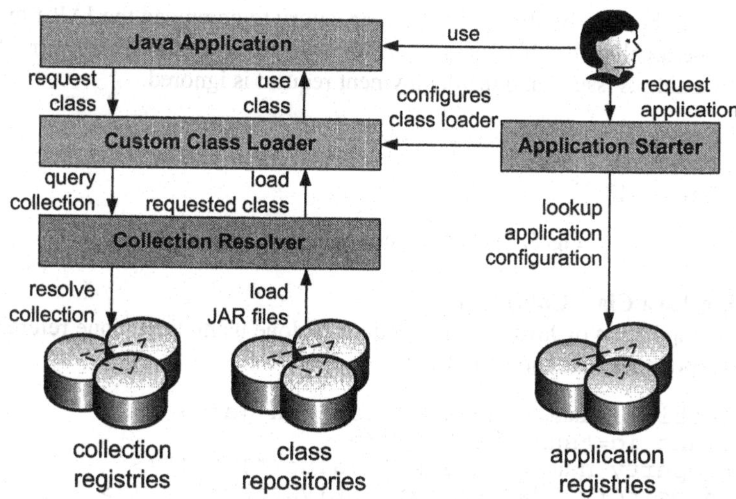

Fig. 3. Custom Class Loader, Collection Resolver and Application Starter

A JAR file is retrieved from the class repositories by the collection resolver but only requested classes are actually downloaded by the custom class loader. Finally, the application can use the class without having been involved in the lookup and download process. A particular application starter is used to start the Java application and to replace the system class loader with the custom class loader, as shown in fig. 4.

```
ClassLoader cl = new CClassCollectionLoader(config);
Class mainClass = cl.loadClass(szMain);
Class t[]={ String[].class };
Method meth = mainClass.getDeclaredMethod("main", t);
meth.invoke(null, arg);
```

Fig. 4. Application Starter Using Custom Class Loader

After the custom class loader `CClassCollectionLoader` has been created, it is used to load the class containing the main method. Due to the class loading strategy of Java, subsequent class loading requests of the main class will use the custom class loader. For further implementation details concerning Java class collections and related custom class loaders we refer to our previous work [11].

3.3 Use

In the following, we briefly illustrate an exemplary work flow covering the deployment of a Java application into an application repository and how it is dynamically installed on an application system.

Uploading Java Class Repositories

First, the upload of a new Java class repository, e.g. a JAR file requires a configuration file as shown in fig. 5. The attribute `id` tags this Java class repository and is later used to reference it within a Java class collection. The attribute `url` denotes the location which may be used by the application repository to download the JAR file and to put it into the local cache. If a class repository with the passed id was already uploaded, a warning is issued and the deployment request is ignored.

```
<repository id="sun-jaf-activation-1.0.1">
  <jarfile url="http://crossware.org/jaf-1.0.1.jar" />
</repository>
```

Fig. 5. Deployment of a Java Class Repository

Registering Java Class Collections

Next, the composition of Java class collections is done using the unique references to Java class repositories, as shown in fig. 6.

```
<collection name="sun-jaf" id="sun-jaf">
 <variant id="sun-jaf-1.0.1">
   <property name="release" value="1.0.1"/>
   <repository id="sun-jaf-activation-1.0.1">
     <class name="com/sun/activation/.*"/>
     <class name="javax/activation/.*"/>
   </repository></variant></collection>
```

Fig. 6. Grouping Java Classes Using Class Collections and Referencing Class Repositories

Similar to the identifier used for Java class repositories, we introduce an attribute id that can be used to reference this Java class collection. In addition, we define a section variant which represents a certain collection of Java classes taken from the specified class repository sun-jaf-activation-1.0.1 and matching the given package pattern, e.g. com/sun/activation/.*. All other classes of the class repository are not included in this class collection. This variant can either be referenced using its unique id sun-jaf-1.0.1 or passing a description of features matched by the property list, e.g. release and 1.0.1. The configuration file is finally uploaded to the collection registry.

Registering Java Application Configurations

Now, the Java class repositories denote the location of Java classes and the Java class collections compose selected classes into custom class sets. In the next step, an application is configured using Java class collections, as shown in fig. 7.

```
<application name="texteditor" id="texteditor">
 <main class="de.fraunhofer.texteditor.Main">
 <property name="version" value="2.1.0"/>
 <collection id="texteditor">
  <property name="release" value="2.1"/>
 </collection> <collection id="sun-jaf">
  <property name="release" value="1.0"/>
 </collection> </application>
```

Fig. 7. Application Configuration Using Java Class Collections

The application configuration contains the attribute `main class` used to start the application, a set of properties describing the application such as `version` and `2.1.0` and a list of collections representing the Java classes required to run the application such as `texteditor`. In the example, the Java class collection `sun-jaf` is not referenced by its id but by a property list, e.g. `release` and `1.0`. In case the application is installed, the application system is free to choose compatible versions of `sun-jaf` as long as the major/minor version numbers are `1.0`, e.g. `1.0.1`.

Customizing Java Application Installation
The self-configuration of the application installation is supported using additional properties which are not only processed using the requirement descriptions of the application but are also evaluated with respect to the capabilities of the current node.

```
<collection name="texteditor" id="texteditor">
  <variant id="console">
   <property name="release" value="2.1"/>
   <property name="screen" value="text_80x50"/>
   <repository id="texteditor-console">
     <class name="crossware/texteditor/.*"/>
   </repository> </variant>
  <variant id="gui">
   <property name="release" value="2.1"/>
   <property name="screen" value="gui_1024x768"/>
   <repository id="texteditor-gui">
     <class name="crossware/texteditor/.*"/>
   </repository> </variant> </collection>
```

Fig. 8. Customizing Java Application Installation

As shown in fig. 8, there are two variants for the collection `texteditor` available with the same release `2.1`. In addition, there is a property `screen` which can be used to select the first variant on nodes offering only a text console and the second one on nodes with a graphical user interface.

Starting Java Applications
While the previous tasks are usually performed by deployers, the customer starts an application using the prepared configurations and uploaded classes. To this end, an extra Java application `CMainStarter` is started with the location of the application configuration file, as shown in fig. 9.

```
java org.crossware.xdk.system.CMainStarter \
 uri=http://crossware.org/jcc/texteditor?version=1.0.0
```

Fig. 9. Starting an Application Using a Remote Configuration File

The parameter `uri` could also point to a locally edited file but in the example above it retrieves a matching application configuration by passing the attribute version 1.0.0 to the application repository on `crossware.org`. As a result, the application repository resolves a suitable application configuration and passes it back to the application system. There, the application configuration is processed and the related class collection configuration files and Java classes are downloaded from the collection registry and class repositories, respectively. After that, the application is started using the main class given in the application configuration. Sometimes it is not possible to start a Java application. For example, the JSP compiler of Jakarta Tomcat is starting a `javac` process which requires passing the classes using CLASSPATH. In this case, we provide a compatibility mode which cannot be dynamically customized but is a workaround for applications that cannot use custom class loaders, as shown in fig. 10.

```
java org.crossware.xdk.system.CJarBuilder \
 uri=http://crossware.org/jcc/texteditor?version=1.0.0\
 > texteditor-1.0.0.jar;
java -jar texteditor-1.0.0.jar
```

Fig. 10. Starting an Application in Compatibility Mode with Native System Class Loader

Instead of starting an extra starter application with a custom class loader, we extract the related Java classes from the class repositories and generate a custom JAR file representing a snapshot of the configured classes. As a result, the Java application can be started without employing a custom class loader but by passing the generated JAR file, as shown at the end of fig. 10.

3.4 Discussion

The presented approach allows to concurrently manage different versions of applications and their components. It supports the distributed deployment and reuse of Java class repositories and hides the actual deployment process among the application repositories. The approach also provides several independent deployment levels and enables the custom definition of application composition without knowing in advance where class repositories have been uploaded and which classes are actually selected. It can be easily applied without modifying legacy Java class repositories or customizing the application code. In comparison with approaches like Sun Java Web Start, it seems to be more complex. This is especially true for small and single application installations. However, regarding large scale scenarios with many nodes and application components, the advantage is the one-time deployment of a certain class repository and the reuse across different applications and repositories. Consequently, the more applications and nodes are involved the better the presented approach releases deployers and customers from details of application deployment and installation, respectively. In addition, it separates the concerns of deployment, composition and configuration without introducing a new programming model. Finally, the approach is not limited to certain application scenarios such as client-side installations and can also be used with applications that do not run with a custom class loader.

4 Application of the Approach

In the following, we briefly present an application of our approach with respect to a so called *Internet Application Workbench* [12] shown in fig. 11. It enables the dynamic employment of Internet applications which have been not installed in advance but are retrieved on-demand using the presented approach.

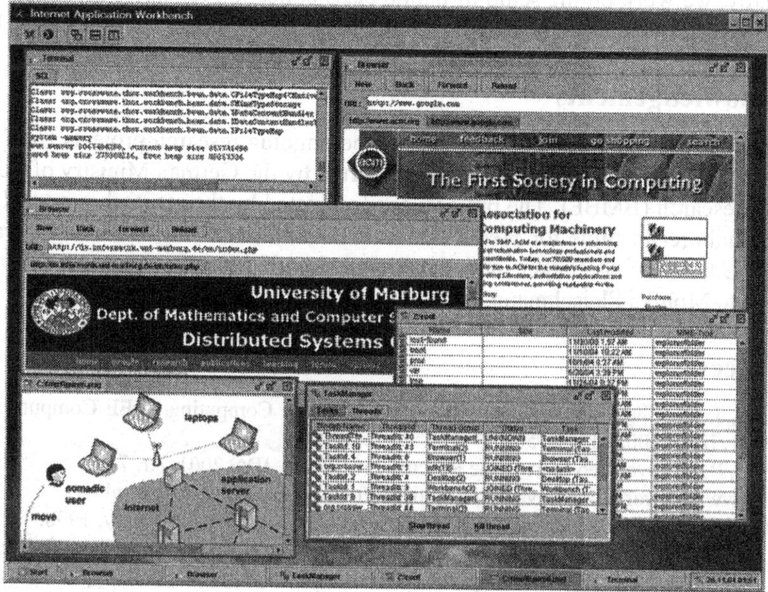

Fig. 11. Internet Application Workbench

In contrast to legacy Java applets or pure Sun JNLP it allows the concurrent execution and sharing of several Java applications in the same Java Virtual Machine [13]. At the initial setup of the workbench on a new Internet node we use Sun Java Web Start and Sun JNLP to deploy a cross-platform application system [14] on the client computer. The application system subsequently utilizes the presented approach to dynamically retrieve and share suitable application classes which match the selected application configurations as well as the capabilities of the current Internet platform. As a result, the Internet Application Workbench can be dynamically extended using remote application configurations and the deployment process is appropriately customized without user intervention.

5 Conclusions

In this paper, we have discussed the objectives and requirements of dynamic software deployment of Java applications in distributed application environments. We have presented our approach using distributed application repositories and Java class collections to dynamically install and update application components on demand without particular user intervention. The realization of the approach and its use were illustrated. Finally, we outlined the application of the approach for deploying an Internet Application Workbench.

There are several areas for future work. First, we currently investigate how to introduce access and composition control of already installed application components. Second, dynamic discovery and integration of application repositories like in peer-to-peer networks and the introduction of self-managing features such as the autonomic selection of compatible collections according to a particularly defined plan are studied. Finally, we work on the setup of public class collection registries for major Java class repositories which can be used to build a global deployment infrastructure [15].

6 Acknowledgements

The presented approach has been applied in the ongoing research projects CAT [16] and AWAKE [17] which are financially supported by the German Ministry of Education and Research (BMBF). The projects are conducted by the research group MARS of the Fraunhofer Institute for Media Communication, Sankt Augustin in cooperation with the University of Siegen and the University of Marburg, Germany. Special thanks go to Monika Fleischmann, Wolfgang Strauss and Jasminko Novak.

References

1. Kephart, J. O., Chess, D. M. The Vision of Autonomic Computing. IEEE Computer. Vol. 36, Nr. 1. IEEE 2003. pp. 41-50.
2. Srinivas, R. N. Java Web Start to the Rescue. JavaWorld. IDG 2001. Nr. 7. http://www.javaworld.com/javaworld/jw-07-2001/jw-0706-webstart_p.html
3. Hunter, J., Crawford, W., Ferguson, P., Java Servlet Programming, O'Reilly, 1998.
4. Paal, S., Kammüller, R., Freisleben, B. Java Class Deployment with Class Collections. Proc. 2003 Conf. on Objects, Components, Architectures, Services, and Applications for a Networked World. LNCS 2591. Erfurt, Germany. Springer 2003. pp. 135-151.
5. Kurzyniec, D., Sunderam, V. Flexible Class Loader Framework: Sharing Java Resources in Harness System. Proc. of International Conference on Computational Science (ICCS). LNCS 2073. Springer-Verlag 2001. pp. 375-384.
6. Liang, S., Bracha, G. Dynamic Class Loading In The Java Virtual Machine. Proc. of ACM OOPSLA.,1998. pp. 36-44.
7. Deploy Directory. http://www.quest.com/deploydirector/
8. Goodwill, J. Apache Jakarta Tomcat. APress. 2001.
9. Apache Server Framework Avalon. http://jakarta.apache.org/avalon/framework/index.html
10. PowerUpdate. http://www.zerog.com/products_pu.html
11. Paal, S., Kammüller, R., Freisleben, B. Customizable Deployment, Composition and Hosting of Distributed Java Applications. Proc. of the 4th Int. Symposium on Distributed Objects and Applications (DOA 2002). LNCS 2519. Irvine, USA. Springer 2002. pp. 845-865.
12. Paal, S., Kammüller, R., Freisleben, B. Supporting Nomadic Desktop Computing Using an Internet Application Workbench. Proc. of the 5th International Conference for Distributed Objects and Applications (DOA 2004). Larnaca, Cyprus 2004. (to appear)
13. Paal, S., Kammüller, R., Freisleben, B. Java Class Separation for Multi-Application Hosting. In Proc. 3rd Conf. on Internet Computing . Las Vegas,. CSREA 2002. pp. 259-266.
14. Paal, S., Kammüller, R., Freisleben, B. Cross-Platform Application System for Nomadic Desktop Computing. Proc. 2004 Conf. on Objects, Components, Architectures, Services and Applications for a Networked World. LNCS 3263. Erfurt, Germany, 2004. pp. 185-200.
15. Crossware - Middleware for Cross-Platform Application Environment. http://crossware.org
16. Fleischmann, M., Strauss, W., Novak, J., Paal, S., Müller, B., Blome, G., Peranovic, P., Seibert, C., Schneider, M. netzspannung.org - An Internet Media Lab for Knowledge Discovery in Mixed Realities. In Proc. 1st Conf. on Artistic, Cultural and Scientific Aspects of Experimental Media Spaces, St. Augustin, Germany. pp. 121-129., 2001.
17. AWAKE - Networked Awareness for Knowledge Discovery. Fraunhofer Institute for Media Communication. St. Augustin, Germany. 2003. http://awake.imk.fraunhofer.de

Semantic Caching of Code Archives

Christoph Pohl[1], Boon Chong Tan[2] and Alexander Schill[3]

[1] SAP AG, Research Center Dresden, Germany
christoph.pohl@sap.com
[2] Siemens AG, ICN EN HS D 513, Munich, Germany
boon.tan@siemens.com
[3] TU Dresden, Chair for Computer Networks, Germany
schill@rn.inf.tu-dresden.de

Abstract In distributed computing environments, clients often need to dynamically download code archives containing program modules from different servers. The hierarchical inner structure of code archives and the partial overlapping between different versions of code archives imposes the applicability of semantic caching approaches, which basically aim at reducing the size of result sets of future queries by intersecting them with results that can already be anticipated from the cache content. This paper devises an extension for an existing cache infrastructure for code archives to adopt notions of semantic caching, allowing it to reason over the discrete contents of its cache store. The logical framework of the implementation is provided by a formal model. A preliminary performance evaluation proves the effectiveness and efficiency in terms of saved bandwith and download times, especially for slow client-server connections.
Keywords: Information Retrieval, Semantic Caching, Web Caching, Code Archives, Java

1 Introduction

The Siemens HiPath 4000 product line [1] provides the network infrastructure for large-scale telecommunication services of numerous customers. The accompanying tools also comprise a large number of network management applications in the form of Java Applets. Figure 1 depicts an exemplary HiPath 4000 network constellation. Siemens *customer service* technicians can access their different customer networks via a

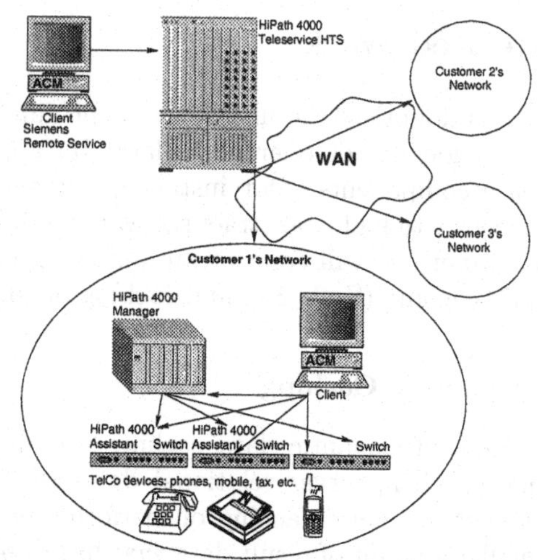

Fig. 1. HiPath 4000 network management model

HiPath Teleservice Server (HTS). Each *customer network* features at least one *HiPath Manager* to control, monitor, and administrate its subsidiary *Assistant* servers in a network of switches. Administrative *client* machines use Web-based tools to operate this infrastructure.

A key element of this client management suite is the *Applet Cache Manager* (ACM) – a software component responsible for reducing redundant Applet downloads. The ACM is thus overriding the page caching features of client Web browsers by providing a proprietary caching service based on versions and origins of Applets. These Applets are packaged in Java ARchives (JAR files) that often differ only slightly between consecutive versions. However, ACM realizes them as totally different cache items, although only small portions of them have actually changed. It cannot recognize these similarities because it lacks vital knowledge regarding the actual contents of JAR code archives. Thus, precious bandwith and time is wasted to transfer mostly redundant files. To remain effective, client caches furthermore bloat in size, even though most of the cache content is partially redundant.

Thus, the idea arose to apply known approaches of semantic caching (see Sect. 2.1) to hierarchical code archives like JAR files with the motivation to save bandwith, to reduce download time, and to minimize cache sizes. The content of a JAR file can be envisaged as a semantic region that formally represents the query for a certain archive, described by its result set.

The remainder of this paper is organized as follows: Section 2 gives a brief overview of related approaches to semantic caching and caching of code archives. Section 3 first introduces our approach of applying principles of semantic caching to code archives and furthermore outlines our prototypical implementation, followed by a brief evaluation of performance benefits in Sect. 4. Finally, we conclude with an outlook.

2 Related Work

Caching is doubtless the most prominent approach to speed up data access by increasing locality of referenced data. Its applications range from the lowest hardware components – for instance, different levels of CPU instruction and data caches – to highly abstract software modules like Web browser page caches. In this paper, we will concentrate on two special fields of caching technology: semantic caching (Sect. 2.1) and caching of code archives (Sect. 2.2).

2.1 Semantic Caching

The notion of semantic data caching was first introduced as a data caching scheme for client-server relational database environments [2, 3]. It has been shown that semantic caching outperforms page and tuple caching because of the smaller amount of result data that has to be transferred. This is achieved by issuing potentially smaller remainder queries after intersecting a client's current cache content with the expected query result.

The principle is depicted in Fig. 2: Let Q be a query $Q = x > x_1 \wedge y \leq y_3$. The current cache content can be described by $V = x < x_2 \vee (y \geq y_1 \wedge y \leq y_2)$. Hence, Q can be split into *probe query* $\mathcal{P}$ and *remainder query* $\mathcal{R}$: $\mathcal{P}(Q, V) = (x > x_1 \wedge x < x_2 \wedge y \leq y_3) \vee (x > x_2 \wedge y \geq y_1 \wedge y \leq y_2$ and $\mathcal{R}(Q, V) = (x \geq x_2 \wedge y < y_1) \vee (x \geq x_2 \wedge y > y_2 \wedge y \leq y_3)$. Semantic caching exploits semantic locality rather than spatial or temporal locality of reference for its cache management meta-data. Individual cache entries are represented by *semantic regions* containing constraint queries as references and lists of data tuples as content.

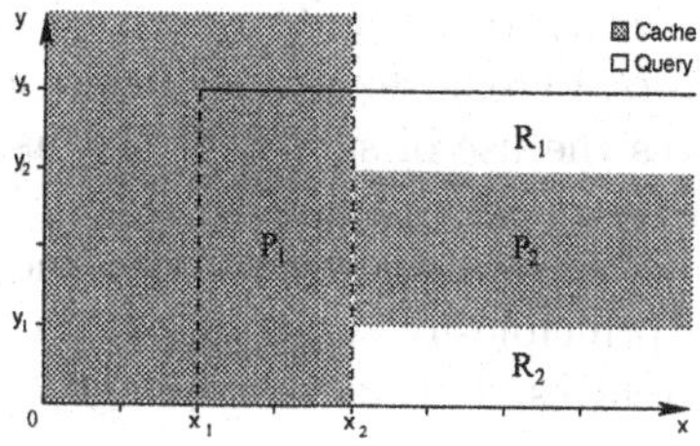

Fig. 2. Semantic caching

The problem of answering queries using views [4] is closely related to the issue of query containment in semantic caching. This in turn leads to the problem of query folding [5] – a technique for rewriting database queries, which is generally applied in data warehouse applications for query optimization, data integration, etc. For instance, [6] investigates this problem with respect to semantic caching. Reducing the search space of query rewritings vs. completeness of possible rewritings is one major issue in this connection.

The main advantages of semantic caching are: *(i)* Clients share query workload, thus increasing scalability of servers; *(ii)* local caches can still partially serve queries of weakly connected clients; *(iii)* approximate answering of aggregate queries; and *(iv)* faster response times, especially when using answer set pipelining.

Semantic caching is particularly advantageous in environments with frequently overlapping or interrelated data queries and intersecting result sets – the hot spots of databases. Semantic caching is also employed within mediator components of distributed heterogeneous database environments to reduce query response times [7, 8]. While [7] proposes to store projection attributes along with condition attributes within the semantic cache, [8] neglects this approach. The application of semantic caching for Web databases in mediators and at wrapper level has also been investigated by [9, 10].

Weakly connected mobile clients especially benefit from semantic caching. [11] introduces semantic caching in mobile computing environments where location dependent data is used.

Semantic locality in client-side caches of hypertext access systems can also be seen as an application for semantic caching. [12] defines semantic regions as a cluster of semantically related logical documents, i.e., subsequently visited, inter-connected documents. This hierarchical nature of this approach is quite similar to our concept of applying semantic caching to code archives.

Attempts to incorporate semantic caching for web queries have been made based on the assumption that form-based web queries can either be translated to SQL with simple predicates over form attributes [6] or reduced to Datalog queries evaluation [13]. Conjunctive web queries, which use only AND and NOT operators, were developed primarily for keyword-based Web meta searching. [13] proposes the use of signature files as the basis for caching in their "Constraint Based Knowledge Broker".

However, no existing work is known to us that tackles the challenge of applying principles of semantic caching to the hierarchical, overlapping nature of code archives. This fact encouraged us to conduct research in this direction.

2.2 Caching of Code Archives

Today's Web browsers typically feature a generic (persistent) cache for objects retrieved via (HTTP) Internet connections, e.g., HTML pages, images, or Java Applets. The principle is quite simple: The Uniform Resource Identifier (URI) [14] of the requested object serves as cache key, the corresponding Web object is saved as a local file for later re-use. However, this mechanism does not recognize, for instance, identical archives from different addresses. It is therefore insufficient for the needs of HiPath ACM.

Since version 1.3 of the Java Plug-in [15], which is part of the Java 2 Runtime Environment, Standard Edition (JRE), there is a parameter `cache_option` that can be handed over to Applets to select between default browser caching for Applets, no caching, or caching Applets within the new Java Plug-in cache. The latter is exclusively reserved for caching Applet code archives in contrast to the browser cache that Applets have to share with all other Web objects. It is furthermore possible to specify a number of JAR files and corresponding required version numbers to control cache management. Although this approach allows more flexibility, it still suffers from the main problem of browser caching: Equivalent versions originating from different servers are still treated as entirely different archives. This issue even persists with JRE version 1.4, despite its numerous novel features. Moreover, some HiPath Applets are yet incompatible with JRE 1.4, thus preventing the use of any exclusive features of this newer platform.

Sun has also launched another technology called Java Web Start [16] for secure, platform-independent, Applet-like deployment of Java applications. Web Start is now part of the standard JRE since version 1.4, but it can also be installed stand-alone for earlier Java versions. Apart from many advantages over standard Applets Java Web Start also features an additional caching module similar to the one of the Java Plug-in. With Java Web Start, it would be possible to implement a functionality similar to what the HiPath ACM did before our improvements. However, it still imposes the limitation of host-name-based caching of JAR files, just like the Java Plug-in and standard browser caching. It furthermore imposes obstacles to backward compatibility of existing deployed applications at Siemens customer sites.

We conclude that all above presented mechanisms for caching of code archives suffer the same limitations, because they all take an "all-or-nothing" approach to caching individual files. There is no concept for considering the inner semantic structure of code archives. Another point against these existing mechanisms is their common notion of a single server being accessed by numerous clients. Contrary, HiPath Clients are few in comparison to the number "servers", i.e., managed active network devices. Hence, a mechanism is needed that does not take the originating server of a code archive into account. This realization was the driving force behind the implementation we will present in the following sections.

3 Implementation

The most prominent conceptual modification of our ACM extension is the additionally introduced cache abstraction, which is depicted in Fig. 3. The *JAR Cache Store (JCS)* manages logical entries for entire code archive versions, thus preserving backward compatibility to the original ACM functionality. Internally, the logical and physical management of these code archives' subcomponents and atoms is done separately by the *Discrete Cache Store (DCS)*. We also refer to this distinction as *component level* (JCS) vs. *document level* (DCS). In the next subsections, we will further investigate the various architectural implications of the abstraction on client and server side.

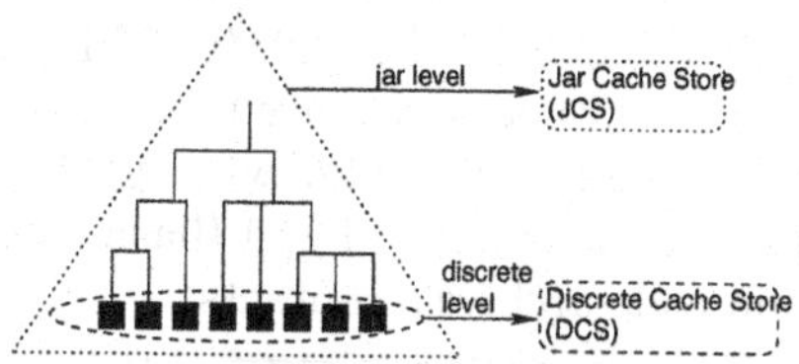

Fig. 3. Cache abstraction

3.1 Semantic Caching Levels

We distinguish four different operating modes of our ACM semantic caching extension: *(i)* no caching (for testing purposes), *(ii)* default caching (original ACM functionality for the sake of compatibility), *(iii)* semantic caching level 1 (**L1**), and *(iv)* semantic caching level 2 (**L2**).

L1 operates on the component level, leveraging only functionality of JCS. Regarding cache containment, JCS considers the sizes and hash values of code archives in contrast to just the originating path and version attributes. Thus, L1 takes especially the fact into account that numerous HiPath 4000 Applets redundantly share identical JAR files with different version numbers and path values, which would otherwise cause them to be cached as different individual components by the original ACM's default caching mode.

In contrast, **L2** operates on the document level, additionally using the DCS module. DCS basically uses the same information as JCS for its cache organization – size, hash value, and link path – but for individual components of code archives, i.e., files and directory (sub-)trees within JAR files. The L2 operating mode involves calculating probe and remainder queries as introduced in Sect. 2.1 based on the actual contents of JAR files. Apart from *total* and *disjoint* matching, we distinguish *structural*, and *document* intersection, as well as *region/component* containment, with respect to (sub-)trees and leafs in Fig. 3 as the semantic regions of our probe and remainder queries. The details of client-server interaction for the L2 operating mode are explained in the next two subsections, followed by the locical framework that forms the theoretical foundation of our cache model in Sect. 3.4.

3.2 Client Side

The most important client-side modules are the *Query Manager* and the *Client Jar Manager*, which closely interact with the above introduced JCS and DCS. Each code archive is accompanied by additional structural meta-data, which we call *Component Info XML*. This meta-data is precomputed at server-side (see Sect. 3.3) and retrieved by the Query Manager the first time an ACM client accesses a yet unknown JAR file. It basically contains the hierarchically structured, accumulated `cid` (hash value), `size`, and `tid` (title) attributes of a certain code archive's contents.

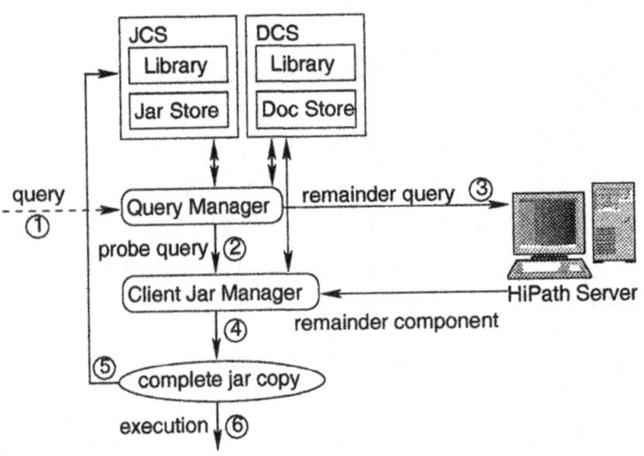

Fig. 4. Schematic client-side interaction

When a query for some code archive *(1)* can not be answered by JCS based on its `cid` and `size` attributes (cf. **L1** in Sect.3.1), the Query Manager intersects the archive's component info with the component info entries in DCS, as depicted in Fig. 4. Thus, it decomposes the query into a probe query to the Client Jar Manager *(2)* and a remainder query to the *HiPath Server (3)*. These queries essentially consist of component info XML fragments. The Client Jar Manager basically handles compression and extraction of code archives. This is necessary to generate physical probe components from DCS contents according to probe queries issued by the Query Manager and also to integrate both probe and remainder components to complete code archives *(4)* for insertion into JCS *(5)* and for client use *(6)*.

The current ACM extension implements a *Least Frequently Used (LFU)* replacement scheme using a replacement value $r = w_{JCS} \times f_{JCS} + f_{DCS}$ for each cache item, where w_{JCS} is a weight factor > 1, f_{JCS} and f_{DCS} are the access frequencies of a particular cache item. Replacement is triggered if the cache size exceeds a certain quota, starting with those items with the lowest value of r.

On the other hand, *cache consistency* is not so much an issue for our implementation in terms of client-server coherence, since code archives are uniquely identified versions that do not expire once they have been released. However, consistency between JCS and DCS must be guaranteed as well. Therefore, we integrated a few fault handling strategies to tackle inconsistencies between these two parts.

3.3 Server Side

The server-side part of our proposed cache architecture comprises several heuristic improvements. In analogy to the Query Manager on client side, the *SCacheManager* module is responsible for serving remainder queries for code archives on the server side as depicted in Fig. 5. It first tries to anticipate an appropriate response from the *Server-side Cache Store (SCS)*, which we introduced for performance reasons to prevent subsequent (re-)generation of popular incomplete code archives, i.e. remainder components. In case of a cache miss in SCS, the *Expanded Package Store (EPS)* is queried next, which contains extracted complete original code archives. This cache store is in turn an optimization to avoid redundant decompression of frequently used code archives. If EPS also produces a cache miss, the SCacheManager uses information from the *Registration service Library (RegLib)* to physically retrieve the original code archive, which is then unpacked by the *JarManager* and stored to EPS. The JarManager also creates the *remainder component* (i.e., the incomplete package), which is stored to SCS before it is sent to the client.

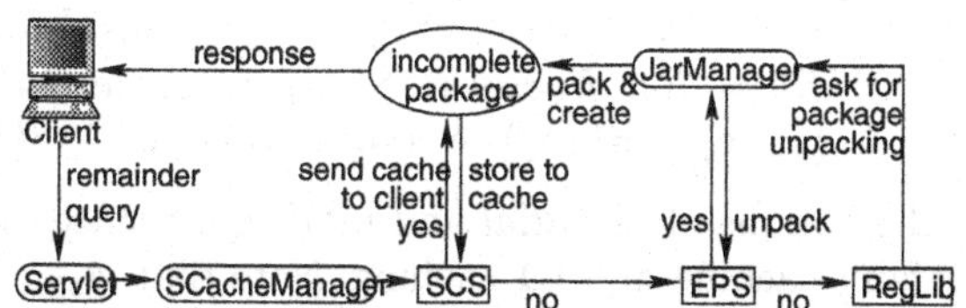

Fig. 5. Schematic server-side interaction

3.4 Formal Model

In the following, we introduce a short outline of the formal model that allows logical reasoning about our semantic cache extensions. The model serves as a formal specification that logically ensures the correctness of the implementation of the semantic cache architecture.

Let a collection of code archives $\mathcal{J} = \{R\}$ be a set of string tuples $\langle Version, Cachepath, \texttt{tid}\rangle$. C_{R_i} represents a physical component referenced by R_i; $D_k^{R_i}$ represents a discrete document of C_{R_i}, $1 \leq k \leq |C_{R_i}|$. Moreover, $\mathcal{C} = \bigcup C_{R_i}$ represents all physical components of C_{R_i} and $\mathcal{D} = \bigcup D_k^{R_i}$ represents all discrete documents of $\mathcal{C}$.

Definition 1. *Given a collection of code archives $\mathcal{J} = \{R_i\}$, we define a* ***semantic region*** *$\mathcal{S}$ as a tuple $\langle R_i, S_{title}, S_{content}\rangle$ where*

$$\begin{aligned} R_i &= \langle Version_{R_i}, Cachepath_{R_i}, \texttt{tid}_{R_i}\rangle \\ S_{title} &= \langle \texttt{tid}, \texttt{cid}, \texttt{size}\rangle \\ S_{content} &= \mathbf{GTT3}(\mathcal{A}_{\texttt{tid}}, \mathcal{A}_{\texttt{cid}}, \mathcal{A}_{\texttt{size}}) \\ &= \mathbf{GTT}(\mathbf{GTT}(\mathcal{A}_{\texttt{tid}}, \mathcal{A}_{\texttt{cid}}), \mathcal{A}_{\texttt{size}}) \end{aligned}$$

GTT3 is a ternary Ground Tree Transducer [17] of three bottom-up Deterministic Finite Tree Automata (DFTA) $\mathcal{A}_{\texttt{tid}}$, $\mathcal{A}_{\texttt{cid}}$, and $\mathcal{A}_{\texttt{size}}$, which is derived from the transitive and composition closures of **GTT**. The detailed definitions of the DFTA $\mathcal{A}_{\texttt{tid}}$, $\mathcal{A}_{\texttt{cid}}$, and $\mathcal{A}_{\texttt{size}}$ have been omitted for brevity.

Definition 2. *Two semantic regions $\mathcal{S}_1, \mathcal{S}_2$ as defined above are **totally equivalent*** iff $R_1 = R_2$. *However, $\mathcal{S}_1, \mathcal{S}_2$ are **essentially equivalent*** iff $(\texttt{cid}_1 = \texttt{cid}_2) \wedge (\texttt{size}_1 = \texttt{size}_2) \wedge (\mathcal{A}_{\texttt{cid}_1} = \mathcal{A}_{\texttt{cid}_2}) \wedge (\mathcal{A}_{\texttt{size}_1} = \mathcal{A}_{\texttt{size}_2})$.

The notions of *essential* and *total* equivalence distinguish types of cache hits of default caching and **L1** caching. Note that $\mathcal{A}_{\texttt{tid}_1}$ and $\mathcal{A}_{\texttt{tid}_2}$ do not contribute to the definition of essential equivalence because they refer to the structure level, which can be easily renamed at the client side.

Definition 3. *Two semantic regions $\mathcal{S}_1, \mathcal{S}_2$ as defined above where*

$$\begin{aligned} \mathcal{S}_{title_1} &= \langle \texttt{tid}_1, \texttt{cid}_1, \texttt{size}_1 \rangle \\ \mathcal{S}_{content_1} &= \mathbf{GTT3}(\mathcal{A}_{\texttt{tid}_1}, \mathcal{A}_{\texttt{cid}_1}, \mathcal{A}_{\texttt{size}_1}) = (Q_1, \Sigma_1, \delta_1, Q_{i_1}, Q_{f_1}) \\ \mathcal{S}_{title_2} &= \langle \texttt{tid}_2, \texttt{cid}_2, \texttt{size}_2 \rangle \\ \mathcal{S}_{content_2} &= \mathbf{GTT3}(\mathcal{A}_{\texttt{tid}_2}, \mathcal{A}_{\texttt{cid}_2}, \mathcal{A}_{\texttt{size}_2}) = (Q_2, \Sigma_2, \delta_2, Q_{i_2}, Q_{f_2}) \end{aligned}$$

*are said to be **disjoint*** iff $\forall q_{\texttt{tid1\_cid1\_size1}} \in Q_{i_1}, q_{\texttt{tid2\_cid2\_size2}} \in Q_{i_2} \cdot \texttt{cid}_1 \neq \texttt{cid}_2 \vee \texttt{size}_1 \neq \texttt{size}_2$.

Definition 3 shows disjoint content of archive components in Discrete Level of **L2**, i.e., no discrete documents, which are represented by automaton states, overlap each other in two components. Then, the two components are said to be disjoint and considered to be potentially cached as different entries.

Definition 4. *A **semantic cache** **SC** $= \{\mathcal{S}\}$ consists of $\mathcal{C}_{JCS}$ and $\mathcal{D}_{DCS}$. $\mathcal{C}_{JCS}$ stores the set of* physical components *referenced by S_i in JCS and D_{DCS} stores the set of* discrete documents *of S_i in DCS.*
$\mathcal{C}_{JCS} = \bigcup_r C_r \mid s = \langle r, s_{title}, s_{content} \rangle \in \mathbf{SC}$
$\mathcal{D}_{DCS} = \bigcup_r D^r_k, 1 \leq k \leq |C_r|$

For the following definitions for query processing we assume a semantic region $\mathcal{S}$ as defined above and a query $\mathcal{Q} = \langle R_Q, \mathcal{Q}_{title}, \mathcal{Q}_{content} \rangle$ where

$$\begin{aligned} \mathcal{S}_{title_S} &= \langle \texttt{tid}_S, \texttt{cid}_S, \texttt{size}_S \rangle \\ \mathcal{S}_{content_S} &= \mathbf{GTT3}(\mathcal{A}_{\texttt{tid}_S}, \mathcal{A}_{\texttt{cid}_S}, \mathcal{A}_{\texttt{size}_S}) = (Q_S, \Sigma_S, \delta_S, Q_{i_S}, Q_{f_S}) \\ \mathcal{Q}_{title_Q} &= \langle \texttt{tid}_Q, \texttt{cid}_Q, \texttt{size}_Q \rangle \\ \mathcal{Q}_{content_Q} &= \mathbf{GTT3}(\mathcal{A}_{\texttt{tid}_Q}, \mathcal{A}_{\texttt{cid}_Q}, \mathcal{A}_{\texttt{size}_Q}) = (Q_Q, \Sigma_Q, \delta_Q, Q_{i_Q}, Q_{f_Q}). \end{aligned}$$

Definition 5. *$\mathcal{Q}$ is **fully answerable** from $\mathcal{S}$ if $\mathcal{Q}$ and $\mathcal{S}$ are* totally equivalent *(i.e., cache hit in default caching) or* essentially equivalent *(i.e., cache hit in **L1** since $\mathcal{S} \in \mathcal{C}_{JCS}$) or* $\forall q_{\texttt{tid1\_cid1\_size1}} \in Q_{i_Q} \cdot \exists q_{\texttt{tid2\_cid2\_size2}} \in Q_{i_S} \cdot \texttt{cid}_1 = \texttt{cid}_2 \wedge \texttt{size}_1 = \texttt{size}_2 \mapsto Q_{i_Q} \subseteq Q_{i_S}$ *(i.e., total discrete cache hit, which is actually equivalent to a cache hit of **L1** above.*

Definition 6. *$\mathcal{Q}$ is* ***partially answerable*** *from $\mathcal{S}$ if* $(\texttt{cid}_S \neq \texttt{cid}_Q \vee \texttt{size}_S \neq \texttt{size}_Q) \wedge \exists q_{\texttt{tid1\_cid1\_size1}} \in Q_{i_S}, q_{\texttt{tid2\_cid2\_size2}} \in Q_{i_Q} \cdot \texttt{cid}_1 = \texttt{cid}_2 \wedge \texttt{size}_1 = \texttt{size}_2$.

Definition 7. *$\mathcal{Q}$ is* ***fully answerable*** *from $\mathcal{D}_{DCS}$ if* $\forall q_{\texttt{tid1\_cid1\_size1}} \in Q_{i_Q} \cdot \exists q_{\texttt{tid2\_cid2\_size2}} \in Q_{\mathcal{D}_{DCS}} \cdot \texttt{cid}_1 = \texttt{cid}_2 \wedge \texttt{size}_1 = \texttt{size}_2 \mapsto Q_Q \subseteq Q_{\mathcal{D}_{DCS}}$ *(i.e., total discrete cache hit in* ***L2****.*

Definition 8. *$\mathcal{Q}$ is* ***partially answerable*** *from $\mathcal{D}_{DCS}$ if* $\exists q_{\texttt{tid1\_cid1\_size1}} \in Q_{i_S}, q_{\texttt{tid2\_cid2\_size2}} \in Q_{i_Q} \cdot \texttt{cid}_1 = \texttt{cid}_2 \wedge \texttt{size}_1 = \texttt{size}_2 \wedge \forall \mathcal{S} \in \mathcal{C}_{JCS} \cdot \texttt{cid}_S \neq \texttt{cid}_Q \vee \texttt{size}_S \neq \texttt{size}_Q$ *(i.e., a case which occurs in* ***L2****).*

Definitions 5–8 explain the idea to verify discrete cache hits in both **L1** and **L2** caching. All the definitions given above helped us to reason about the details of query processing and to establish a solid formal basis for our implementation.

4 Evaluation

To validate the benefits of our implementation, we also conducted several performance tests. Since the major optimization goals of our ACM improvements were *lower transfer volumes* and *reduced response times*, we especially examined these two factors. A representative subset of different versions and originating path values (a–k) was arbitrarily chosen for a number of exemplary Applet code archives. This subset was queried sequentially by a test client using each caching mode individually.

In the following, we will discuss the results of one such Applet test run. Figure 6 compares the transfer volumes for the different cache operating modes as introduced in Sect. 3.1. It clearly shows that while **L1** mode produces only "all-or-nothing" cache hits for different originating paths of binary equivalent code archives, **L2** yields continuous cache hit values [0..1] in terms of $bytes_{cached}/bytes_{transferred}$, due to the semantic decomposition into probe and remainder queries. Thus, while L1 already saves 26 % in comparison to default caching, L2 outperforms L1 by another 27 % adding up to a total saving of 60 % of transfer volumes compared to default caching on average.

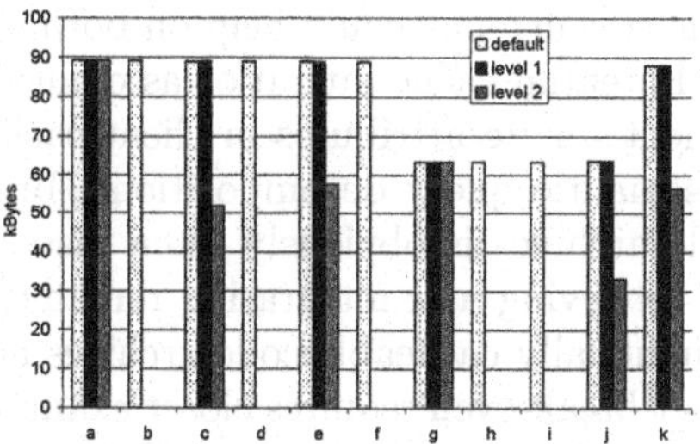

Fig. 6. Transfer volumes

For comparing response times of the three caching modes, we conducted our tests using two different types of client-server connections as depicted in Fig. 7(a) (ISDN/digital) and Fig. 7(b) (modem/analog). It turned out that **L1** outperformed **L2** by 33 % for ISDN connections while L2 only yielded a small saving of 6 % over L1 for modem connections. In other words, the tremendous

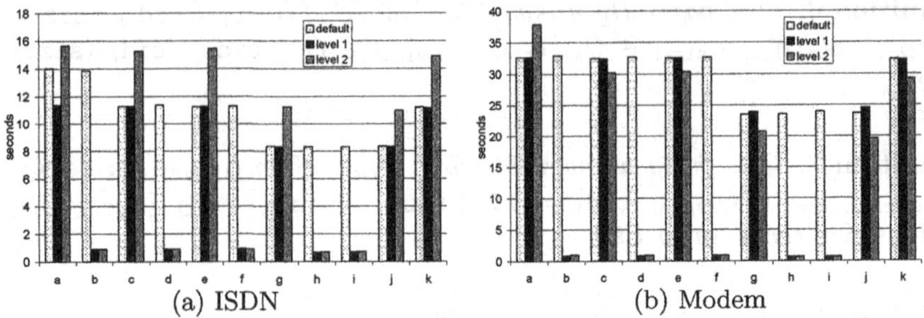

(a) ISDN (b) Modem

Fig. 7. Response times

overhead of semantic query (de-)composition frustrates the achieved benefits in transfer times even for slower connections. This inspired us to further investigate the shortcomings of our prototypical implementation.

We examined the different portions of L2's overhead – which was responsible for roughly half of the overall response time in this operating mode – and thus distinguished the costs for *decomposition* of queries, *preparation* of probe results, *integration* of probe and remainder result sets, and *updating* the cache store at client side, and the cost for *(de-)compression* at server side. We realized that a major part of this time is spent on one hand for preparation, integration, and updating at client side, but on the other hand also for (de-)compression at server side. In the former case, we can make our current XML query/result data handling code responsible for the performance penalty. Whereas in the latter case, the server hardware itself proved to be the bottleneck. Improvements in code concurrency could help on both sides.

Potential cache hit ratios as defined above can be pre-calculated from component's `size` attributes in client cache. This helps to estimate the worthiness of semantic query decomposition: For low ratios, direct download of complete code archives is obviously often faster than the overhead of semantic caching for retrieving and integrating remainder results. Similarly, a minimum size for semantically cacheable code archives also proved to be expedient. However, the exact break-even requires closer examination because it depends on a number of factors like connection speed, client and server performance etc.

We can conclude that our client-side data structures and management code still bears potential for future improvements, while the current implementation prototype is already suitable for environments with higher server performance and slow, expensive network connections.

5 Conclusions and Outlook

Our paper proposed the adoption of semantic caching algorithms to the new application area of code archives. We showed the homomorphic shift of the concept of semantic regions from its traditional background of relational databases towards hierarchical data structures like directory trees in code archives. The viability of this concept was demonstrated with the help of an industry example from the application domain of network management tools. We furthermore outlined the logical foundations of our approach using a formal model.

Initial experiments with real-world data emphasized the practicability and revealed potentials for future enhancements as well as a number of opportunities for immediate improvements of our prototypical implementation. A few of them have already been mentioned at the end of Sect. 4. The next step will be a rewrite of the client side cache store – especially the XML handling portions – for better scalability for large numbers of archives and servers.

We already suggested that our semantic caching approach is also suitable for any other kind of hierarchically structured data. This offers interesting opportunities, e.g., for Web content syndication like it is done using the Resource Description Framework (RDF) [18]. It would also be possible to leverage semantic caching in proxy servers. This means with respect to our example that different clients (i.e., service technicians) would be able use the same semantic cache of code archives for a number of servers (i.e., managed network nodes). These prospects will be subject to our future investigations.

Acknowledgements

Most of the presented work was conducted as part of the HiPath project [1] at Siemens ICN EN HS D 513 and resulted in the graduation of Boon Chong Tan [19] at Dresden University of Technology, Chair for Computer Networks. We would like to express our gratitude to Stefan Beck of Siemens for the inspirations he gave us during countless discussions and for his support during the implementation phase.

References

[1] Siemens AG: (HiPath 4000 Real Time IP System) http:// www.siemensenterprise.com/ prod_sol_serv/ products/ comm_platforms/ hipath4000/ index.shtml.

[2] Keller, A.M., Basu, J.: A predicate-based caching scheme for client-server database architectures. In: Proceedings of the 3rd International Conference on on Parallel and Distributed Information Systems (PDIS'94), Austin, TX, USA, IEEE Computer Society (1994) 229–238

[3] Dar, S., Franklin, M.J., Jónsson, B.T., Srivastava, D., Tan, M.: Semantic data caching and replacement. In Vijayaraman, T.M., Buchmann, A.P., Mohan, C., Sarda, N.L., eds.: Proceedings of the 22th International Conference on Very Large Data Bases (VLDB'96), Mumbai (Bombay), India, Morgan Kaufmann (1996) 330–341

[4] Levy, A.Y., Mendelzon, A.O., Sagiv, Y., Srivastava, D.: Answering queries using views. In: Proceedings of the 14th Symposium on Principles of Database Systems (PODS'95), San Jose, CA, USA, ACM SIGACT-SIGMOD-SIGART, ACM Press (1995) 95–104

[5] Quian, X.: Query folding. In Su, S.Y.W., ed.: Proceedings of the 12th International Conference on Data Engineering (ICDE'96), New Orleans, LA, USA, IEEE Computer Society (1996) 48–55
[6] Luo, Q., Naughton, J.F., Krishnamurthy, R., Cao, P., Li, Y.: Active query caching for database Web servers. In Suciu, D., Vossen, G., eds.: Proceedings of the 3rd International Workshop on Web and Databases (WebDB'00). Volume 1997 of LNCS., Dallas, TX, USA, Springer (2001) 92–104
[7] Li, L., König-Ries, B., Pissinou, N., Makki, K.: Strategies for semantic caching. In Mayr, H.C., Lazansky, J., Quirchmayr, G., Vogel, P., eds.: Proceedings of the 12th International Conference on Database and Expert Systems Applications (DEXA'01). Volume 2113 of LNCS., Florence, Italy, Springer (2001) 284–299
[8] Godfrey, P., Gryz, J.: Answering queries by semantic caches. In Bench-Capon, T., Soda, G., Tjoa, A.M., eds.: Proceedings of the 10th International Conference on Database and Expert Systems Applications (DEXA'99). Volume 1677 of LNCS., Munich, Germany, Springer (1999) 485–498
[9] Lee, D., Chu, W.W.: Conjunctive point predicate-based semantic caching for wrappers in web databases. In Sadri, F., ed.: CIKM'98 First Workshop on Web Information and Data Management (WIDM'98), Bathesda, Maryland, USA, ACM (1998) 45–48
[10] Lee, D., Chu, W.W.: Semantic caching via query matching for web sources. In: Proceedings of the 8th International Conference on Information and Knowledge Management (CIKM'99), Kansas City, Missouri, USA, ACM (1999) 77–85
[11] Ren, Q., Dunham, M.H.: Using semantic caching to manage location dependent data in mobile computing. In Pickholtz, R., Das, S.K., Caceres, R., Garcia-Luna-Aceves, J.J., eds.: Proceedings of the 6th Annual International Conference on Mobile Computing and Networking (MobiCom'00), Boston, MA, USA, ACM Press (2000) 210–221
[12] Cheng, K., Kambayashi, Y.: A semantic model for hypertext data caching. In Spaccapietra, S., March, S.T., Kambayashi, Y., eds.: Proceedings of the 21st International Conference on Conceptual Modeling (ER 2002). Volume 2503 of LNCS., Tampere, Finland, Springer (2002) 276–290
[13] Chidlovskii, B., Borghoff, U.M.: Semantic caching of web queries. The VLDB Journal **9** (2000) 2–17
[14] Berners-Lee, T., Fielding, R., Masinter, L.: Uniform Resource Identifiers (URI): Generic Syntax. IETF. (1998) http://www.ietf.org/rfc/rfc2396.txt.
[15] Sun Microsystems: (Java Plug-in Technology) http://java.sun.com/products/plugin/.
[16] Sun Microsystems: (Java Web Start Technology) http://java.sun.com/products/javawebstart/.
[17] Dauchet, M., Tison, S.: Decidability of confluence for ground term rewriting systems. In Budach, L., ed.: Fundamentals of Computation Theory (FCT'85). Volume 199 of LNCS., Cottbus, GDR, Springer (1985) 80–89
[18] World Wide Web Consortium: Resource Description Framework (RDF). (2004) http://www.w3.org/RDF/.
[19] Tan, B.C.: Efficient storage and retrieval of code archives using semantic caching. Master's thesis, Technische Universität Dresden, Dresden, Germany (2004)

Dezentrale Steuerung verteilter Anwendungen mit rationalen Agenten

Alexander Pokahr, Lars Braubach und Winfried Lamersdorf

Univ. Hamburg, FB Informatik, Verteilte Systeme und Informationssysteme
Vogt-Kölln-Str. 30, 22527 Hamburg
{pokahr, braubach, lamersd}@informatik.uni-hamburg.de

Zusammenfassung. Herkömmliche Methoden für die Steuerung und Koordination verteilter Anwendungen mit weitgehend autonomen Diensten und Prozessen in heterogenen, sich dynamisch ändernden Umgebungen beruhen oft auf *zentralen* Steuerungskomponenten und *statischen* Zustands- und Prozessbeschreibungen. Sie berücksichtigen damit sowohl die Autonomie der Teilprozesse als auch die Dynamik des Anwendungskontextes noch zu wenig. Die *Agententechnologie* wird als ein viel versprechender Ansatz gesehen, Probleme der Konstruktion komplexer verteilter Softwaresysteme in heterogenen Systemumgebungen mit *dezentralen* Steuerungsstrukturen besser beherrschbar zu machen. Durch die naturanaloge Aufteilung des Gesamtproblems in autonome, miteinander interagierende Einheiten lassen sich derartige verteilte Anwendungen adäquat modellieren, simulieren und auch implementieren. Eine *systemtechnische Unterstützung* solcher Anwendungen hat zum Ziel, die aus autonomen Teilaufgaben bestehenden Teilfunktionen und -prozesse rechnergestützt ausführbar und kontrollierbar zu machen. Grundlage dafür sind Middleware-Standards für die Agentenkommunikation sowie entsprechende standardkonforme Plattformen. Zur Realisierung dezentraler Steuerungsprozesse in derartigen Umgebungen ist darüberhinaus die Unterstützung der *Entscheidungsprozesse* (Reasoning) der einzelnen als Agenten modellierten Komponenten besonders wichtig, da diese mangels globaler Sicht oft allein auf Basis lokaler Informationen handeln müssen. Vor diesem Hintergrund stellt das Papier eine im Rahmen eines laufenden DFG-Schwerpunktprogramms entwickelte, agentenbasierte Systemplattform vor, die sowohl die dezentrale Steuerung verteilter Anwendungen als auch die Dynamik der Anwendungsdomäne unter Verwendung *rationaler Agenten* systemtechnisch unterstützt und so die Vorteile erweiterter Middleware-Funktionen mit denen eines agentenorientierten Reasoning-Ansatzes verbindet.

1 Einleitung

Agententechnologie wird heutzutage als ein vielversprechender Ansatz gesehen, Probleme der Konstruktion komplexer Softwaresysteme besser beherrschbar und systemtechnisch umsetzbar zu machen. So kann Agententechnologie z.B. die Modellierung komplexer verteilter Problemstellungen inkl. ihrer Umsetzung in verteilte Softwarelösungen erleichtern, da dabei abstrakte naturanaloge Konzepte als Grundlage einer anwendungsadäquaten Problemlösung verwendet werden. Aufgrund des höheren Abstraktionsgrades bei der agentenorientierten Modellierung solcher Anwendungen können so auch Problemstellungen adressiert werden, die mit herkömmlichen Techniken - wie z.B. der objektorientierten Programmierung - nur schwer handhabbar sind. Als Beleg für diese These können nach Jennings [9] eine Reihe von Argumenten angeführt werden:

1. Agentenorientierte Dekompositionen sind ein effektiver Weg den Problemraum eines komplexen Systems zu partitionieren.
2. Die Schlüsselabstraktionen der agentenorientierten Denkweise sind ein natürliches Mittel, komplexe Systeme zu modellieren.
3. Die agentenorientierte Philosophie zum Modellieren und Verwalten organisationeller Beziehungen ist dazu geeignet, mit den in komplexen Systemen existierenden Abhängigkeiten und Interaktionen besser umzugehen.

Technisch gesehen sind Agenten Softwarebausteine, die über Eigenschaften verfügen, die sie von anderen Komponenten wie z.B. Objekten unterscheiden [11]. Die wichtigsten Eigenschaften sind dabei: Die *Autonomie,* d.h. die Fähigkeit selbstständig und ohne Benutzerinteraktion über einzelne Aktivitäten zu entscheiden, die *Reaktivität,* d.h. die Fähigkeit, die Umgebung wahrzunehmen, und adaptiv auf Ereignisse zu reagieren, sowie die Fähigkeit, ausgehend von abstrakt vorgegebenen Zielen zu jedem Zeitpunkt die jeweils am besten geeignete Handlungsalternative auszuwählen (*zielgerichtetes Verhalten*) und dabei, wenn nötig, auch selbst die Initiative ergreifen zu können (*Proaktivität*). Interaktion zwischen Agenten erfolgt über Nachrichtenaustausch, wobei die Bedeutung des Nachrichteninhalts mittels Ontologien und Sprechakten unabhängig vom konkreten Sender und Empfänger festgelegt wird.

Im Folgenden werden nun Besonderheiten der *agentenorientierten Entwicklung verteilter Softwareanwendungen* näher betrachtet. Dabei werden insbesondere zwei Aspekte der Agententechnologie untersucht: Zunächst werden in Abschnitt 2 Middleware-Standards und konforme Plattformen für Agenten als bereits vorhandene systemtechnische Basis für die Realisierung verteilter Agentenapplikationen vorgestellt. Darauf folgend wird in Abschnitt 3 ein kurzer Überblick über verschiedene Reasoning-Mechanismen für Agenten gegeben. In Abschnitt 4 wird mit der selbst entwickelten Plattformerweiterung Jadex vorgeschlagen, eine direkte Verbindung zwischen Agenten-Middleware und Reasoning herzustellen. Anhand eines Fallbeispieles aus dem Bereich Krankenhauslogistik wird dann in Abschnitt 5 die praktische Anwendbarkeit des Ansatzes aufgezeigt. Kapitel 6 enthält eine Einordnung des Ansatzes in den Kontext verwandter Arbeiten bevor das Papier mit einer Zusammenfassung schließt.

2 Middleware für Agenten

Die Agententechnologie erweitert die Modellierungskonzepte verteilter Systeme und erfordert aufgrund des Paradigmenwechsels hin zu autonomen Softwarebausteinen in offenen verteilten Umgebungen sowohl neue Standards (um die Interoperabilität sicher zu stellen) als auch neue Middleware-Produkte (als systemtechnische Unterstützung um diese Standards umsetzen). Agenten können dabei als Softwarebausteine gesehen werden, die sich auf der Anwendungsebene befinden und mittels Middleware Zugriff auf standardisierte systemtechnische Dienste und Leistungen erhalten.

Für die Interoperabilität von Agenten verschiedener heterogener Plattformen ist derzeit vor allem die Foundation for Intelligent Physical Agents (FIPA) [14] wichtig - eine internationale Non-profit-Organisation, die sich zur Aufgabe gemacht hat, Standards für heterogene interagierende Agenten und Multiagentensysteme (MAS) bereitzustellen. Seit 1997 wurden dazu eine Reihe von Spezifikationen veröffentlicht, die in unregelmäßigen Abständen ersetzt oder ergänzt werden. Dabei konzentrieren sich die Arbeiten auf einerseits Anwendungs- und andererseits Middleware-bezogene Aspekte: Die anwendungsbezogenen Spezifikationen bieten systematisch untersuchte Beispieldomänen mit Dienst- und Ontologiebeschreibungen; die Middleware-bezogenen Spezifikationen behandeln detailliert alle notwendigen Bausteine zur Ausgestaltung einer abstrakten Plattformarchitektur. Dazu gehören sowohl die Mechanismen zur Agentenverwaltung auf der Plattform, als auch Infrastrukturelemente wie Verzeichnisdienste und der Nachrichtentransport. Daneben existieren umfangreiche Spezifikationen auf semantischer und syntaktischer Ebene, welche die Kommunikation zwischen Agenten auf eine einheitliche Basis stellen. Die FIPA-Standards wurden bereits in einer Reihe von Agentenplattformen umgesetzt, welche auch prinzipiell interoperabel sind. Zusätzlich zu den oben aufgeführten Spezifikationsthemen greifen viele dieser Plattformen weitere Middleware-Aspekte auf und bieten spezialisierte Lösungen für z.B. Sicherheits- und Persistenzproblematiken. FIPA-kompatible Middleware-Plattformen ermöglichen es daher, interoperable, offene und zukunftsfähige Systeme zu erstellen.

Dennoch decken weder FIPA-Standards noch die Middleware-Plattformen alle für die Kostruktion verteilter Anwendungen wichtigen Aspekte ab: So erfordern komplexe verteilte Anwendungen häufig nicht nur eine Dekomposition des Gesamtproblems in kleinere Teilprobleme, sondern zusätzlich auch eine adäquate Adressierung der oftmals problemimmanenten Dynamik der Anwendungsdomäne. Nur unter Berücksichtigung dieser Dynamik sowohl auf Modellierungs- als auch auf Realisierungsebene können flexible, adaptive Systeme erstellt werden, die den Ansprüchen komplexer Aufgabenstellungen gerecht werden. Dabei erfordert die für viele verteilte Anwendungen typische Dynamik insbesondere Mechanismen zur Entscheidungsfindung auf Basis der jeweiligen Situation der einzelnen Agenten. Neben der von der Middleware erbrachten Abstraktion von generischen Problemen der Verteilung wird damit also zusätzlich auch eine Abstraktion von Problemen der einzelnen Entscheidungsprozesse notwendig. Für die Beschreibung dieser Entscheidungsprozesse existieren verschiedene Modelle für so genannte *rationale Agenten*, auf die im nächsten Abschnitt näher eingegangen wird.

3 Rationale Agenten

Als rationale Agenten werden Agenten angesehen, die ihre Aktionen auf Grundlage der verfügbaren Informationen fortlaufend neu abwägen und auf Basis kognitiver Fähigkeiten selbständig Entscheidungen treffen können. Dabei beruhen die kognitiven Architekturen auf Theorien zur Beschreibung von Individualverhalten, die ihre Wurzeln in unterschiedlichen Disziplinen wie z.B. der Psychologie, Philosophie oder Biologie haben. Die wichtigsten Konzepte sind in diesem Bereich das Modell Belief-Desire-Intention (BDI) [2,15], die Theorie des Agent Oriented Programming (AOP) [16] und die Unified Theories of Cognition (UTC, SOAR) [10]. Im Folgenden wird speziell auf das BDI-Modell näher eingegangen. Es ist allgemein anerkannt und aufgrund der konzeptuellen Klarheit auch im Bezug auf praktisch eingesetzte Softwaresysteme interessant [8].

Bratman [2] führt im BDI-Modell die Attitüden *Beliefs* (Wissen), *Desires* (Wünsche) und *Intentions* (Absichten) als elementare Bausteine zielgerichteten Handelns ein. Dabei repräsentieren *Beliefs* das subjektiv wahrgenommene Wissen eines Agenten über sich und seine Umwelt und spiegeln somit seine lokal verfügbaren Informationen wider. Diese Informationen sind jedoch kein direktes Abbild der aufgenommenen Reize, sondern zeichnen sich vielmehr durch eine domänenabhängige Abstraktion der Elemente aus, die wichtige Eigenschaften betont und weniger wichtige ausblendet. Dieser Filter- und Interpretationsmechanismus ermöglicht dem Agenten eine persönliche Weltsicht.

Desires repräsentieren die Wünsche eines Agenten, welche die Richtung seines Handelns maßgeblich steuern. Dabei müssen Desires keine konsistente Menge untereinander verträglicher Zielvorgaben sein, sondern können konfligieren und damit nicht gleichzeitig erreichbar sein. Eine konsistente Menge konkreter Ziele wird oft mit dem Begriff *Goals* bezeichnet. Bei einem zielorientierten Vorgehen werden Ziele explizit durch die Angabe von z.B. einem zu erreichenden Zustand formuliert. Dadurch kann nach der Ausführung von Aktionen überprüft werden, ob ein Ziel bereits erreicht wurde, oder Handlungsalternativen gesucht werden müssen. Mit Hilfe von Zielen wird ein Agent in die Lage versetzt proaktiv im Sinne seiner Vorstellungen vorzugehen, anstatt nur auf Ereignisse reagieren zu können.

Ziele versucht ein Agent durch vorgegebene Handlungsfolgen zu erreichen, die in Plänen formuliert werden. Entschließt sich ein Agent ein bestimmtes Ziel mit Hilfe eines Planes zu verfolgen, legt er sich auf die Art und Weise der Zielerfüllung fest. Dieses Festlegen bezüglich der aktuell eingeschlagenen Handlungsstränge wird *Intention* genannt und bildet die dritte Säule des BDI-Modells. In der informatischen Sicht sind die Pläne von vorrangigem Interesse, da sie das Fundament des möglichen Verhaltens bilden. Die Flexibilität im Handeln entsteht bei BDI-Agenten durch die Kombination zweier Facetten. Einerseits ist dies die dynamische Auswahl von Plänen in Bezug auf ein zu erreichendes Ziel. Durch den Prozess des Meta-Level Reasoning kann unter Einbezug auch von Domänenwissen und der aktuellen Informationslage der jeweils am besten geeignetste Plan ausgewählt werden. Scheitert dieser Plan, kann der Auswahlprozess auf Basis der neuen Informationen wiederholt werden, um einen weiteren Plan zu probieren. Andererseits kann die Ausgestaltung der Pläne je nach Bedarf abstrakter oder konkreter ausfallen. Einfache Aktionen können zur Planspezifikation ebenso verwendet werden wie Unterziele, über deren Verfolgungsstrategie erst zur Laufzeit durch das Meta-Level Reasoning entschieden wird.

Grundlage für die meisten Implementierungen von BDI-Systemen ist dabei der abstrakte Interpreter nach Rao und Georgeff (siehe Listing 1). In diesem werden zu Beginn jedes Schleifendurchlaufs die zu einem aufgetretenen Ereignis prinzipiell passenden Pläne bestimmt; danach wird aus diesen verfügbaren Optionen eine Untermenge selektiert (Meta-Level Reasoning), diese der Intentionenstruktur hinzugefügt und schließlich ausgeführt. Alle bis zu diesem Zeitpunkt aufgetretenen externen Ereignisse werden im nächsten Schritt in die Ereignisliste aufgenommen. Abschließend werden die Ziel- und

```
BDI-interpreter
Initialize-state();
repeat
   options := option-generator(event-queue);
   selected-options := deliberate(options);
   update-intentions(selected-options);
   execute();
   get-new-external-events();
   drop-successful-attitudes();
   drop-impossible-attitudes();
end repeat
```

Listing 1. Abstrakter BDI Interpreter aus [15]

Intentionenstrukturen des Agenten aktualisiert indem erfüllte oder unmögliche gewordene Attitüden entfernt werden. In den umgesetzten Systemen existieren zum Teil erhebliche Unterschiede - vor allem hinsichtlich der softwaretechnischen Ausgestaltung der zu Grunde liegenden Konzepte (Beliefs, Goals, Plans). Im Folgenden wird eine konkrete Umsetzung dieser Konzepte im Rahmen einer Erweiterung der standardkonformen Agentenplattform JADE näher beschrieben.

4 Jadex: Eine standardardkonforme BDI-Plattform

Die vorangegangenen Abschnitte motivieren den Bedarf nach einer Agentenplattform, die neben der Interoperabilität auf einer abstrakten Agentenebene durch standardisierte Kommunikation (z.B. nach FIPA) auch die Entwicklung rationaler Agenten durch eine systemtechnische Unterstützung der BDI-Konzepte ermöglicht. Gerade im Bereich der verteilten, aus autonomen Teildiensten bestehenden Anwendungen in dynamischen, d.h. sich laufend ändernden, Umgebungen ist die ausreichende Unterstützung *beider* Aspekte Voraussetzung für eine problemadäqute Anwendungsentwicklung. Im Projekt Jadex [13,3] wird daher der Ansatz verfolgt, bestehende agentenorientierte Middleware-Plattformen um die ihnen bisher fehlenden Konzepte rationaler Agenten zu erweitern. Damit wird ein generisches Framework bereitgestellt, mit dessen Hilfe verteilte Softwaresysteme in unterschiedlichen Anwendungsdomänen unter Verwendung des Agentenparadigmas realitätsnah modelliert und effizient umgesetzt werden können.

Bei der Konzeption wurde deshalb darauf geachtet, den mit dem des BDI-Modell erreichten Abstraktionsgrad auch auf Implementierungsebene möglichst direkt zu unterstützen, um so Anwendungen in möglichst natürlicher d.h. der menschlichen Denkweise ähnlicher Art und Weise modellieren zu können: Anstatt starrer, komplexer Abläufe mit fest vorgegebenen Vorgängen sollen hier nur relativ einfache, in sich geschlossene Funktionalitäten realisiert werden, die die allgemeinen Handlungsmöglichkeiten eines Agenten darstellen. Die Anwendbarkeit dieser Pläne für spezielle Situationen kann dabei über Vorbedingungen näher spezifiziert werden. Derartige Pläne erreichen damit nicht nur einen hohen Grad an Wiederverwendbarkeit, sondern können zudem aufgrund ihrer geringen technischen Komplexität von Domänenexperten verstanden werden. Abstrakte Ziele bilden die Motivation für die Ausführung von

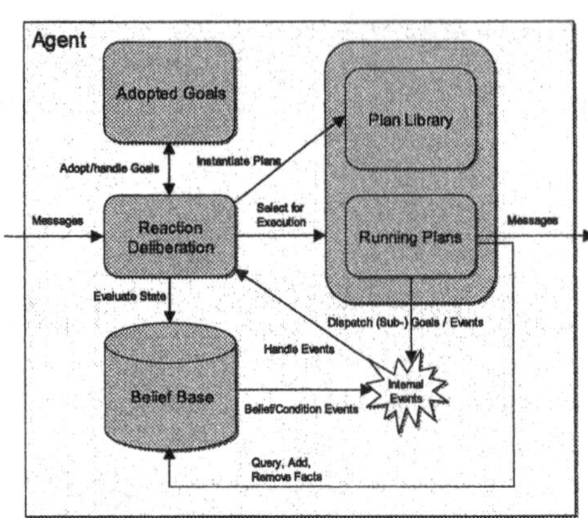

Abb. 1. a: Jadex Architektur

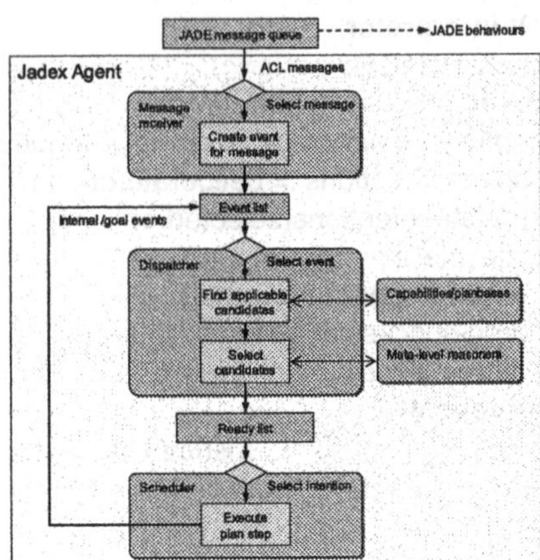

Abb. 1. b: Jadex Verarbeitungszyklus

Plänen. Sie beschreiben einerseits die im System auftretenden Ereignisse, auf die von Agenten reagiert werden muss. Andererseits dienen sie auch der Festlegung allgemeiner Rahmenbedingungen, die vom System automatisch überwacht und im Fehlerfall durch geeignete Maßnahmen wiederhergestellt werden. Das notwendige Wissen zur Ausführung der Pläne und Auswertung von Zielen und Bedingungen wird dabei in der Wissensbasis eines Agenten gehalten und repräsentiert. Unterschiedliche Akteure bzw. Rollen mit spezifischen Zielen, Handlungsmöglichkeiten und Wissen können so auf natürliche Weise durch verschiedene Agenten repräsentiert werden.

4.1 Architektur des Systems Jadex

Abbildung 1.a gibt einen Überblick über die generelle Architektur des auf den oben genannten Grundsätzen realisierten Jadex-Systems: Vom außen betrachtet ist ein Agent eine Black-Box, die lediglich durch Nachrichten mit der Außenwelt kommuniziert und interagiert. Herzstück jedes Agenten ist der Mechanismus zur Reaktion und Deliberation. Ein Agent reagiert auf externe Ereignisse (z.B. Nachrichten anderer Agenten) sowie interne Ereignisse (wie neue Ziele) indem er geeignete Pläne (*Plans*) aus einer entsprechenden Bibliothek auswählt und zur Ausführung bringt. Die Auswahl und Ausführung der Pläne geschieht dabei auf Basis der aktuellen Überzeugungen (*Beliefs*) des Agenten, so dass vor der Ausführung eines Plans überprüfbar ist, ob ein Plan in der aktuellen Situation überhaupt angewendet werden kann, und nach der Ausführung, ob das gewünschte Ergebnis eingetreten ist. Ein Agent ist damit sowohl zu *reaktivem* Verhalten als auch zu *proaktivem* Verhalten, d.h. der Ausführung von Plänen zum Erreichen der eigenen Ziele (*Goals*), fähig.

Der grundlegende Reaktions- und Deliberationsmechanismus wird in Jadex von der sog. *Reasoning Engine* bereitgestellt und ist damit für alle Agenten identisch. Das spezifische Verhalten eines Agenten jedoch wird ausschließlich durch seine konkreten Beliefs, Goals und Plans bestimmt. Im Folgenden wird deshalb näher betrachtet, wie diese drei fundamentalen Konzepte eines BDI-Agenten im Jadex-System realisiert wurden.

Überzeugungen (Beliefs) Im Sinne einer einfachen Verwendbarkeit und Erlernbarkeit verzichtet Jadex auf die (in anderen BDI-Realisierungen übliche) Repräsentation von Beliefs in einer formalen logikbasierten Sprache. Um die Verbindung der objektorientierten Programmierung mit der agentenorientierten Programmierung für den Entwickler so einfach wie möglich zu gestalten, können beliebige Java-Objekte als Beliefs eines Agenten verwendet werden. Damit ist es möglich, von Werkzeugen wie Datenbankschichten und Ontologieentwurfswerkzeugen generierte Klassen direkt im Agenten weiterzuverwenden.

Die Reasoning Engine verwendet die Beliefs als Grundlage zur kontextsensitiven Auswertung von Vor- und Nachbedingungen von Plänen und Zielen. Dazu überwacht die Engine die Beliefs in Bezug auf relevante Änderungen und sorgt automatisch dafür, dass sich diese in den laufenden Zielen und Plänen widerspiegeln. Der Vorteil dieses Modells liegt in der Entkopplung der Manipulation von Daten (Beliefs) an einer Stelle (z.B. in einem Plan) und der dadurch ausgelösten Anpassung des Agenten (durch Erzeugen oder Löschen von Goals und Plans). Daher muss in einem Plan nicht berücksichtigt werden, welche Auswirkungen etwaige Änderungen auf mögliche weitere Ziele bzw. Pläne des Agenten haben. Pläne wie auch Ziele können als in sich geschlossene, wieder verwendbare Komponenten unabhängig voneinander entwickelt werden.

Ziele (Goals) Ziele erlauben die Definition anzustrebender Zustände, ohne dabei bereits konkrete Aktionen festzulegen. Erst zur Bearbeitungszeit werden für Ziele geeignete Pläne ausgewählt und ausgeführt, wobei für jedes Ziel verschiedene alternative Pläne gleichzeitig oder nacheinander ausgeführt werden können bis das Ziel letztendlich erreicht ist. Da ein Agent aber nicht immer alle seine Ziele gleichzeitig verfolgen kann, werden aktive und inaktive Zustände der Zielbearbeitung unterschieden.

In Jadex werden zudem vier verschiedene Arten von Goals unterstützt: Perform-, Achieve-, Query- und Maintain-Goals. Diese Typen unterscheiden sich in der Art und Weise, wann Pläne für diese Ziele ausgeführt werden, und wie entschieden wird, ob ein Ziel erreicht ist. Einzelheiten dazu finden sich in [5]. Diese vier Goal-Typen erlauben es für jede im System vorliegende Aufgabe, die jeweils optimale Repräsentation zu benutzen. So können z.B. für einmalige Aktivitäten Perform-Goals definiert werden, die - basierend auf dem aktuellen Kontext - den richtigen Plan ausführen (z.B. um eine Benachrichtigung per Email oder SMS zu versenden). Achieve- und Query-Goals legen Ergebnisse fest, die benötigt werden bevor weitere Aufgaben fortgesetzt werden können (wie z.B. das Aushandeln eines Termins oder das Finden der Adresse eines Kunden). Mit Maintain-Goals können Bedingungen überwacht werden (z.B. das Einhalten von Fristen durch automatisch vom System ergriffene Maßnahmen - wie etwa die Benachrichtigung des zuständigen Bearbeiters).

Pläne (Plans) Pläne repräsentieren Handlungsalternativen eines Agenten, um Ziele zu erreichen und auf Ereignisse zu reagieren. Dabei besteht ein Plan immer aus zwei Teilen: dem Plankopf (Head) und dem Plankörper (Body). Der Plankörper besteht aus einer Folge von Aktionen und Aktivitäten, und stellt damit im Prinzip ein prozedurales Programm im herkömmlichen Sinne dar. Dagegen ist der Plankopf eine deklarative Beschreibung der Situationen, in denen der Plan eingesetzt werden kann.

Die Auswahl von Plänen erfolgt in einem mehrstufigen Prozess (vgl. Abschnitt 4.2). Dazu wird im Plankopf zunächst angegeben, zur Bearbeitung welcher Ziele oder Ereignisse ein Plan grundsätzlich geeignet ist. Zusätzlich kann die Anwendbarkeit über Vorbedingungen weiter auf einen bestimmten Anwendungskontext eingeschränkt werden. So kann ein Agent z.B. für die Abwicklung einer Bestellung unterschiedliche Pläne auswählen, je nachdem ob es sich um eine externe oder interne Bestellung handelt. Scheitert ein ausgewählter Plan, so werden für das Ziel so lange weitere Pläne ausgeführt bis das Ziel erreicht ist oder keine weiteren Pläne vorhanden sind.

Die eigentliche Anwendungsfunktionalität wird in den einzelnen Plankörpern realisiert. Dies bestehen aus einer Folge von Anweisungen und werden als Java-Klassen implementiert. Dabei kann der Programmierer auf die gesamte Mächtigkeit der Java-Programmiersprache zurückgreifen. Dies vereinfacht die Integration mit bestehenden Anwendungen und Systemen, wo entsprechende Programmbibliotheken oftmals bereits vorliegen.

Agentendefinition Wie gezeigt, besteht ein Jadex Agent aus lose gekoppelten Elementen wie Beliefs, Goals und Plans. Die Zusammenstellung eines Agenten aus seinen initialen Elementen wird in Jadex mittels eines XML-basierten Deskriptors formuliert. Das damit erstellte, so genannte Agent Definition File (ADF) enthält Verweise auf die Java-Klassen, welche z.B. die Belief-Datentypen oder Plankörper implementieren. Alle weiteren Informationen über den Aufbau des Agenten werden deklarativ im ADF angegeben. Dazu gehören die Beschreibungen der Goal-Typen - u.a. mit Parametern und zu erreichenden Zielzuständen - sowie die Planköpfe, die festlegen welche Pläne in welchen Situationen ausgeführt werden können.

4.2 Reasoning Prozess

Die Beliefs, Goals und Plans eines Agenten beschreiben zunächst seine statischen Eigenschaften. Das Verhalten eines Agenten wird dabei maßgeblich durch den Reasoning-Prozess bestimmt, der auf diesen Elementen operiert. Primär dient das Reasoning dazu, auf Ereignisse wie neu entstandene Goals oder eingetroffene Nachrichten durch die Ausführung geeigneter Pläne angemessen zu reagieren.

Abbildung 1.b zeigt den Reasoning Prozess in Jadex. Das Reasoning wird von drei unabhängig voneinander operierenden Komponenten (Message receiver, Dispatcher, Scheduler) durchgeführt. Dennoch ist die Verwandtschaft zum abstrakten Interpreter aus Sektion 3 unverkennbar. Analog zu *get-new-external-events()* verarbeitet der *Message receiver* eingehende Nachrichten und erzeugt entsprechende Ereignisse, die in die Ereignisliste des Agenten eingefügt werden. Der Dispatcher realisiert die Funktionen *option-generator()* und *deliberate(options)* indem er diese und weitere Ereignisse konsumiert, passende Pläne sucht und aus der Menge der passenden Pläne diejenigen auswählt, die zunächst zur Ausführung gelangen sollen. Diese Pläne werden in die Ausführungsliste (*Ready list*) eingetragen und schließlich vom Scheduler im Rahmen der Operation *execute()* schrittweise ausgeführt. Die Ausführung von Plänen kann dabei aufgrund von geänderten Beliefs sowie bearbeiteten oder neu erzeugten Goals zu neuen internen Ereignissen führen, die zur Bearbeitung durch den Dispatcher in der Ereignisliste abgelegt werden.

4.3 Zur Realisierung des Jadex-Systems

Grundlage der Realisierung des Jadex-Systems ist die unter der Führung der Telecom Italia Laboratories (TILab) entwickelte FIPA-konforme Agentenplattform JADE [1]. Aufgrund der breiten Benutzerbasis sowohl im akademischen als auch im industriellen Bereich und der freien Verfügbarkeit unter Open Source-Lizenz bietet die Plattform eine ideale Infrastruktur zur Realisierung verteilter Systeme mit Agenten. Die Plattform legt sich auf keine spezialisierte Technik zur Umsetzung der einzelnen Agenten fest, und bietet somit auch eine gute Ausgangsbasis für Erweiterungen.

Zudem bietet JADE bereits Werkzeuge u.a. zum Abhören der Kommunikation zwischen Agenten an. Im Rahmen des Projekts Jadex wurden weitere Werkzeuge entwickelt, die es z.B. erlauben, den Zustand eines Agenten zur Laufzeit in einer verteilten Umgebung zu überwachen, und auf seine aktuellen Beliefs, Goals und Plans z.B. zu Testzwecken Einfluss zu nehmen. Einzelheiten zur Realisierung des Jadex-Systems findet sich in [13,3]. Das so entstandene System ist unter einer Open Source Lizenz frei verfügbar und wird inzwischen sowohl lokal als auch von anderen Instituten international in verschiedenen Forschungs- und Lehreprojekten eingesetzt.

5 Anwendungsbeispiel

Zur Demonstration der Leistungsfähigkeit der bisher vorgeschlagenen und implementierten Konzepte rationaler Agenten soll abschließend ein Anwendungsbeispiel vorgestellt werden. Dieses stammt aus dem Projekt *MedPAge*, dass im Rahmen des von der Deutschen Forschungsgemeinschaft (DFG) initiierten Schwerpunktprogramms (SPP) *Intelligente Softwareagenten und betriebswirtschaftliche Anwendungsszenarien* [7] durchgeführt wird. Ziel des SPPs mit Beteiligten aus den Gebieten der Wirtschaftsinformatik und der Informatik ist es, Fortschritte auf dem Gebiet der Agententechnologie dadurch zu fördern, dass agentenbasierte Anwendungen in realistischen betriebswirtschaftlichen Szenarien umgesetzt und evaluiert werden. Vor diesem Hintergrund werden im SPP die beiden Anwendungsdomänen Gesundheits- und Fertigungswesen vor allem unter logistischen Gesichtspunkten näher betrachtet.

Dabei setzt sich das in den Anwendungsbereich Krankenhauslogistik einzuordnende Teilprojekt MedPAge (Medical Path Agents) [12] mit der Terminplanung in verteilten, autonomen Krankenhaussystemen auseinander: Angenommen wird dabei, dass Krankenhäuser in viele einzelne teilautonome Funktionsbereiche unterteilt sind, die von den Patienten in Abhängigkeit ihrer jeweiligen Erkrankung durchlaufen werden. Hierbei muss u.a. die Nutzung der verschiedenen Geräten und Ressourcen durch die Patienten nach vorgegebenen Optimierungskriterien vorgeplant werden. Dazu ist es wichtig, jederzeit auch auf unerwartete Ereignisse wie Notfälle und Komplikationen reagieren zu können, um mittels dezentraler Koordination jeweils schnell und flexibel die notwendigen Umplanungen vornehmen zu können. Einen wichtigen Vergleichsmaßstab bei diesen Untersuchungen bilden dabei auch die derzeit in Krankenhäusern verwendeten - meist zentralen - Verfahren zur Terminvergabe.

Vor allem aufgrund der Komplexität derartiger Patientensteuerungsprobleme im Krankenhaus und deren inhärenter Dynamik sollten *dezentralen Steuerungsmechanis-*

men für die verschiedenen (Teil-) Prozesse verwendet werden. Dazu sollte ein Multiagentensystem eingesetzt werden, in welchem alle Koordinationsobjekte wie z.B. Patienten und Krankenhausressourcen als autonome Softwareagenten modelliert werden. Da eine für derartige Zwecke geeignete Agentenplattformen jedoch nicht zur Verfügung steht, wurden bisherige Konzepte erweitert und so das beschriebene System *Jadex* entwickelt und zur Realisierung der genannten verteilten Steuerungsmechanismen eingesetzt. Dabei wird durch die Repräsentation der einzelnen Koordinationsobjekte mit ihren jeweils eigenen Zielen der existierenden verteilten Struktur von Krankenhäusern mit relativ autonomen Teildiensten adäquat Rechnung getragen. Sowohl die Patienten- als auch die Ressourcenagenten treffen lokale Entscheidungen zur Zielerreichung autonom unter Berücksichtigung sowohl ihrer eigenen Ziele als auch der aktuellen Situation (ihren Beliefs) und können damit u.a. sehr flexibel auf Änderungen in der Umwelt (wie z.B. unerwartete Ereignisse) reagieren. So kann z.B. ein Ressourcenagent auf natürliche Art und Weise akute Notfälle oder unvorhergesehene Gerätedefekte berücksichtigen und dementsprechend dynamisch geeignete Umplanungsmaßnahmen einleiten, um das Ziel der jeweiligen Behandlung in jedem Fall bestmöglich zu erreichen. Insbesondere im Zusammenhang mit unerwarteten Ereignissen erweist sich hier der Jadex zugrunde liegende BDI-Mechanismus als sehr vorteilhaft, da z.B. keine starren Verarbeitungsabläufe gespeichert werden. So kann z.B. ein Ressourcenagent ggfs. den Plan zur Durchführung einer Untersuchung wiederholen, wenn zunächst keine relevanten Befunde erzielt wurden. Die Jadex zugrunde liegende FIPA-konforme Agenten-Middleware JADE ermöglicht zudem systemübergreifende Interoperabilität und vereinfacht die Umsetzung der Verhandlungsapekte durch standardisierte Interaktionsprotokolle wie z.B. das FIPA Contract-Net. Weitere Details zur Modellierung und Realisierung des MedPAge-Systems findet man z.B. in [4].

6 Verwandte Arbeiten

Abb. 2 gibt eine allgemeine Übersicht über verschiedene existierende Agentenplattformen, und ordnet diese Systeme mittels der Dimensionen *Einsatzfeld* (Industrie oder Forschung) und *Ausrichtung* (Middleware oder BDI Ansatz) ein.[1] Aus dieser Klassifikation ist ersichtlich, dass eine Verbindung zwischen Middleware-orientierten Systemen und BDI-Systemen derzeit kaum besteht. Insbesondere für eine industrielle Nutzung der Agententechnologie in offenen verteilten Umgebungen ist es aber von entscheidender Bedeutung, dass gleichermaßen Middleware-Aspekte wie z.B. Interoperabilität und Sicherheit sowie rationale Entscheidungsprozesse in adäquater Weise unterstützt werden. Eine Zusammenführung der entsprechenden beiden Forschungsrichtungen erscheint vor diesem Hintergrund besonders interessant.

Zum Schließen dieser Kluft zwischen Middleware und Reasoning gibt es derzeit grundsätzlich zwei unterschiedliche Herangehensweisen: Zum einen setzen Plattformen wie Agentis und Whitesteins TAP1 auf den etablierten Standard *Java J2EE* und integrieren so Agententechnologie in Applikationsserverumgebungen.[2] Die zwei-

[1] Weiterführende Informationen zu den abgebildeten Systemen sind über http://vsis-www.informatik.uni-hamburg.de/projects/jadex/links.php zu erreichen.

[2] http://www.agentissoftware.com/ bzw. http://www.whitestein.com/pages/index.html

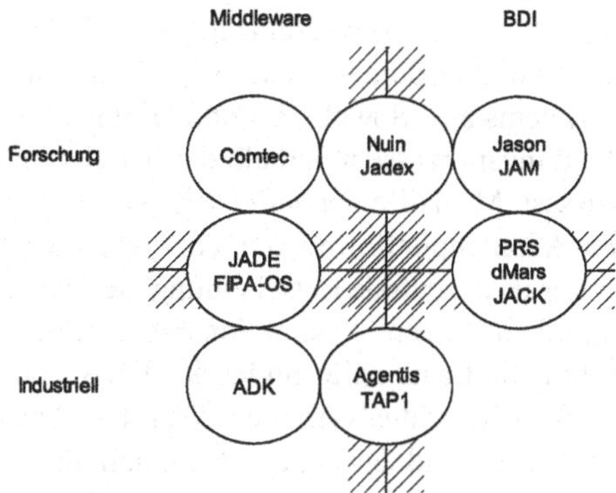

Abb. 2. Klassifikation von Agentensystemen nach Einsatz und Ausrichtung

te Möglichkeit besteht darin, auf bestehende Middleware-Plattformen aufzusetzen und diese um BDI-spezifische Charakteristika zu erweitern. Dieser Ansatz wird von Nuin [6] und dem hier beschrieben Jadex verfolgt. Im Unterschied zu Jadex unterstützt Nuin's Architektur insbesondere Anwendungen aus dem Bereich des Semantic Web.

Beide Integrationsarten bieten unterschiedliche Vor- und Nachteile, so dass nicht pauschal eine Herangehensweise als insgesamt überlegen angesehen werden kann. Vielmehr hängt die Eignung der einen oder anderen Lösung insbesondere von den individuellen Charakeristika des jeweiligen Problemfeldes ab: Generell bietet die Herangehensweise auf der Basis von J2EE Vorteile deshalb, weil sie die Möglichkeit eröffnet, auf etablierte Standards und Werkzeuge zurückgreifen zu können. Problematisch ist dabei ist jedoch, dass diese Standards auf Softwarekomponenten und nicht auf Agenten abzielen und somit starke Anpassungen erfordern. Genau entgegengesetzt verhält es sich bei der Nutzung existierender Middleware-Agentenplattformen, die zwar agentenbasierte Services (z.T. auf Basis von FIPA-Standards) bereitstellen, aber noch nicht den Reifegrad der komponentenbasierten Umgebungen erreicht haben. Für Jadex wurde auch deshalb der letztgenannte Ansatz gewählt, da er näher am aktuellen Stand der Forschung in Bezug auf Agenten-Middleware liegt und es zudem erlaubt, direkt an Fortschritten im Rahmen der aktuellen Standardisierungsbemühungen im Rahmen der der FIPA und der darauf aufbauenden Systemplattformen zu partizipieren.

7 Zusammenfassung

Dieses Papier stellt einen Ansatz zur dezentralen Steuerung und Koordination verteilter Anwendungen vor, der deren steigende Komplexität besser d.h. vor allem problemadäquater zu beherrschen erlaubt indem er neben der Verteilung insbesondere die bisher nur schwer handhabbare Dynamik mit Hilfe der Agententechnologie adressiert. Wichtige Grundlagen dafür bieten *agentenorientierte Middleware-Plattformen*, die Basisdienste z.B. für die Verwaltung und Kommunikation von Agenten zur Verfügung stellen und so Teile der notwendigen Infrastruktur zur Dekomposition komplexer Anwendungen in autonome interagierende Teilkomponenten realisieren. Diese werden im Projekt Jadex um Aspekte der *rationalen Entscheidungsfindung* ergänzt.

Die für die Steuerung autonomer Anwendungsprozesse in verteilten Umgebungen typische Dynamik der Anwendungsdomäne wirkt sich direkt auf die Komplexität des abzubildenden Softwaresystems aus: Sowohl Art und Umfang der Interaktion als auch die notwendigen Entscheidungsprozesse innerhalb der beteiligten Agenten werden dadurch maßgeblich beeinflusst. Mit Hilfe der *Jadex Reasoning Engine*, die als Erweiterung der weit verbreiteten Agentenplattform JADE entwickelt wurde, können Entscheidungsprozesse von Agenten als dezentrale Entscheidungsträger bei einer derartigen Koordination systematisch und auf hohem Abstraktionsniveau formuliert und direkt ausgeführt werden. Konzeptionelle Basis dafür bildet das BDI-Modell zur Beschreibung von rationalem menschlichen Individualverhalten. Damit realisiert das Jadex-System konzeptionell eine Symbiose aus Middleware und Rationalität.

Anhand des Fallbeispiels zur funktionsübergreifenden Terminplanung im Krankenhaus aus dem Projekt MedPAge wurde abschließend kurz exemplarisch verdeutlicht, welche Vorteile der Einsatz zielorientierter Agenten für eine ausgewählte Anwendungsdomäne mit sich bringt und wie die in Jadex vorhandenen BDI-Konzepte angewendet werden können.

Literaturverzeichnis

1. F. Bellifemine, G. Rimassa, and A. Poggi. JADE – A FIPA-compliant agent framework. In *4th Int. Conf. Practical Applications of Agents and Multi-Agent Systems (PAAM-99)*, 1999.
2. M. Bratman. *Intention, Plans, and Practical Reason.* Harvard University Press, 1987.
3. L. Braubach, A. Pokahr, and W. Lamersdorf. Jadex: A Short Overview. In *Net.ObjectDays 2004: AgentExpo*, 2004.
4. L. Braubach, A. Pokahr, and W. Lamersdorf. MedPAge: Rationale Agenten zur Patientensteuerung. *Künstliche Intelligenz*, (2):33–36, 2004.
5. L. Braubach, A. Pokahr, D. Moldt, and W. Lamersdorf. Goal Representation for BDI Agent Systems. In *Proc. 2nd Workshop on Programming Multiagent Systems (ProMAS04)*, 2004.
6. I. Dickinson and M. Wooldridge. Towards practical reasoning agents for the semantic web. Technical Report HPL-2003-99, Hewlett Packard Laboratories, May 15 2003.
7. S. Kirn et al. DFG-Schwerpunktprogramm 1083: Intelligente Softwareagenten und betriebswirtschaftliche Anwendungsszenarien. In *Informatik 2003.* Köllen Druck+Verlag, 2003.
8. M. Georgeff, B. Pell, M. Pollack, M. Tambe, and M. Wooldridge. The Belief-Desire-Intention Model of Agency. In *Agent Theories, Architectures, and Languages (ATAL) '98.* Springer, 1999.
9. N. R. Jennings. An agent-based approach for building complex software systems. *Communications of the ACM*, 44(4):35–41, April 2001.
10. A. Newell. *Unified Theories of Cognition.* Harvard University Press, 1990.
11. J. Odell. Objects and Agents Compared. *Journal of Object Technology*, 1(1), 2002.
12. T. O. Paulussen, N. R. Jennings, K. S. Decker, and A. Heinzl. Distributed Patient Scheduling in Hospitals. In *Proc. 18th Int. Joint Conference on Artificial Intelligence (IJCAI-03)*, 2003.
13. A. Pokahr, L. Braubach, and W. Lamersdorf. Jadex: Implementing a BDI-Infrastructure for JADE Agents. *EXP – in search of innovation*, 3(3):76–85, 2003.
14. S. Poslad and P. Charlton. Standardizing Agent Interoperability: The FIPA Approach. In *Multi-Agent Systems and Applications.* Springer, 2001.
15. A. Rao and M. Georgeff. BDI Agents: from theory to practice. In *Proc. of 1st International Conference on Multi-Agent Systems (ICMAS'95).* The MIT Press, 1995.
16. Y. Shoham. Agent-oriented programming. *Artificial Intelligence*, 60(1):51–92, 1993.

Teil II

Neue Middleware-Ansätze

Dienste zur einfachen Nutzung von Computing Grids

Jürgen Falkner[1] und Anette Weisbecker[2]

[1] Universität Stuttgart, Institut für Arbeitswissenschaft und Technologiemanagement, Nobelstr. 12, D-70569 Stuttgart
Juergen.Falkner@iat.uni-stuttgart.de
[2] Fraunhofer-Institut für Arbeitswirtschaft und Organisation, Nobelstr. 12, D-70569 Stuttgart, Germany
Anette.Weisbecker@iao.fraunhofer.de
http://www.iao.fraunhofer.de

Zusammenfassung. Der folgende Beitrag befasst sich mit Diensten die für die einfache Nutzung von Computing Grids von Bedeutung sind. Unter der einfachen Nutzung wird verstanden, dass es für den Nutzer einer Grid Infrastruktur nicht notwendig ist, auf seinem eigenen System nennenswerte Softwareinstallationen oder spezielle Konfigurationen durchzuführen. Desweiteren soll die Nutzung jederzeit und von überall her möglich sein. Hintergrund dieses Strebens ist es, Grid Technologien einem möglichst breiten Personenkreis zugänglich zu machen und neue Anwenderkreise zu erschließen. Zu diesem Zweck wird im vorliegenden Beitrag der Ansatz eines Web Portals vorgestellt, welches dem Nutzer alle Dienste - inklusive sicherheitsrelevanter Dienste wie Authentifizierung und Autorisation - mit Hilfe von Web Services im Grid und ins Portal integrierten Web Service Clients zur Verfügung stellt.

1 Anforderungen bei der praktischen Nutzung von Computing Grids

Einer der wesentlichen Grundgedanken des Grid Computings ist die sogenannte Virtualisierung von Ressourcen. Darunter wird verstanden, dass es das Ziel sein muss, jegliche Art von Leistungen einer Computer Infrastruktur möglichst immer und überall nutzen zu können ohne wissen zu müssen, wie das System funktioniert. Es wird gerne das Analogon der elektrischen Stromversorgung herangezogen, bei der man weder weiß aus welchem Kraftwerk der Strom nun genau kommt, noch wie das Kraftwerk oder die ganze Infrastruktur zur Weiterleitung des Stroms funktioniert.

Einen ähnlichen Zustand soll nun also Grid Computing im Bereich der Nutzung von Rechenleistung, Datenspeicher, Software und nicht zuletzt den Daten selbst herbeiführen. So wie man das Radio in die Steckdose steckt und einschaltet wenn man Musik hören will, soll man also beliebige Computer an die Netzwerksteckdose stecken und einen virtuellen Knopf drücken können, der bewirkt, dass der Computer die gewünschte Lösung liefert.

Zu diesem Zweck ist es nicht nur notwendig dem Computer bzw. dem Grid beizubringen, die Problemstellungen oder Wünsche eines Menschen zu verstehen, d.h. seine Aufgaben auf die Software-Dienste und Hardwareressourcen im Grid abzubilden und die Ausführung umzusetzen. Man braucht eine Vielzahl an Lösungen für kleine Teilprobleme auf dem Weg zu diesem Idealzustand, die sich oftmals auch als Konsequenz aus anderen Anforderungen ergeben. Die Realität sieht im Moment noch deutlich anders aus, was aber kein Hindernis sein sollte, diesen Zustand anzustreben.

Gegenwärtig findet die Nutzung von Grid-Technologien noch hauptsächlich im wissenschaftlichen Umfeld statt. Der Virtualisierungsgedanke steht dabei nicht primär im Vordergrund, da es zunächst im Wesentlichen darum geht, die Leistung einer Grid Infrastruktur nutzbar zu machen. Das prominenteste Beispiel für diesen sicherlich begründeten pragmatischen Ansatz ist das Large Hadron Collider Grid (LCG) [1], dessen Aufgabe es im Wesentlichen ist, die gigantischen Datenmengen des angeschlossenen Teilchenbeschleunigers zu bewältigen und für die Verarbeitung durch Wissenschaftler in aller Welt zugänglich zu machen.

Dort wo in der Wirtschaft bereits Grid-Lösungen zum Einsatz kommen, sind dies meist spezielle Lösungen für Teilprobleme des Einsatzes von Technologien aus dem Bereich des Grid Computings und speziell für eine bestimmte Unternehmensumgebung angepasst. Es werden beispielsweise im Einzelnen spezielle Clustermanagement-Lösungen eingesetzt, die es ermöglichen, für ganz bestimmte Anwendungen mehr Rechenressourcen zu nutzen als das mit herkömmlichen Lösungen der Fall war [2]. Von der wirklichen Vision eines einfach zu nutzenden Computing Grids, bei dem alle Software, Hardware und Datenressourcen auch für ungeübte Grid-Nutzer jederzeit und von überall her zugänglich sind, ist der größte Teil dieser Lösungen noch weit entfernt.
Inhalt dieses Beitrags sind die Schritte, die nötig sind, um der Vision einer virtualisierten Grid Umgebung ein Stück näher zu kommen und eine Beschreibung wie diese Ansätze im Fraunhofer Resource Grid [3] bereits umgesetzt wurden.

Die Motivation für die Umsetzung der Virtualisierung von Grid Ressourcen ist dabei zum Einen, Grid Technologien einer wesentlich breiteren Nutzerbasis zugänglich zu machen als es bisher der Fall ist. Dies hat seinen Hintergrund in der Tatsache, dass viele Forscher und Entwickler in Wissenschaft und Industrie im Moment einen wesentlichen Teil ihrer Arbeitszeit und ihres kreativen Potenzials dafür aufwenden, die Werkzeuge zu beherrschen, mit denen sie ihre eigentliche Arbeit bewältigen können, anstatt ihre ganze Kraft in Forschungs- und Entwicklungsfragen zu stecken. Im Idealfall sollte es möglich sein auch in Anwendungsbereichen, in die man nicht eingearbeitet ist, schnell und einfach die geeigneten Ressourcen für eine bestimmte Aufgabe zu finden und sie so weit verstehen zu können, um sie anschließend direkt zu nutzen.
Dies führt unmittelbar zur Notwendigkeit der Vereinfachung der Nutzung von Grid Infrastrukturen. Was das Ziel der ständigen Erreichbarkeit von überall her angeht, steht dahinter der Gedanke, dass es auch möglich sein muss, von einem fremden Computer, z.B. in einem Internet Cafe, Arbeiten auf sichere Weise in einer Grid Infrastruktur auszuführen. Dazu ist es erforderlich, den Zugang

zum Grid und seinen Diensten so zu gestalten, dass er mit handelsüblicher und weit verbreiteter Software möglich ist. Es wäre also wünschenswert, wenn die Nutzung eines Grids nicht umfangreiche Installationen und Konfigurationen von Software erfordert - nicht zuletzt deshalb, weil auch dies einen unnötigen Zeit- und Lernaufwand bedeutet.

Um die Vision eines solchen Grids zu verwirklichen müssten primär die im Folgenden genannten Punkte gelöst bzw. vorhanden sein:

- intuitiv zu bedienende Benutzungsoberfläche
- einfaches Auffinden von Diensten, die zur Lösung einer Aufgabenstellung beitragen
- einfaches Erstellen von Job Workflows aus den Teildiensten zur Lösung einer Aufgabenstellung
- einfache Ausführung von solchen Job Workflows
- es soll keine Kenntnis der Ressourcen im Grid nötig sein um den Job Workflow auf die optimalen Ressourcen im Grid zu verteilen. Dies sollte nach unterschiedlichen Prioritäten möglich sein, z.B. schnellstmöglich oder so preiswert wie möglich
- umfangreiche Softwareinstallationen und komplizierte Systemkonfigurationen auf Seiten des Nutzers werden überflüssig; der Rechner des Nutzers muss nicht selbst Teil des Grids sein
- webbasierter Zugriff auf alle Dienste des Grids
- single-logon von jedem herkömmlichen Computer im Internet (Nutzerzertifikat vorausgesetzt)

Die daraus folgende Frage ist, wie diese Anforderungen umgesetzt werden können und was dabei alles an Diensten zur Verfügung gestellt werden muss, um diese Anforderungen in ihrer Gesamtheit abzudecken.

2 Basisdienste für die einfache Nutzung von Grids

Wie Irving Wladawsky-Berger in Ian Fosters und Kesselmans Buch The Grid [4] beschreibt, geht die Entwicklung neuer Technologien üblicherweise in zwei Phasen vonstatten. In der ersten Phase findet die grundlegende Entwicklung der Technologie statt und sie wird im Wesentlichen von den Entwicklern selbst genutzt, da auch für die Nutzung noch umfangreiches Know-How nötig ist. In einer zweiten Phase wird die Nutzung so weit vereinfacht, dass der normale Nutzer nicht mehr wissen muss, wie diese Technologie funktioniert. Dies ist der angestrebte Endzustand.

Die grundlegenden Eigenschaften, die ein modernes Computing Grid ausmachen, sind im Wesentlichen folgende [5]:

- Zugriff auf verteilte Rechenressourcen, also Prozessorleistung
- Zugriff auf verteilte Datenspeicher
- Kopplung technischer Geräte mit verteilten Rechnern und Archivsystemen
- Ermöglichung der kooperativen Bearbeitung großer Datensätze

- sichere Datenübertragung und Authentifikation
- Möglichkeit der Einrichtungen von Virtuellen Organisationen
- Ausführung verteilter Anwendungen, Integration von Anwendungen in Unternehmensinfrastrukturen

Um die Nutzung auch für im Umgang mit dem Grid ungeübte Personen zu ermöglichen und dabei unabhängig von spezieller Infrastruktur und somit mobil zu bleiben, sind desweiteren eine Anzahl an zusätzlichen Voraussetzungen nötig:

- On-Demand Computing, d.h. einen Workflow aus Anwendungen, also einen Grid Job, an das Grid übergeben können, ohne sich um die Details der Ausführung und Verteilung auf konkrete Grid Ressourcen kümmern zu müssen
- einen solchen Workflow definieren können
- die geeigneten Bestandteile eines solchen Workflows finden, um sie dann nach eigenen Vorstellungen zusammenzusetzen
- einfacher Zugang zum verteilten Dateisystem; Daten Up- und Download von außerhalb des Grids
- eigene Inputdaten und Parameter in einen Workflow hineindefinieren können
- Daten im verteilten Datenbestand suchen können, und zwar nach verschiedensten Kriterien (Größe, Alter, Ersteller, Inhalt, Themengebiet, Projekt ...)
- entscheiden können, nach welcher Priorität ein Job ausgeführt wird (Geld, Zeit, Qualität ...)
- Jobqueues einsehen können
- Monitoring eigener Jobs
- Möglichkeit der Definition, wer auf bestimmte Daten/Jobs zugreifen darf
- sicherer Zugang mit der Gewissheit, dass keine unberechtigte Person persönliche Daten einsehen kann
- Home-Bereich im verteilten Dateisystem, wo alle eigenen Daten aufgelistet werden, egal wo sie liegen
- Zugang zu gängigen Best-Practice Anwendungen, die von den Erstellern freigegeben wurden

Für die erfolgreiche Realisierung einer Grid Umgebung, die es ungeschulten Nutzern erlaubt, ohne Kenntnis von Grid Technologien oder gar einzelner Ressourcen letztere zu nutzen, gibt es eine Reihe von Voraussetzungen. Wesentlicher Bestandteil sind dabei die Schaffung bzw. Nutzung von Standards, um eine weite Verbreitung und Kompatibilität zu anderen Grid Infrastrukturen zu ermöglichen, sowie die Einfachheit in der Bedienung und des Zugangs. Dies erfordert jedoch nicht zwangsläufig die Einfachheit der Technologie, die dieses ermöglichen soll. Es ist ganz im Gegenteil zu erwarten, dass die Komplexität der ermöglichenden Technologien mit zunehmendem Bedienungskomfort anwächst.

3 Umsetzung der Basisdienste im Fraunhofer Resource Grid

2001 begann die Fraunhofer-Gesellschaft mit dem Aufbau des Fraunhofer Resource Grids[1] (FhRG) und der Entwicklung von Grid Middleware, um den oben genannten Aspekten gerecht zu werden.

3.1 Die zugrundeliegende Gridinfrastruktur

Die Infrastruktur des Fraunhofer Resource Grids setzt sich zusammen aus einer Reihe von Clustern und Storagesystemen, die sich deutschlandweit an zur Zeit sechs verschiedenen Standorten befinden und über Gigabit-Ethernet ans Internet angeschlossen sind. Die Kommunikation erfolgt über ein Grid-internes VPN um das Grid als Ganzes vor unerwünschten Zugriffen von außen zu schützen. Die Basisplattform, auf der die FhRG-eigene(n) Middleware und Dienste geschaffen wurden, ist das Globus Toolkit [6]. Diese Infrastruktur bietet zunächst nur die Möglichkeit, unter Kenntnis des Globus Toolkits und der Ressourcen im Grid von innerhalb des Grids auf andere Grid Ressourcen zuzugreifen und diese für seine Aufgaben einzusetzen. Durch die FhRG-Middleware, die zu großen Teilen im Open Source Projekt „eXeGrid" [7] unter GPL (General Public License) zur Verfügung gestellt werden wird, werden dem System eine Vielzahl an Modulen hinzugefügt, die beispielsweise Resource Brokerage und Scheduling, Resource Management, Job Mangagement und die Erstellung und Ausführung von Grid-Job Workflows erleichtern. Als Datagrid Lösung kommt der Storage Resource Broker [8] zum Einsatz.

Der eXeGrid Middleware liegt die Grid Application Definition Language (GADL) [9] zugrunde, ein Satz an XML Schemas zur Beschreibung von Grid Ressourcen, Grid Jobs, Daten und Interfaces. Der wichtigste Bestandteil dabei ist die Ressourcenbeschreibungssprache „Grid Resource Description Language" (GRDL). Sie ermöglicht neben der Beschreibung der Ressourcen auch die Definition von Abhängigkeiten zwischen Grid-Ressourcen. Dabei können Grid-Ressourcen sowohl Hardware, Software und Daten als auch abstrakte Klassen solcher Ressourcen sein. Auf diese Weise wird es möglich, ganze Workflows von Grid Jobs automatisch und vor allem dynamisch auf den zum Zeitpunkt der Ausführung am besten geeigneten und verfügbaren Ressourcen ausführen zu lassen [9][10]. Das Entwicklerteam der GADL ist auch im Global Grid Forum (GGF) aktiv und behält dabei stets die Entwicklungen im Auge. Insbesondere die Datenbeschreibungssprache wird mittelfristig der im GGF gegenwärtig entwickelten Data Format Description Language (DFDL) [11] angeglichen werden um die Kompatibilität zu internationalen Standards zu wahren.

[1] Das Fraunhofer Resource Grid wurde im Projekt „I-Lab" mit Förderung des Bundesministeriums für Bildung und Forschung entwickelt; Förderkennzeichen: 01AK928A. Beteiligte Institute: Fraunhofer IAO, ITWM, FIRST, IGD, SIT

3.2 Das Fraunhofer Resource Grid Web Portal

Um dieser Infrastruktur das Wesen der einfachen Nutzbarkeit und allgemeinen Verfügbarkeit hinzuzufügen, wurde die eXeGrid Middleware so konzipiert, dass ihre Dienste auch über das Webportal des Fraunhofer Resource Grids zur Verfügung gestellt werden können. Hilfsmittel wie der Grid Job Builder [12] zum Erstellen von Job-Workflows können direkt aus dem Webportal, ohne nennenswerte Installationen auf dem Client-Rechner, mit Hilfe von Java Webstart[2] verwendet werden und Grid Dienste wie der Grid Job Handler zur dynamischen Ausführung von Grid-Jobs sind über Web Service Clients zu nutzen, die ihrerseits in das Web Portal integriert sind und somit nicht vom End-Nutzer selbst installiert oder gar programmiert werden müssen. Ebenso gibt es zu einzelnen häufiger genutzten Anwendungsworkflows wie zum Beispiel der Umwelt- und Katastrophenschutzsimulation ERAMAS [13] spezielle Weboberflächen, die einen Service-Client zur Eingabe von Simulationsdaten und zur Ausführung über den Grid Job Handler Web Service bereitstellen.

Zweifellos verspricht ein solches Konzept nur dann Erfolg, wenn es bereits einen Dienst im Grid gibt, der zur Lösung der Problemstellung des Nutzer dient. Allerdings sind in der Praxis die allermeisten Anwendungen bereits irgendwo vorhanden und man hat als Nutzer entweder keine Kenntnis von deren Existenz oder man findet sie nicht. Letzteres Problem wird durch das Konzept des Grid Task Mapping [14] im FhRG Web Portal angegangen. Abbildung 1 zeigt das Grundprinzip des Task Mappings.

Zunächst müssen dabei zu allen Grid Ressourcen und zu allen Klassen von Ressourcen, zu denen diese gehören, Ressourcenbeschreibungen in der Grid Resource Defintition Language (GRDL) [15] vorliegen. Bei der Erstellung dieser Ressourcenbeschreibungen können die Ressourcen Aufgabenbereichen zugeordnet werden. Desweiteren enthalten sie detaillierte Beschreibungen der Funktion über die Ressourcen, sowie der technischen Parameter. Durch die Auswahl eines oder mehrerer Aufgabengebiete gibt es so eine klar definierte Menge an Ressourcen, die für die Problemlösung in Frage kommen. Eine Folgeproblematik ist die Optimierung der Ontologien, die der Kategorisierung der Aufgabenfelder zugrunde liegen - insbesondere auch die Anpassung an unterschiedliche User-Communities. Die technische Umsetzung stellt hier allerdings weniger ein Problem dar als die geeignete Wahl der verwendeten Bezeichnungen.

Über die in Abbildung 2 dargestellte Auflösung von Abhängigkeiten zwischen den Ressourcen kann nach der Auswahl der direkt benötigten Dienste oder Anwendungen, die über das Task Mapping gefunden werden, der gesamte Satz an Ressourcen bestimmt werden, der zur Bewältigung einer Aufgabe in Frage kommt.

Die Abbildungen 3 und 4 zeigen eine Übersicht über das Gesamtkonzept der webbasierten Problemlösungsumgebung des FhRG. Dabei bildet das durch eine Sicherheitskomponente geschützte Web Portal die Schnittstelle zwischen Nutzer und Grid, die ihm ermöglicht auf den Task Mapping Dienst zuzugreifen und

[2] Voraussetzung ist lediglich das Vorhandensein eines Java Runtime Environments

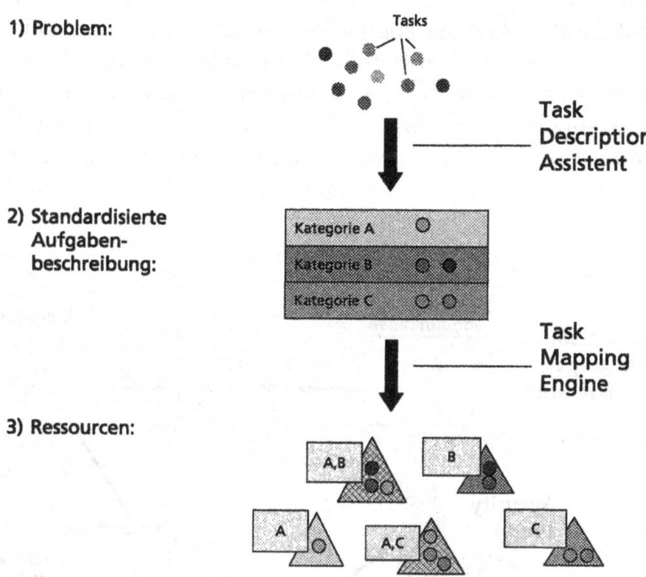

Abb. 1. Grid Task Mapping im FhRG

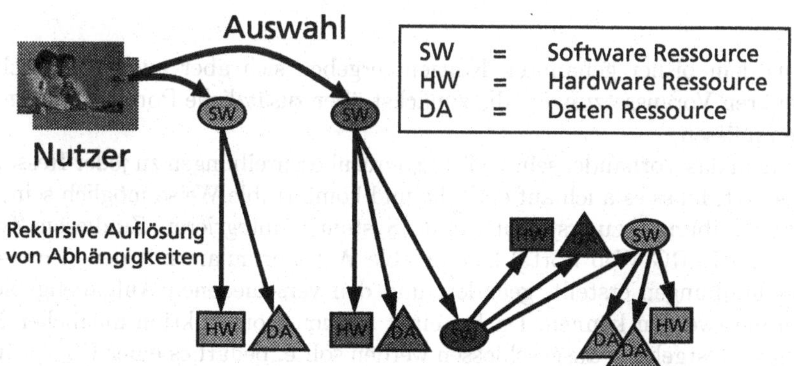

Abb. 2. Auflösung von Abhängigkeiten zwischen Grid Ressourcen

durch die Eingrenzung seiner Aufgabenfelder die passenden Ressourcen für seine Aufgabe zur Verfügung gestellt zu bekommen. Nach Übergabe dieser Auswahl an den Grid Job Builder können komplexe Workflows von Grid Anwendungen erstellt werden, die dem Grid Job Handler Webservice zur Ausführung im Grid übergeben werden. Für die Nutzung aller genannten Dienste ist es im FhRG nicht notwendig, das Webportal zu verlassen. Zur Interaktion mit den Grid Diensten benötigt der Nutzer ausschließlich einen Webbrowser und ein Java Runtime Environment.

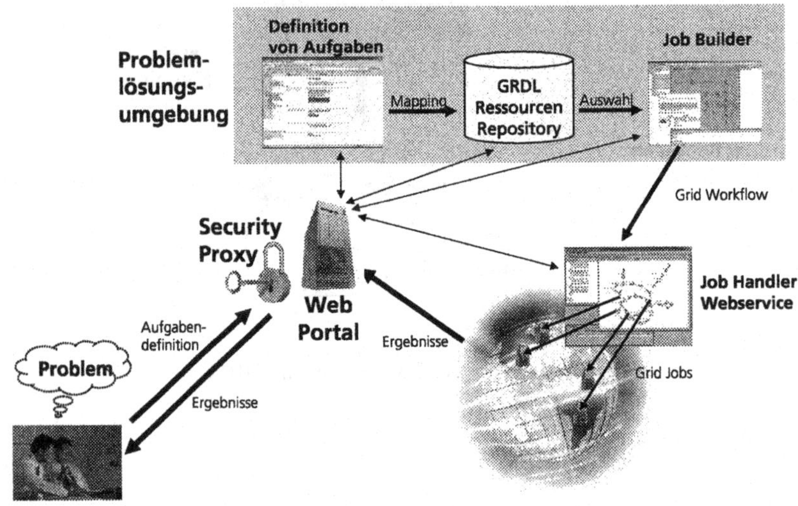

Abb. 3. Überblick über die webbasierte Problemlösungsumgebung des FhRG

Aus dem bisher genannten Konzept ergeben sich aber auch eine Vielzahl an weiteren Voraussetzungen, die zunächst über zusätzliche Portaldienste gelöst werden müssen.
Wenn man das Vorhandensein von Ressourcenbeschreibungen zu jeder Ressource voraussetzt, muss es auch auf einfache und komfortable Weise möglich sein, solche Beschreibungen zu erstellen und ins System zu integrieren. Zu diesem Zweck gibt es am FhRG Web Portal komfortable Web Formulare mit denen Ressourcenbeschreibungen erstellt, geändert und den verschiedenen Aufgabengebieten zugeordnet werden können. Da bei einer solchen Konstruktion möglicher Mißbrauch weitestgehend ausgeschlossen werden sollte, bedarf es einer Überprüfung neuer oder geänderter Ressourcendaten vor ihrer Übernahme in das produktive Task Mapping System. Zu diesem Zweck wurde ein Administrationskonzept entworfen und umgesetzt, das einen dafür zuständigen Personenkreis von Administratoren automatisch über neu eingegangene Ressourcenbeschreibungen informiert und ihnen - ebenfalls am Web Portal - die Möglichkeit zu Reviews und zu

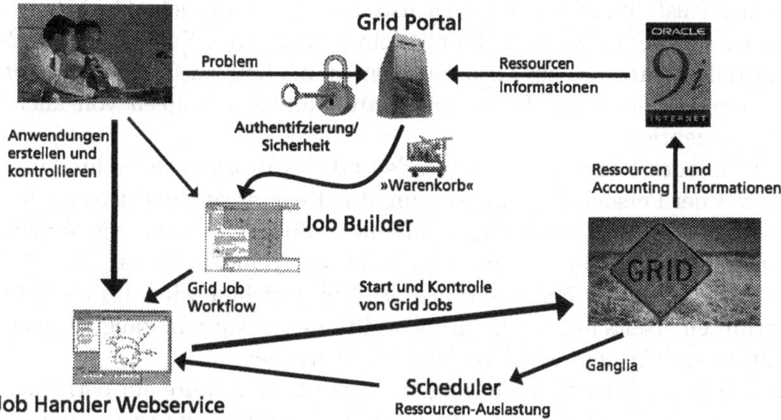

Abb. 4. Schrittweise Nutzung des Web Portals: Task Mapping, Erstellen des Workflows, Ausführung des Workflows

Akzeptanz oder Ablehnung gibt. Die daraus folgenden Aktionen wie das Deployment der Daten in die jeweiligen Datenbanksysteme oder die Benachrichtigung des Erstellers erfolgen dann wieder automatisch durch das System.

3.3 Sicherung des Webportals

Webportale haben sich in vielen Bereichen als einfach zu bedienende Benutzungsoberflächen erwiesen, die bei richtiger Administration eine weitgehend sichere Anwendung gewährleisten und von überall her zugreifbar sind. Den Schutz des FhRG Web Portals übernimmt dabei der vom Fraunhofer SIT entwickelte Security Proxy. Dieser überwacht die Kommunikation auf den für HTTP und HTTPS Kommunikation genutzten Ports des Portal-Rechners und leitet die Anfragen nach erfolgter positiver Überprüfung der Identität des Nutzers an den von außen nicht erreichbaren Webserver bzw. Application Server weiter.

Der Security Proxy überwacht dabei alle Anfragen, die von außen an das Portal gestellt werden und entscheidet aufgrund von Datenbankeinträgen in der Security Datenbank des Grids welcher Nutzer auf welche Dienste des Webportals zugreifen darf. Diese Entscheidungen finden rollenbasiert statt. Der Entscheidungsprozess, der dem Security Proxy zugrunde liegt, ist dabei mehrstufig. Zunächst findet eine Überprüfung des Nutzer-Zertifikats[3] statt. Wenn das Zertifikat gültig ist und als vertrauenswürdig eingestuft wird, werden die zugehörigen User-Daten anhand des Distinguished Names im Zertifikat in der Nutzerdatenbank gesucht. Die Gruppenzugehörigkeit des Nutzers wird mit den Berechtigungen verglichen, die für den angeforderten Portal-Dienst erforderlich sind und somit wird über die Gewährung des Zugriffs entschieden.

[3] zum Einsatz kommen Browser-übliche PKCS12 Zertifikate

Bei der Ausführung von Grid Diensten, also sobald mehr Grid-Ressourcen als nur das Portal involviert sind, findet ein Mapping des Nutzers auf ein Pseudonymzertifikat statt, das zur Grid-internen Anmeldung an Grid Ressourcen und Diensten verwendet wird. Diese Zertifikate werden prinzipiell von allen Grid Diensten akzeptiert.
Aus der zu jeder Ressource existierenden GRDL Ressourcenbeschreibung geht hervor, welcher Personenkreis auf bestimmten Ressourcen Zugriffsrechte hat. Die Durchsetzung dieser Zugangsbeschränkungen obliegt dem für die Ausführung von Grid Job Workflows zuständigen Grid Job Handler Dienst, der über die wirkliche Identität des Nutzers vom Portal unterrichtet wird. Dabei weist sich das Portal seinerseits mit einem für die Grid-interne Nutzung tauglichen eigenen Zertikat gegenüber dem Grid Job Handler Dienst aus.
Für den direkten Zugriff unter Umgehung des Portals wäre ein permanent auf einen bestimmten Nutzer ausgestelltes Zertifikat zur Grid-internen Nutzung notwendig. Somit ist eine Umgehung dieses Sicherheitskonzeptes äußerst schwierig.

Für die Ausführung von Jobs im Grid wird dem Nutzer also ein Pseudonymzertifikat zugewiesen. Dabei wird protokolliert, wann welcher Nutzer unter welchem Pseudonymaccount agiert, was für die spätere Abrechnung der Nutzung ebenso wichtig ist wie für die Zuordnung von Verantwortlichkeiten bei eventuell auftretenden Problemen. Nach Ende der Nutzung wird der Pseudonymaccount komplett bereinigt und alle Daten des Nutzers unter seiner tatsächlichen Identität in das verwendete Datagrid-System[4] [8] verschoben.

3.4 User Management

Will man in einer Grid-Umgebung, in der die Ressourcen nicht alle dem selben Besitzer gehören, erreichen, dass die Vergabe von Rechten auf Ressourcenebene durch den jeweiligen Ressourcen-Besitzer geregelt werden kann, so stellt das hohe Anforderungen an das Grid System und die zugrundeliegende Infrastruktur. Zunächst müssen die Rechte einzeln zu jeder Ressource definierbar sein. Dies ist im FhRG über die GRDL Ressourcenbeschreibung der Fall. Hierbei sollte es aber dem Ressourceneigner vorbehalten sein, die Ressourcenbeschreibung zu editieren.
Weiterhin muss gewährleistet sein, dass jeder Ressourceneigner beliebige Gruppen definieren kann, denen er den Zugriff - gegen Entgelt oder ohne - gewährt. Dazu muss der Ressourceneigner im Bestand der registrierten Grid-Nutzer des gesamten Grids suchen können, um die Nutzer mit ihren dementsprechenden Identifiern, also User IDs, zu der zu definierenden Gruppe hinzufügen zu können. An dieser Stelle treten datenschutzrechtliche Bestimmungen in Kraft, die über Ländergrenzen und möglicherweise generell im Einzelfall verschieden sein können. Um den richtigen eindeutigen Identifier zu finden - es mag in einem Grid mehrere Nutzer mit dem Nachnamen Müller oder Maier geben - ist es nötig, dass der Ersteller einer Gruppe oder virtuellen Organisation Einsicht in weitergehende Nutzerdaten, wie z.B. Geburtsdatum oder Arbeitgeber nehmen kann. Die

[4] Im FhRG wird der Storage Resource Broker verwendet.

Definition solcher Gruppen ist für die Definition von virtuellen Organisationen unabdingbar, da die Zugehörigkeiten zu definieren sein müssen. Dies ist eine der praktischen Problematiken, die sich im Hinblick auf eine einfache Verwendung von Grid Infrastrukturen ergeben, jedoch nicht trivial zu lösen sind.

Neben der rechtlichen Problematik sind die auf Ressourcenebene definierbaren Zugriffsrechte an den dementsprechenden Stellen zu implementieren. So muss der Grid Job Handler beispielsweise die Einhaltung dieser Berechtigungen erzwingen. Ebenfalls sollte das Task Mapping System bereits darauf achten, dass dem Nutzer nur solche Ressourcen zur Lösung seiner Problemstellung angeboten werden, die er auch benutzen darf - gegebenenfalls mit dem Hinweis unter welchen (monetären) Vorraussetzungen er bestimmten Gruppen beitreten kann, um sie benutzen zu dürfen.

4 Ausblick

Wie eingangs festgestellt, ist es einerseits erstrebenswert und liegt es andererseits in der natürlichen Evolution neuer Technologien, dass sie sich zu einfacher Nutzbarkeit, hohen Abstraktionsgraden, und somit im Fall der Grid Technologien, zu einem hohen Virtualisierungsgrad bezüglich der im Grid vorhandenen und zu nutzenden Ressourcen entwickeln. Auf dem Weg zu diesem Virtualisierungsgrad finden weltweit erhebliche Fortschritte statt, beispielspielsweise die Verabschiedung der Open Grid Service Architecture (OGSA) [16] und die Einigung auf das Web Service Resource Framework (WSRF) [17].

Im vorliegenden Beitrag wurden die Arbeiten des Fraunhofer Resource Grids zu den Anstrengungen dargestellt, den Weg zu einer einfachen Nutzung für im Grid ungeübte Nutzer zu beschreiten und die im Grid vorhandenen Dienste ohne nennenswerten Installationsaufwand auf Seiten des Nutzers von überall her nutzbar zu machen. Neben den bereits beschriebenen Aufgaben, die auf dem Weg zum einfach nutzbaren Grid gelöst werden müssen und zum Teil bereits gelöst wurden, gibt es eine Reihe weiterer elementarer Probleme, auf die in diesem Rahmen nicht im Detail eingegangen werden konnte. Dazu zählen Fragen vom Management dezentral gelagerter Daten unter Security-Aspekten, über die Sicherstellung von Ausfallsicherheit und Qualität der Dienste bis hin zur Entwicklung von Entwicklungsumgebungen für diejenigen, die neue Services für das Grid entwickeln möchten oder müssen, da noch keine Lösung für ihr Problem existiert.

Lösungen wie die dynamische Ausführung von Grid Workflows ohne Kenntnis der in Frage kommenden Grid Ressourcen - eine zentrale Grundlage für die Virtualisierung von Grids - kommen im Fraunhofer Resource Grid aber bereits zum Einsatz. Ebenso ist die Nutzung aller FhRG-Grid-Dienste am Webportal möglich; inklusive des Task Mapping Dienstes, der es ermöglicht den Aufgabenstellungen des Nutzers die passenden Ressourcen zuzuordnen und die Abhängigkeiten zwischen den notwendigen Grid-Ressourcen aufzulösen.
Somit ist die Grundlage für die zweite technologische Entwicklungsstufe von Computing Grids [4] bereits gelegt. Das Ziel ist es nun eine weltweite Standardi-

sierung solcher Lösungen zu erreichen und die verbleibenden zahlreichen Detailfragen zu lösen und mittelfristig zu einer Produktreife von Grid-Infrastrukturen und Middleware zu gelangen.

Literaturverzeichnis

1. Large Hadron Collider Computing Grid Project (2004), http://lcg.web.cern.ch/LCG/default.htm
2. Foster, I.: The Grid, COMDEX Las Vegas (2003)
3. Fraunhofer Resource Grid (2004), http://www.fhrg.fhg.de
4. Wladawsky-Berger, I.: The Industrial Imperative, in Foster, I., Kesselman, C.: The Grid 2, Morgan Kaufman Publishers (2004) S.25-34
5. Foster, I., Kesselman, C.: The Grid 2, Morgan Kaufman Publishers (2004) S.37ff
6. Globus Toolkit 2004, http://www.globus.org/toolkit
7. The eXeGrid Open Source Project (2004), http://www.exegrid.org
8. Storage Resource Broker, San Diego Supercomputing Center, http://www.npaci.edu/Research/DI/srb/
9. Hoheisel, A.: Grid Application Definition Language - GADL 0.2, Technical Report (2002), http://www.fhrg.fhg.de/deutsch/Main/downloads/FhRG_GADL0_2.pdf
10. Hoheisel, A., Der, U.: Dynamic Workflows for Grid Applications, Cracow Grid Workshop (2003), http://www.fhrg.fhg.de/deutsch/Main/downloads/Hoheisel_Cracow_2003.pdf
11. Myers, J.: Introduction to DFDL, Global Grid Forum, DFDL-WG (2004) https://forge.gridforum.org/projects/dfdl-wg/
12. Jung, C., Einhoff, M., Noll, S., Schiffner, N.: Grid Job Builder - A Workflow Editor for Computing Grids, ITCC 2004 Conference Proceedings
13. Hoheisel, A., Der, U.: ERAMAS - Environmental Risk Analysis and Management System, Fraunhofer FIRST, Präsentation zur CeBIT (2003), http://www.fhrg.fhg.de/deutsch/Main/downloads/ERAMAS-CeBIT2003_de.pdf
14. Weisbecker, A., Falkner, J.: Zuordnung von Grid Ressourcen zu Problemstellungen für die Komposition von Anwendungsworkflows aus Grid Services, akzeptiertes Paper, DFN Tagung (2004)
15. Grid Resource Definition Language, http://www.fhrg.fhg.de/de/fhrg/schemas/gadl/grdl.xsd
16. Foster, I., Berry, D., Djaoui, A. et al: The Open Grid Services Architecture, Version 1.0, OGSA-WG, Global Grid Forum (2004),
17. Foster, I., Frey, J., Graham, S. et al: Modeling Stateful Resources with Web Services, IBM/HP/University of Chicago (2004)

Ranked Matching for Service Descriptions Using OWL-S

Michael C. Jaeger[1], Gregor Rojec-Goldmann[1], Christoph Liebetruth[1]
Gero Mühl[1] and Kurt Geihs[2]

[1] TU Berlin, Institute of Telecommunication Systems,
FR6-10, Franklinstasse 28/29, D-10587 Berlin
{mcj, gr, trutie}@cs.tu-berlin.de
gmuehl@ivs.tu-berlin.de
[2] Univ. Kassel, FB 16, Wilhelmshöher Allee 73, D-34121 Kassel
geihs@uni-kassel.de

Abstract Semantic Web services envision the automated discovery and selection of Web services. This can be realised by adding semantic information to advertised services and service requirements. The discovery and selection process finds matches between requirements and advertisements according to their semantic description. Based on the Web Ontology Language (OWL) an ontology for Web services (OWL-S) was introduced to standardise their semantic description. There are already some approaches available for matching of service requirements with service advertisements according to such an ontology.
We propose an algorithm, which ranks the matching degree of service descriptions according to OWL-S. Different matching degrees are achieved based on the contravariance of the input and output types for requested and advertised services. Furthermore, additional elements of the service description, such as the service category, are either covered by reasoning processes or, such as quality of service constraints, by custom matching rules. Contrary to mechanisms that return only success or fail, ranked results provide criteria for the selection of a service among a large set of results. With such a discovery mechanism additional Web services can be found that might have normally been ignored.

1 Introduction

The Semantic Web working group of the W3C develops technologies and standards for the semantic description of the Web. The goal of these efforts is to make the Web understandable by machines and to increase the level of autonomous interoperation between computer systems [9]. Several standards and languages were already introduced to address this objective. The most relevant are the *Resource Description Framework (RDF)* [5], and the *Web Ontology Language (OWL)* [11]. The primary purpose of RDF is to structure and describe existing data. Thus, RDF is also called a metadata language. RDF Schema is a vocabulary extension to RDF to describe a semantic network. Based on RDF and RDF Schema, OWL – the successor of the DARPA Agent Markup Language in conjunction with the Ontology Inference Layer, in short DAML+OIL – increases the level of expressiveness with a richer vocabulary but retaining the decidability.

These languages are primarily used to describe content. The next logical step is to describe the semantics of services in order to improve their platform- and organisation-independent interoperability over the Internet. Referring to the Semantic Web, the research field addressing this objective is named *Semantic Web services* [12]. Its vision is the application of semantic description for Web services in order to provide relevant criteria for their automated selection. Based on the predecessor of OWL – DAML+OIL – an upper ontology for the description of Web services named DAML-Services (DAML-S) had been introduced [4]. Using DAML-S, the functionality, execution structure and the binding to existing interface information can be described. Recently DAML-S has been updated and renamed to OWL-S, adapting the evolution of DAML+OIL to OWL [21].

Using OWL-S for the description of Web services can increase the ability of computer systems to find eligible services autonomously. This is important in open environments where provided services can appear and disappear dynamically. Basically a service provider describes his advertised services in an OWL-S compliant ontology and a service requester queries for services with an OWL-S ontology expressing his requirements. In this scenario, matching service descriptions of advertisements with requirements has the purpose to select a suitable service among a set of available ones. Considering known matching approaches that return either mismatch or match, this selection process has the following potential benefits:

- Consider a matching task that returns a large set of services that might meet the requirements. How can a service-seeking agent ensure to choose the optimal service? If the matching process provides ranked results instead of the conclusion that all services "match", the optimal service match is given by the ranking.
- Consider a matching task that returns either a match or mismatch based on a particular threshold of matching degree. If this task returns no services, the service requester might be willing to weaken his requirements in order to find at least one matching service.

Using the OWL-S ontology has particular implications that are reflected in the matching algorithm. For example, a definition about the quality rating in OWL-S could be handled using a rule based mechanism, whereas the conceptualisation of the service category is addressed by reasoning functionality. Therefore, our matching algorithm covers the following aspects:

- We consider the contravariance for the types and their subtypes of the inputs and outputs of a service. This provides another matching degree in addition to the equivalence of concepts.
- Additionally to the inputs and outputs of a service, our matching approach covers the categorisation of the service itself.
- Besides reasoning and type-matching elements of the algorithm, also custom elements are supported addressing individual constrains or requirements, such as quality of service.

The following section 2 provides an overview about the background of this research. It introduces the usage scenarios of a matchmaker and the basics of OWL-S. In section 3

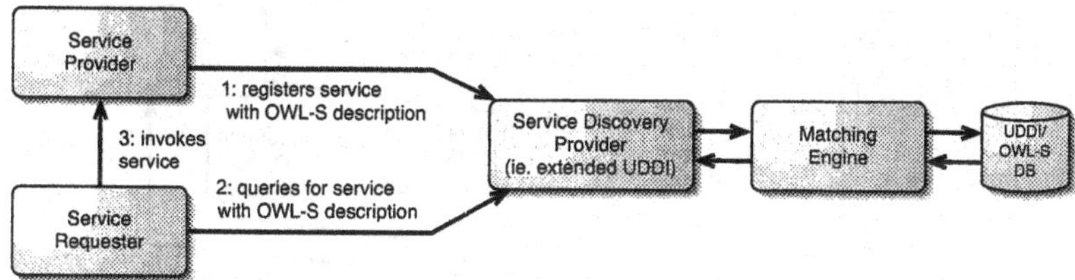

Fig. 1. Matchmaking in a Server-Sided Scenario

we present our novel matching algorithm that is based on OWL-S, and in section 4 we briefly mention some issues with the implementation of the algorithm. The section 5 discusses the algorithm and compares it to related work. At the end, in section 6, we summarize our conclusions and give an outlook to future work.

2 Background

The matchmaking of semantic descriptions is part of the discovery process of Web services. In the architecture description of Web services by the W3C [3] three main discovery scenarios are identified: a centralised registry, an index, and a peer-to-peer (P2P) scenario.

In a registry scenario, a central authority stores service descriptions, which were explicitly submitted by the service providers. An existing specification for such a repository is UDDI [19]. To take also semantic descriptions into account, existing repositories can be extended to be compatible with OWL-S descriptions. When a service requester submits his requirements, the server processes this request by matching the requirements with the description of advertised services. Then, the server returns the found match(es). This scenario is outlined in figure 1. The approach to extend UDDI repositories with semantic description such as DAML-S, is already introduced in [13] and [1].

Another approach is the index scenario. An index just provides the information to find services, whereas service descriptions are provided elsewhere. This approach can be compared with so called crawlers or robots that browse the Web automatically to create an index [8]. The difference between the index and the registry approach is that service providers control what information is put into the registry, whereas the index gathers information on its own, in most cases automatically. In [18] Sycara et. al. explain, how a broker between service requestor and provider finds matches based on OWL-S descriptions. Referring to the basic Web service architecture schemes in [3], a broker stores an index and represents a single point of contact for a service requestor, but acts as an agent to perform the matchmaking of service advertisements and requests.

In a P2P scenario each Web service is being discovered dynamically. A service requester queries other nodes in its network or a specific network domain to find and identify suitable Web services. Depending on the P2P architecture they do or do not have a centralised registry or index. A missing central repository could mean more complexity to identify matching Web services but more reliability and less organisational efforts

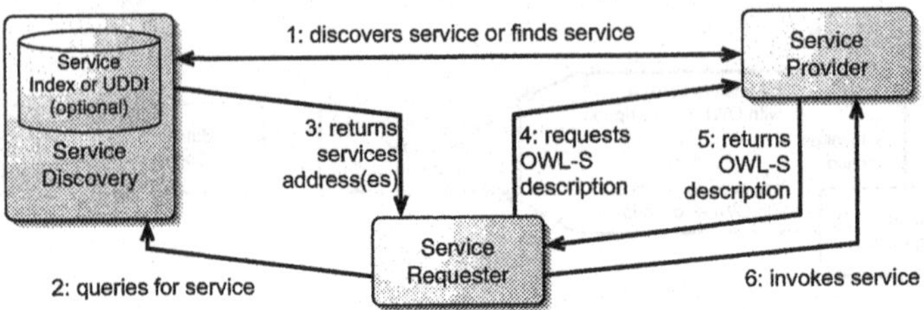

Fig. 2. Matchmaking in a Client-Sided Scenario

to find Web services. Another advantage is that in such an architecture service descriptions are always up to date, whereas a registry or an index might provide outdated information. However, P2P architectures might comprise caching or index mechanisms, or description repositories. If these components are distributed over the P2P network, the validity of the information might be even worse than with using a centralised approach. We presume, that if Web services are discovered in an index scenario or on a P2P basis, the service requester obtains the OWL-S description for eligible services and performs the matching process on its own. Figure 2 outlines a scenario, where the client processes the OWL-S descriptions.

Performing the matchmaking process either on a centralised server or by individual clients has different characteristics. As an advantage of the server-sided scenario, the implementation of a client, which acts as the service requester can be kept very simple. Thus, the effort for finding services on the client side is very low. This issue is a well known criterion for a server-oriented architecture in general.

However, a criterion to prefer the client-sided approach is the following scenario: A service requester wants to use an own matching algorithm instead of the implementation on a central server. These custom modules can define constraints that must be satisfied by the OWL-S description of the advertised service. Only with the client-sided execution of such modules the personalisation of the matching process is possible. Since our approach includes user-customisable modules to enhance the matching algorithm, we have decided in favour of a client-sided scenario. In our approach a service requester queries the OWL-S descriptions from an already obtained list of service descriptions to find the best match. However, our algorithm can also be used on a central repository, if all relevant client information is shipped via the repository interface.

2.1 Short Introduction to OWL-S

The OWL-S ontology defines three basic elements: (1) a service profile to describe the functionality of a service, (2) a process model to describe the structure of the service, and (3) a service grounding to map the abstract interface to concrete binding information. As the focus of this work is on the discovery and selection of Web services, we will concentrate on the service profile, which provides the necessary elements for our matching algorithm.

The profile is divided into three main sections: (a) a textual description and contact information, which is mainly intended for human users, (b) a functional description of the service. This functional description describes the input and output of a service. Additionally, two sets of conditions are defined, namely preconditions, which have to hold before the service can be executed properly, and effects, which are conditions that hold after the successful execution of the service, i.e. postconditions. These four functional descriptions are also referred to as *IOPE* (Input, Output, Precondition, and Effects). In this version of our matching algorithm we will cover only the input and outputs, because preconditions and effects are not yet sufficiently standardised for being considered by a matching algorithm.

The third type (c) is a set of additional properties that are used to describe the features of the service. From these properties we use the service category, which is used to classify the service with respect to some ontology or taxonomy of services. On an optional basis, other properties can also be taken into account, such as the element QualityRating, or custom defined properties, such as the duration of the execution.

3 Ranked Matching for OWL-S Descriptions

The OWL-S specification defines the semantic elements for advertising the functional description of a service with an instance of the class Profile. Although a service can have multiple profiles as a Web service can provide multiple operations, in the following the words service and profile are used synonymously, meaning one specific profile definition. In the class Profile RDF properties point to the IOPE elements Input, Output[1], Precodition, and Effect. Each of the four classes is a subclass of the class Parameter. For the categorisation of their type, each instance is specified with the property parameterType. This property can point to elements of an arbitrary conceptualisation. The OWL-S definition leaves open, whether the definition uses OWL or other conceptualisation languages. A matching algorithm can only support conceptualisations that are covered by a reasoning functionality. Therefore we assume that the conceptualisation is provided in OWL, so that an OWL reasoner can determine a subsumption relation or the equivalence of concepts.

Apart from the IOPEs, a Web service can be described by additional elements like the service category. As found in the definition of the IOPE types, it is also left open, whether the definition for service categories uses OWL or other conceptualisation definitions. So for this case a matching algorithm can only support conceptualisations that are covered by a reasoning functionality as well. Therefore we assume that the conceptualisation of service categories is also provided in OWL.

The conclusion of this consideration is a matching algorithm, which is divided into four stages: (a) the matching of inputs, (b) the matching of outputs, and (c) the matching of the service category. The algorithm determines the matching for each of the stages individually. The results are aggregated with a fourth stage (d), where user-defined constraints or functionality can complete the matching result. The arrangement of these elements is specified in section 3.4, while in the next sections it is explained what is matched by each element of the matching algorithm. Thus, our first task is to classify different relations between two concepts to determine the degree of matching: Let A, B

[1] In fact, OWL-S defines the class ConditionalOutput or its subclass UnConditionalOutput as the possible conceptualisations of outputs.

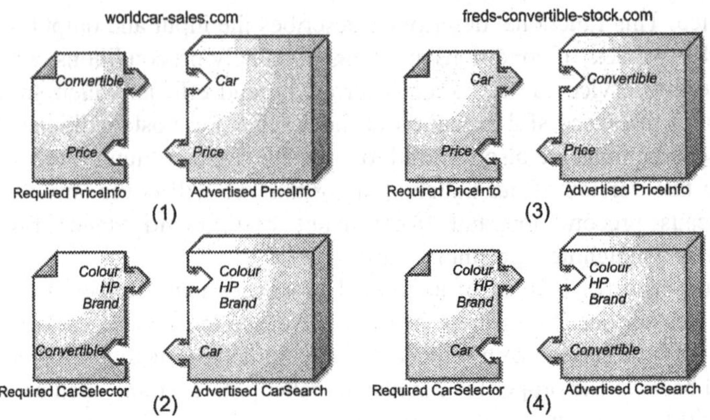

Fig. 3. Contravariance of Input and Output Types

denote two concepts which originate from a given set of ontologies. Then the following three relationships between A and B are considered:

$Fail(A, B)$	The concepts A and B are in no relation with each other.
$Subsumes(A, B)$	The concept B is subsumed by the concept A, meaning that A denotes a more general concept than B.
$Equivalent(A, B)$	A and B are equivalent, meaning that both denote exactly the same concept.

The matching algorithm performs a reasoning over the available conceptualisation to determine the relationship between the concepts.

3.1 Contravariance

For the matching of inputs and outputs, the direction of the subsumption relation is important for (a) the input types to ensure proper execution of the service and for (b) the output types to fulfill the demands of the service requester. Consider an example that is outlined in figure 3: two fictitious car selling services, "worldcar-sales.com" (cases (1) and (2)) and "freds-convertible-stock.com" (cases (3) and (4)), advertise two similar services. One service returns the price of a car and the other provides a search functionality to find a car by some key properties. We assume that the parameter type convertible is defined to be a subclass of the parameter type car in an available OWL ontology.

The input types of service requirements in scenarios (1) and (3) do not match with equivalent ranks to the service advertisements. In case (1) the input type of the requirement is subsumed by the input type of the advertisement, in case (3) vice versa. However, the proper execution of the service can be ensured in case (1) with the assumption, that the contravariance holds for the input type of the advertised service. For case (3) it might happen that the advertised service requires some specific characteristics for the proper execution.

Regarding the output types the subsumption direction between required and advertised service is now reversed. In case (2) the requester is particularly looking for convertibles, but might get all kinds of cars. The requirement cannot be ensured. For case (4) the requester has just looked for cars, and the service returns convertibles only. But in this case the requirements are still met assuming the contravariance for the output type of the service requirement.

3.2 Matching of Inputs, Outputs, and the Service Category

From the four stages of the matching algorithm, the first three stages match the classifications of inputs, outputs and the service category based on subsumption reasoning, because the classifications can be described as concepts of some OWL ontology. In a fourth stage custom matching modules are supported to ensure requirements that cannot be achieved with ontology-based reasoning. The ranks for each of the three first stages are summarised in table 1.

3.3 User-Defined Matching

In addition to the three matching stages also a user-defined matching stage is provided. This matching stage consists of one or more additional modules, which ensure specific requirements or conditions. As a result, each of the modules can return either true, false, or a specific matching degree.

Along with the documentation of OWL-S in the Internet some examples are provided on the OWL-S homepage, which clarify the benefit of this stage. Consider the example service profile of the fictitious Airline Bravo Air named BravoAirProfile.owl found in [20]. It includes a custom parameter such as the geographic radius of a service[2] and an application of the class QualityRating, which can be used to denote a measure for quality of service statements. Applied to this example, custom matching modules can ensure thresholds for the quality rating or the availability of a service at a geographical location.

3.4 Combination of the Four Stages

The result of the matching algorithm is an aggregation of the individual four stages. The simplest approach is to add the ranks of the first three stages and complete the sum with the result of the user-defined module(s). The aggregated result is either a number, which is an abstract measure of the matching quality, or the conclusion, that the descriptions did not match. This aggregation schema is outlined in figure 4.

The algorithm could be modified optionally by assigning weights to the results of the individual stages. For example, the rank of the output matching could be multiplied by two, because the result of a service invocation might be more relevant than its parameterisation. For a sound weighting of the individual stages we propose to test the matching algorithm with sets of training data.

[2] The geographic radius was part of the upper ontology in previous versions of OWL-S. For OWL-S 1.0 this element has been discarded. However – as shown in this example – the geographic radius can be defined as a custom parameter and added to the OWL-S description of a service.

#	Result	Interpretation
Inputs		
0	FAIL	At least one input type of the advertised service has not been successfully matched with one input type of the advertised service. The service cannot be executed properly.
1	UNKNOWN	This matching result is provided, if the used categorisation is not supported by the matching algorithm. However, this result is not the conclusion of an open-world-assumption approach. The reasoning process still follows the closed-world assumption, but due to the lack of understanding the conceptualisation, no conclusion can be drawn.
2	SUBSUMES	For each input type of the advertised service exactly one input type of the required service has been found, which is at least subsumed by the input type of the advertised service. This means that the advertised service might be invoked with a more specific input than expected, assuming the covariance of the input types of the advertise service.
3	EQUIVALENT	For every input type of the advertised service one equivalent input type of the required service is found.
Outputs		
0	FAIL	At least one output of the required service has not successfully been matched with an input of the advertised service.
1	UNKNOWN	This matching result is provided, if the used categorisation is not supported by the matching algorithm. As for the matching of inputs, this result is not the conclusion of an open-world-assumption approach, but due to the lack of understanding the conceptualisation, no conclusion can be drawn.
2	SUBSUMES	The output types of the required service are at least subsumed by or equivalent to the output types of the advertised service. This means that the required service might receive a more specific output type than expected. Assuming the contravariance of the output types of the advertised service, it is still ensured, that the requirement of the service requester are met. Additionally for all output types of the required service a successfully matching counterpart of the advertised service is identified.
3	EQUIVALENT	For each output type of the required service one equivalent output type of the advertised service is found.
Service Categories		
0	FAIL	The two concepts were not successfully matched.
1	UNKNOWN	Either the description of the advertised or the required service is not classified or no reasoning functionality is available to determine matching for the types of categorisation.
2	SUBSUMES	The classification of the advertised service is subsumed by the classification of the required service. This means that the advertised service offers more specific functionality than required.
3	EQUIVALENT	The classification of the advertised service and the classification of the required service are equivalent.

Table 1. Ranking for the Matching of Inputs, Outputs, and Service Categories

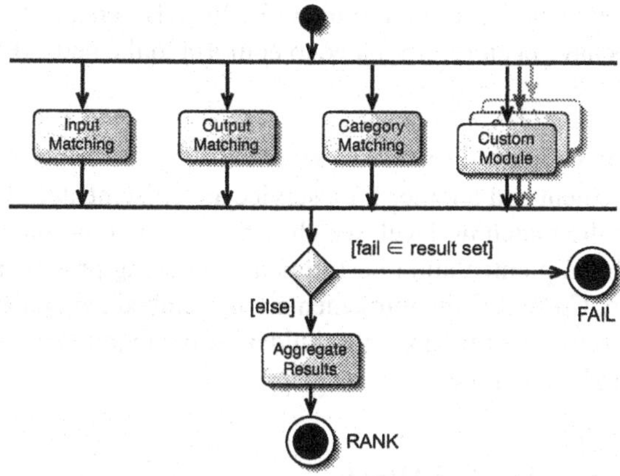

Fig. 4. Combination of the Matching Result

4 Implementation

For testing and demonstration purposes an implementation has been realised in Java, which uses the OWLJessKB reasoner from Joe Kopena[3] for performing the reasoning tasks. The work builds upon a predecessor, which was created for processing DAML-S descriptions [6][4]. The following significant changes have been applied to the existing DAML-S matchmaker to realise the new implementation:

- The handling of files, which contain the service description, has been improved. In the DAML-S version, the tool required three files, which were separated by the different parts of DAML-S *profile, process and grounding* according to its documentation [4]. Examples of this file structure can be found in the example material for DAML-S version 0.9. The new matching implementation calls only the API of the OWLJessKB reasoner component and queries all needed information in the provided knowledge base regardless of the file structure.
- A change from DAML-S to OWL-S is found in referencing concepts, which classify a service parameter. While in DAML-S the concept, which classifies a parameter, is being referenced from both the service profile and the service process model, in OWL-S only the process model references this classification, which can be defined in some OWL ontology. In the service profile a parameter is only pointing to its according description in the process model. Thus, a matchmaker for OWL-S descriptions must also process the service process model and not only the profile as a matchmaker for DAML-S. Additionally, the DAML-S matcher has used the simple subject query methods, which are provided by the DAMLJessKB reasoner

[3] Availble at http://edge.cs.drexel.edu/assemblies/software/owljesskb/

[4] The DAML-S version is available at http://ivs.tu-berlin.de/Projekte/damlsmatcher/, the OWL-S matchmaker at http://ivs.tu-ber.in.de/Projekte/owlsmatcher/. The software is licensed under the LGPL.

API, which have been deprecated in the OWLJessKB version. For these two reasons all queries have been reformulated to conform to the new API of the reasoner component.

The software can be used to select two sets of OWL-S descriptions, one representing a service requirement and another for a service advertisement. In a second step the user can determine the matching level, which is the required minimum for a successful match. Then, the implementation performs the matching process as introduced in the previous section. Currently, the implementation is embedded in a stand-alone Java-based GUI tool, however, the functionality could be also integrated in a service selection environment as introduced in section 2.

5 Discussion and Related Work

Our proposal is a progression from matching approaches for DAML-S ontologies, which were presented in earlier research reports. Our algorithm is based on the new OWL-S standard and provides a fine-grained and tunable ranked matching of service descriptions. A variation of the matching algorithm [10] provides ranking by supporting different reasoning operations, but considers only the categorisation of a service. Our motivation for refining the matching process is that it might easily occur that two profiles will be declared as non-compatible because one (probably less important) property of the category is not matching to a property in the other profile. An optimal matching algorithm should indicate the lack of matching quality, but should not disqualify the advertised service completely.

Furthermore, OWL-S specifications can be arbitrarily complex. By splitting up the profile and determining the matches individually for its subparts, the algorithm can identify matches between service requests and advertisements with a higher precision. The disadvantage of ignoring parts of the profile can be compensated with a proper usage of user-defined modules. For example, a module that evaluates QoS properties could easily be added to the matching algorithm. Another characteristic of our work is the consideration of the direction of the inheritance hierarchy between service requests and advertisements ("which concept subsumes which one"). This issue is not addressed for example in another matching approach that uses a custom ontology and not OWL-S or DAML-S for describing services [22].

The matchmaker ATLAS [14] and the work of Paolucii et al. [13] share our decision to consider the service profile and it's inputs and outputs for determining matches between requests and advertisements. Our matching algorithm can be seen as an extension to these approaches, because our work adds the coverage of the contravariance for the inputs and outputs of a service. A different approach for matching DAML-S descriptions is found in the work of Bansal and Vidal [2]. A matchmaker is proposed that covers only the service model of DAML-S. We did not follow this approach yet, because as described in the introduction of DAML-S, the service model is not primarily provided to express requirements for finding matches with advertisements [4]. The matching of service descriptions is also addressed in other fields, which are not related to Web service or DAML-S. For example in [16] and [15], service descriptions are used, which are based on Conceptual Graphs. An enhanced service trader – the equivalent to a matchmaker – performs comparisons of service specifications and returns a ranking of partial matches. Contra- and covariance rules are applied. This work has been applied for a CORBA trading service: IDL descriptions are translated into a representation using conceptual graphs, which can be processed by the AI-Trader [17]. Another approach for matching capabilities of Web services, which uses a custom RDF ontology, is found in [22].

As already mentioned some approaches also propose the integration of DAML-S descriptions with the UDDI standard, which we have introduced as an application scenario for the matching algorithm ([13] and [1]). For testing our work, the OWL-S descriptions were created by using an XML-Editor. This is by far not as efficient as probably desired by potential users of OWL-S. Thus, we also plan to supplement our work with a methodology and a tool for the creation of OWL-S descriptions as introduced for DAML-S in [7]. A similar GUI tool for the description of services based on Conceptual Graphs was developed for the AI Trader in an earlier project of our research group [15]. Such a methodology supported by a tool for the creation of OWL-S-based descriptions would increase the usability of OWL-S service descriptions, would ensure, that the relevant elements are well defined, and therefore would increase the efficiency of our service matching algorithm.

6 Conclusions

For the matching of semantic Web services we have shown that specific elements of the OWL-S upper ontology can be used to provide a fine grained ranking of matching results rather than flat subsumption reasoning for the service profile description as a whole unit. This work also indicates the potential to provide even finer grained ranks with the consideration of more elements of OWL-S.

The development of the implementation revealed the need for an efficient methodology and tools to create OWL-S descriptions. As a consequence, we have started to design a methodology and a tool. This tool shall facilitate the creation of OWL-S specifications and individual matching constraints, similar to the AI Trader tool mentioned in the previous section. In general, we strongly believe that search facilities and matchmakers will be important components in future service-oriented architectures, but users of OWL-S need tools for the creation of the OWL-S descriptions almost as easy to use as with WSDL.

References

1. Rama Akkiraju, Richard Goodwin, Prashant Doshi, and Sascha Roeder. A method for semantically enhancing the service discovery capabilities of uddi. In *In Proceedings of the Workshop on Information Integration on the Web*, pages 87–92, August 2003.
2. Sharad Bansal and Jose M. Vidal. Matchmaking of web services based on the daml-s service model. In *Proceedings of AAMAS'03*. ACM Press, July 2003.
3. David Booth et al. Web services architecture. Technical report, W3C, http://www.w3.org/TR/ws-arch/, 2004.

4. Anupriya Ankolenkar et al. Daml-s: A semantic markup language for web services. In *Proceedings of 1st Semantic Web Working Symposium (SWWS' 01)*, pages 441–430, Stanford, USA, August 2001. Stanford University.
5. Frank Manola et al. RDF Primer. Technical report, W3C, http://www.w3.org/TR/rdf-primer/, 2004.
6. Michael C. Jaeger and Stefan Tang. Ranked matching for service descriptions using daml-s. In Janis Grundspenkis and Marite Kirikova, editors, *Proceedings of CAiSE'04 Workshops*, pages 217–228, Riga, Latvia, 2004. Riga Technical University.
7. Michael Klein and Birgitta Koenig-Ries. A Process and a Tool for Creating Service Descriptions based on DAML-S. In *Proceedings of 4th International Workshop Technologies for E-Services, TES 2003*, pages 143–154. Springer, September 2003.
8. Mei Kobayashi and Koichi Takeda. Information retrieval on the web. *ACM Computing Surveys*, (2):144–173, June 2000.
9. Marja-Riitta Koivunen and Eric Miller. W3c semantic web activity. In *Semantic Web Kick-Off in Finland*, pages 27–44, November 2001.
10. Lei Li and Ian Horrocks. A software framework for matchmaking based on semantic web technology. In *Proceedings of the 12th International Conference on World Wide Web (WWW2003)*, pages 331–339. ACM Press, May 2003.
11. Deborah L. McGuinness and Frank van Harmelen. Owl web ontology language overview. Technical report, W3C, http://www.w3.org/TR/owl-features/, 2004.
12. Sheila A. McIlraith and David L. Martin. Bringing semantics to web services. *IEEE Intelligent Systems*, 18:90–93, January/February 2003.
13. M. Paolucci, T. Kawamura, T. Payne, , and K. Sycara. Semantic matching of web service capabilities. In *Proceedings of 1st International Semantic Web Conference. (ISWC2002)*, pages 333–347. Springer-Verlag, Berlin, 2002.
14. Terry R. Payne, Massimo Paolucci, and Katia Sycara. Advertising and matching daml-s service descriptions. In *Position Papers for SWWS' 01*, pages 76–78, Stanford, USA, July 2001. Stanford University.
15. A. Puder, F. Gudermann S. Markwitz, and K. Geihs. AI-based Trading in Open Distributed Environments. In *Proceedings of the 5th International Conference on Open Distributed Processing (ICODP'95)*, Brisbane, Australia, February 1995. Chapman and Hall.
16. Arno Puder. *Typsysteme für die Dienstvermittlung in offenen verteilten Systemen*. PhD thesis, Computer Science Department, Johann Wolfgang Goethe University, Frankurt/M., 1997.
17. Arno Puder and Kurt Geihs. Meta-level Service Type Specifications. In *Proceedings of the IFIP/IEEE international conference on Open distributed processing and distributed platforms*, pages 74–84, Toronto, Ontario, Canada, 1997. Chapman and Hall.
18. Katia Sycara, Massimo Paolucci, Julien Soudry, and Naveen Srinivasan. Dynamic discovery and coordination of agent-based semantic web services. *IEEE Internet Computing*, 8(3):66–73, May, June 2004.
19. UDDI Spec TC. Uddi version 3.0.1. Technical report, OASIS, http://www.oasis-open.org/committees/uddi-spec/doc/tcspecs.htm, 2003.
20. The OWL Services Coalition. OWL-S Example Description for Bravo Air. Technical report, http://www.daml.org/services/owl-s/1.0/BravoAirProfile.owl.
21. The OWL Services Coalition. OWL-S: Semantic Markup for Web Services. Technical report, http://www.daml.org/services/, 2004.
22. David Trastour, Claudio Bartolini, and Chris Preist. A semantic web approach to service description for matchmaking of services. In *Proceedings of the 11th international conference on World Wide Web*, pages 89–98, Honolulu, USA, May 2002. ACM Press.

Effiziente Videokodierung von Folienpräsentationen für den eLearning-Einsatz

Zefir Kurtisi, Andreas Kleinschmidt und Lars Wolf

Technische Universität Braunschweig, Institut für Betriebssysteme und Rechnerverbund, Mühlenpfordtstr. 23, 38106 Braunschweig,
{kurtisi|kleinschmidt|wolf}@ibr.cs.tu-bs.de

Zusammenfassung. Präsentationsaufzeichnungen gehören heute zu den verbreitetsten und effektivsten multimedialen eLearning-Materialien. Hierbei werden die verwendeten Folien mit Annotationen, der zugehörigen Sprache des Dozenten und ggf. auch dessen Videomitschnitt aufgenommen und nach einer eventuellen Nachbearbeitung den Studierenden auf Medien-Servern zur Verfügung gestellt. Trotz der Vorteile derartiger Aufzeichnungen existiert dafür kein standardisiertes und breit unterstütztes Format, so dass unterschiedliche und oft proprietäre Lösungen eingesetzt werden. Wir wollen für solche Inhalte mit der ausschließlichen Nutzung offener Standards Aspekte wie Plattformunabhängigkeit und Zukunftssicherheit abdecken und setzen auch für Folienvideos auf MPEG-4-Videokodierung. In diesem Beitrag beschreiben wir Hürden und Lösungen auf dem Weg zu effizienten Folienvideos und dokumentieren die guten Leistungen unserer XviD-Lösung durch Vergleiche mit dem Spezialcodec für Bildschirmaufzeichnungen TSCC.

1 Einleitung / Motivation

Die Aufzeichnung von Lehrveranstaltungen durch Aufnahme der erfolgten Folienpräsentation eines Dozenten mit den dazugehörigen Annotationen, Animationen und seiner Sprache (sowie ggf. auch sein Videobild) stellt eine verbreitete und effektive Form für multimediale eLearning-Materialien dar.

Hieraus ergibt sich die Frage, wie diese Aufzeichnungen am besten kodiert und komprimiert werden können, um für die Endnutzer möglichst einfach und kosteneffizient nutzbar zu sein. Diese Präsentationsaufzeichnungen ähneln dabei Videoaufnahmen bspw. von Nachrichtensendungen, so dass die Idee aufkommt, entsprechende Videokodierverfahren, zum Beispiel aus der MPEG-Familie, einzusetzen. Bei einer genaueren Betrachtung der Charakteristika von Folienpräsentationen erscheint eine Kodierung als reguläre Videos jedoch nicht sinnvoll zu sein. Videos werden beispielsweise durch die statischen Parameter Auflösung und Bildwiederholfrequenz bestimmt und haben über einen bestimmten zeitlichen Bereich, innerhalb von Szenen, einen gewissen kontinuierlichen Verlauf. Eine Folienpräsentation ist hingegen eine ereignisgesteuerte Aneinanderreihung von Standbildern, die um dynamische Elemente wie Annotationen oder Animationen ergänzt werden. Die Kodierung solcher quasistatischen Foliensequenzen mit einem Videocodec erzeugt stark redundante Daten und ist daher ineffizient.

Bislang haben sich kaum andere Arbeiten mit dieser Thematik befasst. So gibt es zwar eine große Zahl an Arbeiten zur Videokodierung, jedoch nicht auf den hier betrachteten, für den Bereich des eLearning sehr relevanten Fall bezogen. Am nächsten vergleichbar sind Tests von Videocodecs, bei denen auch Zeichentricksequenzen berücksichtigt werden (wie in [1]), da es sich dabei auch um synthetische Bildinhalte mit relativ wenig Bewegung handelt.

Auf der anderen Seite würde eine Videokodierung von Präsentationen den Produktionsprozess von multimedialen eLearning-Inhalten stark vereinfachen. Setzt man dabei auf standardisierte und offene Formate, muss man sich nicht mit Aspekten wie Plattform-, Betriebssystem- und Softwarekompatibilität beschäftigen.

Nachdem der MPEG-4-Standard [2] in den letzten Jahren breite Unterstützung und allgemeine Akzeptanz erlangt hat, streben wir für alle produzierten Materialien die Ablage in diesem Format an. Neben der erwähnten Unabhängigkeit von Hard- und Software stellen wir damit auch die Unterstützung künftiger Abspielgeräte sicher. Weiterhin eröffnen wir uns damit die Möglichkeit, die Daten synchron auszuliefern, da mittlerweile alle verbreiteten Streaming-Lösungen MPEG-4 unterstützen. Zuletzt ist für eine langfristige Betrachtung nicht unerheblich, dass Dateien in einem offenen und standardisierten Format auch in Jahren noch verwendbar sein werden.

Im Folgenden diskutieren wir die in diesem Zusammenhang an unserem Institut durchgeführten Arbeiten. Wir beginnen mit den Ergebnissen eines Vergleichstests gängiger Videocodecs. Im nächsten Abschnitt analysieren wir die Daten der MPEG4-Kodierung und beschreiben unsere Ansätze zur Effektivitätssteigerung. Die resultierenden Werte vergleichen wir mit einem auf Bildschirmaufzeichnungen spezialisierten Codec. Wir beschließen diese Untersuchung mit einer Zusammenfassung, in der wir diese Optimierungsmöglichkeiten aufgreifen und auf zukünftige Verbesserungen und Alternativen eingehen.

1.1 Begriffe und Grundlagen

Bevor wir auf die Ergebnisse eingehen, wollen wir die zum Verständnis nötigen Techniken und Termini der Videokodierung kurz erläutern (für weitergehende Informationen siehe bspw. [3]). Videos sind eine Aneinanderreihung von Einzelbildern (auch Frames genannt) mit konstanter Auflösung und konstantem zeitlichen Abstand (Bildwiederholrate, auch Framerate genannt). Die hohe Effizienz von Videocodecs beruht darauf, dass neben der räumlichen (z.B. die JPEG-Kodierung eines Einzelbildes) auch eine zeitliche Kompression der Daten erfolgt. Da aufeinander folgende Frames sich innerhalb einer Szene nur sehr wenig unterscheiden, genügt es, nur die Differenzen zu kodieren. Die Referenz- oder Stützbilder werden dabei I-Frames genannt, da sie intraframe, d.h. unabhängig von anderen Bildern, kodiert sind. Den Kompressionsfaktor und damit die Qualität stellt man bei den meisten Codecs als Quantisierungsfaktor ein, die Werte gehen dabei üblicherweise von Faktor eins für schwache bis Faktor 31 für starke Kompression.

Für die Berechnung der Differenzen werden die Bilder in Makroblöcke unterteilt. Die Bewegung jedes Makroblocks im Vergleich zum Referenzbild wird zusammen mit der Restabweichung als Delta-Frame kodiert. Wird dabei ein vorhergehender Frame referenziert, spricht man von P-Frames (für predicted), berücksichtigt man auch einen nachfolgenden, wird er B-Frame (bidirectional) genannt.

2 Effizienz vorhandener Videocodecs

In einem umfassenden Vergleichstest [4] haben wir als typische eLearning-Inhalte natürliches Video vom Vortragenden und das Folienvideo der Bildschirmpräsentation kodiert und bei den Testkandidaten nach signifikanten Leistungsunterschieden gesucht. Aus den Ergebnissen sind für die weiteren Ausführungen zwei Erkenntnisse herauszustellen. Erstens ist der OpenSource MPEG-4-Videocodec XviD der derzeit für unsere Zwecke geeignetste. Zweitens ist bei der Videokodierung von Bildschirmaufzeichnungen die Anzahl von I-Frames von entscheidender Bedeutung für die erzielte Datenrate. Diese beiden Erkenntnisse wollen wir kurz fundieren.

Für einen Effizienzvergleich haben wir ein Referenzvideo mit einer Auflösung von 1024x768 Pixel und 15 Bildern pro Sekunde bei konstanter Qualität kodiert und anschließend die Abweichung zum Referenzvideo als PSNR (Peak Signal to Noise Ratio) [5] berechnet. Abbildung 1 zeigt die Abhängigkeit der Qualität von der Datenrate bei den untersuchten Videocodecs, wobei ein effizienter Codec sich durch eine niedrige Datenrate bei hohem PSNR-Wert auszeichnet.

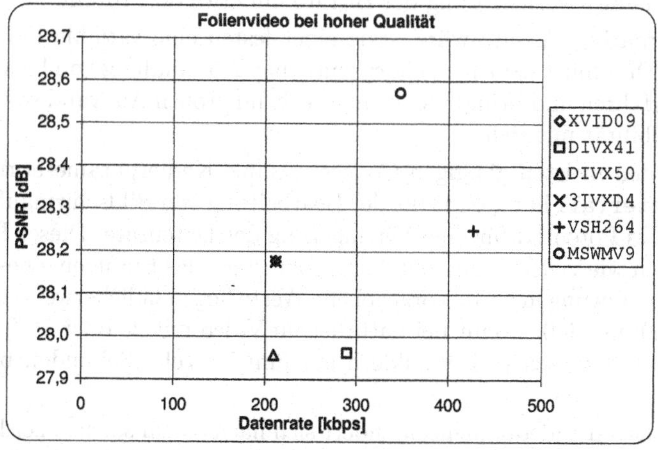

Abb. 1. Datenrate und Qualität von Folienvideos mit aktuellen Videocodecs

Bei den MPEG-4-Kandidaten XviD [6], dem kommerziellen Pendanten 3ivX [7] und DivX 5.0 [8] sind die Datenraten nahezu identisch – bei gleicher Quantisierung und gleichem zugrunde liegenden Verfahren ein erwartetes Ergebnis. Das ältere DivX 4.1 schert bei der Datenrate deutlich aus, da einige Kodierparameter fest vorgegeben und auf unsere spezielle Anwendung nicht anpassbar sind. In dieser MPEG-4-Gruppe heben sich XviD und 3ivX mit einem höheren Qualitätswert von den DivX-Varianten ab.

Deutlich sichtbar ist die höhere Qualität bei Microsofts WMV9 [9], die jedoch mit einer signifikant höheren Datenrate erkauft wird. Eine aktuelle Version des VSS H.264-Videocodecs [10] enttäuscht in dieser Disziplin mit im Vergleich zu XviD nur unwesentlich höherer Qualität bei deutlich höherer Datenrate.

Aufgrund des hohen Anspruchs an die Darstellungsqualität haben Folienvideos bei dieser Kodierung hohe Bitraten. Eine Erhöhung der Quantisierungsparameter führt schnell dazu, dass die Folien unleserlich werden, so dass eine Datenreduktion nur über die Skalierung der räumlichen und zeitlichen Auflösung möglich ist. Beide erweisen sich jedoch als nur bedingt praktikabel: eine Verringerung der räumlichen Auflösung kann den Verlust relevanter Details verursachen und erschwert in jedem Fall die Lesbarkeit der Folien durch eine interpolierte Darstellung. Unter dem Aspekt, dass Präsentationen über weite Bereiche statisch sind (die durchschnittliche Zeit für Folienwechsel liegt im Minutenbereich), bietet sich eine Verringerung der Framerate im Folienvideo als ideale Möglichkeit zur Datenreduktion an. Das trifft jedoch nur dann zu, wenn in der gesamten Präsentation auf dynamische Elemente wie Animationen oder eingebettetes Multimedia verzichtet wird. Wir integrieren in unseren Präsentationen verstärkt handschriftliche Annotationen und wollen auch im Folienvideo die Schriftzüge als solche erhalten. Daher können wir die Framerate nur auf Werte senken, die noch wahrnehmbare Bewegungen ermöglicht. Für die beschriebene Testsequenz ist eine Reduktion der Framerate von 15 auf fünf Bildern pro Sekunde sinnvoll und führt zu einer Verringerung der Bitrate um etwa 40 Prozent.

Ein alternativer Ansatz wäre, statt einer festen eine variable Framerate zu verwenden. Dies führt jedoch zu einer deutlichen Abwandlung von bisherigen Videocodecverfahren und bringt einen entsprechend großen Aufwand sowie Verlust an Kompatibilität mit sich.

Der bei den meisten gängigen Codecs variable Kodierparameter `maximales I-Frame-Intervall` hat gerade bei der Bearbeitung von Bildschirmaufzeichnungen ein großes Potential für eine Verringerung der Datenrate. Dieser Parameter legt fest, nach wie vielen Differenzbildern spätestens das Einfügen eines I-Frames als Stützbild erzwungen wird. Vorgegebene Werte liegen üblicherweise im Bereich zwischen 150 und 300, womit bei natürlichem Video mit 25 oder 30 fps der maximale Abstand zwischen Stützbildern auf fünf bis zehn Sekunden beschränkt wird.

In natürlichen Videosequenzen ändert sich nach einem solchen zeitlichen Abstand der Bildinhalt üblicherweise so stark, dass sich die Verwendung von I-Frames ohnehin aufgrund des Inhalts ergibt und dieses erzwungene Einfügen eines I-Frames nur selten und bei längeren Filmsequenzen ohne Bewegung vorkommt. Die Größe der dadurch redundanten Informationen bleibt so im Vergleich zur Gesamtgröße vernachlässigbar klein. Bei einem Folienvideo ist das Verhältnis von erforderlichen und redundanten I-Frames dagegen ungleich ungünstiger: auch wenn sich der Bildinhalt beispielsweise zwei Minuten lang nicht ändert, werden viele Kopien des Bildes intraframe kodiert. Die dabei eingefügten Daten entsprechen pro I-Frame etwa einem JPEG-Bild bei entsprechender Quantisierung und bilden den ausschlaggebenden Faktor für die geringe Effizienz.

Diese I-Frames sind unter anderem für einen wahlfreien Zugriff auf die kodierten Videodaten nötig, da dabei der jeweils aktuelle Bildinhalt aus allen Frames seit einschließlich dem letzten I-Frame rekonstruiert wird. Damit ist der maximal zulässige Wert für diesen Parameter stark von der eingesetzten Software und der Performance der Hardware abhängig. Wir haben auf verschiedenen Rechner- und Softwarekonfigurationen stichprobenartig Videos mit unterschiedlichen Abständen von Stützstellen durchgeführt und festgestellt, dass bis zu einem I-Frame-Abstand von 400 keine Verzögerungen beim wahlfreien Zugriff bemerkbar sind.

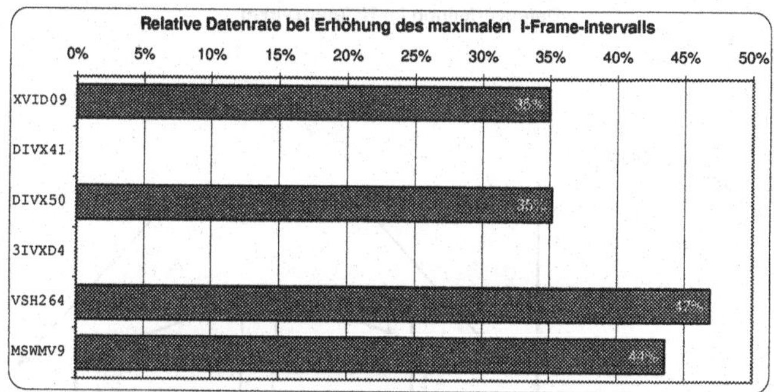

Abb. 2. Datenrate bei Erhöhung des maximalen I-Frame-Intervalls um den Faktor 6

Für die Untersuchung dieses Einflusses haben wir das Folienvideo mit einem verglichen, das mit dem sechsfachen Abstand der Stützbilder kodiert wurde. Auf die Qualität und die Kodierzeit wirkt sich diese Modifikation nicht aus. Dagegen ist der Einfluss auf die Datenrate enorm, wie aus Abbildung 2 hervorgeht. Bei den beiden MPEG-4-Vertretern XviD und DivX 5.0 reduziert sich die Datenmenge auf knapp ein Drittel, Microsofts WMV9 und der VSS H.264 profitieren immerhin mit einer Ersparnis von über 50 Prozent. Bei 3ivX und DivX 4.1 kann dieser Kodierparameter nicht manuell eingestellt werden.

Als Fazit dieser Untersuchung konnten wir eine generelle Praktikabilität von Folienvideos feststellen und XviD als geeigneten Codec empfehlen. Mit der Variation von Framerate und maximalem I-Frame-Intervall kann die Effizienz bei der Videokodierung von Folienpräsentationen deutlich erhöht werden.

3 Vergleich von XviD mit TSCC und Optimierungsansätze

Nach dieser Evaluation gehen wir in diesem Abschnitt mehr auf die technischen Interna der Kodierung ein und stellen mögliche Verbesserungsansätze vor, die wir mit der Wahl geeigneter Kodierparameter und Erweiterungen am quelloffenen XviD erreichen.

Als Maß für die Effizienz vergleichen wir die XviD-kodierten Daten jeweils mit den Werten des auf Bildschirmaufzeichnung spezialisierten TSCC (TechSmith Screen Capture Codec [11]), in dem die Referenzdaten nach einer Aufzeichnung mit TechSmiths Capturing-Tool Camtasia verlustfrei kodiert vorliegen.

Für die Untersuchung der Bitraten und deren Verteilung auf einzelne Elemente des Videostroms verwenden wir den OpenSource Videoeditor VirtualDub [12]. Neben verschiedenen Bearbeitungsfunktionen für Videodaten im verbreiteten Containerformat AVI können damit statistische Informationen abgefragt werden.

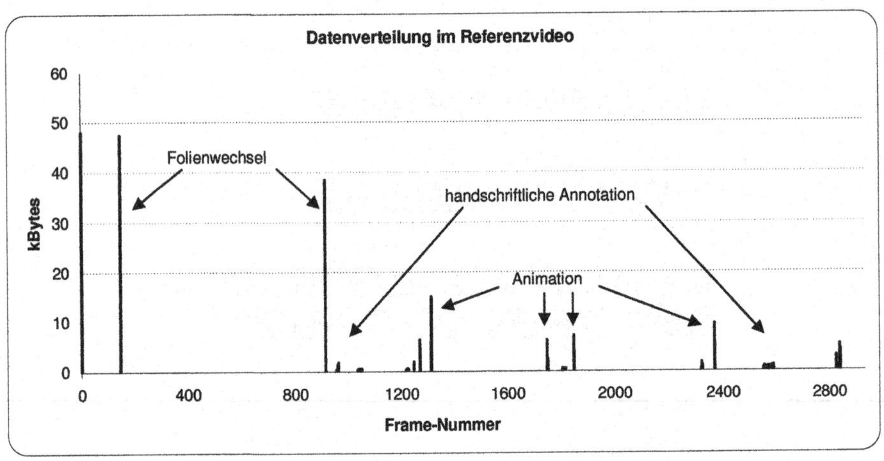

Abb. 3. Datenverteilung im Referenzvideo

Das im Weiteren verwendete Referenzvideo ist eine mit TSCC verlustfrei kodierte Bildschirmaufzeichnung bei einer räumlichen Auflösung von 1024x768 Pixel und 5 Bildern pro Sekunde mit insgesamt 2933 Frames. Inhaltlich setzt es sich aus drei Folien mit unterschiedlicher Charakteristik zusammen. Die Abbildung 3 gibt die im Video enthaltenen Daten für jedes Frame an.

Die Titelfolie ist statisch und umfasst die Frames 0 bis 145. Es folgt eine längere, ebenfalls statische Folie in den Frames 146 bis 913. Die dritte Folie in den Frames 914 bis 2932 enthält Animationen in Form von Text- und Grafikeinblendungen sowie handschriftliche Annotationen. Dabei sind die beiden Folienwechsel mit Bewegungsdaten um 40 kBytes deutlich zu erkennen. Die Daten für

Animationen sind abhängig von der Größe des sich ändernden Bereichs. Sie heben sich deutlich von den Annotationen ab, bei denen sich benachbarte Frames meistens um nur einen Makroblock unterscheiden.

Für dieses Referenzvideo sind die Vergleichswerte in Tabelle 1 in der Spalte (a) aufgeführt. Die durchschnittliche Bitrate von 46 kbps setzt sich dabei aus etwa 3265 kByte für 37 I-Frames und 77 kByte für 2896 P-Frames zusammen. Die Durchschnittsgröße der I-Frames ist 89,1 kByte, wobei die Einzelwerte zwischen 50,9 kByte und 135,4 kByte liegen. Bei den Werten für die P-Frames fällt hier bereits die optimale Differenz-Kodierung auf. Mit der angegebenen minimalen Größe für P-Frames von null Bytes ist eine Kodierung mit variabler Framerate und damit optimale Effizienz bei solchen Inhalten möglich. Die angegebene maximale P-Frame-Größe von 38,1 kByte sollte nicht über den geringen Durchschnittswert von 27 Bytes hinwegtäuschen.

Tabelle 1. Vergleichswerte Videocodierung TSCC vs. XviD

		(a)	(b)	(c)	(d)	(e)	(f)
Codec		TSCC	XviD	XviD	XviD	XviD	XviD
max. I-Frame-Int.			80	80	400	man.	man.
Quantisierung			6	6	6	6	2
	Datenrate[kbps]	46	59	48	14	8	17
I-Frames	Anzahl	37	37	37	8	6	6
	Min[Byte]	52142	48457	48457	48455	48455	103062
	Avg[Byte]	91187	94839	94839	92623	82176	167721
	Max[Byte]	138601	148840	148840	141921	137662	273373
	Summe[kByte]	3265	3396	3396	723	481	982
P-Frames	Anzahl	2896	2896	2896	2925	2927	2927
	Min[Byte]	0	393	7	7	7	7
	Avg[Byte]	27	426	52	101	50	87
	Max[Byte]	38980	47859	47859	47863	10257	18868
	Summe[kByte]	77	1207	150	289	143	250

Da der TSCC als Kodierparameter nur die Wahl zwischen hoher Aufzeichnungsgeschwindigkeit und starker Datenreduktion bietet, können damit keine Videos mit definierten Charakteristiken erstellt werden. Zur direkten Gegenüberstellung der Datenraten von I- und P-Frames haben wir stattdessen bei der XviD-Kodierung schrittweise die Parameter maximales I-Frame-Intervall und Quantisierung angepasst. Die Vergleichswerte dieses Videos sind in Tabelle 1 Spalte (b) wiedergegeben. Während die Anzahl der I-Frames bei einem Abstand von 80 der im Referenzvideo entspricht, stimmt deren Datenmenge bei einer Quantisierung von sechs am besten überein. Die um mehr als 30 Prozent höhere Datenrate bei dieser Einstellung resultiert allein aus der ineffizienten Kodierung der 2896 P-Frames, wobei jedes mindestens 393 Bytes belegt. Ausgehend davon, dass in über 90 Prozent aller Frames überhaupt keine Änderung zum vorhergehenden enthalten ist, summiert sich dieser Overhead auf über drei Megabyte auf und führt zu einer um Faktor 15,7 höheren Datenmenge für die Delta-Frames. Folglich ist dessen Eliminierung für eine effiziente Kodierung von Folienvideos mit XviD zwingend notwendig.

3.1 Reduktion des P-Frame-Overheads

Mit XviD kommt man bei der Effizienz der P-Frame-Kodierung prinzipbedingt an TSCC als Spezialcodec für Bildschirmaufzeichnungen nicht heran: Wie für alle MPEG-Vorgänger ist auch bei MPEG-4 die kleinste Einheit für die Bewegungserkennung ein 16x16-Pixel großer Makroblock (MB). Ändert sich in zwei benachbarten Frames nur ein Pixel, was bei Annotationen der Regelfall ist, muss der gesamte MB kodiert werden.

Abgesehen von dieser Beschränkung ist jedoch im MPEG-4-Visual Standard die Kodierung von Frames ohne Informationsgehalt sehr viel platzsparender möglich als mit den gemessenen 393 Bytes. Bei einem solchen N_VOP, also einem unkodierten Video-Object-Plane (das MPEG-4-Äquivalent zum Frame), wird nur der Header im Bytestrom abgelegt. In der eingesetzten Version von XviD wird diese Funktion zwar unterstützt, muss jedoch erst explizit über den Kodierparameter `Frame drop ratio` eingeschaltet werden. Dieser Wert bestimmt den prozentualen Anteil modifizierter Makroblöcke, bis zu der eine Kodierung als N_VOP zugelassen werden soll.

Für unsere Zwecke ist diese Funktion so nicht geeignet, da schon der minimale Wert von einem Prozent für diesen Parameter unbrauchbare Ergebnisse liefert. Bei einer Auflösung von 1024x768 besteht ein Frame aus 3072 Makroblöcken, so dass Änderungen in bis zu 15 MBs als N_VOPs ignoriert werden. Damit würden nahezu alle Annotationen nicht berücksichtigt.

Wir haben XviD so modifiziert, dass anstatt des relativen Schwellenwerts ein neues Entscheidungskriterium für die Behandlung eines Frames als N_VOP definiert wird: wenn in keinem Makroblock eines P-Frames eine Änderung zur Referenz festgestellt wird, wird es als N_VOP kodiert. Die Vergleichswerte für das mit dieser Modifikation kodierte Video sind in Tabelle 1 Spalte (c) aufgeführt und belegen, dass durch diese Modifikation die Werte für die I-Frames nicht beeinflusst wurden, die Werte für P-Frames hingegen eine signifikante Verbesserung erfahren haben. Die minimale Datenmenge für deren Kodierung ist von 393 auf sieben Bytes gefallen, wodurch sich der Durchschnittswert von 426 auf 52 Bytes pro P-Frame drastisch verbessert und nur noch um weniger als Faktor zwei über den idealen Wert von TSCC liegt. Dadurch rückt die durchschnittliche Datenrate des XviD-kodierten Videos mit 48 kbps sehr nah an den Referenzwert von 46 kbps. Die sieben Bytes für die Ablage eines unveränderten Frames addieren sich erst nach mehreren zehntausend Frames zu der Datenmenge eines I-Frames, so dass der Overhead für diese Kodierung vernachlässigt werden kann. Durch diesen geringen Restaufwand erübrigt sich zudem der Bedarf für eine Lösung mit variabler Framerate.

3.2 Optimierung der Verteilung von I-Frames

Für die Betrachtungen der I-Frame-Kodierung haben wir den Parameter maximales I-Frame-Intervall, entsprechend den Erkenntnissen aus Abschnitt 2, auf 400 angepasst. Dieser Wert empfiehlt sich für solches Ausgangsmaterial und entspricht dem Wert, den wir für die Erstellung von eLearning-Medien an unserem Institut verwenden.

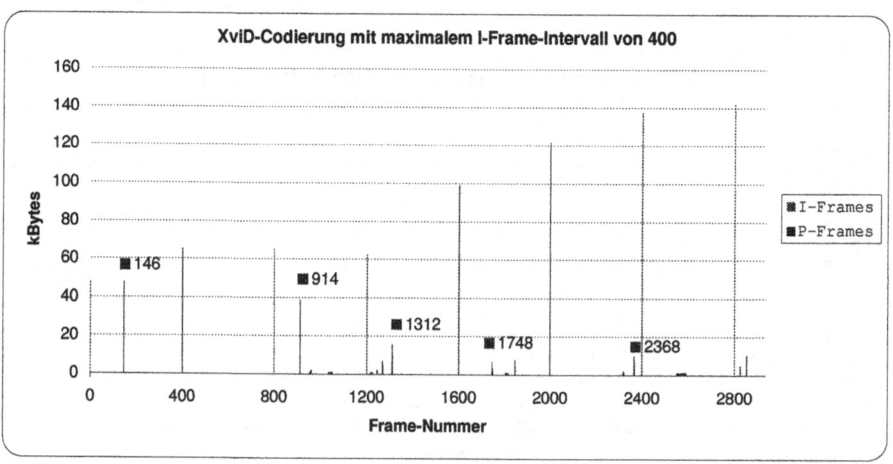

Abb. 4. XviD-Kodierung bei vorgegebenem maximalen I-Frame-Intervall von 400

Die Vergleichswerte dieses Videos sind in Tabelle 1 Spalte (d) aufgeführt, in Abbildung 4 sind die Daten für jedes Frame dargestellt. Deutlich erkennbar ist der hohe Anteil der I-Frames am Datenaufkommen. Zugleich entspricht der maximale I-Frame-Abstand den tatsächlich kodierten, da die Unterschiede zwischen benachbarten Frames im gesamten Video unterhalb der Schwelle liegen, die eine Kodierung als I-Frame auslöst. Die beiden Folienübergänge sind in den P-Frames 146 und 914 erkennbar, die Animationen auf der dritten Folie sind besonders deutlich an den P-Frames 1312, 1846 und 2368 sichtbar. Die ab dem vierten I-Frame steigende Größe resultiert aus schrittweiser Addition von Annotationen und Animationen auf einer anfangs fast leeren Folie.

Von den I-Frames, die über 70 Prozent der Daten ausmachen, ist nur das erste nötig. Die übrigen enthalten redundante Daten, müssen aber zum wahlfreien Zugriff auf den Videostrom eingefügt werden. Mit einer besseren Verteilung der I-Frames lassen sich jedoch Überschneidungen mit nahe liegenden P-Frames vermeiden.

In Abbildung 4 ist eine solche Überlappung der ersten beiden I-Frames mit den beiden durch Folienwechsel bedingten P-Frames 146 und 914 erkennbar. Die Kodierung dieser P-Frames beansprucht ähnliche Datenmengen wie das benachbarte I-Frame. Daher ist es sinnvoll, genau an diesen Stellen I-Frames zu setzen, d.h. jeden Folienwechsel mit einem I-Frame zu beginnen. Für den Fall, dass eine Navigation im Video nicht nur zu den Folienübergängen vorgesehen ist, müssen auch innerhalb einer Folie geeignete Stellen für I-Frames ermittelt werden.

Im vorliegenden Fall besteht die Präsentation der dritten Folie aus über 2000 Frames und dies würde eine Navigation nur mit hoher Verzögerung ermöglichen. Als sinnvolle I-Frames haben wir daher zusätzlich die Animationen in den Frames 1312, 1846 und 2368 ermittelt. Diese Bereiche haben wir dann als Szenen (in XviD über die Funktion `zones`) definiert, die jeweils mit einem I-Frame beginnen.

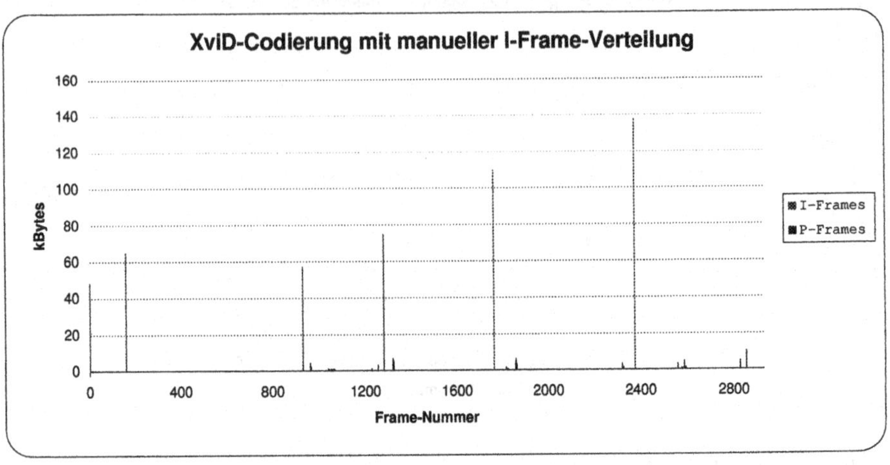

Abb. 5. XviD-Kodierung mit manueller Verteilung der I-Frames

Die Vergleichswerte des resultierenden Videos sind in Tabelle 1 Spalte (e) aufgeführt, die Datenverteilung der Frames in Abbildung 5. Durch das Kodieren der Folienübergänge als I-Frame reduziert sich die Datenmenge der P-Frames um mehr als die Hälfte. Die Datenersparnis bei den I-Frames ergibt sich aus der geringeren Anzahl kodierter Frames. Insgesamt lässt sich mit dieser Optimierung eine weitere Reduktion der Datenrate um bis zu 30 Prozent erreichen. Im Idealfall lassen sich so alle I-Frames auf Folienwechsel verteilen und das Datenaufkommen für P-Frames minimieren. Allerdings erfordert diese Optimierung zum jetzigen Zeitpunkt ein manuelles Eingreifen; nach einigen dafür erforderlichen Änderungen an XviD wollen wir Strategien zur Automatisierung dieses Verfahrens untersuchen.

3.3 Anpassung der Quantisierung

Abseits aller objektiven Messwerte ist der persönlichen Eindruck beim Abspielen der Folienvideos entscheidend für die Akzeptanz der angebotenen Medien. Daher haben wir für eine abschließende Gegenüberstellung auch subjektive Empfindungen berücksichtigt.

Die untersuchte Variation der I-Frame-Intervalle innerhalb der gewählten Grenzen beeinflusst keinen der gebräuchlichen Multimedia-Player, eine Navigation bleibt ohne Zeitverzögerungen möglich.

Allerdings sind nach der verwendeten verlustbehafteten DCT-Kodierung bei Quantisierungsfaktor sechs deutliche Artefakte in hochfrequenten Bildbereichen erkennbar und trüben die Lesbarkeit. Diese verschwinden erst bei einer quasiverlustfreien (und nur so mit TSCC vergleichbaren) Kodierung mit Quantisierungsfaktor zwei. Die Vergleichswerte des so kodierten Videos sind in Tabelle 1 Spalte (f) dargestellt. Zwar verdoppelt sich die durchschnittliche Datenrate im Vergleich zur Quantisierung mit Faktor sechs, allerdings ist das hochauflösende Video einer Bildschirmaufzeichnung bei sehr guter Qualität mit einer Bitrate von 17 kbps immer noch sehr effizient kodiert. Wir konnten bisher noch kein videobasiertes Format finden, das eine ähnliche Qualität bei dieser Bitrate liefert.

4 Zusammenfassung und Ausblick

Wir haben zunächst die generellen Schwierigkeiten einer Videokodierung von quasistatischen Folienpräsentationen untersucht. Dazu haben wir relevante Faktoren analysiert und unter ihrer Berücksichtigung aktuell verbreitete Codecs verglichen. Mit den Ergebnissen dieser Evaluation haben wir den OpenSource MPEG-4-Visual-Codec XviD und dazugehörige Kodierparameter für die Erstellung von Folienvideos empfohlen.

Im Weiteren haben wir die Interna der Videokodierung näher untersucht und Potenziale für eine Erhöhung der Effizienz ermittelt. Unser Minimalziel war dabei eine mit einem auf Bildschirmaufzeichnung spezialisierten Codec vergleichbare Leistung. Durch Modifikationen am XviD-Quellcode war es uns möglich, benachbarte identische Frames sehr sparsam zu kodieren und damit die Effizienz drastisch zu erhöhen. Zusätzlich haben wir gezeigt, dass die Verteilung der I-Frames im Video optimiert und damit die Bitrate noch weiter verringert werden kann.

Diese Verbesserungen führen zu einer Effizienz, die sich mit jeder anderen videobasierten Kodierung messen kann. Absolut betrachtet sind Bitraten ab etwa 18 kbps für das Folienvideo möglich. Im Vergleich dazu ist der begleitende Audiostrom mit Datenraten von mindestens 32 kbps nahezu doppelt so groß. Das absolute Einsparpotential weiterer Optimierungen bei der Videokodierung wird dadurch stark relativiert.

Auch im Vergleich zu Spezialcodecs wie TSCC ist die von uns erreichte Effizienz und Qualität sehr gut. Neben diesen Aspekten und der Offenheit ist ein weiterer Vorteil unseres Ansatzes, dass auf der Nutzerseite reguläre Videoplayer verwendet werden können, so dass die Installation von spezieller Software überflüssig wird und somit, bei einer entsprechend großen Studierendenpopulation, der Beratungs- und Betreuungsaufwand minimiert werden kann. Im Gegensatz zu einigen anderen Werkzeugen, die nur auf spezielle Präsentationswerkzeuge wie Powerpoint ausgerichtet sind, ist unser Ansatz von allgemeiner Natur und unterstützt beliebige Präsentationsanwendungen sowie die Integration von Animationen oder gar Videovorführungen innerhalb einer Präsentation.

Als Fazit stellen wir fest, dass die beschriebene Produktion von Folienvideos, entgegen ersten Annahmen, sehr effizient möglich ist. Dieses ursprünglich als Zwischenlösung geplante Verfahren ist bei uns seit einiger Zeit im regulären Einsatz. Hiermit wurden bereits 357 Lehrveranstaltungsstunden konserviert (siehe bspw. [13]) und diese Aufzeichnungen wurden über 68000 mal von unseren Servern herunter geladen.

Als Motivation für mögliche Änderungen sehen wir weniger den Aspekt der Effizienz, sondern den der Qualität. So bergen insbesondere Verfahren, die Präsentationsfolien nicht pixel- sondern vektorbasiert behandeln, hohes Potential. Breit unterstützte Lösungen sind jedoch erst mittelfristig zu erwarten, so dass wir das beschriebene Verfahren für den unmittelbaren Einsatz als sehr geeignet erachten.

Als einen unserer nächsten Schritte wollen wir die nötigen Änderungen in den offiziellen XviD-Quellcode einbringen. Daneben laufen Arbeiten, die sich mit der Analyse von Aufzeichnungen befassen und Szenen- und Objekterkennung zur optimalen Platzierung von I-Frames zum Ziel haben.

Literaturverzeichnis

1. Doom9. Ausführlicher Vergleich aktueller Videocodecs. `http://www.doom9.org/codecs-203-1.htm`.
2. ISO/IEC. Coding of Audio-Visual Objects. ISO/IEC 14496, 2004.
3. Ralf Steinmetz. *Multimedia-Technologie: Grundlagen, Komponenten und Systeme*. Springer Verlag, October 2000.
4. Zefir Kurtisi and Andreas Kleinschmidt. Evaluation von Video-Codecs für Vorlesungsmaterialien in der ELAN eLearning-Infothek. `http://www.learninglab.de/elan/kb3/index.php?id=296`.
5. V. Ojansivu, O. Silven, and R. Huotari. A technique for digital video quality evaluation. In *Proceedings. 2003 International Conference on Image Processing*, pages III – 181–4 vol.2, September 2003.
6. Christoph Lampert, Edouard Gomez, Michael Militzer, Peter Ross, Radek Czyz, et al. OpenSource MPEG4-Visual Codec XviD. `http://www.xvid.org/`.
7. 3ivX. Kommerzieller MPEG4-Codec von 3ivX. `http://www.3ivx.com/`.
8. DivX. MPEG4-Codecs von DivX. `http://www.divx.com/`.
9. Microsoft. WMV9-Codec. `http://www.microsoft.com/windows/windowsmedia/9series/encoder/default.a%spx`.
10. VSS. Vanguard Software Solutions H.264-Implementation. `http://www.vsofts.com/codec/h264_products.html`.
11. TechSmith. Techsmiths Screen Capture Codec TSCC - Spezialcodec zur Bildschirmaufzeichnung. `http://www.techsmith.com/products/studio/codec.asp`.
12. Avery Lee. OpenSource Video-Editor VirtualDub. `http://www.virtualdub.org/`.
13. Lars Wolf. Vorlesungsaufzeichnung: Mobilkommunikation, SS04. `http://www.ibr.cs.tu-bs.de/lehre/ss04/mk/index.html`.

A Comparison of WS-BusinessActivity and BPEL4WS Long-Running Transaction

Patrick Sauter[1], Ingo Melzer[2]

[1]Universität Ulm, Fakultät für Informatik, 89069 Ulm, Germany
ps9@informatik.uni-ulm.de
[2]DaimlerChrysler AG Research and Technology, Postfach 2360, 89013 Ulm, Germany
paper@ingo-melzer.de

Abstract. Although WS-BusinessActivity and BPEL4WS Long-Running Transaction (LRT) are conceptually very similar and are both designed to support the execution of complex business transactions, they differ in a large number of aspects. This is particularly true because BPEL4WS, unlike WS-BusinessActivity, was not designed to support distributed coordination. This paper comprehensively discusses the similarities and differences between WS-BusinessActivity and BPEL4WS LRT and demonstrates the two concepts on the basis of a joint example. The proposal is to replace BPEL4WS' concept of compensation handlers with a more comprehensive handler type – coordination handlers – that communicate only via SOAP messages and thus make WS-BusinessActivity redundant.

1 Introduction

Within less than three years since its initial release, the Business Process Execution Language for Web Services (BPEL4WS [1]) has gained wide industry and research acceptance. BPEL4WS' goal is to describe, coordinate, and execute complex business processes by combining Web Services with workflow concepts. BPEL4WS will serve as a general framework for composing existing Web Services into coarser-grained, more complex, and possibly long-running applications. The Long-Running Transaction (LRT) coordination protocol is part of the BPEL4WS specification and is a mechanism for dealing with errors during such a long-running activity.

WS-BusinessActivity, on the other hand, is part of the Web Services Transaction Framework (WSTF) which also consists of WS-Coordination [2] and WS-AtomicTransaction [3]. The main purpose of WS-BusinessActivity [4] is to coordinate long-running, compensation-based activities that may consist of several AtomicTransactions.

As a result, it might seem that WS-BusinessActivity and BPEL4WS LRT are rather unrelated approaches to transactions or activities of long duration. The BPEL4WS specification [1] itself states that "the achievement of distributed agreement is an orthogonal problem outside the scope of BPEL4WS, to be solved by using the protocols described in the WS-Transaction specification". (Notice that WS-Transaction now is deprecated and has been split into WS-AtomicTransaction and

WS-BusinessActivity.) In this paper, however, we will argue that the two concepts are not that different after all and can be merged to form a single modeling tool for any kind of long-running transaction.

Therefore, the contribution of this paper is

- the discussion why WS-BusinessActivity and BPEL4WS LRT are neither orthogonal nor contradicting approaches to complex business transactions and
- the description of how their differences can be overcome by fully incorporating WS-BusinessActivity into BPEL4WS.

2 Related Work

Both BPEL4WS and WS-BusinessActivity are relatively new specifications that have emerged during the last few years. Although they clearly are not competing specifications for the same purpose, they share both their underlying transaction model of so-called "open nested transactions" and the idea to invoke explicitly coded compensating actions in the event of failure during the execution of a transaction. These concepts will now be introduced briefly:

In short, an **open nested transaction** is a tree (of arbitrary height) of so-called "subtransactions". Open nested transactions are the generalization of nested transactions which are sometimes also referred to as "*closed* nested transactions". The children of a *closed* nested transaction may commit only when the parent commits. As a result, the overall transaction commits when the root commits, with no individual part of work to be completed (committed) earlier [5, 6]. This limitation does not make sense for long-running, distributed transactions, because it would imply that locks on resources have to be kept for a long period of time until the root commits. Therefore, the subtransactions of an *open* nested transaction (which is mainly used for *distributed* transactions) may commit independently of each other without having to wait for the root transaction to commit.

The next important question on open nested transactions is what the parent transaction should do if one of its child subtransactions has failed. Basically, this behavior is left to the implementor of the transaction – he may decide whether the overall transaction should abort or simply ignore the failed subtransaction. For example, an ordering system that chooses the cheapest supplier might still be able to commit successfully if only one of the suppliers fails during the transaction.

The concept of open nested transactions has not been incorporated into WS-BusinessActivity and BPEL4WS LRT without adaptations. In particular, both are using only a "variant" [1] of open nested transactions and therefore use the terms "nested scopes" (and "nested activities") instead of "subtransactions". A **scope** is the definition of a logical unit of work as well as the smallest unit of error handling and can best be compared with a "try" block in Java. Since scopes can be **nested**, the resulting structure can also be regarded as a tree.

In BPEL4WS, every scope can be assigned a compensation handler. **Compensation** refers to the idea of invoking explicitly coded business logic to undo the effects of a successfully committed action or transaction. A scope's compensation handler therefore contains the appropriate compensation logic, e.g. a WSDL `portType` reference.

Each of these three concepts – open nested transactions, nested scopes, and compensation – has been incorporated into the specifications of both WS-BusinessActivity and BPEL4WS. In particular, the idea of coordinating scopes has been incorporated into BPEL4WS by means of the Long-Running Transaction (LRT) coordination protocol [1, Section 13.2 and Appendix C]. In effect, LRT directly uses the names of states and state transitions of WS-Transaction for coordination among BPEL4WS scopes. The differences of how nested scopes are used by the two specifications will be discussed in the subsequent section.

Apart from WS-BusinessActivity, there are two other important specifications related to transactions for Web Services: WS-Coordination and WS-AtomicTransaction.

In short,

- WS-Coordination provides the protocol for distributing the coordination context of a transaction (e.g. a unique transaction ID) to its participants. For example, WS-Coordination specifies the interface of a transaction manager (a so-called coordinator) for creating a new or joining an already existing transaction. Both WS-AtomicTransaction and WS-BusinessActivity are so-called *coordination types* that are built on top of WS-Coordination.
- A WS-AtomicTransaction is a short-lived (though not necessarily fully ACID-compliant [7]) transaction implementing the two-phase commit (2PC) protocol in terms of Web Services. Typically, an AtomicTransaction is used for locking resources exclusively and sending the `Rollback` notification in the event of failure.

In this context, WS-BusinessActivity can be seen as a framework for putting together a large number of AtomicTransactions (that all share the same `CoordinationContext` as provided by WS-Coordination) that are compensated when the overall BusinessActivity fails. In contrast to an AtomicTransaction, a BusinessActivity is long-running and typically asynchronous. These three specifications are also referred to as the Web Services Transaction Framework (WSTF).

Another noticeable specification related to transactions for Web Services is the Business Transaction Protocol (BTP, [8]) by OASIS. This paper, however, focuses on the WSTF, because it currently is the most widely accepted specification and the two Web Services heavyweights, IBM and Microsoft, are backers of both the WSTF and BPEL4WS.

Moreover, we will analyze the distinction between WS-BusinessActivity and BPEL4WS. The October 2003 paper "The Next Step in Web Services" [9] suggests that these two specifications, among others, should be used in combination. Curbera et al. explicitly consider the combined use of BPEL4WS, WS-Transaction (now: WS-AtomicTransaction and WS-BusinessActivity), and WS-Coordination and state that WS-BusinessActivity (together with WS-Coordination) should be used "in environments where BPEL4WS scopes are distributed or span different vendor implementations". In other words, several BPEL4WS workflows should register as participants to join a BusinessActivity, i.e. BPEL4WS is "smaller" or finer-grained than WS-BusinessActivity. Figure 1 illustrates this idea.

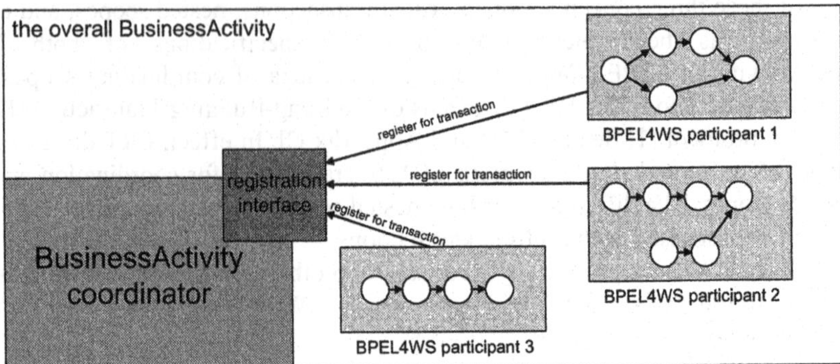

Figure 1 shows the notion of Curbera et al. Here, many "smaller" BPEL4WS instances register for participation in a "large" BusinessActivity.

In the subsequent sections, we will show that there are alternative views on the relationship between BPEL4WS and WS-BusinessActivity.

3 Differences Between WS-BusinessActivity and BPEL4WS LRT

There are several similarities as well as an even greater number of differences between WS-BusinessActivity and BPEL4WS Long-Running Transaction. This section rigorously lists these differences and similarities (the latter are denoted in *italics*) as a table and then discusses the most crucial deviations. We will later argue that the differences can be overcome by simply prescribing the manner in which a BPEL4WS LRT communicates with its nested (child) scopes.

Many of the differences listed in Table 1 are implied by the differing intended purposes of the two specifications – graph-oriented workflow description and execution on the one hand, distributed transactions on the other hand. However, because a coordinated and mutually agreed outcome of an activity is also an important quality aspect of business-critical (BPEL4WS) workflows, the LRT protocol was added to BPEL4WS. Unfortunately, one thing was forgotten: the ability to coordinate *distributed* scopes. LRT supports only the coordination of scopes that are local within the same BPEL4WS engine. As a result, WS-BusinessActivity is still required for all distributed long-running transactions. Figure 2 illustrates this relationship.

WS-BusinessActivity, in turn, has two main problems associated with it:

- It does not offer much additional functionality for coordinating long-running transactions compared to BPEL4WS LRT.
- WS-BusinessActivity is a very simple mechanism intended to support very complex operations. It does not provide mechanisms for dealing with complex activity flows. Consequently, a lot of work is left to the implementor and much of the transaction's business logic has to be hard-coded.

The more complex a transaction is, the more does it make sense to model it as a workflow. For example, a very complex financial transaction that involves debiting and crediting a large number of accounts in a particular order can be modeled more easily as a BPEL4WS workflow than as a BusinessActivity. This is because WS-

BusinessActivity does not provide constructs such as sequences, branches, iterations, etc. that make the actual flow of the transaction's steps more explicit.

Table 1 compares the key features and characteristics of BPEL4WS Long-Running Transaction with those of WS-BusinessActivity.

	BPEL4WS LRT	WS-BusinessActivity
paradigm	orchestrate a flow of Web Services towards a coarser-grained (higher-level) service; act as a wrapper for a flow of "smaller" services	coordinate a set of distributed Web Services (e.g. AtomicTransactions) to reach a mutually agreed outcome; also includes WS-Coordination
number of participants	pre-determined; all potentially involved types of partners (their WSDL descriptions) are known at binding-time	dynamic; participants may join or leave the BusinessActivity at any time as long as they implement the BusinessActivity WSDL interface
error messages	errors (fault and compensation) are handled internally, and no explicit error messages are sent; instead, e.g. a `compensate()` method is called	explicitly described by the specification: error messages (so-called "notifications", e.g. `Compensate`) to the participants are sent as SOAP messages
business error handling concept	*nested scopes and compensation; the unit of error handling is a scope*; a scope is a set of local activities	*nested scopes and compensation; the unit of error handling is a scope*; a scope is a set of distributed activities
fatal error handling concept	the occurrence of a BPEL4WS fault causes the entire scope to exit; the already completed activities are compensated and a fault handler is invoked; similar to try-catch-blocks	go to state `Faulting`; this state cannot be reached directly from the `Completed` state, because compensation has to be tried first; `Faulting` means that a compensation attempt has failed
place to implement the compensation handler	each scope is assigned a dedicated compensation handler that is invoked if the entire scope has to be compensated; therefore, a service might have multiple compensation handlers	the BusinessActivity-compliant service itself must understand and be able to process the `Compensate` notification
short-running transaction support	*may consist of several AtomicTransactions*	*may consist of several AtomicTransaction*
designed for...	*complex long-running transactions* (so-called "activities")	*complex long-running transactions*
scope of the specification	136 pages; complex workflow semantics described; defines its own coordination protocol (LRT)	21 pages; focus not on describing semantics, but on states and state transitions; defines two slightly different coordination protocols
order of activities/ steps	described in detail by the process description, i.e. the `.bpel` file	has to be defined by other means, e.g. has to be hard-coded or the order may even be arbitrary; only the coordination message flow of the overall activity/transaction is pre-defined

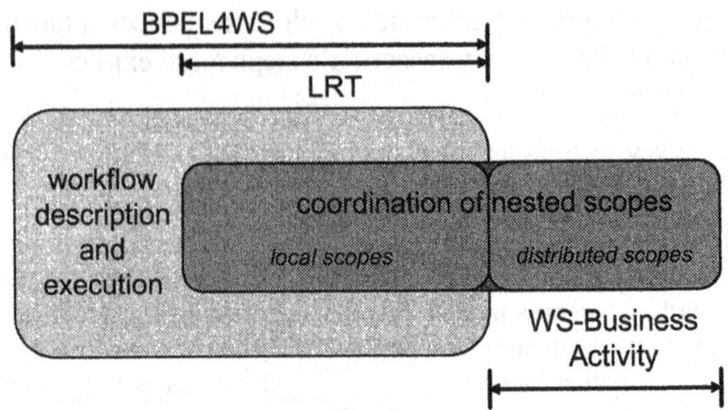

Figure 2 depicts the relationship between BPEL4WS, LRT and BusinessActivity in a set-style notation.

The next section demonstrates the implications of BPEL4WS LRT's lacking distributed coordination support for the implementation of a typical transactional Web Service. Later, in Section 5, we will conclude that this limitation of BPEL4WS can be overcome with little effort, thereby making WS-BusinessActivity redundant.

4 Usage Scenarios and Associated Problems

Reaching distributed agreement is the most important aim of WS-BusinessActivity. In this paper, we will use the example of a patient tracking system in a hospital to demonstrate a typical usage scenario for distributed coordination.

Consider the following situation: A hospital wants to give every stationary patient a unique number, possibly the combination of a person ID with a residence number, and coordinate the treatment by always referencing this number. Part of the treatment might be e.g. appointments in the rehabilitation center or the department of cardiology. Since a hospital essentially is a set of distributed wards interacting with each other, the hospital decides to use Web Service standards for its patient tracking system. They start with providing every patient with a WS-Coordination `CoordinationContext` [2] that consists of his person ID and residence number.

To avoid schedule collisions, every arrangement of an appointment is coordinated by means of WS-AtomicTransaction. For example, whenever a patient must undergo some treatment in multiple wards, the involved wards start an atomic (possibly even ACID) transaction. Furthermore, the treatment within an individual ward might be complex and consist of several sequences, branches, and other typical workflow elements. For example, if the patient's blood pressure is too high, some additional examination steps might have to be performed. Therefore, the wards internally use BPEL4WS implementations (possibly of different vendors) to coordinate the process of treating the patients.

On top of WS-Coordination, WS-AtomicTransaction, and BPEL4WS, the hospital eventually uses WS-BusinessActivity to coordinate the multiple wards' BPEL4WS implementations. For example, if the patient suffers a heart attack during his appointment in the rehabilitation center, the emergency ward (more precisely, its

BPEL4WS instance) joins the overall activity as a participant by registering with the WS-Coordination service and starts the emergency treatment. Moreover, some compensating actions have to be invoked to cancel the (previously successfully committed) appointment with the department of cardiology.

The resulting architecture of the hospital's patient tracking system might be very similar to Figure 1. For example, the participants 1 and 2 shown in Figure 1 might be the department of cardiology and the rehabilitation center, whereas the emergency ward might be the third participant joining the overall BusinessActivity only later, shortly after the patient has suffered the heart attack. In this architecture, all coordination messages are transmitted using dedicated SOAP messages and are WS-BusinessActivity notifications as described in [4].

It is not possible to implement this scenario using only BPEL4WS, because coordination of *distributed* scopes is not supported. Only local scopes, i.e. sets of service invocations, can be coordinated using the LRT protocol of BPEL4WS. In the next section, we will show how BPEL4WS has to be extended to be able to fully implement distributed coordination scenarios such as the hospital example.

5 Fully Incorporating WS-BusinessActivity into BPEL4WS

5.1 The State of the Art

Every BPEL4WS instance is a Web Service that invokes other Web Services. These "smaller" services can therefore also be classified as "nested" or "finer-grained" Web Services. For example, the department of cardiology's BPEL4WS workflow might invoke the Web Service that calculates the costs of the treatment. This computation can be a complex task that might involve several legacy database queries, and so the treatment calculation Web Service might be a (finer-grained) BPEL4WS workflow itself.

The main question now is: Why couldn't the program that coordinates the distributed scopes (up to now: the BusinessActivity coordinator) be a BPEL4WS workflow as well? The answer is quite simple: It could, if only the way in which BPEL4WS coordination signals (e.g. the `compensate()` method invocation) are sent was prescribed to be SOAP notifications and not left to the implementor. If this was the case, no difference would have to be made between local and distributed coordination. To achieve this, we will introduce a new dedicated handler type for coordinating distributed scopes in Section 5.2. BPEL4WS already includes three handler types – event handlers, fault handlers, and compensation handlers.

The first idea might be to use one of the already existing handler types for coordinating distributed scopes, but it turns out that neither of them is suitable for this purpose, because all of them are only required to accept some kind of local "signals" such as implementation-defined method invocations, e.g. `compensate()`. Distributed coordination, however, requires explicit (SOAP) messages instead of local "signals".

The second idea might be to use the most suitable handler type for distributed coordination, the compensation handler, and change the BPEL4WS specification so that the "compensate" signal has to be transmitted by means of a `Compensate` SOAP notification. However, compensation alone is not yet full-fledged distributed coordination.

5.2 The Coordination Handler Concept

Accordingly, a new type of handler is required to process all notifications related to coordination. This handler type will be called a *coordination handler*. Like each of the other handler types, a compensation handler can be attached to either the entire process or to an individual scope. The crucial difference, however, is that coordination handlers accept signals only as explicit SOAP notifications (and not as internal method invocations) that can also be sent from outside the local BPEL4WS instance. As a result of introducing a handler type for all coordination messages including `compensate`, BPEL4WS' compensation handler will become redundant.

Every coordination handler must be able to process the notifications as defined in WS-BusinessActivity. The set of BusinessActivity notifications is subdivided into coordinator-generated and participant-generated messages. In this context, the "coordinator" is the BPEL4WS activity that *calls* a (local or distributed) coordination handler, e.g. the emergency ward's BPEL4WS instance shown in Figure 3. Consequently, these coordinator-generated messages have to be *processed* by every coordination handler, namely: `Completed`, `Fault`, `Compensated`, `Closed`, `Canceled`, `Exit`, `GetStatus`, and `Status`. In turn, every coordination handler must be able to *send* WS-BusinessActivity's participant-generated notifications, more precisely: `Close`, `Cancel`, `Compensate`, `Faulted`, `Exited`, `GetStatus`, `Status`, and maybe also `Complete` (which is only part of the BusinessAgreementWithCoordinatorCompletion protocol of WS-BusinessActivity [4]). These reply messages flow in the reverse direction of the arrows shown in Figure 3.

In order to fully support distributed coordination, it is essential to support not only the set of SOAP notifications specified by WS-BusinessActivity, but also the basic commands of the underlying WS-Coordination specification [2]. These are in particular `Register` and `RegisterResponse`, `CreateCoordinationContext` (to start a new transaction) and `CreateCoordinationContextResponse`. Since probably not all BPEL4WS instances actually require transactional behavior, providing a scope with a coordination handler should be optional.

Since the coordinator and the participant must be able to communicate with each other during the course of the transaction, we suggest using the WS-Notification specification family [10] for establishing the two-way connection of SOAP notifications between the coordinator and the participant. Therefore, it would in particular be required for the WS-Coordination `Register` and `RegisterResponse` notifications to include the contents of a WS-Notification `Subscribe` message, i.e. the coordinator must explicitly register with the participant for the coordinator's coordination messages and vice versa.

5.3 Impact on the Hospital Example

The capability of distributed coordination implies several architectural changes to the hospital example described in Section 4. First of all, the most important simplification is that WS-BusinessActivity, which had been responsible for coordinating the distributed BPEL4WS instances, is no longer used. Instead, the functionality of the Business-Activity-compliant coordination service, probably a hard-coded service surveying the invocations of the registered BPEL4WS instances, is taken over by an explicitly modeled BPEL4WS workflow. Figure 3 shows what this coordinating workflow might look like for the hospital example. Some important aspects of this implementation will now be discussed.

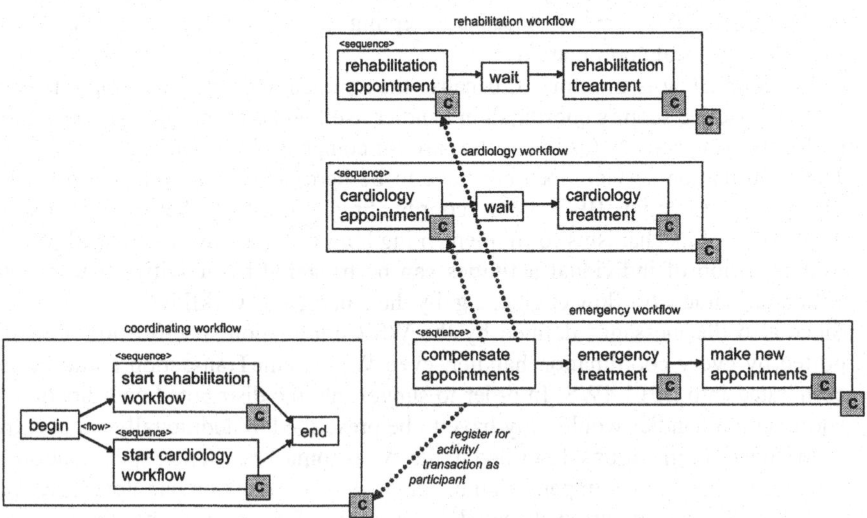

Figure 3 shows a possible architecture of the hospital example as a BPEL4WS workflow with coordination handlers. Boxes with "c" represent the coordination handlers; the dashed arrows indicate the flow of the emergency workflow's SOAP notifications.

Let's first consider the coordination handler of the coordinating (i.e. overall patient treatment) workflow. In order to support the ad-hoc change to its set of active partners when the emergency ward joins the transaction, the overall treatment workflow instance must be able to process the `Register` notification (i.e. "join the existing transaction/activity as a participant"). The emergency ward's workflow then has to compensate all successfully made appointments, call the appropriate heart attack treatment BPEL4WS activities (not shown in Figure 3), and possibly make new appointments.

An important difference to an implementation on the mere basis of BPEL4WS' already specified compensation handlers is as follows: The emergency workflow itself is now able to compensate individual steps of the cardiology and rehabilitation workflows (see the two upper arrows). This would not be possible with compensation handlers, because they only accept signals from within the same workflow engine. As a result, BPEL4WS scopes can now be coordinated even if they are distributed.

5.4 General Advantages

In general, the main advantages of using BPEL4WS with coordination handlers instead of WS-BusinessActivity for coordinating distributed scopes can be listed as follows:

- No distinction has to be made between the implementation of local and distributed scopes; both can be implemented by means of BPEL4WS. A local scope differs from a distributed scope only by the fact that there is no complete implementation of the coordination handler, because accepting the `Compensate` notification is sufficient for local coordination.
- Code redundancy is minimized, because the compensation business logic is kept at the respective scope's coordination handler itself and does not have to be copied to the invoking activity (as this is the case for compensation handlers).
- The coordination service does not have to be hard-coded. Instead, it can be described as an explicit BPEL4WS "coordinating" workflow, thereby minimizing the number of mechanisms for implementing long-running business workflows.
- Compensation of individual activities can be triggered by activities that are not within the same workflow engine, e.g. by the emergency workflow.
- Since also the messages defined by the WS-Coordination specification are supported by every coordination handler, even WS-AtomicTransaction could be incorporated into BPEL4WS. In order to support atomic distributed coordination, a coordination handler would only have to be prescribed to additionally support the set of SOAP notifications described in the WS-AtomicTransaction specification.

As a result, replacing compensation handlers with coordination handlers leverages BPEL4WS LRT to support distributed transactions. Basically, doing so does not change anything about BPEL4WS' underlying workflow and nested scope concept, but only makes BPEL4WS scopes more flexible. When looking at Table 1 again, it becomes obvious that all differences have been overcome by adding the coordination handler concept to BPEL4WS. In particular, the business and fatal error handling concepts have been consolidated, and the number of participants of a BPEL4WS instance has become dynamic since the process' coordination handler now is able to process the `Register` notification.

6 Conclusions

Initially, BusinessActivity and BPEL4WS Long-Running Transaction seemed to be rather orthogonal concepts with different or even incommensurate goals and paradigms. But when having a closer look at the two specifications, the main difference turns out to be BPEL4WS' lacking ability to support *distributed* coordination, although its Long-Running Transaction protocol already supports the coordination of *local* BPEL4WS scopes.

The suggestion of this paper is that BPEL4WS' compensation handlers should be replaced by more powerful *coordination handlers* which accept coordination signals among nested scopes only as SOAP messages. As a result, WS-BusinessActivity is not needed any longer, and we have demonstrated the advantages of using the approach without WS-BusinessActivity on the basis of a hospital's patient tracking system. Moreover, coordination handlers could also be used for reaching atomic agreement among distributed, short-running BPEL4WS scopes and thereby also including the functionality of WS-AtomicTransaction. Eventually, we believe that a single aim – in this case, the implementation of long-running transactional activities – should be pursued by a single powerful mechanism only.

Acknowledgement

This paper was written as part of a Web Services research project at DaimlerChrysler Research and Technology in Ulm, Germany and a diploma thesis at the Department of Applied Information Processing (SAI) of Prof. Schweiggert at the University of Ulm.

References

1. S. Thatte et al. Business Process Execution Language for Web Services. Version 1.1. May 2003. Available at http://www.ibm.com/developerworks/library/ws-bpel/
2. D. Langworthy et al. WS-Coordination specification. September 2003. Available at http://www-106.ibm.com/developerworks/library/specification/ws-tx/#coor
3. D. Langworthy et al. WS-AtomicTransaction specification. September 2003. Available at http://www-106.ibm.com/developerworks/library/specification/ws-tx/#atom
4. D. Langworthy et al. WS-BusinessActivity specification. January 2004. Available at http://www-106.ibm.com/developerworks/library/specification/ws-tx/#ba
5. J. Gray, A. Reuter. Transaction Processing: Concepts and Techniques. Morgan Kaufmann Series in Data Management Systems. 1992.
6. F. Leymann, D. Roller. Production Workflow: Concepts and Techniques. Prentice Hall. 2000.
7. J. Gray. The Transaction Concept: Virtues and Limitations. In Proceedings of the 7th International Conference on Very Large Data Bases. Pages 144-154. September 1981.
8. A. Ceponkus et al. Business Transaction Protocol (BTP). BTP Committee specification. April 2002. Available at http://www.oasis-open.org/committees/business-transactions/
9. F. Curbera, R. Khalaf, N. Mukhi, S. Tai, S. Weerawarana. Service-oriented computing: The next step in Web services. Communications of the ACM, Volume 46 Issue 10. October 2003.
10. S. Graham et al. WS-Notification specification. March 2004. Available at http://www-106.ibm.com/developerworks/library/specification/ws-notification/

Teil III

Drahtlose Netze

Information Dissemination Based on the En-Passant Communication Pattern*

Daniel Görgen, Hannes Frey and Christian Hutter

University of Trier
Department of Computer Science
54286 Trier, Germany
{goergen|frey|hutter}@syssoft.uni-trier.de

Abstract This work presents a communication pattern for high mobile ad hoc networks. En-passant communication uses the short interaction period of passing devices to efficiently synchronize the information of each device. This is achieved by creating peer-to-peer overlays of interest domains. Missing information is determined by exchanging profiles first. As example application `UbiQuiz` is presented, a mobile quiz application. It exchanges questions using the en-passant communication pattern. `UbiQuiz` has been implemented, tested and evaluated within a simulation and on real devices.

1 Introduction

Nowadays, a large variety of more and more powerful mobile devices such as Pocket PCs, PDAs, and smart-phones is available. Since most of these devices are equipped with wireless communication adapters like IEEE 802.11 or Bluetooth, it is reasonable to use these for communication with nearby devices. Communication in ad hoc networks can be classified in single hop communication, where devices communicate with neighboring devices only, and multi hop networks, where messages can pass several hops forwarded altruistically by others.

While it is possible to realize an end-to-end communication over a few hops in dense ad hoc networks by using ad hoc routing mechanisms such as topology based [11] or geographic [5] routing, end-to-end communication will might when network density decreases and network size and mobility increases. In such sparse ad hoc networks infection-based mechanisms work well but degenerate to flooding when the network density increases and may lead to the well known broadcast storm problem [10]. Thus, message exchanging must be reduced to efficient broadcasting mechanisms, where the broadcasting property of wireless networks is utilized to reduce message forwards and not every message is forwarded to every other device. The most critical problem is to decide which message has

* This work is funded in part by DFG, Schwerpunktprogramm SPP1140 “Basissoftware für selbstorganisierende Infrastrukturen für vernetzte mobile Systeme”, Microsoft Research Embedded Systems IFP (Contract 2003-210) and the Luxembourg Ministère de la Culture, de l’Enseignement Supérieur et de la Recherche.

to be forwarded to which device. Thus, the devices have to determine which information is of interest and which is already known to the communicating peer. Classifying devices by domains of interest is achieved by single hop peer-to-peer overlays, where only devices within the same overlay are detected via beaconing and are addressed by a local communication mechanism. The amount of data transferred can be further reduced by exchanging information profiles first. These profiles contain application specific information descriptions and all IDs of known information fitting to this profile. Thus only new information must be sent. This mobility driven information synchronization is termed *en-passant* communication.

Much work has been done in the area of multi hop ad hoc networks in recent years, but only a few real world applications have been implemented. One reason for this is that implementation and testing causes still a high effort since a critical mass of participating devices and test persons are needed. Starting the development with simulations and emulations can reduce the testing overhead and field trials can be reduced to a proof of concept only.

The `UbiQuiz` example is a quiz application helping students preparing for their exams. Questions are shared and exchanged with neighboring devices and disseminated within the ad hoc network. It is very probable, that en-passant communication can be used today in this field, as no connected multi hop ad hoc network is needed. Moreover, creating interest overlays perfectly fits to students behavior, as it is common that they meet fellow-students currently studying for the same exam.

This work is organized as follows: The next Section describes the `UbiQuiz` application and all its parts in detail. It starts with a short application overview, the description of peer-to-peer overlays and information synchronization with neighboring devices. This is followed by a discussion of the applications gaming part and the implementation issues starting with simulation and ending with the real application prototype. The field-trials and the results are presented in Section 3. Section 4 gives a short overview of the related work and finally Section 5 concludes this paper and gives an outlook to future work.

2 The UbiQuiz Application

`UbiQuiz` is a simple quiz game application in the manner of "Who wants to be a millionaire". The user has to answer questions with increasing difficulty by choosing one out of four possible answers. To get help with difficult questions, he is able to use jokers: Discard 50% of the answers keeping the correct one, call a person for help or ask the audience and display a statistic of the results.

`UbiQuiz` is mainly intended to help students preparing their exams. Therefore, it is possible to define different question categories, each covering one learning topic of different subjects, e.g. a lecture on distributed systems in computer science. Students and teachers are able to define own questions and categories in order to create a large and useful question pool. Devices running `UbiQuiz` are able to exchange questions using the en-passant communication pattern.

UbiQuiz maps overlays to question categories. To reduce network load, only devices interested in the same question categories will try to synchronize their question catalogs. This behavior is realized by creating ad hoc peer-to-peer overlays, where only devices interested in the same category are detected and addressed by local communication mechanisms. During the synchronization of question pools, the application aims at efficiently exchanging the missing questions causing a minimum of network load. This is achieved by only sending profiles containing a description of the needed subset and IDs of all known questions fitting to this subset.

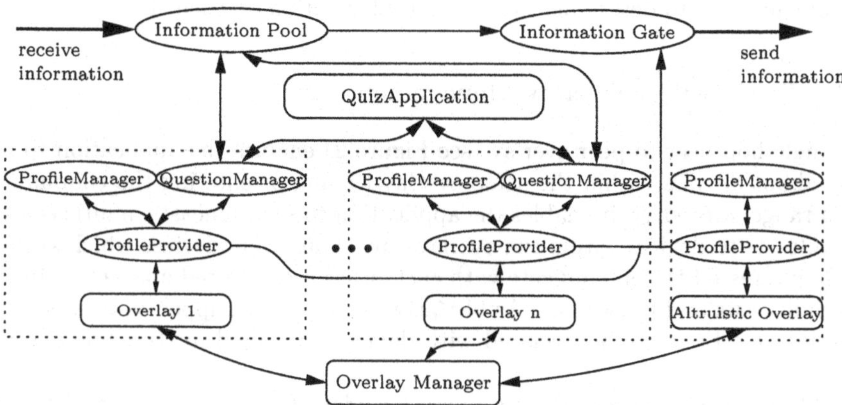

Fig. 1. UbiQuiz P2P communication architecture overview

Figure 1 depicts a simplified overview of the application parts needed for the peer-to-peer ad hoc communication. Each device has one *InformationPool* which stores all known questions and one *InformationGate*, which delivers questions to interested neighboring devices. All received or newly created questions are directly passed to the InformationPool. For each question category the user is interested in, one overlay is created. All overlays are managed by the *Overlay-Manager*. On top of each overlay one *ProfileProvider* is used to send the user profile and all fitting question hashes to devices entering the overlay. The *ProfileManager* manages all known profiles of current neighbors. The *QuestionManager* provides questions to the quiz application and keeps track of all unanswered questions.

To increase the probability that newly created questions are disseminated within the network, each device also stores a fixed amount of questions from other categories altruistically and exchanges them with other devices in an *Altruistic Overlay* as in other overlays but with a lower priority. All devices running UbiQuiz are part of this overlay and also need a ProfileProvider and a ProfileManager for it.

2.1 Information Pool

All received and user created information is stored within the InformationPool. Other application parts are able to register handlers to find out about newly received, created or deleted information. Thus, the application is able to wait for questions of a specific type, e.g. the question category and question difficulty. Additionally, all ProfileProviders are interested in new information in order to send it to interested neighbors. Each information item is addressed with an ID, containing a hash value generated when it is created and a creation timestamp. The hashes are currently generated using an MD5 hash function and are used in the same manner as in the rsync protocol [13], where the hash values are exchanged first to determine the missing information on each site.

2.2 Peer-to-Peer Overlay Management

A single hop peer-to-peer overlay (see Figure 2) enables the application to find out about devices within the same overlay leaving or entering the communication range. Moreover, it enables the application to send unicasts, multicasts and broadcasts to devices within the overlay only. Thus, only devices which are possibly interested to communicate with each other are detected and are addressed by multicasts and broadcasts. As `UbiQuiz` overlays are mapped to question categories, questions are only shared with devices interested in the same question category.

The overlay management uses a periodic adaptive beaconing to broadcast the IDs of all overlays the device currently participates in. The beaconing interval is increased when the number of devices in the direct neighborhood increases. They are counted using the incoming beacon messages. This avoids, that too many beaconing messages are sent within dense networks and too much network bandwidth is used for this service. In sparse networks a smaller beaconing interval is needed to detect single passing devices much earlier. Applications can enter a specific overlay, thus being able to receive enter and leave events of other devices and receive multicast and broadcast messages of an overlay neighbor.

Broadcasts from other overlays are ignored, so that applications only have to consider messages which are of interest to them. Overlay multicasts are used to benefit from the broadcast capability of the network to send one message to all or a subset of all devices within the same local overlay. To increase reliability, in contrast to broadcasts, multicast messages are acknowledged by the receivers. This is achieved by adding all receiver addresses to the multicast message header. This information is also available to the receiving application, so that it can determine the other receivers.

2.3 Profile Based Information Dissemination

One of the most challenging problems when dealing with applications for mobile ad hoc networks is the goal of making all relevant information available to devices

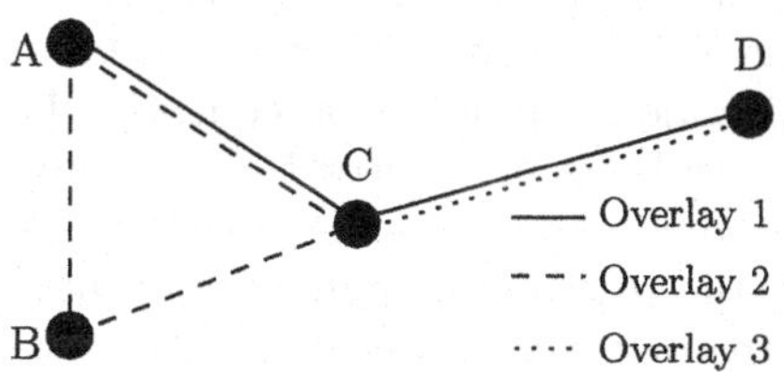

Fig. 2. Devices A, B and C share overlay 2 and are able to communicate. A, C and D are in overlay 1, but A cannot address D directly. C and D are in overlay 3.

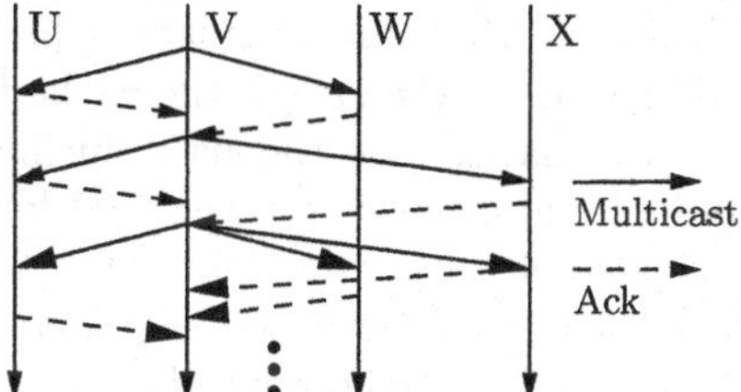

Fig. 3. Device V sends sequentially information items to U,W and X. The next item is sent, after all receivers ACKs the item. The first item is multicasted to U and W, the second to U and X, etc.

interested in them. Thus, it is essential to find efficient strategies for information dissemination.

`UbiQuiz` uses a profile-based approach, where each device determines a description for the subset of information it is interested in. In `UbiQuiz` these profiles currently only distinguish between different question difficulties and creation times, but can be extended easily. Thus, the application is able to request questions of specific difficulties where not enough unanswered questions are left and request all new questions within a specific time delta. Due to the fact that this profile exchange sits on top of an overlay the profiles must only be exchanged with devices within the same question category. To ensure that the receiving devices only send information which is unknown to the profile sending devices, the profile message also contains a set of information keys fitting to the profile. With that, the receiving device can easily determine the set of information to be sent by calculating the difference between all locally known information fitting to the profile and all locally known keys of the other device. Profiles are exchanged by the ProfileProvider whenever another device enters the local overlay. When a profile changes, the device sends a profile update via broadcast to all neighboring devices. Only the difference between the last sent key set and the key set fitting to the new profile has to be included since all devices store the last profile and information keys within their local ProfileManager.

Another reason for storing profile information is that the application can send newly created or received information to interested devices when the local key set does not contain the new key and the information fits to the devices profile.

`UbiQuiz` has been designed to run in cooperative, mobile ad hoc networks. Therefore it features support for general information dissemination realized with an altruistic overlay. The user sacrifices some of his resources like storage capacities, CPU power and communication bandwidth to disseminate data he is not interested in.

The altruistic overlay will also be synchronized with other devices but its internal organization and the synchronization strategy differ from the ones applied to normal overlays. In contrast to the "unlimited" amount of local information stored for them, the size of the cache for the altruistic overlay is restricted and might be changed by the user during application runtime. Consequently the amount of information transmitted for this overlay is in the worst case limited by the size of the cache. When two devices come into communication range, a view of the altruistic cache is transmitted, the receiver computes the optimal cache by adding the content of its cache to the received one and sends the missing elements. Nevertheless it might still occur that transmitted information is discarded. This can happen as the cache might have changed due to information received by other devices not being visible for the sending device.

The cache tries to keep recent data and also aims at being as altruistic as possible. This implies storing data from as many different overlays as possible. Therefore, the altruistic cache is internally organized as two independent caches, one using the timestamps and one using the overlays as an argument to the replacement algorithm. When an information key is deleted from the cache, the corresponding information item is deleted from the InformationPool.

All information data which needs to be sent to interested neighbors is sent by the InformationGate. This is mainly done in a FIFO manner: the information added first is sent first. Due to the fact, that one information can be of interest to more than one device, the FIFO order may be reorganized, so that information addressed to most devices is prioritized. To save network bandwidth, the information is sent via an overlay multicast, so that the information data must only be sent once because a broadcast medium is used (see Figure 3). After all receiving devices have acknowledged the message, the InformationGate sequentially sends the next messages until all information is sent or all receiving devices have left the communication range of the device.

It is possible that not all information is sent to the receiver, because it is always able to leave the communication range. Therefore, it can be necessary to send more important information first and unimportant information last. This ordering can be achieved by adding them in the correct order to the InformationGate, since it sends them in FIFO order. This strategy achieves that the maximum of relevant data can be exchanged even in short interaction periods.

The reception of the information by other devices is communicated to the ProfileManager, so that it does not have to send this information to the receiver again. Moreover, each receiving device can determine all other receivers and is also able to communicate this to its ProfileManager.

2.4 Playing the Game

During an `UbiQuiz` game, the QuestionManager provides questions for the current difficulty level. It keeps track of all answered questions so that it is able to provide only unanswered questions to the user. When it detects that it runs out of unanswered questions, it changes the current profile accordingly and communicates it to the ProfileProvider to announce this change to the neighboring devices. Thus it is possible to receive these questions before no unanswered question is left. To be up to date, the user can adjust the profile so that he always receives the newest questions with a definable age.

It is, of course, possible that no (unanswered) question for a difficulty level is left. In that case, the user can choose to answer a quetsion he answered in a prior game, use a question of a higher difficulty level or wait until a question for this difficulty level is received.

The game can be played offline when enough questions are stored within the QuestionPool. It is also possible to play together with users in the direct neighborhood. In this case, only simple singlehop ad-hoc communication is used. The user is able to choose direct neighbors as a "telephone" or "audience" joker. All active users are listed – this information is already known by the overlay management – and the user is able to select one as telephone joker. Now the other user can answer the question and specify how reliable his answer is. By selecting the audience joker, neighboring devices of the same overlay are addressed via a multicast message and can help the user answering the question. All unicast answers are collected and an answer statistic is provided to the asking user. Another variant is to create a question "on demand". Neighbors are able to create new questions for the playing user who is waiting for receiving questions of the next difficulty step.

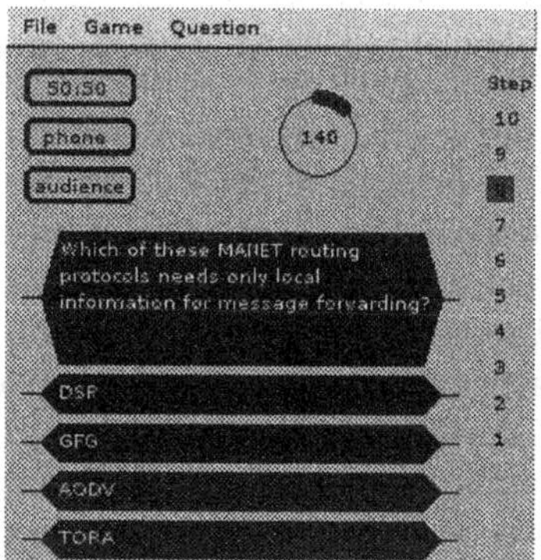

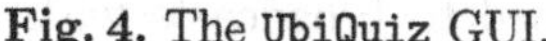
Fig. 4. The `UbiQuiz` GUI.

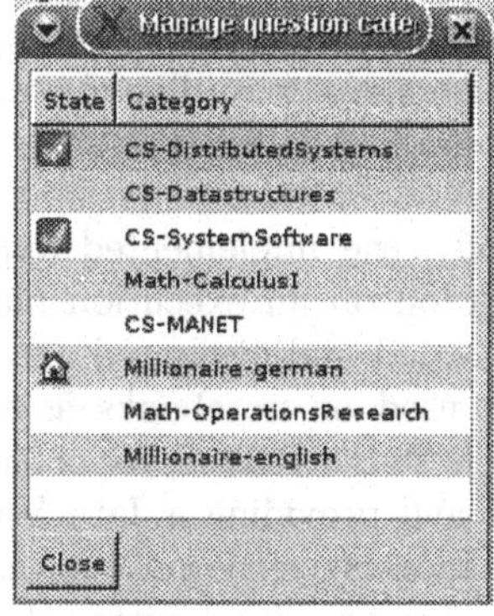

Fig. 5. Manage question categories.

Beside playing the game, the user is able to manage the question categories he is currently able to see. (Figure 5). He can leave or enter each known category. It is also possible to load XML coded question libraries from the file system. These new questions are stored within the local QuestionPool and are disseminated in the ad hoc network from now on. The edit mode allows the user to create new questions for a specific question category and to create new question categories.

2.5 Implementation

The `UbiQuiz` application has been implemented in Java using a workbench for implementing and testing applications for mobile multihop ad hoc networks [6].

In a first step, all information management and exchanging components and protocols were implemented and tested within the workbench's simulator. The second step included the GUI and game logic development process and a testrun in the workbench hybrid mode (see Figure 6). There, real devices can be connected to the simulator and the application can be tested with real user behavior. For such application testing, the devices in the simulator can be moved by clicking on the visualization frame.

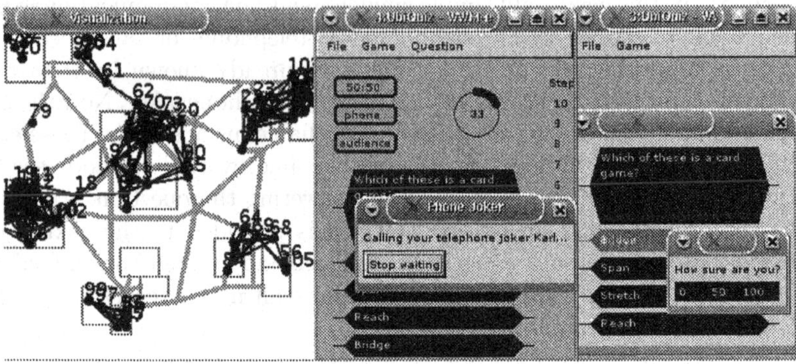

Fig. 6. Two extern devices are connected to the simulator, playing `UbiQuiz` together. Devices are moved according to a path net mobility model.

Finally, the implemented application and GUI code can be used without modification on an execution platform for real devices. Thus, the application can be tested and evaluated on a real hardware platform. The application not only be used on notebooks as used for the field-trials, it is also possible to use it on PocketPCs or other small mobile devices, equipped with a WLAN adapter and providing a Java VM. The execution platform uses UDP unicasts and broadcasts over WLAN for communication. Since multicast communication is realized as broadcast within the lower layers in WLAN (no low level packaging and acknowledgment), the multicasts are mapped to broadcasts with unicast acknowledgments.

3 Evaluation of `UbiQuiz` in Field Trials

In order to estimate the practical applicability of the `UbiQuiz` application, the reference implementation has been investigated in both a static and a mobile "real world" usage scenario. All evaluation runs were performed by using a set of mobile devices consisting of four notebooks and two tablet PCs. Each device is equipped with an IEEE 802.11b interface. If possible, the interface was fixed to the maximum transfer rate and the power save function was disabled.

Each device was running the `UbiQuiz` application, while logging the times of message transmissions and message receipts. For each simulated scenario one device initiated the dissemination of a new set of `UbiQuiz` questions containing 5000 questions, while each question accounting for about 900 – 1000 bytes of message size.

Data rate and error probability were of primary interest in order to judge the performance in both usage scenarios. However, in contrast to traditional evaluation methodology, performance was measured from an application point of view instead of sampling raw data traffic produced by the utilized network protocols. Thus, the presented empirical values were obtained by sampling the data rate and error probability in terms of average number of received question library entries per second and the average number of lost messages during transmission, respectively. The evaluation results presented in the following two sections reflect the typical properties of a wireless communication media. The data rate degrades for both, a growing number of devices utilizing the shared communication media, and an increased distance between sending and receiving device.

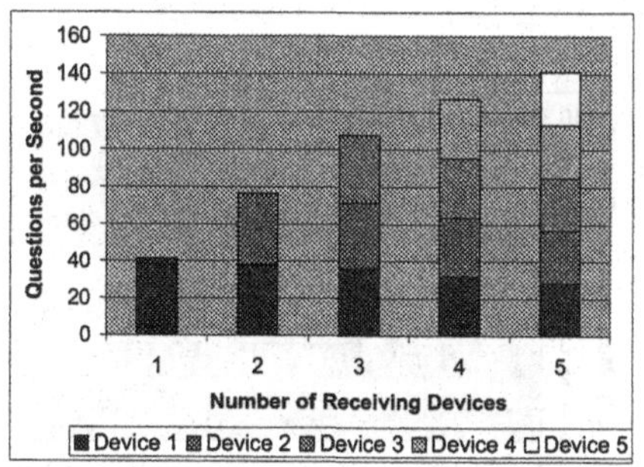

Fig. 7. Question items per second.

Fig. 8. The en-passant communication scenario.

3.1 Evaluating the One-to-Many Scenario

A typical real world application scenario of `UbiQuiz` may be some devices located at a public place, while each device is within the communication range of all others. In order to judge the performance of `UbiQuiz` for such a scenario, three independent trials have been conducted for an increasing number (2-6) of participating wireless devices.

Figure 7 depicts the average number of questions received per second as a function of the number of receiving devices. One can see that the number of received questions per device decreases, when the number of recipients increases. This is due to the application design which requires that acknowledgements of all current recipients have to be received before the next library entry is being sent. Figure 7 also shows that summing the average number of question receipts per device compensates that performance loss. This is due to the fact, that questions are broadcasted to all devices and only the acknowledgments are sent via unicast. Thus, only the small acknowledgement messages leads to a higher protocol overhead, the large question messages has only to be send once to all devices. Implementing such a multicast not within the application layer but in mac layer as the unicast acknowledge my further reduce this acknowledgement overhead.

3.2 Evaluating the En-Passant Scenario

In a second application scenario, the quality of the UbiQuiz application has been investigated with respect to exploiting the limited communication window emerging from two devices passing each other causally as depicted in Figure 8. Again three independent evaluation trials have been conducted, while both test persons passed each other with "almost" the same moving speed. The distance of the starting points was about 150 meter, the meeting point was almost in the middle. In all three evaluation runs the total amount of received messages was about 1300 – 1500 (≈ 14 MByte).

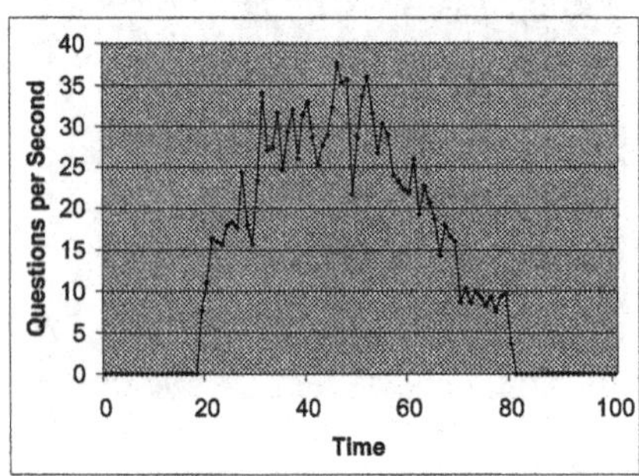

Fig. 9. Data rate during en-passant communication.

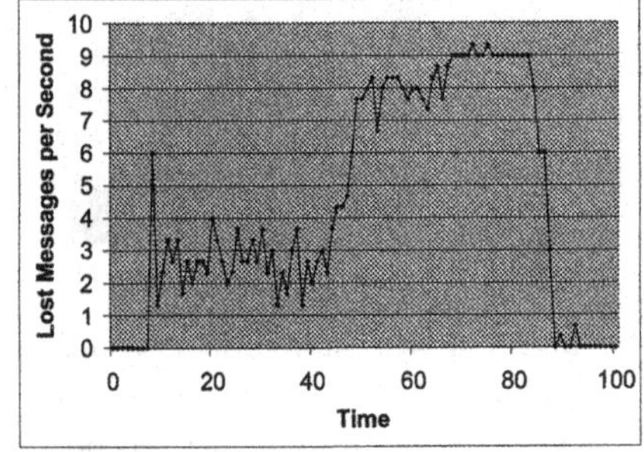

Fig. 10. Message losses during en-passant communication.

The curve progression of the number of transmitted question library entries per second and the number of lost messages was investigated to be nearly the same for all three evaluation runs. Thus, the data rate can be depicted as an average over all three evaluation runs without losing its main characteristics (see Figure 9 and Figure 10). One can see that both devices get in contact for the first time at about 10 sec after starting the experiment. However, signal quality is bad at this time and messages get lost with a high probability. The first message was received successfully about 10 seconds later. The data rate increases and stays around 30 question per second between 30 and 60. The devices met about second 50. There, the data rate drops to 21, probably caused by antenna interference. After passing the meeting point the data rate start to decrease significantly. This is probably due to the test persons hiding the device antennas. The same can also be observed in Figure 9 where the number of lost messages is significantly higher as before the meeting point.

4 Related Work

There are multiple strategies to disseminate information in mobile multi hop ad hoc networks. Beside several flooding algorithms like XCast [7], which uses controlled flooding, e.g. MobiGrid [3] discusses among other ideas the publish subscribe (PS) and the autonomous gossiping (AG) techniques. As `UbiQuiz`, AG also uses en-passant communication and exchanges profiles first. But it neither uses interest overlays, nor efficient information exchanging – date items are always forwarded to neighbors with fitting profiles. PS is used in [1] and works with multi-layer networks to transport the data to the interested parties. A problem when using PS is that a subscription to distant information sources is difficult. Therefore, `UbiQuiz` can be thought of a PS implementation with one hop communication. [4] as a representative of the AG technique broadcasts information items and interested clients can detect and request missing information. Obviously, this might consume a lot of communication bandwidth. Instead of creating information overlays as in `UbiQuiz` it is also possible to use tuple spaces. For instance, [9] spreads tuples in the network according to propagation rules. Thus, the data item "decides" to which device it migrates not the targeted device. XMIDDLE [15] synchronizes information with direct neighbors by using XML trees. Moreover, it is possible to link subtrees to devices were the information is stored, but this leads to a high coupling of devices. Moreover, information access is difficult in larger mobile ad hoc networks.

Many research has been done in the area of efficient flooding protocols [14]. One example are the SPIN [8] protocols which are intended to reduce message overhead in sensor networks. This is also achieved by using information metadata, an application specific information description. New information is offered to all neighbors by sending the metadata and neighbors then request missing information. This causes much more overhead in a mobile environment, since all locally known metadata must be exchanged when a new device is detected in the neighborhood.

Even though the problem of information dissemination/retrieval in mobile ad hoc network has been researched for some time, up to now very few applications have been implemented. [2] is a multi-player adoption of the old single-player "Elite" game. But it still uses central servers and was developed to research social aspects of ubiquitous computer games. The approach made by [12] looks more promising as Opentrek enables rapid game prototyping and delivers easy discovery and integration of players into running games.

5 Conclusion and Further Work

This work introduced `UbiQuiz`, a real world gaming application for multi hop ad hoc networks. Moreover, it introduced an ad hoc information dissemination protocol for efficient information exchanging by reducing the amount of exchanged information to interest domains and profiles. The field-trials performed demonstrated on the one hand the usefulness of using the broadcasting capabilities of wireless communication and the necessity of reducing communication overhead by using interest domains. On the other hand it can be observed, that current system softwares and wireless communication techniques are still not prepared for multi hop ad hoc communication and that still much work has to be done in this area. One example is the lack of reliable communication mechanisms efficiently using the broadcasting facilities of wireless communication.

Since field trials are still very expensive, only a very small subset of necessary tests has been performed. More extensive tests are planned for the nearer future, including the development of a field-trial testbed and a management application helping to reduce the complexity of field-trials.

The `UbiQuiz` application is only one aspect of a larger m-learning environment and should be combined with other m-learning applications. For example combining questions with distributively created scripts and lecture slides disseminated over the ad hoc network to give answering hints is planned. Moreover, it is of course possible to realize more complex applications not only based on simple multiple choice questions.

Another application aspect is the possibility of editing and deleting questions. Currently editing is achieved by simply changing the creation timestamp and keeping the original hash value so that only the newest information survives. Deleting is achieved by propagating deletion information and storing this in a local deletion history. The current work is focused on a distributed information evaluation process, where the user is able to vote for questions. Thus, it is possible to keep a "good" question alive while a "bad" question expires and is deleted.

Finally the application should be put into practice by using it in the context of a system software lecture, since most students are already equipped with mobile devices having wireless communication adapters.

References

1. Emmanuelle Anceaume, Ajoy K. Datta, Maria Gradinariu, and Gwendal Simon. Publish/subscribe scheme for mobile networks. In *Proceedings of the second ACM international workshop on Principles of mobile computing*, 2002.
2. S. Bjork, J. Falk, R. Hansson, and P. Ljungstrand. Pirates! Using the Physical World as a Game Board. In *Conference on Human-Computer Interaction*, 2001.
3. Anwitaman Datta. MobiGrid: P2P Overlay and MANET Rendezvous - a Data Management Perspective. In *CAiSE 2003 Doctoral Symposium*, 2003.
4. Anwitaman Datta, Silvia Quarteroni, and Karl Aberer. Autonomous Gossiping: A self-organizing epidemic algorithm for selective information dissemination in mobile ad-hoc networks. In *International Conference on Semantics of a Networked World*, 2004.
5. Hannes Frey. Scalable geographic routing algorithms for wireless ad hoc networks. *IEEE Network*, 18(4):18–20, July 2004.
6. Hannes Frey, Daniel Görgen, Johannes K. Lehnert, and Peter Sturm. A java-based uniform workbench for simulating and executing distributed mobile applications. In *Proceedings of FIDJI 2003 International Workshop on scientific engineering of distributed Java applications*, Luxembourg, November 27–28 2003.

7. J. Koberstein, F. Reuter, and N. Luttenberger. The XCast Approach for Content-based Flooding Control in Distributed Virtual Shared Information Spaces - Design and Evaluation. In *1st European Workshop on Wireless Sensor Networks (EWSN)*, 2004.
8. J. Kulik, W. Rabiner, and H. Balakrishnan. Adaptive Protocols for Information Dissemination in Wireless Sensor Networks. In *MobiCom*, 1999.
9. Marco Mamei, Franco Zambonelli, and Letizia Leonardi. Tuples on The Air: a Middleware for Context-Aware Computing in Dynamic Networks. Technical report, University of Modena and Reggio Emilia, 2002.
10. S.-Y. Ni, Y.-C. Tseng, Y.-S. Chen, and J.-P. Sheu. The broadcast storm problem in a mobile ad hoc network. *Proc. of the 5th ACM/IEEE Int. Conf. on Mobile Computing and Networking*, pages 151–162, 1999.
11. Elizabeth M. Royer and Chai-Keong Toh. A review of current routing protocols for ad-hoc mobile wireless networks. *IEEE Personal Communications*, pages 46–55, April 1999.
12. Johan Sanneblad and Lars Erik Holmquist. Prototyping mobile game applications, 2002.
13. Andrew Tridgell and Paul Mackerras. The rsync algorithm. Technical report, Australian National University, 1998.
14. B. Williams and T. Camp. Comparison of broadcasting techniques for mobile ad hoc networks. In *Proceedings of the ACM International Symposium on Mobile Ad Hoc Networking and Computing (MOBIHOC)*, pages 194–205, 2002.
15. Stefanos Zachariadis, Licia Capra, Cecilia Mascolo, and Wolfgang Emmerich. XMIDDLE: Information sharing middleware for a mobile environment. In *ACM Proc. Int. Conf. Software Engineering (ICSE02). Demo Presentation.*, Orlando, FL, USA, May 2002.

Hypergossiping: A Generalized Broadcast Strategy for Mobile Ad Hoc Networks

Abdelmajid Khelil, Pedro José Marrón, Christian Becker, Kurt Rothermel

Universität Stuttgart, IPVS/VS, Universitätsstrasse 38, 70569 Stuttgart
{khelil, marron, becker, rothermel}@informatik.uni-stuttgart.de

Abstract. Broadcasting is a commonly used communication primitive needed by many applications and protocols in mobile ad hoc networks (MANETs). Unfortunately, most broadcast solutions are tailored to one class of MANETs with respect to node density and node mobility and are unlikely to operate well in other classes. In this paper, we introduce hypergossiping, a novel adaptive broadcast algorithm that combines two strategies. Hypergossiping uses adaptive gossiping to efficiently distribute messages within single network partitions and implements an efficient heuristic to distribute them across partitions. Simulation results in ns-2 show that hypergossiping operates well for a broad range of MANETs with respect to node densities and mobility levels.

1 Introduction

Mobile ad hoc networks (MANETs) are networks formed on-the-fly by mobile nodes equipped with short range communication capabilities. Such networks are suitable for scenarios where an infrastructure is unavailable and communication must be deployed quickly, e.g. in disaster-rescue or military scenarios.

Broadcasting is a common communication mechanism in MANETs. It is frequently deployed for data dissemination, and for topology discovery and maintenance [1]. Flooding is a common approach to realize broadcasting in MANETs because of its topology independence. In flooding-based approaches nodes forward a received message to all their neighbors. Subsequently, all nodes within the network should receive the message.

But flooding exhibits some serious problems. At the two extremes we can consider dense MANETs and sparse MANETs with respect to the node density, i.e. the number of nodes operating in a given area. While dense MANETs encounter so-called *broadcast storms* [2], where collisions on the Media Access Control (MAC) layer extinguish broadcast messages, sparse MANETs are challenged by frequent *network partitioning*, where messages do not reach every node in one flooding round. Two common strategies can be applied to conquer these extreme cases. First, *selective strategies*, e.g. gossiping [3], cause only subset of nodes to forward a message reducing the probability of broadcast storms. Second, selective *repetition of broadcasts*, e.g. hyperflooding [4,5], can be used to overcome network partitions.

Most broadcasting techniques are unfortunately tailored to one class of MANETs and are likely not to operate well in other classes (see related work section). Our main objective is to provide an adaptive broadcast algorithm for a wide range of MANET operation conditions. The main contribution of this paper is hypergossiping, a novel generalized broadcast mechanism that combines two strategies and provides a configuration depending on the local density of a node, reflected by the number of its neighbors. Using simulation results we show that hypergossiping can be deployed in a wide spectrum of MANETs with respect to node densities and mobility levels.

The remainder of this paper is organized as follows. The next section describes the system model and the requirements on a generalized broadcast strategy for MANETs. In Section 3 we discuss the related work. Section 4 introduces our generalized broadcast strategy, i.e. hypergossiping. In Section 5 we first define the simulation model and the evaluation metrics, then we calibrate the parameters of hypergossiping, evaluate it, and compare it to related work. Section 6 summarizes the paper and gives an overview of ongoing and future work.

2 Preliminaries

This section briefly presents the underlying system model of our approach. Based on the characteristics of the system model we derive some important requirements on our generalized broadcast algorithm.

2.1 System Model

We consider MANETs that are formed by mobile nodes of similar communication capabilities (communication range and bandwidth). We do not assume nodes to have knowledge about their position or speed. The MANET may show very heterogeneous spatial distribution of nodes, from locally very sparse to very dense, and very heterogeneous node mobility pattern: from low mobile to highly mobile. We assume that devices do not change their trajectories for communication purposes.

Broadcast data has typically a temporal and spatial relevance [6]. Broadcast algorithms have to consider this spatio-temporal relevance while broadcasting. In this paper, we consider only the temporal relevance of data and assume that information becomes irrelevant after a certain period of time, i.e. its *lifetime*. Lifetime is application dependent and may be in the range of seconds, minutes, or even hours.

2.2 Requirements

Because node density heavily influences the performance of broadcasting, and MANETs may show a wide range of node densities, the first requirement on a generalized broadcast strategy for MANETs is to adapt to the density of the network, in order to reduce broadcast storms and overcome partitioning. Since global state in MANETs is hard to obtain and spatial distribution of nodes may change continuously, the second requirement on such a strategy is that nodes independently adapt to local MANET characteristics. Third, different instances of the adaptive broadcast strategy have to interoperate in order to deliver messages through the network where different instances are present due to heterogeneity of density.

3 Related Work

Most of existing broadcast algorithms are developed for unpartitioned MANETs, and subsequently break in partitioned ones. They are also optimized for specific scenarios, and subsequently do not support a broader range of MANET situations. In [7] and [8] authors provide two comparative studies for these non-adaptive schemes.

In order to suit these schemes to a broader range of operation conditions, [9] and [10] adapted some of them to local MANET characteristics. In [9] the authors proposed three adaptive schemes, namely, adaptive counter-based (ACB), adaptive location-based (ALB), and neighbor-coverage (NC) scheme. Using simulations the authors derived the best appropriate counter-threshold respectively coverage-threshold for ACB respectively ALB as a function of the number of neighbors. The authors adapted the NC scheme by adjusting dynamically the HELLO interval to node mobility reflected by neighborhood variation, so that the needed 2-hop topology information gets more accurate. Although this optimization, NC scheme still has the main drawback that neighborhood information may be inaccurate in congested networks. The authors showed that these adaptive schemes outperform the non-adaptive schemes and recommend ACB if location information is unavailable and simplicity is required. We will compare our strategy to ACB. [10] introduced the density-aware probabilistic flooding. Nodes use the following forward probability: $p=inf\{1, 11/n\}$, where n is the current number of neighbors. We will also compare our strategy to this scheme. ACB, ALB, NC and density-aware probabilistic flooding support a broad range of dense MANETs but they still show poor performance in partitioned networks.

The first step towards a single solution for all MANET situations was the integrated scheme presented in [5]. We refer to this scheme as integrated flooding (IF). Nodes switch at run-time between three flooding schemes, namely, plain flooding, scoped flooding, and hyperflooding. Authors recognize mobility as main cause of broadcast partitioning [11] and switch between these schemes according to the relative node mobility. To this end, nodes include velocity information (speed and direction) in HELLO beacons. To the best of our knowledge, IF is the single existing adaptive MANET broadcast protocol that considers network partitioning. Unfortunately, IF shows some drawbacks. First, IF adapts to node mobility but not to node density, which makes it break for sparse low-mobile networks that encounter partitions frequently. Second, scoped flooding uses a predefined forward threshold, which makes IF less efficient than the above adaptive schemes in highly dense scenarios. Third, relying on velocity information presents a strong limitation of the deployment of IF. In Section 5.6, we compare our solution to IF.

4 Hypergossiping (HG)

In this section, we present our generalized solution fulfilling the requirements above.

4.1 Approach

In general we can consider a MANET as a set of partitions, which may join or split over time. Thus, we decide to superpose the following two strategies to realize hypergossiping. The first strategy allows an efficient broadcasting within a single partition of the MANET. We refer to this strategy as "intra-partition forwarding" (Fig. 1a)). The second strategy permits an efficient broadcast repetition on partition joins. We call this strategy "broadcast repetition". To this end nodes have to buffer messages during their lifetime and to retransmit an adequate subset of them on partition joins. After broadcast repetition the first strategy can continue to distribute the message to the joining nodes (Fig. 1b)). Note the difference between *forward* and *rebroadcast* explained in Fig. 1. Depending on the mobility of nodes, the node spatial distribution and the lifetime, messages will succeed to other partitions or not.

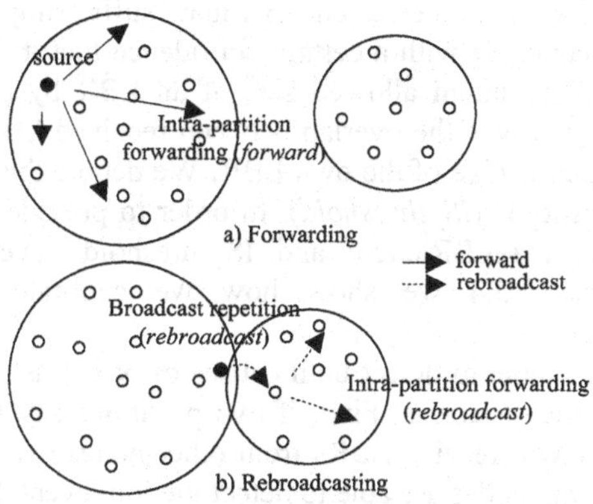

Fig. 1: Approach

In our approach, we assume that each node stores the list of IDs of messages received or originated with their remaining lifetime in a so-called *broadcast_table*. Thus, nodes are capable to decide, whether a received copy of a given message is the first one. Nodes continuously decrement the lifetimes. Nodes purge entries from the broadcast_table and possibly from the buffer, when the correspondent lifetime expires. When a message is forwarded or rebroadcasted, the remaining lifetime is included in the message.

4.2 Intra-partition Forwarding

The analysis of the broadcast storm problem [2] suggests gossiping or probability-based flooding, thus we chose gossiping for intra-partition forwarding.

On receiving the first copy of a given message, gossiping forwards or rebroadcasts the message, with a probability *p*, to all nodes in the receiver's communication range. In order to reduce broadcast storms, we follow a couple of strategies. First, nodes delay each intra-partition-forward for a random time between 0 and *fDelay*, which reduces the number of collisions. Second, we adapt the gossiping probability *p* to the node's current number of neighbors, which reduces forward redundancy, contention, and collisions. For this purpose nodes acquire the number of their neighbors by means of periodic HELLO beaconing.

4.3 Broadcast Repetition

The common strategy to overcome partitioning is the repetition of broadcasting. For this purpose nodes need two mechanisms; one to detect *when* to rebroadcast and a second to decide *what* to rebroadcast. In the following we introduce our novel partition detection heuristic and rebroadcasting protocol.

We let nodes share with their neighbors the IDs of recently received or locally originated packets. We arbitrarily term this list by "Last Broadcast Received" or short *LBR* (Fig. 2). The rational behind this is that two neighboring nodes that belong to the same partition should have received the same broadcasts that had taken place in this partition. By this means nodes are able to conclude whether they are populating the same partition. If a node receives an LBR that "sufficiently" differs from its own LBR, the node can conclude with a certain confidence that it is joining a new partition. We denote the maximum allowed size of an LBR by *maxLBRlength.* Nodes trigger rebroadcasting only if the overlap between received LBR and own LBR does not exceed a given percentage of the own LBR. We denote this percentage threshold by "intersection threshold" (*IS_threshold*). In order to provide an accurate detection of partition joining, maxLBRlength and IS_threshold have to be dimensioned appropriately. In Sec. 5.4 we show how we calibrate maxLBRlength and IS_threshold.

This strategy is suitable to detect both causes of broadcast interruption: Network partitioning and broadcast storms. First, if two partitions say P1 and P2 join, some nodes of partition P1 will receive LBRs from other nodes belonging to the formerly partition P2. In this way nodes are able to detect the join event. Second, if a broadcast stops to progress within a partition due to collision or contention, nodes that received the broadcast may detect this on receiving the LBR of one neighbor that has not yet received the packet.

In order to save bandwidth, nodes exploit the existing HELLO beaconing to share their LBRs. Exchanging the LBRs is only necessary if a new neighbor is detected. Thus we do not include the LBR in each HELLO beacon but only in that beacon that just follows the discovering of a new neighbor. This delays the broadcast repetition until the next discovery of a new neighbor, in case of broadcast interruptions caused by broadcast storms.

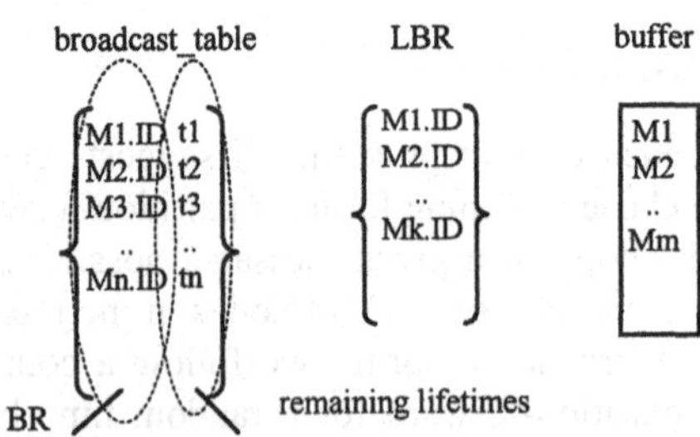

Fig. 2: Definition of BR, LBR and buffer

To allow rebroadcasting nodes should buffer messages that should be rebroadcasted. If not otherwise stated, we assume that nodes buffer all received and originated messages during their lifetimes, i.e. *m*=*n* (Fig. 2). A node triggers rebroadcasting by MAC-broadcasting its *BR list* (Fig. 2). Thus neighbors know which packets the sender has already received and can select from buffer the packets that missed this sender. On receiving these new packets the sender gossips them so they can reach all joining nodes. To increase efficiency nodes schedule the rebroadcasting at a random time between 0 and *rDelay* upon the reception of BR lists. Nodes cancel rebroadcasting if a neighbor starts to rebroadcast before the scheduled time. To reduce the probability of collisions nodes do not rebroadcast all packets at once but wait a random time between 0 and fDelay before rebroadcasting next packet (Fig. 3).

```
Var IS_threshold, maxLBRlength;
Var lifetime, fDelay, rDelay;
List myLBR; myBR; broadcast_table;

On receiving a DATA message (msg) M:
// do gossiping(p):
if(M is received for the first time) {
  deliver M;
  insert a copy of M to buffer;
  insert {M.ID} to myLBR;
  insert {M.ID, lifetime} to broadcast_table;
  if (random(1.0) <= p) {
    wait (random(fDelay));
     send M to all neighbors;
  }
} else {discard M}

On discovering new neighbor:
 insert myLBR to next HELLO beacon;
On expiration of lifetime of M:
if (M in buffer) {delete M from buffer};
if (M.ID in myLBR){delete M.ID from myLBR};
delete entry of M from broadcast_table;

On receiving HELLO with LBR:
// do partition detection:
is=card(myLBR∩recvLBR)/card(myLBR);
if(is <= IS_threshold){
  send BR to neighbors;
}

On receiving HELLO with BR:
// do broadcasting repetition:
Set timeout = random(rDelay);
On receiving msg with ID in (myBR -
recvBR): exit();
On timeout:
Foreach buffered msg M with ID in
(myBR - recvBR){
  wait (random(fDelay));
  rebroadcast M;
}
```

Fig. 3: Pseudo-code for hypergossiping

5 Performance Evaluation

In this section, we introduce the simulation model and define our evaluation metrics. We then study the performance of hypergossiping and compare it to related work.

5.1 Simulation Model

For evaluation we use the network simulator ns-2 [12]. We use as physical layer the TwoRayGround propagation model and as MAC layer the IEEE 802.11 standard. We generate *N* mobile nodes in a 1000mx1000m field, where these nodes move according to the random waypoint mobility model. We use the following communication load model: at the beginning of the simulation *S* nodes initiate broadcasting at a random time between 1 and 3 seconds, and continue to send packets with a constant packet rate. We use a fixed lifetime value during a simulation, i.e. all senders use the same lifetime for all packets they generate. For the same simulation scenario we ran

10 passes with 10 different movement traces and considered the average. Table 1 summarizes the simulation parameters of our experiments, which show a wide range of node density and mobility. Packet rate values cover most of the MANET application scenarios known from the MANET literature.

Table 1. Simulation parameters.

Parameter	Value (s)
Simulation area	1000m x 1000m
Number of nodes	N in {50,100,200,300, 500,800}
Com. range	R = 100m
Com. rate	r = 1 Mbit/s
Data packet size	280 bytes
Movement pattern	Random waypoint
- Max speed	- v in {3, 12.5, 20, 30} m/s
- Pause	- Uniform betw. 0 and 2s
fDelay	10ms
rDelay	100ms
Lifetime	[5 .. 1800] s
Packet rate	[0.001 .. 1] packets/s
HELLO beaconing	Random betw. 0.75s and 1.25s

5.2 Evaluation Metrics

For the evaluation of broadcast protocols the following metrics are typically used:
- *REachability (RE)*: the ratio of mobile hosts receiving the packet to the total number of mobile hosts. This metric measures the delivery reliability of the broadcast algorithm.
- *Delay*: Average end-to-end delay over all receivers.
- *MNF(R)*: Mean Number of Forwards (and Rebroadcasts) per node and packet. MNF(R) is an efficiency metric of the broadcast algorithm.

In Table 2 we illustrate the above metrics for hypergossiping. We denote by t_s the origination time of the packet and by t_i the arrival time of the packet at node *i*. With respect to a given broadcast packet we define the following four sets of nodes:
- *Forwd*: Nodes that forward the packet.
- *Reb*: Nodes that rebroadcast the packet.
- *R(H)*: Nodes reached by means of rebroadcasting.
- *R(HG)*: Nodes reached by HG, i.e. by means of either forwarding or rebroadcasting.

Gain measures the mean number of additionally reached nodes per rebroadcast. It presents a suitable efficiency metric for broadcast repetition strategies.

Table 2. Evaluation metrics.

Metric	Symbol	Value
Reachability	RE	= card{R(HG)} / N
Mean Number of Forwards	MNF	= card{Forwd} / N
Mean Number of Forwards & Rebroadcasts	MNFR	= (card{Reb} + card{Forwd}) / N
Average end-to-end delay over all receivers	delay	$= \frac{1}{card\{R(HG)\}} \sum_{i \in R(HG)} (t_i - t_s)$
Gain or mean number of additionally reached nodes per rebroadcast	gain	= card{R(H)} / card{Reb}

5.3 Adaptation of Gossiping

In this section, we adapt gossiping to local node density by determining the appropriate gossiping probability in function of number of neighbors.

In previous work [13], we have investigated the impact of density on data distribution in a MANET. Based on an epidemic model the optimal gossiping probability was calculated depending on the node density (Fig. 4).

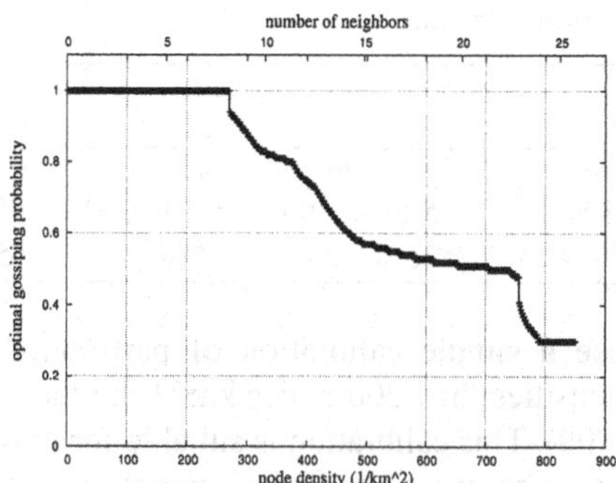

Fig. 4: Adaptation of gossiping

Consistent with our second requirement of generalized broadcasting strategy, we let every node set locally and independently the gossip probability. Given n the number of neighbors and R the communication range, a node computes easily its local density by:

$$d = \frac{n+1}{\pi \times R^2} \tag{1}$$

According to this value the node has to set on-the-fly the gossiping probability. To avoid the computation of local node density, which also assumes that nodes know their communication range, we recommend that nodes select the gossiping probability depending on the current number of neighbors n. We realize that by scaling the x-axis of Fig. 4 using formula (1).

5.4 Calibration of Partition Detection

In this paper, we evaluate our partition detection by measuring the efficiency of rebroadcasting. A suitable efficiency metric for rebroadcasting is the mean number of additionally reached nodes per rebroadcast, i.e. its gain. The higher its gain, the more efficient is rebroadcasting. To dimension the partition detection parameters, i.e. IS_threshold and maxLBRlength, we select the values with maximal gain.

For calibration we arbitrarily fix lifetime to 60s and maximum speed to 30m/s and we vary IS_threshold in {0%, 25%, 50%, 75%, 100%} and maxLBRlength in {1, 5, 10, 25, 50, 100}. For every combination we compute the gain and select the combination that maximizes the gain. LBR serves anyway for the identification of a certain partition until next join. An identification should consider the size of the partition (reflected by number of nodes) and the number of broadcasts originated per unit of time in that partition (reflected by the packet rate). That is why we repeated the calibration process for a wide range of number of nodes and packet rates. The combinations, for which the gain is maximal, are listed in Table 3. We observe that the denser is the network or the more congested it is, the smaller IS_threshold but the higher maxLBRlength should be selected. We repeated these steps for lifetime values of 600s and 1800s and concluded that these combinations are almost independent from the lifetime value.

Table 3. Calibration of partition detection.

N:	50	100	200	300	500
n:	0,57	2,14	5,28	8,42	14,7
1 packet/s	25%, 100	25%, 100	0%, ≥50	0%, 100	0%, 100
0.1 packets/s	50%, 100	25-50%, 100	25-50%, ≥25	≤50%, ≥25	0%, ≥50
0.001 packets/s	25-75%, ≥25	≤75%, ≥25	≤75%, ≥10	≤50%, ≥25	0%, ≥25

In this work, we use a simple calibration of partition detection. We use for MANETs with higher densities than 200 nodes/km^2 the tuple (0%, 100), otherwise we use the tuple (25%, 100). This calibration is suitable for most of simulated scenarios in Table 3. Consistent with our second requirement, we let every node select locally and independently the IS_threshold value: At run-time a node sets IS_threshold to 25% if its current number of neighbors is lower than 6 and 0% otherwise.

5.5 Performance of Hypergossiping

After adaptation and calibration we now investigate the performance of HG for a wide range of node density and mobility levels. We select for all scenarios S=25 senders. If v=0m/s, nodes being static do not discover new neighbors and therefore do not trigger broadcast repetition. That is why HG goes into simple gossiping.

Node mobility contributes to overcome network partitioning. It then follows that the higher is the mobility, the higher is the reachability and the lower is the delay. Fig. 5a) shows that the impact of node mobility on reachability is more significant for lower lifetimes. For very short lifetimes HG reachability is similar to that of simple gossiping. Fig. 5a) illustrates that reachability saturates at around 80%. We explain this as follows: at a sendrate of 0.0005 packets/s every sender originates only 1 packet within lifetimes up to 2000s. So for lifetimes considered in Fig. 5a) only 25 messages are relevant in the MANET. LBRs can store all IDs of these messages. The rebroadcasting condition (IS_threshold<=25%) becomes over time stronger and some partitions could not be detected.

We now set arbitrarily the lifetime to 600s and the sendrate to 0.001 packets/s. Fig. 5b) shows that rebroadcasting can strongly increase reachability in sparse MANETs; For 50 nodes and 3m/s reachability increases from 8% to 68%. Hypergossiping also increases reachability if gossiping reachability drops because of collisions; reachability increases from 63% to 92% for 500 nodes and 3m/s. Hypergossiping keeps the MNFR very low while increasing RE; Nodes namely forward or rebroadcast a given message in average maximal 1.1 times (Fig. 5c)). The bend in reachability and MNFR at 200 nodes is due to the simplicity of our partition detection calibration, where IS_threshold jumps from 25% to 0% by node densities around 200 nodes/km^2 (see Sec. 5.4). In ongoing work, we are looking for smoothing the selection of IS_threshold. Further simulation results, which we could not include due to space constraints, show that for other packet rates hypergossiping provides a comparable performance.

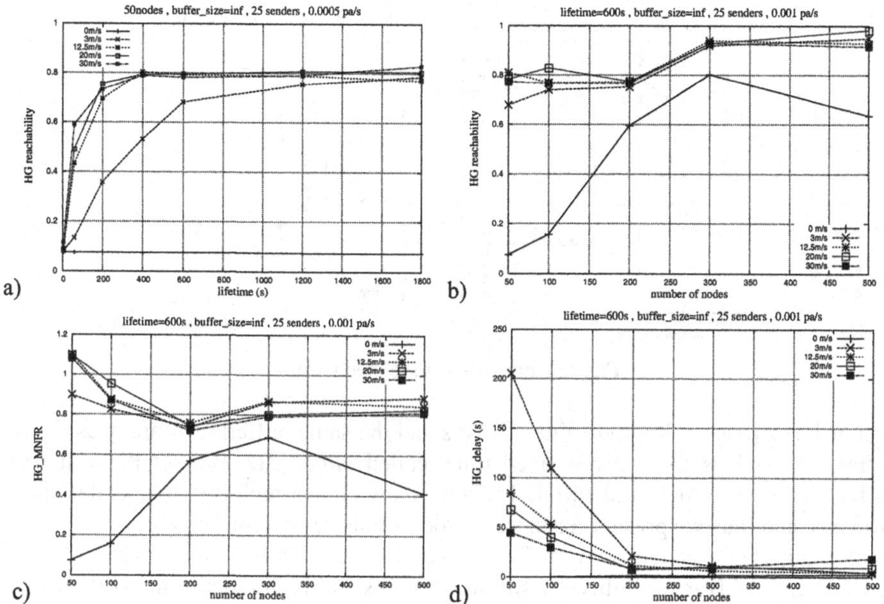

Fig. 5: Impact of lifetime, and node density and mobility.

5.6 Comparison to Related Work

Now we compare hypergossiping to the density-aware probabilistic flooding (PROB-FLOOD) [10], to the adaptive counter-based scheme (ACB) [9] and to the integrated flooding (IF) [5]. For this study we consider 25 senders that send at 0.001 packets/s.

For ACB we use the dynamic threshold given in [9]. ACB uses a random time span to count redundant packet receptions and possibly forwards the message after this span. This time period is comparable to fDelay. We choose the same value for these parameters, i.e. 10 ms, which is also used in [7].

For IF we use the following parameters (most of them are stated in [5]). In scoped flooding a node forwards a new received message, if at minimum 15% of its neighbors are not covered by the sender. We note here that scoped flooding needs 2-hop topology information, which means that nodes have to include their neighbor list in HELLO beacons. Hyperflooding holds packets for fixed time period and rebroadcasts them on discovering a new neighbor. Nodes install scoped flooding if their relative speed to all their neighbors is lower than 10 m/s. If the relative speed is higher than 25 m/s hyperflooding is selected. Otherwise plain flooding is deployed (message is forwarded exactly once by each node). We note that for max speed values until 12.5 m/s, nodes will never reach the higher switching threshold of IF (i.e. 25 m/s) and thus m/s) and thus hyperflooding will never be installed in such configuration. For higher values of max speed hyperflooding will possibly be installed by some nodes, which should increase the reachability of IF. For max speed equals 3 m/s the max relative node speed is 6 m/s, that is why only scoped flooding is installed by IF.

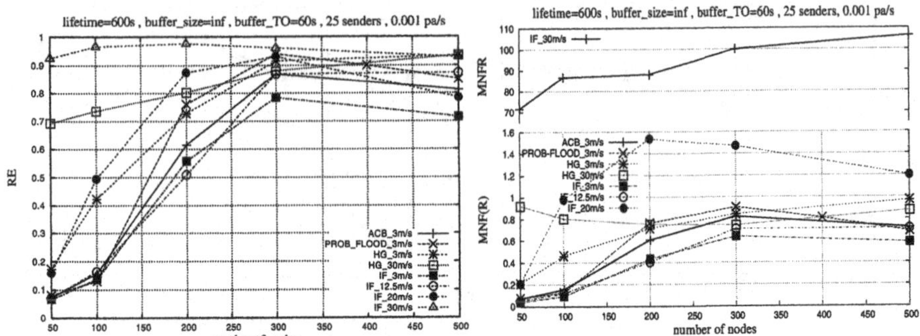

Fig. 6: Comparison to related work

For HG we use a lifetime value of 600 s and the same buffering strategy as IF. IF buffers all packets for a given fixed time, called *buffer_TO*. We set the value of buffer_TO to 60s. ACB and PROB-FLOOD show almost mobility-independent performance and thus we present for these protocols only results for 3m/s.

We can easily conclude from Fig. 6 that HG reachability outperforms PROB-FLOOD and ACB reachability for sparse networks and highly dense networks while keeping MNFR below 1. This is due to that HG remedies both causes of broadcast interruption: Network partitioning and broadcast storms.

Comparing HG and IF we conclude that IF does not provide an efficient partition detection strategy: IF provides namely a very high reachability for highly mobile MANETs, but MNFR ranges from 72 to 106 rebroadcasts per packet and node! (Simulation results show that even for very low buffer_TO values, MNFR is very high for highly mobile scenarios: for buffer_TO=5s and N=100 nodes, MNFR=11). For lower mobility IF installs only scoped flooding and subsequently performs similar to ACB and PROB-FLOOD for sparse networks but worse than these schemes for dense networks, lack of adaptation of scoped flooding to node density.

6 Conclusion and Future Work

In this paper, we introduced hypergossiping, an adaptive MANET broadcast algorithm, which presents our first steps towards a single broadcast solution for a wide range MANET operation conditions. Hypergossiping covers larger MANET densities and mobility levels. We have presented a novel method to adapt gossiping probability to node density and reduce the broadcast storms. Moreover, we presented a novel heuristic for repetition of broadcasts in order to overcome different causes of broadcast interruptions, such as network partitioning.

We are working on more sophisticated adaptation techniques of partition detection parameters. In future work, we will investigate different buffer management strategies to reduce buffer overhead. We expect that these strategies have to take into consideration the residual lifetime of buffered packets and that adapting the buffer capacity to node mobility contributes to reduce the buffering overhead of hypergossiping.

References

1. Z. Cheng, and W.B. Heinzelman, "Flooding Strategy for Target Discovery in Wireless Networks", Proceedings of MSWiM, 2003.
2. S.Y. Ni, Y.C. Tseng, Y.S. Chen, and J.P. Sheu, "The Broadcast Storm Problem in a Mobile Ad Hoc Network", Int. Conf. on Mobile Computing and Networking (MobiCom), 1999.
3. Z.J. Haas, J.Y. Halpern, and L. Li, "Gossip-Based Ad Hoc Routing", INFOCOM, 2002.
4. K. Obraczka, G. Tsudik, and K. Viswanath, "Pushing the Limits of Multicast in Ad Hoc Networks", Int. Conf. on Distributed Computing Systems (ICDCS), 2001.
5. K. Viswanath, and K. Obraczka, "An Adaptive Approach to Group Communications in Multi-Hop Ad Hoc Networks", Int. Conf. on Networking (ICN), 2002.
6. A. Ouksel, O. Wolfson, B. Xu, "Opportunistic Resource Exchange in Inter-vehicle Ad Hoc Networks", IEEE Int. Conf. on Mobile Data Management (MDM), 2004.
7. B. Williams and T. Camp, "Comparison of Broadcasting Techniques for Mobile Ad Hoc Net-works", ACM MOBIHOC, 2002.
8. Y. Yi, M. Gerla, and T.J. Kwon, "Efficient Flooding in Ad hoc Networks: a Comparative Performance Study", IEEE Int. Conf. on Communications (ICC), 2003.
9. Y.C. Tseng, S.Y. Ni, and E.Y. Shih, "Adaptive Approaches to Relieving Broadcast Storms in a Wireless Multihop Mobile Ad Hoc Networks", IEEE Transactions on Computers, V52(5): 545–557, 2003.
10. J. Cartigny, and D. Simplot, "Border Node Retransmission Based Probabilistic Broadcast Protocols in Ad-Hoc Networks", Hawaii Int. Conf. on System Sciences (HICSS), 2003.
11. C. Ho, K. Obraczka, G. Tsudik and K. Viswanath, "Flooding for Reliable Multicast in Multi-Hop Ad Hoc Networks", Proceedings of DIALM, 1999.
12. S. McCanne, and S. Floyd, Ns Network Simulator, http://www.isi.edu/nsnam/ns/.
13. A. Khelil, C. Becker, J. Tian, and K. Rothermel, "Epidemic Model for Information Diffusion in MANETs", Proceedings of MSWiM, 2002.

Improving the Usable Capacity of Ad Hoc Networks

Christian Maihöfer, Tim Leinmüller and Reinhold Eberhardt

DaimlerChrysler AG, Research Vehicle IT and Services,
P.O. Box 2360, 89013 Ulm, Germany
{Christian.Maihoefer|Tim.Leinmueller|Reinhold.Eberhardt}
@DaimlerChrysler.com

Abstract Recent research has shown that multi-hop ad hoc networks suffer from a low capacity and moreover that an individual node's capacity for long-distance communication decreases the more nodes are participating in the ad hoc network. The usable capacity of ad hoc networks is further decreased by the forwarding metric of usual routing protocols, which try to minimize the number of hops or try to minimize the remaining distance to the receiver. This results in traffic concentration at one or several areas in the network, what we will refer to as network center(s), and thus in a decreased usable capacity. Especially in the automotive domain, where road infrastructure and road traffic flow frequently create network centers, solving this issue is of particular interest.
In this paper we will show that the network center is indeed a bottleneck for communication which limits a network's capacity. Then we will present a new forwarding approach, which relieves the network center from handling an excessive part of the traffic. Instead of just trying to minimize the distance to the receiver, this approach additionally tries to avoid routing through the network center. Simulation results show, that the usable capacity of the ad hoc network is increased with this approach by approximately 30%.

1 Introduction

Ad hoc networks are wireless networks of nodes which may be mobile and may work without infrastructure. Such networks provide a convenient, a cheap, and for some scenarios a robust way for communication. That is why ad hoc networks like Bluetooth or IEEE 802.11, which provide both an access point mode and an ad hoc mode, receive more and more attention.

Recently, ad hoc networks are even considered for long distance communication, with senders and receivers outside each others direct wireless communication range. These ad hoc networks are called multi-hop ad hoc networks. This means, some or all nodes of the ad hoc network provide routing functionality (see [1] for an overview of ad hoc routing protocols).

Due to the growing space of large ad hoc networks, which allows spatial reuse of the wireless medium, the total capacity of the network grows. Unfortunately, this is not true for long-distance communication in multi-hop ad hoc networks, as they require cooperation of many nodes. Essentially the broadcast nature of the wireless transmission affects many nodes. All neighboring nodes, i.e. nodes in direct wireless communication range to the initial sender or forwarding node receive the transmission and must not simultaneously transmit themselves. This is a serious problem for multi-hop ad hoc networks, since it limits an individual node's capacity for long-distance communication to a value that decreases the more nodes are joining the ad hoc network.

Although the limited capacity is a serious problem, there are several ways to relax this problem somewhat, i.e. to increase the usable capacity. First of all, if traffic patterns show a high degree of locality between sender and receiver, i.e. if only a small degree of traffic has to be routed over several hops, the usable capacity can be significantly higher and sufficient for many purposes. Another option would be to use the ad hoc network only as an access network and use a wired backbone network to transmit long-distance traffic. However, in this paper we do not want to make such assumptions. Instead we try to increase the usable capacity for long-distance communication inside ad hoc networks by eliminating a serious bottleneck, the area of traffic concentration, i.e. the network center.

In the automotive domain, e.g. in communication scenarios as they have been investigated in the FleetNet project [2], network centers are determined by road networks and road traffic flow. Consequently, network centers are located in areas with high road density and high road traffic flows, e.g. road traffic concentration points in urban areas, whereas the network border lies in direction to areas with lower road traffic flow, for instance rural areas. Therefore we assume network centers can be determined by all nodes by using cartographic data from the navigation system and radio broadcasts on traffic conditions.

The network center is a serious bottleneck particularly for the limited capacity of ad hoc networks in two ways. First of all, most long-distance traffic crosses the network center, since routing protocols often try to minimize the number of hops or try to minimize the remaining distance to the receiver. This leads to an increased traffic concentration at the center of the network which becomes a bottleneck. Second, for long-distance traffic, the usable capacity of the network is limited by the capacity of the center. If the center has a lower capacity than the remaining network, all long-distance traffic suffer from the low center capacity. Note that such a situation is not just a theoretical problem, rather it is quite likely that the capacity of the center is lower than the capacity of other parts of the network. For example, if the node density in the center is above the average node density of the network, instead of increasing the capacity of the center this reduces its capacity.

In this paper we address the problem of the ad hoc network center as a bottleneck which decreases usable capacity. After discussing some related work in the following section, we will start with presenting simulations to validate that such a problem indeed exists in Section 3. Then in Section 4 we present a new routing metric, which relives the center from forwarding most long-distance traffic. Simulation results show, that the usable capacity of the ad hoc network is increased with this approach. Finally, we will conclude with a brief summary.

2 Related Work

Protocols for routing in ad hoc networks can be classified into topology-based and position-based or geographic approaches [3]. Topology-based schemes use only information about existing neighborhood links rather than additional physical (geographical) position information of the participating nodes. Topology-based approaches can be further divided into table-driven and source-initiated on-demand driven protocols [1]. Basically, table driven protocols attempt to maintain consistent and up-to-date routing information among all nodes, while source-initiated on-demand driven protocols create routes only when necessary to deliver a packet. Therefore, the former approach is also known as a proactive routing approach and the latter as a reactive approach.

For geographical routing protocols, three basic forwarding strategies can be identified: 1) greedy forwarding, 2) restricted directional flooding, and 3) hierarchical forwarding. With greedy forwarding a node forwards a packet to a neighbor that is located closer to the destination. If this forwarding strategy fails, since there may be situations in which there is no closer node to the destination than the forwarding node, recovery strategies have to deal with it. Restricted directional flooding is similar to the greedy approach with the modification that a packet is forwarded to some neighbors rather than to just one neighbor. Finally, hierarchical forwarding tries to improve scalability by forming a hierarchy of non-equal nodes. In our simulations in the following sections we will use a greedy routing algorithm.

The capacity of ad hoc networks was analyzed by [4], [5], and [6]. The work in [4] has first analyzed the capacity of ad hoc networks and has shown that the capacity per node in an ad hoc network is $\Theta(1/nlog(n))$, where n is the total number of nodes. This is a quite pessimistic result, since it indicates that large ad hoc networks are not feasible. However, the authors also pointed out that under certain conditions communication with nearby neighbors will be able with constant bit rate independent of the network size.

In [5] the analytical work is extended to reflect the influence of different traffic patterns on scalability of the per node capacity. The authors also determined the influence of forwarding algorithms and 802.11 MAC interaction which resulted in an estimation of missing constants from the previous work of [4].

In [6] the analysis is extended to consider the mobility of nodes. They have shown that long term per node capacity can stay constant. Their presented algorithm makes use of the known result that local communication with constant bit rate is possible. The basic approach is to distribute a packet to many different nodes, which store the packets. Now the nodes' movements will finally bring one of the relaying nodes close to the intended destination of the packet. The packet is then forwarded from the relaying node to the destination node. Therefore, only a constant number of hops is required independent of the network size, thus the

```
Forwarding decision for destination d
(1)  for all neighbors n do
(2)       dist[n] := distance from neighbor n
               to destination d
(3)  od
(4)  select neighbor n with dist[n] ≤ ∀ i : dist[i]
```

Fig. 1. Basic forwarding algorithm

per node capacity stays constant. However, their assumptions will rather not apply to most ad hoc networks and furthermore, packet delivery delays may become infinite.

3 The Network Center Bottleneck

From the results of related work we know that the capacity of ad hoc networks is a critical resource and that we should try to use it very economically. For multi-hop long-distance traffic a particular bottleneck that prevents to use the full theoretical capacity is the center of the network, through which most traffic is routed and which therefore limits the usable capacity. Our first goal is to prove this assumption.

3.1 A Simple Counting Model

In Figure 1 a basic forwarding scheme is shown which is used in the following as the reference approach. This scheme is similar to a greedy forwarding algorithm in position aware networks. For non-position aware forwarding protocols, the used distance metric in the figure is replaced by another metric, e.g. the hop distance to the destination. Although we will assume a position-aware greedy algorithm in this paper, the observations and results will apply for many other protocols, too.

When we apply this basic forwarding scheme to a simple network model with random traffic we can count the number of received packets per node in order to detect a hot spot. This is shown in Figure 2.b with a regular flat network consisting of 10 nodes for each dimension, resulting in 100 nodes in total. It is assumed, that a packet transmission can be received by exactly 8 neighbors, for nodes on the network border accordingly less neighbors (see Figure 2.a). The traffic consists of 2.000 message transmissions between randomly chosen nodes.

The results in Figure 2.b show that there is a traffic concentration at the center of the network, which limits the overall usable capacity of the network and degrades throughput. If we change the system model, e.g. if we assume that a node has only 4 neighbors instead of 8, or if we count the number of forwarded packets per node instead of the number of received packets, the absolute values change but the qualitative results do not.

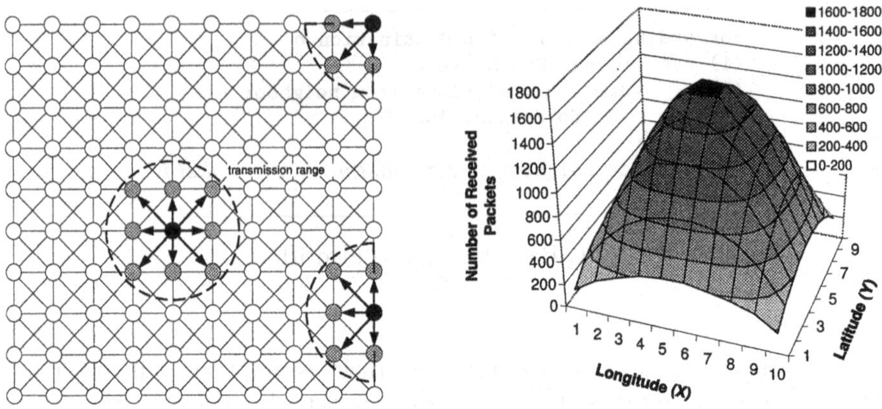

Fig. 2. a) Network model and b) load per node with random traffic

3.2 Simulations of the Network Center Bottleneck

Besides this rather simple approach of analyzing the network load, we have also made extensive simulation studies, which allow deeper insight. With the network simulator NS-2 [7] and the CMU wireless extensions, we were able to run simulations in a quite realistic wireless network scenario. The simulated IEEE 802.11 network was configured to have a 250 m transmission range. It uses the RTS/CTS scheme preceding every data packet exchange and ACKs to confirm successful packet reception. The network was static, i.e. no node movement was considered. We have used a position-based greedy routing algorithm, which was derived from GPSR [8] but lacks the perimeter mode, i.e. no backtracking mechanism is in place if a packet transmission reaches a dead end. In such a case the packet cannot be delivered and is dropped. As we assumed that the position of nodes are known to all other nodes no location service was necessary.

Figure 3.a shows the received link layer packets per node for a similar scenario like Figure 2.b. A regular network of 10x10 nodes and latitudinal and longitudinal distance of 100m between nodes was simulated. The traffic consisted of 2000 message transmissions between random senders and receivers. The figure shows the contour lines from a top to bottom view of the three dimensional graph, which allows better readability. As it can be seen, the qualitative result is identical to the simple counting model, there is a traffic concentration at the center. The quantitative figures are somewhat higher, the center node has to process 2412 packets in the simulation compared to 1673 packets from the numerical approach. This is caused by the higher wireless transmission range, which is 250 m in the simulation, which means that 12 neighbors are within reach of a wireless transmission, while in the numerical approach 8 neighbors are within reach. A decreased transmission range of 150 m in the simulation leads to 8 neighbors within transmission range and a maximum of 1617 received packets for the center, which is quite close to the numerical results.

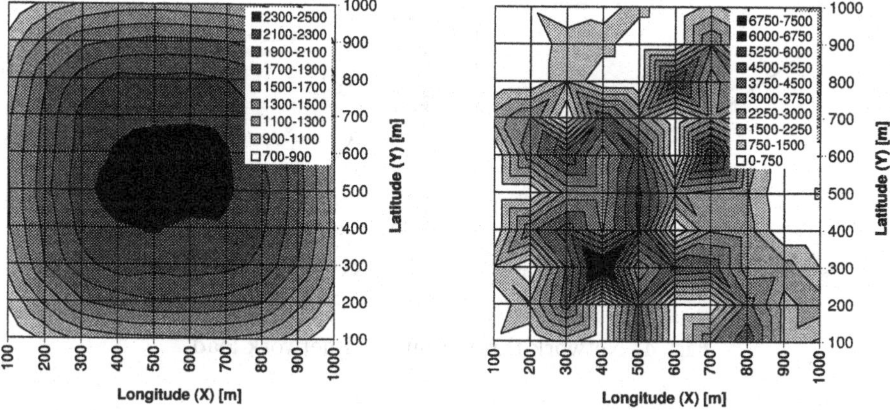

Fig. 3. Network load per node a) regular network and b) network with randomly placed nodes

Figure 3.b shows the results for a non-regular network, consisting of 100 randomly placed nodes in a 1000x1000m^2 area. Although it is more difficult to see a center hot spot, since there are gaps in the network where no node is located, the traffic concentration at the edges is obviously less than the traffic concentration in and around the center.

3.3 Simulations of the Center Density Impact

Now we will prove our second claim from Section 1 that the center, besides being a traffic bottleneck, is moreover likely to have a lower capacity than other parts of the network. A higher node density decreases the capacity of an ad hoc network, since more neighbors are involved in each forwarding step, which is likely for the center of a network.

Figure 4 shows the simulation results for different densities of the center region compared to the average density of a 10x10 network in a grid of 1000x1000m^2 with 250m wireless transmission range. A density below 100% means that the density of the center is lower than the density of other parts of the network, accordingly a density above 100% means that the center density is above average. All 2000 message transmissions were initiated at simulation start (simulation time 0s). Figure 4.a depicts the number of transport layer messages received at the destination at simulation time 1s. For example, with density 100%, from the 2000 transmissions only 77 messages have arrived at the destination, which means that the network is highly congested. In such a congested scenario, the network is at its capacity limit. As a consequence, the measured number of arrived messages corresponds with the usable network capacity. If the center density is increased, the usable network capacity decreases. It increases, if the center density is below the average node density.

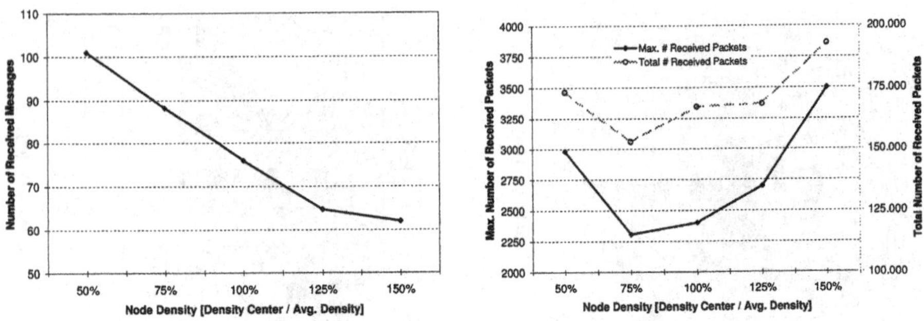

Fig. 4. Network throughput and network load

Figure 4.b shows the the maximum number of received packets at link layer and the aggregated total number of received packets. Both show the expected result that if the node density of the center is above average the number of received packets increase. But they also show that if the node density of the center is below average, the number of received packets increase also. In this case the edges of the network have a node density above normal and hence they cause an increased number of packets. However, as the edges of the network have to forward only a traffic share below average, the network capacity does not decrease, instead it even increases since the center is relieved.

From these results we can conclude that the usable capacity of an ad hoc network is limited by the capacity of the network center. In the following section we will present how the usable network capacity can be increased by a modified forwarding scheme that relieves the center from forwarding load.

4 Increasing the Usable Capacity of Ad Hoc Networks

As the network center limits the usable capacity of an ad hoc network, our goal is to relieve the center from forwarding too many long-distance transmissions.

4.1 A Center-Relieving Forwarding Scheme

The basic forwarding scheme, which was shown in Figure 1, considers only one metric to optimize the forwarding process, the distance to the destination. We modify this forwarding scheme by a second metric, the distance to the center of the network. While we try to minimize with each forwarding step the distance to the destination, we also try to maximize the distance to the network center, which accomplishes that the center is bothered with less traffic. Note that there is surly a trade-off between both metrics.

In Figure 5 we show in detail our modified forwarding scheme. In line (7) it is ensured that each forwarding step makes progress towards the destination. However, if there are several neighbors which are closer to the destination, the

```
Forwarding decision for destination d
(1)  for all neighbors n do
(2)       distdest[n] := distance from neighbor n
              to destination d
(3)       distcent[n] := distance from neighbor n
              to the network center
(4)       forwardmetric[n] := distdest[n]
              - WeightFactor * distcenter[n]
(5)  od
(6)  currdist := current distance to destination d
(7)  select neighbor n with distdest[n] < currdist and
          forwardmetric[n] ≤ ∀ i : forwardmetric[i]
```

Fig. 5. Forwarding algorithm that relives the network center

decision which neighbor is selected depends on both, the progress towards the destination and the distance to the network center. The configuration parameter *WeightFactor* allows to adjust to which extent the network center is to be relieved. If the parameter is set equal to 0, then the distance to the center is not considered and the result of the forwarding scheme is equal to the result of the basic forwarding scheme from Figure 1. On the other hand, if the parameter is set to a value larger than 1, then it is more important to get away from the center than coming closer to the destination. This is not a reasonable forwarding decision, since now too much load is shifted from the center to the borders of the network, which makes the borders a possible bottleneck.

An example for the center-relieving forwarding mechanism is given in Figure 6.a. While the regular forwarding mechanism routes a packet through the network center, the center-relieving mechanism avoids the network center. Figure 6.b shows the contour lines of a NS-2 simulation with the scenario introduced in Section 3.2, i.e. a regular 10 x 10 network with 2000 message transmissions. The *WeightFactor* was set equal to 0.7. Besides resulting in a lower maximum number of received packets compared with Figure 3.a, it also shows that the algorithm is effective in relieving the network center.

4.2 Evaluation of the Usable Capacity Gain

Coming back to our initial goal, improving the usable capacity of an ad hoc network, we evaluate with simulations if and to what extent the center-relieving forwarding can extend the usable network capacity.

We used again the NS-2 simulation environment for IEEE 802.11 wireless LANs introduced in the previous sections. Figure 7 shows the results for a simulation run of 25s and a 2000x2000m^2 network consisting of 500 nodes. Between simulation time 1 and 20s, 5000 message transmissions were initiated between randomly selected senders and receivers. Figure 7.a shows the absolute number

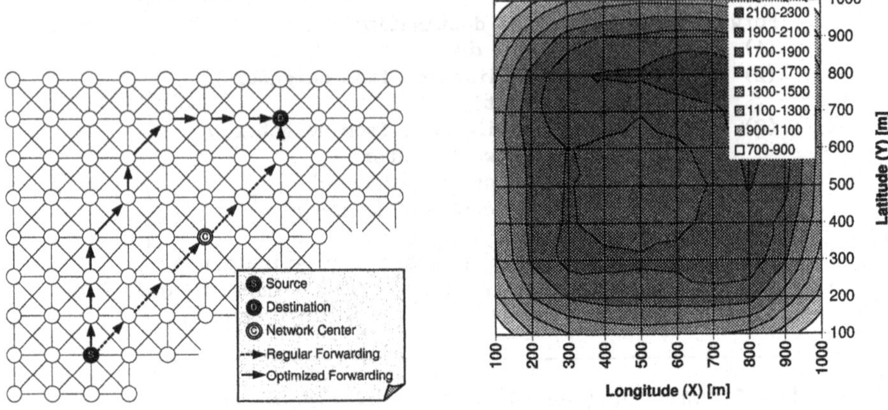

Fig. 6. a) Example for greedy and center-relieving forwarding and b) Effect of center-relieving forwarding on the network load distribution

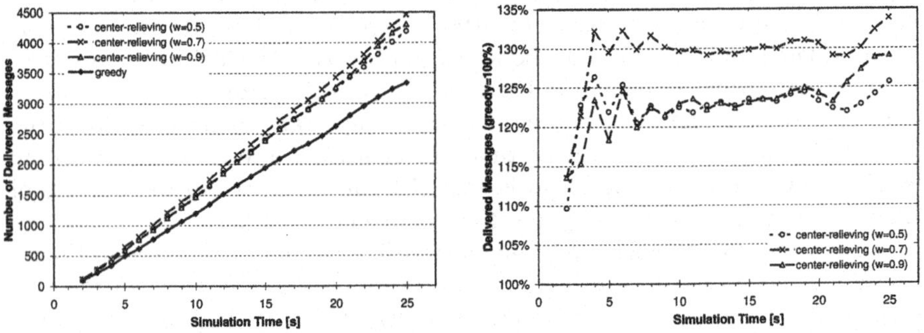

Fig. 7. Capacity comparison of greedy routing and center-relieving routing with respect to simulation time

of delivered messages with respect to the simulation time. The solid line depicts the results for greedy routing. With greedy routing, only 3334 messages out of 5000 can be delivered during the 25s simulation time, because the network center is overwhelmed with packet forwarding.

The center-relieving algorithm can achieve an increased number of delivered messages. The results for center-relieving routing depend on the $WeightFactor$, which was set to 0.5, 0.7, and 0.9, respectively. We can see that if the $WeightFactor$ equals 0.7, with 4463 delivered messages out of 5000 the best results are achieved in this scenario.

In Figure 7.b the relative improvement in delivered messages compared to greedy routing is depicted, which allows a better comparison. After an initial

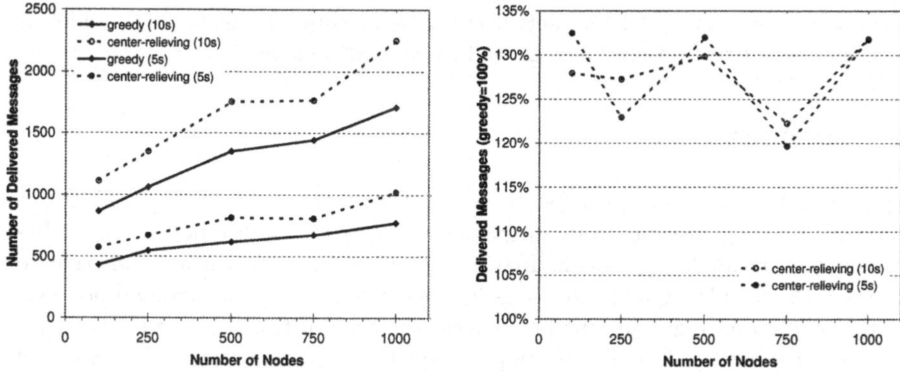

Fig. 8. Capacity comparison of greedy routing and center-relieving routing with respect to network size

increase at simulation start, center-relieving routing is able to achieve a 30% higher delivery rate than greedy routing, which stays roughly constant during the simulation time. Note that this throughput improvement is paid with slightly longer paths from sender to receiver, i.e. increased number of hops and therefore an increased total number of received packets at all nodes in the network. We have measured this increased total number of received packets at all nodes to be approximately 10% in our simulations. Compared to the 30% throughput gain, a 10% increased overall load seems tolerable.

A further comparison of greedy routing with center-relieving routing is shown in Figure 8, with different network sizes of 100, 250, 500, 750 and 1000 nodes. The nodes are randomly placed in a grid of 1000x1000m^2, 1500x1500m^2, 2000x2000m^2, 2500x2500m^2 and 3000x3000m^2, respectively. Again, 5000 message transmissions are initiated between randomly chosen senders and receivers during the time interval of 1 and 20s. The total simulation time was 25s. Center-relieving routing was configured with a $WeightFactor$ of 0.7. The graphs show the results of the received messages in a 5s and a 10s interval after simulation start.

Figure 7.a shows the absolute results, while Figure 7.b shows the relative improvement compared to greedy routing. The increasing number of delivered messages results from the constant number of initiated message transmissions. With more nodes in the network, every one has to process less traffic. More interesting is the comparison between greedy routing and center-relieving routing. The simulation results show that the usable capacity respectively throughput gain of center-relieving routing is in the range of 20%-33%, with different network sizes. Although the observed results are not constant, which results from the random generation of traffic in the simulation, there is no indication that with smaller or larger networks the achieved gain in capacity changes fundamentally. In summary, we have shown that center-relieving routing can increase the usable capacity of ad hoc networks by approximately up to 30%, which is independent of the network size as well as simulation time.

5 Conclusion

Multi-hop ad hoc networks suffer from a low capacity and an individual node's capacity for long-distance communication decreases the more nodes are participating in the ad hoc network. In this paper we have shown an approach to increase the usable capacity for long-distance communication inside ad hoc networks by eliminating a serious bottleneck, the area of traffic concentration, i.e. the network center. Usually, routing protocols try to minimize the number of hops or try to minimize the remaining distance to the receiver, which results in a traffic concentration at the network center, limiting the overall network capacity.

We have presented a new forwarding approach for ad hoc networks, which relieves the center from handling most long-distance traffic. Instead of just trying to minimize the distance to the receiver, our approach additionally tries to avoid routing through the network center. Simulation results show, that the usable capacity of the ad hoc network is increased with this approach by approximately 30%.

In further work we will evaluate the influence of the $WeightFactor$, which determines to what extent the network center is to be relieved from forwarding traffic, in more detail. Also we will include node mobility in our scenarios. Furthermore, we plan to elaborate the results of our work in urban area automotive communication scenarios. On the other hand, we need to investigate mechanisms to determine the network center, without relying on cartographic information.

References

1. E. Royer and C. Toh, "A review of current routing protocols for ad-hoc mobile wireless networks," *IEEE Personal Communications*, vol. 6, no. 2, pp. 46–55, Apr. 1999.
2. W. Franz, R. Eberhardt, and T. Luckenbach, "Fleetnet - Internet on the road," *Eighth World Congress on Intelligent Transportation Systems*, Sydney, Australia, 2001.
3. Martin Mauve, Jörg Widmer, and Hannes Hartenstein, "A survey on position-based routing in mobile ad hoc networks," *IEEE Network*, vol. 15, no. 6, pp. 30–39, Dec. 2001.
4. P. Gupta and P. R. Kumar, "The capacity of wireless networks," *IEEE Transactions on Information Theory*, vol. 46, no. 2, pp. 388–404, Mar. 2000.
5. Jinyang Li, Charles Blake, Douglas S. J. DeCouto, Hu Imm Lee, and Robert Morris, "Capacity of ad hoc wireless networks," in *Proceedings of the ACM/IEEE International Conference on Mobile Computing and Networking (MobiCom)*. Oct. 2001?, ACM Press.
6. M. Grossglauser and D. Tse, "Mobility increases the capacity of ad-hoc wireless networks," *IEEE/ACM Transactions on Networking*, vol. 10, no. 4, Aug. 2002.

7. S. Bajaj, L. Breslau, D. Estrin, K. Fall, S. Floyd, M. Handley P. Haldar, A. Helmy, J. Heidemann, P. Huang, S. Kumar, S. McCanne, R. Rejaie, P. Sharma, K. Varadhan, Y. Xu, H. Yu, and D. Zappala, "Improving simulation for network research," Technical Report 99-702, University of Southern California, USA, 1999.
8. B. Karp and H.T. Kung, "Greedy perimeter stateless routing for wireless networks," in *Proceedings of the Sixth ACM/IEEE International Conference on Mobile Computing and Networking (MobiCom 2000)*, Boston, USA, Aug. 2000, pp. 243–254.

Location-Based Hierarchical Data Aggregation in Vehicular Ad Hoc Networks

Jing Tian, Pedro José Marrón and Kurt Rothermel

University of Stuttgart, Institute for Parallel and Distributed Systems, IPVS
`{tian, marron, rothermel}@informatik.uni-stuttgart.de`*

Abstract Existing road traffic information systems rely on fixed infrastructures to manage traffic data. The deployment and maintenance cost of such infrastructures, however, is very high. With on-board sensors and wireless short range communication, infrastructure-less traffic data management based on inter-vehicle communication will be viable in the near future, with data aggregation being a key issue for data management. In this paper, we review some of the existing data aggregation strategies in wireless ad hoc networks and discuss new data aggregation challenges. Finally, we present a novel location-based hierarchical data aggregation approach, which is scalable and robust with regard to high vehicle mobility.

1 Introduction

Existing road traffic information systems rely on large-scale fixed infrastructures to collect, analyze and disseminate traffic data [12,13]. Stationary sensors, such as induction loops and cameras are installed along the road to collect traffic data, which is sent to a traffic information center for analysis. The results of this traffic analysis, such as accident reports or traffic jam warnings, are delivered to drivers through data broadcast systems or cellular communication networks.

There is, however, a major disadvantage of such infrastructure-based systems, since the deployment and maintenance of large-scale infrastructures is very expensive. Moreover, the traffic information service is only available in the area where infrastructure exists. On the other side, with the widespread deployment of on-board sensors and advances of ad hoc communication, modern vehicles can exchange road traffic data on a peer-to-peer basis, without relying on any infrastructure. A hybrid solution that combines the advantages of infrastructures and the flexibility of peer-to-peer approaches may be more promising than strict infrastructure-based or infrastructure-less solutions. In this paper, we focus on the peer-to-peer approach of data management, and leave the interaction with infrastructure-based systems for future research.

Modern vehicles are equipped with diverse sensors, which continuously monitor the status of the vehicle (e.g., position and speed) as well as the local environment (e.g., obstacles and weather). These vehicles can be viewed as *mobile*

* Jing Tian is supported by the European project CarTALK 2000, contract number IST-2000-28185. http://www.cartalk2000.net

sensor nodes deployed on the road network, which also participate in the road traffic. The sensor data generated by these vehicles are also called Floating Car Data (FCD). Using these vehicles as sensors to collect road traffic data, we can save the high cost of roadside stationary sensors. In addition, through short range radio devices, vehicles can self-organize into a Vehicular Ad Hoc Network (VANET). Based on inter-vehicle communication, vehicles can exchange traffic data with each other on a peer-to-peer basis. Thus, the sensor data can be collected, processed and disseminated among vehicles, without relying on a communication infrastructure such as cellular networks. Some projects have recently investigated cooperating driving systems based on VANETs to improve driving safety and comfort, such as *CarTALK 2000* [11] and *Fleetnet* [3].

With vehicles capable of sensing traffic situations and exchanging sensor data with each other, we are able to build a self-organizing traffic information system, which does not rely on any stationary sensor or communication infrastructure. Fig. 1 illustrates a possible application scenario of such a self-organizing traffic information system based on VANETs. As shown in the figure, there are two possible routes between B and E on the road network. Imagine a vehicle near A wants to drive to F. In order to select the best travel route, it sends a query to both routes for the average vehicle speed in its driving direction. After receiving the query message, vehicles on both routes aggregate their speed data and compute an average value, which is then sent back to the querying vehicle. In this example, we assume a traffic jam on the shorter route (B-E). Based on the received query results, the driver may choose the longer alternative way (B-C-D-E) to avoid the traffic jam.

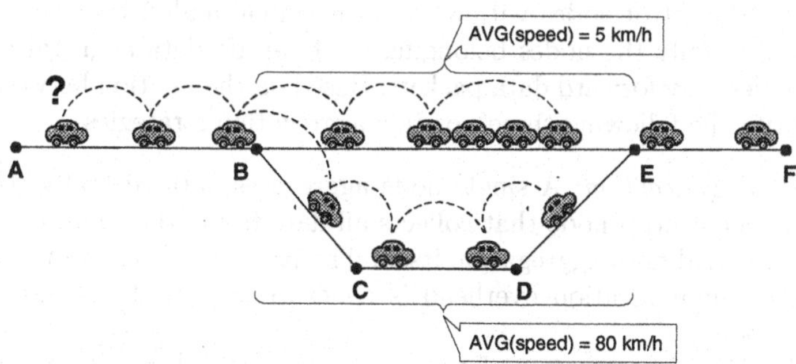

Fig. 1: An application scenario of self-organizing traffic information systems

As shown in the aforementioned example, sensor data from a number of vehicles has to be aggregated to provide a global view of the road traffic situation. Thus, data aggregation plays a central role for the self-organizing traffic information system. In contrast to traditional networks, however, data aggregation in VANETs encounters some new challenges, such as:

- *Large-scale network*: A VANET may contain a very large number of vehicles, with a geographic range of hundreds of kilometers. Thus, scalability is a crucial issue for data aggregation.
- *Dynamic topology*: The network topology changes rapidly due to vehicle mobility. Thus, data aggregation cannot rely on any static network topology as its base structure.
- *Frequent partition*: The network may be frequently partitioned due to the sparse vehicle density or the non-uniform distribution of vehicles. Therefore, aggregation and any other operations on data have to be performed on incomplete data.

Due to these challenges, most existing data aggregation approaches for wireless sensor networks are not suitable for VANETs. In this paper, we present a location-based hierarchical data aggregation approach that is scalable and robust with regard to vehicle mobility.

The remainder of the paper is organized as follows: Section 2 introduces the solution space of data aggregation. In Section 3 we briefly discuss some related work. Section 4 describes the models used by our approach. In Section 5, we present our aggregation mechanism. Some simulation results are presented in Section 6. Finally, Section 7 concludes the paper with a brief summary and a outlook on future work.

2 Data Aggregation Solution Space

In this paper, we focus on the problem of aggregating sensor data within a certain area called *target area*.

Let N be the set of nodes within the target area, and A be a subset of N. We specify that only the nodes belonging to A can do data aggregation, while the other nodes only forward data packets. Based on the relation between A and N, we identify the following three possible aggregation strategies:

1. *centralized aggregation*: A single node aggregates data centrally ($|A| = 1$). There is one central node that collects all data from other nodes within the target area and does aggregation itself. The problem of this strategy is that the data communication overhead is concentrated on the nodes near the central node.
2. *fully distributed aggregation*: Each node aggregates data locally ($A = N$). Each node sends its data to all other nodes within the target area and locally aggregates all the data it receives. Although this strategy is very robust, it does not scale well, since the data communication overhead grows exponentially with the size of N.
3. *group-based aggregation*: Multiple nodes aggregate data in different groups ($A \subset N$ *and* $|A| > 1$). Nodes in the target area are partitioned into a number of *aggregation groups*. Each aggregation group consists of two types of nodes: *group members* and *group leaders*. Only group leaders of each group are responsible for aggregating data from nodes in the group. The aggregation

results from different groups are then aggregated to get the final result. The advantage of this strategy is that data in different groups can be aggregated in parallel, and a hierarchical group structure can significantly reduce the data communication overhead.

Most related work approaches use group-based aggregation strategies, which are discussed in more detail in the next section.

3 Related Work

Many existing data aggregation approaches are based on a group-based strategy, such as [4–6, 8, 9, 16]. These group-based data aggregation approaches, however, can be further classified by the *grouping criteria* used to partition nodes into aggregation groups:

- *routing path*: The routing protocol described in [6, 8, 9] constructs a hierarchical routing tree (or chain) to forward data packets from the data source nodes to the data sink node. This routing tree is then used as the basic group structure for data aggregation.
- *data value*: [16] uses localized information exchange between one-hop neighbors to construct an aggregation tree with the incremental data value of a certain data type (e.g. remaining energy level). Data aggregation functions are then computed in groups based on this aggregation tree.
- *signal strength*: In [5], a number of randomly selected nodes declare themselves to be group leaders and send out advertisement messages throughout the network. Other nodes are then partitioned into different groups based on the signal strength of the received advertisement messages.
- *geographic position*: [4] divides the network space into a hierarchical grid, with the nodes grouped into different grids based on their position.

Most of these data aggregation approaches, however, are designed for wireless sensor networks, and are inadequate for highly dynamic environments. Group structures based on routing path [6,8,9], data value [16] or signal strength [5] rely on a stable network topology, which is not available in VANETs. Furthermore, [4] requires a priori global knowledge of network size and node distribution, which are also not realistic in the road traffic situation.

In addition to wireless sensor networks, some recent papers have also investigated data aggregation in VANETs, such as TrafficView [10] and SOTIS [15]. Nevertheless, the objective of data aggregation in TrafficView is to deliver as many vehicle records as possible in one broadcast message, while in SOTIS, data aggregation is used to monitor traffic situation in a closely surrounding area of each vehicle. The goal of our data aggregation strategy, however, is to support general aggregated queries for traffic situation in an arbitrary road area, as described by the example shown in Fig.1.

4 Models

Before we describe the aggregation approach in detail, we first introduce the system model, the location model and the data model that are used in our aggregation approach.

4.1 System Model

We assume a number of vehicles in the road traffic are equipped with short-range radio devices for inter-vehicle communication. These vehicles self-organize into VANETs as overlay networks on the road. Each vehicle has several on-board sensors monitoring the vehicle itself and the local environment. In addition, we assume that each vehicle in VANETs is equipped with a digital road map and a GPS receiver that allows it to obtain its geographic position and to maintain a global synchronized time.

The geographical ranges of queries are assumed to be based on certain road units, such as road segments or road sections. Moreover, we assume the aggregation functions of the queries to be *decomposable* [9,16], such as the aggregation functions MAX, MIN, AVG, SUM, and COUNT.

4.2 Location Model

In order to support aggregated queries based on road units, we use a location model of the road network [2]. Such a location model can be derived from existing digital road maps, which have the following attributes:

- *Hierarchical structure*: Road units can be classified into different levels, such as road level, section level, and segment level. A road consists of a number of sections, while each section includes a number of segments. In order to support data aggregation at each road level, the location model has to provide support to a road hierarchy.
- *Geometric modeling*: Each road unit can be specified by its geometric attributes, such as its location and shape. For example, a road segment can be specified by a polygon. Geometric modeling of road units is needed to determine whether a sensor data item belongs to the specified target area.
- *Topological modeling*: Road network topology describes the interconnections between road units. Topological modeling can help avoid aggregating traffic data from disjoint road units, which are located within the same geometric area, such as an overpass.

4.3 Data Model

We classify the following three types of messages in our VANET-based traffic information system:

- *Aggregated query message*: generated by the querying vehicle, which is presented by the tuple $Q_{msg} = \{Q_{id}, Q_{area}, F_{agg}, name, Q_{exp}\}$. The message includes a unique Query ID, the target area, the aggregation function, the name of the queried data item, and the expiration time of the query.
- *Raw data message*: generated by an on-board sensor, which is presented by the tuple $\{Q_{msg}, V_{id}, position, time, value\}$. The message includes the original query message, a unique Vehicle ID, the vehicle position, the time of data generation and its value.
- *Aggregated data message*: aggregated from multiple raw data messages, which is presented by the tuple $\{Q_{msg}, AGG_{area}, time, value\}$. The message includes the original query message, the aggregation area covered by the data, the generation time and the value of the data.

5 Location-Based Hierarchical Aggregation

In this section, we briefly describe the Geocast routing protocol as the basis for data query and data aggregation, we then present our aggregation approach, which is based on the hierarchical location model described above.

5.1 Geocast Routing Algorithm

Using Geocast, each node can send a data packet to a certain geographic area, which can be specified by its geometric or topological attributes. Geocast is the routing basis for data operations on higher layers in VANETs, such as data query and data aggregation.

A Geocast packet is first forwarded to the target area hop-by-hop based on the local decision on each intermediate node. The packet forwarding mechanism is based on a greedy strategy: each intermediate node chooses the neighbor that is geographically closest to the target area as the next hop [7]. After reaching the target area, the Geocast packet is locally broadcast within the area. A plain flooding of packet within the area, however, is very expensive and may result in excessive packet collision and contention. Thus, we use a *distance-based rebroadcast* scheme to reduce the communication overhead of local broadcasts [1]. Instead of immediately rebroadcasting the received packet, each node waits for a certain period of time whose length is inversely proportional to its distance to the packet sender. Thus, only the neighbors that are farther away from the sender will rebroadcast the packet, and further rebroadcast within the neighborhood can be saved.

5.2 Data Aggregation Mechanism

Location-Based Grouping After receiving the query message, each vehicle within the target area autonomously performs a location-based grouping process.

The target area is partitioned into a hierarchical group structure based on the location model of the road network, which is assumed to be available on each vehicle. Assuming a vehicle queries for the average vehicle speed in Road *A* and specifies it as the target area in the query message. As shown in Fig. 2, Road *A* can be partitioned into two road sections *A-1* and *A-2*. Section *A-1* can be further partitioned into five road segments from *S-1* to *S-5*, and Section *A-2* into segments from *S-6* to *S-10*.

The group structure of the target area is presented by a hierarchical aggregation tree, whose nodes are *locations*. We assume that the segment level is the lowest level of road units in our location model, thus road segments are leaves in the aggregation tree. Each road segment is the child of the road section it belongs to, which again, is the child of the road that contains the section. The root of the aggregation tree is the target area specified in the query message.

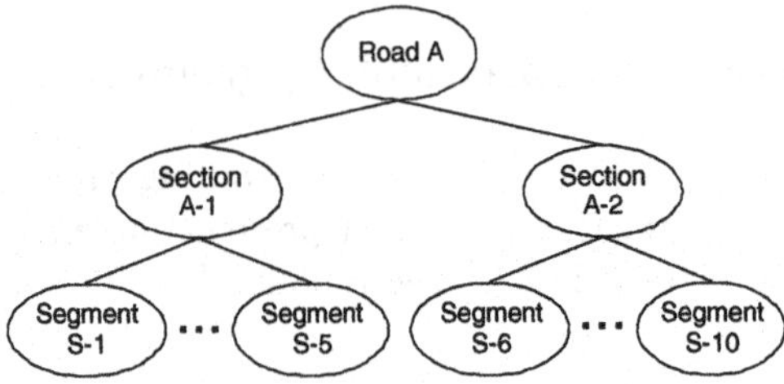

Fig. 2: An example of location-based hierarchical aggregation tree

In contrast to aggregation trees relying on stable network topologies [6,8,9,16], our location-based aggregation tree is insensitive to node mobility. Moreover, there is no membership management for location-based groups. Based on the location model and its current location, each vehicle within the given target area can determine its group membership itself. When a vehicle leaves the current segment and enters a new segment, it automatically switches its group membership to the new segment group.

Hierarchical Aggregation After the fully distributed grouping process, sensor data in the target area is aggregated hierarchically along the location-based aggregation tree.

At the segment level, each vehicle locally broadcasts its raw data within the current segment after a random backoff time. It then starts the *segment aggregation timer* to wait a certain period of time before performing segment-level aggregation. The timeout value of the segment aggregation timer is determined by

$$WT_{agg} = T + rand(0, t) \tag{1}$$

with a basis interval T plus a randomly selected interval between 0 and t. The interval T is selected based on the level of the group and the query expiration time Q_{exp}. The value of t should be selected taking the geographic area of the group and vehicle density into account. During the waiting time, each vehicle listens to the raw data messages sent by other vehicles within the current segment and inserts them into its local storage. The vehicle whose segment aggregation timer first expires declares itself the *group leader* of the current segment and aggregates the raw data in its local storage. The group leader then sends the aggregation result, an aggregated data message, to its parent location in the aggregation tree.

For example, if a group leader in the segment group *S-1* accomplishes raw data aggregation, it sends the aggregation result to the section *A-1*. Thus, the aggregation result of segment *S-1* will be locally broadcast within the section *A-1*, which includes the segment *S-1* itself. After receiving the aggregation result, other vehicles within the segment *S-1* cancel their segment aggregation timer and will not do segment-level data aggregation any more. Thus, the aggregated data message sent by the group leader not only delivers the result to the higher-level group, but also serves to declare the group leadership within the group. Note that only the aggregation result of each segment group is sent to the parent group, while raw data messages may never leave their own segments.

This group leader competition algorithm, however, is not deterministic, since aggregation timers on multiple vehicles in the same group may expire simultaneously despite the randomness in time selection. Thus, there may be more than one leader per segment group. Nevertheless, the additional communication cost due to multiple leaders per group is very limited and does not cause a scalability problem, which is shown by the simulation results in Section 6.

On the higher location group levels, aggregation results from child location groups are aggregated. For example, the results of segments from *S-1* to *S-5* are aggregated for the result of the section *A-1*, while the results of sections *A-1* and *A-2* are aggregated to generate the result of the road *A*. The same group leader competition algorithm is used on higher levels: aggregation timer is used to randomly select group leader(s) in each group on each level. The value of T in formula (1) is proportional to the level of location, but must be less than Q_{exp}.

Finally, on the root of the aggregation tree, the result of the whole target area is computed. The timeout value of the root-level aggregation timer is determined by

$$WT_{agg} = Q_{exp} - rand(0, t) \tag{2}$$

with the query expiration time Q_{exp} minus a randomly selected interval between 0 and t. As for the case of formula 1, the value of t should be selected taking the size of the target area and current network conditions into account ($Q_{exp} = 1s$ and $t = 0.3s$ in our simulation). The group leader of the root level broadcasts the final result within the target area and sends it back to the vehicle that issued the query.

6 Simulations

In order to evaluate the performance of the aggregation protocol presented above, we have simulated the protocol with the ns-2 simulator. In this section, we present the simulation environment and analyze the simulation results.

6.1 Simulation Environment

We choose a part of the street network in Manhattan as the simulation area, as shown in Fig. 3. The simulation area contains 7 streets and 10 avenues in a range of 2500 m × 1700 m, with a total street length of about 33 km. The topology of the street network can be modeled by a graph, with the vertices referring the street intersections and edges denoting the street segments. A *graph-based mobility model* [14] is then used to simulate the vehicles moving in the city: all vehicles are initiated at randomly selected vertices and move along the edges of the graph. Each vehicle chooses another vertex as its destination randomly, and moves along the shortest path along the graph edges to it at a speed randomly chosen in a range from 5 to 15 m/s, which is the normal speed within city limits. After reaching the destination vertex, the vehicle makes a pause randomly selected between 0 and 2 seconds, and then moves to another vertex through random selection. The duration of the pause is at most 2 seconds due to the length of the simulation (50 seconds). Each vehicle repeats this movement behavior for the duration of the simulation.

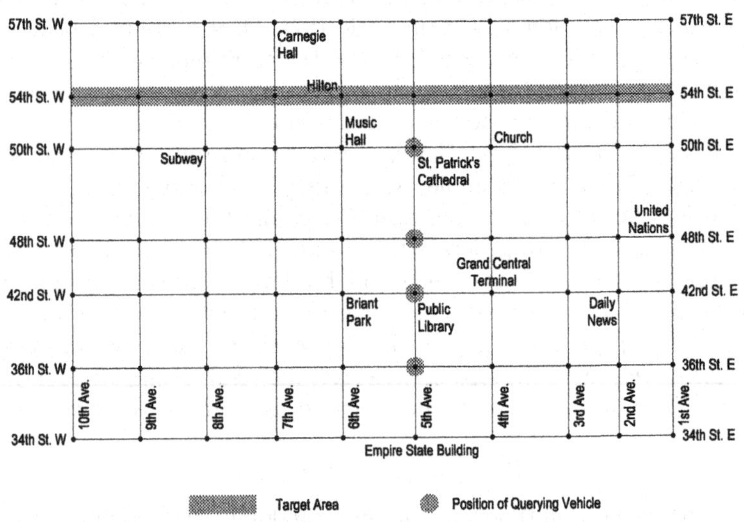

Fig. 3: Manhattan street network as simulation area

In our simulation, we choose 54th St. as the target area, which contains two sections 54th St.W and 54th St.E (divided by the 6th Ave.), and both sections are further partitioned into several segments. The querying vehicle is located on the *street intersections* of the 5th Ave. and sends the query message to the target area. We simulate with different distances between the querying vehicle and the target area, with the position of querying vehicle ranges from the 50th St. to the 36th St. The number of vehicles within the simulation area ranges from 200 to 600. The MAC protocol used corresponds to the ns-2 implementation of the

IEEE 802.11 DCF protocol with a transmission range of 250 meters and two ray ground model for radio propagation. We generate 20 different movement patterns for each density and make 10 simulation runs for each movement pattern. The whole simulation time is 50 seconds, which is more than reasonable for the evaluation of one aggregation query.

6.2 Simulation Results

We evaluate two metrics from the simulation results: the *aggregation completeness* and the *communication overhead.*

Aggregation completeness is defined as the percentage of vehicle sensor data that is included in the final aggregation results. As shown in Fig. 4(a), the vehicle density has a strong impact on the aggregation completeness. The query distance between the query sender and the target area has an obvious effect on the completeness with the low vehicle density (200 vehicles): The completeness is inversely proportional to the query distance, since more packets are lost during forwarding on the longer routing path. Nevertheless, the effect of the query distance is less apparent in higher vehicle densities (400 and 500 vehicles).

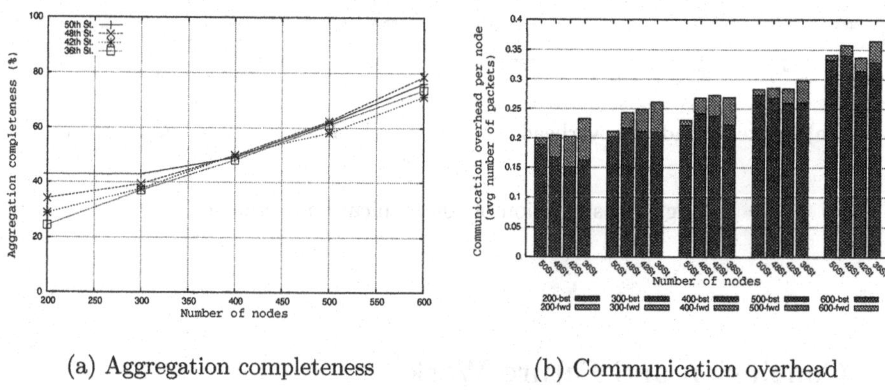

(a) Aggregation completeness (b) Communication overhead

Fig. 4: Aggregation completeness and communication overhead

Communication overhead is measured by the average number of packets transmitted per vehicle for data aggregation. As shown in Fig. 4(b), the communication overhead only increases slowly with the vehicle density. This is because we use the distance-based rebroadcast scheme in the Geocast protocol, which makes the rebroadcast overhead insensitive to vehicle density. Moreover, only aggregation results are sent to the higher level location, which limits the number of packets to be rebroadcast. The query distance does not have a significant effect on the overall communication overhead.

In order to clarify the distribution of the overall communication overhead between *broadcast overhead* and *forwarding overhead*, we present them separately in Fig. 5. As shown in Fig. 5(a), the major part of the overall communication overhead lies in packet broadcasts, which increases with vehicle density. The reason for this is that the number of vehicles within the target area increases with vehicle density, which results in more local broadcast of raw data messages. In contrast, the number of vehicles involved in the processing of queries has no significant effect on the cost of packet forwarding, and the overhead goes down slightly as shown in Fig. 5(b). But, this cost is greater if the distance to the querying vehicle is increased. This is because more hops are needed to deliver the aggregation result back to the querying vehicle.

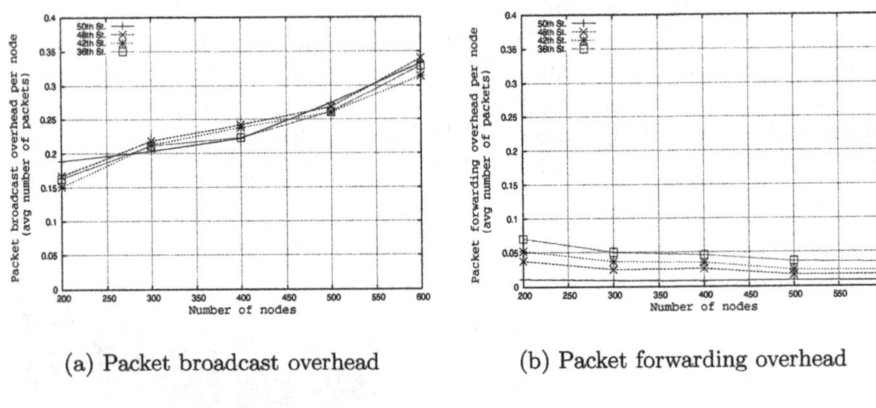

(a) Packet broadcast overhead

(b) Packet forwarding overhead

Fig. 5: Distribution of communication overhead

7 Conclusion and Future Work

In this paper, we introduce a location-based hierarchical data aggregation approach for VANETs. To the best of our knowledge, there is no previous work on data aggregation that supports geographically aggregated queries in highly dynamic infrastructure-less environments. The simulation results show that our approach achieves good completeness and scales well in city scenarios, such as Mannheim or typical American cities, where roads are mostly located in a grid. It remains to show the validity of our approach in typical European cities.

Also as part of future work, we will continue to refine and extend our approach to consider the following issues: Since VANETs may be strongly partitioned with low vehicle density, a vehicle may use *data handover* to overcome the partition by temporally buffering data messages until it meets a new neighbor. We can assign a certain *storage location* to store aggregation results on different levels, in order to avoid the global broadcast cost of aggregation results. Furthermore, we plan to investigate hybrid scenarios, where existing infrastructures are used in combination with VANETs to improve the performance of data aggregation.

References

1. L. Briesemeister and G. Hommel. Role-based multicast in highly mobile but sparsely connected ad hoc networks. In *Proc. of the ACM MobiHOC'00.*
2. F. Duerr and K. Rothermel. On a location model for fine-grained geocast. In *Proc. of the Fifth Intl. Conf. on Ubiquitous Computing*, 2003.
3. W. Franz, R. Eberhardt, and T. Luckenbach. Fleetnet - internet on the road. In *Proc. of the 8th World Congress on Intelligent Transport Systems*, 2001.
4. I. Gupta, R.V Renesse, and K.P. Birman. Scalable fault-tolerant aggregation in large process groups. In *Proc. of The Intl. Conf. on Dependable Systems and Networks (DSN 01)*, 2001.
5. W. R. Heinzelman, A. Chandrakasan, and H. Balakrishnan. Energy efficient communication protocol for wireless micro-sensor networks. In *Proc. IEEE Hawaii Int. Conf. on System Sciences*, 2000.
6. C. Intanagonwiwat, D. Estrin, R. Govindan, and J. Heidemann. Impact of network density on data aggregation in wireless sensor networks. In *Proc. of the 22nd Intl. Conf. on Distributed Computing Systems (ICDCS'02)*, 2002.
7. Brad Karp and H. T. Kung. Gpsr: greedy perimeter stateless routing for wireless networks. In *Proc. of the ACM MobiCom'00*, pages 243–254, 2000.
8. S. Lindsey, C. Raghavendra, and M. Sivalingam. Data gathering algorithms in sensor networks using energy metrics. *IEEE Transactions on Parallel and Distrobuted Systems*, 13(9):924–935, 2002.
9. S. Madden, M. J. Franklin, J. M. Hellerstein, and W. Hong. Tag: a tiny aggregation service for ad-hoc sensor networks. In *Proc. of the Fifth Annual Symposium on Operating Systems Design and Implementation (OSDI)*, 2002.
10. Tamer Nadeem, Sasan Dashtinezhad, Chunyuan Liao, and Liviu Iftode. Trafficview: A scalable traffic monitoring system. In *Proc. of the 5thIEEE Intl. Conf. on Mobile Data Management (MDM)*, 2004.
11. D. Reichardt, M. Miglietta, L. Moretti, P. Morsink, and W. Schulz. Cartalk 2000 - safe and comfortable driving based upon inter-vehicle-communication. In *Proc. of IEEE Intelligent Vehicle Symposium*, 2002.
12. M. H. Ruhe, C. Dalaff, and R. D. Kuehne. Traffic monitoring and traffic flow measurement by remote sensing systems. In *Proc. of the IEEE 6th Intl. Conf. on Intelligent Transportation Systems (ITSC)*, 2003.
13. S. Shekhar and D. Lui. Genesis and advanced traveler information systems. In *Mobile Computing*, pages 699–720, 1996.
14. J. Tian, J. Haehner, C. Becker, I. Stepanov, and K. Rothermel. Graph-based mobility model for mobile ad hoc network simulation. In *Proc. of the 35th Annual Simulation Symposium*, 2002.
15. L. Wischhof, A. Ebner, H. Rohling, M. Lott, and R. Halfmann. Sotis - a self-organizing traffic information system. In *Proc. of the 57th IEEE Vehicular Technology Conf. (VTC)*, 2003.
16. Y. Zhao, R. Govindan, and D. Estrin. Computing aggregates for monitoring wireless sensor networks. In *Proc. of the First IEEE Intl. Workshop on Sensor Network Protocols and Applications (SNPA'03)*, 2003.

Teil IV

Leistungsmessung und -bewertung

Transformation-Based Network Calculus Applying Convex/Concave Conjugates

Markus Fidler[1] and Stephan Recker[2]

[1] Lehrstuhl für Informatik 4, RWTH Aachen, Ahornstr. 55, 52074 Aachen
fidler@i4.informatik.rwth-aachen.de
[2] IMST GmbH, Carl-Friedrich-Gauß-Str. 2, 47475 Kamp-Lintfort
recker@imst.de

Abstract Network calculus has successfully been applied to derive performance bounds for communication networks, whereas a number of issues still remain unsolved or are not well understood yet. Founded on min-plus convolution and de-convolution, network calculus obeys a strong analogy to system theory. However, system theory has been extended beyond the time domain, applying the Fourier transform and allowing for an efficient analysis in the frequency domain. A corresponding dual domain for network calculus has not been elaborated, so far. In this paper we show that in analogy to system theory such a dual domain for network calculus is given by convex/concave conjugates referred to also as Legendre transform. We provide solutions for dual operations and show that min-plus convolution and de-convolution become simple addition and subtraction in Legendre space.

1 Introduction

Network calculus [1,2] is a theory of deterministic queuing systems that allows analyzing various fields in computer networking. Relations and a comparison to classical queuing theory are provided in [3]. Being a powerful and elegant theory, network calculus obeys a number of analogies to classical system theory, however, under a min-plus algebra, where addition becomes computation of the minimum and multiplication becomes addition [2].

System theory applies a characterization of systems by their response to the Dirac impulse, which constitutes the neutral element. A system is considered to be linear, if a constantly scaled input signal results in a corresponding scaling of the output signal and, if the sum of two input signals results in the sum of the two output signals that correspond to the individual input signals. The output of a system can be efficiently computed by convolution of the input signal and the system's impulse response and the concatenation of independent systems can be expressed by convolution of the individual impulse responses.

Network calculus relates very much to the above properties of system theory, while being based on the calculus for network delay presented in [4,5] and on Generalized Processor Sharing in [6,7]. The neutral element of network calculus is the burst function and systems are described by their burst response. Min-plus linearity is fulfilled, if the addition of a constant to the input signal results in an addition of the same constant to the output signal and, if the minimum of two input signals results in the minimum of the two output signals that correspond to the individual input signals. The output of a system is given as the min-plus convolution respective de-convolution of the input signal and the system's burst response and the concatenation of independent systems can be described by min-plus convolution of the individual burst responses. Extensions and a comprehensive overview on current Network Calculus are given in [1,2].

Yet, system theory provides another practical domain for analysis applying the Fourier transform, which is particularly convenient due to its clearness and because the convolution integral becomes a simple multiplication in the Fourier domain. Besides fast algorithms for Fourier transformation exist.

A corresponding domain in network calculus has, however, not been elaborated in depth so far. In [8] it is shown that the backlog bound at a constant rate server is equal to the Legendre respective Fenchel transform [9,10] of the input. A similar concept is used in [11], where the output of a network element is computed in the Legendre domain. Related theories are, however, far more developed in the field of morphological signal processing [12,13] where the slope transform has been successfully applied. Yet, it can be shown that the Legendre transform provides the basis for a new and comprehensive theory, which constitutes a dual approach to network calculus that can be efficiently applied to a variety of problems. As for the Fourier transform, fast algorithms for the Legendre transform exist [14].

The remainder of this paper is organized as follows: First, section 2 briefly summarizes some essential elements of network calculus, including arrival curves for input and output as well as service curves. Then, section 3 introduces the Legendre transform respective convex and concave conjugates and related properties, especially min-plus convolution and de-convolution. In section 4 the derived theory is applied to the elements of network calculus described in section 2. Section 5 concludes the paper.

2 Elements of Network Calculus

The foundations of network calculus are min-plus convolution and de-convolution, where min-plus operations can be derived from the corresponding classical operations by replacing addition by computation of the minimum and multiplication by addition. Consequently the algebraic structure that is used by network calculus is the commutative dioid $(\mathbb{R} \cup \infty, \min, +)$ [2].

Definition 1 (Min-Plus Convolution) *The min-plus convolution is defined in (1), where $t \geq u \geq 0$ is often applied by network calculus.*

$$(f \otimes g)(t) = \inf_u [f(t-u) + g(u)] \tag{1}$$

Definition 2 (Min-Plus De-Convolution) *The min-plus de-convolution is defined in (2), where $t \geq 0$ and $u \geq 0$ is often applied by network calculus.*

$$(f \oslash g)(t) = \sup_u [f(t+u) - g(u)] \tag{2}$$

Note that min-plus convolution is commutative, however, min-plus de-convolution is not. The algebraic structure $(\mathcal{F}, \min, \otimes)$ is a commutative dioid , where $\mathcal{F}$ is the set of wide-sense increasing functions with $f(s) \leq f(t)$ for all $s \leq t$ and $f(t) = 0$ for $t < 0$ that is usually applied by network calculus [2].

Furthermore, in context of network calculus arrival and service curves play an important role. Arrival curves constitute upper bounds on the input and output of network elements, while service curves represent lower bounds on the service offered by network elements. Networks are usually comprised of more than one network element and a network service is generally composed of a concatenation of the services of the individual network elements. This section provides the formal definitions for min-plus convolution and de-convolution, for arrival and service curves, and the computation rules for concatenated service curves and single server output bounds, which will be used in the remainder of this paper.

2.1 Arrival Curves

Flows or aggregates of flows can be described by arrival functions $F(t)$ that are given as the cumulated number of bits seen in an interval $[0, t]$. Arrival curves $\alpha(t)$ are defined to give upper bounds on the arrival functions, where $\alpha(t_2 - t_1) \geq F(t_2) - F(t_1)$ for all $t_2 \geq t_1 \geq 0$.

A typical constraint for incoming flows is given by the leaky bucket algorithm, which allows for bursts of size b and a defined sustainable rate r.

Definition 3 (Leaky Bucket Arrival Curve) *The arrival curve that is enforced by a leaky bucket is given in (3).*

$$\alpha(t) = \begin{cases} 0 & t = 0 \\ b + r \cdot t & t > 0 \end{cases} \tag{3}$$

2.2 Service Curves

The service that is offered by the scheduler on an outgoing link can be characterized by a minimum service curve, denoted by $\beta(t)$. A network element with input arrival function $F(t)$ and output arrival function $F'(t)$ is said to offer the service curve $\beta(t)$ if a time instance s exists for all t with $t \geq s \geq 0$ for which $F'(t) - F(s) \geq \beta(t - s)$ holds.

A special type of service curve is the rate-latency type that is given by (4) with a rate R and a latency T. The rate-latency service curve is defined for $t \geq 0$.

Definition 4 (Rate-Latency Service Curve) *In (4) the rate-latency service curve is defined, where $[\dots]^+$ is zero if the argument is negative.*

$$\beta(t) = R \cdot [t - T]^+ \tag{4}$$

2.3 Concatenation

Networks are usually comprised of more than one network element and a network service is generally composed of a series of individual network element services. The service curve of a concatenation of service elements can be efficiently described by min-plus convolution of the individual service curves.

Theorem 1 (Concatenation) *The service curve $\beta(t)$ of the concatenation of n service elements with service curves $\beta_i(t)$ is given in (5).*

$$\beta(t) = \bigotimes_{i=1}^{n} \beta_i(t) \tag{5}$$

The corresponding proof can be found for example in [1,2].

2.4 Output Bounds

Bounds on the output from a service element can be derived to be the min-plus de-convolution of the bound on the input and the corresponding service curve.

Theorem 2 (Output Bound) *Consider a service element $\beta(t)$ with input that is bounded by $\alpha(t)$. A bound on the output $\alpha'(t)$ is given in (6).*

$$\alpha'(t) = \alpha(t) \oslash \beta(t) \tag{6}$$

The proof can be found for example in [1,2].

3 The Legendre Transform

In this section we show the existence of eigenfunctions in classical and in particular in min-plus system theory. The corresponding eigenvalues immediately yield the Fourier respective Legendre transform. Following the definition of convex and concave conjugates, the two major operations of network calculus, min-plus convolution and de-convolution, are derived in the Legendre domain and finally a list of properties of the Legendre transform is provided.

3.1 Eigenfunctions and Eigenvalues

The output $h(t)$ of a linear time-invariant system with impulse response $g(t)$ and input $f(t)$ is given by the convolution integral in (7).

$$h(t) = f(t) * g(t) = \int_{-\infty}^{+\infty} f(t-u)g(u)du \tag{7}$$

Definition 5 (Eigenfunctions and Eigenvalues) *Consider a linear operator $\mathcal{A}$ on a function space. The function $f(t)$ is an eigenfunction for $\mathcal{A}$, if (8) holds, where λ is the associated eigenvalue.*

$$\mathcal{A}[f(t)] = f(t) \cdot \lambda \tag{8}$$

The functions $f(t) = \mathrm{e}^{\mathrm{j}2\pi st}$ are eigenfunctions for the convolution integral as shown in (9).

$$\mathrm{e}^{\mathrm{j}2\pi st} * g(t) = \int_{-\infty}^{+\infty} \mathrm{e}^{\mathrm{j}2\pi s(t-u)} g(u)du = \mathrm{e}^{\mathrm{j}2\pi st} \cdot G(s) \tag{9}$$

With $G(s)$ according to (10) the Fourier transformation is given [15].

$$G(s) = \int_{-\infty}^{+\infty} \mathrm{e}^{-\mathrm{j}2\pi su} g(u)du \tag{10}$$

In analogy, network calculus applies min-plus convolution to derive lower bounds on the output of network elements, respective min-plus de-convolution to derive upper bounds. For explanatory reasons the following derivation is made applying min-plus de-convolution given in Definition 2. Equation (2) provides an upper bound on the output of a network element with burst response $g(t)$ and upper bounded input $f(t)$. Regarding the eigenfunctions for operators in the min-plus domain we need to take the change from multiplication to addition into account, that is an eigenfunction in the min-plus domain is defined by $\mathcal{A}[f(t)] = f(t) + \lambda$. Consequently, eigenfunctions with regard to min-plus de-convolution are the affine functions $b + s \cdot t$ according to (11).

$$(b + s \cdot t) \oslash g(t) = \sup_u [b + s \cdot (t + u) - g(u)] = b + s \cdot t + G(s) \tag{11}$$

With $G(s)$ defined by (12) the Legendre transform is derived.

$$G(s) = \sup_u [s \cdot u - g(u)] \tag{12}$$

Note that (12) is the Legendre transform respective convex conjugate that applies for convex functions $g(t)$.

3.2 Convex and Concave Conjugates

Before providing further details on the Legendre transform, convexity and concavity are defined as follows:

Definition 6 (Convexity) *A function $f(t)$ is convex, if (13) holds for all u with $0 \leq u \leq 1$.*

$$f(u \cdot s + (1 - u) \cdot t) \leq u \cdot f(s) + (1 - u) \cdot f(t) \tag{13}$$

Definition 7 (Concavity) *A function $g(t)$ is concave, if (14) holds for all u with $0 \leq u \leq 1$.*

$$g(u \cdot s + (1-u) \cdot t) \geq u \cdot g(s) + (1-u) \cdot g(t) \tag{14}$$

If $f(t) = -g(t)$ is convex then $g(t)$ is concave. The sum of two convex or two concave functions is convex respective concave. If the domain of a convex or concave function is smaller than $\mathbb{R}$, the function can be extended to $\mathbb{R}$ while retaining its property by setting it to $+\infty$ respective $-\infty$ where it is undefined [10].

The Legendre transform is defined independently for convex and concave functions. Details can be found in [10]. Further on, set-valued extensions exist that allow transforming arbitrary functions [12,13], which are, however, not used here. Let $\mathcal{L}$ denote the Legendre transform in general, where we for clarity distinguish between convex conjugates $\overline{\mathcal{L}}$ and concave conjugates $\underline{\mathcal{L}}$.

Definition 8 (Convex Conjugate) *The convex conjugate is defined in (15).*

$$F(s) = \overline{\mathcal{L}}(f(t))(s) = \sup_t [s \cdot t - f(t)] \tag{15}$$

Definition 9 (Concave Conjugate) *The concave conjugate is defined in (16).*

$$G(s) = \underline{\mathcal{L}}(g(t))(s) = \inf_t [s \cdot t - g(t)] \tag{16}$$

If $f(t) = -g(t)$ is convex then $\underline{\mathcal{L}}(g(t))(s) = -\overline{\mathcal{L}}(f(t))(-s)$ holds.

3.3 Min-plus Convolution and De-convolution

The foundation of network calculus are min-plus convolution and de-convolution, for which corresponding operations in the Legendre domain are derived here.

Theorem 3 (Min-Plus Convolution in the Legendre domain) *The min-plus convolution of two convex functions $f(t)$ and $g(t)$ in the time domain becomes an addition in the Legendre domain, as already reported in [9,10].*

Proof 1 (Proof of Theorem 3) The min-plus convolution of two convex functions is convex [2]. Thus (17) can be immediately set up.

$$\begin{aligned}
\overline{\mathcal{L}}((f \otimes g)(t))(s) &= \sup_t [s \cdot t - \inf_u [f(t-u) + g(u)]] \\
&= \sup_t [s \cdot t + \sup_u [-f(t-u) - g(u)]] \\
&= \sup_u [\sup_t [s \cdot (t-u) - f(t-u)] + s \cdot u - g(u)] \\
&= \sup_u [\overline{\mathcal{L}}(f(t))(s) + s \cdot u - g(u)] \\
&= \overline{\mathcal{L}}(f(t))(s) + \sup_u [s \cdot u - g(u)] \\
&= \overline{\mathcal{L}}(f(t))(s) + \overline{\mathcal{L}}(g(t))(s)
\end{aligned} \tag{17}$$

Thus, Theorem 3 holds. □

Theorem 4 (Min-Plus De-Convolution in the Legendre domain) *The min-plus de-convolution of a concave function $f(t)$ and a convex function $g(t)$ in the time domain becomes a subtraction in the Legendre domain.*

Lemma 1 (Concavity of the Min-Plus De-Convolution) *The min-plus de-convolution of a concave function $f(t)$ and a convex function $g(t)$ is concave.*

Proof 2 (Proof of Lemma 1) The proof is a variation of a proof provided in [2], where it is shown that the min-plus convolution of two convex functions is convex. Define $\mathcal{S}_{-f(t)}$ and $\mathcal{S}_{g(-t)}$ in (18) to be the epigraphy of $-f(t)$ and $g(-t)$.

$$\begin{aligned}\mathcal{S}_{-f(t)} &= \{(t,\eta) \in \mathbb{R}^2 | -f(t) \leq \eta\} \\ \mathcal{S}_{g(-t)} &= \{(t,\vartheta) \in \mathbb{R}^2 | g(-t) \leq \vartheta\}\end{aligned} \tag{18}$$

Since $-f(t)$ and $g(-t)$ are both convex, the corresponding epigraphy in (18) as well as the sum $\mathcal{S} = \mathcal{S}_{-f(t)} + \mathcal{S}_{g(-t)}$ in (19) are also convex [2,10].

$$\mathcal{S} = \{(r+s, \eta+\vartheta) | (r,\eta) \in \mathbb{R}^2, (s,\vartheta) \in \mathbb{R}^2, -f(r) \leq \eta, g(-s) \leq \vartheta\} \tag{19}$$

Substitution of $r+s$ by t, s by $-u$, and $\eta+\vartheta$ by ξ yields (20).

$$\mathcal{S} = \{(t,\xi) \in \mathbb{R}^2 | (-u,\vartheta) \in \mathbb{R}^2, -f(t+u) \leq \xi - \vartheta, g(u) \leq \vartheta\} \tag{20}$$

Since $\mathcal{S}$ is convex, $h(t) = \inf\{\xi \in \mathbb{R} | (t,\xi) \in \mathcal{S}\}$ is also convex [10].

$$\begin{aligned}h(t) &= \inf\{\xi \in \mathbb{R} | (-u,\vartheta) \in \mathbb{R}^2, -f(t+u) \leq \xi - \vartheta, g(u) \leq \vartheta\} \\ &= \inf\{\xi \in \mathbb{R} | (-u) \in \mathbb{R}, -f(t+u) + g(u) \leq \xi\} \\ &= \inf_u\{-f(t+u) + g(u)\}\end{aligned} \tag{21}$$

From (21) it follows that $(f \oslash g)(t) = \sup_u[f(t+u) - g(u)]$ is concave. □

Proof 3 (Proof of Theorem 4) With Lemma 1 we can set up (22).

$$\begin{aligned}\underline{\mathcal{L}}((f \oslash g)(t))(s) &= \inf_t[s \cdot t - \sup_u[f(t+u) - g(u)]] \\ &= \inf_t[s \cdot t + \inf_u[-f(t+u) + g(u)]] \\ &= \inf_u[\inf_t[s \cdot (t+u) - f(t+u)] + g(u) - s \cdot u] \\ &= \inf_u[\underline{\mathcal{L}}(f(t))(s) + g(u) - s \cdot u] \\ &= \underline{\mathcal{L}}(f(t))(s) - \sup_u[s \cdot u - g(u)] \\ &= \underline{\mathcal{L}}(f(t))(s) - \overline{\mathcal{L}}(g(t))(s)\end{aligned} \tag{22}$$

Thus, Theorem 4 holds. □

Table 1. Properties of the Legendre Transform

Time Domain	Legendre Domain
$f(t)$	$F(s) = \mathcal{L}(f(t))(s)$
$f(t) = \mathcal{L}(F(s))(t)$	$F(s)$
$f(t)$, convex	$F(s) = \overline{\mathcal{L}}(f(t))(s) = \sup_t[s \cdot t - f(t)]$, convex
$f(t)$, concave	$F(s) = \underline{\mathcal{L}}(f(t))(s) = \inf_t[s \cdot t - f(t)]$, concave
$f(t) + c$	$F(s) - c$
$f(t) \cdot c$	$F(s/c) \cdot c$
$f(t) + t \cdot c$	$F(s - c)$
$f(t + c)$	$F(s) - s \cdot c$
$f(t \cdot c)$	$F(s/c)$
$f(t) = g(t) \otimes h(t)$, g convex, h convex	$F(s) = G(s) + H(s)$, G convex, H convex
$f(t) = g(t) \oslash h(t)$, g concave, h convex	$F(s) = G(s) - H(s)$, G concave, H convex

3.4 Properties of the Legendre Transform

The Legendre transform exhibits a number of useful properties of which Table 3.4 lists the most relevant ones. More details can be found in [10].

The Legendre transform is self-dual, that is it is its own inverse. More precisely $\mathcal{L}(\mathcal{L}(f))(t) = (\text{cl}f)(t)$, where $(\text{cl}f)(t)$ is the closure of $f(t)$ that is defined to be $(\text{cl}f)(t) = \liminf_{s\to t} f(s)$ for convex functions and $(\text{cl}f)(t) = \limsup_{s\to t} f(s)$ for concave functions. Thus, if $f(t)$ is convex then $(\text{cl}f)(t) \le f(t)$ and if $f(t)$ is concave then $(\text{cl}f)(t) \ge f(t)$. If $(\text{cl}f)(t) = f(t)$ then $f(t)$ is said to be closed. The Legendre transform of a convex function is a closed convex function, respective the Legendre transform of a concave function is a closed concave function.

For arbitrary functions $f(t)$ the convex conjugate follows as $\overline{\mathcal{L}}(f(t))(s) = \overline{\mathcal{L}}(\text{cl}(\text{conv}f)(t))(s)$, where the convex hull $(\text{cl}(\text{conv}f))(t)$ of $f(t)$ is the greatest closed convex function majorized by $f(t)$. It can be seen as the pointwise supremum on all affine functions majorized by $f(t)$ such that $(\text{cl}(\text{conv}f))(t) = \sup_{b,r}\{b+r\cdot t : (\forall s : b+r\cdot s \le f(s))\}$, thus $(\text{cl}(\text{conv}f))(t) \le f(t)$. For the concave conjugate $\underline{\mathcal{L}}(f(t))(s) = \underline{\mathcal{L}}(\text{cl}(\text{conc}f)(t))(s)$ holds, where the concave hull follows as $(\text{cl}(\text{conc}f))(t) = \inf_{b,r}\{b+r\cdot t : (\forall s : b+r\cdot s \ge f(s))\}$ and $(\text{cl}(\text{conc}f))(t) \ge f(t)$.

4 Network Calculus in the Legendre Domain

After the introduction of concave and convex conjugates and of the dual min-plus operations in the Legendre domain we can derive the dual operations to the network calculus concatenation theorem and output theorem. However, the prerequisite for application of the Legendre domain network calculus is a transformation of arrival and service curves into this domain, which will be presented first. Each of the following sub-sections presents the dual element in the Legendre domain that corresponds to the element of network calculus presented in the pertaining sub-section of section 2.

4.1 Arrival Curves

According to Definition 3 arrival curves of leaky-bucket type are concave and defined for $t \geq 0$. We apply the concave extension described in section 3.2 by setting $\alpha(t) = -\infty$ for $t < 0$. Note that the extended arrival curve does not belong to the set $\mathcal{F}$, where $f(t) \in \mathcal{F}$ implies $f(t) = 0$ for $t < 0$, which is usually applied by network calculus in the time domain. Then we can derive the concave conjugate of a leaky-bucket arrival curve according to Corollary 1.

Corollary 1 (Conjugate Leaky Bucket Arrival Curve) *The concave conjugate of the leaky bucket constraint given in Definition 3 can be computed according to (16) and is given in (23).*

$$A(s) = \inf_t [s \cdot t - \alpha(t)] = \begin{cases} -\infty & s < r \\ -b & s \geq r \end{cases} \tag{23}$$

In [16] the burstiness curve is defined to be the maximal backlog at a constant rate server with rate s and input $\alpha(t)$, whereby it has been pointed out in [8] that the burstiness curve is actually the Legendre transform $-\underline{\mathcal{L}}(\alpha(t))(s)$. Thus, we obtain a very clear interpretation of $A(s)$.

Generally the concave hull of an arbitrary arrival curve is a valid arrival curve, since $\mathrm{cl}(\mathrm{conc}\,\alpha)(t) \geq \alpha(t)$ for all t. Note that the hull must not be derived explicitly in the time domain, since it follows immediately from $\underline{\mathcal{L}}(\mathrm{cl}(\mathrm{conc}\,\alpha)(t))(s) = \underline{\mathcal{L}}(\alpha(t))(s)$.

4.2 Service Curves

The rate-latency service curve according to Definition 4 is convex and defined for $t \geq 0$. The convex extension described in section 3.2 allows setting the curve to $+\infty$ for $t < 0$. However, in this context it is more meaningful to set the service curve to zero for $t < 0$ which results in a convex function that belongs to $\mathcal{F}$.

Corollary 2 (Conjugate Rate-Latency Service Curve) *The convex conjugate of the rate-latency service curve given in Definition 4 can be computed based on (15) and follows immediately according to (24).*

$$B(s) = \sup_t [s \cdot t - \beta(t)] = \begin{cases} +\infty & s < 0 \\ s \cdot T & s \geq 0,\, s \leq R \\ +\infty & s > R \end{cases} \tag{24}$$

The conjugate $B(s)$ of the service curve $\beta(t)$ can be interpreted as the backlog bound that holds, if a constant bit rate stream with rate s is input to the respective network element.

Generally the convex hull of an arbitrary service curve is a valid service curve, since $\mathrm{cl}(\mathrm{conv}\,\beta)(t) \leq \beta(t)$ for all t. Note that the hull must not be derived explicitly in the time domain, since it follows immediately from $\overline{\mathcal{L}}(\mathrm{cl}(\mathrm{conv}\,\beta)(t))(s) = \overline{\mathcal{L}}(\beta(t))(s)$.

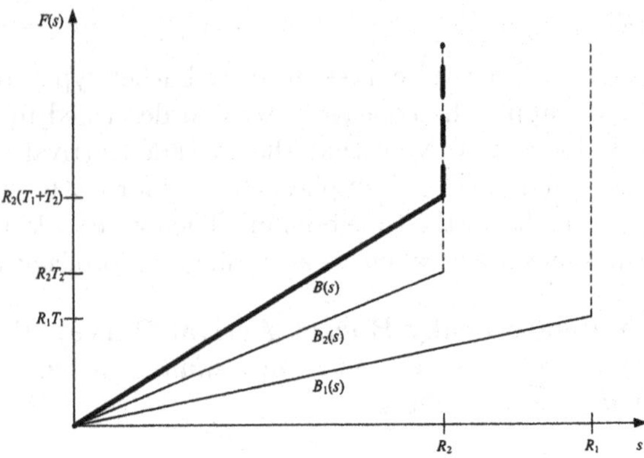

Fig. 1. Conjugate concatenated service curve

4.3 Concatenation

A concatenation of service elements, can be represented by min-plus convolution of the individual service curves according to Theorem 1. With Theorem 3 we can immediately formulate the following corollary.

Corollary 3 (Conjugate Concatenation) *In (25) the conjugate service curve $B(s)$ of the concatenation of n service elements is given as the sum of the individual conjugate service curves $B_i(s)$.*

$$B(s) = \sum_{i=1}^{n} B_i(s) \tag{25}$$

Since $\overline{\mathcal{L}}(\overline{\mathcal{L}}(\beta))(t) = \overline{\mathcal{L}}(B(s))(t) = (\text{cl}(\text{conv}\,\beta))(t) \leq \beta(t)$ we find that $\overline{\mathcal{L}}(B(s))(t)$ is generally a valid service curve.

Here, we provide an example for the concatenation of rate-latency service elements. Consider n service elements in series with service curves $\beta_i(t) = R_i \cdot [t - T_i]^+$ for all t. The corresponding conjugates are $B_i(s) = s \cdot T_i$ for $0 \leq s \leq R_i$ and $+\infty$ else. The sum is $B(s) = s \cdot \sum_i T_i$ for $0 \leq s \leq \min_i[R_i]$ and $+\infty$ else. An example for $n = 2$ is shown in Figure 1.

The result is convex and deriving the convex conjugate of $B(s)$ we find $(\text{cl}(\text{conv}\,\beta))(t) = \overline{\mathcal{L}}(B(s))(t) = \min_i[R_i] \cdot [t - \sum_i T_i]^+$. The result is exact since $(\text{cl}(\text{conv}\,\beta))(t) = \beta(t)$, where $\beta(t) = \bigotimes_{i=1}^{n} \beta_i(t)$. The same service curve can be found by min-plus convolution in the time domain.

4.4 Output Bounds

For the output bound defined in Theorem 2 we can formulate the following corollary by applying Theorem 4.

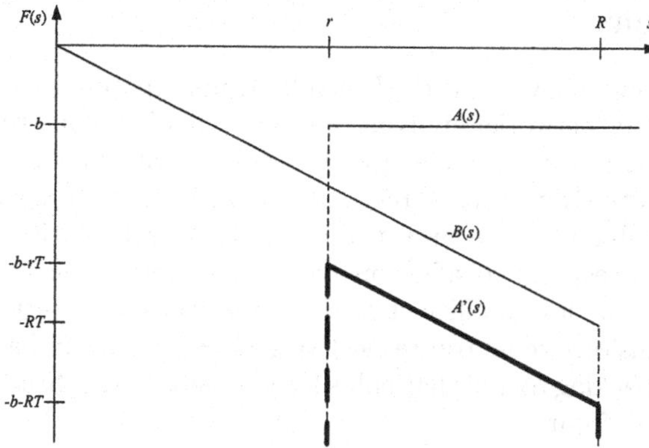

Fig. 2. Conjugate output arrival curve

Corollary 4 (Conjugate Output Bound) *The conjugate output bound $A'(s)$ of a service element with conjugate service curve $B(s)$ and constrained input with conjugate input bound $A(s)$ is provided in (26).*

$$A'(s) = A(s) - B(s) \tag{26}$$

Since $\underline{\mathcal{L}}(\underline{\mathcal{L}}(\alpha'))(t) = \underline{\mathcal{L}}(A'(s))(t) = (\text{cl}(\text{conc}\,\alpha'))(t) \geq \alpha(t)$ we find that $\underline{\mathcal{L}}(A'(s))(t)$ is generally a valid output arrival curve.

As an example consider the output bound that can be derived for a rate-latency service element with service curve $\beta(t) = R \cdot [t - T]^+$ for all t and leaky bucket constrained input with arrival curve $\alpha(t) = b + r \cdot t$ for $t \geq 0$, zero for $t = 0$ and $-\infty$ for $t < 0$. The respective conjugates are $B(s) = s \cdot T$ for $0 \leq s \leq R$ and $+\infty$ else and $A(s) = -b$ for $s \geq r$ and $-\infty$ else. The difference is $A'(s) = -b - s \cdot T$ for $r \leq s \leq R$ and $-\infty$ else. The example is shown in Figure 2.

The result is concave according to Lemma 1 and the concave conjugate of $A'(s)$ becomes $(\text{cl}(\text{conc}\,\alpha'))(t) = \underline{\mathcal{L}}(A'(s))(t) = b + r \cdot (t + T)$ for $t \geq -T$ and $(\text{cl}(\text{conc}\,\alpha'))(t) = \underline{\mathcal{L}}(A'(s))(t) = b + R \cdot (t + T)$ for $t < -T$. Again our solution is exact since $(\text{cl}(\text{conc}\,\alpha'))(t) = \alpha'(t)$, where $\alpha'(t) = \alpha(t) \oslash \beta(t)$. The result is well known for $t \geq 0$ from min-plus de-convolution in the time domain. Further on, it is shown in [2] that the result of min-plus de-convolution is also valid for $t < 0$. Note that min-plus de-convolution in the time domain as well as in the Legendre domain is not closed in $\mathcal{F}$, where $f(t) \in \mathcal{F}$ implies $f(t) = 0$ for $t < 0$. In contrast, the output arrival curve $\alpha'(t)$ is strictly positive for $0 > t > -T - b/R$. The usual approach applied by network calculus in the time domain is to truncate functions for $t < 0$ implicitly by allowing only values $t \geq u \geq 0$ in min-plus convolution (1) respective $t \geq 0$ and $u \geq 0$ in min-plus de-convolution (2). Here, we require an explicit truncation of the output arrival curve $\alpha'(t)$ for $t < 0$ before interpreting the result of the Legendre transform $\underline{\mathcal{L}}(\alpha'(t))(s)$ as a meaningful backlog bound for a virtual subsequent constant rate network node.

5 Conclusions

In this paper we have shown that the Legendre transform provides a dual domain for analysis of data networks applying network calculus. Our work is a significant extension of the known analogy of system theory and network calculus where the Legendre transform corresponds to the Fourier transform in system theory. In particular we have proven that min-plus convolution and min-plus de-convolution correspond to addition respective subtraction in the Legendre domain, which allows for an efficient analysis and fast computation. In addition the Legendre transform of arrival respective service curves can be intuitively interpreted as the backlog bound that holds for a constant bit rate server respective a constant bit rate input.

References

1. Chang, C.-S., *Performance Guarantees in Communication Networks*, Springer, TNCS, 2000.
2. Le Boudec, J.-Y., and Thiran, P., *Network Calculus A Theory of Deterministic Queuing Systems for the Internet*, Springer, LNCS 2050, 2002.
3. Schmitt, J., *On Average and Worst Case Behaviour in Non-preemptive Priority Queueing*, Proceedings of SCS SPECTS, pp. 197-204, 2003.
4. Cruz, R. L., *A Calculus for Network Delay, Part I: Network Elements in Isolation*, IEEE Transactions on Information Theory, vol. 37, no. 1, pp. 114-131, 1991.
5. Cruz, R. L., *A Calculus for Network Delay, Part II: Network Analysis*, IEEE Transactions on Information Theory, vol. 37, no. 1, pp. 132-141, 1991.
6. Parekh, A. K., and Gallager, R. G., *A Generalized Processor Sharing Approach to Flow Control in Integrated Services Networks: The Single-Node Case*, IEEE/ACM Transactions on Networking, vol. 1, no. 3, pp. 344-357, 1993.
7. Parekh, A. K., and Gallager, R. G., *A Generalized Processor Sharing Approach to Flow Control in Integrated Services Networks: The Multiple-Node Case*, IEEE/ACM Transactions on Networking, vol. 2, no. 2, pp. 137-150, 1994.
8. Naudts, J., *Towards real-time measurement of traffic control parameters*, Elsevier Computer Networks, vol. 34, no. 1, pp. 157-167, 2000.
9. Baccelli, F., Cohen, G., Olsder, G. J., and Quadrat, J.-P., *Synchronizaition and Linearity, An Algebra for Discrete Event Systems*, Wiley, 1992.
10. Rockafellar, R. T., *Convex Analysis*, Princeton, 1972.
11. Hisakado, T., Okumura, K., Vukadinovic, V., and Trajkovic, L., *Characterization of a Simple Communication Network Using Legendre Transform*, Proceedings of IEEE Internationl Symposium on Circuits and Systems, pp. 738-741, 2003.
12. Dorst, L., and van den Boomgard, R., *Morphological Signal Processing and the Slope Transform*, Elsevier Signal Processing, vol. 38, no. 1, pp. 79-98, 1994.
13. Maragos, R., *Slope Transform: Theory and Application to Nonlinear Signal Processing*, IEEE Transactions on Signal Processing, vol. 43, no. 4, pp. 864-877, 1995.
14. Lucet, Y., *A fast computational algorithm for the Legendre-Fenchel transform*, Computational Optimization and Application, no. 1, pp. 27-57, 1996.
15. Ohm, J.-R., Lüke, H. D., *Signalübertragung: Grundlagen der digitalen und analogen Nachrichtenübertragungssysteme*, Springer, 9. Auflage, 2004.
16. Low, S., and Varaiya, P., *Burst reducing servers in ATM networks*, Queueing Systems, Theory and Applications, vol. 20, no. 1-2, pp. 61-84, 1995.

Measuring Large Overlay Networks – The Overnet Example

Kendy Kutzner and Thomas Fuhrmann

System Architecture Group, Universität Karlsruhe (TH), 76128 Karlsruhe, Germany
{kendy.kutzner|thomas.fuhrmann}@ira.uka.de

Abstract Peer-to-peer overlay networks have grown significantly in size and sophistication over the last years. Meanwhile, distributed hash tables (DHT) provide efficient means to create global scale overlay networks on top of which various applications can be built. Although filesharing still is the most prominent example, other applications are well conceivable. In order to rationally design such applications, it is important to know (and understand) the properties of the overlay networks *as seen from the respective application*.

This paper reports the results from a two week measurement of the entire Overnet network, the currently most widely deployed DHT-based overlay. We describe both, the design choices that made that measurement feasible and the results from the measurement itself. Besides the basic determination of network size, node availability and node distribution, we found unexpected results for the overlay latency distribution.

1 Description of Overnet and Kademlia

Overnet is a popular peer-to-peer filesharing network, currently used by more than 10^6 unique servants (i.e. server-clients). It is based on Kademlia [8], a general peer-to-peer routing algorithm that can be used to implement distributed hash tables (DHT). Its service is similar to that of other popular DHT routing algorithms like Chord [15], CAN [11], or Pastry [14]. In all these DHTs, participating nodes are assigned a unique identifier, usually a 128 or 160 bit long unsigned integer. In Overnet, the ID is 128 bits long, generated randomly (uniformly) during first node startup, and saved permantently for consecutive starts. These identifiers can be viewed as addresses in an overlay network that extends the functionality of the underlying network infrastructure [3]. Unlike classical networks, these overlays are organized in a way that *every* address maps to a node participating in the overlay network. Thus, these addresses can be used for hashing arbitrary keys to the network's nodes. Hence, the term distributed hash table.

With Kademlia, this address-to-node mapping assigns each address the closest node where closeness is defined by the XOR-metric, i. e. $d(a, b) = a \oplus b$. This metric has the benefit of symmetry, i. e. when node B is close to node A, then also node A is close to node B.

In order to provide routing in this address space, Kademlia nodes have to maintain overlay links to other Kademlia nodes. To this end, all nodes have so-called buckets each holding k different *(Kademlia-address, IP-transport-address)* pairs representing these overlay links. The assignment of pairs to the buckets is based on Kademlia-address prefixes: For each (shortest) prefix that is *not* a prefix of the respective node's address, there is one bucket. As an example, a node with ID 110100 would maintain a bucket for nodes whose addresses are starting with 0, 10, 111, 1100, 11011 and 110101. (Clearly, some of these buckets will be empty, since typically for large prefixes no appropriate overlay links are available.) For routing, a message then simply is forwarded to one of the peers from the longest prefix bucket.

Overnet employs this to create a filesharing network. We do not address any of the aspects associated with that particular use, but rather study the properties of the Overnet network resulting from this general overlay mechanism. Our results can therefore be expected to reflect fundamental aspects of such large overlay networks.

This paper is structured as follows: After discussing related work in section 2, we describe our measurement setup in section 3. We especially focus on general issues that are likely to occur with future peer-to-peer protocols, too. Section 4 summarizes our measurement results. Besides the determination of the fundamental parameters of the Overnet network, we report some astonishing findings which we cannot fully explain at the moment. In section 5, we conclude with an outlook to future work.

2 Related Work

Although there already is a multitude of peer-to-peer measurement studies, they rarely explore the global view of a large scale overlay network as seen from inside. Many studies are concerned with query patterns (user perspective) and Internet traffic properties (provider perspective), whereas we are interested in the global overlay's performance with respect to node availability and message routing delays (application perspective). E.g. RTT distributions *on the overlay layer* are an important parameter when judging the feasibility of certain peer-to-peer applications, like instant messaging, distributed filesystems, etc. To the best of our knowledge, no sufficiently significant measurement study of this property exists, so far.

The measurement study that comes closest to ours probed node availability in Overnet [1]. However, at that time Overnet seems to have been significantly smaller than today. (Only about 40 000 concurrent nodes were discovered there. We saw 4 – 5 times as many.) Moreover, the design of that measurement did not aim at gathering the global picture of the network. (They probed only a small subset of the discovered nodes.) Especially, the authors did not measure application layer latency. [7] address the problem of overlay-layer latency. But their measurement included only 25 nodes. [9], too, mentioned that problem, but do not provide any measurements.

[4] reviews many measurements of interarrival times, transfer times, burst sizes and burst lengths. The authors found some evidence for heavy-tailed distributions in burst sizes, but less evidence for such a distribution in interarrival times. That result is somehow expected in the light of the well-studied self-similarity in the Internet. Our finding of a power-law RTT distribution on the overlay layer, however, is unexpected from these earlier Internet results. It seems to be in fact a genuine overlay effect.

3 Measurement Setup

The aim of our measurement was twofold: On the one hand, we wanted to get an up-to-date picture of a large overlay-network. On the other hand, we wanted to gain experience in measuring such large networks in general. We focused our measurements on the distribution of the overlay nodes in the underlying network and the round-trip-times (RTT) as experienced by the overlay application. The content (=files) users are sharing with Overnet were outside the scope of this study.

Such a measurement study requires a large base of overlay nodes capable of constantly probing the network. We used PlanetLab [2, 10] to host the probing instances. This gave us more than 300 points in the Internet from which we could probe the Overnet network. Special care had to be taken to not degrade PlanetLab's network connectivity by our measurement traffic. Conversely, we had to take precautions to keep measurement artifacts caused by other PlanetLab users as small as possible.

3.1 The Probing Application

For our measurements we implemented a very reduced version of an Overnet servant. As described above, the search for nodes close to a given key is an elementary operation in Overnet/Kademlia. We used exactly this functionality to probe the network for nodes and at same time measure the RTT to these nodes. Hence, our measurement application could only send messages of type *search*, which Overnet servants use to discover other peers. The respective answer, a *search_next* message, then contains pointers to other servants in the network. These pointers are *(Kademlia-address, IP-transport-address)* pairs which could be used to iteratively search for more servants in the network.

The probing application maintained a ring buffer of all known Overnet clients. It continiously sent a *search* message to each of them. Every received *search_next* message was parsed and the sender of that message was marked alive. The round trip time (RTT) between sending and receiving was recorded. All previously unknown Overnet Clients from the received message were added to the ring buffer. During this process, addresses from special purpose IP ranges ([13, 12, 5]) were excluded. Also sites which previously complained about traffic from PlanetLab nodes were not added. The full source code of the application is available from the authors on request.

Our probing application employs two complementary probing modes. It queries either for

- the address of the queried node itself. This makes a node respond with a list of all its neighbors in the overlay. This mode ensures that all nodes have a chance to be found.

or

- a randomly generated bit string. Although the queried node is probably not very good at answering that query (it is not close in Kademlia terms), only this mode of querying ensures that the whole overlay address space will be covered. Moreover, this keeps the different probing applications from following the same trail through the network and thereby allows a simple parallelization of the measurements.

The queries were tailored so that answers fit in a 1400 octet UDP message: The above mentioned *(Kademlia-address, IP-transport-address)*-pair is encoded in 23 octets, and every probe sent queried for 60 such pairs. The Overnet message transporting these pairs has an encoded size of 19 octets.

A local Overnet node was continiously running the original Overnet P2P file sharing program. It's transport address (i. e. IP-address and port number) was hard-coded in the probing application and it was used as bootstrapping node. Even all probing applications started from the same bootstrapping node, by querying for random bit strings, their paths into the Overnet network quickly diverged.

3.2 Flow Control and Congestion Avoidance with UDP

Overnet uses UDP as transport protocol, i.e. there is no inherent flow and congestion control mechanism. An interesting problem was thus how to do flow and congestion control without modifying the given Overnet protocol. To this end, we reverted to two simple mechanisms:

1. Probes were sent either after a fixed timeout t or immediately after receiving a response to the previous probe. This ensured a rate bound by the timeout and the RTT value. The timeout was set to one second.
2. Results were constantly sent back to our central data collection facility using a TCP connection. If this connection stalled due to congestion on the PlanetLab link (a frequent event), we stopped further probing until this reporting traffic was flowing again.

The latter made our probing application TCP-friendly, but only on the probing site local links. Rate limitation for the probed Overnet servants didn't have to be considered in particular, since we probed an extremely large set of nodes from only 300 measurement nodes. Thus the rate there was at least three orders of magnitude below that at the probing sites.

Nevertheless, the probing application performed an emergency halt as soon as one of the following conditions became true:

- The number of nodes that responded is smaller than 10 percent of the probes sent.
- All known nodes have been tried at least once, regardless of whether they answered or not.
- The application ran out of credits. For every probe received the credit was set to c_{max}. For every probe sent, the credit was decreased by one. During deployment, we initialized the credit value to 500 and used a c_{max} of 100.
- The application ran for more than one hour.

The motivation behind these stop rules is that we wanted to prevent the probing application to overload the local network when our security measures descibed above failed to work. One scenario where this could occur is a local admistrator installing a firewall to block the probing application during runtime of the prober. Without these additional measures the prober would run forever.

3.3 Deployment

As stated above, we used PlanetLab as basis for our measurements. During our preparations we encountered a few minor issues that could be solved by software upgrades in the respective operating systems, but that we nevertheless believe worth reporting here, since they shed light on potential problems that can occur with future similar measurement studies.

We started our development with Linux 2.4.26/i386. Its protocol stack keeps a table with IP destinations. This table is, e.g., used to cache routing decisions and to store results of path MTU discovery. Since our application uses many different destination addresses, this table filled more quickly than Linux could garbage collect this table. Thus the maximum probing rate we achieved with the above platform was only about 300 different IP destinations per second. (Meanwhile, kernel 2.6.7 solved this issue.)

A similar limitation was encountered at the faculty firewall whose connection tracking mechanism did not clean its table quick enough for our measurements. Unlike with the Linux kernel problem, here, the firewall machine just crashed and had to be disabled for further measurements. Although our actual measurements deployed with PlanetLab did not use such a high rate as we did in the initial trials from within the faculty network, the problems came up there, too. At the University of Waterloo, Canada, e.g., the large number of destination addresses triggered a security alarm, and we had to exclude this site from our experiment.

From this experience we conclude that for further deployment of peer-to-peer techniques, firewall and intrusion detection system manufacturers need to modify their software, in order to be able to cope with peer-to-peer traffic. Note that we consider traffic with a large number of different IP destinations an inherent characteristic of peer-to-peer systems, not an artifact of our measurements. Moreover, even 300 messages per second is not a high rate.

4 Results

The measurement described in the previous section was run continiously for two weeks in July 2004. During that time the system was able to perform 482 912 462 RTT measurements and collect 2 943 223 different Kademlia addresses (with 9 549 043 different IP addresses) of the participating nodes (The difference between these numbers is explained below in section 4.2). Typically, between 200 000 and 265 000 Overnet nodes were concurrently present worldwide.

4.1 Performance of the Probing Application

Figure 1 shows the number of successfully received reports plotted over the rank of the respective PlanetLab node. Most nodes received almost 2 million reports each, corresponding to a rate of about 1.6 reports per second. Not all PlanetLab nodes were available all the time, hence the differences in figure 1. Remarkably, about 30 nodes only have ca. 20 000 reports. These nodes are part of the *Internet2* [6] and have limited connectivity to the rest of the Internet, so that they weren't able to collect as many reports as the rest of PlanetLab.

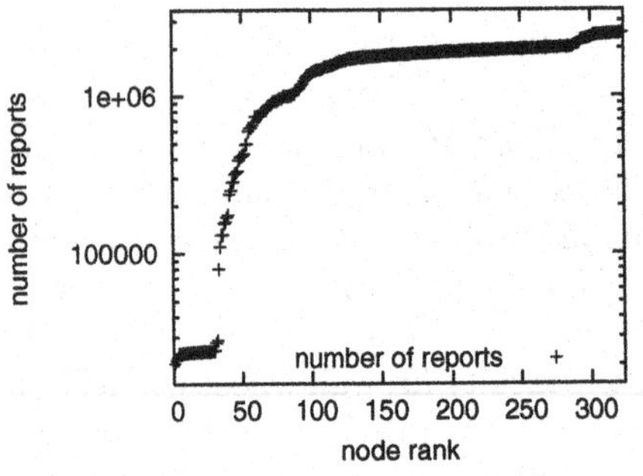

Fig. 1. Rank plot of reports per PlanetLab node

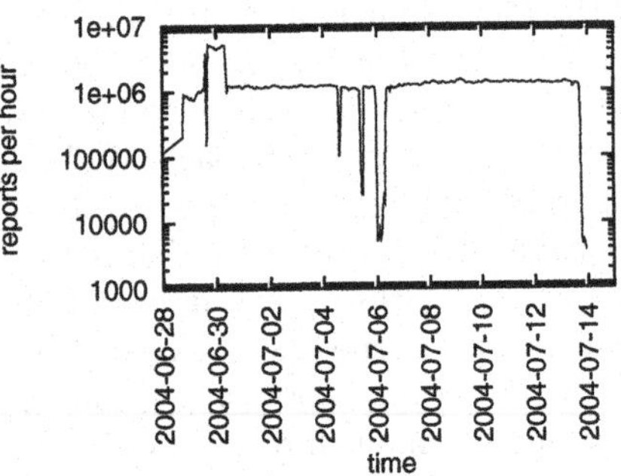

Fig. 2. Reports per hour

As stated above, the whole experiment ran for 14 days at the beginning of July 2004. Figure 2 shows the number of reports the entire measurement system received per hour. Typically, the system ran very smoothly at its design rate of 1 million reports per hour. Taking the mentioned number of an average of almost 250 000 Overnet node, this means that each Overnet servant was probed on average every 15 minutes.

In the initial phase, before July 1st, we experimented with different rate limits and adjusted them in accordance with feedback from the PlanetLab community. Except for one site (Waterloo, Canada) all sites were happy with the traffic the experiment created. (As explained above, the problem was not the bandwidth usage of this experiment but its address cache usage in the firewalls and intrusion detection systems.)

Arround July 5th, we experienced local network problems which kept us from storing the reports in our central data collection facility. Hence the seemingly lower rate.

4.2 Usage Patterns

While the above analysis was concerned with the performance of our measurement application, the collected data reveils also temporal effects caused by the Overnet users.

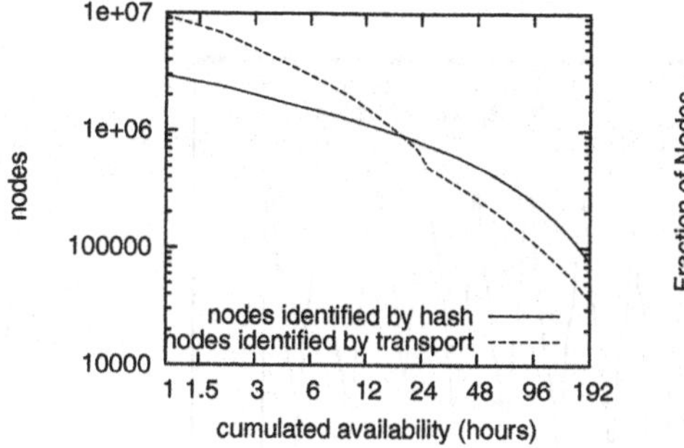

Fig. 3. Cumulated Node Availability

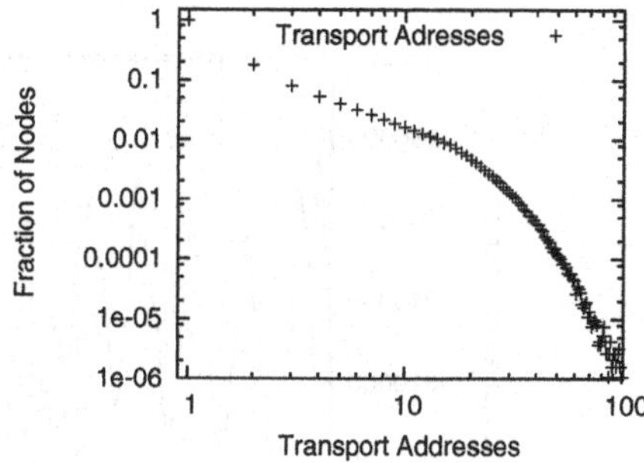

Fig. 4. Transport Addresses seen per Hash Value

Figure 3 shows the availability of servants. In this double-logarithmic plot, the number of nodes is plotted against the nodes' observed cumulated availability. According to our measurement scheme we cannot determine uninterrupted uptime, but only availability defined as time-interval during which we did not discover an outage. To prevent packet loss from spoiling the result, we define a node available if we receive at least one response within an hour of measurement. We chose one hour as sampling interval because the probing application were restarted after that time.

The plot shows two lines. The dashed lines corresponds to the transport addresses (i. e. IP-address and port number pairs), the normal line to the Kademlia overlay addresses. This distinction is necessary because of the use of dynamic IP addresses. I.e. an Overnet node may come and go, each time bearing a different transport address. Accordingly the transport address line is skewed against the line showing the availability of overlay addresses. Even though a transport connection breaks, e.g. by a modem hang-up, the node may be constantly available through an immediate re-dial. [1] calls the differences created by distinct ways to identify a node the *aliasing effect.*

This skew effect that is caused by the typically home users with dial-up connectivity to the Internet is also clearly demonstrated by the curve's elbow at 24 hours which is caused by those DSL providers who cut connections after 24 hours. Nodes behind such an access cannot have uptimes beyond 24 hours. Thus the transport address uptime actually is the combination of a 24h limited distribution and an unlimited distribution.

Figure 4 shows the number of transport addresses seen per Kademlia address. Most nodes have static IP addresses, but others appeared with more than 100 different addresses within our measurement period.

Cum grano salis, the up-time is power-law distributed. 50% of the nodes are available for up to (more than) 6 hours. 18% of the nodes were available for more than 48 hours. It is unclear whether there is a cut-off on the order of one or two weeks. (This could not be decided by a two week measurement.)

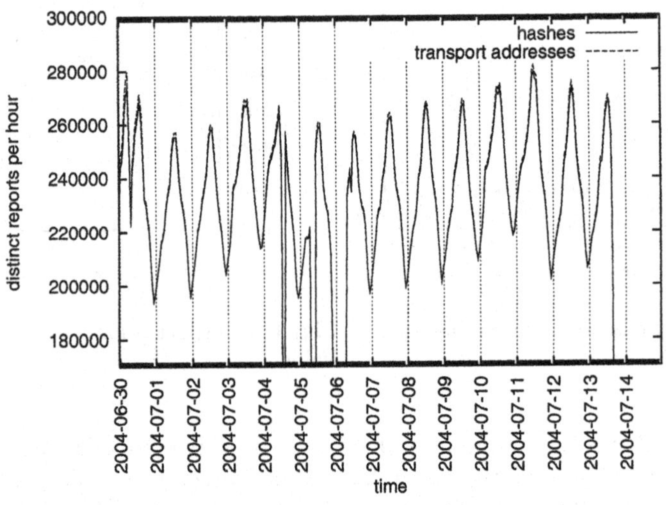

Fig. 5. Number of Hash Values and Transport Addresses seen per hour

Figure 5 shows the number of distinct nodes available at a given hour (time in GMT). There is a strong diurnal pattern with respect to both the transport and overlay addresses, but no significant difference between the two types of addresses. The above mentionend aliasing effect is not visible here because in any given hour, a node is likely to be online with a single transport address.

Figure 6 explains why this pattern is visible even without correction for local timezones. The figure shows that most Overnet nodes are located in Asia. Note the log-scale of the plot. IP addresses were mapped to time zones in two steps. First we used a snapshot of BGP data from `www.routeviews.org` to map the address to an AS number. To map AS numbers to time zones, we utilized the longitude column of `http://netgeo.caida.org/aslatlong.txt`. Of course this method is far from perfect, but it gives an rough overview of node distribution.

One source of error is that all addresses are mapped to the headquarter of their origin AS. Furthermore the routing table used did not contain entries for all prefixes. But in summary we were only unable to locate 796136 (8.3%) of all addresses.

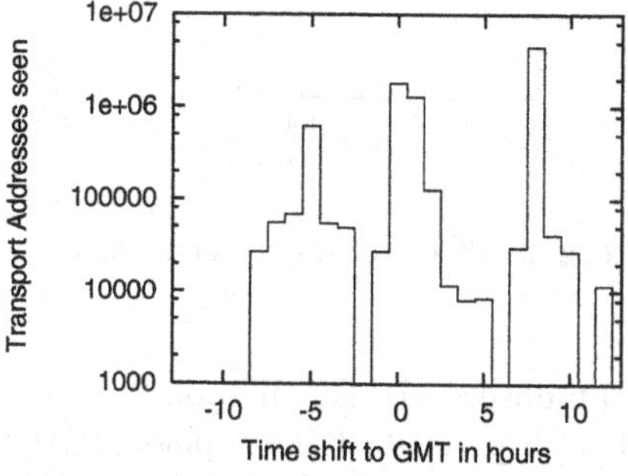

Fig. 6. IP Addresses per time zone

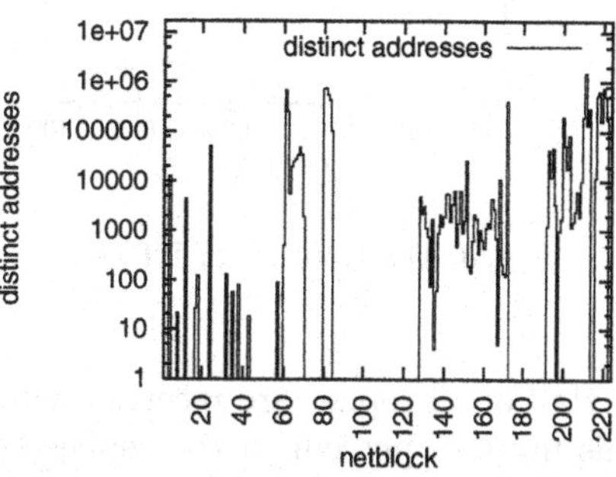

Fig. 7. Number of distinct transport addresses per /8 netblock

4.3 Overnet Node Distribution

During the entire measurement over 9 million distinct transport (=underlay) addresses were encountered. The difference between the number of overlay and underlay addresses is again due to the presence of machines with dynamic IP addresses.

Figure 7 shows the distribution of the encountered IP addresses over the IP address space. (Addresses were binned into /8 prefixes.) One can clearly see the large currently unassigned chunks between 89/8 and 126/8, as well as between 173/8 and 190/8. The usage of the remaining net-blocks shows huge deviations. (Note the logarithmic axis of ordinates.) The most densely populated regions remain only about one order of magnitude behind the theoretical maximum (upper edge of the plot box). Typically, the regions bear between 100 and 100 000 Overnet nodes.

4.4 Round-Trip Times

Figure 8 depicts the distribution of experienced round-trip times, and figure 9 the CCDF thereof. The resolution for the binning of values was 10 milliseconds. Note that these are application-level round-trip times, i.e. they include all processing done in the underlying operating systems as well as the time the application needs to create the reply. The peak in this graph is at arround 250 ms, which appears to be a typical round trip time between two Overnet applications across the Internet.

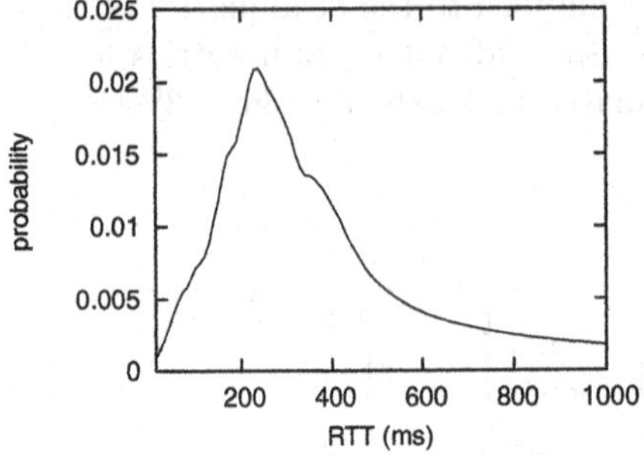

Fig. 8. Distribution of RTTs

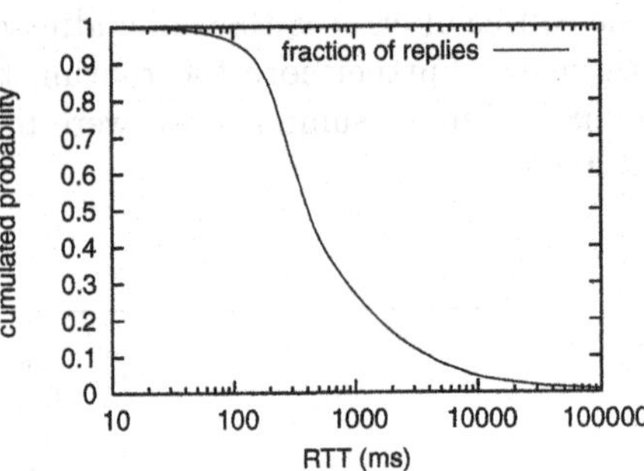

Fig. 9. CCDF of RTT distribution

Half of all replies are received within 410 milliseconds. But it took 8.71 seconds until 95 percent of the replies arrived. 1.15 percent of the replies arrived after one minute and later. A few valid replies even arrived after more than one hour! Such extremes are typical for power-law distributions. The double-logarithmic plot of the results (figure 10) in fact suggests that round-trip times above 250 milliseconds follow a power-law distribution, with no cut-off being visible after two weeks of measurement. Only a longer measurement could reveal where the cut-off appears.

This result is astonishing since we do not know of any obvious reason that would cause a rather sharp on-set of a pretty exact power-law distribution that spans over at least five orders of magnitude. We can only speculate about over-dimensioned application layer message queues, processes delayed by swapping the system memory, and scheduling peculiarities.

If analyzed in detail, the RTT measurement provides more surprises. E.g., there is a distinct dip in figure 8 at arround 320 milliseconds for which we do not have an explanation at the moment. The same holds for the three small bumps between 2.5 and 50 seconds in figure 10. We can again only speculate about interference of the Overnet application's message queue with the underlying operating system.

5 Conclusion and Outlook

In this paper, we presented a measurement study of the Overnet network. With the help of more than 300 PlanetLab nodes, we probed every hour 1 million Overnet servants for a period of two weeks. We described both, the design of our measurement application and the problems we encountered when setting up the measurement. These problems are rooted in the fact that although we measured at a very low rate (1.6 messages per second for the probing nodes, 4 messages per hour for the probed nodes), we communicated with a considerable number of destinations. Since we expect such communication patterns to become more and more common with the spread of more sophisticated peer-to-peer applications,

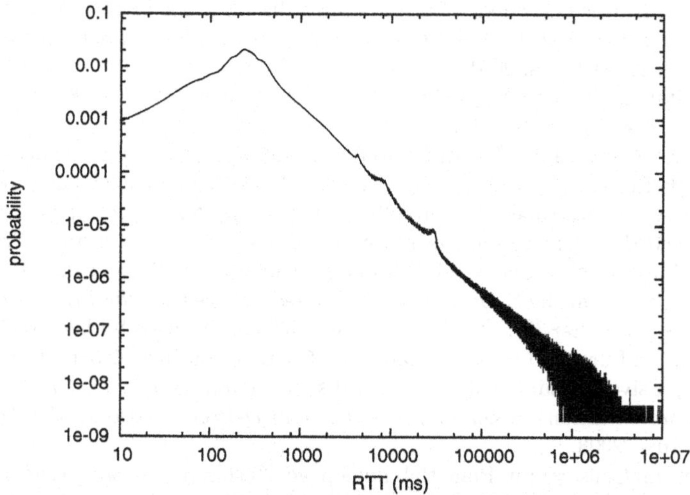

Fig. 10. Distribution of RTTs

we recommend addressing this problem in operating systems, as well as in firewall and intrusion detection software.

Concerning the measurement results, we determined the fundamental parameters of the Overnet network: network size, node availability, and node distribution. Unlike most measurement studies in the field of peer-to-peer networking, we successfully documented the global view on two weeks in the life of a heavily used file-sharing network. Moreover, we collected more than a total of 480 million RTT measurements from hundreds of measurement sites worldwide. Currently, we are still analyzing that data to localize Overnet nodes with the help of network tomography methods. This analysis is complicated by the fact that our approach was to capture the actual overlay RTTs, not the Internet RTTs typically measured by the *ping* tool. Besides that, we are still investigating the unexpected peculiarities that we found in the RTT distribution.

References

[1] Ranjita Bhagwan, Stefan Savage, and Geoffrey Voelker. Understanding availability. In *Proceedings of the 2003 International Workshop on Peer-to-Peer Systems (IPTPS)*, Berkeley, CA, February 2003.

[2] Brent Chun, David Culler, Timothy Roscoe, Andy Bavier, Larry Peterson, Mike Wawrzoniak, and Mic Bowman. PlanetLab: An Overlay Testbed for Broad-Coverage Services. *ACM SIGCOMM Computer Communication Review*, 33(3):00–00, July 2003.

[3] Curt Cramer and Thomas Fuhrmann. On the Fundamental Communication Abstraction Supplied by P2P Overlay Networks. *European Transactions on Telecommunications.* To be published.

[4] Allen B. Downey. Evidence for long-tailed distributions in the internet. In *Proceedings of the First ACM SIGCOMM Workshop on Internet Measurement*, pages 229–241. ACM Press, 2001.

[5] C. Huitema. An anycast prefix for 6to4 relay routers. RFC 3068, Internet Engineering Task Force, June 2001.

[6] Internet2 Consortium. Internet2 homepage, 2004. `http://www.internet2.edu`.

[7] Karthik Lakshminarayanan and Venkata N. Padmanabhan. Some findings on the network performance of broadband hosts. In *Proceedings of the 2003 ACM SIGCOMM conference on Internet measurement*, pages 45–50. ACM Press, 2003.

[8] Petar Maymounkov and David Mazières. Kademlia: A Peer-to-Peer Information System Based on the XOR Metric. In *Revised Papers from the First International Workshop on Peer-to-Peer Systems*, pages 53–65. Springer-Verlag, 2002.

[9] Hirokazu Miura and Miki Yamamoto. Content routing with network support using passive measurement in content distribution networks. *IEICE Transactions on Communications, Special Issue on Content Delivery Networks*, E86-B(6):1805–1811, June 2003.

[10] PlanetLab Consortium. Planetlab homepage, 2004. `http://www.planet-lab.org`.

[11] Sylvia Ratnasamy, Paul Francis, Mark Handley, Richard Karp, and Scott Shenker. A Scalable Content-Addressable Network. In *Proceedings of the SIGCOMM 2001 conference*, pages 161–172. ACM Press, 2001.

[12] Y. Rekhter, B. Moskowitz, D. Karrenberg, G. J. de Groot, and E. Lear. Address allocation for private internets. RFC 1918, Internet Engineering Task Force, February 1996.

[13] J. F. Reynolds and J. B. Postel. Assigned numbers. RFC 1700, Internet Engineering Task Force, October 1994.

[14] A. Rowstron and P. Druschel. Pastry: Scalable, distributed object location and routing for large-scale peer-to-peer systems. In *Proceedings of the IFIP/ACM International Conference on Distributed Systems Platforms (Middleware) 2001*, Heidelberg, Germany, November 2001.

[15] Ion Stoica, Robert Morris, David Karger, M. Frans Kaashoek, and Hari Balakrishnan. Chord: A scalable peer-to-peer lookup service for internet applications. In *Proceedings of the SIGCOMM 2001 conference*, pages 149–160. ACM Press, 2001.

Adjusting the ns-2 Emulation Mode to a Live Network*

Daniel Mahrenholz and Svilen Ivanov

University of Magdeburg, Universitätsplatz 2, D-39106 Magdeburg, Germany
mahrenho@ivs.cs.uni-magdeburg.de

Abstract The network simulator ns-2 implements both wireless networks and *emulation* – a feature that allows to simulate a network environment among real stations. In contrast to a discrete event simulation an emulation is affected by various system parameters. The understanding of the impact of those parameters is crucial to obtain valid results from an emulation experiment. In this paper we evaluate a modified version of the ns-2 that has been optimized for emulations. We analyze the effect of different parameter settings in various experiments and compare the results with measurements in a live network.

1 Introduction

Real-time simulation (*emulation*) is a modeling technique where simulator objects reproduce a timing behavior similar or equal to the timing behavior of the simulated entities. This technique is used to simulate a desired application environment during an application development process. So it allows testing of different simulated environments with relatively small effort. The main goal is that an application can interact with the simulated environment during the development phase the same way as it would with the real one and so can be deployed later without modification.

The network simulator ns-2 [12] is a widely accepted discrete event network simulator, actively used for wired and wireless network simulations. It has an *emulation* feature [7], i.e. the ability to simulate an arbitrary network in real-time. Discrete event simulation assumes that event execution does not take any (simulation) time. In [10] we showed the problems that arise when the simulation clock runs in real-time. This is because event execution times now have to be considered. We also explained the weaknesses of the current ns-2 implementation that lead to an unpredictable timely behavior and so result in wrong simulation results (especially for wireless networks). We presented some generic modifications to the ns-2 to solve these problems and to highly improve its emulation abilities (s. section 2.1 for a brief overview). In this paper we will study the effects of various system and simulation parameters on the performance and

* This work has been supported by the German Research Foundation (DFG), grant no. NE 837/3-1

correctness of the simulation results. We also take a closer look onto the scaling limits of our approach.

The remainder of our paper is structured as follows. Section 2 describes our emulation environment – the hard- and software setup we are using and the modifications made to improve the ns-2 emulation mode. Section 3 investigates various parameters of the emulation environments and their impact on the performance of the simulator and the accuracy of the emulation results. Section 4 discusses related projects and finally section 5 gives some conclusions and an outlook on further work.

2 Emulation Environment

Our emulation environment consists of a host running a modified version of the ns-2 simulator (s. section 2.1) and a number of Linux machines, one for each node in the simulation. The *live* network in our setup is a virtual network among the Linux machines running the node software. To reduce the number of physical Linux hosts needed for an experiment we use *User-Mode-Linux* (UML) virtual machines. UML is an extended Linux kernel which runs as an application process on top of a Linux host. It has its own network interface and appears as a full-featured operating system for an application running inside. Figure 1 depicts the current setup.

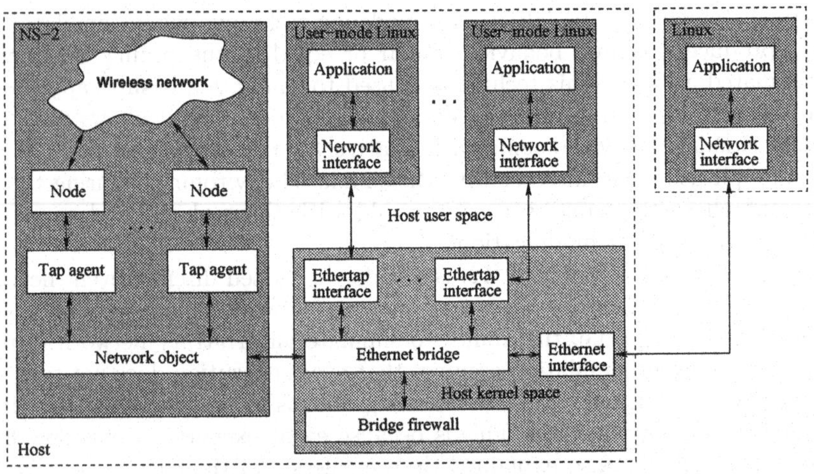

Fig. 1. Emulation Environment Setup

To connect the Linux machines we use separated Ethernet interfaces for the physical hosts and the TAP virtual Ethernet device for the UML machines. To build the virtual network we created an Ethernet bridge in the ns-2 host kernel that connects all TAP devices and the physical Ethernet device into a single

Ethernet network. This virtual network enables all machines to communicate directly with each other. But our goal is to route all traffic through the simulation. So we have to block direct communication using a firewall and only allow traffic through the simulation.

2.1 NS-2 Modifications

Ns-2 already provides an emulation facility, but it proved to be unsuited for the emulation of wireless networks because of various reasons. The major reason is, that event execution times are not considered in the real-time scheduler used for the emulation mode. Additionally the simulator makes excessive use of operating system functions inside the real-time critical event execution loop for the time synchronization and the event logging. These system calls can block the simulator for an unpredictable time – often longer than the timeouts defined in different protocols. This falsifies the execution of the simulation model or even makes it impossible – especially for wireless networks.

Implementation Improvements: This section details the changes made to the ns-2 to improve its overall performance and to increase the accuracy of the virtual simulation clock. These changes can be divided into performance improvements and some changes to the execution of the simulation model. A more detailed explanation can be found in [10].

Time measurement: To synchronize event execution with the system time the ns-2 real-time scheduler uses the system call gettimeofday(). This system call is called very often during a simulation which consumes a lot of time. So we replaced this system call by a function that uses the CPU cycle counter to measure times. Together with the CPU frequency we get $Timestamp = \frac{\#Cycles}{Frequency}$. Such a cycle counter is available in many current CPUs. Of course our approach is only feasible for CPUs that run on a constant frequency or can be configured to do so which is possible in most cases.

Precise Waiting: Before executing the next event the real-time scheduler has to wait until the moment in time the event was planned for. For this it uses a combination of busy waiting and blocking. If the time to the next event t_w is below a certain threshold t_t (1ms by default) the scheduler performs busy waiting. Otherwise it sleeps for t_w. The problem now is that the process does not regain control of the CPU exactly at the planned time but with a delay of d_w. To increase the precision we now change the sleeping time to $(t_w - d_{wmax})$. We chose d_{wmax} such that it is greater than a considerable part of the wakeup delays and perform busy waiting afterwards. This additional busy waiting introduces a higher CPU utilization and so there is a tradeoff between precision and CPU load (s. section 3.4).

Disk I/O reduction: The simulator stores information about events happening during a simulation to disk. This event logging is implemented as part of the event execution. Although the simulator maintains a memory buffer to accumulate trace information before writing them to disk, disk writes are still performed as part of the event execution. These I/O operations block the simulator process for a certain time and so can delay the execution of events. To solve this problem we divided the simulator into two processes – a high priority process that executes the events and a low priority process that collects the trace data and stores them to disk. Both communicate through a non-blocking ring buffer in a shared memory segment. So the logging cannot longer block the simulator directly. But the disk I/O still can interfere with the execution of the simulator process. So in order to reduce the number of write operations during the simulation or to avoid them at all in many scenarios, the logging process compresses the data before storing it using the zlib library.

Time Correction: The performance improvements described in the previous section increase the accuracy of real-time simulations and increase the overall event throughput. But these improvements cannot avoid delays in the event execution, especially under a high system load or when simulating complex scenarios. Furthermore, regardless how big these delays are, they all lead to an incorrect execution of the simulation model. This and our proposed solution will be explained in the following.

The simulation model is executed using the time of the virtual clock (t_{Vc}) which is constantly updated in the main loop of the simulation scheduler. Everytime the scheduler checks whether it can execute a new event from the event queue, it reads the current time from the system clock and updates the virtual clock. Now consider an event E_1 that should be executed at t_{E_1}. The scheduler waits until that moment and then executes the event. Because of the high resolution of the used timer, the event is executed with a measurable delay at $(t_{E_1} + \Delta t_{E_1})$. Now assume that E_1 schedules another event E_2 with a time difference of $\Delta p_{1,2}$. Because all simulation objects assume that all events are executed at the exact moments in time, events are scheduled relatively to the current time (t_{Vc}). But compared to the system clock E_2 is scheduled for $(t_{E_1} + \Delta t_{E_1} + \Delta p_{1,2})$ and will be executed at $(t_{E_1} + \Delta t_{E_1} + \Delta p_{1,2} + \Delta t_{E_2})$. This clearly shows that the current method accumulates the delays inside a chain of dependent events. This delay accumulation is even more serious in overload situations. If we have more than one concurrent chain of events then it is likely that the delay in different chains increases differently. This can lead to changes in the chronological order of events and so falsifies the simulation model. To solve this problem we use the planned execution time that is stored inside the event object. When an event is executed, we set t_{Vc} to the planned time. So dependent events will be scheduled relatively to the planned execution time defined by the simulation model. This does not avoid a late execution, compared to the system clock, but prevents the accumulation of errors. Furthermore, if the CPU is not constantly overloaded, it reduces previous delays.

3 Emulation Tuning

Before we can tune the parameters of the emulation environment we have to understand their impact on the setup. In this section we will first explain the experimental setup used to run all the tests. Then we will look on the parameters that need to be determined and setup in order to adjust the emulation to the behaviour of a live network. Afterwards we discuss the impact of various parameters on the performance of the simulator and the accuracy of the emulation results. From this we finally derive some guidelines to handle the tradeoff between accuracy and performance.

3.1 Experimental Setup

Figure 1 already showed the principle experimental setup. Now we will have a closer look onto the used hard- and software. All emulation experiments were run using the User-Mode-Linux machines. On the one hand this requires the most resources on the simulation host but on the other hands allows the most accurate measurements. This is because of two reasons. First we have a highly precise and perfectly synchronized clock in all components because all access the cycle counter of the same CPU. Second we can ignore the transmission overhead caused by the virtual Ethernet. We measured the overhead and it was below 1.5% of the end-to-end transmission time. Our simulation host was a AMD XP 2400+ with 512 MB of RAM running the vanilla 2.6.1 Linux kernel. We used ns-2 version 2.27 as the basis for our modifications. We setup all the UML machines to use at most 32MB of RAM and the logging process of the simulator to use 100MB for the compressed trace file. So we avoided all disk I/O operations during a simulation run because all trace data fit into the compressed in-memory file. Inside the UML machines we used the same 2.6.1 Linux kernel as on the host system.

For the live-network measurements we used different combinations of laptops running Linux kernel version 2.4.25 and 2.6.3 with different 802.11b wireless network cards to compensate for driver specific effects. Our traffic generator was a slightly modified ping version. We added a command line option to specify a deadline for the receiving of the response packet and some statistic extensions. All packets that meet the deadline are counted as *on-time packets.*

3.2 Initial Parameter Setup

The first step to adjust the emulation to the real-world is a careful parameter setup. The most important parameters are the transmission bit rate, the error probability, the transmission power, and the retransmission counters. Additionally the node distance and the traffic pattern are important for the simulation scenario. The transmission bit rate, transmission power, and retransmission counters are values that can be simply specified in the simulator setup and on the network interface. For all experiments we used a bit rate of 2Mbit/s and set the transmission power and retransmission counters to the standard values reported by the wireless network adapter. The node distance was set to 2m in our tests. The value for the error probability can not be setup that easy. It has to be measured in the real world and then can be specified in the emulation.

Ns-2 allows to generate errors on the sender or the receiver side. Because we try to model errors on the wireless medium we decided to generate errors at the receiver. So a packet send as broadcast is not received by all or none nodes but by any possible number. To measure the error rate we use ICMP echo request/response packets and count transmitted and received packets. To measure the raw packet loss rate we have to make sure that there are no retransmissions on the MAC layer. An effective way to enforce this is to use broadcast packets. The ping command can send echo requests to a broadcast address, but normally responses are send to the unicast address of the requesting host. To circumvent this behaviour we specify a broadcast MAC address on both hosts as the MAC address of the opposite host. So when using a ping with an unicast IP address, the packets are send as broadcasts in both directions. With this setup we send 100.000 packets with a rate of 100 per second and counted the received packets. From these numbers the raw packet error rate can be computed. Assume the ICMP error rate is $p_{ICMP} = \frac{\#Received}{\#Send}$. We only receive an echo response if both packets does not get lost. So we can compute

$$p_{ICMP} = 1 - (1 - p_{raw})(1 - p_{raw})$$
$$p_{raw} = 1 - \sqrt{1 - p_{ICMP}}$$

We ran several measurements with small (8 byte payload) and large (1000 byte payload) packets in an undisturbed and a normal office environment and obtained the numbers shown in table 1 that then were used for the following experiments.

Environment	p_{ICMP}	p_{raw}
office, small packets	0.046%	0.022%
office, large packets	0.6%	0.3%
undisturbed, small packets	0%	0%
undisturbed, large packets	0%	0%

Table 1. Wireless error probabilities

As the first experiment we ran a ping with an adaptive transmission rate of at least 100 packets per second. Adaptive means that we send a new packet at least every 10ms or immediately after receiving a response before this time. This way we performed a bandwidth measurement. Because of the adaptive sending the value can be above 100 packets per second. We additionally specified a deadline of 5ms for this test and counted all packets as *on-time packets* where we got a response within this time. The deadline has no effect on the trasmission of packets, it is only used for statistics. Table 2 shows the result for the measurement with small packets and no RTS/CTS (s. section 3.3 for more details).

Measurements for large packets and other parameter settings will be presented below.

	Emulation	Live network
Bandwidth [pkt/s]	286.85 (±0.290)	307.17 (14.58)
average RTT [ms]	3.34 (±0.003)	2.77 (0.017)
on-time [%]	99.84 (±0.000)	99.66 (0.180)

Table 2. Comparison Emulation/Live network ping

All emulation test were run with the method of independent replications. The presented numbers for the live network are the average calculated over 30 tests and the root-mean-square deviation (its square-root for better readability in brackets). For the emulation we give a 95%-confidence interval also calculated over the 30 different tests. The bandwidth is the number of successfully transmitted packets per second. The average round-trip-time (RTT) is the average time difference between sending the request packet and receiving the response. Each test run for either at least 10 minutes or 100.000 packets to get a broad result set.

The results show that we get comparable results in the emulation and in the live network. The throughput is slightly smaller in the emulation and we have larger runaway results. We can also see that the confidence interval in the emulation is small.

3.3 Parameter Impact on the Simulator Performance

In this section we will take a closer look on the effects that different parameters have on the performance and the results of the emulation. We have chosen the scenarios so that we could verify all the results in a real-world measurement. Understanding these effects is crucial to get usable results from an emulation because choosing a wrong set of parameters can falsify an emulation. So the following experiments should help to identify an erroneous simulator behaviour. The next chapter will then discuss possible corrections to obtain usable results at the cost of lesser accuracy.

The first parameter we want to discuss is the use of the RTS/CTS frame exchange sequence in the 802.11b MAC layer. The RTS/CTS mechanism tries to overcome the hidden-station problem. If two senders are far away, but want to sent to the same or colocated stations, they cannot sense each other on the medium due to being out of range of each other, so their transmissions would collide at the receiver. With RTS/CTS, the sender issues a small RTS frame, which is answered by the receiver with a small CTS frame. As both frames contain the length of the transmission that is about to be started, all receivers of any of these frames know about this transmission and do not interfere with it.

To measure the effect of the RTS/CTS usage we used the modified ping with large packets (1000 byte payload) and an adaptive transmission rate with at least 100 packets per second. Because of the large packet size we increased the deadline to 15ms. The raw error rate was set to the one measured in the office environment (0.3%). We ran both measurements with and without RTS/CTS each 30 times. We used large packets for this experiment because RTS/CTS makes no sense for small packets in a live network.

	CTS/RTS enabled		CTS/RTS disabled	
	Emulation	Live network	Emulation	Live network
Bandwidth [pkt/s]	78.17 (±0.030)	74.02 (0.020)	86.24 (±0.020)	80.36 (1.130)
average RTT [ms]	12.55 (±0.002)	13.46 (0.003)	11.42 (±0.001)	12.38 (0.020)
on-time [%]	99.83 (±0.010)	99.93 (0.050)	99.86 (±0.000)	99.99 (0.020)
CPU utilization	44.82 (±0.020)	—	39.67 (±0.020)	—

Table 3. 1000 byte payload; 15ms deadline; office environment

The table 3 shows the results from this experiment. In both cases the emulation delivers a slightly higher throughput than the live network. When we look back to the results in table 2 we see that the emulation delivers a lower throughput for very small packets. So for the average case the throughput will be the same in both scenarios. The on-time packets are almost the same in all measurements. Furthermore we can see that the use of RTS/CTS has the same effect in the emulation and the live network. In both cases it results in an about 10% decrease of the throughput. But we can also see that the use of RTS/CTS increases the CPU utilization of the simulator by about 12% due to the fact that it now has to simulate a larger number of events.

The second experiment tests the effect of different error rates. We compare the measurements of the previously used office scenario (0.3% error rate) with an artificial scenario (*Noisy*) with a much higher value of 5%. For both scenarios we run the adaptive ping test with small and large packets and a 15ms deadline.

	8 byte payload		1000 byte payload	
	Office (0.3%)	Noisy (5%)	Office (0.3%)	Noisy (5%)
Bandwidth [pkt/s]	286.85 (±0.290)	240.27 (±0.130)	86.24 (±0.020)	74.08 (±0.060)
average RTT [ms]	3.34 (±0.003)	3.69 (±0.001)	11.42 (±0.001)	12.60 (±0.008)
on-time [%]	99.84 (±0.000)	99.78 (±0.000)	99.86 (±0.000)	81.92 (±0.100)
CPU utilization	80.2 (±0.070)	74.75 (±0.090)	39.67 (±0.020)	37.45 (±0.020)

Table 4. no RTS/CTS; 15ms deadline

The table 4 shows the results for these measurements. We notice several things in this experiment. First that the throughput decreases – an expected result because we lose more packets. Second that the average RTT increases. This is due to the fact that we now have more retransmissions on the MAC layer. As a consequence the percentage of on-time packets drops in the second measurement because the average is already short below the deadline. A more surprising result is the reduced CPU utilization. It seams that the reduced overall number of transmitted packets outweighs the simulated retransmissions which increase the number of events to simulate.

The third test will investigate the effects caused by one of our modifications to the ns-2 simulator. As described in section 2.1 we introduced a correction time to compensate for imprecise system calls – the blocking sleep in our case. We reduce the blocking time and use busy waiting up to the starting time of an event. This busy waiting increases the CPU load. As a result other processes in the system receive less CPU time to work because the simulator process runs with a high priority. This especially effects the UML machines running on the same host because they are blocked by the simulator. We ran the test with large packets, no RTS/CTS and a deadline of 15ms. To get a high precision we set d_{wmax} (s. section 2.1) to 2ms. Then we reduced this value to 0.2ms which results in a lower precision.

	high precision	low precision
Bandwidth [pkt/s]	86.24 (±0.020)	88.02 (±0.030)
average RTT [ms]	11.42 (±0.001)	11.18 (±0.002)
on-time [%]	99.86 (±0.000)	99.86 (±0.010)
CPU utilization	39.67 (±0.020)	5.25 (±0.020)

Table 5. no RTS/CTS; 1000 byte payload; 15ms deadline

The results from this experiment are shown in table 5. From this values we clearly see that the low precision settings result in a significantly lower CPU utilization. All other values are almost equal. So the lower precision of the emulation does not effect our ping application. In section 3.4 we take a closer look on the internal behaviour of the simulator and show that this setting really results in a lower precision although it can not directly be seen in these results.

The last experiment will test the scalability of our solution. Now we increase the number of nodes from two to six and run the same ping tests pairwise. In the simulation we configured the three node pairs to use different wireless channels. So they should not interfere with each other and the results of each pair should be comparable to the two node scenario. As in the third test we run the six node scenario twice, first with a high precision and second with the lower one. In both cases we transmitted large packets using RTS/CTS and compare the results with the two node measurement in the live network (s. table 3).

The results of this experiment can be seen in table 6. The first measurement delivers results completely different from the live network. The bandwidth is roughly the half and the on-time packets are only a tenth. The CPU utilization is also very high. This clearly shows that we caused an overload situation. The second measurement with a lower precision in contrast delivers results that match the reference values. The reasons for these results will be discussed in the next

	high precision		low precision	
	6 nodes	2 nodes	6 nodes	2 nodes
Bandwidth [pkt/s]	45.41 (±0.070)	74.02 (0.020)	75.43 (±0.040)	74.02 (0.020)
average RTT [ms]	18.54 (±0.014)	13.46 (0.003)	12.74 (±0.004)	13.46 (0.003)
on-time [%]	9.64 (±0.010)	99.93 (0.050)	98.73 (±0.020)	99.93 (0.050)
CPU utilization	73.94 (±0.060)	—	45.12 (±0.060)	—

Table 6. RTS/CTS; 1000 byte payload; 15ms deadline

section. One might wonder why six nodes do not work at a CPU utilization of the simulator of about 75% because table 4 clearly shows that we run a valid emulation with 80%. The answer is simple if we look on the remaining CPU time available for the UML machines. In the previous experiment the remaining 20% were distributed to two machines so each virtual machine could use about 10%. In this experiment the remaining 25% distributes to six virtual machines – about 4% for each, which obviously is not enough. With the decreased precision we now have about 9% per virtual machine left which is sufficient.

3.4 Trading Accuracy for Performance

As seen in the previous section we can improve the simulator throughput and so the scalability by adjusting the compensation (safe) time for imprecise system calls. We also said that this reduces the precision of the emulation. By only looking at the results of the experiment this statement is questionable. So we will present some more measurements that will prove it. With the precision or accuracy of the emulation we mean the difference between a planned and the actual execution of an event. The planned time is the time defined by the simulation model. To measure the difference between both times we extended the scheduler to record the planned execution time and the time of the system clock of every event that it executes. We ran this measurement for the two and six node scenario. The results look similar but we will only discuss it for the six node scenario because it makes an important difference there.

The figure 2 shows the distribution of delays. With the high safe time we have an upper bound of $100\mu s$ and more than 90% of all events with a delay below $30\mu s$. With the reduced safe time we still have about 67% of all events delayed less than $30\mu s$ but now 28% with a delay of $100\mu s$ up to 1ms and even some events with a delay of more than 1ms. For our applications such delays are not a serious problem. But transmitting packets with larger delays to the receiving application increases the likelihood of changes in the application behavior. So the application running on top of the emulation system defines bounds for the precision of the simulator.

After looking at the results of this measurement we will explain the reasons for this simulator behaviour. A high CPU utilization is mainly caused by the busy waiting inside the scheduler. So reducing the busy waiting time decreases the CPU utilization. Busy waiting is required if the execution of the next event is scheduled for a time below the threshold where we safely could use a blocking

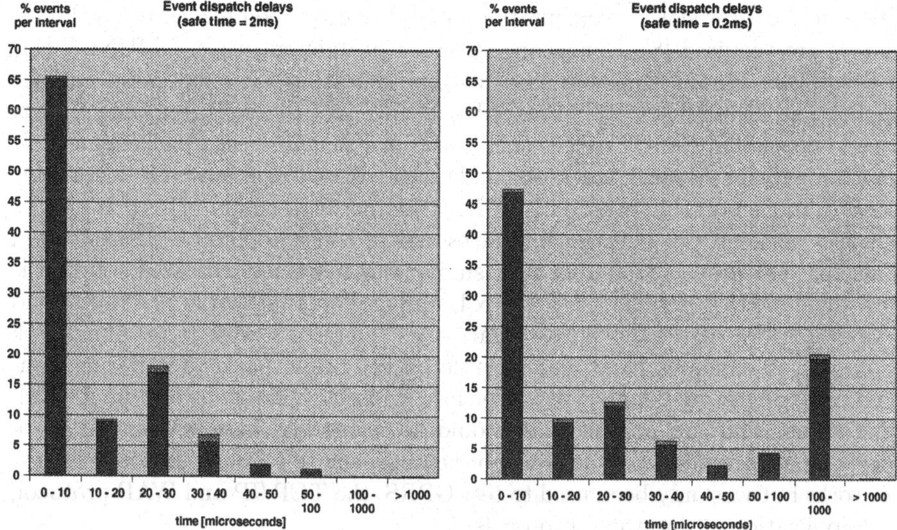

Fig. 2. Delay distribution with high/low safe time

wait and some busy waiting afterwards. Increasing the number of nodes not only increases the number of packets to simulate. It also significantly increases the probability that the starting time of two consecutive events differ less than the safe value. So just placing a new event between two others can convert a lot of sleeping time into busy waiting time which highly increases the CPU utilization. As a side effect this leads to less remaining CPU time for the virtual machines because they are blocked during the busy waiting of the simulator. So the busy waiting places restrictions on the event throughput and on the scalability of our approach especially when using multiple virtual machines on the same host. Solutions to this scalability problem are the use of multiple CPU systems and the distribution of the applications to external hosts.

4 Related Work

There are a lot of network simulators available. They all differ in their purposes and technologies. The majority of all network simulators are discrete event simulators that determine the network behavior on different detail levels. NS-2 is widely used but there are other universal network simulators like SWiMNet [2], GloMoSim [6]. They provide an important method to test network protocols and topologies but share some major problems. They use their own protocol implementations and so cannot be used to test the interaction and behaviour of actual protocol implementations used in operating systems and network devices used in live networks. Additionally they cannot be directly used with the traffic generated by different applications. To overcome these problems in order to study actual protocol implementations under realistic conditions network emulators are required [8]. Emulators can work in different ways. EMUNET [11] is a software library that simulates a communication network inside an user application. Dummynet [13] (FreeBSD), x-SIM [3] (x-kernel), and the Hitbox pseudo-device [5] (SunOS) are kernel extensions that intercept packets on their way through the network stack to simulate the effects experienced in a real network. A more portable solution is ONE (Ohio network emulator) [1]. It acts as a router between two network interfaces and provides adjustable transmission, queueing and propagation delays. A similar but more sophisticated solution is provided by NIST Net [4]. It is a Linux kernel module that works as a router and is optimized for high bandwidth scenarios and supports a wide range of network protocols. It emulates fixed and variable packet delay; packet reordering; random and congestion-dependent packet loss; packet duplications and bandwidth limitations. The last project that should be mentioned here is Seawind [9], a wireless network emulator. It is a generic approach to emulate various wireless networks but was only been used to test GPRS, the TCP/IP and WAP protocol, and applications using these protocols.

5 Conclusion and Further Work

In this paper we showed that the combination of the flexibility of a discrete event simulation with real applications in a general-purpose environment is feasible even for simulated wireless networks. We presented some changes to the widely used ns-2 simulator to optimize its behavior in the emulation mode. In several experiments we measured the impact of different parameter settings on the performance of the emulation system and the accuracy of the measured results. We proposed a method to configure the simulation using real-world parameters and verified by experiment that the emulation behaves the same way as the live network. We also recognized that our current setup imposes some tight limitations on the scalability of the simulation complexity. So future work will mainly focus on a distributed setup. In a first step we distributed the applications running on top of the simulated network to separated hosts. This already significantly increased the number of possible nodes in the simulation. Later we will study the distribution of the simulator itself, either by a separation and distribution of independent parts of a simulated network to different simulator instances (as in the six node scenario) or possibly by applying our modifications to the parallel distributed version of ns-2.

References

[1] M. Allman and S. Ostermann. One: The Ohio Network Emulator. Technical report, Ohio University, 1996.

[2] Azzedine Boukerche, Sajal K. Das, and Alessandro Fabbri. SWiMNet: A Scalable Parallel Simulation Testbed for Wireless and Mobile Networks. *Wireless Networks*, 7(5):467–486, 2001.

[3] Lawrence S. Brakmo and Larry L. Peterson. Experiences with Network Simulation. In *Measurement and Modeling of Computer Systems*, pages 80–90, 1996.
[4] Mark Carson and Darrin Santay. NIST Net: a Linux-based network emulation tool. *SIGCOMM Comput. Commun. Rev.*, 33(3):111–126, 2003.
[5] P. Danzig, Z. Liu, and L. Yan. An Evaluation of TCP Vegas by Live Emulation. In *Proceedings of ACM SIGMetrics '95*, 1995.
[6] Lokesh Bajaj et al. GloMoSim: A Scalable Network Simulation Environment. Technical Report 990027, 13, 1999.
[7] K. Fall. Network emulation in the VINT/NS simulator. *Proceedings of the fourth IEEE Symposium on Computers and Communications*, 1999.
[8] S. Floyd and V. Paxson. Difficulties in simulating the Internet. *IEEE/ACM Transactions on Networking*, 9(4):392–403, August 2001.
[9] M. Kojo, A. Gurtov, J. Mannner, P. Sarolahti, T. Alanko, and K. Raatikainen. Seawind: a wireless network emulator, 2001.
[10] Daniel Mahrenholz and Svilen Ivanov. Real-Time Network Emulation with ns-2. In *Proceedings of DS-RT'04*, Budapest, Hungary, October 2004.
[11] Xiannong Meng. EMUNET: Design and Implementation - A Debugging Aid for Distributed Programs in TCP/IP Based Network.
[12] The Network Simulator ns-2. http://www.isi.edu/nsnam/ns/.
[13] Luigi Rizzo. Dummynet: a simple approach to the evaluation of network protocols. *ACM Computer Communication Review*, 27(1):31–41, 1997.

Exploiting Regular Hot-Spots for Drive-thru Internet

Jörg Ott and Dirk Kutscher

Technologiezentrum Informatik (TZI), Universität Bremen,
Postfach 330440, 28334 Bremen, Germany
{jo|dku}@tzi.uni-bremen.de

Abstract IEEE 802.11 WLAN technology has become an inexpensive, yet powerful access technology that is targeted at mobile users that remain within reach of the hot-spot. Such hot-spots are usually provided by a wireless Internet service provider (WISP) in locations often frequented by travelers. Past measurements have shown that WLAN is even able to support mobile users passing by without stopping and "hopping" from one hot-spot to the next. The Drive-thru Internet project develops a disconnection-tolerant architecture that enables such unconventional usage of WLAN technology. In this paper, we focus on two prime aspects relevant for interworking with existing hot-spot installations: we investigate the impact of auto-configuration and authentication and present performance results for a driving user accessing the Internet via a hot-spot using different access link technologies. We finally suggest enhancements to hot-spot architectures to facilitate Drive-thru Internet access.

1 Introduction

Mobile users and nomadic computing are today supported by two classes of networks: On one hand, cellular networks (GSM, GPRS, UMTS) aim at providing ubiquitous connectivity, even across different service providers. However, their price-performance ratio is rather poor and temporary disconnections may occur despite the wide coverage for a variety of reasons. On the other hand, IEEE 802.11 WLAN hot-spots do not aim at seamless connectivity; their limited reach implies disconnection periods while the user is moving between locations. Usually, manual user interaction is required, e.g., to suspend and resume communication applications but also for reconfiguration [OK04c]. Nevertheless, the availability of high data rates at acceptable cost render WLAN technology an attractive alternative for mobile usage scenarios. Because of unlicensed operation and low investment and operational cost, WLAN has become an inexpensive commodity and the number of public WLAN hot-spot installations is ever-increasing: besides hotels, cafés and the like particularly airports, train stations, gas stations, and service areas are covered, i.e., places serving commuters and travellers on the road. [1]

Numerous approaches are pursued that combine access to different service providers or integrate WLANs and cellular networks to enhance connectivity (particularly for WLANs), improve the achievable data rate, and minimize cost (for cellular networks) to keep users *always best connetced* [RCC+04] [ZWS+03] [Lei01]. While

[1] Examples include Agip gas stations and MAXI service areas in Germany, Neste A24 gas stations in Estonia, and Texaco service stations in the UK as well as truck stops in the US.

such approaches render existing wireless technologies more attractive to users, the issue of temporary disconnection (from an affordable high performance link) remains.

In the Drive-thru Internet project [OK04a], we leverage conveniently located WLAN hot-spots to provide Internet services to mobile users moving at high speeds (in vehicles). The objective of Drive-thru Internet is to enable service access by using *intermittent connectivity*, i.e., connectivity that is only temporarily established while a user traverses the coverage area of a WLAN hot-spot. We have developed an architecture that allows (existing) applications to take advantage of such potentially short and unpredictable periods [OK04b]. A key requirement for Drive-thru Internet is the ability to operate in today's *existing* WLAN infrastructure, which mostly consists of public hot-spots. We allow for incremental deployment by avoiding dependencies on specific service providers and hot-spot architectures. To achieve this independence, we need to take the characteristics of commercial hot-spot installations into account and develop support functions that allow us to use an existing hot-spot "as is" for Drive-thru Internet.

This paper explores the issues related to obtaining Internet access from existing WLAN hot-spots in a way suitable for Drive-thru Internet: we investigate implications of access link characteristics and analyze steps towards efficient user authentication and access authorization. In section 2, we review representative architectures for commercial hot spots and outline the Drive-thru Internet concept in section 3. Related work concerning these two fields is discussed in the respective sections. We then report on our findings from real and experimental hot-spot settings and introduce our approach towards enabling the use of commercial hot-spots in section 4 where we also derive desirable hot-spot properties. Section 5 concludes this paper and suggests future work.

2 Wireless LAN Hot-Spots

Early WLAN hot-spot installations concentrated on connectivity and did generally not provide sophisticated user authentication mechanisms. However, emerging regulatory requirements, identified WLAN security issues and, in particular, commercial interests have led to the development of *WLAN hot-spot architectures* that provide a whole set of functions beyond the basic provisioning of network access. [HKR+03] provides an overview of typical hot-spot features including: *enabling WLAN access* (WLAN association etc.), *provisioning the hot-spot* (device and user authentication), *IP layer management* (auto-configuration, DNS, NAT, etc.), *providing access to a hot-spot LAN for local information services*, *providing WAN access*, and *providing accounting information*.

How these functions are distributed across different components in a hot-spot depends on its specific architecture. An example is shown in figure 1: The wireless access link can be composed of a *service set* of WLAN access points providing coverage for the hot-spot area. In addition, there is an access controller that controls client access and a local access router (e.g., a DSL router) among other network elements. The *user authentication* function consists of a local front end in the hot-spot and, for larger hot-spot operators, usually an external AAA server. So far, no common authentication method has been established. Instead, different incompatible methods are in use, such as web-based login, SIM-cards [ACDS03], and IEEE 802.1X. For commercial hot-spots, the most common method is *web-based login* which is recommended by the Wi-Fi Alliance [ABS03] under the name *Universal Access Methods* (UAM) and works as follows:

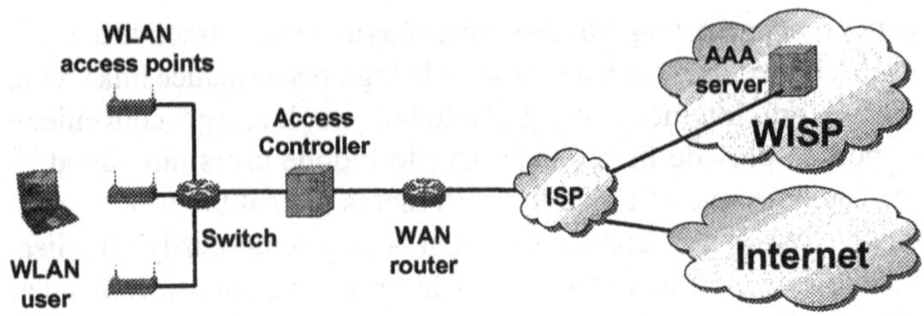

Fig. 1. Sample hot-spot architecture

The user's mobile device connects to the hot-spot WLAN that has SSID broadcast enabled and does not use WEP. A DHCP server supplies the necessary IP and DNS parameters but access to the Internet is still disabled at this point. The hot-spot access control function intercepts the first HTTP request from the user's device and redirects the user's web browser to the operator's login page. The login page prompts the user to enter her credentials. If the user is authorized network access is granted, typically enforced by means of MAC or IP address filtering. Terminating the use of a hot-spot (and thus stopping accounting) may also be done via the web browser and is usually complemented by inactivity detection. The advantage of UAM is that it imposes very little requirements on user equipment. The user can use commodity WLAN NICs and is not required to install any special-purpose software, e.g., VPN clients. [2]

WLAN roaming is still not generally available. However, there is an increasing number of hot-spots where the local operator is not identical to the actual WISP. E.g., at some airports the user is presented a selection of WISPs in the initial UAM web page and can select the preferred WISP before logging in. So called hot-spot aggregators [Wir03] such as *Boingo Wireless* and *iPass* have roaming agreements with selected hot-spot operators and offer some form of international roaming – at selected hot-spot sites.

For commercial hot-spots, one of the more important characteristics with respect to mobile usage scenarios is the *tariff model* employed by the WISP. Essentially three different models can be distinguished: volume-based, connection-time-based and flat-rate tariffs. In most countries, true flat-rate access is currently rather uncommon.[3] With respect to billing, pre-paid and post-paid models can be differentiated: Mobile phone operators that run a larger hot-spot network often apply accounting models for GSM-based Internet access to WLAN: network usage is accounted for on a time basis, and

[2] It should be noted that different strategies for providing users with credentials for the UAM login exist: For example, users may purchase vouchers that carry an authentication code that has to be entered into the HTML form of the login page. For operators with existing business relationships with their WLAN users, e.g., for mobile phone operators, it is considered beneficial to bill the user on her regular mobile phone bill; therefore the credentials are sent in text messages (SMS) to the user's GSM phone.

[3] In some countries, e.g., the US, flat-rate WLAN access is already available. In addition hot-spot aggregators often offer flat-rate tariffs, however with some restrictions with respect to specific hot-spots. E.g., Boingo Wireless offer flat-rates in general, but many international, i.e., outside the US, hot-spots are considered *premium sites* where additional charges apply.

the user is billed on the regular mobile phone bill For the pre-paid model, there are significant differences with respect to the accounting granularity: For voucher-based authentication, the user is typically authorized to use the WLAN at a location for a certain duration, e.g., one hour, without being able to suspend the session. In contrast to this one-time access model, some WISPs allow for using the time budget more flexibly, in multiple sessions. The granularity differs and ranges from one minute to one hour.[4]

Summarizing, we can state that, while more and more WLAN hot-spots are established, there are still some open technological and deployment challenges that have to be overcome in order to use WLAN hot-spots as a ubiquitous infrastructure. The existing infrastructure does, in general, not provide global roaming and relies on a set of different authentication, accounting and billing strategies.[5]

3 Drive-thru Internet

In the Drive-thru Internet project, we exploit WLAN connectivity from hot-spots along the road to provide Internet access to mobile users passing by who will experience intermittent connectivity. Our past work concentrated on the WLAN link: we carried out extensive laboratory and field measurements investigating the communication characteristics between a mobile node in a car and a fixed one co-located with the access point(s) under a variety of conditions. The results were convincing and clearly proved the feasibility of WLAN as last hop access even at higher speeds: in our current IEEE 802.11g setup we are able to obtain some 1800 m of connectivity [OK04b].

Throughput measurements showed a bell-shaped curve that led us to identify a *three-phase model*: during the *entry* and *exit phases* communication is possible at limited performance due to low link layer bit rate, link layer retransmissions, and packet losses. A *production phase* with stable connectivity and constantly high throughput approaching stationary conditions is available for up to 1000 m [OK04a] [OK04b]. With link data rates of 54 Mbit/s for large parts of the production phase, we achieved transfer volumes of more than 70 MB in a single pass at 120 km/h. While traffic (and weather) conditions influenced the performance, we obtained a mininum of 20–30 MB across all measurement settings. Further experiments with UDP and TCP background traffic and with two mobile nodes in different cars showed that the TCP flows to the mobile nodes obtained a reasonable share of the available link capacity. Congestion control adapted quickly to the changing link and traffic conditions. Altogether, our past measurements showed that IEEE 802.11 WLAN is a suitable communication substrate for providing high-performance network access to fast moving mobile nodes.

Nevertheless, the short and unpredictable connectivity periods pose various challenges to applications usually built under the assumption of rather stable network access conditions [OK04c]. We have devised the Drive-thru architecture [OK04b] to deal with unstable connectivity as well as transport and application layer timeouts. As shown in

[4] For example, Deutsche Bahn offers a pre-paid tariff, where users purchase a budget of 8 hours that can be used at different Deutsche Bahn hot-spots with a granularity of one minute. However, most WISPs account for network usage at a coarser granularity.

[5] A detailed discussion of challenges and future directions for hot-spots is provided in [BVB03].

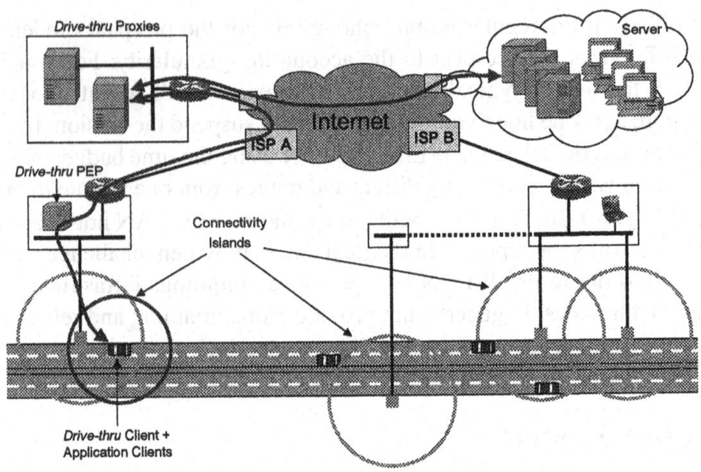

Fig. 2. Overview of the Drive-thru Internet Architecture

figure 2, we apply an enhanced variant of *connection splitting* [BKG+01] and introduce two intermediaries: The *Drive-thru client* is co-located with the mobile node and the *Drive-thru proxy* is placed somewhere in the fixed network. An additional *Performance Enhancing Proxy* (the Drive-thru PEP) in a hot-spot may be used to decouple the link layer characteristics of the WLAN and the access link/backbone [BKG+01]. Drive-thru client and server terminate transport (and application) connections to the application client (e.g., an e-mail client or a web browser) and the corresponding server, respectively, and protect the application entities from the intermittent nature of connectivity. They use a TCP-based "session" protocol—the *Persistent Connection Management Protocol* (PCMP) [OK05]—to provide transport connections that persist across connectivity islands and allow for continuous exchange of larger data volumes.

Drive-thru Internet differs fundamentally from other approaches using wireless (LAN) technologies for communication to and between mobile users in vehicles: Often users in airplanes, buses, or trains [TMC04] are served as a group via classic WLAN with WWAN connectivity to the outside. MAR [RCC+04] and IPonAir [ZWS+03] implement the seamless integration of different networks for individual users, as mentioned in the introduction. Fleetnet [BFW03] requires a dedicated wireless infrastructure with specific lower layer protocols, primarily targets new applications and does not address short-lived connectivity whereas Drive-thru Internet leverages existing WLAN hot-spots for existing applications. Other approaches such as Hocman [EJÖ02] focus on occasional very short inter-vehicle communications without fixed network access. Finally, in its support for disconnected operation, the Drive-thru Internet approach bears similarities to *Disruption/Delay-tolerant Networking (DTN)* [Fal03] and Drive-thru clients and proxies conceptually resemble DTN routers. The major difference is that DTN fundamentally assumes an asynchronous communications model (for newly developed applications) while we focus on *existing* applications and particularly need to embrace synchronous and interactive communications as much as possible.

4 Real-World Hot-Spots in Drive-thru Environments

Our past measurements assumed an ideal hot-spot environment to validate basic operation: a predefined SSID and static IP addresses were used, we did not perform any authentication with the access point, and we assumed that the Drive-thru proxy was located in the hot-spot so that the data did not need to pass through an access link that could become a bottleneck in communications. This section presents our investigations and findings when moving towards real-world hot-spot architectures: In experiments with hot-spots in airports, train stations, and other locations in different cities, we have traced packet exchanges from entering a hot-spot to completion of the authentication process to measure contents and timing of packet exchanges, and we have collected login pages from different WISPs to analyze authentication forms. We have simulated different types of access links. We have finally replicated parts of a hot-spot infrastructure (using the web-based authentication engine *NoCat*) in the lab and on the road.

4.1 Hot-Spot Access

Accessing a network through a hot-spot incurs several steps: Firstly, the mobile node needs to detect a radio carrier and determine the SSID(s) of the available WLANs (*association*). Next, DHCP is used for *IP auto-configuration*. Packet traces from different commercial hot-spots have shown that DHCP completes in 0.1–2s if no retransmissions are needed (those may add up to 5s each), with another 0.5–2s for subsequent ARP requests. The total delay incurred by DHCP in static scenarios is usually less than five seconds. We have validated the applicability of DHCP in our Drive-thru environment by measurements on the road at 120km/h and have observed some 2–8s for DHCP.

Finally, the mobile node needs to authenticate with a hot-spot service provider (*authentication*) as described in section 2. For basic hot-spot architectures (a single WISP, UAM-based authentication [ABS03]), we are able to perform automated authentication with rather simple means (see section 4.3). Packet traces of web-based authentication processes in commercial hot-spots show that DNS lookup, HTTP redirection, TLS setup, and login page retrieval complete fairly quickly as does the authorization once the user credentials are submitted (less than 6s in total). Our experiments with an automated tool confirm these observations: access to a hot-spot is usually granted or denied in less than five seconds including DNS requests and redirection of the initial HTTP request (together usually less than 0.5s) as well as retrieval of the login page, form submission, and retrieval of the confirmation page. Altogether, automatic configuration and authentication using standard procedures may easily complete within 5–10s (i.e. during the entry phase) and hence leave all of the production phase for user data exchange.

4.2 Hot-Spot Communications

After completing authentication, the Drive-thru client on a mobile node starts exchanging data with its peer, i.e., the Drive-thru proxy in the fixed network. Without any access link constraints, the throughput characteristics follow the three phase model outlined in section 3. To determine the impact of different access links on the communication characteristics in a Drive-thru environment, we have created the setup depicted in figure

3a): A mobile node (a laptop with two Ethernet interfaces) with a fixed node (another laptop with an Ethernet interface). The link simulator runs a software link-layer bridge (*satnat*) for which delay, data rate, and queue size can be configured independently in each transmission direction. For reference measurements without simulator the latter one is bypassed (dashed line in the figure). Mobile and fixed node both run the *tcpx* tool (short for *TCP eXchange* [OK04a]) developed by us that carries out a configurable data exchange pattern with its peer (here: sending or receiving only at the maximum achievable rate using 1460 byte segments).

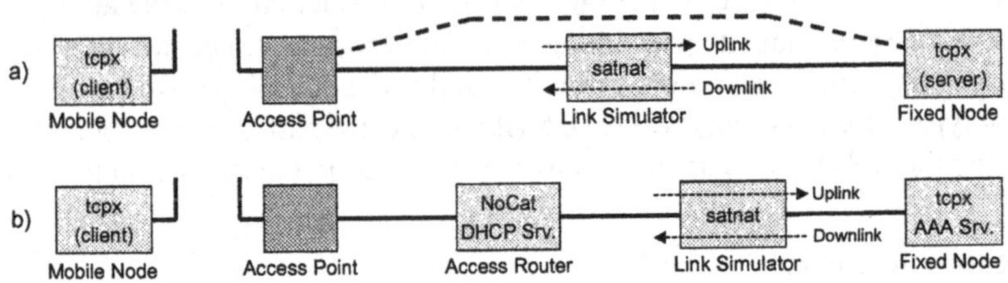

Fig. 3. Measurement setup for investigating the impact of access links

We have chosen seven different settings and measured each with a fixed and a mobile sender: a reference setting with no access link constraints (*LAN*), dial-up access (*ISDN BRI*), a leased line equivalent (*ISDN PRI*), *DSL* access at two rates, and bi-directional satellite links without rate limits (*satellite 1*, to investigate the influence of pure delay) and at a low DSL rate (*satellite 2*, as available from DVB-RCS satellite service providers). The data rate limits (*uplink* and *downlink*) are defined from the hot-spot's viewpoint as indicated in figure 3. We have carried out two measurements for each direction on the road resulting in 28 measurements and one measurement each in the lab. These settings are listed on the left hand side of table 1: downlink and uplink limit refer to the data rate limit on the access link from and to the Internet, respectively; and RTT was measured in the lab on an uncongested simulated link using *ping*. The measurements on the road were taken at a speed of 120 km/h. The access point was connected to an external antenna mounted on a fence pole at about 2 m height, the WLAN card of the mobile node was connected to an omni-directional antenna on the car's rooftop. These tests were carried out between 10:00 and 14:00 on a weekday. Varying traffic conditions have influenced individual measurements (e.g., led to lower goodput in one transmission direction) but have not affected the general observations.

On the right hand side, the table shows a summary of the measurement results: *duration* indicates the average length of the connectivity period at the tcpx level, i.e., from connection setup to the last received segment; *volume* shows the average net data volume transferred in a single pass and *rate* the resulting effective net data rate for a single hot-spot. Finally, we define a degree of effectiveness (*effect.*) to denote the ratio of the result on the road compared to an ideal static lab setting in order to quantify the performance loss due to vehicle mobility.

As can be seen from the table, the duration of the TCP connection remains roughly constant at 60–70 s per pass (the connectivity island extends to some 2 km, see also fig-

Parameters					*Results*			
Link type	Sender	Downlink limit	Uplink limit	RTT	Duration	Volume	Avg. Rate	Effect.
LAN	fixed	—	—	1 ms	60s	59.1 MB	7.9 Mbit/s	54%
LAN	mobile	—	—	1 ms	64s	51.4 MB	6.4 Mbit/s	69%
ISDN BRI	fixed	64 kbit/s	64 kbit/s	30 ms	69s	498 KB	58 kbit/s	97%
ISDN BRI	mobile	64 kbit/s	64 kbit/s	30 ms	63s	447 KB	56 kbit/s	92%
ISDN PRI	fixed	1920 kbit/s	1920 kbit/s	20 ms	60s	11.1 MB	1.5 Mbit/s	80%
ISDN PRI	mobile	1920 kbit/s	1920 kbit/s	20 ms	62s	12.6 MB	1.6 Mbit/s	88%
DSL 1	fixed	768 kbit/s	128 kbit/s	50 ms	61s	5.3 MB	700 kbit/s	95%
DSL 1	mobile	768 kbit/s	128 kbit/s	50 ms	64s	821 KB	102 kbit/s	83%
DSL 2	fixed	4096 kbit/s	384 kbit/s	37 ms	68s	16.5 MB	1.95 Mbit/s	63%
DSL 2	mobile	4096 kbit/s	384 kbit/s	37 ms	59s	2.45 MB	335 kbit/s	91%
Satellite 1	fixed	—	—	515 ms	71s	1.66 MB	188 kbit/s	72%
Satellite 1	mobile	—	—	515 ms	63s	929 KB	118 kbit/s	89%
Satellite 2	fixed	768 kbit/s	128 kbit/s	515 ms	66s	1.68 MB	205 kbit/s	83%
Satellite 2	mobile	768 kbit/s	128 kbit/s	515 ms	65s	611 KB	76 kbit/s	67%

Table 1. Overview of measurement settings and results

ure 4). From the degree of effectiveness, we observe that mobility does not appear to have a negative impact on the overall performance: despite the highly variable connectivity, the access link is kept filled most of the time and a moving vehicle will exploit on average 80% of its capacity. Only when the available bandwidth grows beyond several megabits per second (as in settings LAN and DSL 2)[6] and makes up a significant fraction of the available WLAN capacity, the poor performance of the entry and exit phases gain weight. The reason can be seen from figure 4 showing a few representative plots: if the access link's capacity amounts only to a small fraction of the WLAN's itself, even the low performance in the entry and exit phases suffice to fill the access pipe—which is the case almost immediately after the TCP connection is established. The temporary throughput drops seen in the figure also contribute to the lower effectiveness; they are due to link layer retransmissions and packet losses caused by other vehicles blocking signals or causing interference. Nevertheless, such losses are recovered quickly as long as the RTT is sufficiently low—which holds for all scenarios except for satellites.

Several conclusions can be drawn from these observations: Today's available terrestrial access technologies are suitable to provide Drive-thru Internet services in regular WLAN hot-spots. As long as queues in the access routers (both at ISPs and in the hot-spot) are kept short so that the RTT remains low, there is no need for performance enhancing proxies (PEPs) in the Drive-thru connectivity island: with terrestrial access networks, the variations of the wireless link's communication characteristics can be handled "end-to-end", i.e., between Drive-thru client and proxy. This is of particular importance because it implies that a regular hot-spot may be used "as is" and dependencies on WISPs are avoided. Only for satellite links, it is advisable to use PEPs to

[6] For the setting DSL 2 with a fixed sender, the maximum transmission rate was limited by the RTT and the small TCP default window size of 16 KB on the receiving machine so that even under ideal conditions only a maximum transmission rate of some 3 Mbit/s was possible.

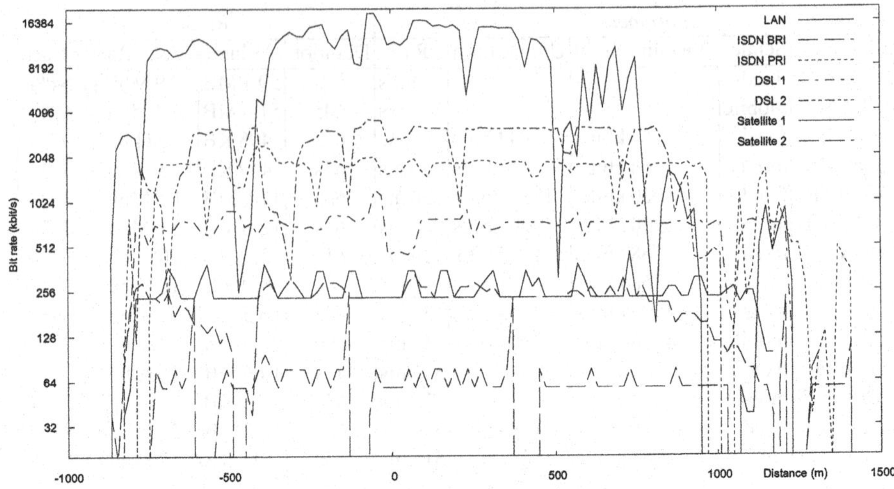

Fig. 4. Measured data rate (fixed sender, 120 km/h)

decouple the WLAN from the satellite link characteristics and provide optimized repair strategies for the long latency link, particularly because of non-congestion induced packet losses on the access link (as further experiments have confirmed).

Finally, we have validated a complete hot-spot scenario using a setup as depicted in figure 3b)—which includes another Laptop with two Ethernet interfaces to act as an access router and an authentication server. Our measurements for the DSL 1 setting showed that DHCP and automated authentication always completed in 5s and that the subsequent data exchange yielded results similar to the above (duration 63s, volume 5.2 MB, avg. rate 658 kbit/s): the incurred goodput penalty appears smaller than the usual performance variation (of up to 1 MB). In summary, automatically accessing a UAM-compliant hot-spot is feasible and takes less than ten seconds and thus completes in the entry phase leaving the production phase available for actual data exchange.

4.3 Implementation

Based upon our findings, we have developed a number of software components for the mobile node. They support the Drive-thru client in its task to manage connectivity with the Drive-thru proxy in existing hot-spots. The *ConnectivityDetector* monitors the network interfaces in the mobile node to determine when link layer connectivity becomes available and when it disappears. It distributes information about available access points, their SSIDs, and the signal strength locally. An *enhanced DHCP client* is triggered by the *ConnectivityDetector*, performs auto-configuration, and signals the completion of the IP stack configuration to other components. The *AutoAuthenticator* is triggered by the *ConnectivityDetector* and the DHCP client and is responsible for obtaining network access. It attempts to create an HTTP connection to the Drive-thru Proxy in order to check for Internet connectivity. As soon as the retrieval succeeds, authentication is considered complete. Usually, the initial request is redirected to a local web page via HTTP/TLS, which is retrieved and analyzed to find the UAM-compliant login submission form. In addition to the SSID and DHCP-assigned domain name, the authentication server certificate and the login page are used as hints to identify the WISP which is then matched against a local database. If found, the *AutoAuthenticator* submits the form with the corresponding credentials filled in. It checks the response and performs the necessary further actions (such as maintaining a connection for a logout page) to keep the access enabled. The *AutoAuthenticator* continuously sends local notifications about (changes to) the authentication status of a hot-spot.

The *Drive-thru client* is independent of the underlying connectivity establishment process. But it takes the above triggers about connectivity as hints when to attempt to set up a new connection to its Drive-thru Proxy and when to wrap up communications for a connectivity island. If a WLAN link becomes available it initiates/resumes communications right away (rather than waiting for a particular SNR threshold to be reached) and continues until connectivity is lost again.

Our implementation is currently tailored to work with the most common hot-spot scenarios. Laboratory tests of the individual software components, first non-mobile tests of the *AutoAuthenticator* with real-world hot-spots, and field tests using our experimental hot-spot setup have been successful. Nevertheless, various issues remain to be addressed: enhancing the AutoAuthenticator to deal with more complex login pages, supporting selected WEP-protected networks and integrating 802.1x-based authentication. Two further open issues are user policies defining when to use which hot-spots and which WISP and, as a prerequisite, to unambiguously (and quickly) identify which WISPs are available in a given hot-spot—these are subject to our current research.

4.4 Desirable Hot-Spot Properties

From the above discussions, we can devise a set of desirable properties to be considered for future hot-spot installations. At the WLAN link layer, dedicated access points with antennae mounted outdoor, e.g. on the roof of a building, are needed to offer sufficient connectivity. Directional antennae may be used pointed towards the road, and separate access points with non-overlapping channels are recommended to serve stationary users without interference. At the IP layer, traffic of stationary and Drive-thru users may be separated on the access link, e.g., by means of diffserv classes (or even different access links) to ensure a guaranteed bandwidth share for passing users. In most cases, it should be easy to satisfy these requirements and "upgrade" an existing hot-spot by simply adding dedicated access points and traffic management functions.

Furthermore, hot-spot service identification and user authentication aspects are crucial elements for successful deployment. A Drive-thru node must be able to automatically determine 1) whether or not a hot-spot is meant meant for public access; 2) which services are offered[7]; and 3) from which WISPs Internet access is available at what cost. While our AutoAuthenticator shows that parsing HTML pages is workable for selected hot-spot operators, this short-term solution may fail if web pages do not follow the UAM conventions or contain JavaScript code, if multiple WISPs are offered via

[7] Such services might include *Internet access* but also local services, e.g., availability of a Drive-thru PEP, download of local resources, advertisements, pre-selected content, etc.

a single web page, or if the initial redirect does not lead to the login page. However, other authentication mechanisms may need to be supported as well which ultimately requires implementing a trial-and-error decision chain to determine the access method and WISP—which takes precious time to complete and is error-prone. It is preferable to have the hot-spot operator disseminate information about available services, service providers, tariff models, and access methods using a standardized protocol and service description language. The Wi-Fi Alliance suggests a *smart client* authentication protocol that uses service announcements [ABS03]; other approaches to optimized service announcements are in discussed, e.g., in [BWSF03] and [KO03].

Finally, tariff models for WLAN access and accounting practices need to match the short hot-spot access periods, even special terms for short access durations (e.g., less than 120s) could be offered, and, of course, flat-rate service plans. Roaming agreements between WISPs would improve accessibility of hot-spots for individual users.

5 Conclusions

Drive-thru Internet introduces a new paradigm for mobility support and enhances the use of WLAN infrastructure previously restricted to stationary users. While initial measurements of WLAN performance in mobile scenarios have already shown the potential of the Drive-thru approach, in this paper, we have validated that our approach is workable with real-world hot-spot installations. We have proven that autoconfiguration and even "manual" authentication procedures can be completed in an automated fashion within a few seconds. Our measurements have shown that data rate adaptation to the changing WLAN characteristics is achievable end-to-end across common terrestrial access links. In summary, today's exising hot-spots are, in principle, usable without fundamental modification. But we have also identified areas for improvements: of particular interest are service announcements that allow a mobile node to unambigously determine the available WISPs, authentication methods, and tariff options—and to allow a hot-spot operator to provide this very information to attract customers. Furthermore, most current (time-budget-based) tariff models are suboptimal for the usually short Drive-thru access periods, and WLAN roaming is still not generally available.

On the hot-spot side, our future work includes providing service announcements, considerations for Drive-thru PEPs beyond plain connection splitting, and proper traffic differentiation. For the mobile node, we are advancing our *AutoAuthenticator* to understand service announcements, allow for policy-based WISP selection, and support additional authentication methods to achieve widespread applicability. Future measurements will include mobile user and background traffic via access links modeled following web and emails access traffic patterns. Ultimately, simulations are needed to assess the overall system behavior with many hot-spots and mobile users.

As the pervasiveness of 802.11 is still increasing—meanwhile the technology is considered as a low-cost area-wide network infrastructure for cities [Mooc04]—it is likely that the mobile usage scenario we have developed in the Drive-thru Internet project will gain popularity. With support for automated hot-spot association and disconnection-tolerant networking at hand, WLAN hot-spots could easily evolve into connectivity oases for stationary *and* mobile users.

References

[ABS03] B. Anton, B. Bullock, and J. Short. Best Current Practices for Wireless Internet Service Provider (WISP) Roaming, Version 1.0. Wi-Fi Alliance, February 2003.

[ACDS03] Ahmad A, R. Chandler, A. A. Dharmadhikari, and U. Sengupta. SIM-Based WLAN Authentication for Open Platforms. *Technology@Intel Magazine*, 2003.

[BFW03] Marc Bechler, Walter J. Franz, and Lars Wolf. Mobile Internet Access in FleetNet. In *13. Fachtagung Kommunikation in verteilten Systemen, Leipzig*, 2003.

[BKG+01] J. Border, M. Kojo, J. Griner, G. Montenegro, and Z. Shelby. Performance Enhancing Proxies Intended to Mitigate Link-Related Degradations. RFC 3135, June 2001.

[BVB03] A. Balachandran, G. M. Voelker, and P. Bahl. Wireless Hotspots: Current Challenges and Future Directions. In *Proceeding of WMASH'03*, 2003.

[BWSF03] Marc Bechler, Lars Wolf, Oliver Storz, and Walter J. Franz. Efficient Discovery of Internet Gateways in Future Vehicular Communication Systems. In *Proceedings of the 57th IEEE VTC 2003 Conference), Jeju, Korea*, 2003.

[EJÖ02] Mattias Esbjörnsson, Oskar Juhlin, and Mattias Östergren. The Hocman Prototype - Fast Motor Bikers and Ad-hoc Networking. Proceedings of MUM, 2002.

[Fal03] Kevin Fall. A Delay-Tolerant Network Architecture for Challenged Internets. Proceedings of ACM SIGCOMM 2003, 2003.

[HKR+03] John Hammond, Bart Kessler, Juan Rivero, Chad Skinner, and Tim Sweeney. Wireless Hotspot Deployment Guide. Technical report, Intel, December 2003.

[KO03] Dirk Kutscher and Jörg Ott. Dynamic Device Access for Mobile Users. In *Proceedings of the 8th Conference on Personal Wireless Communications*, 2003.

[Lei01] Gosta Leijonhufvud. Multi access networks and Always Best Connected, ABC. November 2001. MMC Workshop.

[Mooc04] Philadelphia Mayor's office of communications. Mayor John F. Street Announces Appointment Of Wireless Philadelphia Executive Committee. Press release, 2004.

[OK04a] Jörg Ott and Dirk Kutscher. Drive-thru Internet: IEEE 802.11b for „Automobile" Users. In *Proceedings of the IEEE Infocom 2004 Conference, Hong Kong*, 2004.

[OK04b] Jörg Ott and Dirk Kutscher. The "Drive-thru" Architecture: WLAN-based Internet Access on the Road. In *Proceedings of the IEEE Semiannual Vehicular Technology Conference May 2004, Milan*, May 2004.

[OK04c] Jörg Ott and Dirk Kutscher. Why Seamless? Towards Exploiting WLAN-based Intermittent Connectivity on the Road. In *Proceedings of the TERENA Networking Conference, TNC 2004, Rhodes*, June 2004.

[OK05] Jörg Ott and Dirk Kutscher. A Disconnection-Tolerant Transport for Drive-thru Internet Environments. In *Proceedings of the IEEE Infocom 2005 Conference*, 2005.

[RCC+04] P. Rodriguez, R. Chakravorty, J. Chesterfield, I. Pratty, and S. Banerjee. MAR: A Commuter Router Infrastructure for the Mobile Internet. In *Proceedings of ACM Mobisys 2004*, June 2004.

[TMC04] TMCnet.com. Clic TGV Brings Wifi Onboard France's High Speed Trains. available online at http://www.tmcnet.com/usubmit/2004/Jan/1022655.htm, January 2004.

[Wir03] Boingo Wireless. Toward Ubiquitous Wireless Broadband. White Paper, 2003.

[ZWS+03] M. Zitterbart et al. IPonAir – Drahtloses Internet des nächsten Generation. PIK, Vol 26, No 4, October 2003.

Wireless Inter-System Quality-of-Service: A Practical Network Performance Analysis of 3G and Beyond

Peter Reichl[1*], Norbert Jordan[2], Joachim Fabini[2], Reinhard Lauster[3], Martina Umlauft[1], Werner Jäger[3], Thomas Ziegler[1], Peter Eichinger[3], Günther Pospischil[4], Werner Wiedermann[4]

[1] Forschungszentrum Telekommunikation Wien (ftw.), Donaucitystr. 1, A-1220 Wien
[2] Technische Universität Wien, Institut für Breitbandkommunikation (IBK), Favoritenstr. 9/388, A-1040 Wien
[3] Kapsch CarrierCom AG, Am Europlatz 5, A-1120 Wien
[4] Mobilkom Austria AG & Co KG, Obere Donaustrasse 29, A-1020 Wien

Abstract. The provisioning of Quality-of-Service and the interworking between heterogeneous mobile environments will be of vital importance for the future economic success of mobile telecommunications. This paper presents a strictly practical performance evaluation of live and lab UMTS/GPRS/WLAN networks as performed within the project WISQY – Wireless Inter-System Quality-of-Service. We report on experiments using Mobilkom Austria's UMTS/GPRS live network and compare the results to lab trials results. Moreover, a novel IPv6-based mobility management approach is evaluated through extensive measurements in a dedicated WLAN testbed. Our performance evaluation results provide quantitative information which might be especially useful for the correct calibration of simulation scenarios for 3G and beyond networks.

1 Introduction and Overview

During the next few years, the successful deployment of 3G networks like UMTS and their seamless interplay with Wireless LAN (WLAN) hotspot solutions will be of vital importance for the future economic success of mobile telecommunications. Hence, the provision of Quality-of-Service (QoS) as well as the interworking between heterogeneous mobile environments provides an important step towards All-IP mobile networks and will be one of the crucial prerequisites for launching new services in 3G and beyond networks.

In contrast to the huge variety of related work and projects investigating this research area more from a conceptual point-of-view, the project WISQY – "Wireless Inter-System Quality-of-Service" [11] is focused on a strictly practical performance evaluation of live UMTS/GPRS/WLAN networks. The results presented in this paper concentrate on two key aspects, i.e. (1) the quantitative behaviour of live and lab

* corresponding author: reichl@ftw.at; phone: +43 1 5052830-31; fax: +43 1 5052830-99

UMTS/GPRS networks for various measurement scenarios, and (2) optimized IP-based mobility management in a dedicated IEEE 802.11b WLAN testbed.

Therefore, our first main focus concerns the analysis of the overall user experience of QoS in live UMTS networks compared to the (already wide-spread) GPRS networks. Employing an application end-to-end perspective, we focus on the network impact on the application layer, measuring round-trip time (RTT), HTTP, SMTP, POP3, FTP upload and download (including DNS lookup) for connection establishment, data transfer etc. The experiments have been performed using the A1 network, i.e. the live network of Mobilkom Austria, Austria's market leader in mobile communications. Note that already in August 2000, Mobilkom Austria launched the world's first full-coverage GPRS network in Europe, and in September 2002, it became the first European network operator to launch a national UMTS network, with the customer launch in April 2003. Based on this rich experience, the A1 network has turned out to be an ideal testbed for our live measurements.

The GPRS/UMTS live measurements have been repeated in a dedicated lab environment in order to compare the live results with an undisturbed environment. To this end we used the GPRS/UMTS Lab of Kapsch CarrierCom (KCC), a system synnovator of communication technology solutions for fixed, mobile and data network operators. Due to the long-term system integration relationship between Mobilkom Austria and KCC, hard- and software of the GPRS/UMTS Lab is almost identical to the A1 network. The KCC test system is a simple but complete and fully functional GSM/GPRS and UMTS Network (conforming to 3GPP R99 specifications) applicable for end-to-end tests, which can be performed with real GSM/GPRS or UMTS equipment.

Our evaluation results are especially relevant for existing and future simulator developments, as simulation tools for wireless networks require careful calibration with real-world network performance measurements, involving the transfer of huge amounts of data and the associated costs for live network tests. The results also emphasize the need for optimization of highly interactive protocols to handle the high delay of wireless networks in a way that is acceptable to the end user.

Secondly, as far as the optimization of IP-based mobility management is concerned, the main contribution of this paper concerns the performance evaluation of Mobile IPv6 (MIPv6) mechanisms in a multi-operator WLAN environment. The increasing popularity of IEEE 802.11-based WLANs available through hotspot ISP providers, combined with the upcoming 3G cellular network technology, has created the urgent need to coordinate the utilization of these two complementary wireless IP access technologies in order to open their respective advantages for mobile customers. While the link-layer handles the horizontal handover (intra-WLAN or intra-3G) with no need to change the configuration at the IP layer, vertical (inter-technological) handovers between WLAN and 3G require more sophisticated solutions, e.g. the application of MIPv6. In this paper we deal with the reduction of WLAN link-layer Handover (HO) latency, and present a performance comparison between baseline MIPv6 and enhanced Fast MIPv6 approaches.

The remainder of the paper is structured as follows: After Section 2 has introduced the testbed architecture and measurement scenarios, in Section 3 we will take a quick look at the employed measurement tools. Section 4 presents the UMTS/GPRS live and lab performance evaluation results, followed by an overview on our Fast MIPv6 approach for WLAN-based networks in Section 5. Section 6 concludes the paper with a couple of summarizing remarks.

2 Testbed Architecture and Measurement Scenarios

2.1 GPRS/UMTS Experiments

In our GPRS/UMTS experiments, the mobile client consists of a WindowsXP notebook connected via serial (for GPRS) or USB (for UMTS) cable to UMTS/GPRS mobiles, thus preventing bandwidth bottlenecks and other potential disturbances due to IrDA or Bluetooth connections. All application servers (HTTP, SMTP, POP3, FTP) are running on a SUSE Linux-based server. Our live client has been located at the Institut für Breitbandkommunikation (IBK), a department of the Technical University of Vienna situated close to the city centre of Vienna. The Linux Application Server was connected via the TU Vienna's intranet and through other ISP's to Mobilkom Austria's Gi LAN interface.

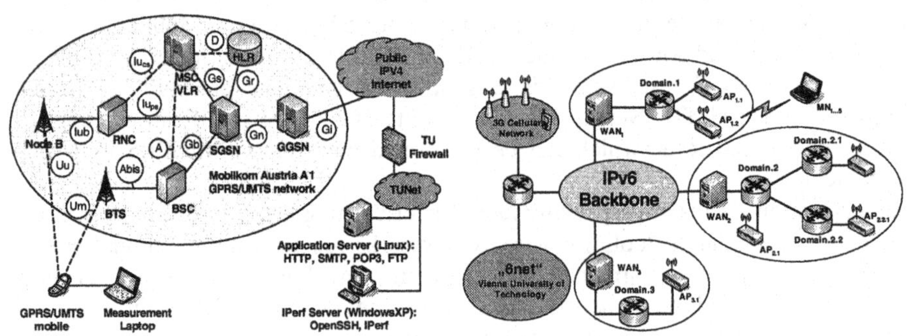

Fig. 1: Setup for A1 Live UMTS Network (left) and MIPv6 Wireless Testbed (right)

As already mentioned, we tested the live Mobilkom A1 UMTS network with standard APN (DCH: DL 384 kbit/s, UL 64 kbit/s). A Nokia 6650 UMTS phone was connected to the mobile client (laptop HP Omnibook 6000 with Windows XP SP1) via USB cable. Figure 1 left shows the setup used for our experiments; for a more general introduction into the basic building blocks of GPRS/UMTS networks we refer to 3GPP TS23.060 R99. RNC, SGSN, GGSN, VLR, and HLR were located in the A1 network environment (for live measurements) and the KCC UMTS test network environment (for lab measurements). In the lab environment, both ALONE and IPerf servers were connected directly to the Gi LAN. The DNS server required for the ALONE test suite was installed on the Suse Linux application server. For our measurements, we used GPRS mobile phones like Siemens S55 or TelMe T919 which support GPRS class 10 (total of 5 timeslots, dynamically 4+1 or 3+2).

All tests at KCC were run as exclusive single-user tests, i.e. no other mobile phones could allocate any resources within the mobile network and/or originate any interfering traffic. Additionally, the mobiles were put into an RF shield box to guarantee undisturbed radio conditions. Moreover, the Gi LAN was fully dedicated to test server operation and free of external traffic influences.

2.2 Mobile IPv6 Studies

For the MIPv6 performance evaluation, we have implemented an enhanced IPv6 testbed connected to the worldwide native "6net" infrastructure. As sketched in Figure 1 right, a couple of subnetworks are attached to a central backbone network. Between each pair of different network providers we implemented WAN emulators thwarting all IPv6 packets transmitted. Thus we are able to tune the link-delay individually, depending on the analyzed scenarios. Both IEEE 802.11b and IEEE 802.11g technologies are deployed in the overall wireless hotspot infrastructure.
Three independent network operator domains are deployed, one of them including the Home Agent for the mobile node experiments. Another network operator domain includes some kind of a hierarchical structure in order to allow a performance comparison with the alternative Hierarchical MIPv6 approach. All hosts have RedHat Linux 8.0 with Kernel 2.4.22 installed. For the MIPv6 basic functionality we utilized MIPL 1.0, provided by Helsinki University of Technology (HUT) [3]. The Linux driver for all WLAN activities is based on the HostAP project [4], a very flexible tool for fast link-layer triggering.

3 Evaluation Tools

ALONE. For measuring the end-to-end application-layer performance for TCP/IP-based application protocols over UMTS and GPRS networks we used the ALONE tool suite. ALONE (Application Oriented Network Evaluation) is a NSPR-library based measurement tool, which implements RFC-compliant clients for HTTP/1.0, SMTP, POP3 and FTP. The ALONE client connects to RFC-compliant application servers, opens a protocol session and exchanges data with these servers according to the selected protocol. It records the success or failure of the protocol session along with the duration of DNS lookup, end-to-end connection establishment, data transfer and total session duration. ALONE's data exchange is file-based, i.e., the ALONE client uploads or downloads files according to the selected protocol. Our tests transfer zip-compressed files to exclude server-side optimizations (data compression) in the mobile operator's network.
For SMTP, POP3, and FTP ALONE supports multiple data transfers within one protocol session. E.g., the ALONE FTP client opens a connection to an FTP server, authenticates itself once and then transfers the user-specified data file n times. This 1:n data transfer model extends the 1:1 model commonly used for performance tests.

IPerf (TCP/UDP). The ALONE-measured application-level network performance is compared against the raw UMTS/GPRS TCP/IP network throughput as reported by IPerf 1.7.0 for TCP. We also measured UMTS network streaming performance using IPerf 1.7.0 in UDP mode and ICMP packet round-trip times using the standard ping utility with varying payload size.
ALONE, IPerf and Ping have been invoked by means of Perl wrapper scripts. The scripts automate our tests by starting clients and servers locally and remotely with the

pre-configured range of parameters like tested protocol, file name, file size, payload size, timeout values, etc. Moreover, they implement automated dial-in and disconnect procedures, log the duration of these commands, and parse, process and log the output of third-party tools like IPerf. Local and remote systems are synchronized via SSH client/server communication.

WebSim. For more detailed HTTP measurements we used the WebSim traffic generator tool developed at FTW [2] for simulating HTTP/1.0 traffic according to the SURGE model [1]. WebSim consists of a server simulating an HTTP server, and a client simulating user behavior. The client requests typical pages (consisting of several files) by opening a new TCP session for each requested file, thus allowing for multiple simultaneous (parallel) TCP sessions, and simulates user think times between page requests and parsing times of the browser. Pages typically consist of an HTML document with several embedded objects. The server responds with files whose file size distribution corresponds to the SURGE model. For further information on the WebSim traffic generator we refer to [2].

i-Motion. i-Motion is our new tool for reducing the link-layer disruption in WLAN environments [6]. It aims at minimizing the considerable service interruption period between the interface card disconnecting from the previous link and the Mobile Node arriving and reestablishing at the new Access Point (AP). Initial analysis of the IEEE 802.11 link-layer handover process has already been performed in [8], [9] and [10], suggesting how to reduce its duration. There, it is demonstrated that the HO latency can vary between 500 and 1500 ms, depending on the deployed equipment. The major latency problem with HOs is caused by the firmware inside the interface-card detecting the lack of radio connectivity only after several unsuccessful frame transmissions. Therefore, in our WLAN testbed we implemented i-Motion as an enhanced mobility management tool that continuously monitors the radio signal quality of the attached AP and starts searching for alternative APs already before any frame has been dropped. In this way the overall HO time can already be reduced by 50 % compared to traditional implementations [6].

4 Results

As pointed out before, our mobile network performance analysis reflects the current status of GPRS and UMTS networks from an end-user perspective, both in live networks and in test laboratory environments. We measured raw TCP/IP throughput, application-layer throughput for HTTP, SMTP, POP3 and FTP, UDP bandwidth, packet loss and jitter, and ICMP packet round-trip-time. All measurements in the live network were evenly distributed over at least one week to reflect a representative load in the live GPRS/UMTS network.

According to the technical specifications, UMTS networks should outperform GPRS networks by at least one order of magnitude both in terms of throughput and round-trip-time. On the other hand, GPRS networks are already highly optimized while UMTS networks have just started to operate. Our measurements analyze the benefit end-users can expect from a high-performance infrastructure like UMTS compared to GPRS. We point out potential performance limitations due to the design of applica-

tion protocols under specific traffic situations which may have a negative impact on the user acceptance of UMTS and other wireless network technologies.
Note finally that all our tests rely on a strict end-user view of the mobile network. We regard the GPRS/UMTS network as a black box with no user-configurable parameters. Optimization was restricted to selection and configuration of mobile devices and to the fine-tuning of operating system parameters.

4.1 Raw Network Performance: TCP and UDP

Starting with TCP, we tested 30-second TCP/IP throughput bursts with IPerf 1.7.0 in the UMTS and GPRS network as a reference for our application-level measurements. According to our measurement results the TCP window size has visible but minor impact on the throughput.

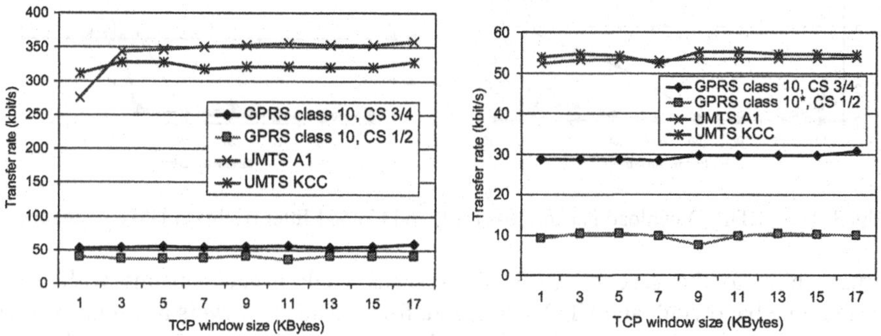

Fig. 2: IPerf TCP/IP: Download Transfer Rate (left) and Upload Transfer Rate (right)

Figure 2 shows that the TCP/IP throughput of GPRS networks depends on the number of GPRS timeslots allocated for upload and for download and the GPRS coding scheme, but not on channel conditions, user equipment etc. The number of timeslots available to the user for data transfer depends on the mobile devices' GPRS class, on the maximum number of GPRS timeslots that the operator grants to one mobile device and on the current mobile network load. The A1 GPRS network fully supports mobile phones up to GPRS class 10. This enables allocation of a total of 5 timeslots, either as 4 download + 1 upload or as 3 download + 2 upload. The allocation changes dynamically depending on the predominant data transfer direction. From Figure 2 we can see that the A1 network uses the (4+1) scheme for TCP/IP download and switches to (3+2) for TCP/IP-based upload. Combined with GPRS coding scheme CS 3/4 the A1 network transfers an average of up to 60 kbit/s.
We compared these results against measurements within the KCC GPRS test network. The KCC network was configured to support CS 1/2 (in order to allow a comparison to CS 3/4 in the live network), a maximum of 4 timeslots for download and 1 timeslot for upload. Figure 2 left shows the difference in download throughput over GPRS networks for 4 timeslots using CS 3/4 and 4 timeslots using CS 1/2. The performance gain of GPRS CS 3/4 compared to CS 1/2 is remarkable both in upload and download direction.

UMTS outperforms GPRS both in TCP/IP upload and download direction. UMTS upload throughput peaks at 55 kbit/s, which is about twice the throughput of a GPRS mobile with CS 3/4 and full operator support (two timeslots in upload direction). Finally, our live network UMTS download measurements report a peak of 357 kbit/s goodput, which is close to the theoretical feasible throughput for UMTS network micro cells. Note that the KCC UMTS Lab network configuration was not optimized for maximum throughput leading to slightly lower download results. The UMTS download throughput amounts to six times the maximum GPRS download performance.

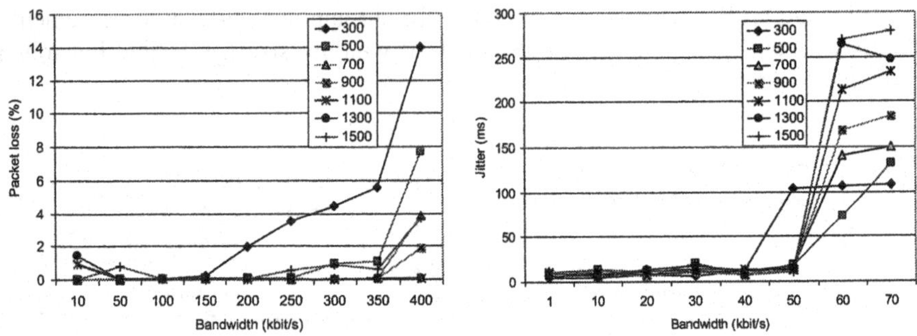

Fig. 3: IPerf UDP: Download Packet Loss (left) and Upload Jitter (right) in UMTS networks

Turning now to the case of UDP, IPerf sends UDP packet streams with user-configurable bandwidth and UDP packet size from clients to servers and reports jitter and packet loss for the stream. We tested all possible combinations of packet lengths between 300 and 1500 bytes (step 200 bytes) and stream bandwidths between 1-70 kbit/s (step 10K) for upload and 10-400 kbit/s (step 50K) for download. During one UDP stream test of 30 sec the bandwidth and packet parameters were kept constant.

Figure 3 left displays the packet loss for UDP stream downloads over UMTS networks. The packet loss increases with increasing bandwidth; above 300 kbit/s the loss becomes significant for all UDP packet sizes. Small UDP packet streams are more likely to suffer from packet loss than streams transfering large UDP packets because of the significant UDP/IP overhead associated with small UDP packets. 300-byte payload UDP packet streams waste roughly 10 % of the available bandwidth for overhead, whereas for 1500-byte payload streams, overhead becomes less than 2%.

The jitter in upload direction increases to values above 150ms when the upload bandwidth exceeds 50 kbit/s as shown in Figure 3 right. Like in download direction streams consisting of small UDP packets are more severely affected by jitter.

4.2 Ping ICMP Round-Trip Time

In the next experiment, we measured average ICMP packet round-trip times (RTTs) for varying packet payloads. The payload was verified to be identical for sent and returned packets. Figure 4 left shows the average ICMP RTT for GPRS and UMTS networks. We executed the complete ICMP test 65 times for any payload size between 100 and 1450 bytes, distributed over a one-week interval. Any of these meas-

urement points averages the result of 20 ping packets. The results are a good approximation of RTTs to be expected for UDP packets over GPRS and UMTS networks.
The round-trip performance that we measured for UMTS networks is excellent compared to GPRS. UMTS ranges from less than 150 ms for 32 byte and 160 ms for 100 byte packets to 537 ms for 1450 byte packets while GPRS round-trip-time peaks at 2142 ms for 1450 byte packets. Typical SIP/IMS messages carrying a payload of around 800 bytes will incur an UMTS RTT of approximately 360 ms.

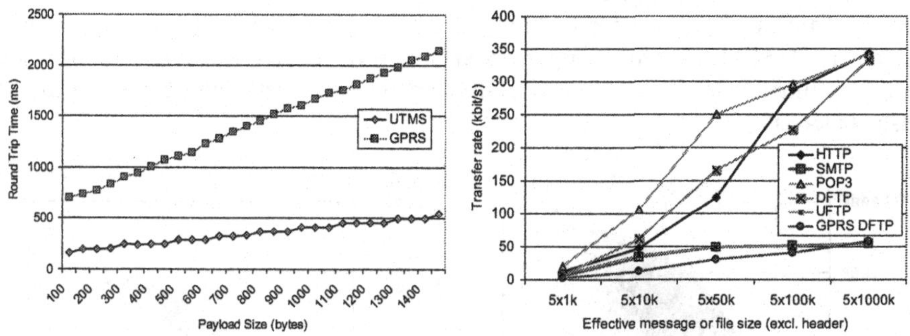

Fig. 4: ICMP Ping RTT (left) and Application-Level Transfer Rate (right) for UMTS

4.3 Application-Level Performance

The IPerf measurements approximate the optimum transfer rate and round-trip-time for the tested GPRS and UMTS networks. Mechanisms implemented in the layers positioned between network layer and end-user require part of this available network resource. Examples include application protocol headers, application server delays, handshakes, round-trip delays, etc. and optimization techniques like TCP slow start and Nagle algorithm – to name just a few. End-users do not gain the full benefit of the network performance except for some huge file transfers or streams.
We measured application-layer performance using ALONE and WebSim and compared the results against network performance measured with IPerf. We evaluated the impact of specific application protocols on the network performance offered to the end-user. Our conclusion is that existing protocols waste a huge part of the available network resources and must be explicitly optimized for the use in wireless networks.
Figure 4 right depicts the application-level, end-to-end transfer rate of the application protocols HTTP, SMTP, POP3, Download FTP and Upload FTP. The diagram shows that the user gains full benefit of the UMTS network download performance only for files exceeding 1MByte of size. FTP download is outperformed by HTTP and POP3 because of the round-trip times that are required to start and end a FTP file transfer. The chart is based on the true payload that is transferred by HTTP, SMTP and POP3 and ignores protocol-specific headers added to the message or file. It must be stated that POP3 and SMTP are both not capable of transferring binary files while FTP

copes well with both, text and binary files. The transfer of binary files using POP3 or SMTP results in part of the available bandwidth being wasted for encoding.
Figure 5 shows more detailed results for HTTP/1.0, i.e. the transfer rate over web page size (including embedded objects) for the UMTS (left) and GPRS (right) live network. Due to the delay incurred at every connection establishment the user perceived transfer rate varies according to file size. Also, because HTTP/1.0 opens a new TCP session for each embedded file, pages made up of several small files suffer a significant decrease in transfer rate. On the other hand we observed performance near the theoretical maximum of UMTS for files of 1 MB and above (approx. 335 kbit/s). For GPRS we measured a maximum of around 60 kbit/s. This results in min. page download times of 0.3 sec for UMTS and 1.3 sec for GPRS which shows the improvement UTMS brings for user perceived QoS of interactive web applications since responses times below 1 sec are typically perceived as "fast" and below 300 ms as "instantaneous".

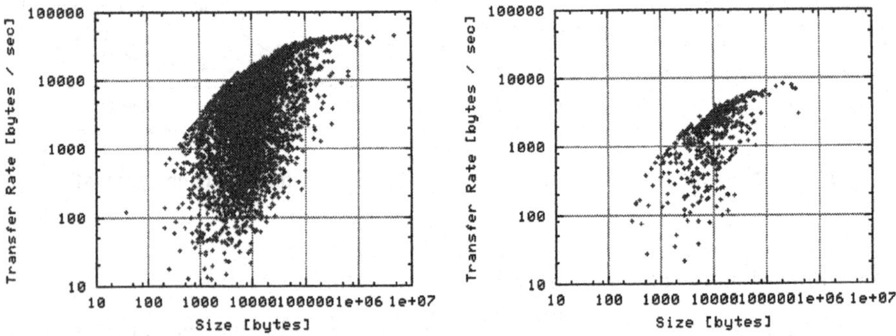

Fig. 5: User Perceived Transfer Rates for HTTP/1.0: UMTS (left) and GPRS (right)

Our measurements indicate that TCP/IP connection establishment and synchronization handshakes are major penalty factors. POP3 uses one single TCP/IP connection for the transfer of all 5 messages and performs best of all tested protocols, especially for small files. HTTP 1.1 should perform significantly better than HTTP 1.0 for pages made up of several small files because of TCP/IP connection re-use.

5 Mobility Management for All-IP Networks

5.1 Basics of Fast MIPv6

Using Mobile IPv6, a mobile node can effectively maintain its IP-layer connectivity to the Internet while changing its point-of-attachment. During the accomplishment of the handover, the mobile node is unable to send or receive IPv6 packets because of its L2 and L3 handover operations. This high handover latency is unacceptable to real-time applications or delay sensitive traffic. Each time a mobile client moves, it is necessary to perform movement detection by its current point-of-attachment. In Mobile IPv6 [5], the movement detection algorithm relies on the periodic sending of router advertisements in order to enable the mobile node to determine its current location. The only way to improve the detection performance is to broadcast router advertisements at a faster rate, which may result in a poor link utilization. For that reason, a fast handover protocol is designed to achieve a seamless handoff when mobile nodes switch from one subnet to another.

The Fast Mobile IPv6 approach enables a Mobile Node to quickly detect at IP-layer that it has moved to a new subnet by receiving link-related information from the link-layer and furthermore gathering anticipative information about the new Access Point and the associated subnet prefix when the Mobile Node is still connected to its previous subnet. It is also possible to initiate vertical handovers between different wireless access technologies. In the mobile-initiated and anticipated fast-handover scenario described in [7], the mobile node first sends a Router Solicitation for Proxy (RtSolPr) message to the current access router containing any Access Point specific identifiers. The trigger for sending the initiating RtSolPr message can be derived directly from a link-layer specific event, e.g. an imminent movement to an AP providing better signal-quality. Consequently, the MIPv6 protocol assumes that the link-layer protocol is capable of delivering the L2 identifier of the new access point to the mobile node. For seamless handover initiation it is more important that the current AR must be able to map the new L2 identifier into the IP address of the target AR. In the remainder of this section we will present first testbed results, which demonstrate the beneficial behavior of the Fast Handover approach for Mobile IPv6 in Wireless LAN based networks.

5.2 Performance Evaluation of Link-Layer HO

Figure 6 left presents the results for link-layer HO with and without our i-Motion monitoring tool for a client with maximum throughput at each AP and demonstrates the reduced HO latency behavior in comparison to conventional WLAN switching.

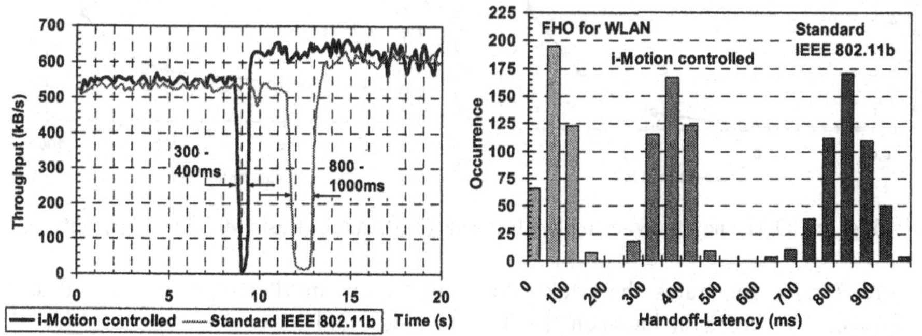

Fig. 6: IEEE 802.11b Handover Latency

For further optimization of the HO latency, we remove the firmware-based Active-Scanning procedure during the execution-phase. An Active-Scan is a procedure in which a WLAN station searches for all APs (on all available channels) in range. Each AP can be addressed by a specific Service-Set ID (SSID). As the i-Motion monitoring tool in our scenario already knows the exact SSID for the selected AP, it does not make sense to restart an Active-Scan once more. Scanning all channels takes time and is not desirable when the execution of movement to another AP is going on. For that reason we re-developed the WLAN hardware drivers to achieve switching without active-scanning. Figure 6 right demonstrates the result for a WLAN station moving in between two APs: we observe that the delay without any optimization is about 800ms, the handoff delay is about 350ms for predictive mode of i-Motion, whereas for the same experiment with enabled i-Motion monitoring tool and skipped active-scanning phase, the overall delay is only about 80ms. This is an excellent outcome for these initial optimization approaches. However it should be noticed that the presented HO results for IEEE 802.11 are obtained through measurements in our testbed and carried out for only 4 WLAN station at the respective APs. It is expected that the HO delay might slightly increase for scenarios with additional user activity.

5.3 Performance Evaluation

This section presents our evaluation results for the implemented basic Mobile IPv6 wireless testbed. Furthermore, interesting results will be demonstrated for the application of enhanced fast HO mechanisms for MIPv6. All measurements consist of roughly 1000 samples averaged for each individual point.

Figure 7 left demonstrates the functionality of the IPv6 Router Discovery mechanism. It shows the dependence of the overall handoff latency (L2 and L3) on the frequence of sent Router Advertisements (RA). Obviously, the HO latency decreases as RA messages are sent more frequently.

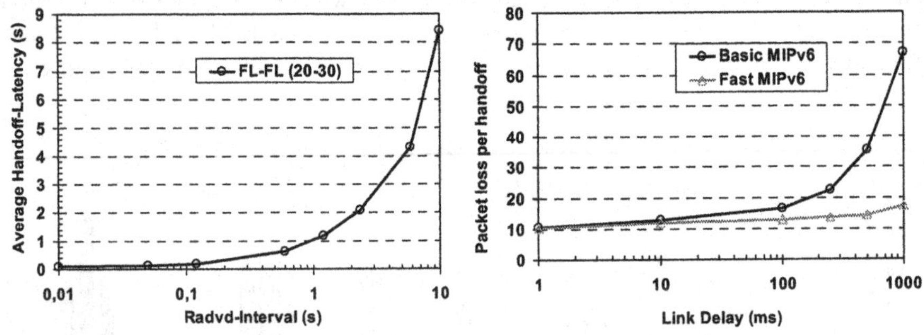

Fig. 7: HO Latency for Varying RA Intervals (left) and for Basic Mobile IPv6 (right)

Figure 7 right illustrates the packet loss results for an IPerf-generated UDP-data stream of 160 kbit/s in between the Mobile Node and its correspondent node. As already mentioned, we deployed WAN emulators in order to be able to delay packets in between each provider subnet and the core network.

As can be observed, the packet loss during the HO between different network operators highly increases for basic MIPv6. In contrast, the Fast Handover approach shows a lower increase for the whole range of wired link-delays. These results show that the Fast Handover approach for WLAN based networks may provide acceptable performance in a realtime multimedia infrastructure (e.g., VoIP over WLANs).

6 Summary and Conclusions

This paper is dedicated to a couple of central results achieved within the application-oriented project WISQY. We have investigated two important topics in the general context of performance analysis for UMTS/GPRS/WLAN networks: first, we provide a quantitative evaluation of live and lab UMTS/GPRS networks with respect to several important parameters which are extremely relevant e.g. for the correct calibration of future simulation tools for heterogeneous wireless environments. Secondly, a novel IP-based WLAN mobility management approach has been introduced and evaluated with respect to optimized IEEE 802.11b HO latencies.

Future work in this area includes QoS and performance evaluations of IP Internet applications for mobile networks, especially investigating the planned introduction of the 3GPP IMS (IP Multimedia Subsystem) architecture.

Acknowledgements

This work has been funded by the Austrian Kplus competence center program.

7 References

1. P. Barford, M. E. Crovella: *Generating Representative Workloads for Network and Server Performance Evaluation.* ACM Sigmetrics '98, pp. 151-160, Madison (WI), 1998.
2. E. Hasenleithner, H. Weisgrab, T. Ziegler: *A0 Deliverable 5-2, Final Report Testbed Phase 1, Hardware & Software Setup, Dummynet, QoS Demonstration.* FTW Technical Report A0 D 5-2, Vienna, Austria, Feb. 2002.
3. Mobile IPv6 for Linux, version 1.0, Software and Documentation URL: http://www.mobile-ipv6.org.
4. Host AP Driver for Intersil Prism2/2.5/3 and WPA Supplicant, Jouni Malinen, 2004, Software and Documentation URL: http://hostap.epitest.fi.
5. D. B. Johnson, C. E. Perkins, J.Arkko: *Mobility Support for IPv6.* RFC 3775, IETF Network Working Group, June 2004.
6. N. Jordan, R. Fleck, C. Ploninger: *Fast Handover Support in Wireless LAN based Networks.* Proc. Fifth IFIP-TC6 International Conference on Mobile and Wireless Communication Networks (MWCN 2003), Singapore, October 2003.
7. R. Koodli: *Fast Handovers for Mobile IPv6.* Internet-Draft, IETF Mobile IP Working Group, < draft-ietf-mipshop-fast-mipv6-02.txt>, July 2004.
8. A. Mishra, M. Shin, W. Arbaugh: *An Empirical Analysis of the IEEE 802.11 MAC Layer.* Technical Report CS-TR-4395, University of Maryland, 2002.
9. H. Velayos, G. Karlsson: *Techniques to Reduce IEEE 802.11b MAC Layer Handover Time,* KTH Technical Report, ISSN 1651-7717, Stockholm, April 2003.
10. H. Velayos, G. Karlsson: *Techniques to Reduce IEEE 802.11b Handoff Time.* Proc. IEEE ICC'04, Paris, France, June 2004.
11. A3-WISQY: Wireless InterSystem QoS. URL: www.ftw.at/projects/A3_engl.html.

Teil V

Methoden und Werkzeuge

A Honeypot Architecture for Detecting and Analyzing Unknown Network Attacks

Patrick Diebold, Andreas Hess and Günter Schäfer

Telecommunication Networks Group, Technische Universität Berlin, Germany,
dakkonbb@cs.tu-berlin.de, [hess, schaefer]@tkn.tu-berlin.de

Abstract In this paper, we propose a honeypot architecture for detecting and analyzing unknown network attacks. The main focus of our approach lies in improving the "significance" of recorded events and network traffic that need to be analyzed by a human network security operator in order to identify a new attacking pattern. Our architecture aims to achieve this goal by combining three main components: 1. a packet filter that suppresses all known attacking packets, 2. a proxy host that performs session-individual logging of network traffic, and 3. a honeypot host that executes actual network services to be potentially attacked from the Internet in a carefully supervised environment and that reports back to the proxy host upon the detection of suspicious behavior. Experiences with our first prototype of this concept show that it is relatively easy to specify suspicious behavior and that traffic belonging to an attack can be successfully identified and marked.

1 Introduction

Recent experiences with attacks in the Internet and especially the tremendous increase in the propagation speed of self-distributing attacks clearly show that the problem of exploiting vulnerabilities of hosts connected to the Internet can not be countered appropriately with an approach that is only aiming to defend from attacks against end systems by fixing security holes when patches become available. In order to overcome this situation, various researchers are working on network based intrusion prevention (examples of existing open-source IPS are Snort-Inline [2], Hogwash [9], IBAN [3] and FIDRAN [5, 6]).

However, in order to realize an efficient intrusion prevention system (IPS), relatively detailed knowledge about potential attacking patterns is needed. Most of the systems in use today, therefore, work with a set of so-called *attack signatures*, that describe attacking patterns in sufficient detail for identifying ongoing attacks automatically. However, the specification of such signatures usually needs to be done by experienced network security analysts by either monitoring an existing network and extracting the relevant information as new attacks are launched and get detected, or by directly analyzing new attacking tools, worms, etc. as they become available.

In order to support this task, the use of so-called *honeypots* has been proposed in recent years. One common definition of this term is: *"a honeypot is an information system resource whose value lies in unauthorized or illicit use of that resource"* [13].

As stated in this definition, a honeypot is a system that is built and set up in order to be hacked. Honeypots can be used as intrusion detection facility (burglar alarm), defense- or response mechanism. Apart from this, honeypots can be deployed in order to consume the resources of the attacker or distract him from the valuable targets and slow him down, so that he wastes his time on the honeypot instead of attacking production systems.

The fundamental principle of the honeypot idea is that every connection (even an attempt) or scan, respectively, which is destined to a honeypot can be considered suspicious. A honeypot is not a production system and consequently, nobody has reasons to contact it. According to this, the amount of traffic that is sent to a honeypot is assumed to be manageable and of high significance to intrusion detection. However, as we experienced in an experimental setup (see below), traffic volume received by a honeypot still lies in a rather high range, so that a more intelligent way than just analyzing all received traffic is required.

We therefore developed a honeypot architecture that allows to obtain more significant traffic logs of suspicious behavior by combining filtering of already known attacks with session-individual traffic logging and marking of suspicious sessions based on evidence gained on an actual honeypot host. The remainder of this paper is organized as follows: in session 2 we give some background information on honeypots, review related work and report on our experience with traffic volume received by a honeypot in an experimental setting. Section 3 describes our concept, and in section 4, we describe our prototype implementation of this concept and discuss first results. In the final section 5, we draw some conclusions and give an outlook to future work.

2 Honeypots

Honeypots are often categorized by their level of interaction [13]. So-called *low interaction honeypots* are defined as simulated services, i.e. anything from an open port to a fully-simulated network service. Most of the low interaction honeypots use simple script-based languages to describe the honeypots reactions to attacker inputs. Low interaction honeypots are easy to set up and because of the limited capabilities they are quite secure. The drawbacks are that they are easy to detect for attackers, because the service's reactions are not implemented completely. The information gained is limited as well, because no real vulnerabilities can be distinguished from attack attempts. Its use is restricted to the logging of automated attacks and intrusion detection.

So-called *high interaction honeypots* — we emphasize here that we do not make a distinction between medium and high interaction honeypots — are real services which are usually executed in a secured environment. The attacker communicates with an actual service implementation but theoretically he does not achieve total system control in case of a successful attack if the honeypot is well designed. One advantage of this approach is that a high interaction honeypot is difficult to unmask. Actually, the attacker should not be able realize that he interacts with a honeypot because a real service is used. Of course, the honeypot system can be only as secure as its sandbox subsystem — in case that it comprises such functionality.

Another important factor for the usefulness of a honeypot is accessibility. Obviously, it is only useful if it gets attacked. Moreover, in order to gather the intrusion related information, logging and sniffing techniques must be integrated into a honeypot architecture. Accordingly, the question arises how to realize a honeypot which resembles a vulnerable system, but which can not be exploited, and which beyond this possesses intrusion detection capabilities, in order to inform the administrator about the occurrence of an attack.

2.1 Related Work

Honeyd [12] is a low-to-medium-interaction honeypot system. Installed on a Unix system it listens on the network interface card (NIC) for incoming ARP requests. If an ARP request is detected *Honeyd* initiates an ARP request itself. If no response to the own ARP request is given and a rule for the requested IP exists in the configuration file, *Honeyd* overtakes the IP and starts pre-configured services on the specified ports. The honeypot comes with some shell scripts that emulate services (e.g. a WWW server). *Honeyd* is able to emulate the behavior of most common IP-stack implementations (Windows, Linux, etc.) that can be detected by the tools *nmap* [4] and *x-scan* [15] by using the same rule base as the scanners. *Honeyd* is open source and has been successfully used on the Cebit 2003 by the heise publisher (see article [17]).

Bait'n'Switch [18] is a honeypot response mechanism that redirects the attacker from valuable targets to a honeypot system. *Bait'n'Switch* is realized as a *Snort* [2] in-line extension. Whenever a successful attack is detected, the IDS drops the packets of the first attack and all further traffic from the host that initiated the attack is rerouted to a dedicated honeypot host. This process is hidden from the attacker so that he does not realize that he is not communicating with the original target anymore. The attacker's further interaction with the honeypot can later be analyzed and the production system is protected from the attacker's further actions. The system reacts on attacks that are described in an IDS signature database and can therefore only react on previously known attacks.

The *Intrusion Trap System* [14] is an improved version of *Bait'n'Switch*. In case that *Snort* detects an attack, the *Intrusion Trap System* is able to directly redirect the attack to a honeypot host. This way, even the traffic of the first attack can be handled by a honeypot and the attacker is unable to notice that he is not communicating with the production system. However, the approach has the same limitation to known attacks as *Bait'n'Switch*.

Honeycomb [8] is realized as a *Honeyd* extension. It is based on the idea that any traffic directed to the honeypot can be considered an attack. *Honeycomb* automatically generates *Snort* and *Bro* [10] signatures for all incoming traffic. New signatures are created if a similar pattern does not yet exist. Existing signatures are updated whenever similar traffic has been detected, so the quality of the signatures is increased with each similar attack session. Signatures can be updated to match mutations of existing attacks. For each mutation a more generic description for the signature is generated, so that the original attack and the mutation are both matched. This way the signature base is kept small. The mechanism creates signatures for all traffic directed to the honeypot. Unfortunately the attacks are not verified to be successful in any way. Therefore, it suffers of false positives if any non-attack traffic is directed to the honeypot like e.g. the IPX protocol. A computer connected to the Internet especially on a dial-up connection is addressed even by non attack traffic. Whenever a search engine tries to mirror the host or a peer to peer program tries to connect, a signature is generated. Signatures must be checked manually afterwards whether they were created for an attack or for something else. An approach to verify the attack patterns is desirable. The signature generation mechanism could be used to create IDS signatures if an appropriate attack traffic is identified and directed to the system.

Finally, the idea of so-called *honeynets* [11] exist. Instead of simulating a single vulnerable host, a honeynet tends to simulate a complete network by the deployment of a set of honeypots.

The central idea of honeypots is, that any traffic directed to the honeypot, is considered an attack. The state of the art shows that on the one hand the gathering of attack related information currently requires the manual analysis of the log files and on the other hand the approach to generate signatures that match any incoming traffic leads to false positives that have to be eliminated manually. Furthermore, honeypot approaches that only react to known signatures do not gather any information valuable for identifying new signatures. Summarizing, the existing approaches do not provide sufficient support for the (semi-)automatic detection and analysis of unknown attacks.

2.2 Field-Test

As described in section 2.1 the open-source low-interaction honeypot *Honeyd* is able to simulate several host identities and in addition, it offers scripts that simulate network services. We configured *Honeyd* such that it represents a typical Linux installation (with one IP-address) which runs a WWW- and a SSH-server. For four days we connected the setup to the Internet and we logged each connection. The corresponding log file grew to a size of $18MByte$. A consecutive evaluation of the log file showed that a big part of the conncections were caused by known attacks (see table 1).

Table 1. *Honeyd* field-test results

Event	No of occurrences
Nimda	8871
CodeRed	2155
CodeRed II (3 versions)	2626
MyDoom	1369
W32/Welchia.D	1674
Attempts to access the IIS-samples	645
Attempts to get '/etc/passwd'	168
Attempts to execute cmd.exe	123245

Apart from the attacks enlisted in table 1, many entries were enregistered that were caused by browser connections or by "talkative" protocols like NetBIOS, IPX, etc. The conducted experiment clearly shows that even in case of a honeypot with an "unadvertised" IP-address assigned to it, the amount of logged (attacking) traffic is immense.

Since the focus of our work on honeypots is towards the detection and analysis of unknown network security attacks, further measures to increasing the significance of logged traffic are required. In the next section, we describe our approach to this problem.

3 Concept

The goal of our approach is the design and realization of a generic high interaction honeypot framework that allows to (semi-)automatically identify application layer based attacks (e.g. buffer overflows, format string attacks, etc.). Figure 1 depicts an example scenario that includes two attackers, a firewall / intrusion prevention system (IPS)

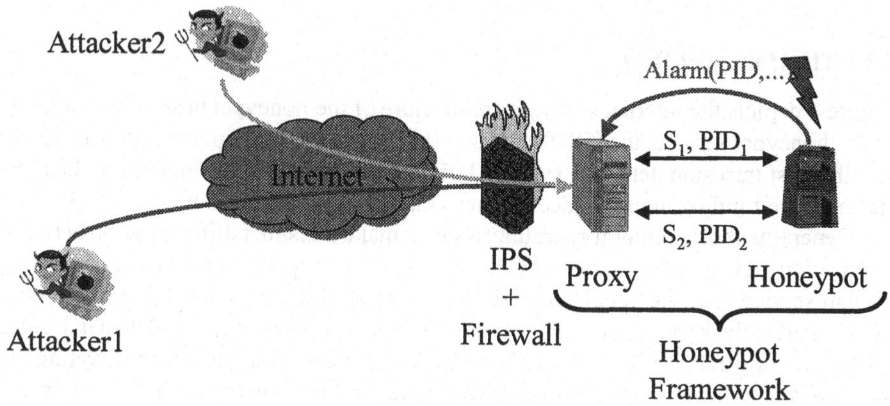

Fig. 1. An example scenario

and our honeypot framework. The purpose of the IPS / firewall is to filter the incoming traffic for known attacks. The honeypot framework itself consists of a proxy and a honeypot host. The proxy host is responsible for the session-individual logging of the network traffic that was sent to the honeypot. Furthermore, in case of a detected attack the proxy provides a mechanism to replay a specific previously logged session. An advantage of the bipartite approach is that the honeypot and the log files are kept on separate hosts so that in case of a complete system takeover of the honeypot host by an attacker the log files remain save. Besides this, the replay mechanism that is integrated in the proxy can be used to analyze a discovered attack in detail, as well as to test if other system configurations are just as vulnerable as the honeypot service to the attack.

The honeypot host consist of a honeypot service, namely a real service, and a host intrusion detection system (HIDS). The running service is the bait that attracts worms respectively hackers whereas the HIDS supervises the honeypot service. The realized detection mechanism is generic and allows the detection of attacks on the basis of system-call signatures. The reasoning behind this approach is that the main part of current attacks exploit a vulnerability that is specific for a software (e.g. a buffer overflow vulnerability of a WWW-server). In case of a successful attack, the hacker will sooner or later exploit its newly gained authorizations which most often results in an observable system change. An example for this would be an attacker that tries to open a new network socket in order to download further hacking utilities. Or another popular example is a worm that starts on each infected system an email relaying server which it uses for its further spreading. On the system-call level both examples can easily be monitored. The interface between honeypot service and HIDS is generic such that is possible to exchange or add a honeypot service in an easy and flexible manner.

As depicted in figure 1, it might occur that a honeypot service is running two or more process entities (parent + children processes) simultaneously. For example, if the honeypot system was running a WWW-server as a honeypot service, the server parent process would create a child process for each HTTP-session.

3.1 The Honeypot Host

Figure 2 depicts the internal software architecture of the honeypot host, which consists of the honeypot service, the HIDS-manager (hidsmgr), the honeypot monitor (monitor) and the host intrusion detection system (HIDS). Honeypot service, monitor and HIDS-manager are running in user-space, whereas the HIDS is located in the kernel space.

Generally, most common operating systems make a distinct differentiation between application and operating system. Each time a user-space process requires an operating system service (e.g. the opening of a network socket) the service must send the proper system call to the kernel. The kernel checks the request of the process and then it decides whether to fulfill it or not. By inserting a HIDS into kernel-space and by redirecting the system-calls to the HIDS, it is possible to extend the functionality of the kernel. In our case, it is possible to monitor on the basis of system-call level what a process in user-space does. In addition, it is possible to introduce more detailed decision criteria in the kernel to determine whether the desired action is allowed or not (a similar mechanism has also been proposed for performing access control on active networking nodes; see also [7]).

The general method of system call interception is depicted in figure 3 and shows the interception of the *socket* system call. The user process uses the *socket()* command to create a socket for network communication. A process must execute a system call to gain access to the operating system services. Normally, this is done by wrapper functions which are part of standard libraries. The wrapper function puts the variables to be submitted into the correct order, and then executes the proper system call. At the entry point into the kernel, the kernel uses a table — the so-called system call table — for the forwarding of the incoming system calls to the corresponding functions. By changing the destination of a pointer inside the system call table, we can redirect a defined system call to another function, in our case to the HIDS. That checks if the service is authorized to use a specific operating system service. If this test is passed, the HIDS then calls the standard kernel function belonging to the system call.

The HIDS is realized as a Linux Kernel Module (LKM) and it detects intrusions on system-call-level. Whenever a user space process tries to execute a series of system-

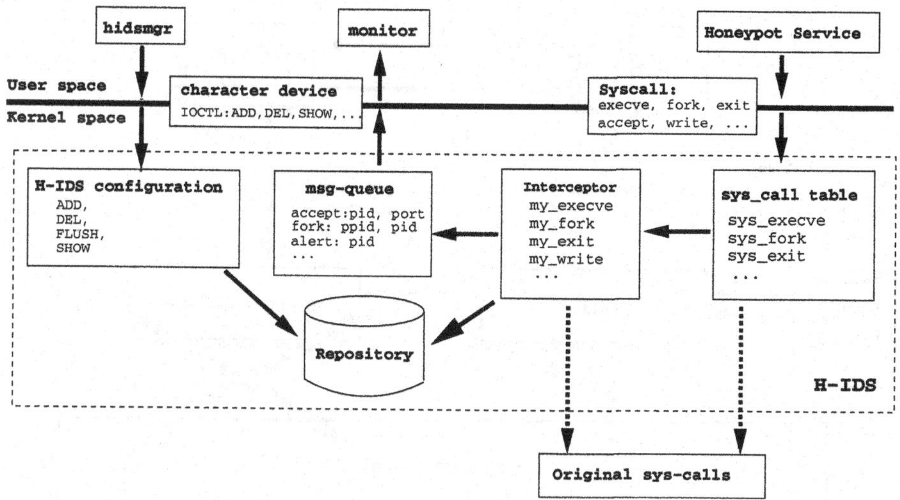

Fig. 2. The honeypot host

calls that matches an attack signature a security alert is raised. Furthermore, the HIDS refuses to forward the last requested system-call to the operating system in order to prevent the honeypot system from being harmed. Consecutively, the HIDS triggers the monitor process to send an alarm message to the logging proxy. The attack signatures are specified inside the repository as a series of system-calls or simply as a black-list of disallowed system-calls. Besides this, it is also possible to configure the HIDS such that the execution of a specific group of applications (e.g. common gateway interface - CGI) is authorized. The user space front-end monitor handles the synchronization of local process ID and remote session ID between honeypot and proxy server.

The HIDS checks for each observed system-call, whether or not it is executed by a process under supervision. The access to the operating-system is either granted or not, depending on the policy. Moreover, if necessary a message is sent to the monitor and then forwarded to the logging component.

Finally, the HIDS-manager can be used to reconfigure the HIDS at runtime. It provides a set of functions which first can be used to add, delete or modify existing attack patterns. Second, the manager also allows to modify the list of services that must be observed by the HIDS.

3.2 The Logging Proxy

The logging proxy listens for connection requests to the honeypot service which originate from a potential hacker. Next, the proxy server acts itself as a client on behalf of the user / attacker and forwards the request (using its own IP address) to the honeypot service. Besides forwarding, the proxy server also creates for each forwarded session (session ID) an individual log file which in addition, contains the IP-address of the

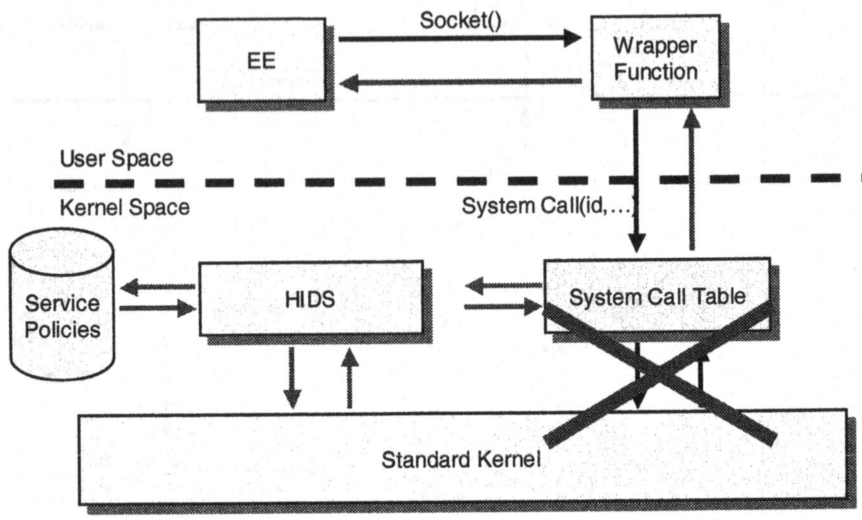

Fig. 3. Interception of a system call

attacker, the connection ports and a timestamp. To the attacker, the proxy server is invisible; all honeypot service requests and returned responses appear to be directly from the proxy host.

The proxy logs the connection data of the honeypot service. A difficulty thereby is to match attack session and PID of the corresponding process on the honeypot host, as one host keeps the logs while the other one detects the attacks. If a new client connection is initiated by an attacker, the proxy sends the new session ID via the control channel to the monitor on the honeypot monitor. This one acknowledges the successful connection of the proxy to the honeypot service by sending a message to the proxy server, which contains the PID of the corresponding child process and the ports of the incoming connection. The ports are used to track which connection and session ID belong together. Furthermore, the proxy server maintains a list of currently established connections to the honeypot service. On a fork of the honeypot service a new PID message is automatically sent by the honeypot service monitor to the proxy server. In case that a process tries to execute a series of an unauthorized system-calls (attack signature), the honeypot monitor triggers an alert and sends a corresponding message to the proxy server. The alert-message contains the PID of the honeypot service process that violated the security policy and the kind of violation. By the means of the alert message the proxy server tags the corresponding session and adds the alert information to the proper log file. In addition, the proxy server is able to stop the ongoing attack session — if specified so in its local security policy.

Process ID Tracking Generally, processes can be identified by their unique process identification number, the PID. As already mentioned, many networking services —

that can be used as the honeypot service — create a new process environment for each connection that they accept. Accordingly, a mechanism is required to keep track of the processes that must be observed by the HIDS. Figure 4 depicts our principle of PID tracking. Initially, we open a *shell* which we subsequently add — with the help of the HIDS manager — to the list of processes that are monitored by the HIDS. Next, the chosen honeypot service is started from inside the shell, which automatically assigns it to the group of services that must be observed by the HIDS.

Normally, a new process is created by a networking service through the execution of the *fork()* system-call (other possibility *clone()*). In this case the operating system creates a new process environment and assigns a new process ID to it. Now, in case that an attacker connects to the honeypot service, then the operating system creates the new process by executing the *fork()* command and returns two values. One value, which is the PID of the newly created process, is returned to the parent process, whereas the newly created child process receives a zero as return value. Whenever a process that is member of the list of services that must be observed by the HIDS creates a child process, then the newly created child process is automatically assigned to be a member of the list.

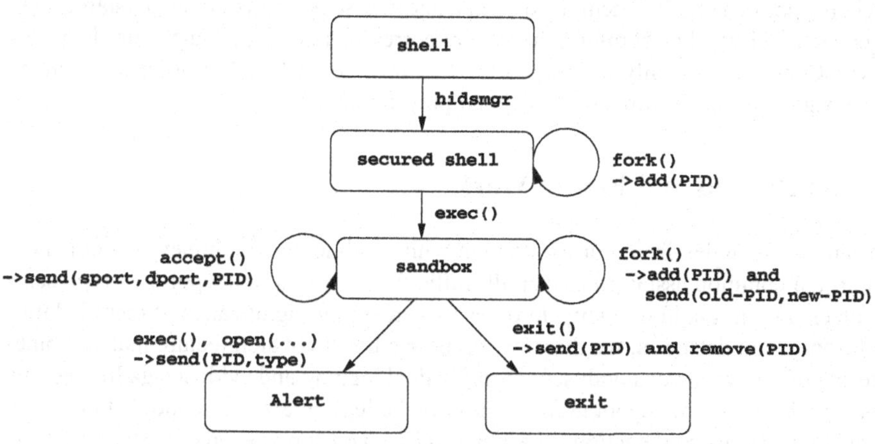

Fig. 4. Process ID (PID) tracking

3.3 Replay Mechanism

The session-specific log-files that are created by the proxy server can be used by the replay tool, that is part of the proxy server, to repeat a selected (attack) session. In case that the honeypot service is stateless and deterministic, the attacker can be replaced by the replay tool and each suspicious log-file can be replayed in sequence. This allows to analyze attacks in detail as well as to test if other systems are equally vulnerable to an attack.

4 Proof of Concept

We realized a Linux-based prototype of the described honeypot architecture. In order to test its functionality we setup a testbed, which consists of three Pentium III 800 machines running Linux 2.4.24, and which are connected via Ethernet. The middle host — equipped with two network interface cards — is running the proxy server. The remaining hosts are used as attacker and honeypot.

The Dune Web Server [1], which is known to contain several security holes, was chosen as honeypot service. Furthermore, we downloaded the according exploitation tool *xdune* [16] from the Internet. *Xdune* is a tool that can be used to remotely exploit a buffer overflow vulnerability of the *Dune* web server. We started our honeypot system with the *Dune* server as honeypot service. Before starting the *Xdune* tool, we simultaneously started several harmless HTTP sessions in order to check if the honeypot system is capable to automatically identify and tag the attacking session.

The normal order of events — without the intervention of a HIDS — would be as follows. First *Xdune* searches in a brute-force manner for the correct return address that directs the process execution to the injected code. If successful, the injected shell code opens a listener and executes the command */bin/sh*. With the HIDS running on the honeypot system, the attempts to open a network socket respectively to start a shell triggered an alarm. Furthermore, the system correctly tagged the log-file on the proxy server. Consequently, only the tagged log-file must be analyzed in order to create an attack signature for an intrusion detection / prevention system.

5 Conclusions and Future Work

As can be concluded from our experiment with a public domain honeypot implementation, the common assumption that all traffic destined to a honeypot host represents an attack does not hold in reality. In order to increase the significance of recorded traffic for intrusion detection, we therefore propose a honeypot architecture that combines filtering of known attacks with session-individual logging and evidence gathering on a honeypot host. Our honeypot in fact combines the high interaction honeypot idea with a host based intrusion detection system that is based on supervision of system calls. As most attacks coming in from the Internet sooner or later try to perform a "suspicious" action like starting a shell process, accessing specific files, etc. our approach is able to operate effectively even with rather simple signatures of "suspicious" behavior. By marking the session logs of traffic streams that resulted in suspicious behavior, a significant reduction of traffic to be evaluated is attained, so that forensic analysis of recorded traffic is considerably simplified. In our future work, we plan to improve the ability of our system call supervision functionality to track state (e.g. allowing incremental evidence gathering as compared to simple call sequences), in order to be able to specify more complex behaviors as suspicious. Furthermore, the logging proxy could be augmented with further measures to reduce the amount of input data to forensic analysis by aggregating instances of identically looking attacking sessions.

References

[1] Baris. Dune. http://freshmeat.net/projects/dune/, 1999.

[2] J. Beale, J. C. Foster, J. Posluns, R. Russell, and B. Caswell. *Snort 2.0 Intrusion Detection.* Syngress, 2003.

[3] W. La Cholter et al. IBAN: Intrusion Blocker Based on Active Networks. In *Proc. of Dance 2002.*

[4] Fyodor. The Art of Port Scanning. *Phrack Magazine*, 7, 1997.

[5] A. Hess, M. Jung, and G. Schäfer. FIDRAN: A Flexible Intrusion Detection and Response Framework for Active Networks. In *Proc. of 8th IEEE Symposium on Computers and Communications (ISCC'2003)*, July 2003.

[6] A. Hess and G. Schäfer. ISP-Operated Protection of Home Networks with FIDRAN. In *First IEEE Consumer Communications and Networking Conference (CCNC'2004)*, January 2004.

[7] A. Hess and G. Schäfer. Realizing a Flexible Access Control Mechanism for Active Nodes based on Active Networking Technology. In *IEEE International Conference on Communications (ICC 2004)*, Paris, France, June 2004.

[8] C. Kreibich and J. Crowcroft. Honeycomb - Creating Intrusion Detection Signatures Using Honeypots. In *2nd Workshop on Hot Topics in Networks (HotNets-II)*, 2003.

[9] J. Larsen. Hogwash. http://hogwash.sourceforge.net/docs/overview.html.

[10] V. Paxson. Bro: a System for Detecting Network Intruders in Real-Time. *Computer Networks (Amsterdam, Netherlands: 1999)*, 31(23–24):2435–2463, 1999.

[11] The Honeynet Project. *Know Your Enemy.* Addison-Wesley, 2002.

[12] N. Provos. Honeyd - A Virtual Honeypot Daemon. In *10th DFN-CERT Workshop*, Hamburg, Germany, Februrary 2003.

[13] L. Spitzner. *Honeypots: Tracking Hackers.* Addison-Wesley, 2003.

[14] Takemori, Rikitake, Miyake, and Nakao. Intrusion Trap System: An Efficient Platform for Gathering Intrusion Related Information. Technical report, KDDI R and D Laboratories Inc., 2003.

[15] Xfocus Team. X-Scan Version 3.1 English. http://www.xfocus.org, 2004.

[16] Vade79. Xdune an Exploit for the Dune HTTP Server. http://downloads.securityfocus.com/vulnerabilities/exploits/xdune.c, 2003.

[17] von Raison, A. and Grunwald, L. Wireless Honeypot auf der Cebit, Messe-Trend Mobile Hacking. *iX*, 5:16, 2003.

[18] J. Whitsitt and A. Gonzalez. Bait'n'Switch. Technical report, Team Violating. http://baitnswitch.sf.net.

Methodik und Software zur Erstellung und Konsum von MPEG-21 Digital Items*

Harald Kosch und Alexander Arrich

Institut für Informationstechnologie, Universität Klagenfurt, Österreich
harald.kosch@itec.uni-klu.ac.at
http://www-itec.uni-klu.ac.at/~harald/MPEG/

Zusammenfassung. Im MPEG-21 Multimedia Framework Standard spielt das Digital Item als fundamentale Transaktions- und Austauscheinheit eine zentrale Rolle. Dieser Artikel beschreibt eine Methodik und Software zur Erstellung und den Konsum von Digital Items. Das Softwarewerkzeug setzt sich aus zwei Teilen zusammen: Der *DI Builder* erlaubt es Benutzern MPEG-21 Digital Items zu erstellen, die mit dem *DI Consumer* konsumiert werden können. Die Software demonstriert Teile des MPEG-21 Standards, im speziellen Teil 2-Digital Item Declaration, Teil 3-Digital Item Identification, Teil 5-Rights Expression Language, Teil 6-Rights Data Dictionary und Teil 7-Digital Item Adaptation.

1 Einleitung

MPEG-21 [1] ist der fünfte Standard der Moving Pictures Experts Group (MPEG). Während es sich bei MPEG-1, MPEG-2 und MPEG-4 um reine Kodierungsstandards handelt [2], hat MPEG mit MPEG-7 [3] einen Beschreibungsstandard für Multimedia Inhalte entwickelt[1]. Mit MPEG-21 will man nun ein so genanntes 'Multimedia-Framework' schaffen, welches das Austauschen von Multimedia-Daten und Inhalten interoperabel, benutzerfreundlich und fairer macht [4]. *Digital Items(DIs)* spielen im MPEG-21 Multimedia Framework Standard als Transaktions- und Austauscheinheit eine zentrale Rolle. In diesem Artikel werden eine Methodik und Software für die Erstellung und den Konsum von MPEG-21 Digital Items beschrieben. Die Erstellung von Digital Items basiert auf der partiellen Abbildung der Digital Item Declaration Language (DIDL) auf eine Objektstruktur, welche die Erstellung, Verarbeitung und Benutzung von Digital Items erstmalig ermöglicht. Die zwei entwickelten Softwarewerkzeuge *DI Builder* und *DI Consumer* erlauben die Erstellung bzw. den Konsum von Digital Items, wobei der Konsum das Abspielen von Mediendateien und das Betrachten der Metadaten des Digital Items umfasst.

* Dieses Projekt wurde teilweise aus Mitteln des FWFs (Fonds zur Förderung der wissenschaftlichen Forschung) unter der Projektnummer P14789 finanziert.

[1] Überblick über die MPEG-Standards unter: http://www.chiariglione.org/mpeg/standards.htm

Im nächsten Teil wird der MPEG-21 Standard eingeführt. Den Schwerpunkt des Artikels bilden Kapitel 3 und 4, welche die Methodik und Software zur Erstellung und Konsum von Digital Items beschreiben.

2 MPEG-21 Standard

Die beiden zentralen Konzepte eines MPEG-21 verteilten Multimediasystems sind das *Digital Item* und der *Benutzer* [1,4]. Das Digital Item ist die vom Benutzer verwendete Austausch- und Transaktionseinheit des Systems. Benutzer sind alle Entitäten, die im MPEG-21 System interagieren bzw. Digital Items erzeugen und verwenden.

Das *Digital Item* ist ein strukturiertes und hierarchisch aufgebautes Objekt, das Multimediaressourcen und Metadaten kapselt. Die Metadaten eines Digital Items beschreiben einerseits das Digital Item und dessen Gebrauch, andererseits aber auch die Ressourcen des Digital Items.

Der *Benutzer* ist jede Entität, die am MPEG-21 System teilnimmt bzw. Digital Items verwendet. Es fallen daher Einzelpersonen, Personengruppen, Konsumenten und auch Organisationen gleichermaßen unter den Begriff *Benutzer*. In diesem Sinn folgt MPEG-21 dem Peer-to-Peer-Paradigma mit gleichberechtigten Teilnehmern [5] und nicht dem Client/Server-Paradigma, bei dem Benutzer klar definierte und festgelegte Rollen einnehmen [6]. Die Rolle eines Benutzers wird durch die Interaktion mit anderen Benutzern bestimmt, das heißt beispielsweise, dass ein Benutzer in einer Transaktion die Rolle des Konsumenten und in einer anderen Transaktion die Rolle des Produzenten übernehmen kann. Abbildung 1 veranschaulicht die Beziehungen zwischen Benutzern, Digital Items und den Kernelementen des MPEG-21 Multimediasystems.

2.1 Teile des MPEG-21 Standards

Der MPEG-21 Standard umfasst inzwischen schon *16 Teile*, die nachfolgend zusammen mit einer kurzen Beschreibung aufgelistet sind. Die in der Arbeit verwendeten Teile werden gesondert näher beschrieben[2].

- Teil 1: Visionen, Technologien und Strategien von MPEG-21.
- Teil 2: Digital Item Declaration (DID) zur Darstellung von Digital Items.
- Teil 3: Digital Item Identification (DII) zur Identifikation von Digital Items und seiner Komponenten.
- Teil 4: Intellectual Property Management and Protection (IPMP) zum Schutz von Inhalten und den damit verbundenen Rechten (in Bearbeitung).
- Teil 5: Rights Expression Language (REL) zur Spezifikation von Rechten in Bezug auf die Verwendung von Multimediainhalten.
- Teil 6: Rights Data Dictionary (RDD) stellt eine Menge an Begriffen bereit, die von der REL verwendet werden.

[2] siehe auch `http://www.chiariglione.org/mpeg/working_documents.htm`

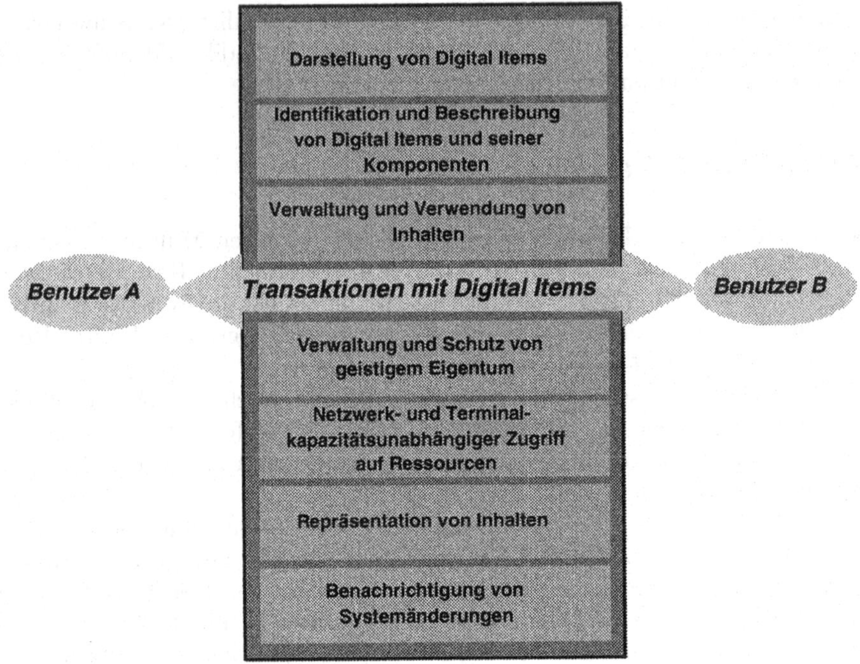

Abb. 1. Die konzeptuellen Hauptelemente des MPEG-21 Standards

- Teil 7: Digital Item Adaptation (DIA) zur Anpassung von Ressourcen und Metadaten an verfügbare Netzwerk- und Terminalkapazitäten.
- Teil 8: Referenzsoftware zur Validierung der Vorschläge für die Teile 1-7.
- Teil 9: Ein Dateiformat zum effizienten Speichern und Zugriff auf Digital Items (in Bearbeitung).
- Teil 10: Digital Item Processing umfasst eine Menge von Operationen zur Konfiguration und Manipulation von Digital Items (in Bearbeitung).
- Teil 11: Persistent Association Tools umfasst Methoden und Techniken zur dauerhaften Verknüpfung von Informationen und ihrer Identifikation und zur Beschreibung von Inhalten mit den Inhalten (z.B. Wasserzeichen) selbst (in Bearbeitung).
- Teil 12: Resource Delivery Test Bed ist eine Testumgebung für MPEG-21 Anwendungen.
- Teil 13: Scalable Video Coding sucht Techniken und Methoden zur skalierbaren Kodierung von Videoströmen (in Bearbeitung).
- Teil 14: Conformance Testing (in Bearbeitung).
- Teil 15: Event Reporting für die Meldung von Systemänderungen (in Bearbeitung).
- Teil 16: Binary Format zur kodierten Darstellung von MPEG-21 Digital Items (in Bearbeitung).

Digital Item Declaration (DID) Die Digital Item Declaration Language (DIDL) ist das wichtigste Ergebnis der DID Arbeitsgruppe und stellt ein XML Schema dar, das die Struktur von Digital Items bestimmt. Die Bestandteile eines Digital Items sind Ressourcen und Metadaten. Die DIDL bestimmt, wie diese Ressourcen und Metadaten auf eine strukturierte Weise zu einem XML-basierten Digital Item integriert werden. Abbildung 2 zeigt ein einfaches Beispiel. Das DIDL-Element ist das Wurzelement eines Digital Items. Es beinhaltet in einfacher Form ein oder mehrere *item-Elemente*, welche die Grundeinheit einer zusammenhängenden MPEG-21 Beschreibung darstellen. Diese können hierarchisch angeordnet werden. Ein item-Element enthält neben Beschreibungskomponenten (*Descriptor-Elemente*, z.B. MPEG-7 oder Dublin Core Beschreibungen) ein *Component-Element*, welches die Ressource als Referenz spezifiziert oder inline trägt. Digital Items lassen sich durch *Auswahlstrukturen* konfigurieren. Kapitel 3.1 zeigt ein einfaches Beispiel.

Digital Item Identification (DII) Die Digital Item Identification (DII) Spezifikation erlaubt die Assoziation von eindeutigen Bezeichnern mit Digital Items bzw. Teilen eines Digital Items unabhängig vom Typ und der Granularität des spezifischen Teils. Zur Identifikation von Digital Items bzw. Komponenten eines Digital Items nützt DII die Uniform Resource Identifiers. Zur Differenzierung zwischen XML Schemata nützt DII den XML Namespace-Mechanismus. Unterschiedliche Arten von Digital Items wie Content Digital Items und Method Digital Items werden unterschieden, indem der Typ des Digital Items angegeben wird. Ein weiteres Entwurfsmerkmal von MPEG-21 DII ist, dass nicht versucht wurde, bestehende Identifikationssysteme zu ersetzen, sondern dass deren Nutzung explizit ermöglicht wurde.

Rights Expression Language (REL) Die Rights Expression Language (REL) ist eine Sprache zur Darstellung von Rechten an digitalen Inhalten und an Metadaten. Die REL benutzt zur Beschreibung von Rechten Begriffe aus dem Rights Data Dictionary (MPEG-21 RDD), einer erweiterbaren Sammlung von Definitionen [7]. Durch die Rights Expression Language können digitale Inhalte geschützt und Rechte, Bedingungen und Gebühren für die Verwendung digitaler Inhalten spezifiziert werden. Das Kernelement der REL ist die Berechtigung (Grant), die es einem Rechteinhaber bzw. -herausgeber erlaubt, einem Rechtenehmer Rechte in Form von erlaubten Aktivitäten an einer Ressource zuzuerkennen. Die Ausübung von Rechten durch den Rechtenehmer kann von Bedingungen, die der Rechteinhaber definiert, abhängen. Das REL Datenmodell wurde als eigenes XML Schema verwirklicht.

Digital Item Adaptation (DIA) Ein Ziel des MPEG-21 Multimediasystems ist der transparente Zugriff auf Multimediainhalte, unabhängig von Netzwerk- und Terminalkapazitäten. Dieses Ziel erfordert, dass Digital Items bzw. die darin gekapselten Ressourcen und Metadaten beim Erkennen von Kapazitätsengpässen angepasst werden können. Bei der Adaptierung von Digital Items werden die Ressourcen und Metadaten durch Digital Item Adaptation Tools an gegebene Netzwerk- und Terminalkapazitäten angepasst. Dabei wird ausgehend vom Originalitem ein adaptiertes Ergebnisitem erzeugt, indem die

```
<?xml version="1.0" encoding="UTF-8"?>
<DIDL xmlns:targetNamespace="urn:mpeg:mpeg21:2002/01-DIDL-NS"
      xmlns:xsi="http://www.w3.org/2001/XMLSchema-instance">
   <ITEM>
      <DESCRIPTOR>
         <STATEMENT>Spiderman-Film in unterschiedlichen Auflösungen</STATEMENT>
      </DESCRIPTOR>
      <ITEM>
         <DESCRIPTOR>
            <STATEMENT>Spiderman-Film in niedriger Auflösung für einen schnellen
                       Download
            </STATEMENT>
         </DESCRIPTOR>
         <COMPONENT>
            <DESCRIPTOR>
               <STATEMENT>Spiderman-Film in Auflösung 320x240</STATEMENT>
            </DESCRIPTOR>
            <RESOURCE REF="www.online-films/spiderman_low.mpg"/>
         </COMPONENT>
      </ITEM>
      <ITEM>
         <DESCRIPTOR>
            <STATEMENT>Spiderman-Film in sehr hoher Auflösung</STATEMENT>
         </DESCRIPTOR>
         <COMPONENT>
            <DESCRIPTOR>
               <STATEMENT>Spiderman-Film in DVD - Qualität</STATEMENT>
            </DESCRIPTOR>
            <RESOURCE REF="www.online-films/spiderman_high.mpg"/>
         </COMPONENT>
      </ITEM>
   </ITEM>
</DIDL>
```

Abb. 2. Einfaches Digital Item

Ressourcen in einer Resource Adaptation Engine und die Metadaten in einer Description Adaptation Engine angepasst werden. Der Anpassungsprozess wird in beiden Engines durch DIA Tools gesteuert [8]. Die DIA Tools umfassen Beschreibungen und formatunabhängige Mechanismen zur Steuerung des Anpassungsprozesses.

Ein Beispiel eines DIA Tools ist die von uns entwickelte standardisierte Generic Bitstream Definition Language (gBSDL) [9]. Die gBSDL beschreibt die Struktur einer Ressource (z.B. die Frames eines Videos) in einer generischen Weise, wobei diese Beschreibung in XML ausgedrückt wird. Eine Adaptation Engine verwendet diese Beschreibung als Grundlage für die Anpassung eines Videos, beispielsweise zum Entfernen von Frames, um die Bandbreitenanforderung zu reduzieren. Der DI Consumer beinhaltet eine Adaptation Engine.

Beispiele für weitere DIA Tools sind Beschreibungen des Benutzers, der Gebrauchsumgebung, des Netz-werkes und der Fähigkeiten von Endgeräten. Diese Beschreibungen werden dazu verwendet, um den Adaptierungsprozess zu steuern. In unserem Framework kann der Benutzer den Adaptierungsprozess mit Hilfe einer Auswahlliste möglicher Adaptierungsmethoden direkt steuern.

2.2 MPEG-7 Beschreibung im MPEG-21 Digital Item

MPEG-7 ist ein MPEG Standard zur Beschreibung von audiovisuellen Inhalten durch Metadaten [3]. Es können sowohl syntaktische und semantische Eigenschaften von Multimediadaten durch Metadaten beschrieben werden. Die beschreibbaren Eigenschaften von audiovisuellen Inhalten sind im Standard in Form von XML Schema-Konstrukten, so genannten Deskriptoren, definiert. Ein Beispiel einer syntakti-schen Eigenschaft ist etwa die Beschreibungen der Farbverteilung eines Bildes, ein Beispiel einer semanti-schen Eigenschaft ist die Beschreibung der Objekte und ihrer Beziehungen, die im Bild sichtbar sind. Zu bemerken sei noch, dass der Standard zwar die XML Schema-Konstrukte normativ vorgibt, die Extraktion und der Ähnlichkeitsvergleich von Beschreibungen aber als Gegenstand des Firmenwettbewerbs belassen wurden.

Die übliche Methode, externe Metadaten in Digital Items einzubinden ist, die Metadaten als DIDL Deskriptor-Element ins Digital Item einzufügen. Wie der Name impliziert, ist das DIDL Deskriptor-Element die primäre Wahl, Digital Items bzw. deren Ressourcen zu beschreiben. Beispiele für Beschreibungen sind etwa Ressourcenbeschreibungen, Lizenzen, Bezeichner und ähnliches. In unserer Arbeit haben wir beispielsweise den MPEG-7 GoF/GoP-Deskriptor als Ressourcenbeschreibung implementiert. Der MPEG-7 Group-of-Frames/Group-of-Pictures (GoF/GoP)-Deskriptor erstellt ein HSV-Farbhistogramm für eine Gruppe von (Video-)Frames, beispielsweise die Frames einer abgeschlossenen Szene [10]. Er wurde beispielhaft verwendet, um ein Content-Based Retrieval (CBR) auf Digital Items zu ermöglichen und Ähnlichkeitsabfragen zwischen Videos und zwischen Videos und Bildern zu unterstützen [11]. Unsere Softwarelösung stellt die notwendigen Engine-Container für CBR auf den GoF/GoP-Deskriptoren zur Verfügung, auf die dann entsprechende Retrieval- und Datenbankanwendungen, wie z.B. unsere MPEG-7 Multimediadatenbank [12], zugreifen können.

2.3 Resumée

MPEG-21 ist ein relativ junger MPEG Standard, viele Teile werden oder wurden in diesem Jahr veröffentlicht (u.a. Definition eines Digital Items, Ressourcenadaptierung, Rechtesprache), andere befinden sich in Arbeit (u.a. Intellectual Property Management)[3]. Für einige Teile von MPEG-21 gibt es kleine Referenzimplementierungen, aber es gab bisher keine Methodik Software, mit der sich Digital Items erstellen, verarbeiten und konsumieren lassen. Eine manuelle Erstellung der XML-Daten mit Hilfe gängiger Editoren, erweist sich natürlich als mühsam und vor allem fehleranfällig, insbesondere dann, wenn extern vorhandene Ressourcenbeschreibungen eingefügt werden müssen. Ein erster Ansatz, die Struktur von Digital Items im Erstellungsprozess abzubilden, stellt die Software DICreator von Enikos.com[4] dar. Allerdings muss exklusiv XML-Code eingegeben werden. Ebenso wie im Bereich MPEG-7, sind Werkzeuge wünschenswert, welche die Konzepte hinter dem XML-Schema visualisieren (z.B. Übersetzung des Schemaelemente in graphische Menüführungen) und sich nicht nur auf den XML-Code alleine konzentrieren.

[3] siehe auch `http://www.chiariglione.org/mpeg/workplan.htm`
[4] `http://www.enikos.com/products.shtml`

3 Erstellung von MPEG-21 Digital Items

Der DI Builder erlaubt die einfache und transparente Erstellung von MPEG-21 Digital Items in einer graphischen Oberfläche. Die Methodik zur Erstellung von Digital Items basiert auf der partiellen Abbildung des Digital Item Declaration (DID) Items auf eine Objektstruktur und die Generierung eines Digital Items aus der Objektstruktur.

3.1 Methodik zur Erstellung von MPEG-21 Digital Items

Die Methodik für die Erstellung von Digital Items basiert auf der Abbildung des DID Items auf eine Objektstruktur, die semantisch und strukturell der Digital Item Declaration Language (DIDL) entspricht.

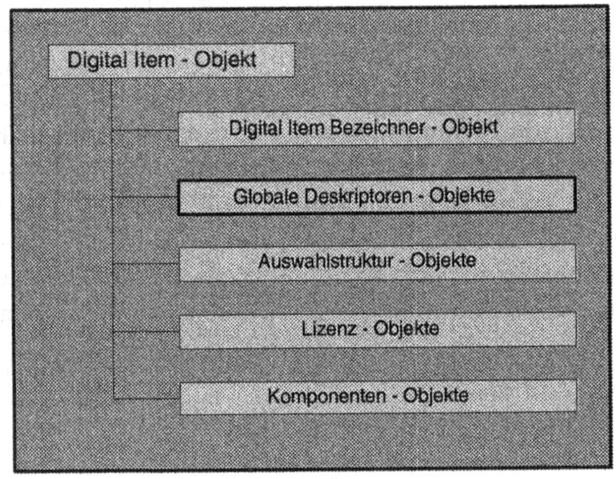

Abb. 3. DID Modellkonforme Objektstruktur

Die Objektstruktur (siehe Abbildung 3) umfasst Objekte für den Bezeichner des Digital Items, für Deskriptoren des Digital Items, Lizenzen, Auswahlstrukturen (DIDL Choices) und Komponenten des Digital Items, wobei Komponenten aus Videodateien sowie MPEG-7 und MPEG-21 DIA Beschreibungen der Videodateien bestehen. Die Objekte sind in der Objektstruktur den DID Items entsprechend angeordnet, wodurch aus der Objektstruktur direkt ein MPEG-21 Digital Item abgeleitet bzw. erzeugt werden kann. Jedes Objekt der Objektstruktur erstellt ein voll- und selbständiges DIDL XML-Fragment aus seinen Daten.

Das Digital Item-Objekt Das Digital Item-Objekt dient als Behälter für andere Objekte und ist das Basisobjekt der Objektstruktur. Das Digital Item-Objekt setzt die DIDL XML-Fragmente seiner Komponenten zu einem Digital Item zusammen. Das Digital Item-Objekt ist auch für die Erzeugung des Headers verantwortlich, wofür es die XML Namespaces, die von seinen Komponenten benötigt werden, abfrägt. Jedes Objekt muss die XML Namespaces, die es benötigt, bekannt geben.

Das Digital Item Bezeichner-Objekt Das Digital Item Bezeichner-Objekt wird zur Erzeugung des Bezeichners eines Digital Items verwendet. Der generierte Bezeichner ist ein Uniform Resource Name (URN), dessen Zweck die dauerhafte und ortsunabhängige Bezeichnung von Digital Items ist. Der Bezeichner startet mit dem Header "urn:mpeg21", es folgt die Systemzeit, die Stringrepräsentationen der numerischen IP-Adresse des Benutzerrechners und eine dreistellige Pseudozufallszahl.

Deskriptoren zur Beschreibung des Digital Items Globale Deskriptoren werden zur allgemeinen Beschreibung des Digital Items benutzt, das heißt, mit globalen Deskriptoren wird der Verwendungszweck des Digital Items in textueller Form angegeben. Ein Objekt für einen globalen Deskriptor besteht aus dem Namen, dem Typ und dem Inhalt eines globalen Deskriptors. Der Typ des globalen Deskriptors beschreibt die Ausprägungsform des Inhalts, beispielsweise reiner Text oder Information, in XML Notation. Das Objekt eines globalen Deskriptors erstellt aus dem Namen, dem Typ und dem Inhalt ein DIDL Descriptor-Fragment.

Lizenzen des Digital Items Zu jeder Videodatei eines Digital Items muss im DI Builder eine Lizenz erstellt werden. Eine Lizenz besteht aus der URL einer Videodatei, dem Rechtevergeber, dem Rechtenehmer, dem Recht und Bedingungen, denen die Ausübung des Rechts unterliegen. Als Bedingungen können der Zeitraum, in dem die Ausübung des Rechts erlaubt ist und die maximale Anzahl erlaubter Rechteausübungen angegeben werden. Ein Lizenzobjekt erzeugt aus seinen Daten ein REL License-Fragment. Die REL License-Fragmente der Lizenzen werden zu einem REL LicenseGroup-Fragment zusammengefasst und in ein DIDL Descriptor-Fragment eingebunden.

Beispiel: Betrachten wir folgendes vom DI Builder erzeugtes REL XML-Fragment. Im ersten Teil wird der Rechtenehmer (`Edith`) mit dem keyHolder-Element[5] spezifiziert. Danach erfolgt die Bekanntgabe ihrer Rechte, hier das Recht, die Ressource, identifiziert durch die DII `urn:harald-1`, abzuspielen. Es folgt eine Nebenbedingung, die aussagt, dass dieses Recht nur im Jahr 2004 ausgeübt werden kann. Danach identifiziert sich der Rechtenehmer (`Harald`) z.B. über seine Digitale Signatur.

```
<license xmlns="http://www.xrml.org/schema/2002/05/xrml2core"
xmlns:mx="urn:mpeg:mpeg21:2002:01-REL-NS">
 <!--Lizenz vergeben für Edith -->
 <grant>
 <keyHolder licensePartId="Edith">
  <info> <!-- Digitale Signatur von Edith --> </info>
 </keyHolder>
 <mx:play/>
```

[5] definiert in XrML (the eXtensible Markup Language), einem allgemeinen Digital Right Language Standard, siehe `http://www.xrml.org/`.

```
  <mx:diReference>
   <mx:identifier>urn:harald-1</mx:identifier>
  </mx:diReference>
  <validityInterval>
   <notBefore>2004-01-01T00:00:00</notBefore>
   <notAfter>2004-12-31T12:59:59</notAfter>
  </validityInterval>
 </grant>
 <!--Die Lizenz ist von Harald ausgestellt-->
 <issuer>
  <keyHolder>
   <info> <!-- Digitale Signatur von Harald --> </info>
  </keyHolder>
 </issuer>
</license>
```

Auswahlstrukur des Digital Items Das Auswahlstrukturobjekt entspricht dem DIDL Choice-Fragment und umfasst Name, Typ, Frage und Alternativen einer Auswahlstruktur. Der Name identifiziert die Auswahlstruktur innerhalb des Digital Items eindeutig. Der Typ legt die Anzahl an wählbaren Alternativen. Die Frage zeigt dem Benutzer an, was er in dieser Auswahlstruktur auswählen kann. Die Alternativen einer Auswahlstruktur werden intern durch einen Namen und dem Benutzer gegenüber durch eine Beschreibung repräsentiert. Ein Auswahlstrukturobjekt erzeugt aus seinen Daten ein DIDL Choice-Fragment.
Das folgende XML-Fragment zeigt eine mögliche Auswahlstruktur zwischen zwei Videoauflösungen.

```
<Choice minSelections="1" maxSelections="1">
 <Descriptor>
  <Statement mimeType="text/plain">
   Welche Auflösung bevorzugen Sie?
  </Statement>
 </Descriptor>
  <Selection select_id="MPEG_klein_FORMAT">
    ...
  </Selection>
  <Selection select_id="MPEG_gross_FORMAT">
    ...
  </Selection>
</Choice>
```

Diese Auswahlstruktur ist an die Auswahl der Ressourcen wie folgt geknüpft:

```
<Component>
 <Condition require="MPEG_klein_FORMAT"/>
```

```
 <Resource mimeType="video/mpeg" ref="video1.mpeg"/>
</Component>
...
<Component>
 <Condition require="MPEG_gross_FORMAT"/>
 <Resource mimeType="video/mpeg" ref="video2.mpeg"/>
</Component>
```

Das Komponenten-Objekt Ein Komponentenobjekt besteht aus der URL einer Videodatei, einer Bedingung für die Verwendung der Komponente beim Konsum des Digital Items und optionalen Beschreibungen der Videodatei. Eine Komponente wird beim Konsum des Digital Items nur dann verwendet bzw. verarbeitet, wenn die Bedingung der Komponente wahr ist. Eine Bedingung ist die Konjunktion von mehreren internen Namen von Alternativen (siehe Auswahlstrukturobjekt) und ist dann wahr, wenn alle Alternativen, auf die sich die internen Namen der Bedingung beziehen, durch den Benutzer ausgewählt werden. Zu einer Videodatei können optional eine MPEG-7 GoF/GoP-Beschreibung und eine MPEG-21 DIA gBSDL-Beschreibung erstellt werden. Die Beschreibungen der Videodateien werden als eigenständige DIDL Descriptor-Fragmente eingebunden. Das Komponentenobjekt erstellt ein DIDL Component-Fragment, in das es die DIDL Descriptor-Fragmente der Videodateibeschreibungen integriert.

3.2 Ablauf zur Erstellung eines Items

Die Erstellung eines Digital Items umfasst drei Schritte. Im ersten Schritt werden die Objekte der Ob-jektstruktur mit den Daten, die der Benutzer über die graphische Schnittstelle eingegeben hat, initialisiert. Nach diesem Schritt steht die Objektstruktur zur weiteren Verarbeitung bereit. Zur Erstellung des Digital Items aus der Objektstruktur wird jedes Objekt dazu aufgerufen, sein DIDL XML-Fragment zu erstellen. Diese XML Fragmente sind die Bausteine, aus dem das Digital Item generiert wird. Nachdem jedes Objekt sein DIDL XML-Fragment erstellt hat, können die einzelnen DIDL Fragmente zu einem Digital Item zusammengefügt werden. Außerdem muss noch der Header des Digital Items erzeugt werden. Der Header besteht aus den vom Digital Item und dessen Komponenten verwendeten XML Namespaces, wobei die Namespaces von den Objekten der Objektstruktur abgefragt werden. Nachdem der Header erzeugt wurde, werden der Reihe nach das DIDL Fragment für den Bezeichner des Digital Items, die DIDL Fragmente für die globalen Deskriptoren, das DIDL Fragment für den Lizenzdeskriptor, die DIDL Fragmente für die Auswahlstrukturen und Komponenten zu einem Digital Item zusammengefügt. Das Ergebnis dieses Schrittes ist ein Digital Item in XML Notation. Anzumerken ist in diesem Zusammenhang auch, dass wenn sich das XML Schema für die Digital Item Declaration Language ändern würde, nur der Teil der Objekte geändert werden müsste, der das XML Fragment generiert.

3.3 Der DI Builder

Der DI Builder als *signiertes* Applet realisiert, erlaubt die einfache und transparente Erstellung von MPEG-21 Digital Items in einer graphischen Oberfläche. Daneben unterstützt der DI Builder den Transfer per FTP von Digital Items und Mediendateien auf Server wie auch den Download von Mediendateien ins lokale Dateisystem des Benutzers. Abbildung 4 zeigt die Maske zur Erstellung der Lizenzen. Linker Hand werden Name und zu schützende Ressource angegeben, während rechter Hand die Eigenschaften der Lizenzierung spezifiziert werden. Der DI Builder (und DI Consumer) kann unter:
`http://www-itec.uni-klu.ac.at/~harald/MPEG-21/` getestet werden.

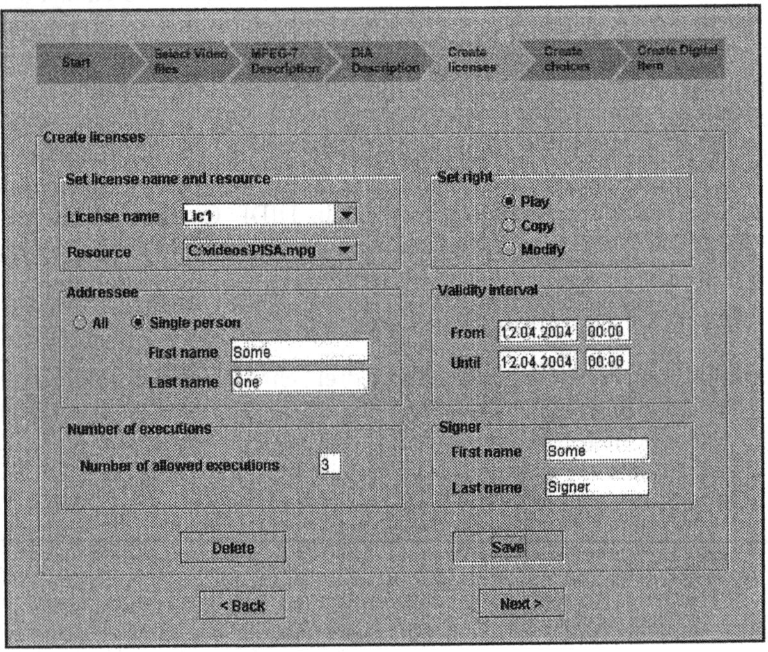

Abb. 4. Die Create Licenses-Maske zur Angabe von Lizenzen

Der DI Builder ist in zwei logische Teile gegliedert, die graphische Oberfläche zur Eingabe der Daten für die Erstellung von Digital Items und den Logikteil, dessen Hauptkomponente die Objektstruktur ist. Die Erstellung eines Digital Items ist in drei Schritte unterteilt. Im ersten Schritt füllt der Benutzer in der graphischen Oberfläche ein Eigenschaftsobjekt mit Eigenschaft-Wert-Paaren. Beispiele für eine Eigenschaft ist die FTP-Adresse an welche die Mediendateien transferiert werden sollen. Im Logikteil wird das Eigenschaftsobjekt geparst und daraus die Objektstruktur erstellt. Abschließend wird aus der Objektstruktur ein MPEG-21 konformes Digital Item generiert. Die Kommunikation zwischen

Oberfläche und Logikteil beschränkt sich auf die Übergabe des Eigenschaftsobjekts. Eine Callback-Funktion wird zur Anzeige des Fortschritts bei der Erstellung des Items in der graphischen Oberfläche benötigt. Durch diese Trennung ist der Logikteil unabhängig vom Implementierungsteil der Oberfläche.

4 Konsum von MPEG-21 Digital Items

Die *DI Consumer*-Software erlaubt den Konsum von Digital Items u.a. solche, die mit dem DI Builder erstellt wurden. Der Konsum umfasst dabei die Auswahl von Videodateien des Digital Items, das Abspielen der Videodateien und das Betrachten des Digital Items in einem XML Viewer. Sowohl das Abspielen der Videodateien als auch das Betrachten der Metadaten des Digital Items hängt vom Besitz einer gültigen Lizenz ab, das heißt, nur wenn im Digital Item eine Lizenz mit den notwendigen Rechten integriert ist, darf der Benutzer die Aktionen ausführen. Die Verarbeitung des Digital Items geschieht in so genannten Engines. Die Aufgabe der Engines ist die Verarbeitung von Digital Items mit und ohne Hilfe des Benutzers. Das Ergebnis der Verarbeitung ist abhängig von der jeweiligen Engine und umfasst beispielsweise die Auswahl der Ressourcen aus einem Digital Item oder auch das Überprüfen von Benutzerberechtigungen.

4.1 Methodik zum Konsum von MPEG-21 Digital Items

Der Hauptbestandteil des logischen Teils des DI Consumers sind die *Engines* zur Verarbeitung eines Digital Items. Eine Engine übernimmt ein Digital Item und verarbeitet das Digital Item bzw. Teile des Digital Items mit oder ohne der Hilfe des Benutzers. Der DI Consumer besteht aus drei Engines. Die *ChoiceEngine* verarbeitet die Auswahlstrukturen eines Digital Items mit Hilfe des Benutzers und füllt einen globalen Ressourcenbuffer mit den Videodateien an, die durch die gewählten Alternativen bestimmt werden. Danach wird das Digital Item an die ProcessingEngine weitergeleitet. Die *ProcessingEngine* adaptiert die Videodaten auf Wunsch, spielt sie dann in einem Videoplayer ab und zeigt das Digital Item in einem XML Viewer an. Vor der Anzeige eines Videos bzw. des Digital Items ruft die ProcessingEngine die LicenseEngine auf. Die *LicenseEngine* prüft, ob der Benutzer das Video und das Digital Item ansehen darf. Nur wenn die LicenseEngine ein positives Evaluierungsergebnis liefert darf der Benutzer das Video abspielen. Der Fluss eines Digital Items durch die einzelnen Engines ist in Abbildung 5 festgehalten. Im folgenden beschreiben wir die Aufgaben der Engines.

Aufbau und Funktionalität der Engines Die DI Consumer-Software besteht aus einer graphischen Oberfläche, Engines zur Verarbeitung von Digital Items und einer zentralen Schnittstellenkomponente zur Interaktion zwischen der graphischen Oberfläche und den Engines des DI Consumers. In der graphischen Oberfläche wird der Konsum von Digital Items durch den Benutzer gesteuert, wobei die Komponenten der graphischen Oberfläche über die Schnittstellekomponente auf die Engines und deren Funktionalität zugreifen. Die Aufgabe der

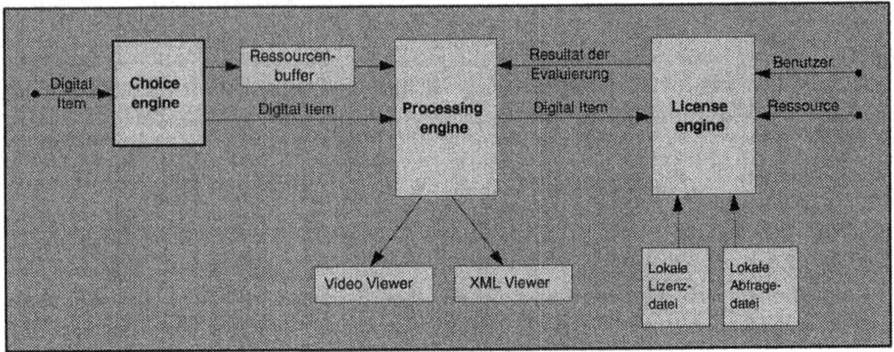

Abb. 5. Engines des DI Consumers

Engines ist es, ein Digital Item zu übernehmen und zu verarbeiten, wobei der Verarbeitungsschritt von der spezifischen Engine abhängt. Jede Engine implementiert ein Interface mit einer Methode zur Verarbeitung eines Digital Items.

Funktionsweise der ChoiceEngine Die ChoiceEngine verarbeitet die Auswahlstrukturen eines Digital Items mit Hilfe des Benutzers und füllt den globalen Ressourcenbuffer des DI Consumers. Der Ressourcenbuffer enthält nach der Verarbeitung der Auswahlstrukturen alle Mediendateien, die den Auswahlkriterien des Benutzers entsprechen. Die Auswahlstrukturen lassen sich sehr gut in der graphi-schen Oberfläche darstellen (mit Hilfe von Radiobuttons bzw. Checkboxen). Der Benutzer sieht nur die Frage und die Alternativen der Auswahlstruktur.

Funktionsweise der ProcessingEngine Die ProcessingEngine spielt ein Video ab und stellt ein Digital Item in einem XML Viewer dar. Bevor ein Video durch den Benutzer abgespielt werden darf, wird von der ProcessingEngine die LicenseEngine aufgerufen. Die LicenseEngine prüft, ob der Benutzer zum Abspielen des ausgewählten Mediendatei berechtigt ist. Nur wenn die LicenseEngine ein positives Evaluierungsergebnis liefert, wird die Mediendatei abgespielt und der XML Viewer aktiviert. Die ProcessingEngine integriert auch eine *AdaptationEngine*, welche eine Ressource vor dem tatsächlichen Konsum auf Benutzeranforderung adaptiert. Die AdaptationEngine verwendet die BSDL-Beschreibung des Digital Items für die Anpassung eines Videos, beispielsweise zum Entfernen von Frames, um die Bandbreitenanforderung zu reduzieren. Der Benutzer kann um eine solche Adaptierung ansuchen, wenn Betriebsmittelengpässe vorliegen.

Funktionsweise der LicenseEngine Die LicenseEngine überprüft, ob der aktuelle Benutzer eine gewählte Mediendatei zum aktuellen Zeitpunkt abspielen darf. Darunter fällt auch die Prüfung, ob der Benutzer die Anzahl erlaubter Wiedergaben noch nicht überschritten hat. Nur wenn die LicenseEngine ein positives Resultat liefert, wird die Mediendatei im DI Consumer wiedergegeben und es dem Benutzer erlaubt, das Digital Item in einem XML Viewer anzusehen.

4.2 Software zum Konsum von MPEG-21 Digital Items

Der *DI Consumer* ermöglicht den Konsum von MPEG-21 Digital Items. Der Konsum eines Digital Items umfasst die Auswahl von Mediendateien, das Abspielen der Mediendateien und das Betrachten der Metadaten des Digital Items. Das Abspielen der Mediendateien und das Betrachten der Metadaten durch den Benutzer hängt davon ab, ob der Benutzer durch die in den Digital Item spezifizierten Lizenzen dazu berechtigt wurde.
Der Konsum eines Digital Items wird über die graphische Oberfläche des DI Consumers gesteuert. Um das zuvor erwähnte Anwendungsszenario zu unterstützen, wurde ein HTTP-Downloader integriert, mit dem Digital Items von öffentlichen Servern heruntergeladen werden können.

Die DI Consumer-Software besteht aus einer graphischen Oberfläche, Engines zur Verarbeitung von Digital Items und einer zentralen Schnittstellenkomponente zur Interaktion zwischen der graphischen Oberfläche und den Engines des DI Consumers. In der graphischen Oberfläche wird der Konsum von Digital Items durch den Benutzer gesteuert, wobei die Komponenten der graphischen Oberfläche über die Schnittstellenkomponente auf die Engines und deren Funktionalität zugreifen.

5 Schlussfolgerungen

MPEG-21 ist der "Multimedia-Framework" Standard, welcher den Austausch von Multimedia-Daten und Inhalten benutzerfreundlicher, transparenter und fairer gestalten soll. Ein Digital Item ist dabei die grundlegende Entität zur Verteilung von Informationen im Multimedia-Framework. Es ist eine Zusammenfassung von Ressourcen (z.B. ein Video) und Metadaten (z.B. eine Beschreibung der Farbverteilungen im Video). Die ersten Teile von MPEG-21 sind kürzlich veröffentlicht worden, oder werden bis Jahresende zur Verfügung stehen. Werkzeuge zur Erstellung und Verarbeitung von Digital Items, welche dem Framework-Gedanken von MPEG-21 folgen, sind deswegen unerlässlich.

In diesem Zusammenhang stellt unser Artikel eine Methodik und Software zur Erstellung und zum Konsum von MPEG-21 Digital Items zur Verfügung. Die entwickelte Methodik zur Erstellung von Digital Items, insbesondere die Abbildung eines Digital Items in einer Objektstruktur, ist einfach zu handhaben, weiters allgemein und leicht erweiterbar. Die zwei entwickelten Softwarewerkzeuge *DI Builder* und *DI Consumer* ermöglichen einerseits das (transparente) Erstellen und den Konsum von Digital Items für Anwender, und zeigen andererseits eine allgemeine Methodik zur Verarbeitung von Digital Items auf.

Wir planen zur Zeit gerade die Verknüpfung unserer Softwarewerkzeuge mit Caliph and Emir [13][6], einem MPEG-7 Bildannotierungswerkzeug, welches es uns ermöglicht, auch für Bilder MPEG-7 Beschreibungen zu generieren.

[6] siehe auch `http://caliph-emir.sourceforge.net/`

Literaturverzeichnis

1. Burnett, I. Van de Walle, R. Hill, K. Bormans, J. Pereira, F.: "MPEG-21: Goals and Achievements", IEEE MultiMedia 10(4):60-70, Oct-Dec 2003.
2. Watkinson, J.: "MPEG Handbook", Focal Press, 395 pages, Sep 2001. ISBN: 0240516567.
3. Kosch, H. Heuer, J.: "MPEG-7", Aktuelles Schlagwort, Informatik Spektrum, 26(2):105-107, April 2003.
4. Pereira, F.: "The MPEG-21 Standard: Why an Open Multimedia Framework?". In the Proceedings of the 8th International Workshop on Interactive Distributed Multimedia Systems (IDMS 2001), LNCS 2158, Springer Verlag, pp. 219-220, Lancaster, UK, September 2001.
5. Xu, D. Hefeeda, M. Hambrush, S. Bhargava, B. : "On Peer-to-Peer Media Streaming". In Proceedings of IEEE International Conference on Distributed Computing Systems (ICDCS'02), Vienna, Austria, pp. 363-373, July 2002.
6. Mühlhäuser, M. Gecsei, J.: "Services, Frameworks, and Paradigms for Distributed Multimedia Applications", IEEE MultiMedia, 3(3):48-61, 1996.
7. Rights.com: "The MPEG-21 Rights Expression Language", White Paper der Rightscom Ltd, Jul 2003. Verfügbar unter `http://www.rightscom.com/Portals/0/whitepaper_MPEG21-RELCB.pdf`.
8. Vetro, A.: "MPEG-21 digital item adaptation: enabling universal multimedia access", IEEE MultiMedia 11(1):84-87, Jan-Mar 2004.
9. Panis, G. Hutter, A. Heuer, J. Hellwagner, H. Kosch, H. Timmerer, C. Devillers, S. Amielh, M.: "Binary Resource Adaptation Using XML Bitstream Syntax Description", EURASIP Signal Processing: Image Communication, 18(8):721-747, September 2003.
10. Sikora, T.: "The MPEG-7 Visual Standard for Content Description-An Overview", IEEE Transactions on Circuits and Systems for Video Technology, 11(6):703-315, June 2001.
11. Kosch, H.: "Distributed Multimedia Database Technologies supported by MPEG-7 and MPEG-21", CRC Press, 248 pages, November 2003. ISBN: 0-849-31854-8.
12. Döller, M. and Kosch, H.: "An MPEG-7 Multimedia Data Cartridge". In Proceedings of the SPIE Conference on Multimedia Computing and Networking 2003 (MMCN03), Santa Clara, CA, January 2003.
13. Lux M., Klieber W., Becker J., Tochtermann K., Mayer H., Neuschmied H., Haas W.: "XML and MPEG-7 for Interactive Annotation and Retrieval Using Semantic Meta-data", Journal of Universial Computer Science, 8(10):965-984, Okt. 2002.

Methode für das Design von SLA-fähigen IT-Services

Christian Mayerl[1], Stefan Link[2], Matthias Racke[2], Stefan Popescu[2], Tobias Vogel[2], Oliver Mehl[2], Sebastian Abeck[2]

[1] Universität Karlsruhe (TH), Fakultät für Informatik, Dekanat, Arbeitsgruppe Lehrunterstützung, Postfach 6980, 76128 Karlsruhe
mayerl@ira.uka.de

[2] Universität Karlsruhe (TH), Fakultät für Informatik, Institut für Telematik, Cooperation & Management, Postfach 6980, 76128 Karlsruhe
[link | racke | popescu | vogel | mehl | abeck]@cm-tm.uka.de

Zusammenfassung. Da es sich bei IT-Services um immaterielle Produkte von IT-Betreibern handelt, basieren SLA-Verhandlungen zwischen Dienstleistern und Dienstnehmern auf IT-Service-Beschreibungen. Derartige Beschreibungen müssen als Kriterien erfüllen, dass die Funktionalitäten und Qualitäten der angebotenen IT-Services mit den verfügbaren Ressourcen des IT-Dienstleisters realisiert und entsprechend den Beschreibungen ausgehandelte SLAs nach Abschluss überwacht und erfüllt werden können. Wenngleich bestehende Ansätze Strukturen für die Beschreibung von IT-Services und SLAs aufzeigen, so fehlt bis jetzt ein systematisches Vorgehen, nach dem auf Basis technischer und ablauforganisatorischer Ressourcen IT-Services und deren Beschreibungen entwickelt werden können. Der vorliegende Beitrag zeigt eine Service-Design-Methode als Prozess kooperierender Rollen eines IT-Dienstleisters zur Gewinnung von IT-Service-Beschreibungen auf. Ziel der Methode ist die Definition SLA-fähiger IT-Services, anhand deren Beschreibungen Verhandlungen zwischen IT-Dienstleistern und Dienstnehmern geführt werden können.

1 Einleitung

Heutige Betreiber von Informationstechnologien (IT) positionieren sich als Dienstleister gegenüber Anwendern von IT, die als Dienstnehmer im Kontext ihrer Geschäftsprozesse Information verarbeitende Funktionalität mit definierter Qualität nachfragen. Gegenstand der Kooperation zwischen IT-Dienstleister und Dienstnehmer sind IT-Services, bzgl. derer Leistungs- und Qualitätseigenschaften verhandelt und *Service Level Agreement* (SLA) vereinbart werden. Das Spektrum der IT-Services reicht von IT-Kerndiensten, die Funktionen zur Verarbeitung von Informationen bereitstellen und auf Funktionen von Netz-, System- und Anwendungssoftwaretechnologien zurückzuführen sind, bis hin zu Zusatzdiensten, die Informations-, Beratungs-, Schulungs-, Problembehebungs-, Änderungsdurchführungsleistungen usw. umfassen und durch definierte Betriebsprozesse innerhalb eines IT-Dienstleisters erbracht werden [7]. Im Zusammenhang mit den gewünschten Services werden Qualitätsanforderungen einerseits an die zu betreibende technische Service-Infrastruktur und andererseits an die durchzuführenden Betriebsprozesse des IT-Dienstleisters gestellt.

Nach Abschluss von SLAs steht ein IT-Dienstleister in der Pflicht, die definierten Services mit der vereinbarten Qualität den jeweiligen Dienstnehmern zur Verfügung zu stellen [14]. Sowohl Dienstnehmer als auch Dienstleister sind an einem Nachweis der SLA-Erfüllung und damit an einer Qualitätsüberwachung interessiert. Folglich setzt die garantierte Einhaltung von SLAs eine Überwachung der IT-Services voraus, deren Leistungs- und Qualitätseigenschaften auf den zur Verfügung stehenden Ressourcen des IT-Dienstleisters beruhen, deren technische und ablauforganisatorische Eigenschaften gemessen werden können. Umgekehrt werden diese wiederum auf die Eigenschaften der bereitzustellenden Services abgebildet. Mit dem Ziel, abgeschlossene SLAs überwachen und erfüllen zu können, ist ein IT-Dienstleister deshalb bereits beim Design der Services an einem strukturierten Vorgehen interessiert, mit dessen Hilfe die verfügbaren Leistungsmöglichkeiten als Angebot gegenüber den Dienstnehmern beschrieben und zur Verfügung gestellt werden können.

Bestehende Ansätze im Bereich *IT Service Management* [2] zeigen Lösungen für die Beschreibung und Verwaltung von IT-Services auf, anhand derer SLAs verhandelt und abgeschlossen werden können. Probleme bei der Überwachung und Einhaltung von abgeschlossenen SLAs lassen sich jedoch oft auf ein nicht durchgängig strukturiertes Vorgehen bei der Konstruktion der angebotenen IT-Services zurückführen, das eigentlich von den technischen sowie ablauforganisatorischen Möglichkeiten eines IT-Dienstleisters ausgehen sollte. Es fehlt ein methodisches Vorgehen, wie ein IT-Dienstleister bereits beim Design auf Basis seiner Ressourcen seine verfügbaren Leistungen erfassen und entsprechende IT-Services entwickeln kann.

In diesem Beitrag wird eine Methode vorgestellt, mit deren Hilfe ein IT-Dienstleister auf der Basis seiner vorhandenen technischen und ablauforganisatorischen Möglichkeiten Leistungen als IT-Services beschreiben kann. Die so erstellten Service-Beschreibungen abstrahieren von den zugrunde liegenden Ressourcen und stellen so den fundierten Ausgangspunkt für den Abschluss von SLAs dar, deren Einhaltung und Erfüllung überwacht und nachgewiesen werden kann. Im nächsten Abschnitt werden hierzu zunächst bestehende Ansätze diskutiert und bewertet. Im darauf folgenden Abschnitt wird die Service-Design-Methode als kooperativer Prozess verteilter Betreiberrollen definiert. Es schließt sich ein Abschnitt über Service-Management-Werkzeuge zur Unterstützung der Methode an. Der Beitrag endet mit einer Zusammenfassung der wichtigsten Erkenntnisse und einem Ausblick auf aktuell anstehende Weiterentwicklungen.

2 Bestehende Ansätze

Im IT-Lebenszyklus endet die Phase der Entwicklung mit der Auslieferung des fertig gestellten IT-Produkts [13]. Unter der Prämisse, dass die Funktionalität einer IT als Service produktiv genutzt werden soll, schließt sich an die Entwicklung der IT die Einführung und Integration des IT-Produkts in das Betriebsszenario eines IT-Dienstleisters an. Neben der technischen Installation, Konfiguration und Integration müssen die Leistungs- und Qualitätseigenschaften der neuen Technologie erfasst und die den Dienstnehmern anzubietenden, immateriellen IT-Services entworfen werden.

Im noch jungen Forschungsbereich *Service Engineering* wird das Service-Design als Entwurfsphase für immaterielle Produkte und Geschäftsbeziehungen zwischen Organisationen in Analogie zum Entwurf materieller Produkte gesehen [1, 8]. Dabei beschäftigt sich die Service-Design-Phase mit der Gestaltung wahrnehmbarer Eigenschaften von Dienstleistungen [11]. Wenngleich bestehende Ansätze im Bereich *Service Engineering* ein ingenieurmäßiges Vorgehen zu Analyse, Design, Bereitstellung und Ablösung von Services als notwendig ansehen, so fehlt eine Konkretisierung der Ansätze insbesondere im Bereich von IT-Services.

Die wohl umfangreichste Sammlung von Vorgehensbeschreibungen im Bereich *IT Service Management* (ITSM) stellt die *IT Infrastructure Library* (ITIL) dar [13]. ITIL gilt als De-facto-Standardwerk für die Definition von IT-Betriebsprozessen, an dem sich neben IT-Dienstleistern auch viele Entwickler von Management-Werkzeugen zur Unterstützung der Prozesse orientieren. Beiträge für die Bereitstellung von IT-Services liefert ITIL mit den Empfehlungen zum *Service Support* und *Service Delivery*, und hier insbesondere mit der Definition des Prozesses für das *Service Level Management* (SLM). Dieser beginnt mit der Identifikation von Kundenwünschen und dem Aushandeln von Services und SLAs und endet mit der SLA-Überwachung und der Erstellung eines Qualitätsnachweises. Der SLM-Prozess legt den Hauptfokus auf die Interaktion zwischen einem IT-Dienstleister und einem Dienstnehmer. Obwohl erwähnt wird, dass die Anforderungen seitens des Dienstnehmers mit den Leistungsmöglichkeiten des IT-Dienstleisters abgeglichen werden müssen, schweigt sich die ITIL über ein konkretes Vorgehen im Bereich IT-Service-Design aus.

[15] beschäftigt sich mit Fragen des Betriebs und des Managements speziell von Telekommunikationsdiensten und -infrastrukturen. Ziel ist die Automatisierung der Geschäftsprozesse im Telekommunikationsbereich. Ein wesentliches Ergebnis dieser Arbeit ist die *enhanced Telecom Operations Map* (eTOM), in welcher Betriebsprozesse von Telekommunikationsunternehmen beschrieben werden [5, 6]. Neben den Prozessdefinitionen stellt die *Next Generation Operations Systems and Software* (NGOSS) ein von der Industrie anerkanntes Rahmenwerk zur Entwicklung betreibergerechter Systeme dar. NGOSS folgt den aus der Lehre der Softwaretechnik bekannten Schritten zur Softwareentwicklung (Geschäftsbereichsanalyse, Systemanalyse, Systementwurf und Systemtest) und liefert Ansätze für die Entwicklung von Management-Werkzeugen, welche die entstehenden IT-Lösungen und die darauf aufbauenden IT-Services qualitätsgesichert betreibbar machen. Jedoch fehlt bei eTOM eine systematische Herleitung und Dokumentation der Prozesse, wie z.B. für das Service-Design.

Aktuelle Forschungsarbeiten tragen zu ausgewählten Teilfragestellungen in den Bereichen *Service Engineering* und *IT Service Management* bei. [4] stellt beispielsweise ein strukturiertes Dienstmodell vor, welches die vereinheitlichte Basis für weitere Konzepte des *IT Service Managements* bildet. Das Modell unterscheidet zwischen einer kundenspezifischen, einer betreiberspezifischen und einer seitenunabhängigen Sicht auf einen Service. Der kundenspezifische Anteil beschreibt die für den Dienstnehmer über einen definierten *Service Access Point* abrufbare Funktionalität. Der betreiberspezifische Anteil ergänzt Service-Informationen, die für den Betrieb und weniger für den Dienstnehmer relevant sind. Eine ausführliche Beschreibung des Dienstmodells findet sich in [5]. [9] zeigt den Zusammenhang zwischen der Modellierung von IT-Services und dem Abschluss von SLAs auf. Jedoch fehlt auch in den aktuellen Forschungsergebnissen ein systematischer Ansatz, der beschreibt, wie ausgehend von den Anforderungen an IT-Services diese auf Basis der Leistungsmöglichkeiten eines IT-Dienstleisters entworfen werden können.

3 Service-Design-Methode

Ziel der Service-Design-Methode ist die systematische Konstruktion von Service-Beschreibungen auf Basis vorhandener Ressourcen eines IT-Dienstleisters. Da ein IT-Service eine immaterielle, nicht lagerbare Leistung darstellt, liefern Service-Beschreibungen die Grundlage für SLA-Verhandlungen zwischen IT-Dienstleistern und IT-Dienstnehmern. Neben einer dienstnehmergerechten Abstraktion von den IT-Services zugrunde liegenden Ressourcen muss ein IT-Service Kriterien wie technische und ablauforganisatorische Realisierbarkeit, Abrechenbarkeit sowie Überwachbarkeit erfüllen. Beispielhaft soll im Folgenden der IT-Service Backup zur Datensicherung betrachtet werden.

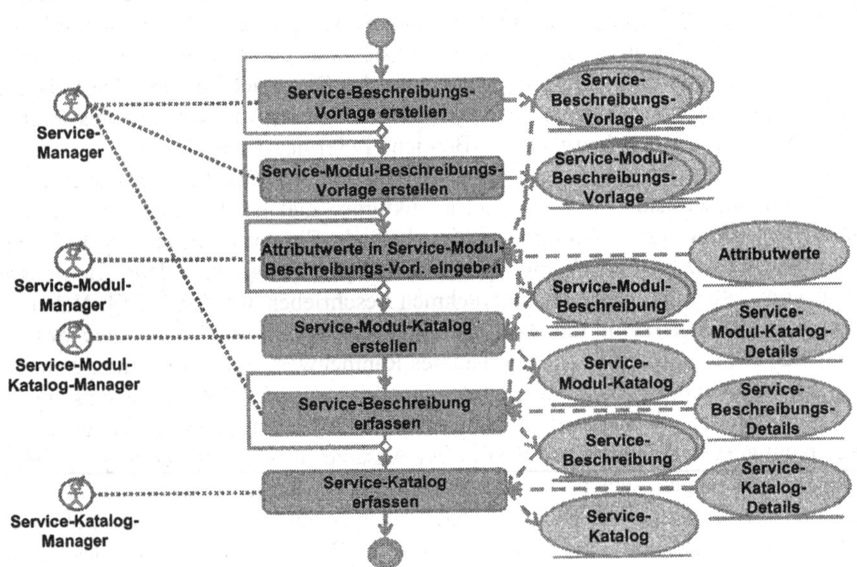

Abbildung 1 – Aktivitäten der Service-Design-Methode

Ausgehend von einer zeitlich vorangegangenen Analyse der grundlegenden Anforderungen an IT-Services, in welcher der IT-Dienstleister ein Verständnis über die Bedürfnisse und die Sichtweise der Dienstnehmer aufbaut, erstellt der Service-Manager mit den gewonnenen Erkenntnissen Vorlagen für eine einheitliche und strukturierte Beschreibung der IT-Services (vgl. Abbildung 1). Bei der Erstellung der Vorlagen ist zu berücksichtigen, dass die späteren, darauf aufbauenden Service-Beschreibungen von Dienstnehmern verstanden werden, die beschriebenen IT-Services einen Mehrwert für den Dienstnehmer liefern, die versprochene Funktionalität und Qualität überwachbar ist, für jeden Service ein Verantwortlicher benannt wird, die Inanspruchnahme eines Service einem intuitiven Ablauf folgt und mit einem klar definierten Preis ausgezeichnet werden kann. Für die Beschreibung eines Service werden in der

Service-Beschreibungs-Vorlage Attribute definiert, die sich in die folgenden Attributgruppen einteilen lassen:

- **Identifikationsattribute** identifizieren einen IT-Service innerhalb des Gesamtangebots eines IT-Dienstleisters eindeutig: `Name`, `ID`, `Version`, `Varianten-Name` `usw.`
- **Statusattribute** geben Auskunft über die Vorlaufzeit für die Bereitstellung und den Zustand eines IT-Service im Rahmen seines Lebenszyklus: `in Planung`, `Pilotphase`, `in Produktion`, `in Ablösung`, `im Archiv` `usw.`
- **Organisationsattribute** beschreiben organisatorische Randbedingungen rund um die Erbringung eines IT-Service: `Verantwortlicher`, `Stellvertreter`, `Organisationseinheit` `usw.`
- **Leistungsattribute** spezifizieren die (funktionale) Leistung eines IT-Service: `Kurz- und Langbeschreibung`, `Leistungseinheit`, `Liefererergebnis`, `Voraussetzungen`, `benötigte Service-Module`, `Ausschlüsse`, `Risiken` `usw.`
- **Qualitätsattribute** beschreiben die Qualität der Dienstleistung: `Verfügbarkeit`, `Speicherkapazität`, `Reaktionszeit` `usw.`
- **Kostenattribute** zeigen die Kosten bzw. den Preis eines IT-Service bzw. dessen Inanspruchnahme auf: `Zielkostensatz`, `Verrechnungspreis`, `Einrichtungskosten`, `Kostenmodell`, `Kostentreiber` `usw.`

Um die Service-Beschreibung auf ein technisches und ablauforganisatorisches Fundament zu stellen, erhebt der Service-Manager Informationen über die Teilleistungen, sog. Service-Module, die in einen IT-Service und dessen Service-Beschreibung eingehen. Aufgrund der Verteilung und Komplexität heutiger IT, fallen Informationen über die Teilleistungen ebenso verteilt z.B. über unterschiedliche organisatorische Abteilungen an. Zudem lassen sich an der Technologie und an herstellerspezifischen Produkten ausgerichtete Organisationseinheiten für die Bereiche Netzwerke, (Server-) Systeme und Anwendungssoftware erkennen. Um weitestgehend einheitliche Service-Modul-Beschreibungen zu erhalten, erstellt der Service-Manager Vorlagen für die Service-Modul-Beschreibungen. Da Service-Modul-Beschreibungen zu Service-Beschreibungen verarbeitet werden, bauen die beschreibenden Attribute eines IT-Service auf den Attributen von Service-Modulen auf und ähneln sich in ihrer Struktur. Zusätzlich muss ein Service-Modul als eigenständige Einheit überwachbar und ganzheitlich im Kontext eines Service genutzt werden können.

Mit Hilfe einer Service-Modul-Beschreibungs-Vorlage beschreibt ein Service-Modul-Manager z.B. innerhalb seiner Abteilung die für einen IT-Service notwendige Teilleistung. Der Beispiel-IT-Service Backup setzt sich aus den Service-Modulen Backup-Server aus dem Bereich Server-Systeme und Backup-Zugang aus dem Bereich Netzwerke zusammen. Durch die Belegung der durch die Vorlage abgefragten Attribute mit Attributwerten nimmt der jeweils zuständige Service-Modul-Manager eine abstrakte Beschreibung der technischen Ressourcen und der ablauforganisatorischen Teilprozesse als Service-Modul vor. Die abgegebenen Attributwerte definieren die vorhandenen Leistungsmöglichkeiten einzelner Bereiche des IT-Dienstleisters, z.B. technologischer Bereiche oder Abteilungen.

Fertig gestellte Service-Modul-Beschreibungen werden in einem Service-Modul-Katalog zusammengeführt, der in seiner Gesamtheit die technischen und ablauforganisatorischen Leistungsmöglichkeiten eines IT-Dienstleisters beschreibt. Der Service-

Modul-Katalog wird anhand von Kriterien basierend auf den Attributen und Attributwerten der Modul-Beschreibungen zur Weiterverarbeitung strukturiert und durch Service-Modul-Katalog-Details, wie z.B. Gültigkeit, Geschäftsjahr usw. näher spezifiziert. Sinnvolle und technisch realisierbare Modul-Kombinationen spannen zudem den Raum für Service-Varianten auf.

Die Service-Modul-Beschreibungen im Service-Modul-Katalog stellen das vorhandene Fundament für die Definition von IT-Services dar. Mit der technischen Installation, Konfiguration und Integration der IT geht die Zusammenführung der beteiligten Service-Modul-Beschreibungen zu IT-Service-Beschreibungen einher. Dabei müssen einzelne Attributwerte der Service-Beschreibung je nach Attributgruppe aus den Attributwerten der beteiligten Service-Modul-Beschreibungen berechnet, zusammengesetzt oder als Service-Beschreibungs-Details individuell hinzugefügt werden. Vorschriften für Identifikationsattribute des IT-Service sind allenfalls für die Art und Weise der Bezeichnung festzulegen. So kann sich ein Service-Varianten-Name des IT-Service `Backup` an den Qualitätsattributen seiner Service-Module, z.B. Speicherkapazität des Moduls `Backup-Server` in Verbindung mit Datendurchsatz des Moduls `Backup-Zugang`, orientieren. Auf jeden Fall müssen die Identifikationsattribute eindeutig gegenüber den Dienstnehmern definiert werden. Statusattribute verschiedener Service-Module können aufeinander abgebildet werden. Beispielsweise kann sich die Vorlaufzeit des IT-Service `Backup` aus der größten Vorlaufzeit der beteiligten Service-Module ergeben, falls beide Module weitestgehend parallel eingerichtet werden können. Der Zustand des konstruierten IT-Services entspricht dem Zustand mit der geringsten Qualitätssicherung der verbauten Service-Module; eine Verarbeitung eines Service-Moduls im Zustand `in Ablösung` oder `im Archiv` ist nicht mehr möglich, wohl aber im Zustand `Pilotphase`. Organisationsattribute müssen, ähnlich wie Identifikationsattribute, individuell festgelegt werden. Die Beschreibung der Leistung eines IT-Service kann aus der Summe der Teilleistungen der beteiligten Service-Module gewonnen werden. Die Korrelation der Qualitätsattribute von Service-Modulen zu Qualitätsattributen von IT-Services ist bezogen auf die in den SLAs auszusprechende Garantie der Attributwerte ein nicht trivialer Aspekt. Neben der Berechnung von Qualitätsattributwerten nach komplexen Korrelationsvorschriften hat sich die Zusammenführung von an Service-Modulen gemessenen Erfahrungswerten, z.B. nach statistischen Prinzipien, bewährt. Hierbei können Ansätze zur Anwendung kommen, die den schlechtesten bzw. geringsten Wert als den maximal garantierbaren Wert darstellen (pessimistischer Ansatz). Als Erfahrungswerte gewonnene Verfügbarkeiten der Service-Module `Backup-Service` von 99,9% und `Backup-Zugang` von 95% führen beispielsweise zu einer garantierbaren Verfügbarkeit des IT-Service `Backup` von 95%. Qualitätsattribute, wie z.B. Speicherkapazität des `Backup-Servers` in Verbindung mit Datendurchsatz des `Backup-Zugangs`, deren Werte sich nicht unmittelbar miteinander vergleichen oder aufeinander abbilden lassen, können für eine erhöhte Transparenz der verbauten Service-Module nebeneinander in die Service-Beschreibung aufgenommen werden. Die Kostenattribute des IT-Service werden nach betriebswirtschaftlichen Gesichtspunkten aus den Kosten der Service-Module berechnet.

In der letzten Aktivität der Service-Design-Methode werden die IT-Service-Beschreibungen in einem Service-Katalog zusammengefasst. Der Service-Katalog ist in erster Linie für die Auswahl der IT-Services und die SLA-Verhandlungen mit den Dienstnehmern ausgelegt. Entsprechende Strukturierungs- und Sortiermöglichkeiten, z.B. nach bestimmten Attributen, werden durch Service-Katalog-Details festgelegt und vereinfachen die Suche nach gewünschten IT-Services.

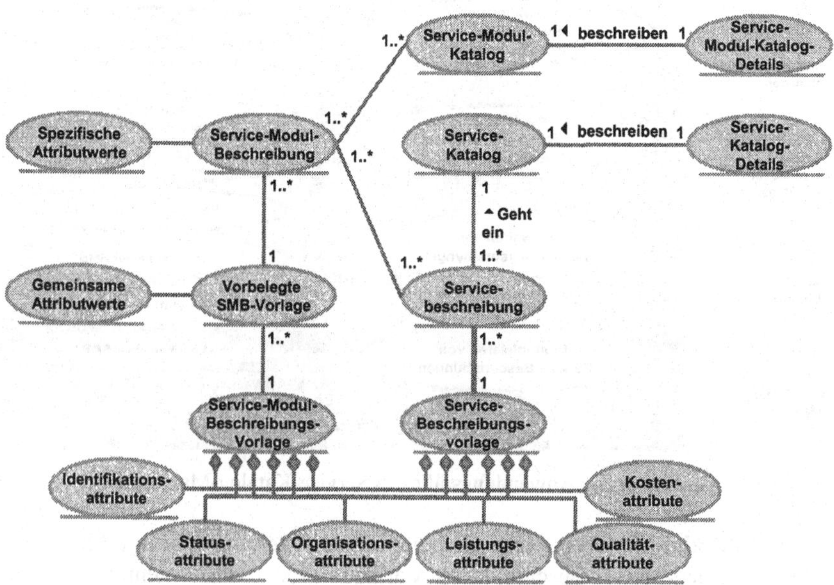

Abbildung 2 – Geschäftsobjekte im Kontext der Service-Design-Methode

Abbildung 2 fasst die Geschäftsobjekte zusammen, die im Kontext der Service-Design-Methode zum Einsatz kommen und die für die Entwicklung von unterstützenden Service-Management-Werkzeugen verfeinert und auf eine geeignete Werkzeug-Architektur abgebildet werden müssen.

4 Unterstützende Werkzeuge

In Analogie zum eTOM-Ansatz wurden für eine effiziente Anwendung der Service-Design-Methode unterstützende Service-Management-Werkzeuge entwickelt: Der Service-Katalog-Manager (SKM) unterstützt Aktivitäten von der Erhebung der Service-Modul-Beschreibungen bis hin zur Verwaltung von IT-Service-Beschreibungen im Service-Katalog. Der Anteil des Service-Katalogs, der für die Kommunikation mit den Dienstnehmern benötigt wird, wird über ein Service-Portal (SP) veröffentlicht, das zwischen IT-Dienstleister und den Dienstnehmern positioniert ist.

Die Benutzer des SKM lassen sich aus dem Aktivitätsdiagramm der Service-Design-Methode ableiten (vgl. Abbildung 1). Neben dem Service-Modul-Manager und dem Service-Manager werden die Rollen zweier Katalog-Manager unterschieden, die für die Katalogisierung der Service-Modul- und der Service-Beschreibungen zuständig sind.

Beispielhaft wird im Folgenden der Ablauf zum Verwalten der Service-Modul-Beschreibungen vertieft. Die Erstellung einer Service-Modul-Beschreibung kann in zwei Schritten erfolgen:

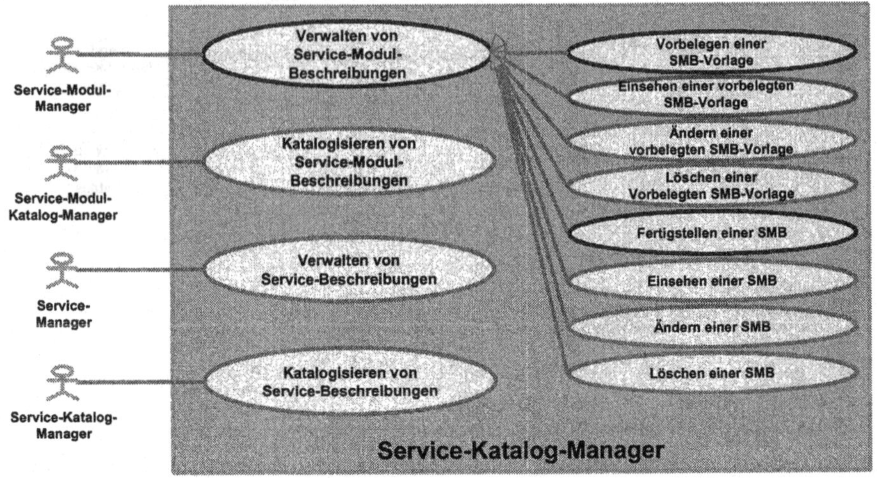

Abbildung 3 – Anwendungsfälle des Service-Katalog-Managers

Der Service-Modul-Manager – z.B. als Leiter einer Abteilung – belegt Attributwerte in der Service-Modul-Beschreibungs-Vorlage vor, die mehreren Modul-Beschreibungen gemeinsam sind. Dies können z.B. Organisationsattribute sein, die allen Beschreibungen einer Abteilung gleichen. Die Vorbelegung erhöht die Effizienz bei der Erstellung der Modul-Beschreibungen und sorgt für ein hohes Maß an Einheitlichkeit.

Eine individuelle Service-Modul-Beschreibung wird dann durch Angabe der spezifischen Attributwerte vervollständigt. Zu den spezifischen Attributen zählen neben eindeutigen Identifikationsattributen insbesondere Leistungs- und Qualitätsattribute, die sich z.B. aufgrund herstellerspezifischer Eigenheiten der eingesetzten und zu betreibenden Technologien ergeben.

Die grundlegende Architektur des Service-Katalog-Managers (vgl. Abbildung 4) folgt einer Drei-Schichten-Architektur mit einer Trennung zwischen Präsentations-, Geschäftslogik- und Datenhaltungsschicht. Zusätzlich kommt das Prinzip eines *thin client* zum Einsatz. Beide Architekturprinzipien erhöhen die Flexibilität bei der Weiterentwicklung des SKM und vereinfachen dessen Integration in die Management-Werkzeug-Umgebung eines IT-Dienstleisters.

Die Aufgaben der SKM-Komponenten sind wie folgt zu verstehen: Die `ServiceCatalogManagerBusinessProcessControl` (`SCMBPC`) koordiniert Geschäftsprozesse, die sich über mehrere Systemanwendungsfälle erstrecken. Wird von der `SCMBPC` ein Anwendungsfall wie etwa die Verwaltung von Service-Modul-Beschreibungen identifiziert, so wird die Abwicklung der anfallenden Aufgaben an die entsprechende Anwendungsfallsteuerungskomponente (`UseCaseControl`, `UCC`) delegiert. Diese steuert den Ablauf eines Anwendungsfalls, der während der Analyse durch ein anwendungsfallbeschreibendes Aktivitätsdiagramm festgelegt wurde. Um diesen Ablauf zu realisieren, kooperieren `UCCs` mit der Funktionalität der Dialogsteuerungskomponenten (`DialogControl, DC`) und der Fachkomponenten (`BusinessObject, BO`). `DCs` bilden die Brücke zwischen der Präsentations- und Geschäftslogikschicht der Drei-Schichten-Architektur. Für jeden Hauptanwendungsfall (vgl. Abbildung 3) existiert eine eigene `UCC`: `SCMAdministrationOfSmdsUCC` für das Verwalten von Service-Modul-Beschreibungen, `SCMCatalogOfSmdsUCC` für das Katalogisieren von Service-Modul-Beschreibungen, `SCMAdministrationOfSdsUCC` für das Verwalten von Service-Beschreibungen, `SCMCatalogOfSdsUCC` für das Katalogisieren von Service-Beschreibungen.

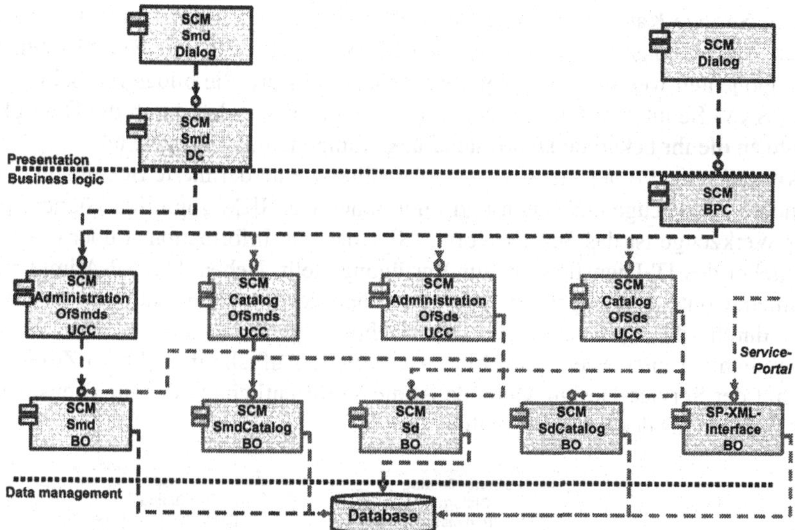

Abbildung 4 – Architektur des Service-Katalog-Managers

Die Fachkomponenten realisieren die für den entsprechenden Anwendungsfall benötigte, geschäftsobjektbezogene Funktionalität. Sie sind damit hauptsächlich für die Verarbeitung der Daten verantwortlich: Sei es, die von der Anwendungsfallsteuerungskomponente übergebenen Daten zu speichern, die von ihr geforderten Daten zu liefern oder sonstige Berechnungen durchzuführen. Ein weiterer Grund, dazu separate Komponenten in der Geschäftslogikschicht zu entwerfen, besteht darin, die Datenbank vom Rest der Anwendung abzukapseln und anderen Komponenten höherwertige Schnittstellen anzubieten. Dies hat den Vorteil, dass Zugriffe auf das Persistenzmedium nur in Fachkomponenten realisiert werden müssen und sich andere Komponenten nicht darum kümmern müssen, wie die Daten der Geschäftslogik entsprechend abgelegt oder wieder aufbereitet werden. Folgende Fachkomponenten wurden entworfen: `SCMSmdBO` und `SCMSmdCatalogBO` für das Verwalten und Katalogisieren der Service-Modul-Beschreibungen, `SCMSdBO` und `SCMSdCatalogBO` für das Verwalten und Katalogisieren der Service-Beschreibungen sowie `SPXMLInterfaceBO` als XML-konforme Schnittstelle.

Für jede Anwendungsfallsteuerungskomponente existiert eine entsprechende Fachkomponente, da jeder Anwendungsfall andere Funktionalitätsanforderungen hat und somit für jeden Fall eine eigene Fachkomponente modelliert werden muss. Dies bedeutet jedoch nicht, dass jede `UCC` nur eine Fachkomponente ansteuert. So nutzt die Anwendungsfallsteuerungskomponente `SCMCatalogOfSmdsUCC` auch Funktionen der Fachkomponente `SCMSmdBO`. Als Beispiel ist hier das Einsehen der Service-Modul-Beschreibungen zu nennen.

In der Präsentationsschicht steuert die Dialogsteuerungskomponente komplexere Dialoge, die unabhängig von der Anwendungsfallsteuerung aufgebaut und gesteuert werden können. Die Hauptaufgaben dieser Komponente sind die Abfolge von Dialogen zu steuern sowie syntaktische Eingabevalidierungen durchzuführen. Bisher wurde beim Service-Katalog-Manager der Fokus auf die Dialogsteuerungskomponente für den Anwendungsfall „Verwalten von SMB", `SCMSmdDC`, gelegt. Mit den Dialogkomponenten werden die Dialogoberflächen realisiert. Sie bilden die Schnittstelle zu den SKM-Benutzern. Die Eingaben des Benutzers werden durch die Dialogkomponente an die ihr bekannte Dialogsteuerungskomponente weitergeleitet.

Die Komponente `SPXMLInterfaceBO` realisiert eine definierte Schnittstelle, über die andere Werkzeuge auf Daten und Funktionen des SKM zugreifen können. Eines dieser Werkzeuge ist das Service-Portal (SP), das u.a. Informationen über das Service-Angebot des IT-Dienstleisters zur Verfügung stellt. Neben dem SP-Administrator und einem Content-Manager, der über den Inhalt des Portals wacht, wird das SP vor allem durch die (potenziellen) Dienstnehmer genutzt, die an den Service-Beschreibungen interessiert sind. Eine wesentliche Aufgabe des SPs im Zusammenhang mit der Service-Design-Methode ist die Veröffentlichung des für Dienstnehmer gedachten Anteils des Service-Katalogs.

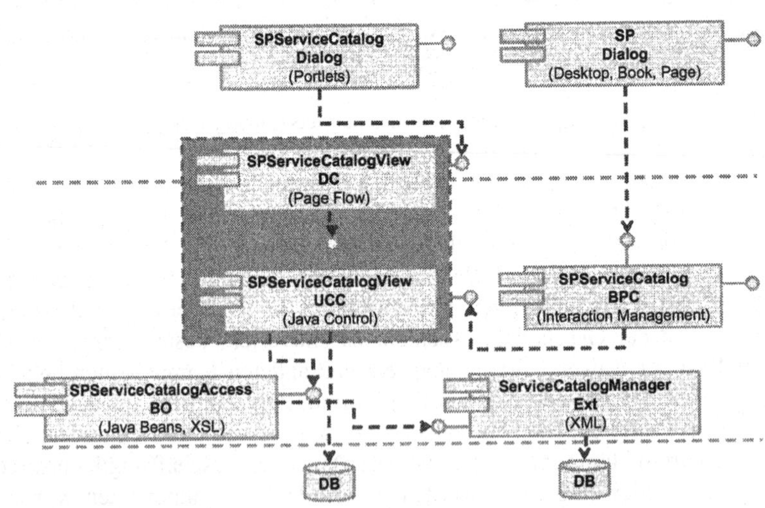

Abbildung 5 – Architektur des Service-Portals (SP)

Wie der SKM folgt auch das Service-Portal (SP) einer Drei-Schichten-Architektur (vgl. **Abbildung 5**). Neben Dialog- und Dialogsteuerungskomponenten verfügt auch das SP über eine UCC, die den Dienstnehmern den Zugriff auf die Inhalte des Service-Katalogs ermöglicht: `SPServiceCatalogViewUCC`. Um redundante Datenhaltung und damit Konsistenzprobleme zu vermeiden, werden innerhalb des Portal-Systems ausschließlich Portal-spezifische Daten, wie z.B. Rollen und Zugriffsrechte usw., gespeichert. Die Service-Beschreibungen werden über eine Zugriffskomponente (`SPServiceCatalogAccessBO`) realisiert, die auf die Schnittstelle des SKM (`ServiceCatalogManagerExt`) zugreift. Für die Darstellung der Inhalte des Service-Katalogs werden die Struktur des Katalogs an sich, mit deren Hilfe ein Dienstnehmer im Katalog navigieren kann, sowie nach Auswahl eines IT-Service dessen Beschreibung vom SKM an das SP übertragen. Der Austausch der Daten an dieser Schnittstelle erfolgt mittels XML.

Die SKM-Implementierung wurde mit Hilfe der J2EE-Technologie realisiert. Der Prototyp wird auf einem *Sun Java System Application Server 8* betrieben. Als Entwicklungsumgebung kam die IDE *Eclipse* in Verbindung mit dem UML-Modellierungswerkzeug *Enterprise Architect 3.6* zum Einsatz. Für die Implementierung des Service-Portals hingegen stand im Szenario die Portal-Entwicklungsumgebung von BEA zur Verfügung. Beide Technologie-Umgebungen wurden für die Implementierung der Prototypen beibehalten, um die Integrationsfragestellung zu untersuchen und zu lösen.

5 Zusammenfassung und Ausblick

Die Service-Design-Methode sowie die unterstützenden Management-Werkzeuge wurden in Kooperation mit IT-Dienstleistern entwickelt, deren Ziel die Bereitstellung qualitätsgesicherter Netz-, System- und auch Anwendungsdienste ist. Ausgehend von der allgemeinen Konzeption der Service-Design-Methode wurden Konkretisierungen der Methode in den jeweiligen Szenarien vorgenommen. Unter Berücksichtigung Szenarien-abhängiger Anforderungen wurden Prototypen der prozessunterstützenden Werkzeuge als Machbarkeitsstudien der Methode entwickelt.

Eine wesentliche Erkenntnis der Arbeiten im Zusammenhang mit der Service-Design-Methode ist die Tatsache, dass es sich beim Entwurf von SLA-fähigen IT-Services um einen grundlegenden Geschäftsprozess verteilter und kooperierender Rollen innerhalb von IT-Dienstleistern handelt. Ziel der Methode ist die Beschreibung von IT-Services auf der Basis aufgezeigter bestehender Ansätze, die einerseits ein technisches und ablauforganisatorisches Fundament in den Leistungsmöglichkeiten des IT-Dienstleisters finden und andererseits als Ausgangspunkt für SLA-Verhandlungen dienen können, deren Erfüllung nach Abschluss auch überwacht und nachgewiesen werden kann.

Neben einer Verfeinerung der Methode, insbesondere im Bereich der Zusammenführung von Service-Modulen zu IT-Services, steht die Einbettung der Service-Design-Methode in den sonstigen Betrieb eines IT-Dienstleisters an und hier vor allem die Identifikation von Querbeziehungen zu anderen Betriebsprozessen. Die Definition von ablauforganisatorischen wie auch technischen Schnittstellen soll zur Schärfung der Methode selbst beitragen und vermindert Akzeptanzprobleme bei Mitarbeitern des IT-Dienstleisters. Beispielsweise werden Zusammenhänge zu Prozessen des Konfigurationsmanagements untersucht, innerhalb derer bereits die Konfiguration zu betreibender IT-Ressourcen mittels standardisierter Informationsmodelle, wie dem *Common Information Model* (CIM) [3], beschrieben werden [12]. An der Schnittstelle hin zum Dienstnehmer werden auf Basis des Service-Katalogs die Prozesse im Bereich *Service Level Management* (SLM) weiter ausgebaut.

[10] beschreibt eine integrierte Service-Management-Architektur (SMA), die neben IT-Management-Komponenten zur Überwachung und Steuerung der zu betreibenden IT auch Komponenten zur Unterstützung der kooperativen Betriebsprozesse sowie des IT-Service-Managements vorsieht. Die in diesem Beitrag vorgestellten Management-Werkzeuge sollen in eine SMA-konforme Gesamtinfrastruktur eines IT-Dienstleisters integriert werden. Da sich ausgehend von den sich ändernden Anforderungen an die IT-Services auch die Betriebsprozesse und mit ihnen die Anforderungen an die einzusetzenden Management-Werkzeuge ändern, soll die Integration der einzelnen Management-Werkzeuge über eine lose Kopplung der sonst selbständigen Werkzeuge bewerkstelligt werden. Dabei soll untersucht werden, inwieweit sich das Paradigma Service-orientierter Architekturen (SOA) auch auf die Entwicklung und Integration von Management-Werkzeugen anwenden und etablieren lässt.

6 Literatur

1. T. Böhmann, M. Junginger, H. Krcmar: Modular Service Architectures – A Concept and Method for Engineering IT services, International Conference on System Sciences (HICSS'03), Hawaii, 2003.
2. J. v. Bon, G. Kemmerling, D. Pondman: IT Service Management – An Introduction, Van Haren, 2002.
3. Distributed Management Task Force (DMTF): Common Information Model (CIM) Specification: Version 2.2, 1999; CIM Schema: Version 2.8.1, 2004.
4. G. Dreo Rodosek, A Generic Model for IT Services and Service Management. Symposium on Integrated Network Management (IM 2003), Colorado Springs, 2003.
5. G. Dreo Rodosek, H.-G. Hegering: IT-Dienstmanagement, Herausforderungen und Lösungsansätze, PIK, K.G. Saur, 2004.
6. enhanced Telecom Operations Map (eTOM) – The Business Process Framework For The Information and Communications Services Industry, GB921 v4.0, 2004.
7. H.-G. Hegering, S. Abeck, B. Neumair: Integrated Management of Networked Systems: Concepts, Architectures, and Their Operational Application: Morgan Kaufmann, 1999.
8. A. Keller, H. Ludwig: Defining and Monitoring Service Level Agreements for dynamic e-Business, System Administration Conference (LISA 2002), Philadelphia, 2002.
9. C. Mayerl, S. Abeck, M. Becker, A. Köppel, O. Mehl, B. Pauze: Dienstbeschreibung und –modellierung für ein SLA-fähiges Service-Management, KIVS 2003.
10. C. Mayerl, Z. Nochta, M. Müller, M. Schauer, A. Uremovic, S. Abeck: Specification of a Service Management Architecture to Run Distributed and Networked Systems, Trends towards a Universal Service Market (USM'2000), München, 2000.
11. J. McConell: Practical Service Level Management – Delivering High-Quality Web-Based Services, Cisco Press, 2004.
12. O. Mehl, M. Becker, A. Köppel, P. Paul, D. Zimmermann, S. Abeck: A Management-Aware Software Development Process Using Design Patterns, Symposium on Integrated Network Management (IM 2003), Colorado Springs, 2003.
13. Office of Government Commerce (OCG): IT Infrastructure Library (ITIL) – Service Support (ISBN 0113300158), 2000; Service Delivery (ISBN 0113300174), 2001; Planning to Implement Service Management (ISBN 0113308779), 2002; Application Management (ISBN 0113308663), 2002.
14. R. Sturm, W. Morris, M. Jander: The Heart of the Matter: Service Level Agreements, 2001.
15. TeleManagementForum: TeleManagementForum-Portal, http://www.tmforum.org, 2004.

CURE: Eine Reparaturheuristik für die Planung ökonomischer und zuverlässiger Kommunikationsnetzwerke mit Hilfe von heuristischen Optimierungsverfahren

Dirk Reichelt[1] und Franz Rothlauf[2]

[1] Institut für Wirtschaftsinformatik, Technische Universität Ilmenau
Dirk.Reichelt@tu-ilmenau.de
[2] Lehrstuhl für ABWL und Wirtschaftsinformatik, Universität Mannheim
rothlauf@uni-mannheim.de

Zusammenfassung. Dieser Beitrag beschäftigt sich mit dem Aufbau kostengünstiger Kommunikationsnetzwerke unter Zuverlässigkeitsrestriktionen. Für den Aufbau des Kommunikationsnetzes stehen je Verbindung verschiedene Leitungstypen mit unterschiedlichen Zuverlässigkeiten und Kosten zur Verfügung. Im Rahmen der Planung ist das Netzwerk so aufzubauen, dass das resultierende Gesamtnetz kostenminimal ist und eine geforderte minimale Gesamtzuverlässigkeit garantiert werden kann. Aufgrund der hohen Komplexität des Problems (NP-vollständig) werden üblicherweise heuristische Optimierungsverfahren zur Lösung eingesetzt. Um sicherzustellen, dass die dadurch ermittelten Lösungen die geforderte Zuverlässigkeit aufweisen, werden in den meisten Ansätzen unzulässige Lösungen, welche die geforderte Zuverlässigkeit nicht erfüllen, durch die Verwendung von Straftermen schlechter bewertet. Der vorliegende Beitrag ersetzt diese Strafterme durch eine Reparaturheuristik (CURE). CURE stellt sicher, dass heuristische Optimierungsverfahren nur zulässige Lösungen erzeugen und keine Strafterme für invalide Lösungen mehr notwendig sind. Experimentelle Untersuchungen der Leistungsfähigkeit von heuristischen Optimierungsverfahren am Beispiel eines genetischen Algorithmus zeigen, dass durch CURE im Vergleich zu Ansätzen mit Straftermen deutlich bessere Lösungen mit geringerem Aufwand gefunden werden können.

1 Einleitung

Bei der Planung von Netzwerktopologien zum Aufbau verteilter Systeme müssen in der Regel mehrere (oft auch konfligierende) Kriterien wie Kosten des Netzwerks und Ausfallsicherheit beachtet werden. Für den Planer stellt sich die Aufgabe, eine Netzwerkstruktur zu finden, welche möglichst kostengünstig ist, trotzdem aber eine vorgegebene Gesamtzuverlässigkeit erfüllt. Für den Aufbau eines derartigen Kommunikationsnetzes stehen üblicherweise Leitungstypen mit unterschiedlichen Zuverlässigkeiten (und entsprechenden Kosten) zur Verfügung.

In der Regel nehmen die Kosten einer Leitung mit der zugesicherten Ausfallsicherheit (Zuverlässigkeit) der Verbindung zu. Ein gebräuchliches Maß für die Messung der Gesamtzuverlässigkeit eines Kommunikationsnetzwerkes ist die *All-Terminal Zuverlässigkeit.* Dieses Maß berechnet sich aus den vorgegebenen Zuverlässigkeiten der einzelnen Leitungen, welche im Netzwerk eingesetzt werden, und gibt die Wahrscheinlichkeit dafür an, dass sämtliche Knoten des Netzwerks miteinander kommunizieren können. Das Problem des Findens einer kostenminimalen Netzwerkstruktur bei vorgegebener Gesamtzuverlässigkeit zählt zu den NP-harten Problemen [1, S.207]. Aufgrund der hohen Komplexität des Problems wurden in der Vergangenheit überwiegend heuristische Optimierungsverfahren wie z.B. genetische Algorithmen zur Lösung des Problems eingesetzt [3-7,9]. Der vorliegende Beitrag stellt ein Verfahren zur Ermittlung einer kostenminimalen Netzwerkstruktur bei Berücksichtigung einer vorgegebenen Gesamtzuverlässigkeit des Netzwerkes vor. Als Verfahren zur Ermittlung kostenminimaler Netzwerkstrukturen wird ein genetischer Algorithmus eingesetzt. Der Hauptunterschied zu bisherigen Ansätzen liegt in der Art und Weise, in der die geforderte minimale Gesamtzuverlässigkeit des Netzwerkes berücksichtigt wird. Im Gegensatz zu den meisten bisherigen Arbeiten, bei welchen Netzwerkstrukturen, welche die geforderte Zuverlässigkeit nicht erfüllen, durch die Einführung von Straftermen (Penalties) schlechter bewertet werden [3,7], wird im vorliegenden Beitrag eine Reparaturheuristik (CURE) eingesetzt. Durch CURE wird sichergestellt, dass sämtliche Lösungen, welche durch das heuristische Optimierungsverfahren generiert werden, zulässig sind und die geforderte Gesamtzuverlässigkeit für das Netzwerk aufweisen. Zusätzliche Strafterme sind damit nicht mehr notwendig. Die Leistungsfähigkeit von CURE wird anhand von drei Benchmarkproblemen aus der Literatur untersucht. Die Ergebnisse zeigen, dass durch die Verwendung von CURE deutlich bessere Lösungen gefunden werden können, als mit herkömmlichen Straftermansätzen.

2 Problembeschreibung

2.1 Ökonomische Netzwerkplanung unter Zuverlässigkeitsrestriktionen

Ziel des Planungsprozesses ist es, eine Netzwerkstruktur mit minimalen Kosten zu finden, welche einer vorgegebenen Zuverlässigkeitsanforderung genügt. Ein Netzwerk wird hierbei als ein ungerichteter Graph $G(K, E)$ modelliert. K ist die Menge der Knoten und E die Menge der Kanten im Graphen. Durch jede Kante bzw. Knoten wird eine Verbindung bzw. ein Knoten des zugehörigen Netzwerkes repräsentiert. Es wird davon ausgegangen, dass die Position der Knoten fest vorgegeben ist und deren Installationskosten für die Planung nicht relevant sind. Für jede Kante $e_{ij} \in E$ zwischen Knoten i und j besteht die Auswahlmöglichkeit zwischen verschiedenen Zuverlässigkeitsoptionen l_k $(k = 1 \dots n)$, welche sich hinsichtlich Kosten $c(l_k(e_{ij}))$ und Ausfallsicherheit $r(l_k(e_{ij}))$ unterscheiden. Dabei entspricht $l_k(e_{ij})$ der aktuell für die Kante e_{ij} gewählten Option k. Weiterhin gelten die Annahmen, dass die Knoten zuverlässig arbeiten, jede Kante sich entweder im Zustand $s_{e_{ij}}$ „operational" ($s_{e_{ij}} = 1$) oder „failed" ($s_{e_{ij}} = 0$) befindet, die Ausfallwahrscheinlichkeiten der einzelnen Leitungen unabhängig voneinander sind, die Verbindungen bidirektional sind und Reparaturen ausgefallener Verbindungen nicht berücksichtigt werden. Die Lösung des Optimierungsproblems wird durch den Subgraph $G_N(K, E_N \subset E)$ dargestellt. Die Zielfunktion für das Optimierungsproblem lautet:

$$\begin{aligned} C(G_N) = \sum_{e_{ij} \in E_N} c(l_k(e_{ij})) \rightarrow min \\ \text{mit: } R(G_N) \geq R_0 \end{aligned} \tag{1}$$

Dabei sind $C(G_N)$ die Gesamtkosten des Netzwerkes, welche sich aus den Kosten $c_k(l(e_{ij}))$ der aktuell gewählten Optionen für die Kanten e_{ij} zusammensetzen. $R(G_N)$ ist die Gesamtzuverlässigkeit des Netzwerks, die eine minimal geforderte Zuverlässigkeit R_0 nicht unterschreiten darf.

Lösungsansätze für dieses Optimierungsproblem wurden bereits in verschiedenen früheren Arbeiten entwickelt. In [8] wird ein Branch and Bound Algorithmus vorgestellt, der die Netzwerkkosten unter Beachtung einer Zuverlässigkeitsschranke minimiert. Smith et al. stellen in [3,7] genetische Algorithmen vor, bei denen die Zuverlässigkeitsnebenbedingung über einen Strafterm direkt in die Zielfunktion integriert wird. Die Autoren arbeiten in [7] lediglich mit einer Option pro Kante. In [3] wird der Ansatz auf Probleme mit unterschiedlichen Optionen pro Kante erweitert. Eine Erweiterung des Ansatzes aus [7] für größere Probleminstanzen erfolgt in [9] durch den Einsatz von parallelen genetischen Algorithmen. Eine parallele Betrachtung von Zuverlässigkeit und Kosten als multikriterielles Optimierungsproblem erfolgt in [5,6].

2.2 Zuverlässigkeit von Netzwerktopologien

Die Bewertung der Zuverlässigkeit der Kommunikation zwischen allen vorhandenen Knoten eines Netzwerks erfolgt durch die All-Terminal Zuverlässigkeit R_{All} [2-8]. Diese ist definiert als die Wahrscheinlichkeit, dass zwischen jedem Knotenpaar des Netzwerks ein funktionierender Kommunikationspfad existiert [10]. R_{All} kann als die Wahrscheinlichkeit interpretiert werden, dass in dem Netzwerk mindestens ein funktionierender Baum existiert, welcher sämtliche Knoten des Netzwerks miteinander verbindet [2, S. 3]. Die allgemeine Berechnungsvorschrift der All-Terminal Zuverlässigkeit für ein Netzwerk G_N lautet:

$$R_{All}(G_N) = \sum_{s_i \in S} \Phi(s_i) \cdot Pr(s_i) \tag{2}$$

Ein Zustand s_i repräsentiert dabei einen möglichen Zustand des Netzwerks G_N bei dem ein Teil der Kanten ausgefallen ist. Ein Zustand s_i gilt dabei als „operational" ($\Phi(s_i) = 1$), wenn der resultierende Graph immer noch verbunden ist. Falls der dem Zustand s_i entsprechende Graph nicht mehr verbunden ist, gilt $\Phi(s_i) = 0$. $Pr(s_i)$ entspricht der Eintrittswahrscheinlichkeit der einzelnen Zustände s_i. Ein Beispiel für die Berechnung von R_{All} wird in Abschnitt 2.3 gegeben. Die exakte Berechnung der All-Terminal Zuverlässigkeit zählt zu den NP-harten Problemen [2, S. 3]. Daher wurden für die Berechnung und Approximation von R_{All} in den vergangenen Jahren eine Reihe unterschiedlicher Methoden entwickelt. Ein einfaches Verfahren zur Bestimmung einer oberen Grenze für R_{All} wird in [11] beschrieben. Eine exakte Berechnung von R_{All} kann mit Hilfe von dem in [10] beschriebenen Dekompositionsansatz erfolgen. Bei zunehmender Netzwerkgröße ist allerdings der Einsatz von exakten Berechnungsverfahren auf Grund der langen Laufzeiten und dem damit verbundenen hohen Ressourcenbedarf nicht mehr praktikabel. An Stelle einer exakten Berechnung von R_{All} treten dann zunehmend Schätzverfahren, wie z.B. Monte-Carlo Simulationen [2,4-7]. Das Grundprinzip sämtlicher Monte-Carlo Techniken ist identisch. In mehreren unabhängig voneinander durchgeführten Stichproben generiert das Verfahren jeweils einen Zustand s_i des Netzwerks und untersucht, ob der entsprechende Graph verbunden ist. Aus einer Vielzahl von Stichproben wird anschließend eine Schätzung für die tatsächliche All-Terminal Zuverlässigkeit vorgenommen.

2.3 Ein Beispiel zur Bestimmung der Gesamtzuverlässigkeit und Kosten eines Kommunikationsnetzwerks

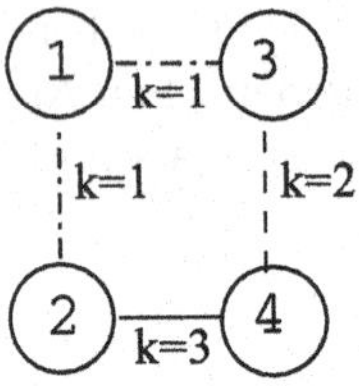

	$l_1(e_{ij})$		$l_2(e_{ij})$		$l_3(e_{ij})$	
	$r(l_1(e_{ij}))$	$c(l_1(e_{ij}))$	$r(l_2(e_{ij}))$	$c(l_2(e_{ij}))$	$r(l_3(e_{ij}))$	$c(l_3(e_{ij}))$
e_{12}	0,8	10	0,9	20	0,95	40
e_{24}	0,8	14	0,9	28	0,95	56
e_{34}	0,8	24	0,9	48	0,95	96
e_{13}	0,8	12	0,9	24	0,95	48

Abb. 1. Beispielnetzwerk zur Bestimmung von Netzwerkkosten und -zuverlässigkeit

An Hand des in Abb. 1 gezeigten Beispielnetzwerks wird die Berechnung der Netzwerkkosten sowie der All-Terminal Zuverlässigkeit demonstriert. Das abgebildete Netzwerk besteht aus 4 Knoten und 4 Kanten (e_{12}, e_{24}, e_{34} und e_{13}). Für jede der vier Kanten (Leitungen) können jeweils drei verschiedene Optionen (l_1 mit Zuverlässigkeit $r(e_{ij}) = 0,8$, l_2 mit Zuverlässigkeit $r(e_{ij}) = 0,9$ und l_3 mit Zuverlässigkeit $r(e_{ij}) = 0,95$) mit jeweils unterschiedlichen Kosten gewählt werden. Für die vier Leitungen wurden die folgenden Optionen ausgewählt: $l_1(e_{12})$, $l_3(e_{24})$, $l_2(e_{34})$ und $l_1(e_{13})$. Die Kosten für das Netzwerk werden nach (1) als $C(N) = c(l_1(e_{12})) + c(l_3(e_{24})) + c(l_2(e_{34})) + c(l_1(e_{14})) = 10 + 56 + 48 + 12 = 126$ berechnet. Die Berechnung der All-Terminal Zuverlässigkeit erfolgt mit Hilfe einer vollständigen Enumeration sämtlicher Zustände s_i nach Formel 2. Für die Berechnung sind nur die fünf Zustände von Interesse, für die das Netzwerk verbunden ist. Die möglichen Zustände hierfür sind 1) keine Kante ausgefallen 2) e_{12} ausgefallen 3) e_{13} ausgefallen 4) e_{34} ausgefallen und 5) e_{24} ausgefallen. Da bei einem gleichzeitigen Ausfall von mehr als zwei Kanten das Netzwerk nicht mehr verbunden ist, müssen die anderen Zustände für die Berechnung von R_{All} nicht mehr berücksichtigt werden. Damit berechnet sich R_{All} aus der Summe der Wahrscheinlichkeiten der Einzelzustände als $R_{All} = (0,8 * 0,95 * 0,9 * 0,8) + (0,2 * 0,95 * 0,9 * 0,8) + (0,8 * 0,05 * 0,9 * 0,8) + (0,8 * 0,95 * 0,1 * 0,8) + (0,8 * 0,95 * 0,9 * 0,2) = 0,9104$. Damit ist das Netzwerk mit einer Wahrscheinlichkeit von ca. 91% komplett verbunden.

3 Ein Ansatz zur Planung von Netzwerkstrukturen unter Kosten- und Zuverlässigkeitsaspekten

3.1 CURE – Eine Schnittbasierte Reparaturheuristik

Mit der Reparaturheuristik CURE (CUt based REpair heuristic) wird ein Verfahren vorgestellt, welches in der Lage ist, beim Entwurf ökonomischer und zuverlässiger Netzwerktopologien Kosten und Zuverlässigkeit gleicher Maßen zu berücksichtigen. Die Reparaturheuristik CURE verwendet Netzwerkstrukturen, welche durch ein heuristisches Optimierungsverfahren erzeugt wurden und verbessert diese solange bis die All-Terminal Zuverlässigkeit des Netzwerkes größer als eine minimal geforderte Schranke R_0 ist. CURE geht dabei prinzipiell so vor, dass in einem ersten Schritt versucht wird, die Zuverlässigkeit von einzelnen Kanten zu erhöhen. Die Zuverlässigkeit der einzelnen Kanten wird dadurch erhöht, dass für eine Kante e_{ij} eine Option l_k mit einer höheren Ausfallsicherheit $r(l_k(e_{ij}))$ gewählt wird. Falls für jede mögliche Kante die maximal mögliche Zuverlässigkeit $r(l_k(e_{ij}))$ gewählt ist und das geforderte R_0 noch nicht erreicht ist, werden in einem zweiten Schritt zusätzliche Verbindungen in das Netzwerk eingefügt. Durch diese Vorgehensweise stellt CURE sicher, dass stets eine Netzwerkstruktur erzeugt wird, welche die Zuverlässigkeitsnebenbedingung $R_{All} \geq R_0$ erfüllt. Der Einsatz einer solchen Prozedur in einem heuristischen Optimierungsverfahren wie z.B. einem genetischen Algorithmus (GA) ermöglicht es, ungültige Lösungen, welche im Laufe des Optimierungsprozesses entstehen, hinsichtlich der gestellten Zuverlässigkeitsnebenbedingung zu reparieren.

Für die Auswahl der Kanten, deren Zuverlässigkeit im ersten Schritt von CURE vergrößert wird, wird die Theorie der minimalen Schnitte in Graphen verwendet. Ein Schnitt $C \subset K$ in einem Graphen G ist eine nichtleere Teilmenge der Knoten K. Jeder Menge C an Knoten wird die Menge E_C an Kanten e_{ij} zugeordnet, für die gilt $\forall e_{ij} \in E_C : i \in C$ und $j \notin C$. Löscht man nun alle Kanten E_C aus G so zerfällt G in zwei Subgraphen, welche jeweils aus den Knotenmengen C und $K \setminus C$ bestehen. Das Gewicht eines Schnittes C ist die Summe der Gewichte der Kanten E_C. Ein minimaler Schnitt ist der Schnitt mit dem geringsten Gewicht. Beim Entwurf zuverlässiger Netzwerktopologien kann das Konzept der minimalen Schnitte zum Finden der Verbindungen in einem Netzwerk genutzt werden, deren Ausfall das Netzwerk trennen würde. Für die Anwendung der CURE Heuristik wird jede Kante des Graphen G_N mit den

Kosten $c(l_{k+1}(e_{ij}))$ der nächst zuverlässigeren Option $l_{k+1}(e_{ij})$ bewertet. Durch die Wahl von Kanten, die zu einem Schnitt gehören, wird sichergestellt, das die Elemente des Graphen verbessert werden, durch deren gemeinsamen Ausfall das Netzwerk nicht mehr verbunden wäre. Durch die Verwendung des minimalen Schnittes wird die Kantenmenge gefunden, bei deren Verbesserung der geringste Kostenzuwachs entsteht. Im Folgenden wird der Ablauf von CURE beschrieben:

Prozedur CURE
Input: $G_N(K, E_N)$, $G(K, E)$, R_0
Queue $Q = \emptyset$, Q.append(G_N)
while (!Q.empty) & ($R_{All}(G_N) < R_0$)) do begin
  G_{work} = Q.first()
  assign weights (costs) to $e_{ij} \in G_{work}$: $c(l_k(e_{ij})) = \begin{cases} c(l_{k+1}(e_{ij})) & \text{if } k < k_{max} \\ c(l_k(e_{ij})) & \text{if } k = k_{max} \end{cases}$
  C = MinCut(G_{work}) (using the weights $c(l_k(e_{ij}))$
  increase reliability $\forall e_{ij} \in E_C : l_k(e_{ij}) = \begin{cases} l_{k+1}(e_{ij}) & \text{if } k < k_{max} \\ l_k(e_{ij}) & \text{if } k = k_{max} \end{cases}$
  calculate $R_{All}(G_N)$
  $G_{N_1} = G_{work} \setminus \{C\}, G_{N_2} = C$
  if number of nodes in $(G_{N_1}) > 1$
    Q.append(G_{N_1})
  if number of nodes in $(G_{N_2}) > 1$
    Q.append(G_{N_2})
  Q.remove(G_{work})
  if (Q.empty) & ($\exists e_{ij} \in E_N$: $k < k_{max}$)
    Q.append(G_N)
end
if ($R_{All}(G_N) < R_0$) begin
  add $e_{ij} \in E \setminus E_N$ to G_N, $\forall e_{ij} \in G_N : l_k(e_{ij}) = l_1(e_{ij})$
  call CURE
end

Im ersten Schritt werden sämtliche Kanten aus G_N mit den Kosten $c(l_{k+1}(e_{ij}))$ der nächst zuverlässigeren Option bewertet. k gibt hierbei die Nummer der aktuellen Option an. Ist für eine der Kanten bereits die Option mit der höchsten Zuverlässigkeit gewählt ($k = k_{max}$), so wird die Kante mit den Kosten der aktuellen Option bewertet. Die Bewertung für das in Abbildung 1 vorgestellte Netzwerk zeigt Abb. 2. Der zu verbessernde Graph wird anschließend in die Queue eingestellt.

Während des Verbesserungsprozesses wählt die Prozedur jeweils den Graphen G_{work} der Queue und ermittelt für diesen die Kanten des minimalen Schnittes (MinCut). Zum Finden des minimalen Schnittes C wird das Verfahren aus [12] genutzt. Anschließend wird für alle Kanten des minimalen Schnittes die Zuverlässigkeit auf die nächste Option erhöht und die Kanten E_C aus G_{work} entfernt, so dass zwei Subgraphen G_{N_1} und G_{N_2} entstehen. Jeder Subgraph mit $|K| > 1$ wird am Ende der Queue angefügt. Wird durch die erste Verbesserung die geforderte Zuverlässigkeit R_0 nicht erreicht, so werden auf diese Weise rekursiv die neu entstanden Subgraphen G_{N_1}, G_{N_2} ebenfalls mittels CURE verbessert. Wenn die Queue leer ist und noch nicht für sämtliche Kanten die höchste Zuverlässigkeitsoption ($k = k_{max}$) gewählt wurde, so wird der komplette Graph erneut in die Queue eingestellt und CURE erneut gestartet. Reichen die in G_N enthaltenen Kanten mit ihrer maximal möglichen Zuverlässigkeit nicht aus um die geforderte Zuverlässigkeit R_0 zu erfüllen, so wird eine neue Kante aus G in G_N eingefügt und CURE erneut gestartet. Details zur Auswahl einer geeigneten Kante sind in [4] beschrieben.

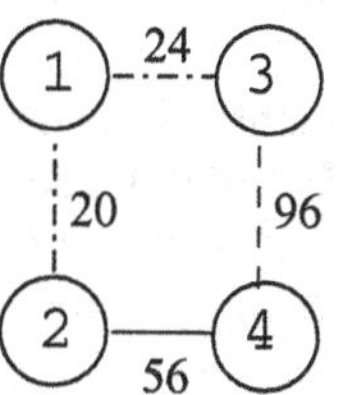

Abb. 2. Verbindungsbewertung für Netzwerk aus Abb. 1

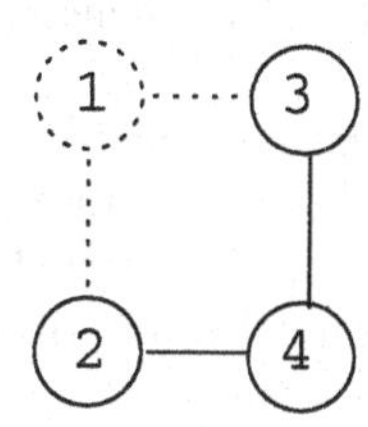

Abb. 3. Subgraph G_{N_1} für Netzwerk aus Abb. 1

Der Ablauf von CURE soll am Beispiel des Graphen G_N aus Abb. 2 erläutert werden. In Abb. 3 werden der Schnitt C sowie die Kanten E_C gepunktet dargestellt. Als minimaler Schnitt wird $C = \{1\}$ mit $E_C = \{e_{12}, e_{13}\}$ mit einem Gewicht von 44 ermittelt. Für die Kanten e_{12} und e_{13} wird die nächst bessere Option ($l_2(e_{12})$ und $l_2(e_{13})$) ausgewählt und diese anschließend aus G_N gelöscht. Nach dem Löschen entstehen die Subgraphen G_{N_1} mit den Knoten $\{2,3,4\}$ und G_{N_2} mit dem Knoten $\{1\}$. Da G_{N_2} nur einen Knoten besitzt, wird der Subgraph durch CURE nicht weiter betrachtet. Konnte durch die Verbesserung der Kanten e_{12} und e_{13} die geforderte Zuverlässigkeit R_0 nicht erreicht werden, so wird das Verfahren rekursiv auf G_{N_1} angewendet.

3.2 Entwurf eines genetischen Algorithmus unter Verwendung der CURE-Reparaturheuristik

Genetische Algorithmen [13] adaptieren die Prinzipien der Evolution (survival of the fittest) für die computergestützte Problemlösung. Dabei werden Suchoperatoren (Rekombination und Mutation) auf eine Menge (Population) von Problemlösungen über mehrere Iterationen (Generationen) angewendet. In jeder Generation wird die Qualität (Fitness) jedes Individuums mittels einer Zielfunktion (hier Formel (1)) bewertet. Über einen Selektionsoperator werden schlechte Lösungen aus der Population entfernt. GA verwenden als Hauptsuchoperator die Rekombination. Im vorliegenden Beitrag wird ein Uniform-Crossover Operator für die Rekombination eingesetzt. Durch den Mutationsoperator können zusätzlich kleine Veränderungen eines Individuums durchgeführt werden. Eine umfassende Erläuterung zu GA findet man in [13]. Durch die Operatoren des GA kann allerdings nicht sichergestellt werden, dass für sämtliche in der Population enthaltenen Lösungen gilt, dass $R_{All} \geq R_0$. Für das hier betrachtete Problem können durch die Suchoperatoren Lösungen erzeugt werden, die eine zu geringe

Gesamtzuverlässigkeit R_{All} aufweisen. Wird während des Suchprozesses ein solches Individuum erstellt, so wird dieses während der Bewertung der Fitness mit Hilfe der CURE Reparaturheuristik in eine valide (gültige) Lösung überführt.

4 Experimentelle Ergebnisse

4.1 Probleminstanzen

Die Leistungsfähigkeit des im vorherigen Abschnitts vorgestellten genetische Algorithmus soll an Hand von drei unterschiedlichen Testproblemen aus der Literatur untersucht werden:

Testproblem Jan5 - 5 Knoten Das einfachste hier untersuchte Netzwerk aus [3] besitzt 5 Knoten. Die optimalen Lösungen für $R_0 = \{0{,}85; 0{,}9; 0{,}93125; 0{,}95; 0{,}99; 0{,}995; 0{,}999\}$ sind aus [3] bekannt. Als „Proof of Concept" soll mit diesem Problem die Fähigkeit von CURE zum Finden optimaler Lösungen untersucht werden.

Testproblem Detter10 - 10 Knoten Das aus [3] entnommene Testproblem besitzt zehn Knoten, die zufällig auf einer 100x100 Fläche platziert wurden. Es werden optimale Lösungen für $R_0 = 0.95$ gesucht. Für das Problem sind $4^{10*9/2} = 1,237e27$ Lösungen möglich und eine optimale Lösung ist nicht bekannt. Als Kosten für die beste gefundene Lösung wird in [3] 5 881,42 angegeben.

Testproblem Türkei19 - 19 Knoten Dieses Problem ist das größte, welches in [3] untersucht wurde. Das Netzwerk muss mindestens eine All-Terminal Zuverlässigkeit R_0 von 0,99 aufweisen. Die Kosten der besten gefundenen Lösung werden in [6] mit 1 755 474 angegeben.

4.2 Experimentierumgebung

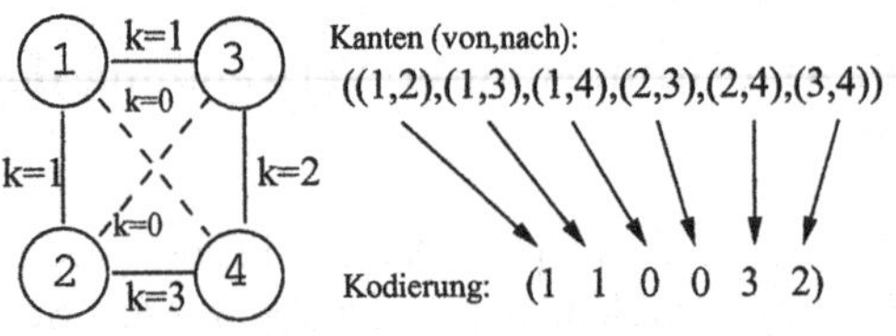

Abb. 4. Kodierung des Netzwerks aus Abb. 1 als Genom

Für die Experimente wurde ein genetischer Algorithmus mit überlappenden Populationen unter Verwendung der in Abschnitt 3.1 beschriebenen Reparaturheuristik CURE implementiert. Eine mögliche Lösung (Netzwerk) wird im GA als ein Vektor ganzer Zahlen der Länge $|K| * |K - 1|/2$ kodiert. Hierbei gibt jede Zahl des Vektors an, welche Option $l_k(e_{ij})$ mit $0 < k \leq k_{max}$ für die jeweilige Kante e_{ij} verwendet wird. Eine Null gibt an, dass keine Verbindung zwischen Knoten i und j existiert. Abb. 4 zeigt die Kodierung des Netzwerks aus Abbildung 1. Nicht vorhandene Verbindungen sind gestrichelt dargestellt. Alle Experimente wurden mit einer Populationsgröße $M = 200$ durchgeführt. Die Initialisierung der Netzwerke für die erste Generation erfolgt zufallsbasiert. Das Initialisierungsverfahren erstellt mit 40% Wahrscheinlichkeit eine Verbindung zwischen zwei Knoten. Wurde eine Verbindung erstellt, wird gleichverteilt eine der zur Verfügung stehenden Optionen für die Zuverlässigkeit der Kante gewählt. Genügt ein durch das Initialisierungsverfahren erstelltes Netzwerk nicht den Zuverlässigkeitsanforderungen, so wird dieses mittels CURE repariert. Der GA arbeitet mit Uniform-Crossover, einem Flip-Mutator und einer Mutationswahrscheinlichkeit 0,01. Ein GA-Lauf wird nach maximal 1000 Generationen oder wenn in den letzten 20 Generationen keine bessere Lösung gefunden wurde abgebrochen. Die Bewertung der All-Terminal Zuverlässigkeit erfolgt für die Probleme Jan5 und Deeter10 mit Hilfe des exakten Verfahrens aus [10]. Für das Problem Türkei19 ist dieses Verfahren auf Grund der Netzwerkgrößen nicht mehr einsetzbar. Stattdessen wird hier eine einfache Monte-Carlo Simulation genutzt. Für jedes Problem wurden jeweils zehn voneinander unabhängige GA-Läufe durchgeführt. Für den Vergleich der mit CURE gewonnenen Ergebnisse mit bisherigen Ansätzen wurde der in [3] vorgestellte Strafterm-Ansatz implementiert.

4.3 Auswertung

Tabelle 1 fasst die Ergebnisse für das Problem Jan5 für unterschiedliche R_0 zusammen. Die Tabelle vergleicht die Reparaturheuristik CURE mit dem Strafwertansatz von [3] bezüglich den durchschnittlichen Kosten der jeweils gefundenen besten Lösung (min. Kosten), der Wahrscheinlichkeit P_{succ}, dass die optimale Lösung gefunden wird, und der durchschnittlichen Anzahl (⊘ Eval) der hierfür notwendigen Bewertungen von Lösungen. Für $R_0 = 0,85$ und $R_0 = 0,90$ wird in allen zehn Läufen die optimale Lösung bereits bei der Initialisierung der ersten Population gefunden. Darüber hinaus findet mit Ausnahme von $R_0 = 0,995$ der GA die optimale Lösung in mindestens drei von zehn Läufen. Für $R_0 = 0,995$ wird in allen zehn Läufen lediglich eine suboptimale Lösung mit den minimalen Kosten 4 382 gefunden. Ein Vergleich der notwendigen Fitnessbewertungen zwischen CURE und dem Strafwertansatz aus [3] zeigt, dass ein GA mit CURE deutlich weniger Fitnessbewertungen bei gleicher Lösungsqualität benötigt. Dies ist besonders positiv hervorzuheben, da die Bewertung von Lösungen (Berechnung von R_{All} sowie Ermittlung der Kosten) für größere Netzwerke sehr rechenaufwendig ist und im Vergleich dazu der Aufwand für CURE vernachlässigt werden kann. Zusammenfassend lässt sich für das einfache Problem Jan5 feststellen, dass ein GA mit der Reparaturheuristik CURE in der Lage ist, optimale bzw. nahezu optimale Lösungen zu finden. Tabelle 2 vergleicht die Leistungsfähigkeit des GAs für die Probleme Deeter10 und Türkei19. Es sind der Mittelwert der Kosten (⊘ Kosten) der besten gefundenen Lösungen über alle 10 Läufe, die Kosten des besten gefundenen Netzwerks (min. Kosten), die durchschnittliche Anzahl der pro Lauf durchgeführten Fitnessbewertungen (⊘ Eval.) und die durchschnittlich benötige Laufzeit (t_{conv}) jeweils für CURE und dem Strafwertansatz aus [3] angegeben. Als beste Lösung wurde unter Verwendung von CURE für das Problem Deeter10 ein Netzwerk mit den Kosten von 4 385,99 gefunden. Die mittleren minimalen Kosten gemittelt über alle 10 Läufe betragen 4 439,40. Beide Ergebnisse liegen deutlich unter den mit Hilfe eines Strafterms erzielten Lösungen.

Tabelle 1. Ergebnisse für Testproblem Jan5

R_0	Kosten opt. Lsg.	CURE			Ansatz von [3]		
		min. Kosten	P_{succ}	⊘ Eval	min. Kosten	P_{succ}	⊘ Eval
0,999	5 522	5 522	0,3	360	5 522	0,8	40 560
0,995	4 352	4 382	0	-	4 352	0,4	23 200
0,99	3 754	3 754	1	1 560	3 754	1	31 400
0,95	2 634	2 634	1	270	2 634	1	118 880
0,93 125	2 416	2 416	1	1 170	2 416	1	25 560
0,9	2 184	2 184	1	200	2 184	1	26 160
0,85	1 904	1 904	1	200	1 904	1	4 640

In den Abbildungen 5(a) und 5(b) werden für die Probleme Deeter10 und Türkei19 die durchschnittlichen Kosten der jeweils gefundenen besten Lösung über die Anzahl der Generationen des GA dargestellt. Die Kurven beschreiben somit, wie sich die Qualität der besten gefundenen Lösungen während der GA-Läufe verändert. Die Ergebnisse zeigen, dass durch den Einsatz von CURE deutlich bessere Startlösungen ermittelt werden können und auch im weiteren Verlauf der Optimierung die Kosten der besten gefundenen Netzwerke beim Einsatz von CURE stets kleiner sind als beim Einsatz von Straftermen. Eine Analyse des Fitnessverlaufs zeigt, dass ein GA bei der Verwendung von CURE deutlich schneller konvergiert und somit zum Finden besserer Lösungen weniger Fitnessbewertungen als der straftermbasierte Ansatz benötigt. Es ist festzuhalten, dass der Strafterm-GA zwar teilweise weniger Bewertungen benötigt und stets eine kürzere Laufzeit hat, die Qualität der gefundenen Lösungen jedoch deutlich schlechter ist. Analysiert man die in Tabelle 2 für das Problem präsentierten Ergebnisse, so erfolgt durch den CURE-GA eine deutliche Verbesserung der bisher gefundenen besten Lösungen. Im Vergleich zu [6], wo die Kosten des besten gefundenen Netzwerkes für das Problem Türkei19 mit 1 755 474 angegeben wurde, konnte durch den Einsatz von CURE eine Netzwerkstruktur mit Kosten 1 577 755 ermittelt werden (eine Verringerung der Kosten um mehr als 10% bei gleichem R_0). Gegenüber der besten in [3] veröffentlichten Lösung (7 694 708) konnte sogar eine Verbesserung um zirka 80% erreicht werden.

	Deeter10		Türkei19	
	CURE	Strafterm	CURE	Strafterm
min. Kosten	4 385,99	4 948,79	1 577 755	2 499 080
⊘ Kosten	4 439,40	5 239,90	1 720 994	2 763 670
⊘ Eval.	4 830	6 190	33 330	20 550
t_{conv}	1 508	773	25 200	8 100

Tabelle 2. Vergleich der Ergebnisse für Testproblem Deeter10 und Türkei 19

Beim Problem Deeter10 konnten die Kosten der optimalen Lösung von 5881 auf 4386 bei gleichem R_0 verringert werden (eine Verbesserung von ca. 25%). Da das hier betrachtete Planungsproblem keinen Echtzeitanforderungen unterliegt, ist der zusätzliche Aufwand, der durch den Einsatz der Reparaturheursitik entsteht, in Anbetracht der deutlich höheren Lösungsqualität vertretbar.

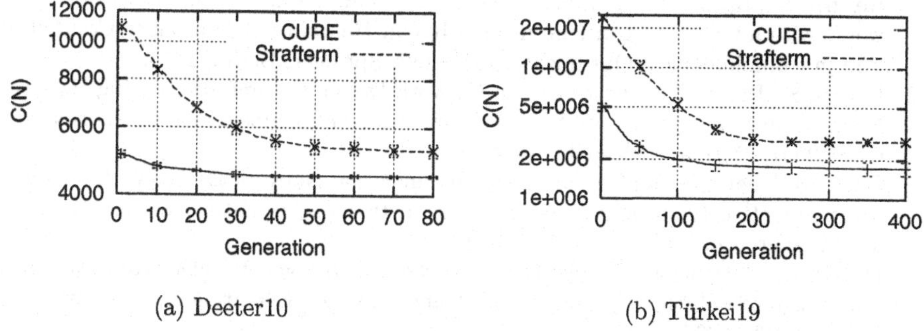

(a) Deeter10 (b) Türkei19

Abb. 5. Kosten $C(N)$ der besten gefundenen Lösungen in Abhängigkeit von der Anzahl der Generationen des eingesetzten GAs. Ein GA findet bei der Verwendung von CURE deutlich bessere Lösungen als beim Einsatz des Strafkostenansatzes.

5 Zusammenfassung

Dieser Beitrag beschäftigt sich mit der Planung von Netzwerkstrukturen unter Kosten- und Zuverlässigkeitsaspekten. Hierbei werden zum Ermitteln von kostenoptimalen Netzwerkstrukturen, welche eine vorgegebene minimale Gesamtzuverlässigkeit R_0 aufweisen, heuristische Optimierungsverfahren eingesetzt. Im Gegensatz zu bisherigen Forschungsarbeiten, bei welchen Netzwerke, welche die geforderte Zuverlässigkeit R_0 nicht erfüllen, durch die Einführung von Straftermen schlechter bewertet werden, wird im vorliegenden Beitrag eine Reparaturheuristik CURE entwickelt und eingesetzt. CURE bestimmt mit Hilfe der minimalen Schnitte für ein Netzwerk die für eine Reparatur relevanten Kanten und liefert eine Netzwerkstruktur, welche die vorgegebene Zuverlässigkeitsrestriktion erfüllt. Die Reparaturheuristik CURE wurde in einem genetischen Algorithmus implementiert und deren Leistungsfähigkeit im Rahmen einer experimentellen Studie mit dem bisher üblichen Straftermansatz verglichen.

Die Leistungsfähigkeit von CURE wurde für drei Probleminstanzen aus der Literatur mit unterschiedlicher Komplexität getestet. Die Ergebnisse zeigen, dass CURE mit geringem Aufwand durchweg bessere Lösungen findet als der bisherige Straftermansatz. Bei den zwei praktisch relevanten Problemstellungen konnten durch den Einsatz von CURE Netzwerkstrukturen gefunden werden, welche um bis zu 25% geringere Kosten bei gleicher Gesamtzuverlässigkeit aufweisen.

Literatur

1. Garey M. R., Johnson D. S.: Computers and Intractibility: A Guide to the Theory of NP-Completeness. W. H. Freeman and Company, San Fransisco, 1979.
2. Colbourn, C.: The Combinatorics of Network Reliability. Oxford University Press, Oxford, 1987.
3. Deeter D., Smith A.: Economic Design of Reliable Networks. IIE Transcations, Special Issue on Economics of Reliable Engineering 30:1161–1174, 1998.

4. Reichelt D., Rothlauf, F., Gmilkowsky P.: Designing Reliable Communication Networks with a Genetic Algorithm using a Repair Heuristic. Evolutionary Computation in Combinatorical Optimization:177–187, Springer, Berlin, 2004.
5. Duarte S., Barán B.: Multiobjective Network Design Optimisation Using Parallel Evolutionary Algorithms. In XXVII Conferencia Latinoamericana de Informática CLEI'2001, Merida, Venezuela, 2001.
6. Barán B.,Duarte S.,Benítez D.: Telecommunication Network Design with Parallel Multi-objective Evolutionary Algorithms. In IFIP/ACM Latin America Networking Conference, La Paz, Bolivia, 2003.
7. Dengiz B., Altiparmak F., Smith A.E.: Local search genetic algorithm for optimal design of reliable networks. IEEE Transactions on Evolutionary Computation 1(3):179–188, 1997.
8. Jan R. H., Hwang F.J., Cheng S.T.: Topological optimization problem of communication networks subject to a reliability constraint. IEEE Transactions on Reliability 42:63–70, 1993.
9. Baran B.,Laufer F.: Topological optimization of reliable networks using a-teams. In World Multiconference on Systemics, Cybernetics and Informatics - SCI 99 and ISAS 99, Vol 5, 1999.
10. Yunbin C., Jiandong L., Jiamo C.: A new algorithm for network probabilistic connectivity. In IEEE military communication conference, 1999.
11. Konak A., Smith. A.: An improved general upperbound for all-terminal network reliability. Technical report, University of Pittsburgh, 1998.
12. Stoer M., WagnerF.: A Simple Min Cut Algorithm. Algorithms. In Algorithms - ESA '94 Second Annual European Symposium:141–147, Springer, Berlin, 1994.
13. Goldberg D. E.: Genetic algorithms in search, optimization, and machine learning. Addison-Wesley, Reading, 1989.

An Integrated Simulator for Inter-domain Scenarios

Matthias Scheidegger, Florian Baumgartner and Torsten Braun

Institute of Computer Science and Applied Mathematics
University of Bern, Neubrückstrasse 10, 3012 Bern, Switzerland
(mscheid|baumgart|braun@iam.unibe.ch)
Tel: +41-31-63189557 Fax: +41-31-6313261

Abstract The simulation of large-scale inter-domain networks is useful for various aspects of network planning and management. It is also a challenge due to its scalability problems, and the often incomplete knowledge about the network in question. Automatic configuration of the simulator based on network measurements may also be required. None of the many proposed approaches to network simulation are suitable for all possible simulation scenarios. A combination of several approaches provides much more flexibility. We describe a hybrid network simulator capable of combining packet-based simulation with a wide variety of other simulation approaches. A combination of packet-based simulation with analytical models is presented. This simulator is part of Intermon, an integrated system for the collection, processing, modeling, simulation and visualization of inter-domain data. The collected information is used for simulations allowing a "what-if" analysis of real networks. This paper describes the architecture and the underlying analytical models, and it evaluates the hybrid simulator.

1 Introduction

With the growing Internet and increased customer demands for quality of service, systems and tools for the monitoring and management of networks become more and more indispensable. This includes tools to monitor traffic within the network, and tools to analyze the gathered measurements in order to identify present and potential future problems in the network. Simulation is a powerful tool for predicting network performance but there are a number of problems that must be overcome to make it usable in the inter-domain context.

First and foremost is the problem of scalability. Classical network simulators like ns2 do not scale to the network sizes and traffic volumes of today's inter-domain networks. Much research has gone into making simulators more scalable. Furthermore, simulation scenarios must be carefully configured if they should accurately predict the effects of changes in the real network. This should ideally be done automatically from measurement data. A simulator should thus provide a mechanism to support this task. Another problem is that many existing simulators assume perfect knowledge of the network's topology and traffic flows, which is rarely the case because of technical and political reasons. Even if an ISP has measurement data available it is very unlikely to publish it, as this could present a competitive advantage to other ISPs. Simulators should thus also be able to model parts of the network based on coarse-grained information obtained using network tomography tool, for example.

The "advanced architecture for INTER-domain quality of service MONitoring, modeling and visualization" (Intermon) project aims to develop an architecture for monitoring, modeling, simulation, prediction and the visualization of inter-domain quality of service. This includes tools for the monitoring process itself as well as the development of models and simulators to predict the behavior of inter-domain networks.

Within this project the Hybrid Simulator has been developed and implemented. It is based on the observation that none of the various simulation approaches that have been proposed in the literature fulfill all requirements from above. Instead, a combination of several approaches may provide much greater flexibility. The hybrid simulator extends the packet-based simulator `ns2` with other simulation approaches by using a hot-plug mechanism that can insert modules into the `ns2` topology. These modules simulate parts of the network using other, more adequate approaches.

A first plug-in implements an analytical modeling approach for multi-domain networks, which is based on the assumption that, at a given time, the Internet can be divided into areas where congestion is negligible, interconnected by bottleneck links. Congestion free areas are treated as black boxes with several ingress and egress points. Packet loss and delay caused by excessive queuing are only in the bottleneck links. Creating models for congestion free areas has the advantage that the simulation of packet losses and excessive queuing can be restricted to a small part of a simulation scenario (the bottleneck links), thus greatly reducing the complexity of the scenario as a whole. In fact it is sufficient to model congestion free areas using quasi-stationary delay distributions. Apart from its scalability advantage this approach may be useful to model network areas of which we do not know the exact topology. Moreover, a mechanism has been implemented that can automatically configure scenarios using measurement data provided by the Intermon architecture.

Suggested application areas for the hybrid simulator include end-to-end QoS evaluation of single flows – simulated using traditional packet-based models – over a complex backbone network, or the effect of changes in a backbone network (e.g. addition/removal of links, capacity changes, big changes of network load due to new SLAs, etc.) on flows traversing the network.

The remainder of this document is structured as follows: In Section 2 the Intermon architecture, the integration of the simulator in the system, and the hybrid simulator itself are described. Section 3 gives an overview about the analytical models used by the hybrid simulator. In Section 4 the simulation results are compared with measurements from a laboratory network, and Section 5 concludes the paper.

2 Architecture

The Intermon architecture (Fig. 1) has been designed as a highly distributed system. Measurements, data storage, simulation and visualization can all be hosted on individual systems. The communication elements are implemented in Java using the Java Messaging Standard API (JMS) as a communications middleware.

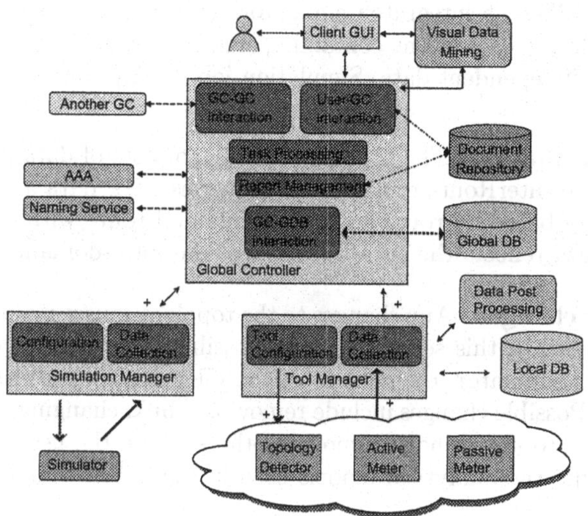

Fig. 1. A global view of the Intermon architecture

A central goal of the Intermon project is the integration of the different components into a single Intermon toolkit architecture. The integrated tools cover mechanisms for structure discovery of inter-domain topologies, as well as for measurement, modeling, simulation, and visual data mining of inter-domain traffic [1]. The key elements of the system are a global controller (GC), which accepts and forwards user requests, and the tool managers, which control the tools and convert messages between tool and GC into the appropriate format.

Since the Intermon system is distributed and depends on intense communication between the components, security issues have to be taken into account. Accordingly, all Intermon components communicate through a dedicated Virtual Private Network (VPN). Another advantage of the VPN is the simplified configuration of firewalls which may exist between the different hosts in the Intermon VPN.

2.1 Generating and Processing Simulation Jobs

Many applications of the Intermon toolkit, like "what-if" scenarios for example, require the use of simulation. A set of four distinct simulators, one of which is the hybrid simulator described below, has been implemented and integrated into the Intermon system in order to be able to adequately solve different simulation tasks and to study the advantages of different simulation approaches [2]. All integrated simulators can be interactively configured and controlled through a common graphical user interface, which can also be used to configure the meters deployed throughout the network gathering measurement data, and to visualize the simulation results.

A generic XML-based simulation job description format has been developed to control the different integrated simulators in a common way. This format separates the data into sections containing simulator-specific data and sections with simulator-independent data. Simulation job descriptions are structured as follows:

Topology information: The topology usually consists of data previously collected by the InterRoute tool [3], which queries BGP data and reconstructs the topology based on route advertisements and route withdrawals. Therefore this data reflects the current status of the inter-domain scenario to be simulated.

User applied changes: Any changes to the topology a user makes through the GUI are listed in this section. As the possible actions differ depending on the selected simulator, the content of the GUI dialogs is different for every simulator. Possible changes include removing a link, changing its capacity, or adding flows to the scenario, amongst others. Here, the user can also select and configure the analytical models used in the hybrid simulator described below.

Simulator specific parameters: Each simulator has some simulator specific parameters that are not related to the topology. They are encoded within this section. This allows the user to supply general instructions and parameters to the simulator. Examples of such parameters are the duration of the simulation and the granularity of the results.

The XML job description is generated by the graphical user interface and sent via the global controller to the tool manager of the appropriate simulator.

Since network simulations can require a lot of computing power and also can produce a huge amount of data, scalability was a central aspect during the design and the implementation of the hybrid simulator's tool manager and its underlying tool chain (see Fig. 2). The system supports the processing of simulation requests in parallel and thus supports multiprocessor computers as well as computer clusters.

The first steps in job processing consist of converting the XML simulation job description into configuration files for the hybrid simulator, and then starting the simulator. This is done by the demultiplexer component. After the simulation has finished, the multiplexer components takes care of processing the simulator tracefiles and stores the results in a data repository. Finally, it returns a message telling the system by which URL the results can be obtained.

The messages returned by the hybrid simulator's tool manager include some descriptive comments on the content of the reply and indicate the processing

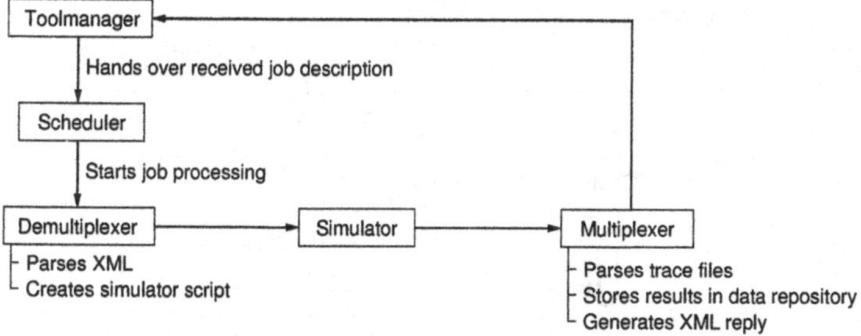

Fig. 2. The hybrid simulator's tool chain for the automatic processing of simulation requests

time and the status (e.g. running, ok, canceled, broken) of the simulation job. As the simulators may produce several different types of results, multiple result sections may be included in the reply, one for each desired measure (e.g. time series of throughput, or of end-to-end delay on a certain path). The sub-results have their own descriptive comment and a type identifier to help visualization.

2.2 Hybrid Simulator

The hybrid simulator aims to combine packet-based simulation with other simulation approaches to increase modeling flexibility and to overcome the limitations of the single simulation approaches used. In order to be able to integrate other simulation approaches with packet-based simulation, the `ns2` network simulator has been modified and extended. The main changes apply to the `ns2` node, whose structure is shown in Fig. 3. The typical node structure consists of an address classifier, a port classifier and a set of agents acting as traffic sources and sinks. The address classifier routes incoming packets either directly to outgoing links or to a port classifier forwarding the packets to an appropriate agent. We added a mechanism to the node structure to defer the delay and loss behavior of a node to loadable external modules, which can be implemented using arbitrary simulation approaches.

While the internal predictor module implements some minimal functionality to apply delay patterns to passing packets, its main function is to defer the respective computation to dynamically loadable external modules. In this case the predictor only provides an interface to the external module and takes care of delaying or dropping the packet inside the simulator.

Apart from the functions allowing for dynamic loading and unloading as well as initialization and configuration of the module, a predictor module only has to provide a single function `process_packet`, which is called for each arriving packet. Depending on the return value, the module interface within the node either delays or discards the packet (for values ≥ 0 or < 0, respectively). With each call to the this function, the predictor gets information about the packet itself, the previous and the next hop, and the simulation time. If the module

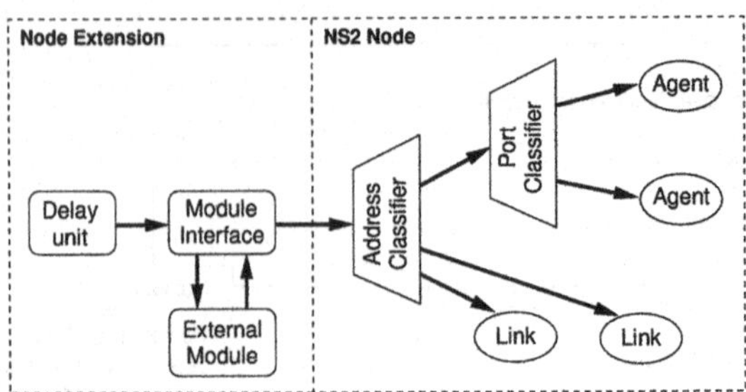

Fig. 3. Extension of the ns2 nodenetwork simulator with an interface for delay and loss predictor modules

requires another representation it has to generate it by itself, based on the events it receives. For example, if the module uses fluid flow representation internally, it will have to convert the packet arrival events into an estimate of current bandwidth.

3 An Analytical Modeling Extension for ns2

The extension mechanism described in Section 2.2 allows to load arbitrary modules into ns2 nodes. A first fully useable extension module is based on a set of analytical models, which can be used to scalably model the behavior of whole inter-domain networks. In this section we introduce the ideas and concepts these models are based on and describe how they can be applied to improve the scalability of inter-domain simulation scenarios.

Scalability is often an issue when simulating large-scale computer networks. Especially packet-based simulators like ns2 do not scale to scenarios with large topologies and high traffic volumes because of the large number of events to be processed. Many approaches to this scalability problem have been proposed. While parallel simulation [4,5] is arguably the most prominent one, alternatives include approaches such as fluid flow simulation [6,7,8], time stepped hybrid simulation [9] and packet trains [10], to name a few. Scalability in network simulation is generally achieved by reducing the level of detail (or accuracy) of the simulation scenario or of the simulation algorithm. Carefully chosen, such abstractions can considerably reduce the complexity of large-scale simulations without significantly distorting the results. However, an abstraction suitable for one task is not necessarily the right choice for other tasks. For the Intermon project a simulator was needed that can scalably simulate inter-domain networks while allowing for automatic measurement-based configuration, and which provides adequate abstractions for parts of the network where the topology cannot be determined.

We propose a model that is based on the assumption that, over certain time spans, networks like the Internet can be divided into areas where congestion is negligible, and which are interconnected by bottleneck links. We treat congestion free areas as black boxes, which we call *domain models*. Modeling congestion free

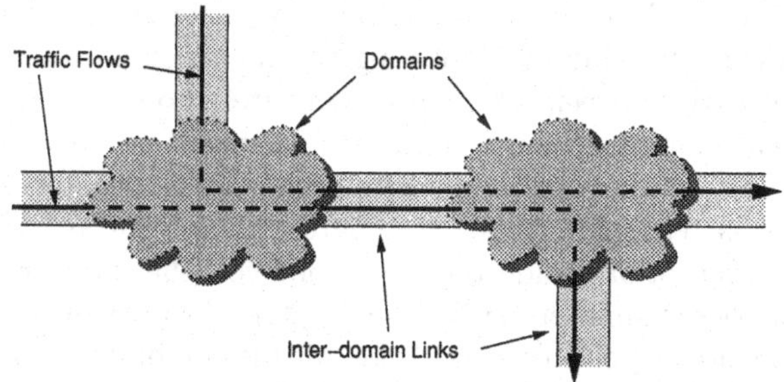

Fig. 4. The basic modeling view

areas has the advantage that we can neglect packet losses and excessive queuing in large parts of the network and restrict the model to quasi-stationary delay behavior. Apart from its scalability advantage this approach is primarily useful to model network areas of which we do not know the exact topology. Domain models can be based on empirical cumulative distribution functions (ECDFs) to simulate the delays of packets crossing the domain. The ECDF is chosen depending on the ingress and egress points on which the packet enters and leaves the domain, respectively. A big advantage of this concept is that delay measurements from a real network can be directly used to configure a domain model. It is important to note that ECDF models, while giving good reproductions of observed first and second-order moments in measurements, ignore any non-stationarity of the sample.

The bottleneck links between two domains of a simulation scenario are represented by *inter-domain link models.* Here, packet loss and queuing delay are simulated. The basic parameters of an inter-domain link model are similar to those of a link in a packet-based simulator. Nonetheless, inter-domain link models are not event-driven but rely on parameters like offered load and link capacity. Figure 4 shows this modeling view.

Traffic in the network is modeled using *application traffic models*, which serve as scalable models for large aggregates of application traffic like VoIP, Video, HTTP, etc. They take the form of a function $f(t)$ that yields the load generated by the traffic aggregate given a (monotonously rising) point in time. Also, traffic caused by `ns2` packets passing the extended node is also modeled by application traffic models.

By combining domain, inter-domain link and application traffic models we create a *multi-domain model*, which can then be inserted into the extended `ns2` simulator. We refer to this combination of analytical models and packet-based simulation as *hybrid simulation.* To determine how to handle a packet when it reaches the multi-domain model through the extension interface we have to update and inspect the model at the time of the packet arrival. This is done in three steps: First, the application traffic models must be updated, which includes the bandwidth estimators that convert between packet arrival events and load estimates. Second, any changes in traffic load have to be distributed through the multi-domain model. Then, we can decide whether to drop the packet or to delay it by a certain value by inspecting the domain and inter-domain link models along the path between the ingress and egress points of the packet.

One useful partitioning scheme for the above approach is to model autonomous systems (ASs) as domains, and their border links as inter-domain links. This partitioning is reasonable since the ingress routers of an AS may police flows to prevent congestion inside the AS. Moreover, the interior links usually have bigger capacities than inter-AS links, and internal routes may be changed to distribute traffic load. A possible application of this combination of fine grained packet-based simulation and coarse grained analytical models could be scenarios like a multi-site virtual private network. The local networks would then be modeled inside ns2, while the network in between would be modeled as a multi-domain model.

3.1 Modeling of Delay and Packet Loss

Packet loss and delay depends on the interaction of links and traffic flows in the network. We chose to model inter-domain links with the simple M/M/1/K queue, that is, an analytical queue with Poisson arrival and service processes, a single server (the physical link) and system capacity K. The arrival and service rates λ and μ depend on the offered load on the link and the link's capacity, respectively. The system capacity K, if unknown, can be set to a typical value (for example, 128-packet buffers are rather common in routers). Recent work [11] suggests that the arrival process would be better modeled as a Batch Markovian Arrival Process (BMAP). Also, sophisticated techniques like traffic-based decomposition [12] or the decomposition approach in Sadre et al. [13] could be used. These techniques also consider the effect of correlations in network traffic, which the M/M/1/K queue clearly ignores. However, while these approaches use traffic models that statistically describe traffic behavior over long time periods, the traffic models in our approach only describe the state of traffic sources at specific time instants – when a packet arrives at the multi-domain model. Correlations are thus only ignored on the small time-scale. The system's behavior in the long run is not modeled but rather simulated and hence also includes the effects of correlations.

In order to model the behavior of the inter-domain link we have to find the probability p_i of the system to be in state i, where state K means the queue is full, and state 0 means the system is empty and does not send. The M/M/1/K queue is a birth and death process with arrival and departure rates λ and μ, respectively. For a birth and death process of this kind the probabilities p_i are given by

$$p_i = \begin{cases} \frac{1-\lambda/\mu}{1-(\lambda/\mu)^{K+1}}, & i = 0 \\ (\lambda/\mu)^i p_0, & i > 0 \end{cases} \tag{1}$$

if $\lambda \neq \mu$, and

$$p_0 = p_1 = \ldots = p_K = \frac{1}{K+1} \tag{2}$$

if $\lambda = \mu$. As stated above, p_K is the probability of the system being full. Therefore, p_K is also the loss ratio of the link. The functional representation of the inter-domain link used in the section about multi-domain models above can thus be written as $L(\lambda) = (1 - p_K)\lambda$, with p_K calculated according to formulas 1 and 2. From the probabilities p_i we can further construct a discrete density function of the link's delay distribution. The number of bytes that are in the system when another byte arrives is proportional to the time this byte has to wait before it is sent to the link. δ_{pr} is the propagation delay on the link, which depends on physical properties of the link, e.g. its length. The discrete delay distribution looks like this

$$\begin{pmatrix} p_0 & \cdots & p_{K-1} & p_K \\ \delta_{pr} + \frac{1}{\mu} & \cdots & \delta_{pr} + \frac{K}{\mu} & \infty \end{pmatrix} \quad (3)$$

The infinite delay in the case of a full queue indicates that this packet is effectively lost.

Using the above results we can compute the loss ratio by multiplying the forwarding probabilities $(1 - p_K)$ of all the inter-domain links on the path. Similarly, the time it takes for a packet to traverse a path P can be described as a random variable δ_P with

$$\delta_P = \sum_{i=1}^{n} \delta_{L_i} + \sum_{i=1}^{n-1} \delta_{L_i, L_{i+1}} \quad (4)$$

where δ_L is the random variable of the delay caused by inter-domain link L, and $\delta_{L,K}$ is the random variable of delay in the domain between the inter-domain links L and K ($\delta_{L,K}$ is only defined if L is a predecessor of K). Having a random variable of a path's delay further allows to easily calculate values like the path's mean delay or jitter.

4 Evaluation

A first evaluation experiment for the hybrid simulator was done by comparing measurements from a testbed network to the results from the corresponding simulation scenario. The testbed was set up using the extended cross traffic topology shown in Fig. 5(a), which is useful to evaluate the performance of the inter-domain link and multi-domain models as well as the ns2 toolchain. A comparison of domain models to real network behavior is less useful as these models are directly based on measurements from these networks. All nodes were Intel-based Linux systems, interconnected by 100 mbit ethernet links.

A reference flow was sent from A to H, and cross traffic was sent from B to G and from C to G. All three traffic sources consisted of multiple 1 mbit/s CBR streams with Pareto interarrival times and exponential hold times. The traffic load produced by these sources can be seen in Fig. 5(b). For reference, the theoretical maximum capacity of the the links is indicated as a line in the Figure.

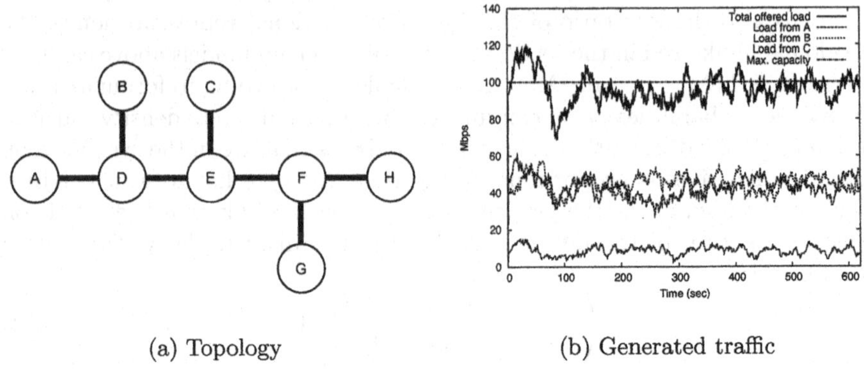

(a) Topology (b) Generated traffic

Fig. 5. Testbed setup

As the delay introduced by the nodes was expected to be minimal we chose to model them by domain models with zero delay. The ethernet links were modeled with inter-domain link models. Interfaces to `ns2` were attached at A and H, and a reference stream generated by `ns2` was sent along the path A-D-E-F-H to determine delay and loss ratio as well as to test the interface code itself.

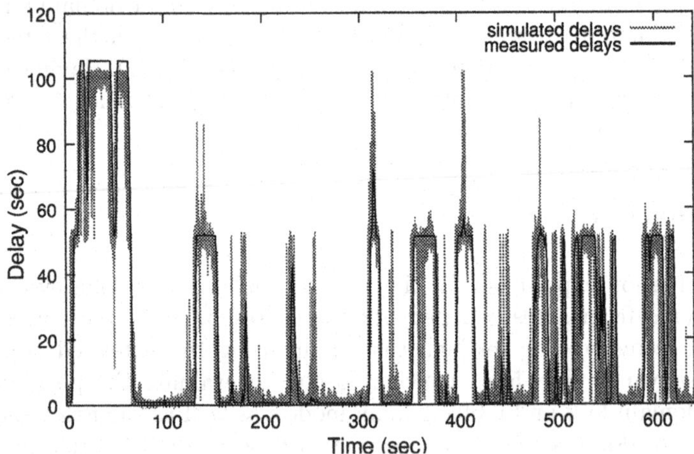

Fig. 6. Comparison of delays from testbed and simulation scenario

Figs. 6 and 7 show a comparison of the measurements and the simulation results. The delays in the testbed showed very little variance even with full queues, which is due to the CBR characteristic of the generated traffic. Consequently, the inter-domain link models, expecting Poisson arrivals, overestimated the traffic's burstiness. However, the mean of delay was similar in both, testbed results and simulator traces. As can be seen in Fig. 6 both graphs match rather well. Only when nodes E and F are under full load, packet forwarding in the routers begins to slow down slightly, which leads to the small gap between simulated and measured delays.

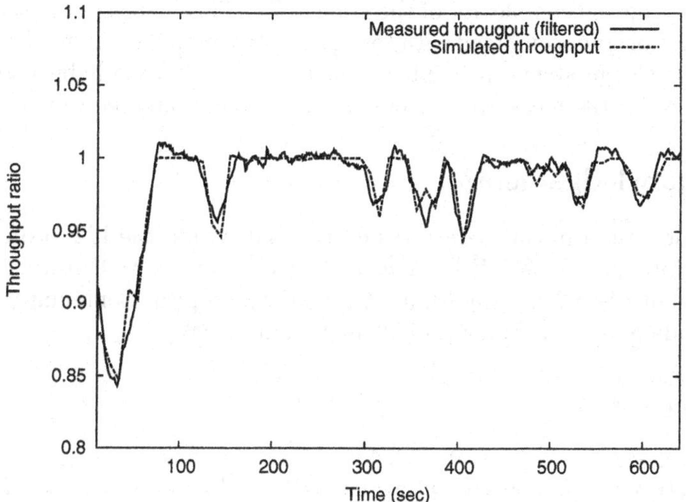

Fig. 7. Comparison of throughput from testbed and simulation scenario

In contrast to delay the throughput in the testbed proved to be rather bursty, probably because of interrupt timing in the routers. This didn't have much effect on the delay as the effect was hardly noticeable in comparison with queuing delay. However, the resulting small transient queues caused the throughput graph to be rather noisy. The graph in Fig. 7 was therefore smoothed using a box filter. Nonetheless, it can be seen that the simulated values closely match the testbed measurements.

5 Summary

In this document we presented a hybrid simulator for the scalable analysis of inter-domain networks. Measurements from other tools in the Intermon toolkit can be used to automatically generate scenarios, which makes the system suitable for "what-if" analysis. A tool chain handles the XML simulation job descriptions coming from the GUI, converts them to a local format, and generates an XML reply based on the simulation results.

The simulator itself is based on the combination of packet-based simulation with other simulation approaches to increase flexibility and scalability. A plug-in mechanism extension to the ns2 simulator allows to attach arbitrary extension modules to a ns2 node. A plug-in module enhances ns2 by providing scalable analytical and stochastic models for the modeling of inter-domain networks. The evaluation showed that delay and throughput values obtained by the simulator are very similar to direct measurements in a laboratory test network.

Since the underlying network can be abstracted by an appropriate network model (e.g. the presented analytical), the size of the network does not have a direct impact on the complexity of the simulation. This increases the scalability of the simulation and, combined with the capability to simulate networks without an exact knowledge about their internal structure, makes the hybrid simulator a perfect tool for the measurement based simulation of large network scenarios.

A Acknowledgements

The work presented in this paper was carried out within the IST project "Advanced Architecture for INTER-domain Quality of Service MONitoring, modeling and visualization" (Intermon), funded by the European Community and the Swiss "Bundesamt für Bildung und Wissenschaft (BBW)."

References

1. Gutiérrez, P.A.A., Malone, P., Ofoghlu, M. et al.: Acquisition, modelling and visualisation of inter-domain routing data. IPS'04, Budapest, Hungary, 2004
2. Bartoli, M., Baumgartner, F., Scheidegger, M. et al.: The intermon simulation framework. IPS'04, Budapest, Hungary, 2004
3. Gutiérrez, P.A.A., et. al.: Integrating inter-domain routing analysis in novel management strategies for large scale ip networks. NEW2AN'04, St.Petersburg, Russia
4. Chandy, K.M., Misra, J.: Asynchronous distributed simulation via a sequence of parallel computations. Communications of the ACM **11** (1981) 198–205
5. Ammar, M.H., Riley, G.F., Fujimoto, R.M.: A generic framework for parallelization of network simulations. MASCOTS'99, College Park, MD (1999)
6. Yan, A., Gong, W.B.: Fluid simulation for high speed networks with flow-based routing. IEEE Transactions on Information Theory (1999) 1588–1599
7. Liu, B., Guo, Y., Kurose, J., Towsley, D., Gong, W.: Fluid simulation of large scale networks: Issues and tradeoffs. PDPTA'99, 2136–2142
8. Liu, B., Figueirido, D.R., et al.: A study of networks simulation efficiency: Fluid simulation vs. packet-level simulation. Proceedings of IEEE Infocom (2001)
9. Guo, Y., Gong, W., Towsley, D.: Time-stepped hybrid simulation (TSHS) for large scale networks. Proceedings of IEEE Infocom (2000)
10. Ahn, J.S., Danzig, P.B.: Packet network simulation: speedup and accuracy versus timing granularity. IEEE/ACM Transactions on Networking **4** (1996) 743–757
11. Klemm, A., Lindemann, C., Lohmann, M.: Modeling ip traffic using the batch markovian arrival process. Performance Evaluation (2003) 149–173
12. Heindl, A., Telek, M.: Output models of MAP/PH/1(/K) queues for an efficient network decomposition. Performance Evaluation (2002) 321–339
13. Sadre, R., Haverkort, B., Ost, A.: An efficient and accurate decomposition method for open finite and infinite-buffer queueing networks. Proceedings of the Third International Workshop on Numerical Solution of Markov Chains (1999) 1–20

Teil VI

Preisträger

Durchsatzmaximierung von Wireless-LAN-Netzen
Parameteranalyse des Standards IEEE 802.11b

Matthias Lenk

AMD Saxony LLC & Co.KG, Wilschdorfer Landstraße 101, 01109 Dresden
matthias.lenk@amd.com

Zusammenfassung. WLAN-Netze sind aufgrund der Kanaleigenschaften inhärent fehleranfällig. Der WLAN-Standard IEEE 802.11 sieht eine Reihe von Mechanismen vor, um diese Probleme anzugehen. Mit Hilfe von analytischen Modellen und einer Simulationsumgebung sowie Zuhilfenahme aufgezeichneter Fehlerdaten wurden die wichtigsten Parameter dieser Mechanismen in Bezug auf Auswirkungen auf den Durchsatz untersucht und Algorithmen entworfen, die den Durchsatz einer drahtlosen Mobilstation unter schlechten Kanalbedingungen deutlich verbessern können.

1 Einleitung

Drahtlose lokale Netzwerke (WLAN) haben in den letzten Jahren vielfach Einzug gehalten in Firmen, Privathaushalte und öffentliche Einrichtungen. Ein Ende dieser Entwicklung ist nicht abzusehen. Die entscheidenden Vorteile dieser Technologie gegenüber traditionellen drahtgebundenen Netzwerken sind zweifelsohne die MobilitäT der Teilnehmer sowie die Vermeidung von aufwändingen und teuren Verkabelungen in Gebäuden. Jedoch gibt es neben Sicherheitsrisiken weitere signifikante Nachteile wie limitierte Bandbreite und Reichweite durch Effekte wie Mehrwegeausbreitung, Interferenz und Verlust von Signalstärke mit zunehmender Entfernung. Zudem entsteht nicht zu vernachlässigender Overhead durch die verwendeten Protokolle, die besondere Mechanismen enthalten, um den genannten Effekten Rechnung zu tragen.

Daher ist es wichtig, die vorhandenen Mechanismen optimal einzusetzen, um die verfügbare Bandbreite auszunutzen.

Im Folgenden wird zunächst der WLAN-Standard IEEE 802.11b kurz vorgestellt und in Abschnitt 3 analysiert. In Abschnitt 5 werden zum Zwecke der Maximierung des Durchsatzes und damit der Kanaleffizienz geeignete Algorithmen entwickelt, die im Rahmen der durch den Standard gegebenen Möglichkeiten bleiben.

2 Der Standard IEEE 802.11

Der Standard IEEE 802.11 [1] beschreibt die unteren beiden Schichten des ISO/OSI-Schichtenmodells für drahtlose lokale Netze, die physikalische Schicht und einen Teil der Sicherungsschicht, die Mediumzugriffsschicht (MAC). Zudem wird zwischen verschiedenen Operationsmodi unterschieden. Zum einen gibt es ad-hoc-Netze, in denen sich spontan mehrere Mobil-Stationen zu einem drahtlosen Netzwerk zusammenschließen. Des Weiteren sind Infrastrukturnetze vorgesehen, in denen ein sogenannter Access Point (AP) Zugang zu einem drahtgebundenen Netzwerk bietet. In diesem Fall läuft jegliche Kommunikation von und zu am AP angemeldeten Mobilstationen über den AP. In beiden Modi sind physikalische Schicht und Medienzugriff identisch.

2.1 Die physikalische Schicht

Die physikalische Schicht beschreibt die Übertragung von Rohdaten von einer Station zur anderen. Die am weitesten verbreitete Methode sieht die Modulationen BSPK (Binary Phase Shift Keying) und QPSK (Quadrature Phase Shift Keying) im 2,4 GHz-Band in 14 Kanälen vor, bei denen die Phase der Trägerfrequenz 2 bzw. 4 Zustände einnehmen kann und somit 1 oder 2 Bits pro Phasensprung übertragen werden können. Zusätzlich wird die sogenannte Spread-Spectrum-Methode (Frequenzspreizung) angewendet.

Die Erweiterung IEEE 802.11b ergänzt die physikalische Schicht um zwei weitere Modulationsschemata, die sich in der Symbolrate und der Kodierung der Frequenzspreizung unterscheiden. Somit werden die Datenraten 1, 2, 5,5 und 11 Mbps unterstützt. Zusätzlich wird optional ein kürzerer Header (Short Preamble) eingeführt, so dass mehr Zeit für die eigentliche Datenübertragung zur Verfügung steht. Im Grunde können Datenrate und Präambel von der sendenden Station frei gewählt werden, sofern die empfangende Station diese unterstüzt.

2.2 Die MAC-Schicht

Im Gegensatz zu drahtgebundenen Technologien wie Ethernet können Kollisionen, also das gleichzeitige Senden mehrerer Stationen, nicht festgestellt werden. Deshalb wird für den Medienzugriff ein CSMA/CA (Carrier Sensing Multiple Access with Collision Avoidance) Schema eingesetzt. Bevor eine Station senden darf, muss sie den Kanal beobachten und darf erst senden, wenn der Kanal frei ist und sie eine Backoff-Prozedur erfolgreich durchgeführt hat. Diese Prozedur verteilt den Zugriff auf das gemeinsame Medium nach einem stochastischen Muster. Jede Station im drahtlosen Netz wählt dazu eine zufällige Zeitspanne, die gleichverteilt in einem bestimmten Intervall liegt. Die Station mit der kleinsten Zeitspanne darf zuerst senden. Eine Station, die nicht zum Zuge gekommen ist, wählt beim nächsten Versuch keine neue Zeitspanne, sondern darf die bereits gewartete Zeit von der gewählten Zeitspanne abziehen. Sollte eine Übertragung fehlschlagen, so wird das Intervall, in dem die Zeitspanne gewählt wird, größer.

Die zu übertragenden Daten werden in Rahmen zu je maximal 2304 Byte eingeteilt. Zusätzlich wird ein Header angefügt, der Adress- und Längeninformationen sowie eine Prüfsumme enthält. Alle Unicast-Rahmen werden durch einen ACK-Rahmen bestätigt, so dass festgestellt werden kann, ob eine Übertragung

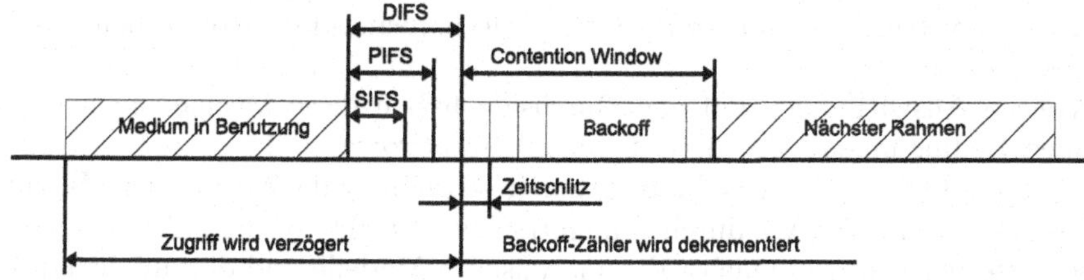

Abb. 1. Medienzugriff nach IEEE 802.11

erfolgreich war oder nicht. Die Rahmenlänge kann durch einen Fragmentierungsmechanismus verkürzt werden. Jedes einzelne Fragment eines Rahmens wird dann einzeln bestätigt, und nur das erste Fragment muss den Backoff-Prozess durchlaufen. Bei schlechten Kanalbedingungen müssen somit nur die Fragmente wiederholt gesendet werden, die nicht übertragen werden konnten, und nicht der gesamte Rahmen.

Ein weiteres Verfahren, das insbesondere die Auswirkungen von Kollisionen verringern soll, ist der RTS/CTS-Handshake. Bevor ein Rahmen oder Fragment gesendet werden darf, muss zunächst ein RTS-Rahmen (Request to Send) gesendet werden, der vom Empfänger mit einem CTS-Rahmen (Clear to Send) bestätigt werden muss.

Fragmentierung und RTS/CTS werden durch Schwellen-Parameter geregelt. Das heißt man kann festlegen, ab welcher Rahmengröße fragmentiert wird bzw. ab welcher Fragmentgröße der RTS/CTS-Mechanismus genutzt wird. Neben den genannten gibt es eine Reihe weiterer Parameter, die zum großen Teil offensichtlich keine Auswirkung auf den Durchsatz haben. Weitere potentiell wichtige Parameter sind insbesondere die Retry-Limits, welche festlegen, wie oft versucht wird einen Rahmen erneut zu senden, wenn er fehlschlägt.

3 Parameteranalyse

Wie bereits erwähnt, ist die drahtlose Übertragung geprägt von inhärenten Schwächen. Mehrwegeausbreitung und geringe Signal-Rausch-Abstände erschweren den Empfang von Datenpaketen. Dazu kommt noch die Möglichkeit der Kollision und Interferenz durch andere Geräte. Kollisionen entstehen, wenn viele Stationen an einem WLAN teilnehmen und senden wollen. Eine weitere Ursache ist das sogenannte Hidden-Terminal-Problem. Sind zwei Stationen A und B so weit voneinander entfernt, dass sie einen Sendevorgang von der jeweils anderen Station nicht mehr detektieren können, jedoch eine Station C existiert, zu der der Abstand gering genug für erfolgreiches Senden von beiden Station A und B ist, so kann es zu Kollisionen kommen, da Kollisionsvermeidung hier nicht mehr greift.

Für diese Probleme sieht der Standard entsprechende Maßnahmen vor: Die verschiedenen Datenraten sind unterschiedlich robust gegenüber schlecher Signalqualität und -stärke. Fragmentierung hilft wiederholte Übertragungen durch

Bitfehler zu verringern, und der RTS/CTS-Mechanismus hilft Kollisionen zu vermeiden.

Welche Auswirkungen auf den Durchsatz haben diese Mechanismen unter welchen Bedingungen? Um diese Frage zu beantworten, gibt es zwei Ansätze. Zum einen gibt es analytische Modelle zur Beschreibung des Medienzugriffs, zum anderen kann ein WLAN durch Simulation untersucht werden. Die folgenden Abschnitte beleuchten zunächst die analytischen Modelle und darauffolgend die verwendete Simulationsumgebung sowie die gewonnenen Resultate.

3.1 Analytische Modelle

Die meisten analytischen Modelle des Medienzugriffs nach IEEE 802.11 basieren auf der folgenden Gleichung:

$$S = \frac{E[L]}{E[T]} \quad (1)$$

Der Durchsatz S (Systemdurchsatz) wird ermittelt, indem man den Erwartungswert der Datenmenge pro Paket durch den Erwartungswert der dafür benötigten Zeit dividiert. Nach dem Modell von Quao und Choi [2] werden die genannten Größen durch einfache Methoden der Wahrscheinlichkeitsrechnung ermittelt. Demnach ist der Erwartungswert der Datenmenge pro Paket gegeben durch

$$E[L] = P_F\Big(L_P, f_c\Big) \cdot L_P + \Big(1 - P_F\Big(0, f_c\Big)\Big) \cdot 0 = P_F\Big(L_P, f_c\Big) \cdot L_P \quad (2)$$

wobei P_F die Wahrscheinlichkeit der erfolgreichen Übertragung eines Paketes der Länge L_P bestehend aus f_c Fragmenten ist. P_F ergibt sich aus der Betrachtung, dass keines der Fragmente des Pakets öfter wiederholt werden darf, als es das Wiederholungslimit vorschreibt, sowie aus dem Fehlermodell, das die Wahrscheinlichkeit beschreibt ob ein einzelnes Paket erfolgreich gesendet wird. Auf ähnliche Weise ermittelt man den Erwartungswert für die Übertragungsdauer eines Paketes.

$$E[T] = T_O + \overline{f_c} \cdot T_F\Big(\frac{L_P}{f_c}\Big) - P_F\Big(L_P, f_c\Big) \cdot T_{SIFS} \quad (3)$$

$\overline{f_c}$ in der obigen Formel beschreibt die mittlere Anzahl von Fragmenten, T_O die Zeit, die für den Protokolloverhead immer anfällt. T_F steht für die mittlere Zeit, die für die Übertragung eines Fragments benötigt wird, und T_{SIFS} ist die Zeitdauer eines sogenannten Short Interframe Space zwischen Rahmen und Bestätigungsrahmen. Mit etwas Aufwand ließe sich auch der RTS/CTS-Mechanismus durch ähnliche Herangehensweise abbilden.

Dieses Modell beschreibt allerdings nur den Durchsatz bei einer sendenden Station. In der Regel werden jedoch mehrere Stationen in einem Netz aktiv sein. Um dieses Phänomen zu beschreiben muss der Backoff-Prozess analytisch modelliert werden. Nach Bianci [3] wird dies durch einen zwei-dimensionalen Markow-Prozess erreicht. Auf diese Weise lassen sich die Wahrscheinlichkeiten ermitteln, ob es zu Kollisionen aufgrund von Mehrfachsendung kommt. Damit lässt sich auf ähnliche Weise wie in dem Modell von Quao und Choi [2] der Systemdurchsatz beschreiben. Hier geht man jedoch davon aus, dass, sofern keine Kollisionen auftreten, die Übertragung fehlerfrei verläuft. Ebenso geht man von unfragmentierter Übertragung aus. Ohne diese Vereinfachungen werden allerdings grundlegende Annahmen des Modells ungültig, oder das Markov-Modell lässt sich nur noch mittels aufwendiger numerischer Verfahren lösen.

3.2 Analyse durch Simulation

Die Beschränkungen der analytischen Modelle lassen sich nur durch geeignete Simulationsmodelle umgehen. Dazu verwendet man in der Regel diskrete Ereignissimulatoren, die dadurch gekennzeichnet sind, dass eine Liste von Ereignissen abgearbeitet wird. Ein Ereignis kann dann wieder neue Ereignisse hervorrufen und in die Liste der Ereignisse einfügen. Ein solcher Simulator ist NS-2 [4], das von einer Vielzahl von Institutionen entwickelt und erweitert worden ist. Es enthält unter anderem auch ein Modell des IEEE 802.11 Standards, jedoch zum Zeitpunkt der Untersuchung nur der ersten Standard-Version und mit eingeschränktem Funktionsumfang.

Um größtmögliche Genauigkeit zu erreichen, wurde das NS-2 um einige Fähigkeiten erweitert. Dazu zählen die Unterstützung von Datenraten des IEEE 802.11b Standards, Fragmentierung, Funkwellenausbreitungsmodelle und insbesondere Fehlermodelle.

Ebenso wesentlich für exakte Simulationergebnisse sind Fehlermodelle, die über Fehlerwahrscheinlichkeiten und -verteilungen entscheiden. Je nach Komplexität des Simulationsszenarios sind einfache Bitfehlermodelle, bei denen eine feste Bitfehlerrate vorgegeben ist, oder exakte, durch Messwerte gegebene Fehlermodelle ausreichend. Bei den letztgenannten Modellen wird durch Emulation oder Messungen an existierenden Geräten die Fehlerhäufigkeit beim Empfang von Paketen in Abhängigkeit von Signalstärke, Signalqualität, Paketgröße und Datenrate aufgezeichnet. Im Simulator sind die genannten Größen beim Empfang eines Paketes bekannt, und somit lässt sich mittels Pseudozufallszahlen realitätsnahes Fehlerverhalten approximieren. Um zusätzlich die räumliche oder zeitliche Korrelation des Fehlerverhaltens zu simulieren, wurde die Methode von Punnoose, Nikitin und Stancil [5] implementiert, die insbesondere die Effekte der Mehrwegeausbreitung effektiv approximiert.

In dieser Simulationsumgebung wurden die folgenden Parameter näher untersucht:

- Schwellenparamter für Fragmentierung und RTS/CTS
- Datenrate (Modulationsschemata) nach IEEE 802.11b
- Short und Long Retry Limit
- Präambel-Typ (kurz oder lang)

Die folgende Tabelle 1 zeigt weitere Parameter, wie sie als Standardwerte für die Untersuchungen verwendet wurden, sofern das jeweilige Szenario nicht andere Werte erforderte.

Tabelle 1. Standardparameterwerte für die Analyse per Simulation

Parameter	Wert
Ausbreitungsmodell	Two ray ground (eine Reflexion)
Paketgröße (MSDU) / Verkehrsmodell	VBR, gleichverteilte Größe in [20, 2304]
Verkehrsfluß	UDP zur jeweils nächsten Station
Anzahl der Stationen	10
Short Retry Limit	7
Long Retry Limit	4
Fragmentierungsschwelle	2346
RTS-Schwelle	2347
Datenrate	11 Mbps short preamble
Simulationszeit	15 s

4 Resultate

Als erster Parameter wurde der Präambel-Typ unter Zuhilfenahme des analytischen Modells von Quao und Choi [2] und eines exakten AWGN-Fehlermodells (Additive White Gaussian Noise) analysiert. Dieses Fehlermodell berücksichtigt keine Reflexionen im Signal und wurde aus Daten erstellt, die durch Emulation von existierenden Basisband-Lösungen gewonnen wurden.

Die Präambel dient zur Erkennung eines Rahmens in der physikalischen Schicht. Eine längere Präambel erhöht also die Chancen einen Rahmen auch bei Störung des Signals zu erkennen. Eine kürzere Präambel spart dagegen wertvolle Zeit, in denen der Kanal für die eigentliche Datenübertragung genutzt werden kann. Wie sich im weiteren Verlauf der Untersuchungen bestätigte, ist die lange Präambel nur in seltenen Fällen performanter, so dass sich die Zeitersparnis deutlicher auswirkt als die etwas höhere Erkennungsrate der Rahmen. Die kurze Präambel kann also generell bevorzugt werden, da selbst im Falle einer performanteren langen Präambel der Vorteil nur sehr gering ist.

Das AWGN-Fehlermodell eignet sich ebenso sehr gut um die Auswirkungen von schwachen Signalpegeln auf den Durchsatz von verschieden Datenraten zu analysieren. Offensichtlich sind höhere Datenraten und die damit verbundenen Modulationsschemata anfälliger für schlechte Kanalbedingungen. Das bestätigt sich beim Blick auf Abbildung 2.

Mit zunehmendem Abstand zwischen den Stationen bricht der Durchsatz der hohen Datenraten schnell zusammen, während die niedrigen Datenraten noch immer akzeptable Werte liefern. An dieser Stelle zeigt sich eine wesentliche Anforderung für einen potentiellen Algorithmus: Bei schlechten Kanalbedingungen sind niedrigere Datenraten zu bevorzugen.

Wie bereits erwähnt, ist im Standard der Fragmentierungsmechanismus vorgesehen als eine weitere Option zur Verringerung der Auswirkung von Bit- bzw. Paketfehlern. Um die Effektivität des Mechanismus zu prüfen wurde eine mittlere Datenrate fest gewählt (2 Mbps) und die Fragmentierungsschwelle unter verschiedenen Bitfehlerraten variiert. Das Ergebnis ist in Abbildung 3 zu sehen.

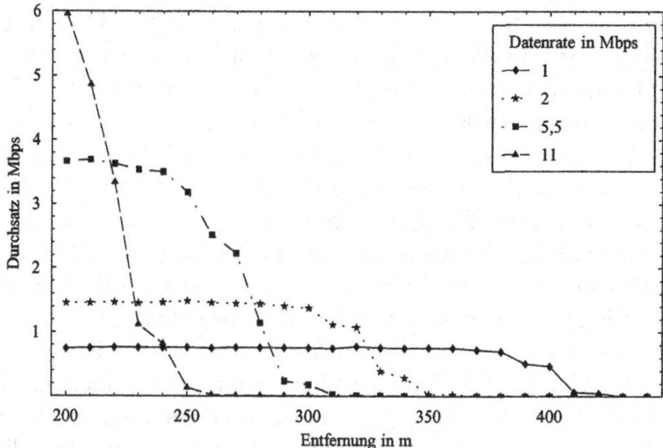

Abb. 2. Durchsatz verschiedener Datenraten bei gegebenem Abstand zwischen Stationen

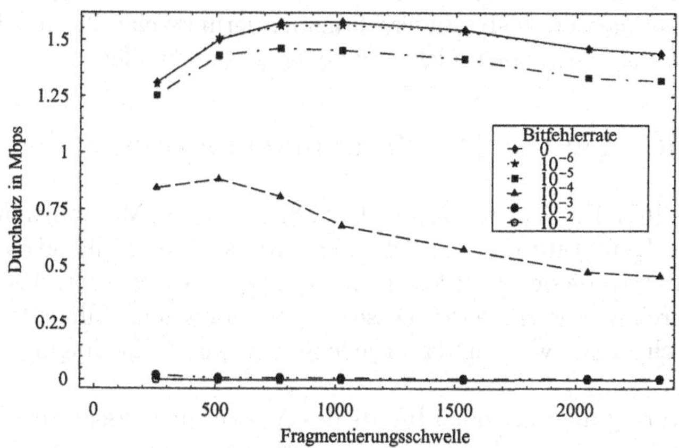

Abb. 3. Effekt von Fragmentierung bei Bitfehlern

Bei Bitfehlerraten um 10^{-4} ist eine signifikante Verbesserung des Systemdurchsatzes zu erkennen. Beachtenswert ist, dass selbst bei idealen Kanalbedingungen Fragmentierung für Pakete größer als 800 bis 1000 Byte besseren Durchsatz ergibt als ohne Fragmentierung. Dieses Ergebnis ist der Tatsache geschuldet, dass ein Netzwerk mit 10 Stationen verwendet wurde, und somit bereits Kollisionen auftreten. Bei höheren Datenraten kehrt sich dieser Effekt jedoch um, da aufgrund kürzerer absoluter Paketübertragungszeiten der Overhead der Fragmentierung die Oberhand gewinnt. Fragmentierung ist also in der Regel nur für niedrige Datenraten und bei vielen Stationen oder schlechten Kanalbedingungen geeignet.

Führt man den gleichen Test bei Variation der RTS/CTS-Schwelle anstatt der Fragmentierungsschwelle durch, so zeigt sich eine kaum wahrnehmbare Schwankung des Durchsatzes. Wesentlich deutlicher sind die Auswirkungen jedoch, wenn statt Bitfehlern Kollisionen auftreten. Bei 100 sendenden Stationen lässt sich der Durchsatz selbst bei 11 Mpbs um 1,5 Mbps steigern wenn eine RTS/CTS-Schwelle um 400 gewählt wird. Entsprechend deutlicher ist der Effekt bei geringeren Datenraten. Ein interessanter Effekt ist, dass der Systemdurchsatz bei 5 Stationen höher ist als bei 2 Stationen. Dies lässt sich damit erklären, dass bei 5 Stationen die durchschnittliche Dauer des Backoff-Prozesses geringer ist als bei 2 Stationen und zusätzlich die Kollisionswahrscheinlichkeit noch relativ gering ist. Des Weiteren bestätigt sich die Vermutung, dass der RTS/CTS-Mechanismus das Hidden-Terminal-Problem effektiv vermeiden kann.

In Abschnitt 2.2 wurden die Retry-Limits als Parameter erwähnt, die möglicherweise Einfluss auf den Durchsatz haben. Es zeigte sich, dass diese Größen bei den im Standard vorgeschlagenen Standardwerten jeweils das Durchsatzmaximum erreicht haben, sowohl bei Fragmentierung als auch bei Kollisionen oder Bitfehlern und RTS/CTS.

Neben den genannten Ergebnissen zeigen sich auch Abhängigkeiten der Parameter untereinander. Insbesondere Fragmentierungsschwelle und RTS/CTS-Schwelle sind im Allgemeinen nicht unabhängig voneinander.

5 Algorithmen zur Durchsatzmaximierung

Die vorgestellten Ergebnisse zeigen deutlich, dass ein Mechanismus benötigt wird, der die Datenrate und die Schwellenparameter in Abhängigkeit von den äußeren Bedingungen des drahtlosen Kanals adaptiv so einstellt, dass der größtmögliche Durchsatz erzielt wird. Dieser Algorithmus muss für jede Zielstation getrennt durchgeführt werden, da für jede Station andere Bedingungen vorliegen können.

Die zur Verfügung stehenden Inputs des Algorithmus lassen sich in zwei Kategorien einteilen. Zum einen können statistische Informationen über den bisherigen Datenverkehr zur Zielstation gesammelt werden. Zum anderen gibt es messbare Größen wie Signalstärke und -qualität, die ausgewertet werden können. Die letztere Gruppe von Daten ist jedoch nur bedingt einsetzbar, denn es können nur die Signaleigenschaften von Paketen gemessen werden, die von der Zielstation ausgegangen sind, und nicht die Signaleigenschaften der Pakete, die zur Zielstation gesendet werden. Nur wenn die Sendeleistung der Zielstation mit der zu optimierenden Station übereinstimmt, zusätzlich noch eine ähnliche Mehrwegeausbreitung vorliegt und die Rausch- und Interferenzstärken für beide Stationen auf gleichem Niveau liegen, sind diese Daten ohne Einschränkung nutzbar. Zu den statistischen Daten, die gewonnen werden können, zählen insbesondere die Paketfehlerrate und die Anzahl der sendenden Stationen. Der gemessene Durchsatz ist von geringerer Bedeutung, da er nicht nur von den Kanalbedingungen abhängt, sondern auch von der von den oberen Protokollschichten angebotenen Last (Offered Load).

Aus den beschriebenen Information lassen sich die Soll-Parameterwerte für Datenrate, Fragmentierungs- und RTS/CTS-Schwelle im Allgemeinen nicht direkt bestimmen, denn die maximal mögliche Datenrate ist abhängig von Faktoren, die nicht gemessen werden können, wie z.B. die Anzahl von Hidden Terminals. Aus diesen Grund sind klassische Verfahren wie Regelkreise nicht anwendbar. Es muss also eine Heuristik verwendet werden, die in möglichst vielen Situationen gute Durchsätze ermöglicht.

Eine weitere Anforderung an dem Algorithmus ist, dass die Anpassung an die Kanalbedingungen sehr schnell erfolgt, denn aufgrund der Mehrwegeausbreitung können sich Größen wie Signalstärke in Bruchteilen von Sekunden signifikant ändern.

5.1 Statistikbasierte Ansätze

Eckhard und Steenkiste [6] beschreiben einen einfachen Algorithmus, der basierend auf statistischen Informationen einen Parameter adjustiert. Wenn zwei Pakete in Folge nicht erfolgreich übertragen werden können, wird ein Parameter entsprechend angepasst. Im Falle von 3 erfolgreichen Übertragungen wird der Parameter in die entgegengesetzte Richtung modifiziert. Als Parameter sind Paketlänge und Stärke der Fehlerkorrektur vorgesehen, wobei letztere in IEEE 802.11 nicht unterstützt wird. Dieser Ansatz wurde nun im Rahmen der Arbeit verallgemeinert, indem man ein Signal y_i bestimmt, das sich durch einen Filter aus p_i mit

$$p_i = \begin{cases} 1 & \text{falls Paket } i \text{ erfolgreich} \\ -1 & \text{falls Paket } i \text{ verloren} \end{cases} \tag{4}$$

berechnet. Überschreitet y_i einen oberen Schwellwert, so wird der gewählte Parameter auf eine bestimmte Weise modifiziert. Unterschreitet y_i einen unteren Schwellwert, so wird der Parameter in die andere Richtung angepasst. In beiden Fällen wird der Filter zurückgesetzt. Ausgehend von der durchgeführten Parameteranalyse ist die Datenrate der Parameter mit der größten Wirkung. Ein verwendeter Filter ist

$$y_{i+1} = \beta y_i + \alpha p_i \tag{5}$$

mit empirisch bestimmten $\beta = 0.9$ und $\alpha = 1.0$. Des Weiteren wurde ein Mittelwertfilter über die Pakete einer bestimmten Zeitspanne verwendet, um die aktuelle Paketfehlerrate zu bestimmen. Beide Filter liefern mit geeigneten Schwellwerten ähnlich gute Ergebnisse. In die Berechnung der Paketfehlerrate gehen jedoch auch Kollisionen ein, da sie sich nicht von Bitfehlern unterscheiden lassen. Mittels folgender Formel lässt sich dies jedoch bereinigen.

$$per_c = \frac{per - P_C}{1 - P_C} \tag{6}$$

P_C bezeichnet die Kollisionswahrscheinlichkeit, die sich mittels des analytischen Modells von Bianchi [3] oder durch Simulationdaten aus der geschätzten Anzahl von sendenden Stationen berechnen läßt. Abbildung 5 zeigt den Durchsatz in einem Szenario, in dem sich zwei Gruppen von Stationen auseinander bewegten und sich schließlich wieder aufeinander zu bewegten. Die Referenzwerte ergeben sich aus dem besten Wert einer beliebigen fest eingestellten Datenrate ohne Fragmentierung und RTS/CTS (Abbildung 4).

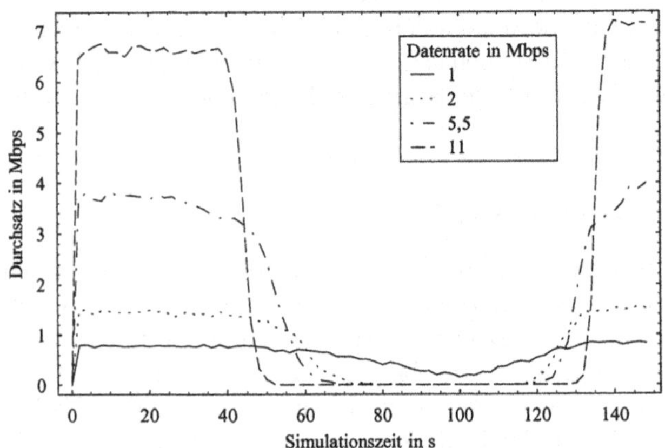

Abb. 4. Referenzdurchsatz verschiedener Datenraten ohne Mehrwegeausbreitung in Szenario 1

5.2 Signalbasierte Ansätze

Ein weiterer in der Arbeit implementierter Ansatz besteht darin die Signalparameter auszuwerten, von Paketen, die von der jeweiligen Zielstation stammen. Zusätzlich wird die Information über die Anzahl der sendenden Stationen verwendet. Mittels der in der Simulation gewonnenen Daten lassen sich nun die optimalen Werte der Ausgabeparameter interpolieren. In der verwendeten Simulation mit dem bereits besprochenen Szenario (Szenario 1) liefern diese offensichtlich die besten Ergebnisse, wie in Abbildung 5 zu erkennen ist. Die Referenzwerte werden teilweise übertroffen, da hier die Schwellenparameter optimal eingesetzt werden.

Die Schwächen des Algorithmus liegen, wie eingangs erwähnt, auf der Hand: Nur wenn die Kanalbedingungen bei Zielstation und zu optimierender Station ähnlich sind und zudem die Empfangseigenschaften beider Stationen vergleichbar sind, liefert dieser Algorithmus optimale Werte.

Um die Schwächen der vorgestellten Ansätze zu überwinden, wurden beide Ansätze kombiniert. Der erste Weg besteht darin den signalbasierten Ansätz um statistische Funktionen zu erweitern. Wenn die gemessende Paketfehlerrate nicht der entspricht, die das verwendete Fehlermodell vorgibt, dann wird ein positiver

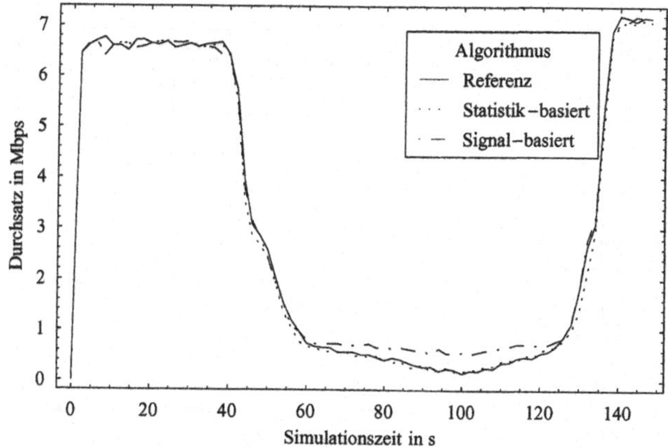

Abb. 5. Durchsatz verschiedener Algorithmen in Szenario 1

oder negativer Offset auf die gemessene Signalstärke addiert. Somit lassen sich Unterschiede in der Sendeleistung kompensieren.

Der andere Weg addiert Informationen aus der Parameteranalyse zu der Datenratenanpassung durch statistische Größen. Konkret heißt das, dass in Abhängigkeit von der Paketfehlerrate, der Anzahl von Stationen und der gewählten Datenrate die in der Parameteranalyse besten Werte für die Schwellenparameter gewählt werden.

Beide Methoden bringen messbare Verbesserungen gegenüber den einfachen Ansätzen. Alle bisher vorgestellten Algorithmen teilen jedoch eine Schwäche: Sobald Hidden Terminals im Spiel sind, bricht der Durchsatz ein, da Hidden Terminals nur schwer zu detektieren sind. Eine einfache Modifikation bringt jedoch eine deutliche Verbesserung. Wird die Datenrate in Abhängigkeit von der Paketfehlerrate gewählt, so kann die RTS/CTS-Schwelle auf einen Wert fest eingestellt werden, der Hidden Terminals effektiv behandelt, sobald die Höchstdatenrate von 11 Mbps verlassen werden muss. Auf diese Weise wird bei optimalen Kanalbedingung eine Degradierung des Durchsatzes vermieden. Sind die Kanalbedingungen suboptimal und damit geringere Datenraten bevorzugt, ist der Overhead durch den RTS/CTS-Mechanismus weniger ausgeprägt. Abbildung 6 zeigt die Ergebnisse mit und ohne die Modifikation.

In dem dargestellten Szenario (Szenario 2) bewegen sich zwei Gruppen von Stationen von einer dritten Gruppe weg und schließlich wieder zur dritten Gruppe hin.

Somit können die vorgestellten Algorithmen den Durchsatz deutlich verbessern, insbesondere bei schlechten Kanalbedingungen. Für die aktuellen Standards IEEE 802.11g und IEEE 802.11a lassen sich diese Algorithmen in ähnlicher Form offensichtlich ebenfalls anwenden.

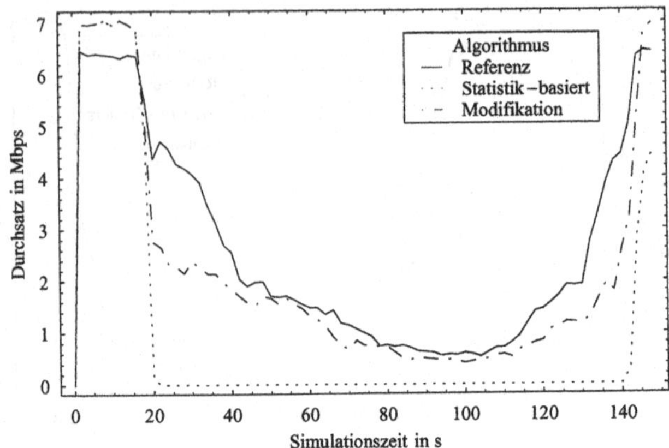

Abb. 6. Durchsatz bei Hidden-Terminal-Szenario (Szenario 2)

6 Danksagung

Dieser Beitrag fasst die Ergebnisse der Diplomarbeit „Untersuchung und Implementierung von Algorithmen zur Durchsatzmaximierung von drahtlosen Kommunikationssystemen unter Berücksichtigung der Kanaleigenschaften und unter Auswertung spezifischer Parameter der MAC-Schicht" zusammen, die am Lehrstuhl Rechnernetze und verteilte Systeme von Prof. Dr. K. Irmscher am Institut für Informatik der Universität Leipzig in Kooperation mit AMD Saxony LLC & Co.KG entstanden ist. Besonderer Dank gilt den Betreuern der genannten Einrichtungen.

7 Literatur

1. Die Herausgeber von IEEE 802.11: Wireless Lan Medium Access Control (MAC) And Physical Layer (PHY) Specifications.
2. Quao Daji, Choi Sunghyun: Goodput Enhancement of IEEE 802.11a Wireless LAN via Link Adaption. IEEE Conference on Communications, 2001.
3. Bianchi G: Performance Analysis of the IEEE 802.11 Distribution Coordination Function. IEEE Journal on selected areas in communication 3:535–547, 2000
4. NS-2 Homepage: http://www.isi.edu/nsnam/ns/index.html
5. Punnoose R, Nikitin P, Stancil D: Efficient simulation of Ricean fading within a packet simulator. IEEE-VTS Vehicular Technology Conference, 2000.
6. Eckhardt D, Steenkiste P: Improving wireless LAN performance via adaptive local error control. 6th Conference on Network Protocols, 1998.

A Dynamic Network Architecture for Cellular Access Networks

Parag S. Mogre

Multimedia Communications Lab (KOM), Technische Universität Darmstadt,
Merckstrasse 25, 64283 Darmstadt, Germany

Abstract High user mobility coupled with high bandwidth demands and bursty nature of traffic is expected in beyond 3G cellular access networks. Such a scenario leads to the creation of highly congested areas or hot-spots in these cellular access networks. The location and duration of existence of these hot-spots is closely related to the mobility patterns of the users and varies over time. We observe heavy loss, high delay, and congestion in parts of the cellular access network as a result of the mobility induced load variation, although the network as a whole can support the user load. This paper proposes a novel dynamic network architecture (*DNA*), which enables better distribution of load and can adapt the network topology dynamically to provide relief to congested areas in the network. Our mechanism outlined here is online, distributed, and does not require advance knowledge of traffic demand.

1 Introduction

The evolution of networks beyond 3G leads to a heterogeneous set of access technologies. In such a scenario, there are several challenging issues, including more efficient utilization of the available bandwidth, low power consumption and provisioning of QoS guarantees. In particular, we see a need for flexible, distributed network architectures, which can achieve higher throughput and are capable of dynamically responding to high variation in traffic demand over time. QoS provisioning is crucial for future cellular access networks to enable voice and multimedia applications to be supported. The high bandwidth requirements of such applications coupled with the mobility of end-users leads to fluctuation of the required bandwidth in individual cells over a period of time. This leads in turn to the creation of highly congested areas in the cellular access networks, so called hot-spots, despite the fact that the overall capacity of the network may be greater than the total load offered to the network at a given point in time.

Hollick et al. [1] provide a detailed study of the changes in traffic demands as a function of user mobility. In general, we observe that congestion develops in parts of the network due to an uneven distribution of the load. In a cellular network, partial relief from this phenomenon can be provided by relaying some traffic from heavily loaded cells to some neighbouring cells which may be less loaded. This enables a more even distribution of the load. Our dynamic network architecture, *DNA*, builds on relaying concepts similar to the work of Wu et al. [2]. However, we believe that a simple relaying mechanism alone is not enough. Therefore we introduce and propose a wireless relay router (*WRR*), which works in close co-operation with our QoS-routing mechanism presented in [3]. Our framework enables dynamic modification of the network topology in response to congestion in parts of the network. This alleviates the need for heavy overprovisioning of resources in all parts of the cellular access network. At the same time, this mechanism enables additional bandwidth to be made available wherever and whenever it is required.

The remainder of this paper is organized as follows. In Section 2 we give a short overview of the related work. Then, in Section 3 we outline our proposed architecture and also define the roles of the individual network components in detail. This is followed by a description of the functions of the individual components. We outline the mechanism by which the network architecture adapts itself in response to the likely build up of congestion in parts of the network. Finally we present a summary of this work, also giving an outlook for a real implementation of our proposed *DNA*.

2 Related Work

As has been highlighted in the introduction, the beyond 3G scenario requires us to design smart technology which has the ability to handle high data traffic, at the same time enabling provision of QoS. The work [1] models the user mobility for the case of a city. The results clearly highlight the creation of transient hot-spots in the network. The work also shows that the location of these hot-spots varies over time. Given the above observation, it is necessary to manage the very high variation in the offered load. However, it is expensive to overprovision network resources. Besides, despite a high overprovisioning factor, it is possible that transient bursts of traffic lead to congestion in parts of the cellular access networks. Therefore, we believe that the network should be flexible enough to allow an on-demand dynamic allocation of resources.

A promising approach to address the congestion problem arising due to unbalanced traffic in a cellular network is proposed by Wu et al. [2]. They propose the use of ad hoc relaying stations (*ARS*) to relay traffic from a heavily loaded cell to a less loaded cell dynamically. This increases the overall load that the system can handle. They identify three different relaying mechanisms, namely primary relaying, secondary relaying and cascaded relaying.

The primary relaying and secondary relaying mechanisms are shown in Fig. 1. For example, with respect to Fig. 1(a), a mobile subscriber X wants to set up a new call in a heavily loaded cell A. However, the call fails due to the unavailability of channels in the cell. In such a case the mobile subscriber X switches to an alternative radio interface and the call will be relayed through the (*ARS*) to a neighbouring cell B that has less load. The authors describe this mechanism as primary relaying. Fig. 1(b) shows the secondary relaying mechanism. Here, as in the case of primary relaying, the mobile subscriber X wants to establish a new call in a highly loaded cell A. The call initially cannot

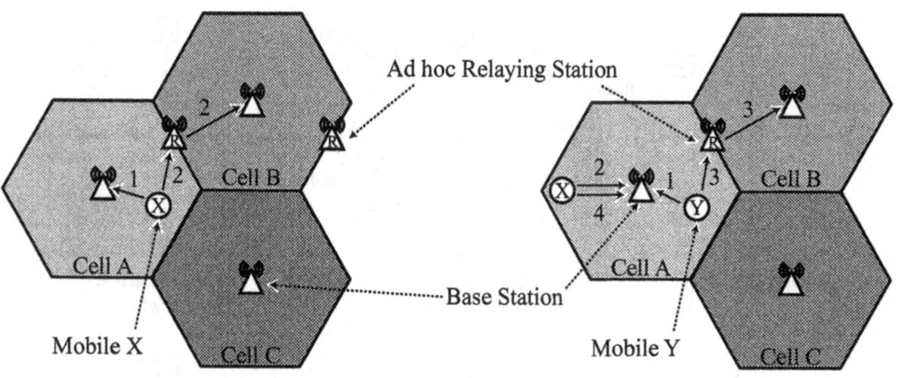

Fig. 1. Overview of relaying mechanisms

be setup due to unavailability of channels in the cell A. In this case, however, the mobile subscriber is not within the range of a suitable *ARS*. The base station for cell A then transfers an existing call, in this example that of mobile subscriber Y, via an *ARS* to a neighbouring cell. This frees up channels which can then be used to permit mobile subscriber X to set up the new call. The third relaying mechanism, cascaded relaying, described in [2] is a combination of both primary relaying and secondary relaying. In summary, the authors describe a mechanism, which enables an even distribution of load. They show that the overall load supported by the system is maximized if the load per cell is equal.

In our work [3], we develop a near-optimal multiclass, multipath, minimum-delay routing algorithm. The routing algorithm is distributed in nature and computes for a given destination a next-hop set and a corresponding load distribution along various paths to that destination. Fig. 2 gives an overview of the routing mechanism. Consider a router i, as shown in Fig. 2, and its neighbours. At time $n * T_l + p * T_s$ the routing table at router i has as next-hop, for some destination, the set of neighbours k_2, k_3 and k_4. The numbers besides the links show the fraction of traffic for the destination under consideration at router i, which is to be sent along that link to a neighbour in the next-hop set. As shown in figures 2(b)-2(f), the routing algorithm operates at two timescales. At every time interval T_l, the next-hop set for a destination is updated; whereas, at a smaller time interval T_s, the fraction of traffic sent to individual neighbours in the next-hop set is adjusted. This enables an efficient load-balancing mechanism which takes into account both, the long term delay along paths to the destination (by changing the next-hop set) as well as the short term transient changes in delay along individual paths to a destination (by adjusting the fraction of traffic sent along individual paths). The routing mechanism in [3] utilizes as the link cost, the incremental delay that is experienced by traffic along the link. Here, by link we refer to a directed link, i.e. the cost if link (i,k) may not be the same as the cost of link (k,i) at a given point of time. Incremental delay as link cost was introduced by Gallager [4]. He presents the optimal routing problem and also

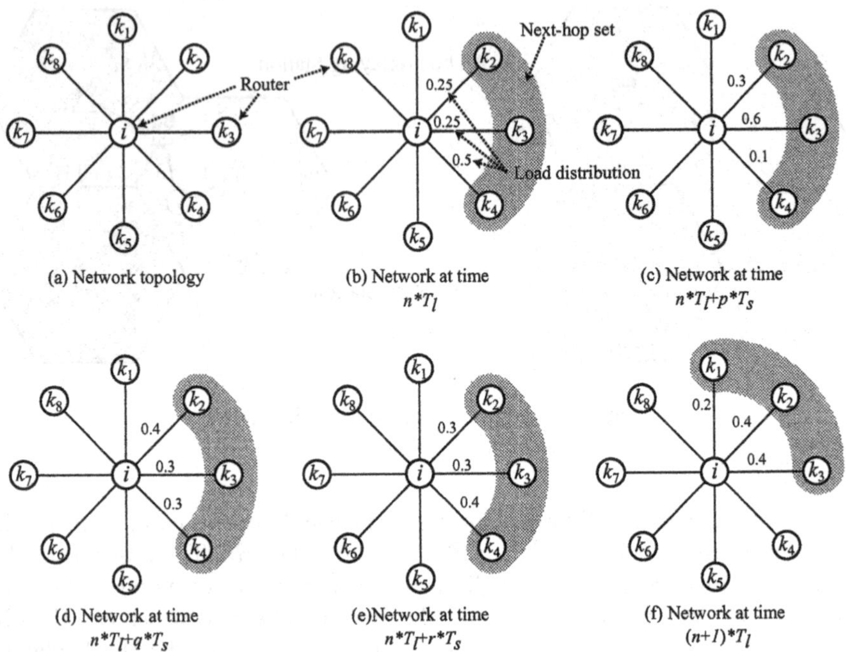

Fig. 2. Overview of routing mechanism used by Mogre [3]

proposes a solution to this problem. The work by Vutukury et al. [5] extends [4] so that it is applicable in real networks. We, in our work [3], extend and improve on [5], so that it is QoS aware and can cater to different classes of traffic and their varying tolerances of loss and delay. We show through an extensive simulation study that our routing mechanism gives excellent results with respect to both average delay and overall throughput in the network.

The work [6] by Lin et al., presents a new architecture (MCN) for wireless communications. The goal of this work is to either reduce the number of base stations needed to service a given area or to reduce the transmission power and range of individual base stations. To reach the above goals, the work makes use of multi-hop relaying mechanisms involving mobile user nodes. However, the usage of end-user nodes in the system makes it difficult to guarantee improved coverage or throughput. Hence, in our work here, we avoid the usage of the end-user nodes at the time of design of our proposed *DNA*.

The work [7] by Lott et al., discusses a possible scenario to handle communications beyond 3G. It discusses the possibility of a hierarchical overlay of multi-hop communication or WLAN, HiperLan/2 and UMTS, GSM/GPRS, and satellite systems. Such a vertical handover mechanism is also possible in our network architecture. In [7], the authors also discuss the use of multi-hop enabled nodes or extension points in order to extend coverage. Similar to the work [6], they assume that these extension points can be mobile end-systems.

The work by Yeh et al. [8], advocates that a completely novel approach is needed to deal with challenges thrown up by multi-hop cellular networks. They propose a complete overhaul of existing architecture and routing mechanisms. They propose a selective table-driven integrated routing with different roles for different mobile devices in the system, depending on the capacity and the ability of the node in question. An implementation of this mechanism makes radical changes necessary both at the end-user nodes and in the provider infrastructure. Although, such an overhaul may be inevitable, we in our work design our architecture to be more easily implementable given current infrastructure. At the same time the architecture we develop also serves the needs of future applications.

3 Dynamic Network Architecture for Cellular Networks

The focus of our architecture is to support load balancing and QoS routing in a beyond 3G network. We build up on the work of Hollick et al. [9] to derive the network architecture shown in Fig. 3.

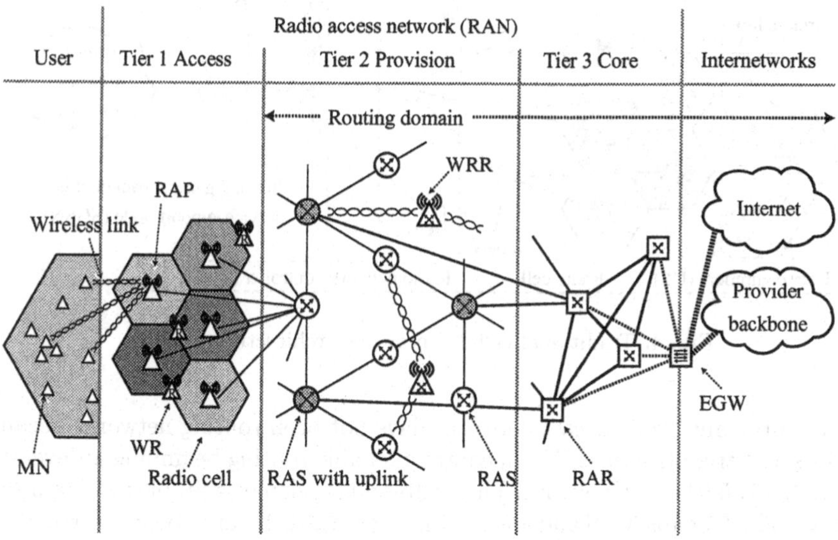

Fig. 3. Proposed dynamic network architecture (*DNA*)

Similar to the work of Hollick et al. [9], we assume a three tier architecture. The mobile nodes or terminals (*MNs*) are associated to the wireless base stations, the so called radio access points (*RAPs*), representing the last hop of the provision network. The function of the first tier can thus be described as radio access. The balancing of load between neighbouring radio cells is performed by the wireless relays (*WRs*). The *WRs* are supposed to have a functionality similar to that outlined for *ARSs* in the work by Wu et al. [2]. The second tier of the radio access network comprises of radio access servers *RASs* and the wireless relay routers (*WRRs*). *RASs* are used to attach multiple *RAPs*. The *RASs* are partially meshed with additional connectivity being provided by the (*WRRs*). As in [9], we assume our network to be a routing network beginning at the *RAS* level. Some of the *RASs* have uplinks to the so called radio access routers (*RARs*), which together with the edge gateways (*EGWs*) form the third tier of the proposed *DNA*, and are assumed to be fully meshed. A crucial point is the distributed and decentralised nature of the topology instead of the traditional tree-structured ones in telecommunication networks like GSM or UMTS (see Fig. 4).

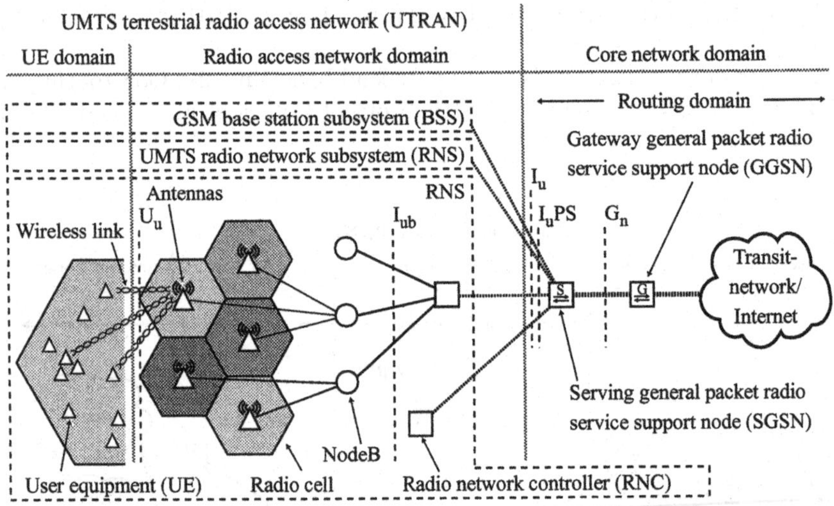

Fig. 4. Traditional cellular network architecture UMTS

Traditionally, radio access networks have not been routing networks because of the strict tree structure. We, in contrast, enable routing beginning at level two (ie. *RAS*/*WRR*) of the network. This enables us to deploy suitable routing mechanisms, which enable QoS and load balancing in the cellular network starting at a much lower level in the hierarchy as compared to traditional telecommunication networks.

3.1 Dynamic Behaviour of the *DNA*

In the following we discuss the dynamic behaviour of our proposed architecture (*DNA*) in response to congestion in the network. Dynamic reaction to congestion in the network is enabled by the wireless relay (*WR*) and the wireless relay router (*WRR*), respectively. We next give an overview of the working of the *WR* and the *WRR*.

The *WR* operates at tier one of the proposed *DNA*. The goal of the *WR* is to distribute load from a heavily loaded cell to some neighbouring cells. In our scenario it enables load balancing between neighbouring *RAPs*. We assume that the *WR* is able to support all the relaying mechanisms which may be supported by the *ARS* proposed in [2]. Consequently, the *WR* is assumed to be able to support primary relaying, secondary relaying as well as a cascaded relaying mechanism. However, we assume that the *WR* is part of the provider network and not an ad hoc end-user node. Thus, the *WR* enables the *DNA* to achieve a higher call acceptance ratio as compared to a traditional cellular network, by enabling a more even amount of load per cell.

The other dynamic component of our proposed *DNA*, which enables dynamic action in face of congestion in the network, is the *WRR*. The *WRR* operates at tier two of our proposed *DNA*. The function of the *WRR* is to adapt the actual network topology in response to congestion in the network. We assume the *WRR* to be located such that it can reach a number of *RASs* by means of wireless links. The *RASs* are assumed to have a suitable wireless interface to interact with the *WRR*.

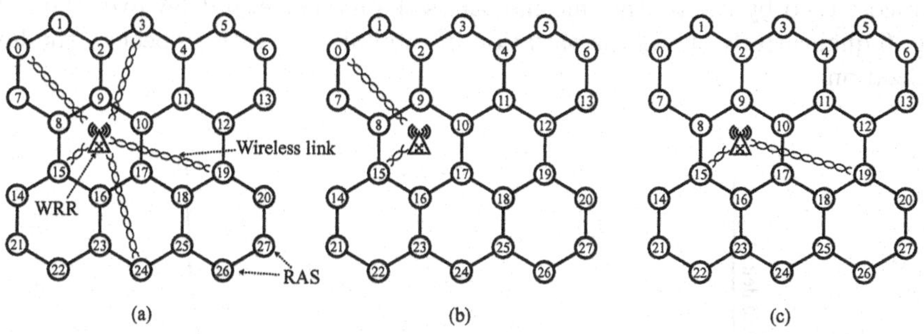

Fig. 5. WRR mechanism

Fig. 5(a) shows a sample instantiation of the second tier of the *DNA*. Here, the lines from the *WRR* to the individual *RASs* denote that the *WRR* is able to reach these *RASs*, which have a suitable wireless interface capable of interacting with the *WRR*. The solid lines connecting individual *RASs* indicate wired links between the respective *RASs*. Also, in order to enable a higher number of *WRRs* to be deployed in the network, we assume that the wireless links are established by means of directional antennas, thus reducing the resulting interference. These wireless links are assumed to be high bandwidth links, and may permit duplex data transfer. Fig. 5(a) shows that the *WRR* is able to communicate with a number of *RASs* in its range, but need not and may not be able to support high bandwidth simultaneous data transfer with all these *RASs*. For the purpose of this paper, without loss of generality, we assume that the *WRR* is able to simultaneously support high capacity, duplex links using directional antennas to a minimum of two other entities (either both *RASs* or both *WRRs* or a combination of a *RAS* and a *WRR*). Given the limited number of wireless links with the *RASs* that the *WRR* can simultaneously support, the mechanism we develop works to provide this additional bandwidth where it is most needed in the network. This mechanism works with the aid of feedback from the routing mechanism developed in [3]. For example as shown in Fig. 5(b) at a given time t_1 the *WRR* may enable the wireless links to *RAS* 0 and *RAS* 15, thereby providing a virtual link between *RASs* 0 and 15. While at some other time t_2, based on the network traffic conditions and feedback from the routing algorithm, the *WRR* enables the wireless links to *RASs* 15 and 19, thus providing a virtual link between the *RASs* 15 and 19. Thus, it can be seen that the *WRR* should adapt the network topology (provide virtual links between pairs of *RASs*) in response to feedback from the routing mechanism. The interworking of the topology changes with the routing mechanism is crucial for the understanding of our architecture. As already introduced, the routing mechanism used in [3] computes multiple loop-free paths, possibly of unequal costs, to a destination at each router in the network. This route computation is done at time interval T_l. On a smaller timescale T_s, the amount of traffic sent along individual paths is adjusted so that more load is sent along low cost paths than along higher cost paths. The link cost used by the routing mechanism is the incremental delay over the link. Fig. 6 qualitatively shows the variation in the link cost with respect to the link utilization.

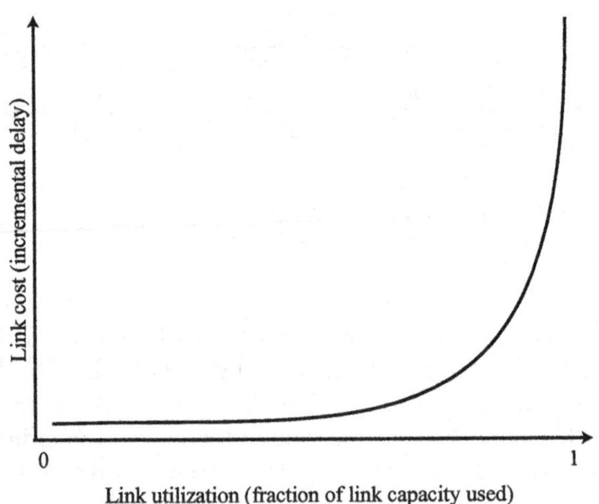

Fig. 6. Variation in link cost with the utilization of the link

As can be observed from Fig. 6, the link cost starts increasing exponentially as the traffic on the link approaches the link capacity. With the incremental delay as link cost more than an order of magnitude increase in the link cost is observed as the link utilization moves from 0.7 to 0.9. This region corresponds to the build up of congestion at that link. For the wireless links through the *WRR* on the other hand we keep the link cost a constant value and set it to be more than the average wired link cost observed in the network at 0.7 link utilization. We call this constant cost for the wireless links through the *WRR* as *threshold-cost*. We return to Fig. 5 for the following discussion. Consider Fig. 5(a), the *WRR* at startup discovers the set of *RASs* in its range having a suitable interface for communication with the *WRR*. In this example it would be the set of *RASs* 0, 3, 15, 19 and 24. It then transmits this neighbourhood information to the above *RASs*. As mentioned, these *RASs* have a suitable radio interface for communication with the *WRR*. The data transmission and reception over this interface is handled by an agent called the virtual interface proxy (*VIP*).

On receipt of this connectivity information by the *RAS* 0 (for example) with the aid of the *VIP*, the *RAS* 0 updates its set of neighbours to 1, 7, 3, 15, 19 and 24. Here, it should be noted that *RAS* 0 has permanent wired links to *RASs* 1 and 7 but may only sometimes be able to communicate with *RASs* 3, 15, 19 and 24 via the *WRR*, depending on whether the required wireless links are enabled or not. Hence, we denote these wireless links as virtual links (in the sense that they are not always existent). Here, the links (0,3), (0,15), (0,19), and (0,24) are virtual links. As we mentioned previously, these virtual links are advertised as *threshold-cost* links. Due to their high cost as compared to the normal wired links in the network, these virtual links are normally not used for forwarding data by the routing tables computed at the individual *RASs*. However, with the increase of load in parts of the network, the cost of some of the wired links may increase exponentially and at a point in time, a path through the virtual link may become cheaper in cost and will then be used by the routing tables at the individual *RASs*. An indication as to which of the virtual links are to be activated is closely coupled to the feedback of the routing mechanism. Here, the *VIP* at the *RAS* plays a significant role. It is responsible for periodically requesting the *WRR* to activate a particular virtual link based on whether it has data to transfer over the virtual link, which is triggered by the routing algorithm at the *RAS*.

The *VIP* at a *RAS* periodically transmits requests for activation of a virtual link to the *WRR* along with a measure of how much traffic has to be sent along the virtual link. The *WRR* then analyzes all the currently pending requests (based on which virtual link has to carry more traffic), and decides on which virtual link to activate next.

In case the *VIP* receives data for some destination to be transfered over a virtual link that is not currently active, then the data is distributed over the other neighbours in the next-hop set for that destination. For example, consider Fig 5(b). Here, the virtual link (0,15) is active, i.e. data can be sent via the *WRR* from *RAS* 0 to *RAS* 15. Now consider that the next-hop set at *RAS* 0 for the destination 4 is $\{1, 3\}$ (here *RAS* 3 is connected via a virtual link (0,3) to *RAS* 0 and is said to be a virtual neighbour of *RAS* 0). If the routing algorithm at this point sends some data intended for *RAS* 4 for transfer over the virtual link (0,3) it is handled first by the *VIP* at *RAS* 0. In this case the *VIP* detects that the required virtual link is currently unavailable and distributes the data, where possible, over the other members in the next-hop set for the destination 4. In our example, this data will be transmitted over the interface to *RAS* 1. At this point the *VIP* also sends a request for activation of virtual link (0,3) to the *WRR* along with related information about what fraction of traffic at *RAS* 0 is to be sent along link (0,3). The information about the fraction of traffic to a particular neighbour can be computed from the routing tables as used in [3].

The *WRR* selects periodically the next virtual link to be activated based on which virtual link has to carry the maximum amount of traffic. For seamless interworking with the routing algorithm, we also have to determine an appropriate frequency for the switching between the various virtual links to be activated by the *WRR*. As already explained, the routing mechanism updates the routing tables at a time interval T_l and at a smaller time interval T_s adjusts the fraction of traffic to be sent along individual paths. Hence, we decide to choose the virtual link switching interval to be some multiple of T_s but less than T_l. This enables the *WRR* to respond to transient congestion as well as long term overload in parts of the network. Detailed protocols and heuristics to be run by the *VIP* and the *WRR* are given in [3].

4 Conclusion

In this paper we have given an overview of a part of our work in [3]. We have discussed our dynamic network architecture and have highlighted the roles of the individual components. We also described our mechanism to provide additional bandwidth in the network where it is required. In order to enable such a dynamic bandwidth allocation and topology adaptation in the network we rely on feedback from the routing mechanism. We have outlined a distributed mechanism by which this can be achieved. We believe that the concept of the *WRR* may be implemented using currently available standard technologies. For example to enable high capacity, long range wireless links for the *WRR* we envision the use of components based on IEEE 802.16-2004 standards [10].

The ultimate goal for such topology adaptation mechanisms, as also discussed by Kleinrock [11], is to achieve optimization goals such as minimization of delay or maximization of throughput.

5 Acknowledgements

This work was partially funded by Siemens AG, CT IC 2, and the DAAD. We would like to thank Dipl.-Ing. M. Hollick, Dipl.-Inf. T. Krop, Prof. Dr.-Ing. J. B. Schmitt, Prof. Dr.-Ing. R. Steinmetz, and Prof. G. Barua for their guidance and support.

6 References

1. Hollick M., Krop T., Schmitt J.B., et al.: Modeling mobility and workload for wireless metropolitan area networks. Computer Communications, vol. 27, 751–761, 2004.
2. Wu H., Qiao C., De S., et al.: Integrated cellular and ad hoc relaying systems:iCAR. IEEE Journal on Selected Areas in Communications, vol. 19, 2105–2115, 2001.
3. Mogre P.S.: Near-optimal multiclass minimum-delay routing for cellular networks with variable topology, M.Tech. thesis, Dept. of CSE, IIT Guwahati; Multimedia Communications Lab, Dept. of ETIT, TU-Darmstadt, 2004.
4. Gallager R.G.: A minimum delay routing algorithm using distributed computation, IEEE Trans. on Communication, vol 25, 73–84, 1977.
5. Vutukury S.: Multipath routing mechanisms for traffic engineering and quality of service in the Internet, PhD. thesis, Univ. of California Santa Cruz, 2001.
6. Lin Y.D., Hsu Y.C.: Multihop cellular: a new architecture for wireless communications, IEEE INFOCOM 2000,1273–1282, 2000.
7. Lott M., Weckerle M., Zirwas W., et al.: Hierarchical cellular multihop networks, EPMCC03, 2003.
8. Yeh C.H.: Acenet: architectures and protocols for high throughput, low power and qos provisioning in next-generation mobile communications, IEEE PIMRC 2002, 2002.
9. Hollick M., Krop T., Schmitt J.B., et al.: Comparative analysis of quality of service routing in wireless metropolitan area networks, IEEE LCN 2003, 470–479, 2003.
10. IEEE 802.16-2004: IEEE standard for local and metropolitan area networks – part 16: air interface for fixed broadband wireless access systems, 2004.
11. Kleinrock L.: Queueing Systems, vol 2: computer applications. Wiley Interscience, 1976.

Modellierung der Leistungsregelung zur Planung von Wideband CDMA Systemen

Kenji Leibnitz

Graduate School of Information Science and Technology, Osaka University,
1-5 Yamadaoka, Suita, Osaka 565-0871, Japan
leibnitz@ist.osaka-u.ac.jp

Zusammenfassung. Das Ziel dieser Arbeit ist die Herleitung analytischer Modelle, um eine Leistungsbewertung von Mobilfunksystemen der dritten Generation (3G) zu ermöglichen. Als eine der wichtigsten Einflussfaktoren wird das dynamische Verhalten der Sendeleistungsregelung (engl. *power control*) erachtet. Die Aufgabe von Power Control ist es, die Leistung der Sendestation derart einzustellen, dass sie möglichst minimal ist, jedoch auch den Mindestanforderungen für die empfangene Signalleistung genügt. Durch dieses dynamische Verhalten entsteht eine Wechselwirkung zwischen der Zellgröße, Kapazität und der Dienstgüte im System. Es ist daher von entscheidender Wichtigkeit vor der Einführung dieser neuen Systeme die Systemstabilität zu untersuchen und alle Einflussfaktoren zu identifizieren.

1 Einführung in UMTS und WCDMA

Derzeit vollzieht sich ein Paradigmenwechsel bei der Entwicklung von Mobilfunksystemen. Der Übergang von Systemen, die nur reine Sprachdienste anbieten, zu den sogenannten Systemen der dritten Generation (3G) steht unmittelbar bevor oder hat bereits in einigen Ländern begonnen. Dies ermöglicht die Einführung neuer Dienste im Mobilfunk, die bisher nur im Festnetzbereich verfügbar waren. Die steigende Bedeutung von Internetanwendungen, wie Browsen im World Wide Web oder das Senden und Empfangen von Electronic Mail, hat es erforderlich gemacht, dass viele Benutzer von überall her Zugang zu diesen Diensten haben wollen, wie sie es von der Benutzung eines Mobiltelefons gewohnt sind.

Jedoch erfordern diese neuen Anwendungen auch eine höhere Bandbreite als Sprachverkehr und benötigen somit die Einführung neuer Technologien, die eine Übertragung von durchschaltevermitteltem und paketorientiertem Verkehr ermöglichen. Die Tendenzen, die hier gesehen werden können, führen zu einer allmählichen Konvergenz des Internets und des Mobilfunkbereichs. Bisher existiert im Mobilfunk eine Vielzahl heterogener Systeme, die von den Anbietern in den verschiedenen Ländern oder Kontinenten mit unterschiedlichen Zugriffstechnologien angeboten werden. Zum Beispiel werden in Europa fast ausschließlich GSM-Dienste angeboten, während in den USA nur eine eingeschränkte Versorgung mit GSM stattfindet und andere Systeme, wie z.B. AMPS oder cdmaOne, hauptsächlich in Gebrauch sind. Eine der Ziele der Standardisierungsgremien für

3G war es daher ein einheitliches System zu schaffen, das ein globales Roaming unterstützt.

Für 3G wird mit Wideband CDMA eine neue Technologie für die Luftschnittstelle eingeführt [1], die eine höhere Kapazität als schmalbandige Systeme hat. Jedoch erfordern die signifikanten Unterschiede zwischen Wideband CDMA und den konventionellen Systemen der zweiten Generation auch neue Paradigmen bei der Dimensionierung und Planung der Netze. Anders als bei GSM ist die Kapazität bei CDMA-basierten Netzen nicht fest und diese „weichen" Kapazitätsgrenzen (engl. *soft capacity*) führen zu einer Neudefinition des Begriffs der Zellgröße. Sie ist bei CDMA Netzen nicht mehr lediglich von den Ausbreitungsbedingungen festgelegt, sondern bildet sich vielmehr aus der Interaktion zwischen Versorgung, Kapazität und Dienstgüte.

Im Anschluss folgt eine kurze Einführung in die Grundprinzipien der CDMA Technologie und es werden die wichtigsten Einflussfaktoren bei der Bewertung der Systemkapazität vorgestellt. Dies wird im Abschnitt 2 gefolgt von der Herleitung der analytischen Modelle der Regelkreisläufe bei der Sendeleistungsregelung in CDMA. Nach der Leistungsuntersuchung für einen Nutzer, wird die Untersuchung in Abschnitt 4 auf die Bewertung des gesamten Systems ausgeweitet. Ein Modell mit einem räumlichen Punktfeld wird verwendet um die zufälligen Nutzerpositionen zu charakterisieren. Die gewonnen Ergebnisse können als Hinweise für eine verkehrs-orientierte Funknetzplanung verstanden werden.

1.1 Prinzipien von Code Division Multiple Access

Bei jedem Kommunikationssystem, bei dem viele Benutzer gleichzeitig eine gemeinsame Ressource nutzen, ist ein Mehrfachzugriffsverfahren erforderlich. Alle Teilnehmer konkurrieren um einen oft nur begrenzten Vorrat an Ressourcen, z.B. eine begrenzte Anzahl an Funkkanälen. Dies trifft vor allem bei der Kommunkation in Mobilfunksystemen zu, bei denen das Nutzsignal auf einen Funkträger in einem sehr begrenzten Frequenzspektrum aufmoduliert wird. Das Mehrfachzugriffssystem wird benötigt, um die Bandbreite effizient zu nutzen und eine hohe Systemkapazität zu erreichen, siehe Abb. 1.

Im Gegensatz zu herkömmlichen Zugriffsverfahren wie F/TDMA (Frequency/Time Division Multiple Access) bei GSM, bei dem ein Zeitschlitz in einem Frequenzband einem Benutzer für die gesamte Dauer seiner Übertragung zur Verfügung steht, verwendet CDMA (Code Division Multiple Access) orthogonale Codes, um die einzelnen Verkehrskanäle zu trennen. CDMA basiert auf der *Spread Spectrum* Technologie und wurde in der Mitte der 1950er Jahre ursprünglich für militärische Anwendungen entwickelt, aufgrund seiner Robustheit gegenüber Störung und seiner hoher Abhörsicherheit [7].

Die Signalspreizung wird in CDMA durch Modulation des Nutzsignals auf einen rausch-ähnlichen Träger mit einer höheren Frequenz durchgeführt. Der Vorteil bei der Verwendung eines Rausch-Trägers liegt darin, dass das Signal robuster gegenüber Störung wird. Jedoch, da das Signal jedes Nutzers auf der Luftschnittstelle als Rauschen erscheint, trägt es auch somit zur gesamten Interferenz bei. Da die Verbindung eine Mindestqualität hinsichtlich *bit-energy-to-*

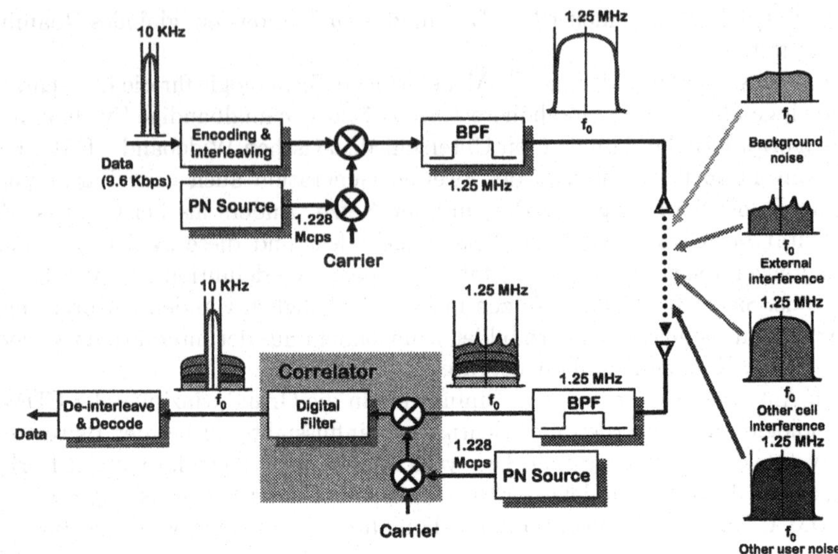

Abb. 1. Das CDMA Übertragungsprinzip

noise ratio (E_b/N_0) erfordert, limitiert somit die Interferenz im Endeffekt die Kapazität von CDMA Systemen.

1.2 Power Control

Alle Benutzer in einem CDMA System teilen sich das Frequenzband und interferieren miteinander. Weiterhin befinden sich die Mobilstationen (MS) auf unterschiedlichen Positionen mit unterschiedlichen Entfernungen zur Basisstation (BS). Falls jeder Benutzer mit der gleichen Signalstärke übertragen würde, würden näher an der BS gelegene Teilnehmer über die weiter entfernten dominieren. Dies ist in der Literatur als *Near-Far Effect* bekannt. Um effizient ablaufen zu können, erfordert CDMA, dass alle Teilnehmer mit nahezu gleichen Signalstärken an der BS empfangen werden. Dafür wurde eine Sendeleistungsregelung (engl. *Power Control*) implementiert, bei dem der Empfänger die Signalleistung des Senders regelt, um eine vorgegebenen Signalgüte an empfangener E_b/N_0 einzuhalten.

Bei CDMA Systemen werden zwei Arten von Power Control auf dem Uplink (MS-BS Verbindung) verwendet: *Open Loop* und *Closed Loop*. Bei Open Loop Power Control verwendet die MS die empfangene Signalstärke des Pilotkanals der BS als Schätzwert für den Ausbreitungsverlust und setzt die Sendestärke dementsprechend. Zusätzlich dazu arbeitet Closed Loop in Wechselwirkung zwischen MS und BS, um die Fluktuationen auf dem Funkkanal zu überwinden. Die Closed Loop Schleife besteht aus *Inner Loop* und *Outer Loop*, siehe Abb. 2.

Innerhalb der Inner Loop überprüft die BS andauernd die Verbindungsqualität durch den empfangenen E_b/N_0-Wert und vergleicht ihn mit einem Schwellwert. Falls der empfangene Wert zu hoch ist, wird die MS angewiesen ihre Sendestärke zu verringern. Andernfalls, ist die Verbingunsqualität nicht ausreichend und ein *Power-Up* Kommando wird übertragen. Die Zeiteinheit für diese Power Updates wird als Power Control Groups (PCG) bezeichnet und beträgt bei UMTS 0.67 ms.

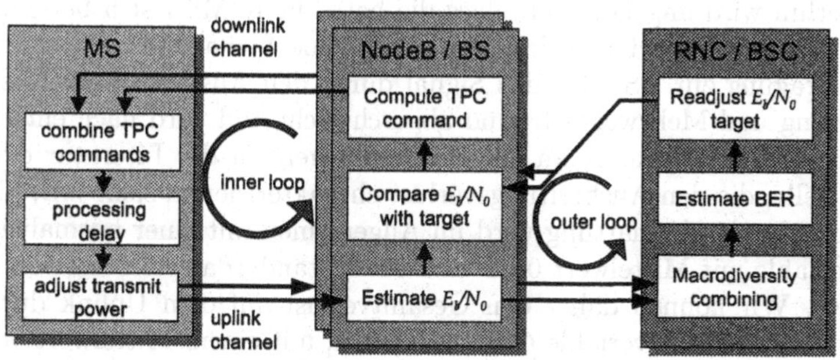

Abb. 2. Kreislauf der Closed Loop Power Control bei UMTS

Nachdem ein kompletter Rahmen übertragen worden ist, geht der Power Control Algorithmus in die Outer Loop über. Deren Hauptaufgabe ist es eine akzeptable Rahmenfehlerrate (*frame error rate*, FER) durch die Anpassung des E_b/N_0 Schwellwertes nach jedem Rahmen zu erreichen.

1.3 Das Universal Mobile Telecommunication System (UMTS)

Das *Universal Mobile Telecommunication System* (UMTS) ist der europäische Beitrag zur 3G Standardisierung. Es ist Teil von dem Ansatz der ITU um eine globale Familie von 3G Systemen als IMT-2000 (International Mobile Telephony) zu vereinheitlichen. Das Hauptziel ist es die Systeme der zweiten Generation zu ersetzen und schnelle, paket-orientierte Mobilfunkverbindungen zu ermöglichen.

Die Luftschnittstelle von UMTS wird bezeichnet als UTRA (UMTS Terrestrial Radio Access) und verwendet WCDMA (Wideband CDMA) bei Datenraten zwischen 12.2 kbps bei Sprache bis hin zu 2 Mbps für Multimediaanwendungen. UMTS unterstützt Power Control auf dem Up- und Downlink.

2 Analytische Modellierung von Power Control

2.1 Modell der Inner Loop

Die Sendestärke der betrachteten MS wird im Folgenden mit dem abstrakten Index $j, 0 \leq j \leq J$ bezeichnet. Sei $P^{(n)}$ eine Zufallsvariable für die Sendestärke der MS zum Zeitpunkt n.

Das ursprüngliche Signal wird auf dem Uplink durch den Kanalverlust abgeschwächt. Im vorliegenden Modell wird der Kanalverlust stochastisch mit der Zufallsvariable $G^{(n)}$ beschrieben. Die Wahrscheinlichkeit für Power-Up und Power-Down Kommandos unter der Bedingung, dass die betrachtete MS zum Zeitpunkt n mit Stärke j sendet, ist gegeben durch

$$p_u^{(n)}(j) = Pr\left[\varepsilon^{(n)} \leq \theta \mid P^{(n)} = j\right] \tag{1}$$

und $p_d^{(n)} = 1 - p_u^{(n)}$.

Weiterhin wird angenommen, dass die betrachtete MS i sich bei einer Entfernung von x zu der BS befindet und mit eine Signalstärke P_i sendet. Bei der Übertragung zur BS wird das Signal durch den Ausbreitungsverlust $L(x)$, Abschattung und Mehrwegeschwund abgeschwächt und wird nach einer Verzögerung δ mit der Stärke S_i an der BS empfangen. In der Literatur existieren viele Modelle, die den Ausbreitungsverlust charakterisieren, siehe z.B. [6, 9].

Verlust durch Abschattung wird im Allgemeinen mit einer normalverteilten Zufallsvariable mit Mittelwert 0 dB und einer Standardabweichung von 7–8 dB modelliert. Wir können daher den Gesamtverlust auf dem Uplink durch eine normalverteilte Zufallsveriable $G^{(n)}$ annehmen, mit einem Mittelwert von $L(x)$ abhängig von der Distanz zwischen MS und BS und der Standardabweichung σ_G.

Mit Hilfe des Multi-Access Interference (MAI) Faktors φ lässt sich E_b/N_0 in einer sehr vereinfachten Form als

$$\varepsilon^{(n)} = P^{(n)} + G^{(n)} + (W - R - N + \varphi)\,, \tag{2}$$

darstellen, wobei W die Frequenzbandbreite, R die Datenrate und N das Hintergrundrauschen sind und die letzten vier Elemente als konstant betrachtet werden.

Die Wahrscheinlichkeit, dass ein Power-Up Kommando zum Zeitpunkt n gesendet wird, kann dadurch berechnet werden, indem $\varepsilon^{(n)}$ mit θ verglichen werden.

$$p_u^{(n)}(j) = Pr\left[G^{(n)} \leq \theta - j\right] \tag{3}$$

2.2 Modell der Outer Loop

Der Schwellwert der Outer Loop wird erhöht falls der Rahmen fehlerhaft ist, ansonsten wird er verringert. Sei B die Anzahl von Bits pro Rahmen. Ein fehlerhafter Rahmen tritt auf, wenn mindestens ein Bit im Rahmen einen Fehler hat. Daher kann die Wahrscheinlichkeit $q_u(i)$ für eine Erhöhung und $q_d(i)$ für eine Verringerung des Schwellwerts θ von Stufe i durch eine Binomial-Verteilung angenommen werden.

$$q_u(i) = 1 - (1 - p_b(i))^B \tag{4}$$
$$q_d(i) = 1 - q_u(i). \tag{5}$$

Diese Gleichungen beruhen auf der Annahme, dass ein Interleaving den Auftritt von Bitfehlern innerhalb eines Rahmens unabhängig voneinander macht. Zwecks Vereinfachung wird weiter angenommen, dass der E_b/N_0 Schwellwert durch einen maximalen Wert M beschränkt wird.

2.3 Markov-Ketten Modell

Um ein Modell herzuleiten, das beide Schleifen beinhaltet, wird eine Markov-Kette mit zwei-dimensionalen Zuständen $z(i,j)$ betrachtet, wobei $1 \leq i \leq M$ und $1 \leq j \leq J$. Der erste Index i beschreibt den E_b/N_0 Schwellwert und j den Pegel der Sendestärke. Die Übergänge zu und von einem Zustand $z(i,j)$ sind in Abb. 3 abgebildet.

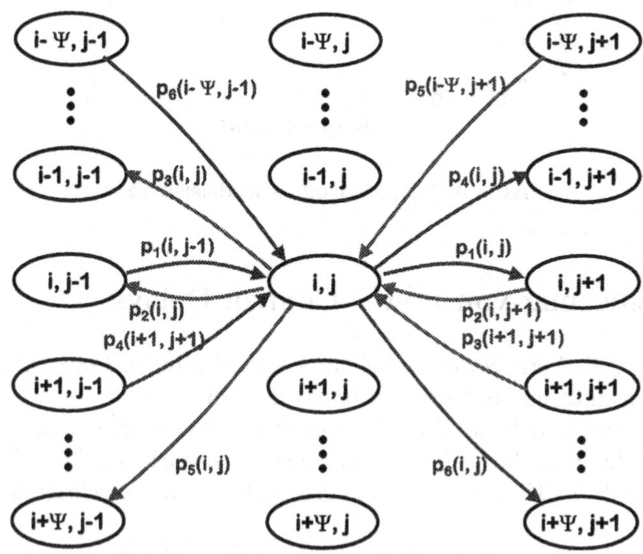

Abb. 3. Zustandsübergänge

Analog zu Gl. (1) wird die Sendeleistung erhöht und verringert mit $p_u(i,j)$ bzw. $p_d(i,j) = 1 - p_u(i,j)$ und kann in einer geschlossen Form angegeben werden unter Berücksichtigung der Normalverteilungsannahme.

$$p_u(i,j) = \frac{1}{2} + \frac{1}{2}\, erf\left(\frac{i-j-\mu_G}{\sqrt{2}\sigma_G}\right) \tag{6}$$

Es können nun die Übergänge zu und von einem bestimmten Zustand $z(i,j)$ in Abb. 3 beschrieben und eine Übergangswahrscheinlichkeitsmatrix im stationären Zustand erstellt werden. Anhand Standardverfahren aus der Verkehrstheorie wird die stationären Zustandsverteilung $z(i,j)$ bestimmt.

Ein beispielhaftes Ergebnis ist in Abb. 4 dargestellt. Es gibt drei wichtige Effekte, die in dieser Abbildung zu sehen sind. Erstens, ein Benutzer mit größerem Abstand zur BS benötigt eine höhere Sendeleistung. Weiterhin bewirkt eine Erhöhung der Last in der Zelle oder der Datenrate eine Verringerung der Zellgröße und schließlich führt diese Tatsache zu einer Wechselwirkung zwischen Größe und Kapazität der Zelle, was in Abschnitt 4 vertieft wird.

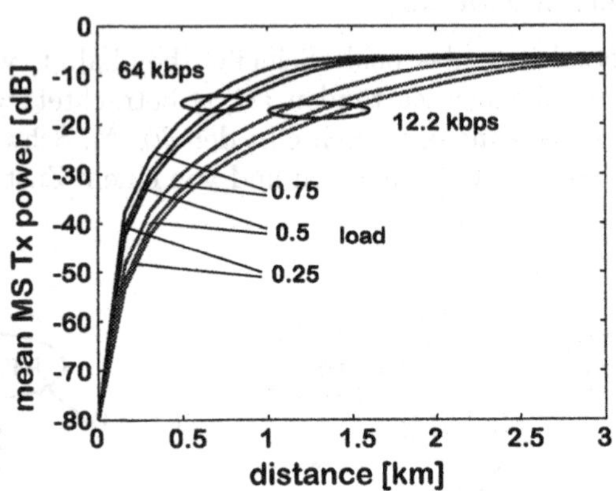

Abb. 4. Mittlere Uplink-Sendeleistung

3 Modellierung von Power Control Delays

Bisher wurden die Verzögerungen bei der Verarbeitung der Power Control Kommandos vernachlässigt und angenommen, dass diese sofort im nächsten Zeitschritt nach dem Erhalt des Signals ausgeführt werden. In einem tatsächlichen System wird das zeitliche Verhalten der Inner Loop stark von dieser Verzögerung beeinflusst und das Kommando wird erst nach $\delta = 3$ Zeitschritten tatsächlich ausgeführt.

Die Übergänge von einem (diskreten) Sendepegel zum nächsten finden in jedem PCG statt und werden nur zwischen benachbarten Pegel durchgeführt. Die Abhängigkeiten zwischen den Sendepegeln um einen bestimmten Pegel j zu erreichen sind in Abb. 5(a) dargestellt.

Abb. 5(a) zeigt, dass das Power-Up Kommando für Level j zur Zeit n von den Wahrscheinlichkeiten für Power-Up der vier möglichen Zustände abhängt, d.h. Sendepegel, die vor 3 PCG angenommen werden konnten ($j+3$, $j+1$, $j-1$, $j-3$ zum Zeitpunkt $n-3$). Es soll angemerkt werden, dass es nicht möglich war vor drei Zeitschritten im gleichen Zustand gewesen zu sein.

Da die Wahrscheinlichtkeit für jeden Zustand zum Zeitpunkt $n-3$ sich gleichermaßen aus einer derartigen Baum-Struktur herleitet, besteht ebenfalls eine Abhängigkeit diese Zustände zum Zeitpunkt $n-3$ zu erreichen. Daher kann in diesem Fall nicht einfach angenommen werden, dass die $p_u^{(n)}(j)$ die Übergangswahrscheinlichkeiten bilden, sondern es müssen auch noch die Pfade berücksichtigt werden, um diese Zustände zu erreichen. Es werden nun Makro-Zustände $\bar{z}^{(n)}(j_1, j_2, j_3)$ definiert, die eine Abfolge von drei Sendepegeln beschreiben.

$$\bar{z}^{(n)}(j_1, j_2, j_3) = Pr\left[P^{(n)} = j_3 \mid P^{(n-1)} = j_2, P^{(n-2)} = j_1\right] \tag{7}$$

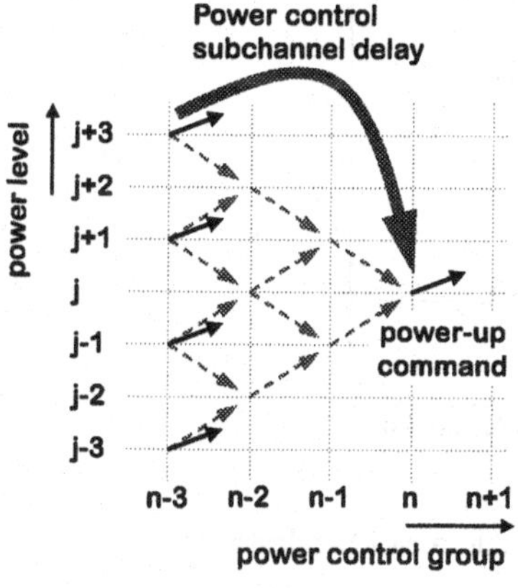

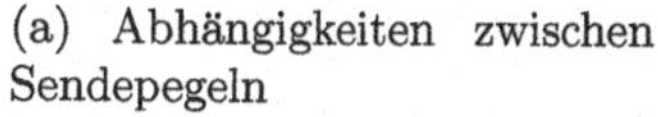
(a) Abhängigkeiten zwischen Sendepegeln

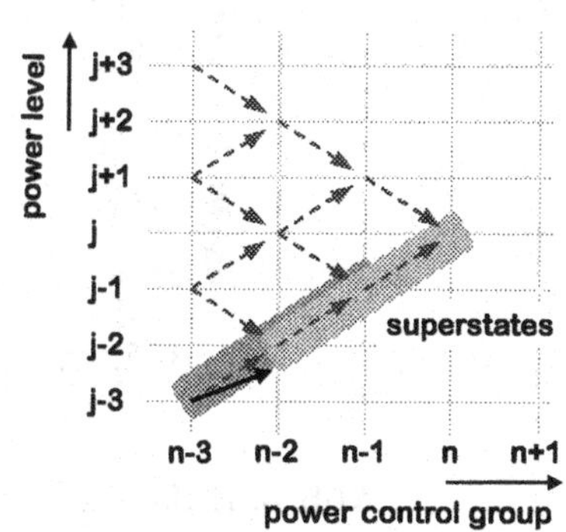

(b) Übergänge zwischen Makro-Zuständen

Abb. 5. Zustandsübergänge im Power Control Modell

Die Übergänge zwischen den Makro-Zuständen sind in Abb. 5(b) dargestellt. Die Übergangswahrscheinlichkeiten zum Zeitpunkt n können in einer Matrix $\mathbf{Q}^{(n)}$ angeordnet werden und anhand des Zustandsgleichungssystems gelöst werden.

3.1 Instationäre Analyse der Dynamik von Power Control

Es wird nun ein instationärer Fall betrachtet bei dem, ausgehend von einer Anfangsverteilung für die Sendestärke $P^{(0)}$ zur Zeit $n = 0$, iterativ die nachfolgende Verteilung der Sendeleistung $P^{(n)}$ berechnet wird. Die Berechnung erfolgt anhand des o.a. Schemas mit der Betrachtung der Pfade. Die neuen Zustandswahrscheinlichkeiten $P^{(n+1)}$ werden aus $P^{(n)}$ berechnet indem zuerst der korrespondierende Makro-Zustand $\bar{Z}^{(n)}$ bestimmt wird und dann aufeinanderfolgend mit der Übergangsmatrix $\mathbf{Q}^{(n)}$ multipliziert wird.

$$\bar{Z}^{(n+1)} = \bar{Z}^{(n)} \cdot \mathbf{Q}^{(n)}.$$

Die Transformation von $\bar{z}^{(n+1)}(j_1, j_2, j_3)$ nach $z^{(n+1)}(j)$ liefert die neuen Zustandswahrscheinlichkeiten. Dies wird durch die Summe über alle Makro-Zustände mit gleichem Endzustand erreicht.

$$z^{(n+1)}(j) = \sum_{j_1, j_2} \bar{z}^{(n+1)}(j_1, j_2, j), \qquad j = 0, \ldots, J.$$

Um das dynamische Systemverhalten zu untersuchen, wird die Zeit betrachtet, die benötigt wird um von einem stabilen Zustand zum nächsten zu gelangen.

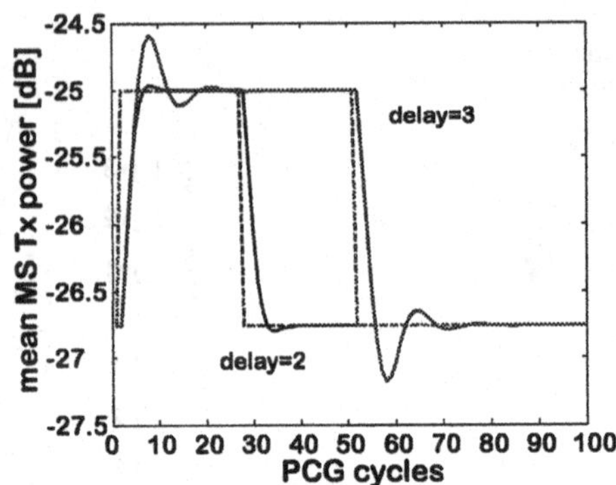

Abb. 6. Einfluss des Delays auf die mittlere MS Sendestärke

Der Schwerpunkt liegt dabei auf dem Einfluss der Zelllast auf die Dauer der Konvergenz in dieser Zelle.

Die Wahl des Startvektors zum Zeitpunkt $n = 0$ hat einen großen Einfluss auf die Geschwindigkeit der Konvergenz. Um zu gewährleisten, dass das System sich am Anfang in einem eingeschwungenen Zustand befindet, wird anhand einer stationären Analyse eine Verteilung der Sendestärke ermittelt, die als Startvektor für die instationären Untersuchungen gewählt wird.

Die Ergebnisse in Abb. 6 zeigen, dass der Mittelwert der MS Sendestärke nicht vom Delay abhängt. Jedoch wird die transiente Phase deutlich verlängert, wenn der Delay von 2 auf 3 PCG erhöht wird. Dies wird durch die verzögerte Reaktion des Systems auf die Power Control Kommandos verursacht und wird deutlich in der Oszillation um den theoretischen Mittelwert. Die Studie zeigt, dass eine Verringerung des Delays von 3 PCG (wie im cdmaOne System) auf 2 PCG ein deutlich stabileres System bei Schwankungen in der Zelllast bewirken würde.

4 Planung von WCDMA Netzen mit räumlichem Verkehr

In den bisherigen Abschnitten wurde das Verhalten von Power Control eines einzigen Nutzers betrachtet und die weiteren Teilnehmer wurden nur implizit durch die Last berücksichtigt. In diesem Abschnitt wird das Modell erweitert um eine räumliche Verteilung der Nutzer anhand von räumlichen Punktprozessen [3] mathematisch zu charakterisieren.

Allgemein ist ein räumlicher Punktprozess die Erweiterung eines eindimensionalen Punktprozesses auf eine zweidimensionale Fläche, wobei die Punkte durch ihre Koordinaten gekennzeichnet sind. Ähnlich ihrem eindimensionalen Gegenstück, werden sie durch das erste Moment beschrieben, das als *Intensitätsmaß* bezeichnet wird. Im einfachsten Fall eines homogenen Poisson-Prozesses besteht dieses Intensitätsmaß aus einem Skalar λ, das die mittlere Anzahl

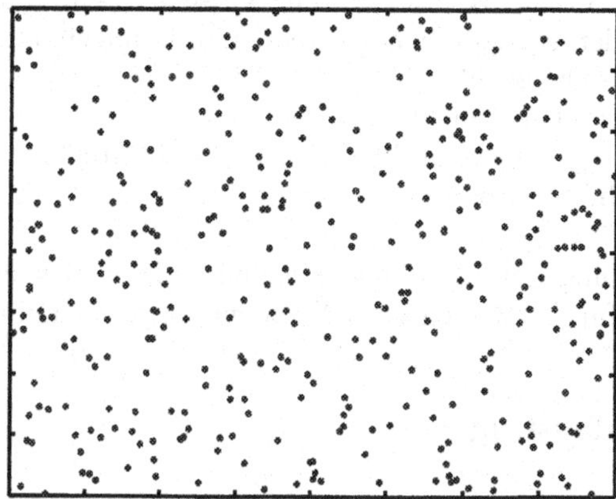

Abb. 7. Realisierung eines homogenen Poisson Prozesses

von Punkten (hier Teilnehmern) auf einer Einheitsfläche beschreibt. Die Realisierung eines homogenen Poisson-Prozesses ist in Abb. 7 gegeben.

Die folgende Untersuchung behandelt die Wechselwirkung zwischen Zellradius und Kapazität, d.h. die mittlere Anzahl der Teilnehmer ξ in einer Zelle. Es wird eine maximale Schranke p^*_{out} für die Ausfallswahrscheinlichkeit (engl. *Outage Probability*) angenommen, welche die Dienstgüte beschreibt und die nicht unterschritten werden darf. Durch Auflösen der Gleichung für die Ausfallwahrscheinlichkeit, die aus dem Modell gewonnen werden kann, kann der maximale Zellradius ermittelt werden, bei dem p^*_{out} eingehalten werden kann.

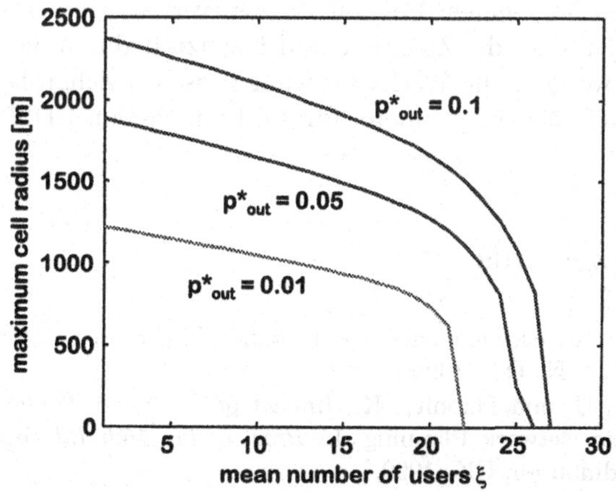

Abb. 8. Wechselwirkung Zellgrößen gegenüber Kapazität

Die Ergebnisse für die Wechselwirkung zwischen Zellradius und Kapazität sind in Abb. 8 wiedergegeben. Je höher die Anforderungen an die Ausfallsicherheit werden, d.h. je kleiner p^*_{out} ist, umso kleiner wird der maximale Zellradius bei der gleichen Anzahl an Teilnehmern. Daher können bei einer CDMA Zelle die Größe der Versorgungsgebiete und die Kapazität als Größen angesehen werden, die eher durch Stabilitätskriterien bestimmt werden als durch die tatsächlichen Ressourcen.

Unter Verwendung der bisherigen Ergebnisse lässt sich ein einfacher Planungsalgorithmus für CDMA-basierte Netze wie in [2] formulieren.

5 Zusammenfassung

Die Arbeit beschäftigt sich mit der analytischen Modellierung des Power Control Kreislaufs in einem CDMA-basierten Mobilfunksystem und der Leistungsuntersuchung in Anbetracht einer räumlichen Benutzerverteilung. Es wurde ein analytisches Markov-Ketten Modell der Inner und Outer Loop hergeleitet. Das vorrangige Ziel war eine mathematische Beschreibung der Sendeleistung einer beliebigen MS zu erhalten. Als Kriterium für die Leistungsfähigkeit des Systems wurde die Ausfallwahrscheinlichkeit berechnet als die Wahrscheinlichkeit, dass die maximal mögliche Sendeleistung nicht ausreicht, um eine gewünschte Dienstgüte zu erreichen.

Eine Erweiterung des Modells beinhaltet die Verarbeitungsverzögerung und die Abhängigkeit der Sendepegel, die durch Aggregation der Pfade zu Makro-Zuständen ebenfalls in das Modell eingebaut werden konnten. Es wurden Studien durchgeführt, die das Systemverhalten bei einer plötzlichen Veränderung der Verkehrslast aufzeigten.

Nach der Betrachtung einer einzelnen Verbindung beinhaltete der nächste Schritt eine Berücksichtigung der gesamten Zelle bei dem die Teilnehmer nach einem räumlichen homogenen Poisson Prozess verteilt sind. Die Ergebnisse in der Arbeit zeigten, dass die Zellgröße und Kapazität durch die Verkehrsverteilung beeinflusst werden. Die Wechselwirkung zwischen Zellgröße und Kapazität erweist sich als nützlicher Parameter für die Planung von CDMA Mobilfunksystemen.

Literaturverzeichnis

[1] 3GPP: Radio resource management strategies. Technical Specification TR25.942. 3GPP, TSG RAN. Dec. 1999.

[2] Ehrenberger, U. und Leibnitz, K. Impact of Clustered Traffic Distributions in CDMA Radio Network Planning In *Proc. of the 16th International Teletraffic Congress*, Edinburgh, UK. 1999.

[3] Frey, A. und Schmidt, V.: Marked point processes in the plane I - a survey with applications to spatial modeling of communication networks. *Advances in Performance Analysis.* 1(1):65–110. 1998.

[4] Leibnitz, K.: Impacts of power control on outage probabilities in CDMA wireless networks. In *Proc. of IFIP 5th International Conference on Broadband Communications*, Hong Kong. 1999.

[5] Leibnitz, K., Tran-Gia, P. und Miller, J. E. Analysis of the dynamics of cdma reverse link power control. In *Proc. of IEEE GLOBECOM*, Sydney, Australia. 1998.

[6] Rappaport, T. S.: *Wireless Communications - Principles & Practice.* Prentice Hall. Upper Saddle River, NJ. 1996.

[7] Viterbi, A. J.: *CDMA - Principles of spread spectrum communications.* Addison–Wesley. Reading, MA. 1995.

[8] Veeravalli, V. V., Sendonaris, A., und Jain, N.: CDMA coverage, capacity and pole capacity. In: *Proc. of IEEE VTC'97.* S. 1450–1454. Phoenix, AZ. May 1997.

[9] Walke, B.: *Mobile Radio Networks, Networking and Protocols.* Wiley. 1998.

Router Aided Congestion Avoidance with Scalable Performance Signaling

Michael Welzl

Institute of Computer Science, University of Innsbruck, Austria

Abstract This paper justifies using explicit performance signaling in support of congestion control by means of a simple yet efficient scheme called "Congestion Avoidance with Distributed Proportional Control (CADPC)". It thereby contradicts a common belief that no additional forward traffic should be sent by such mechanisms. CADPC, which solely relies on rare bandwidth feedback from routers, is shown to outperform several TCP-friendly mechanisms and TCP "flavors" in various aspects in simulations; its robustness against RTT fluctuations and loss from link noise makes it particularly well suited for heterogeneous network scenarios.

1 Introduction

TCP causes congestion in order to avoid it. Since it bases its decisions on a binary congestion signal — traditionally packet loss, more recently the ECN flag — a sender can only react when it is already too late (or almost too late, as with ECN). This behavior repeatedly causes the bottleneck queue to grow, which leads to increased delay and eventually causes packets to be dropped. Therefore, it must be a goal to *avoid* congestion (keep queues small and prevent loss) while efficiently using the available bandwidth in order to obtain good performance. To this end, an entirely different approach may be necessary.

We present one such alternative: "Congestion Avoidance with Distributed Proportional Control" (CADPC). Our mechanism only uses rare bandwidth querying packets to calculate the rate and needs no other feedback. Since it does not depend on the loss ratio or the round-trip time (RTT), the (very simple) rate calculation can be performed by any network node which sees acknowledgments from the receiver; also, other than TCP, RTT deviations due to link layer retransmissions and packet loss from link noise do not hinder the convergence of the mechanism. Our scheme has a number of additional advantages:

- it quickly reaches a stable state instead of a fluctuating equilibrium
- it has a smooth rate
- it showed greater throughput than TCP, almost no loss and a small queue length over a wide range of parameters in simulations
- it realizes precise max-min fairness in a fully distributed manner
- while it requires an occasional forward signaling packet, it generates a significantly smaller number of feedback messages from the receiver to the sender than TCP, leading to better behavior across highly asymmetric links

Signaling is carried out with the *Performance Transparency Protocol (PTP)*, which resembles ATM ABR explicit rate feedback, but is scalable and lightweight: the code to be executed in routers is reduced to the absolute minimum and does not involve any per-flow state — all calculations are done at end nodes. PTP is briefly explained in the next section (for an in-depth description of the protocol, the reader is referred to [1] and [2]). In section 3, we motivate the design of the endpoint control law and show that, assuming a fluid model and equal RTTs, our mechanism converges to an asymptotically stable equilibrium point. We present simulation results in section 4 and describe related and future work in section 5; section 6 concludes.

2 The Performance Transparency Protocol (PTP)

PTP is designed to efficiently retrieve any kind of performance related information (so-called "performance parameters" — these could be the average bottleneck queue length, the "Maximum Transfer Unit (MTU)" of the path or the maximum expected bit error ratio, for example) from the network. In order to facilitate packet detection, the protocol is layered on top of IP and uses the "Router Alert" option [3]. In *Forward Packet Stamping* mode, PTP packets carrying information requests are sent from the source to the destination and updated by intermediate routers. The receiver builds a table of router entries, detects the relevant information and feeds it back to the sender. PTP packets must not be fragmented and will not exceed the standard 576 byte fragmentation limit on typical Internet paths.

CADPC needs information regarding the available bandwidth in the network. With PTP, this means that intermediate routers have to add the following information:

- The address of the network interface
- A timestamp
- The nominal link bandwidth (the "ifSpeed" object from the "Management Information Base (MIB)" of the router)
- A byte counter (the "ifOutOctets" or "ifInOctets" object from the MIB of the router)

At the receiver, two consecutive such packets are required to calculate the bandwidth that was available during the period between the two packets. Then, the nominal bandwidth $\mathcal{B}$, the traffic λ and the interval δ of the dataset which has the smallest available bandwidth are fed back to the sender, where they are used by the congestion control mechanism.

3 Congestion Avoidance with Distributed Proportional Control (CADPC)

3.1 Fluid Flow Model Design

CADPC is a distributed variant of the "Congestion Avoidance with Proportional Control" (CAPC) ATM ABR switch mechanism by Andrew Barnhart

[4]. Roughly, while CAPC has the rate increase or decrease proportional to the amount by which the total network traffic is below or above a predefined "target rate", CADPC does the same with the relationship between the rate of a user and the available bandwidth in the network. In mathematical terms, the rate $x(t+1)$ of a sender is calculated as

$$x(t+1) = x(t)\Big(2 - \frac{x(t)}{\mathcal{B}(t)} - \frac{\lambda(t)}{\mathcal{B}(t)}\Big) \tag{1}$$

whenever new feedback arrives. The old rate, $x(t)$, can be arbitrarily small but it must not reach zero.

Assuming a fluid-flow model, synchronous RTTs and n users, equation 1 becomes

$$x(t+1) = x(t)\big(2 - x(t) - nx(t)\big) \tag{2}$$

(normalized to $\mathcal{B} = 1$), which is a form of logistic growth and is known to have an unstable equilibrium point at $\overline{x} = 0$ (hence the rule that the rate must not reach zero) and an asymptotically stable equilibrium point at $\overline{x} = 1/(1+n)$ [5]. Thus, the total traffic in the network converges to

$$n\overline{x} = \frac{n}{1+n} \tag{3}$$

which rapidly converges to 1 as the number of users increases. We decided that this convergence behavior is acceptable because it is very unlikely that only, say, two or three users would share a high capacity link, and eqn. 3 already yields very high values for 10 or more users. In fact, this may be a more "natural" way of allocating bandwidth; users tend to be very dissatisfied if their performance is degraded significantly due to new users entering the network. CADPC can also be expected to properly adapt to background traffic: if we assume constant background load b, the measured traffic becomes $nx(t) + b$, which yields the equilibrium point $(1-b)/(1+n)$ for the rate of a user. The total traffic then converges to $1-b$ as the number of users grows.

Simulation results indicate that the stability property of the control remains intact in the face of asynchronous RTTs; in fact, its convergence does not depend upon the RTT at all, rendering the mechanism robust against a broad range of potentially harmful effects in heterogeneous environments (e.g., delay spikes from link layer ARQ). In order to speed up the behavior at the beginning of a connection (similar to "Slow Start" in TCP), an alteration of the rate update rule which temporarily allows a flow to be slightly more aggressive was designed; further details can be found in [1].

3.2 Discrete Model Design

In the case of a real network with packets and queues, some additional details need to be taken into account. Two of them quickly became evident in early simulations; they are i) the rate update frequency and ii) operational limitations due to packet sizes.

Update Frequency Receiving and reacting to feedback more often than every RTT (as calculated from the departure and arrival times of PTP packets) causes oscillations. This is a natural phenomenon: as a fundamental principle of control, one should only use feedback which shows the influence of one's actions to control a system [6]. Since CADPC differs from TCP in that it reacts more drastically to precise traffic information, increasing the rate earlier can cause the traffic to reach a level where the control law tells the source that it should back off and vice versa. RTTs fluctuate — thus, the update frequency should be chosen large enough to ensure that it is larger than a RTT; as a general rule of thumb, four times the RTT is such a value.

As an alternative, it may seem to be a good idea to calculate the rate update frequency similar to the TCP retransmit timeout, which uses an exponentially weighted moving average process; this function appropriately weighs the most recent measurement against the history of measurements. However, in the case of CADPC, the situation is different because measurements are only received at the approximate rate of TCP retransmit timeouts — thus, the most recent measurement is much more important. In simulation experiments, using the TCP timeout calculation led to undesirable traffic phase effects [7] when all flows were started at the same time.

Operational Limitations The fact that a calculated rate cannot be reached precisely (because the rate granularity depends on the packet size) causes oscillations, rendering the mechanism potentially unstable. Consider a single link and a single flow traversing it: if, for example, the calculated rate is 2.5 packets per measurement interval, there will be an interval with 2 and another interval with 3 packets. Following the interval with 2 packets, the calculated rate will be much higher, causing the mechanism to overshoot the point of convergence. During the next interval, chances are that there will be too many packets, leading to a severely reduced rate and so on. These fluctuations are hard to come by and may not be so bad in the long run: on average, the source sends at the appropriate rate.

Yet they narrow the operational range of the mechanism — it can become unstable if there are too many flows, the smoothness parameter a is set too high or packets are too large with respect to the link bandwidth. In other words, the stability of the mechanism is directly proportional to the link bandwidth and indirectly proportional to packet sizes, the number of flows and a.

With a fixed value of 0.5 for a, the packet size imposes a lower limit on the bottleneck bandwidth and an upper limit on the number of users that CADPC can support. For values beyond these limits, oscillations lead to growing queues (and, thus, larger delay) and packet loss — in other words, the quality of the mechanism is significantly degraded. This is illustrated in fig. 1: in cases with a small bandwidth and a large number of flows, the packet loss ratio grows — in the extreme case of 100 flows traversing a 1 Mbit/s link, half of the packets are lost. The increased loss ratio coincides with an increased average queue length. Figure 2 shows the same scenario with a packet size of 500 instead of 1000 bytes;

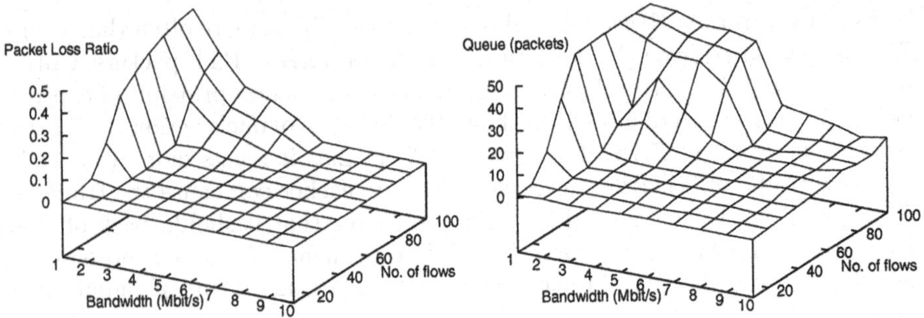

Fig. 1. Packet loss ratio (left) and average queue length (right) of CADPC

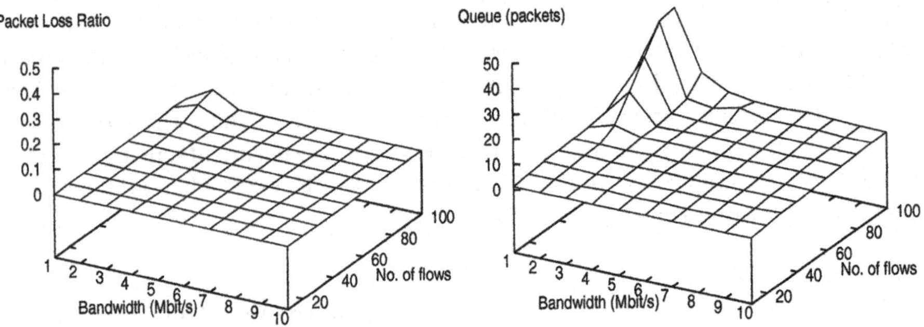

Fig. 2. Packet loss ratio (left) and average queue length (right) with smaller packets

obviously, the region with a packet loss ratio and queue length close to 0 grows as the packet size is decreased. Instead of changing the packet size, it would also be possible to choose a smaller value for a at the cost of having a less responsive system.

4 Performance Evaluation

The Performance Transparency Protocol was implemented for Linux (both configured as a router and as an end system) for simple functionality tests. So far, CADPC performance evaluations were only carried out using the *ns* network simulator[1]; except otherwise noted, simulation parameters were always set according to table 1. This includes the simulations in the previous section.

4.1 Dynamic Behavior

Two simulation examples are shown in fig. 3: the diagrams depict the total throughput of 10 CADPC and 10 TCP flows (only flows of one kind at a time, two simulations per scenario) sharing a 10 Mbit/s and a 100 Mbit/s bottleneck

[1] Linux and *ns* code is available from http://www.welzl.at/ptp

Table 1. Default simulation parameter values

Parameter	Value
Topology	Dumbbell
Packet size	1000 byte
Bottleneck link bandwidth	10 Mbit/s
Bandwidth of all other links	1000 Mbit/s
Link delay	50 ms each
Queuing discipline	Drop-Tail
Duration	long-term: 160 seconds
All flows start after	0 seconds
Flow type	greedy, long-lived (FTP in the case of TCP)
Number of flows	short-term: 10, long-term: 100
CADPC update frequency	4 RTTs
CADPC smoothness factor a	0.5
CADPC startup enhancement	active
TCP "flavor"	TCP Reno
ECN	active for all TCP "flavors"

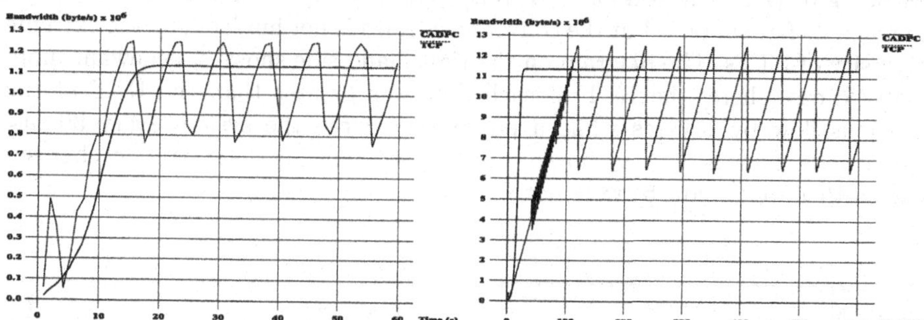

Fig. 3. CADPC vs. TCP with a 10 Mbit/s (left) and a 100 Mbit/s bottleneck (right)

link, respectively. Clearly, the rate of CADPC is smoother than the rate of TCP. Also, in the case of TCP, the speed of convergence and bandwidth utilization decreases in the case of higher link capacities whereas CADPC is always capable of rapidly converging to its steady rate.

The diagram on the left-hand side of figure 4 depicts the rates of 10 flows that were started at the same time but had a different RTT. It was obtained by increasing the update frequency by 4 with the number of the flow, leading to rate updates of 4, 8, 12 ... RTTs. Clearly, the rates even converge towards their fair share of approximately 10 Mbit/s / $(1 + n)$ = 113636 byte/s in this very extreme example — neglecting queuing delay, the rate update frequency of flow no. 0 was 4*300=1200 ms and the frequency of flow no. 9 was 12000 ms, which is similar to changing the RTT from 300 to 3000 ms. This result additionally shows that it is possible for a flow to "artificially prolong" its RTT by updating the rate slower than every 4 RTTs. This is an important feature of CADPC,

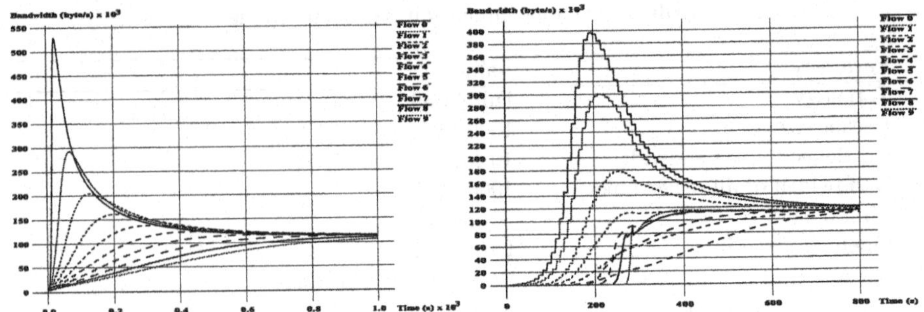

Fig. 4. Fairness with heterogeneous RTTs

as it enables imposing an upper limit on signaling traffic and therefore ensures scalability of the mechanism.

It can be seen that the enhanced startup behaviour almost degrades to regular logistic growth in this example — it takes flow no. 9 approximately 1000 seconds to reach its fair share — but the convergence itself is not hindered by the extreme diversity of RTTs. The diagram on the right-hand side shows a somewhat more realistic case; here, the RTT of each flow was greater than the RTT of the previous flow by 117 ms while a new flow entered the system every 30 ms. Apparently, some flows (e.g., flow 8) were capable of using the startup mechanism while others (e.g., flow 5) were not.

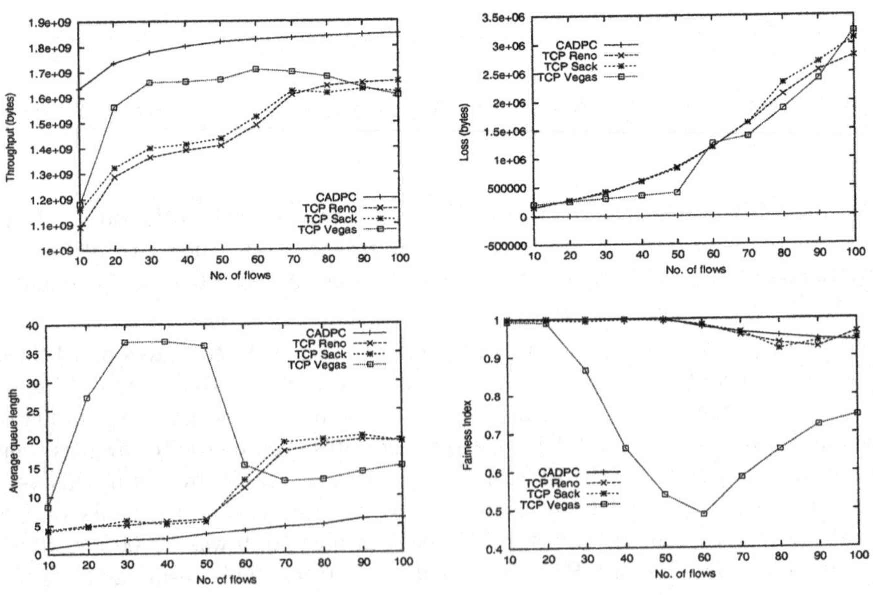

Fig. 5. CADPC and TCP, bottleneck 100 Mbit/s

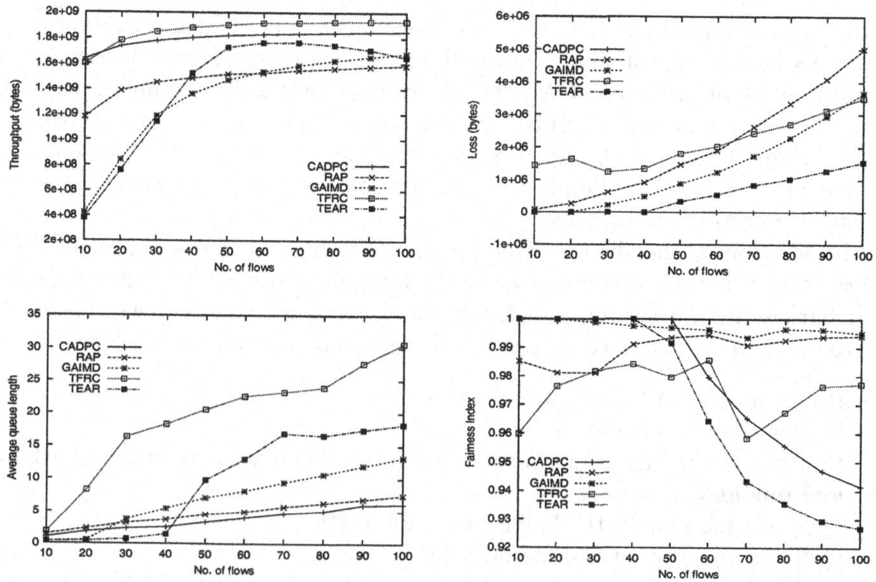

Fig. 6. CADPC and TCP-friendly mechanisms, bottleneck 100 Mbit/s

4.2 Long-Term Performance Evaluation: CADPC Vs. TCP(-friendly) Congestion Control

In oder to evaluate the performance of CADPC, its behavior was compared with TCP Reno, TCP SACK and TCP Vegas (each combined with ECN) and several TCP-friendly congestion control protocols in simulations — RAP [8], GAIMD [9] with $\alpha = 0.31$ and $\beta = 7/8$ (which was realized by tuning RAP parameters), and the slowly-responsive TFRC [10] and TEAR [11]. Flows of one particular kind at a time shared a single bottleneck link in a "dumbbell" topology. For all the results in figures 5 and 6, the simulation time was 160 seconds and link delays were 50 ms each, which, neglecting queuing delays, accounts for a RTT of 300 ms — thus, a simulation took approximately 500 RTTs when the network was lightly loaded. PTP was used in a mode where packets have an initial size of 32 bytes and grow by 16 bytes at each router [2]. Only the payload flow is shown in the figures.

Note that in our simulation scenario, unresponsive senders which transmit at a high data rate would always achieve the greatest total throughput; therefore, high throughput can only be considered a good sign if the packet loss ratio is low. For example, the high throughput of TFRC is not necessarily a good sign because it corresponds with high loss. Yet, TFRC appears to work better with many flows than RAP because RAP shows less throughput as well as more loss.

CADPC outperformed its competitors in our simulations: it achieved more throughput than almost all other mechanism while maintaining a very low loss ratio. Also, while CADPC is the only mechanism that does not acknowledge every packet, it almost always showed the smallest average queue size — it should be no surprise that CADPC also worked very well in simulations with active queue management, which we did not include due to space restraints. Interestingly, CADPC achieves these results based on a single PTP packet that is sent every 4 RTTs while all other mechanisms acknowledge each and every packet that reaches the receiver.

In addition to the shown examples, the following scenarios were simulated (here, "QoS" is used synonymously for throughput, loss, average queue length and fairness in comparison with TCP Reno, Sack and Vegas, RAP, GAIMD, TFRC and TEAR) and led to good results (details can be found in [1]):

- Robustness against fast path changes
- Mixing of converged flows
- Convergence to "max-min-fairness" with two different bottlenecks ("parking lot" topology)
- QoS as a function of the bottleneck bandwidth
- QoS as a function of end-to-end delay
- QoS with the active queue management mechanisms *RED*, *REM* and *AVQ*.

We also examined the performance of the mechanism with varying web-like background traffic; since such traffic is much more dynamic than CADPC by nature, the mechanism cannot react in time. Thus, this was the only scenario that yielded unsatisfactory results.

5 Related and Future Work

The advantage of moving a step further from binary to multilevel feedback is outlined in [12]. Actual ABR-like signaling based on RTCP is used with per-flow state in the "Adaptive Load Service" (ALS) [13] and with a window-based approach, no per-flow state but somewhat strenuous router calculations where the header of every payload packet is examined in XCP [15]. In [14] and [16], the focus is on the interaction between ABR-like signaling and DiffServ.

Among these approaches, XCP is particularly noteworthy, as it resembles CADPC in several aspects: both quickly saturate the available capacity, converge to max-min fairness (which facilitates applying weights at the edges in order to realize service differentiation) and require router support. Also, both mechanisms require their traffic to be isolated from TCP flows ([15] describes a method to separate flows via two different queues in routers in order to achieve TCP-friendliness).

Table 2 shows the most important differences between the two mechanisms. Briefly put, we believe that CADPC imposes less burden on routers at the cost of responsiveness; however, XCP is clearly a better choice in highly dynamic environments. CADPC, on the other hand, could also utilize SNMP to retrieve the relevant information. Such an implementation would be slightly less efficient but could be deployed without installing a software update in routers. The CADPC

Table 2. Differences between XCP and CADPC

Property	XCP	CADPC
Feedback	in payload packets	extra signaling
Routers examine...	every packet	1 packet every 4 RTTs
Convergence to...	bottleneck capacity	capacity*users/(users+1)
"web mice" bg traffic	works well	does not work well

requirement for long-lived flows seems to make the mechanism a particularly good match for bulk data transfers in computational Grids; we are currently investigating such usage scenarios, where we intend to isolate CADPC traffic from the rest by exclusively placing it in a DiffServ class [17]. Other envisioned future work includes:

- CADPC converges to max-min fairness — such a rate allocation can also be attained by maximizing the linear utility function of all users. Although this may in fact suit certain special applications, common network services like file transfer and web surfing are known to have a logarithmic utility function; as of yet, it remains an open question whether CADPC could be extended to support such utility functions and converge to proportional fairness [18].
- So far, CADPC was designed to strictly rely on PTP feedback and not include any additional signaling. It is planned to extend the mechanism with regular per-packet acknowledgments and see whether it can be tuned to be TCP-friendly; also, this variant may be rendered gradually deployable by allowing the mechanism to use a default TCP-like behaviour in the absence of complete path information from PTP.
- Possible extensions for non-greedy flows and multicast scenarios should also be examined.
- Most importantly, gradual deployment methods should be pursued. In addition to the aforementioned idea of mandating CADPC behavior within a DiffServ class, it might be possible to utilize PTP signaling between edge routers of a domain and have these devices control traffic aggregates instead of end-to-end flows. This could be done in support of traffic engineering, or as dynamic resource allocation scheme for DiffServ.

6 Conclusion

In this paper[2], a novel approach to congestion control based on explicit and lightweight feedback was presented. The control law converges to a fixed and stable point, which accounts for higher throughput, less loss, reduced fluctuations and therefore better performance than TCP. Moreover, the rate calculation is simple and can be performed wherever feedback packets are seen; it is easy to enforce appropriate behavior and implement load-based and differentiated

[2] This paper is an overview of [1], which contains further details on the design rationale, extensive simulation results and a complete specification of the PTP protocol.

pricing. While our mechanism has the obvious drawback of requiring router support, we believe that future work on gradual deployment can lead to a service that is fit for the Internet.

References

1. Welzl M: Scalable Performance Signalling and Congestion Avoidance. Kluwer Academic Publishers, Boston, 2003. ISBN 1-4020-7570-7.
2. Welzl, M: A Stateless QoS Signaling Protocol for the Internet. Proceedings of IEEE ICPADS'00, July 2000.
3. Katz, D.: IP Router Alert Option. RFC 2113, February 1997.
4. Barnhart, A. W.: Explicit Rate Performance Evaluations. ATM Forum Technical Committee, Traffic Management Working Group, Contribution ATM Forum/94-0983 (October 1994).
5. Luenberger, D. G.: Introduction to Dynamic Systems - Theory, Models, and Applications. John Wiley & Sons, New York, 1979.
6. Jain, R., Ramakrishnan, K. K.: Congestion Avoidance in Computer Networks with a Connectionless Network Layer: Concepts, Goals and Methodology. Computer Networking Symposium, Washington, D. C., April 1988, pp. 134-143.
7. Floyd, S., Jacobson, V.: On Traffic Phase Effects in Packet-Switched Gateways. Internetworking: Research and Experience, V.3 N.3, September 1992, p.115-156. Earlier version: Computer Communication Review, V.21 N.2, April 1991.
8. Rejaie, R., Handley, M., Estrin, D.: RAP: An End-to-end Rate-based Congestion Control Mechanism for Realtime Streams in the Internet. Proceedings of IEEE Infocom 1999, New York City, March 1999.
9. Yang, Y. R., Lam, S. S.: General AIMD Congestion Control. Technical Report TR-2000-09, Dept. of Computer Sciences, Univ. of Texas, May 2000.
10. Floyd, S., Handley, M., Padhye, J., Widmer, J.: Equation-Based Congestion Control for Unicast Applications. Proceedings of ACM SIGCOMM 2000.
11. Rhee, I., Ozdemir, V., Yi Y.: TEAR: TCP emulation at receivers – flow control for multimedia streaming. Technical Report, Department of Computer Science, North Carolina State University.
12. Durresi, A., Sridharan, M., Liu, C., Goyal, M., Jain, R.: Traffic Management using Multilevel Explicit Congestion Notification. Proceedings of SCI 2001, Orlando Florida 2001.
13. Sisalem, D., Schulzrinne, H.: The Adaptive Load Service: An ABR-like Service for the Internet. IEEE ISCC'2000, France, July 2000.
14. Li, N., Park, S:, Li, S.: A Selective Attenuation Feedback Mechanism for Rate Oscillation Avoidance. Computer Communications 24 (1), pp. 19–34, Jan. 2001.
15. Katabi, D., Handley, M., Rohrs, C.: Internet Congestion Control for Future High Bandwidth-Delay Product Environments. ACM SIGCOMM 2002, Pittsburgh, PA, 19-23 August 2002.
16. Kim, B. G.: Soft QoS Service (SQS) in the Internet. Proceedings of SCI 2001, Orlando Florida 2001.
17. Welzl, M., Mühlhäuser, M.: Scalability and Quality of Service: a Trade-off? IEEE Communications Magazine Vol. 41 No. 6, June 2003, pp. 32-36.
18. Kelly, F.: Charging and rate control for elastic traffic. European Transactions on Telecommunications, 8. pp. 33-37. An updated version is available at http://www.statslab.cam.ac.uk/frank/elastic.html

Index der Autoren